QUICK REFERENCE GUIDE

Looking at Diversity

In Real Life

Ethical Challenges

Cengage Advantage Books

LOOKING OUT
LOOKING IN

FIFTEENTH EDITION

Ronald B. Adler
Santa Barbara City College

Russell F. Proctor II
Northern Kentucky University

CENGAGE
Learning®

ralia • Brazil • Mexico • Singapore • United Kingdom • United States

Cengage Advantage Books: Looking Out Looking In, Fifteenth Edition
Ronald B. Adler, Russell F. Proctor II

Product Director: Monica Eckman

Product Manager: Kelli Strieby

Senior Content Developer: Marita Sermolins

Senior Content Developer: Jessica Badiner

Associate Content Developer: Karolina Kiwak

Product Assistant: Colin Solan

Marketing Manager: Sarah Seymour

Senior Content Project Manager: Corinna Dibble

Senior Art Director: Marissa Falco

Manufacturing Planner: Doug Bertke

IP Analyst: Ann Hoffman

IP Project Manager: Sarah Shainwald

Production Service and Compositor: Cenveo Publisher Services

Cover Designer: Sarah Bishins

Cover Image: © Teresa Arévalo de Zavala/Design Pics/Corbis

Text Designer: Alisha Webber, Cenveo Publisher Services

Library of Congress Control Number: 2015951609

ISBN: 978-1-305-64534-9

Cengage Learning
20 Channel Center Street
Boston MA 02210
USA

Cengage Learning is a leading provider of customized learning solutions with employees residing in nearly 40 different countries and sales in more than 125 countries around the world. Find your local representative at **www.cengage.com.**

Cengage Learning products are represented in Canada by Nelson Education, Ltd.

To learn more about Cengage Learning Solutions, visit **www.cengage.com.**

Purchase any of our products at your local college store or at our preferred online store **www.cengagebrain.com.**

To
Neil Towne
whose legacy continues in these pages.

Printed in the United States of America

Print Number: 01   Print Year: 2015

BRIEF CONTENTS

CONTENTS

3

COMMUNICATION AND IDENTITY: CREATING AND PRESENTING THE SELF   61

4

PERCEPTION: WHAT YOU SEE IS WHAT YOU GET   103

12

MANAGING INTERPERSONAL CONFLICTS   379

PREFACE

Listening is arguably the most important communication skill of them all. That's certainly been true as we developed this new edition of *Looking Out Looking In*. Listening to our users has helped us refine the book you're holding, so it will address the concerns of both professors and students.

Before we began work on this 15th edition, we asked current and prospective users what we could do to best meet their needs. They told us they want an introduction to interpersonal communication that's clear, engaging, and concise. They said their text must reflect the way communication operates in today's world. And it has to be priced fairly.

You spoke, we listened, and you are now seeing the results.

New to This Edition

Users of *Looking Out Looking In* will find that the new edition has been improved in several ways while remaining true to the approach that has served more than one million students over four decades.

- **More Affordable Price**

  We applaud Cengage Learning for making *Looking Out Looking In* more affordable to make it more accessible for students, especially at a time when budgets are tight and the costs of higher education are rising.

- **Extensive Coverage of Social Media**

  The new Chapter 2 is entirely devoted to the role of mediated communication in interpersonal relationships. Topics include differences between mediated and face-to-face communication, the benefits and costs of social media, how gender and age influence the uses of mediated communication, and how to use social media competently to achieve personal and relational goals.

  In addition to Chapter 2, new coverage of social media is integrated throughout the book. Topics include online impression management (Chapter 3), the impact of social media on emotion perception and expression (Chapter 5), nonverbal communication in mediated messages (Chapter 6), giving and receiving support online (Chapter 8), how social media shapes the rise and fall of close relationships (Chapter 9), and the role of social media in communication in families, friendships, and romantic relationships (Chapter 10).

- **New Examples from Popular Culture**

  This edition is loaded with illustrations—now integrated into every chapter—of how communication operates in a variety of relationships. Television profiles include comedies like *Louie* and *Blackish* and dramas such as *Scandal* and *House of Cards*. Many other profiles come from popular films including *Boyhood, Dear White People, The Imitation Game,* and *The Disappearance of Eleanor Rigby.* Captioned photos of figures from the news also highlight how communication principles operate in today's world.

- **New Magazine-Style Readings**

  Compelling readings have always distinguished *Looking Out Looking In*. This edition features a new lineup that shows how principles in the text operate in a wide range of settings and relationships. New readings explore whether software can communicate competently, how to juggle commitments with friends and romantic partners, how loneliness can be pervasive in a hyperconnected world, instagramming to project an idealized identity, saving lives by texting support, and how posting photos online can strengthen close relationships. Now, each reading is followed by a series of "Reflect" questions that help readers connect the material to their everyday lives.

- **Research Updates**

  To reflect the latest communication scholarship, new research is cited throughout the book. Among the updated and expanded topics addressed are the expression of positive emotions (Chapter 5), striking a balance between power and politeness (Chapter 6), giving and receiving social support (Chapter 7), and the communication of love, commitment, and affection in romantic relationships (Chapter 10).

Interactive Learning with MindTap

MindTap for *Looking Out Looking In* is a fully online, highly personalized learning experience built upon *Looking Out Looking In*. MindTap combines student learning tools—readings, multimedia, activities, and assessments—into a singular Learning Path that guides students through the course. Instructors personalize the experience by easily customizing the existing content and learning tools with their own materials. The result: An easy-to-use learning system that is exactly right for your own unique situation.

- **Learning Path.** The MindTap experience begins with a chapter- specific Learning Path built around key student objectives. This intuitive navigator guides students to master the subject matter and provides immediate access to the resources they need along the way. MindTap delivers a suggested Learning Path right "out of the box," ready for you to personalize your course. You control what students see and when they see it. Use it as-is or match to your syllabus exactly—hide, rearrange, add, and create your own content. Customize your Learning Path by:

  - changing due dates
  - reordering content
  - renaming course sections
  - moving or hiding chapters you don't use
  - removing unneeded activities
  - engaging students by inserting campus- or course-specific resources, like handbooks, school catalogs, and web links, your favorite videos, activities, current events materials, or any resource you can upload to the Internet

Students see "Counts for a grade" flags to alert them to assignments due and personalized resources you add appear inline for a seamless experience that keeps students focused while they are in your course.

- **MindTap Reader.** The MindTap Reader is more than a digital version of a textbook. It is an interactive, learning resource built to create a digital reading experience based on how students assimilate information in an online environment. Videos and activities bring the book concepts to life. The robust functionality of the MindTap Reader allows learners to make notes, highlight text, and even find a definition right from the page. After completing the reading, students can review vocabulary with the flashcards and check their comprehension with chapter quizzes.

- **MindApps.** This suite of learning tools gives instructors the ability to manage and customize their course and students the tools they need to prepare for a course or exam—all from a single platform. Examples of apps include:

  - **ReadSpeaker®**, an online text-to-speech application that vocalizes, or "speech-enables," the MindTap content
  - **Merriam-Webster MindApp**, which allows students to look up a word simply by highlighting it and selecting "Dictionary" on the contextual menu
  - **Notebook App** that captures notes and highlights students create in the MindTap Reader and links to the popular Evernote web-based note taking platform.
  - **MindTap Analytics**, a visual dashboard fueled by powerful analytics, allows educators to track learner engagement and class progress, while empowering students with information on where they stand and where they need to focus. Instructors can instantly access an in-depth analysis of each student to understand how engaged he or she is in the course, how often the student is accessing the solution, and what progress has been made within the course activities. Students can quickly see where they stand.
  - **ConnectYard App** allows you to bring in "virtual speakers" to discuss important issues with students. You can invite other classes—even outside your school—to join in.
  - **The RSS Feed App** can be used to bring current event topics into the classroom, making book content even more relevant.

If you want your students to have access to MindTap for this text, these resources can be bundled with every new copy of the text or ordered separately. Students whose instructors do not order these as a package with the text may purchase access to them at cengagebrain.com.

MindTap® Look for the MindTap icon in the pages of *Looking Out Looking In* to find MindTap resources related to the text.

What's Familiar

As always, the user-friendly approach of *Looking Out Looking In* connects scholarship and everyday life. Virtually every page spread contains an attention-grabbing assortment of materials that support the text: articles from print and online sources, poetry, cartoons, photographs, and profiles of popular films and television shows. A prominent treatment of ethical issues helps readers explore how to communicate in a principled manner. An extensive package of ancillary resources (described below) aims at helping students learn and instructors teach efficiently and effectively.

Looking Out Looking In presents communication not as a collection of techniques we use *on* others, but as a process we engage in *with* them. Readers also learn that even the most competent communication doesn't always seek to create warm, fuzzy relationships, and that even less personal interaction usually has the best chance of success when handled in a constructive, respectful manner.

The discussion of gender and culture is integrated throughout the book, rather than being isolated in separate chapters. The treatment of these important topics is nonideological, citing research that shows how other variables are often at least as important in shaping interaction. The basic focus of the chapters has remained constant, and Chapters 2 through 12 can be covered in whatever order works best for individual situations.

In-Text Learning Resources

Every chapter contains a variety of resources to help students understand and use the principles introduced in the text. These include:

Looking at Diversity **profiles** provide first-person accounts by communicators from a wide range of cultural, physical, ethnic, and occupational backgrounds. For example, new profiles in this edition describe a successful arranged marriage and how police officers can better understand and serve communities of color. These profiles help readers appreciate that interpersonal communication is shaped by who you are and where you come from.

On the Job features in every chapter highlight the importance of interpersonal communication in the workplace. Grounded in scholarly research, these features equip readers with communication strategies that enhance career success. New features in this edition discuss how to manage a professional identity, repair damaged workplace relationships, stay humble, and choose workplace battles wisely.

In Real Life **transcripts** describe how the skills and concepts from the text sound in everyday life. Seeing real people use the skills in familiar situations gives students both the modeling and confidence to try them in their own relationships. Dramatized versions of many of these transcripts are featured in the MindTap for *Looking Out Looking In*.

Activities in every chapter help readers engage with important concepts. Activities are labeled by type:

- *Pause and Reflect* boxes help readers understand how theory and research apply to their own lives.
- *Skill Builders* help readers improve their communication skills.
- *Ethical Challenges* offer wisdom about dilemmas that communicators face as they pursue their own goals.

Other Teaching and Learning Resources

Along with the text itself, *Looking Out Looking In* can be bundled with an extensive array of materials that make teaching and learning more efficient and effective.

- The **Advantage Edition of *Looking Out Looking In*** is available for instructors who are interested in an alternate version of the book. Part of the Cengage Learning Advantage Series, this paperback, black-and-white version of the complete book additionally offers a built-in student workbook at the end of each chapter that has perforated pages so material can be submitted as homework.

- The **Student Activities Manual** has been revised by Sheryll Reichwein of Cape Cod Community College. It contains a wealth of resources to help students understand and master concepts and skills introduced in the text and will be available through the Instructor Companion Site.

- A comprehensive **Instructor's Resource Manual,** revised by Sheryll Reichwein, Cape Cod Community College, provides tips and tools for both new and experienced instructors. The manual also contains hard copy of over 1,200 class-tested exam questions, indexed by page number and level of understanding.

- **Instructor's Companion Website.** This website is an all-in one resource for class preparation, presentation, and testing for instructors. Accessible through Cengage.com/login with your faculty account, you will find an Instructor's Manual, Chapter-by-Chapter PowerPoint presentations, and Cengage Learning Testing files powered by Cognero.

- **Cengage Learning Testing, powered by Cognero.** Accessible through Cengage.com/login with your faculty account, this test bank contains multiple choice, true/false, and essay questions for each chapter. Cognero is a flexible, online system that allows you to author, edit, and manage test bank content. Create multiple test versions instantly and deliver them through your LMS platform from wherever you may be. Cognero is compatible with Blackboard, Angel, Moodle, and Canvas LMS platforms.

- Communication **Scenarios for Critique and Analysis Videos** include additional scenarios covering interviewing and group work. *Contact your Cengage Learning sales representative for details.*

- ***Communication in Film III: Teaching Communication Courses Using Feature Films*** by Russell F. Proctor II, Northern Kentucky University, expands on the film tips in each chapter of *Looking Out Looking In.* This guide provides detailed suggestions for using classic films to illustrate communication principles introduced in the text.

- Cengage Learning Engagement Services—**a full portfolio of support for students, instructors, and institutions alike**—is made possible through a dedicated staff of experienced, highly credentialed professionals. Proactive, start-to-finish support helps you get trained, get connected, and get the resources you need for the seamless integration of digital resources into your course. This unparalleled technology service and training program provides robust online resources, peer-to-peer instruction, personalized training, and a customizable program you can count on.

- Create a text as unique as your course. Learn more about **custom learning materials** at http://services.cengage.com/custom/.

Acknowledgments

We are grateful to the many people who helped bring you this new edition. Thanks are due to the colleagues whose reviews helped shape this new edition:

Marlene Adzema, Red Rocks Community College; Renee Aitken, Park University; Keith Allen, Mott Community College; Randall Allen, Bay de Noc Community College Bay; Alicia Andersen, Sierra College; Kim Ards, Amberton University; Diane Auten, Allan Hancock College; Pat Baker, Davidson College; Jim Bargar, Missouri Western State University; Amy Bessin, Taylor University; Francesca Bishop, El Camino College; Nancy Bixler, Skagit Valley College; Ellen Bland, Central Carolina Community College; Beth Brooks, Bucks County Community College; Cynthia Brown, El Macomb Community College; Susan Cain, A-B Tech Community College; Kelly Champion, Northern Illinois University; Tammy Christensen, Central Christian College of the Bible; Marlene Cohen, Prince George's Community College; Dolly Conner, Radford University; Sarah Contreras, Del Mar College; Diana Crossman, El Camino College; Patricia Cutspec, Asheville Buncombe Technical Community College; Nicholas Dahl, Clark College; Alexis Davidson, California State University, Sacramento; Kathryn Dederichs, Normandale Community College; Karen DeFrancesco, Bloomsburg University; Sherry Dewald, Red Rocks Community College; Erica Dixon, South Puget

Sound CC; Cassandra Dove, Central Maine Community College; Mike Dunn, Austin Peay State University; Steve Epstein, Suffolk Community College; Nancy Fraleigh, Fresno City College; Ann Gross, Napa Valley College; Jill Hall, Jefferson Community and Technical College; Benjamin Han, Concordia University Wisconsin; Yael Hellman, Woodbury University; Aimee Herring, Amberton University; Ronald Hochstatter, Mclennan Community College; Jenny Hodges, St. John's College; Caryn Horwitz, Miami Dade College; Karen Huck, Central Oregon Community College; Rae Ann Ianniello, Ohlone College; Kati Ireland, San Jose City College; Joann Kaiser, Indiana University Kokomo; Stefanie Kelly Armstrong, Atlantic State University; Chris Kennedy, Western Wyoming Community College; Howard Kerner, Polk State College; Karyl Kicenski, College of the Canyons; April Kindrick, South Puget Sound Community College; Mark Knapik, Lake Erie College; Norman Komnick, Pierce College; Meg Kreiner, Spokane Community College; Janet Kucia, Mississippi College; Julie Kusmierz, Hilbert College; Jorge Luna, William Jessup University; Nancy Luna, Woodbury University; Ross Mackinney, College of the Redwoods; Jennifer Marks, Northeast Lakeview College; Barbara Mayo, Northeast Lakeview College; Floyd McConnell, San Jacinto College North; Chikako McLean, Oakton Community College; Connie McKee, West Texas A&M University; Che Meneses, Ohlone College; Kendra Mitchell, West Kentucky Community and Technical College; M Moe-Lunger, Lee University; David Moss, Mt. San Jacinto College; Anjana Mudambi, Randolph-Macon College; Lynnette Mullins, University of Minnesota Crookston; Kay Neal, University of Wisconsin Oshkosh; Carel Neffenger, Green River Community College; Larry Neuspickle, Beckfield College; Katherine Oleson, Bellevue College; Cindy Peterson, MidAmerica Nazarene University; Sandra Poster, Borough of Manhattan Community College; Tracey Powers, GateWay Community College; Jennifer Ramsey, Odessa College; Heidi Reeder, Boise State University; Sheryll Reichwein, Cape Cod Community College; Rebecca Richey, Middle Tennessee State University; Laura Ringer, Piedmont Technical College; Rebecca Roberts, University of Wyoming; Nicole Roles, Williston State College; Linda Seward, Middle Tennessee State University; Jay Sieling, Alexandria Technical and Community College; Cheryl Skiba-Jones, Trine University; Linda Smith, Skagit Valley College; Tim Soulis, Transylvania University; Kalisa Spalding, St. Catharine College; Elizabeth Stephens, Middle Tennessee State University; Antonia Taylor, Saint Mary-of-the-Woods College; Mary-Beth Taylor, Central Maine Community College; Michelle Thiessen, Rock Valley College; Catherine Thompson, University of Hawaii Maui College; Melinda Tilton, Montana State University, Billings; Juleen Trisko, Northwest Technical College; Jayne Turk, College of the Siskiyous; Desrene Vernon-Brebnor, Andrews University; Shawna Warner, Crown College; Joyce Webb, Shepherd University; Frank Wells, Dunwoody College of Technology; Dan West, Rochester Community and Technical College; Colene White, Everett Community College; Ellen White, Mt. Hood Community College; Katherine Woodbury, Central Maine Community College; Sandra Wu-Bott, University of Hawaii at Manoa; Marguerite Yawin, Tunxis Community College; Paul Zietlow, Concordia University Wisconsin

We are grateful to Brandi Frisby of the University of Kentucky, author of the bonus chapter on military communication that accompanies this edition. We continue to appreciate the contributions of David DeAndrea of Ohio State University and Stephanie Tom Tong of Wayne State University, whose work started the evolution of the current chapter on social media. Thanks also to Sheryll Reichwein of Cape Cod Community College for her work on the revisions of the Instructor's Manual, Student Activities Manual, and MindTap activities.

Our thanks also go to the hardworking team at Cengage Learning who have played a role in this edition from start to finish: Nicole Morinon, Sue Gleason Wade, Jessica Badiner, Lisa Boragine, Colin Solan, and Corinna Dibble. Special thanks goes to Marita Sermolins, whose ongoing help kept this project on track. In addition, we are grateful to Jean Finley for her work on this edition. We are especially indebted to Sherri Adler for selecting the evocative photos that help make *Looking Out Looking In* unique.

Ronald B. Adler
Russell F. Proctor, II

ABOUT THE AUTHORS

Since this is a book about interpersonal communication, it seems appropriate for us to introduce ourselves to you, the reader. The "we" you'll be reading throughout this book isn't just an editorial device: It refers to two real people—Ron Adler and Russ Proctor.

Ron Adler lives in Santa Barbara, California, with his wife, Sherri, an artist and photo researcher who selected most of the images in this book. Their three adult children were infants when early editions of *Looking Out Looking In* were conceived, and they grew up as guinea pigs for the field testing of many concepts in this book. If you asked them, they would vouch for the value of the information between these covers.

Ron spends most of his professional time writing about communication. In addition to helping create *Looking Out Looking In*, he has contributed to six other books about topics including business communication, public speaking, small group communication, assertiveness, and social skills. Besides writing and teaching, Ron teaches college courses and helps professional and business people improve their communication on the job. Cycling and hiking help keep Ron physically and emotionally healthy.

Russ Proctor is a professor at Northern Kentucky University, where his sons RP and Randy both attended. Russ's wife, Pam, is an educator too, training teachers, students, and businesses to use energy more efficiently.

Russ met Ron at a communication conference in 1990, where they quickly discovered a shared interest in using feature films as a teaching tool. They have written and spoken extensively on this topic over the years, and they have also co-authored several textbooks and articles. When Russ isn't teaching, writing, or presenting, his hobbies include sports (especially baseball), classic rock music (especially Steely Dan), and cooking (especially for family and friends on his birthday each year).

1

A FIRST LOOK AT INTERPERSONAL COMMUNICATION

AFTER STUDYING THE TOPICS IN THIS CHAPTER, YOU SHOULD BE ABLE TO:

1. Assess the needs (physical, identity, social, and practical) that communicators are attempting to satisfy in a given situation or relationship.

2. Apply the transactional communication model to a specific situation.

3. Describe how the communication principles and misconceptions identified in this chapter are evident in a specific situation.

4. Describe the degree to which communication (in a specific instance or a relationship) is qualitatively impersonal or interpersonal, and describe the consequences of this level of interaction.

5. Diagnose the effectiveness of various communication channels in a specific situation.

6. Determine the level of communication competence in a specific instance or a relationship.

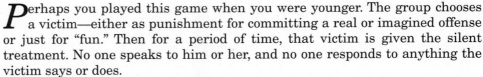

MindTap READ AND UNDERSTAND ...

the complete chapter text online in a rich interactive platform.

*P*erhaps you played this game when you were younger. The group chooses a victim—either as punishment for committing a real or imagined offense or just for "fun." Then for a period of time, that victim is given the silent treatment. No one speaks to him or her, and no one responds to anything the victim says or does.

If you were the subject of this silent treatment, you probably experienced a range of emotions. At first you might have felt—or at least acted—indifferent. But after a while, the strain of being treated as a nonperson probably began to grow. If the game went on long enough, it's likely you found yourself either retreating into a state of depression or lashing out with hostility—partly to show your anger and partly to get a response from the others.

Vicky Kasala/Getty Images

Adults, as well as children, have used the silent treatment in virtually every society throughout history as a powerful tool to express displeasure and for social control.[1] We all know intuitively that communication—the company of others—is one of the most basic human needs, and that lack of contact is among the cruelest punishments a person can suffer. In fact, workplace studies show that employees would rather get negative attention from bosses and coworkers than receive no attention at all. It hurts to be picked on, but it's worse to be ostracized.[2]

Besides being emotionally painful, being deprived of companionship is so serious that it can affect life itself. Frederick II, emperor of Germany in the 13th century, may have been the first person to prove the point systematically. A medieval historian described one of his significant, if inhumane, experiments:

> He bade foster mothers and nurses to suckle the children, to bathe and wash them, but in no way to prattle with them, for he wanted to learn whether they would speak the Hebrew language, which was the oldest, or Greek, or Latin, or Arabic, or perhaps the language of their parents, of whom they had been born. But he labored in vain because all the children died. For they could not live without the petting and joyful faces and loving words of their foster mothers.[3]

Fortunately, contemporary researchers have found less barbaric ways to illustrate the importance of communication. In one study of isolation, subjects were paid to remain alone in a locked room. Of the five subjects, one lasted for eight days. Three held out for two days, one commenting, "Never again." The fifth subject lasted only two hours.[4]

The need for contact and companionship is just as strong outside the laboratory, as individuals who have led solitary lives by choice or necessity have discovered. W. Carl Jackson, an adventurer who sailed across the Atlantic Ocean alone in fifty-one days, summarized the feelings common to most loners:

> I found the loneliness of the second month almost excruciating. I always thought of myself as self-sufficient, but I found life without people had no meaning. I had a definite need for somebody to talk to, someone real, alive, and breathing.[5]

WHY WE COMMUNICATE

You might object to stories like this, claiming that solitude would be a welcome relief from the irritations of everyday life. It's true that all of us need solitude, often more than we get, but each of us has a point beyond which we do not want to be alone. Beyond this point, solitude changes from a pleasurable to a painful condition. In other words, we all need relationships. We all need to communicate.

Physical Needs

Communication is so important that its presence or absence affects physical health. In extreme cases, communication can even become a matter of life or death. When he was a Navy pilot, U.S. Senator John McCain was shot down over North Vietnam and held as a prisoner of war for six years, often in solitary confinement. He and his fellow POWs set up clandestine codes in which they sent messages by tapping on walls to laboriously spell out words. McCain describes the importance of keeping contact and the risks that inmates would take to maintain contact with one another:

> The punishment for communicating could be severe, and a few POWs, having been caught and beaten for their efforts, had their spirits broken as their bodies were battered. Terrified of a return trip to the punishment room, they would lie still in their cells when their comrades tried to tap them up on the wall. Very few would remain uncommunicative for long. To suffer all this alone was less tolerable than torture. Withdrawing in silence from the fellowship of other Americans … was to us the approach of death.[6]

Other prisoners have also described the punishing effects of social isolation. Reflecting on his seven years as a hostage in Lebanon, former news correspondent Terry Anderson said flatly, "I would rather have had the worst companion than no companion at all."[7]

The link between communication and physical well-being isn't restricted to prisoners. Medical researchers have identified a wide range of health threats that can result from a lack of close relationships. For instance:

- A meta-analysis of nearly 150 studies and over 300,000 participants found that socially connected people—those with strong networks of family and friends—live an average of 3.7 years longer than those who are socially isolated.[8]

- A lack of social relationships jeopardizes coronary health to a degree that rivals cigarette smoking, high blood pressure, blood lipids, obesity, and lack of physical activity.[9]

- Socially isolated people are four times more susceptible to the common cold than are those who have active social networks.[10]

- Divorced, separated, and widowed people are five to ten times more likely to need mental hospitalization than their married counterparts. Happily married people also have lower incidences of pneumonia, surgery, and cancer than do single people.[11] (It's important to note that the quality of the relationship is more important than the institution of marriage in these studies.)

By contrast, a life that includes positive relationships created through communication leads to better health. As little as ten minutes per day of socializing improves memory and boosts intellectual function.[12] Conversation with others reduces feelings of loneliness and its accompanying maladies.[13] Stress hormones decline the more often people hear expressions of affection from loved ones.[14]

Research like this demonstrates the importance of having satisfying personal relationships. Not everyone needs the same amount of contact, and the quality of communication is almost certainly as significant as the quantity. The key point is that personal communication is essential for our well-being.

Identity Needs

Communication does more than enable us to survive. It is the way—indeed, the only way—we learn who we are. As Chapter 3 explains, our sense of identity comes from the way we interact with other people. Are we smart or stupid, attractive or plain, skillful or inept? The answers to these questions don't come from looking in the mirror. We decide who we are based on how others react to us.

Deprived of communication with others, we would have no sense of ourselves. A dramatic example is the "Wild Boy of Aveyron," who spent his early childhood without any apparent human contact. The boy was discovered in January 1800 digging for vegetables in a French village garden. He showed no behaviors that one would expect in a social human. The boy could not speak but rather uttered only weird cries. More significant than this lack of social skills was his lack of any identity as a human being. As one author put it, "The boy had no human sense of being in the world. He had no sense of himself as a person related to other persons."[15] Only with the influence of a loving "mother" did the boy begin to behave—and, we can imagine, think of himself— as a human.

Like the boy of Aveyron, each of us enters the world with little or no sense of identity. We gain an idea of who we are from the way others define us. As Chapter 3 explains, the messages we receive in early childhood are the strongest, but the influence of others continues throughout life.

Social Needs

Besides helping to define who we are, communication provides a vital link with others. Researchers and theorists have identified a whole range of social needs that we satisfy by communicating. These include pleasure, affection, companionship, escape, relaxation, and control.[16]

Research suggests a strong link between effective interpersonal communication and happiness. In one study of more than 200 college students, the happiest 10 percent described themselves as having a rich social life. (The very happy people were no different from their classmates in any other measurable way such as amount of sleep, exercise, TV watching, religious activity, or alcohol consumption.)[17] In another study, women reported that "socializing" contributed more to a satisfying life than virtually any other activity, including relaxing, shopping, eating, exercise, TV, or prayer.[18] Married couples who are effective communicators report happier relationships than less skillful husbands and wives—a finding that has been supported across cultures.[19]

Despite knowing that communication is vital to social satisfaction, a variety of evidence suggests that many people aren't very successful at managing their interpersonal relationships. For example, one study revealed that a quarter of the more than 4,000 adults surveyed knew more about their dogs than they did about their neighbors' backgrounds.[20] Research also suggests that the number of friendships is in decline. One widely recognized survey reported that, in 1985, Americans had an average of 2.94 close friends. Twenty years later, that number had dropped to 2.08.[21] It's worth noting that educated Americans reported having larger and more diverse networks. In other words, a higher education can enhance your relational life as well as your intellect.

∧ In his TV show *Louie*, comedian Louie CK is a relational pessimist who is chronically unlucky in love. Nonetheless he keeps trying because life without companionship is too lonesome to bear. How well does your communication fulfill your needs for connection? How can you use the information in this book to help you meet your social needs?

Because connections with others are so vital, some theorists maintain that positive relationships may be the single most important source of life satisfaction and emotional well-being in every culture.[22] If you pause now and make a mental list of your own relationships, you'll probably see that, no matter how successfully you interact with friends, at home, at school, and at work, there is plenty of room for improvement in your everyday life. The information that follows will help you improve the way you communicate with the people who matter most to you.

Practical Goals

Besides satisfying social needs and shaping our identity, communication is the most widely used approach to satisfying what communication scholars call **instrumental goals**: getting others to behave in ways we want. Some instrumental goals are quite basic: Communication is the tool that lets you tell the hair stylist to take just a little off the sides, lets you negotiate household duties, and lets you convince the plumber that the broken pipe needs attention *now*!

Other instrumental goals are more important. Career success is the prime example. As the On the Job box in this section shows, communication skills are essential in virtually every career. They can even make the difference between life and death. The Los Angeles Police Department cited "bad communication" among the most common reasons for errors in shooting by its officers.[23] The ability to communicate effectively is just as essential for doctors, nurses, and other medical practitioners.[24] Researchers discovered that "poor communication" was the root of more than 60 percent of reported medical errors—including death, serious physical injury, and psychological trauma.[25] Research published in the *Journal of the American Medical Association* and elsewhere revealed a significant difference between the communication skills of physicians who had no malpractice claims against them and those with previous claims.[26]

On The JOB

Communication and Career Success

No matter what the field, research confirms what experienced workers already know—that communication skills are crucial in finding and succeeding in a job. Communication skills often make the difference between being hired and being rejected. In one widely followed annual survey, employers list the skills and qualities for their ideal candidate. Communication skills always top the list, ahead of technical skills, initiative, analytical ability, and computer skills.[a]

In another survey, managers across the country rated the abilities to speak and listen effectively as the two most important factors in helping college graduates find jobs in a competitive workplace—more important than technical competence, work experience, and specific degree earned.[b] When 170 well-known business and industrial firms were asked to list the most common reasons for *not* offering jobs to applicants, the most frequent replies were "inability to communicate" and "poor communication skills."[c]

Once you have been hired, the need for communication skills is important in virtually every career.[d] Engineers spend the bulk of their working lives speaking and listening, mostly in one-to-one and small-group settings.[e] Accountants and the firms that hire them consistently cite effective communication as essential for career success.[f] One executive at computer giant Sun Microsystems made the point forcefully: "If there's one skill that's required for success in this industry, it's communication skills."[g] Writing in *The Scientist*, a commentator echoed this sentiment: "If I give any advice, it is that you can never do enough training around your overall communication skills."[h]

Psychologist Abraham Maslow suggested that the physical, identity, social, and practical needs we have been discussing fall into five hierarchical categories, each of which must be satisfied before we concern ourselves with the less fundamental needs.[27] The most basic of these needs are *physical:* sufficient air, water, food, and rest, and the ability to reproduce as a species. The second of Maslow's needs is *safety:* protection from threats to our well-being. Beyond physical and safety needs are the *social needs* we have mentioned already. Beyond these, Maslow suggests, each of us has *self-esteem* needs: the desire to believe that we are worthwhile, valuable people. The final category of needs described by Maslow is *self-actualization:* the desire to develop our potential to the maximum, to become the best person we can be. As you read on, think about the ways in which communication is often necessary to satisfy each level of need.

THE PROCESS OF COMMUNICATION

We have been talking about *communication* as though the meaning of this word were perfectly clear. Communication scholars have argued for years about communication definitions. Despite their many disagreements, most would agree that, at its essence, communication is about using messages to generate meanings.[28] Notice how this basic definition holds true across a variety of contexts—public speaking, small groups, mass media, etc. Before going further, we need to explain systematically what happens when people exchange messages and create meanings in interpersonal communication. Doing so will introduce you to a common working vocabulary and, at the same time, preview some of the topics that are covered in later chapters.

A Linear View

In the early days of studying communication as a social science, researchers created models to illustrate the communication process. Their first attempts resulted in a **linear communication model**, which depicts communication as something a sender "does to" a receiver. According to the linear model in Figure 1.1,

> A **sender** (the person creating the message)
> **encodes** (puts thoughts into symbols and gestures) a
> **message** (the information being transmitted), sending it through a
> **channel** (the medium through which the message passes) to a
> **receiver** (the person attending to the message) who
> **decodes** (makes sense of the message), while contending with
> **noise** (distractions that disrupt transmission).

Notice how the appearance of and vocabulary in Figure 1.1 are similar to how radio and television broadcasting operate. This isn't a coincidence: The scientists who created it were primarily interested in early electronic media. The widespread use of this model has affected the way we think and talk about communication. There is a linear, machine-like quality to familiar phrases, such as "We're having a communication breakdown" and "I don't think my message is getting through." While this is sometimes the case in mediated forms of communication, these familiar phrases (and the thinking they represent) obscure some important features of human communication. Does interpersonal communication really "break down," or are people still exchanging information even when they're not talking to each other? Is it possible to "get a message through" to someone loudly and clearly, but still not get the desired reaction? Here are some other questions to consider about the shortcomings of the linear model:

- When you're having a face-to-face conversation with a friend, is there only one sender and one receiver, or do both of you send and receive messages simultaneously?

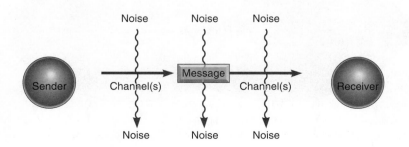

< **FIGURE 1.1**
Linear Communication Model
© Cengage Learning

- Do you purposely encode every message you send, or do you engage in some behaviors unconsciously that still communicate messages to others?

- Even when you send a message electronically (e.g., through texting or email), is the message's meaning affected by larger factors such as culture, environment, and relational history?

These and other questions have led scholars to create models that better represent interpersonal communication. We will look at one of these models now.

A Transactional View

A **transactional communication model** (Figure 1.2) updates and expands the linear model to better capture communication as a uniquely human process. Some concepts and terms from the linear model are retained in the transactional model, whereas others are enhanced, added, or eliminated.

The transactional model uses the word *communicator* instead of *sender* and *receiver*. This term reflects the fact that people typically send and receive messages simultaneously and not in a unidirectional or back-and-forth manner, as suggested by the linear model. Consider, for example, what might happen when you and a housemate negotiate how to handle household chores. As soon as you begin to hear (receive) the words sent by your housemate, "I want to talk about cleaning the kitchen...," you grimace and clench your jaw (sending a nonverbal message of your own while receiving the verbal one). This reaction leads your housemate to interrupt defensively, sending a new message: "Now wait a minute...."

A transactional model also shows that communicators often occupy different **environments**—fields of experience that affect how they understand others' behavior. In communication terminology, *environment* refers not only to a physical location but also to the personal experiences and cultural background that participants bring to a conversation.

Consider just some of the factors that might contribute to different environments:

- Person A might belong to one ethnic group, and person B to another.

- Person A might be rich, and B poor.

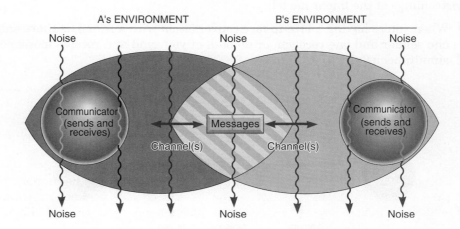

FIGURE 1.2 >
Transactional
Communication Model
© Cengage Learning

- Person A might be rushed, and B have nowhere to go.

- Person A might have lived a long, eventful life, and B might be young and inexperienced.

- Person A might be passionately concerned with the subject, and B indifferent to it.

Notice how the model in Figure 1.2 shows that the environments of persons A and B overlap. This area represents the background that the communicators have in common. As the shared environment becomes smaller, communication usually becomes more challenging. Consider a few examples in which different perspectives can make understanding difficult:

- Bosses who have trouble understanding the perspectives of their employees will be less effective managers, and workers who do not appreciate the challenges of being a boss are more likely to be uncooperative (and probably less suitable for advancement).

- Parents who have trouble recalling their youth are likely to clash with their children, who have never known and may not appreciate the responsibility that comes with parenting.

- Members of a dominant culture who have never experienced how it feels to be marginalized may not appreciate the concerns of people from minority co-cultures, whose own perspectives make it hard to understand the cultural blindness of the majority.

Communication channels retain a significant role in the transactional model, as they did in the linear model. Although it's tempting to see channels simply as neutral conduits for delivering a message, a closer look reveals the important role they play.[29] For instance, should you say "I love you" in person? Over the phone? In a text message? By renting space on a billboard? By sending flowers and a card? Via email? In a voicemail? On a Facebook wall? Mediated channels have become so important that Chapter 2 is devoted to explaining the role they play in interpersonal relationships.

The transactional model also retains the concept of noise but with a broader focus. In the linear model, the focus is on noise in the channel—what is known as *external noise*. For instance, loud music or too much cigarette smoke in a crowded room might make it difficult for you to pay attention to another person. The transactional model shows that noise also resides *within* communicators. This includes *physiological noise*, which involves biological factors that interfere with accurate reception: illness, fatigue, hearing loss, and so on. Communicators can also encounter *psychological noise:* forces within that interfere with the ability to understand a message accurately. For instance, a student might become so upset upon learning that she failed a test that she would be unable (perhaps *unwilling* is a better word) to understand clearly where she went wrong. Psychological noise is such an important communication problem that we have devoted much of Chapter 11 to investigating its most common cause, defensiveness.

For all the insights they offer, models can't capture some important features of interpersonal communication. A model is a "snapshot," while communication more closely resembles a "motion picture." In real life it's

difficult to isolate a single discrete "act" of communication from the events that precede and follow it.[30] Consider the "Zits" cartoon seen here. If you read only the final frame, it appears that Jeremy is the victim of his mother's nagging. If you then read the first three frames, you might conclude that if Jeremy were more responsive to his mother, she might not need to be so persistent. And if you watched the two of them interact over the days and weeks preceding the incident in this cartoon, you would have a larger (but still incomplete) picture of the relational history that contributed to this event. In other words, the communication pattern that Jeremy and his mother have created together contributes to the quality of their relationship.

This leads to another important point: Transactional communication isn't something that we do *to* others; rather, it is an activity that we do *with* them. In this sense, interpersonal communication is rather like dancing—at least the kind of dancing we do with partners. Like dancing, communication depends on the involvement of a partner. And like good dancing, successful communication doesn't depend only on the person who takes the lead. A great dancer who forgets to consider and adapt to the skill level of his or her partner can make both people look bad. In communication and dancing, even having two talented partners doesn't guarantee success. When two skilled dancers perform without coordinating their movements, the results feel bad to the dancers and look foolish to an audience. Finally, relational communication—like dancing—is a unique creation that arises out of the way in which the partners interact. The way you dance probably varies from one partner to another. Likewise, the way you communicate almost certainly varies from one partner to another.

▼ The movie *Boyhood* chronicles the life of Mason (Ellar Coltrane) from early childhood until he enters college. Shot over a 12-year period with actors who aged with the story, the film illustrates the irreversible, unrepeatable, and transactional nature of interpersonal communication. How have events from your upbringing affected the way you communicate today?

IFC Films/Photofest

Now we can summarize the definition of interpersonal communication that we have been developing. **Interpersonal communication** is a transactional process involving participants who occupy different but overlapping environments and create meaning and relationships through the exchange of messages, many of which are affected by external, physiological, and psychological noise. Whether or not you memorize this definition is a matter for you and your instructor to decide. In any case, notice how it reflects a more sophisticated view of the process than you might have had before reading this far. With this definition in mind, let's look at how interpersonal communication differs from less personal kinds of interaction.

Interpersonal and Impersonal Communication

Scholars have characterized interpersonal communication in a number of ways.[31] The most obvious definition focuses on the number of people involved. A *quantitative* definition of interpersonal communication includes any interaction between two people, usually face to face. Social scientists call two interacting people a **dyad**, and they often use the adjective *dyadic* to describe this type of communication. So, in a quantitative sense, the terms *dyadic communication* and *interpersonal communication* can be used interchangeably. Using a quantitative definition, a salesclerk and customer or a police officer ticketing a speeding driver would be examples of interpersonal acts, whereas a teacher and class or a performer and audience would not.

You can probably see the problems with a quantitative definition of interpersonal communication. For example, consider a routine transaction between a salesclerk and customer, or the rushed exchange when you ask a stranger on the street for directions. Communication of this sort hardly seems interpersonal—or personal in any sense of the word. In fact, after transactions like this, we commonly remark, "I might as well have been talking to a machine."

The impersonal nature of some two-person exchanges and the personal nature of others have led some scholars to argue that *quality*, not quantity, is what distinguishes interpersonal communication.[32] Taking a *qualitative* approach, interpersonal communication occurs when people treat one another as unique individuals, regardless of the context in which the interaction occurs or the number of people involved. When quality of interaction is the criterion, the opposite of interpersonal communication is **impersonal communication**, not group, public, or mass communication.

Several features distinguish qualitatively interpersonal communication from less-personal communication.[33] The first feature is *uniqueness*. Communication in impersonal exchanges is determined by social *rules* (e.g., laugh politely at others' jokes, don't dominate a conversation) and by social *roles* (e.g., the customer is always right, be especially polite to senior citizens). Qualitatively interpersonal relationships are characterized by the development of unique rules and roles. For example, in one relationship you might exchange good-natured insults, whereas in another you are careful never to offend your partner. Likewise, you might handle conflicts with one friend or family member by expressing disagreements as soon as they arise, whereas the unwritten rule in another relationship is to withhold resentments until they build up and then clear the air periodically. Communication scholars use the term *relational culture* to describe people in close relationships who create their own unique ways of interacting.[34]

A second feature of qualitatively interpersonal relationships is *irreplaceability*. Because interpersonal relationships are unique, they have no substitute. This explains why we usually feel so sad when a close friendship or love affair

ETHICAL *Challenge*

Martin Buber's I and Thou

Martin Buber is arguably the most influential advocate of qualitatively interpersonal communication, as defined in this section. His book *Ich und Du* (*I and Thou*) is a worldwide classic, selling millions of copies since its publication in 1922.[a]

Buber states that "I-It" and "I-Thou" represent two ways in which humans can relate to one another. "I-It" relationships are stable, predictable, detached. In an "I-It" mode we deal with people because they can do things for us: pump gas, laugh at our jokes, buy products we are selling, provide information or amusement. "I-It" is also the approach of science, which attempts to understand what makes people tick in order to explain, predict, and control their behavior. Buber would have regarded advertisers as operating in an "I-It" mode, crafting messages that lead people to buy their products or services. "I-It" relationships exist in personal relationships as well as impersonal ones: On an everyday basis, parents and children, bosses and employees, service providers and customers—even lovers—deal with one another as objects ("I wish she would leave me alone." "Can you pick me up after work?" "How can I get him/her to love me?").

In profound contrast to "I-It" relationships, Buber described an "I-Thou" way of interacting. "I-Thou" relationships are utterly unique. Because no two teachers or students, parents or children, husbands or wives, bosses or employees are alike, we encounter each person as an individual and not as a member of some category. An "I-Thou" posture goes further: Not only are people different from one another, but they change from moment to moment. An "I-Thou" relationship arises out of how we are now, not how we might have been yesterday or even a moment ago. In an "I-Thou" relationship, persuasion and control are out of the question: We certainly may explain our point of view, but ultimately we respect the fact that others are free to act.

Buber acknowledges that it is impossible to create and sustain pure "I-Thou" relationships. But without this qualitatively interpersonal level of contact, our lives are impoverished. To paraphrase Buber, without "I-It" we cannot exist, but if we live only with "I-It," we are not fully human.

MindTap APPLY ... the ethical principle(s) introduced here by answering the following questions, either here or online.

Think of your most important relationships:

1 To what degree can they be described as "I-Thou" or "I-It"?

2 How satisfied are you with this level of relating?

3 What obligation do you have to treat others in an "I-Thou" manner?

Based on your answers to these questions, how might you change your style of communication?

---

cools down. We know that no matter how many other relationships fill our lives, none of them will ever be quite like the one that just ended.

Interdependence is a third feature of qualitatively interpersonal relationships. At the most basic level, the fate of the partners is connected. You might be able to brush off the anger, affection, excitement, or depression of someone you're not involved with personally, but in an interpersonal relationship the other's life affects you. Sometimes interdependence is a pleasure, and at other times it is a burden. In either case, it is a fact of life in qualitatively interpersonal relationships. Interdependence goes beyond the level of joined fates. In interpersonal relationships, our very identity depends on the nature of our interaction with others. As psychologist Kenneth Gergen puts it: "One cannot be 'attractive' without others who are attracted, a 'leader' without others willing to follow, or a 'loving person' without others to affirm with appreciation."[35]

A fourth feature of interpersonal relationships is often (though not always) the amount of *disclosure* of personal information. In impersonal relationships we don't reveal much about ourselves, but in interpersonal relationships we feel more comfortable sharing our thoughts and feelings. This doesn't mean that all interpersonal relationships are warm and caring, or that all self-disclosure is positive. It's possible to reveal negative, personal information: "I'm really angry with you." The point is, we tend to reserve these kinds of disclosures—both positive and negative—for our more personal relationships.

A fifth feature of interpersonal communication is *intrinsic rewards*. In impersonal communication, we seek payoffs that have little to do with the people involved. You listen to instructors in class or talk to potential buyers of your used car in order to reach goals that usually have little to do with developing personal relationships. By contrast, you spend time in qualitatively interpersonal relationships with friends, lovers, and others because you find the time personally rewarding. It often doesn't matter *what* you talk about: The relationship itself is what's important.

Because relationships that are unique, irreplaceable, interdependent, disclosing, and intrinsically rewarding are rare, qualitatively interpersonal communication is relatively scarce. We chat pleasantly with shopkeepers or fellow passengers on the bus or plane; we discuss the weather or current events with most classmates and neighbors; we enjoy bantering with online acquaintances on social networking websites. However, considering the number of people with whom we communicate, personal relationships are by far in the minority.

Most relationships aren't *either* interpersonal *or* impersonal. Rather, they fall somewhere on a continuum between these two extremes. Your own

PAUSE *and* REFLECT

How Personal Are Your Facebook Relationships?

MindTap REFLECT ... on your own communication by answering the following questions, either here or online.

If you're a Facebook user, scroll through your list of friends on that site. Consider how personal (or impersonal) your relationships are with those people:

- How many would you regard to be "highly personal"? How many are "highly impersonal"? (Perhaps you can rank them on a scale of 1 to 10.)

- Which factors noted in this section (unique, irreplaceable, interdependent, disclosing, and intrinsically rewarding) affect your appraisals?

- What percentage of your communication with these people occurs exclusively on Facebook? Through other mediated channels (phone, text, email)? Face to face? How does this ratio affect your friendships?

experience probably reveals that there's often a personal element in even the most impersonal situations. You might appreciate the unique sense of humor of a familiar blog poster or connect on a personal level with the person cutting your hair. And even the most tyrannical, demanding, by-the-book boss might show an occasional flash of humanity.

Just as there's a personal element in many impersonal settings, there is also an impersonal element in our relationships with the people we care most about. There are occasions when we don't want to be personal: when we're distracted, tired, busy, or just not interested. Sometimes all we want to know about certain friends is what they post on social media sites. In fact, interpersonal communication is rather like rich food—it's fine in moderation, but too much can make you uncomfortable.

Most of us don't have the time or energy to create highly personal relationships with everyone we encounter, either in person or via social media. In fact, the scarcity of qualitatively interpersonal communication contributes to its value. Like precious jewels and one-of-a-kind artwork, interpersonal relationships are special because of their scarcity.

COMMUNICATION PRINCIPLES AND MISCONCEPTIONS

Now that we've looked at definitions and approaches to communication, it's important to identify some principles of interpersonal interaction—and what communication can and can't accomplish.

Communication Principles

It's possible to draw several important conclusions about communication from what you have already learned in this chapter.

Communication Can Be Intentional or Unintentional Some communication is clearly intentional: You probably plan your words carefully before asking the boss for a raise or offering constructive criticism. Some scholars argue that only intentional messages like these qualify as communication. Others contend that even unintentional behavior is communicative. Suppose, for instance, that a friend overhears you muttering complaints to yourself. Even though you didn't intend for her to hear your remarks, they certainly did carry a message. In addition to these slips of the tongue, we unintentionally send many nonverbal messages. You might not be aware of your sour expression, impatient shifting, or sigh of boredom, but others view them nonetheless. Scholars have debated without reaching consensus about whether unintentional behavior should be considered communication, and it's unlikely that they will ever settle this issue.[36] In *Looking Out Looking In*, we will look at the communicative value of both intentional and unintentional behavior.

It's Impossible Not to Communicate   Because both intentional and unintentional behaviors send a message, many theorists agree that it is impossible not to communicate. Whatever you do—whether you speak or remain silent, confront or avoid, act emotional or keep a poker face—you provide information to others about your thoughts and feelings. In this sense, we are like transmitters that can't be shut off.

Of course, the people who decode your message may not interpret it accurately. They might take your kidding seriously or underestimate your feelings, for example. The message that you intend to convey may not even resemble the one that others infer from your actions. Thus, when we talk about "a communication breakdown" or "miscommunication," we rarely mean that communication has ended. Instead, we mean that it is inaccurate, ineffective, or unsatisfying.[37]

This explains why the best way to boost understanding is to discuss your intentions and your interpretations of the other person's behavior until you have negotiated a shared meaning. The perception-checking skills described in Chapter 4, the tips on clear language offered in Chapter 6, and the listening skills introduced in Chapter 8 will give you tools to boost the odds that the meanings of messages you send and receive are understandable to both you and others.

Communication Is Unrepeatable   Because communication is an ongoing process, it is impossible to repeat the same event. The friendly smile that worked so well when meeting a stranger last week might not succeed with the person you meet tomorrow. It might feel stale and artificial to you the second time around, or it might be wrong for the new person or occasion. Even with the same person, it's impossible to re-create an event. Why? Because neither you nor the other person is the same person. You've both lived longer. Your feelings about each other may have changed. You need not constantly invent new ways to act around familiar people, but you should realize that the "same" words and behavior are different each time they are spoken or performed.

Communication Is Irreversible   We sometimes wish that we could back up in time, erasing words or acts and replacing them with better alternatives. As the cartoon here points out, such reversal is impossible. Sometimes, further explanation can clear up another's confusion, or an apology can mollify another's hurt feelings. Other times no amount of explanation can erase the impression you have created. It is no more possible to "unreceive" a message than to "unsqueeze" a tube of toothpaste. The same is true of most electronic messages: Once you hit "send," they can't be taken back. Words said, messages sent, and deeds done are irretrievable.

"We can pause, Stu—we can even try fast-forwarding—but we can never rewind."

Communication Has a Content and a Relational Dimension   Practically all exchanges operate on two levels. The **content dimension** involves the information being explicitly discussed: "Turn left at the next corner." "You can buy that for less online." "You're standing on my foot." In addition to this sort of obvious content, messages also have a **relational dimension** that expresses how you feel about the other person: whether you like or dislike the other person, feel in control or subordinate, feel comfortable or anxious, and so on.[38] For instance, consider how many different relational messages you could communicate by simply saying, "I'm busy tonight, but maybe some other time" in different ways.

Sometimes the content dimension of a message is all that matters. For example, you may not care much about how the customer service rep feels about you as long as you get a technician scheduled to fix your car. At other times, though, the relational dimension of a message is more important than the content under discussion (consider times when a customer service rep has spoken to you in a tone that seemed dismissive or rude). This explains why arguments can develop over apparently trivial subjects such as whose turn it is to wash the dishes or how to spend the weekend. In cases like this, what's really being tested is the nature of the relationship. Who's in control? How important are we to each other? Chapter 9 will explore these key relational issues in detail.

R. Jerome Ferraro/Getty Images

Communication Misconceptions

It's just as important to know what communication is *not* as to know what it is.[39] Avoiding the following misconceptions can save you a great deal of personal trouble.

More Communication Is Not Always Better   Whereas not communicating enough can cause problems, there are also situations when *too much* communication is a mistake. Sometimes excessive communication is simply unproductive, as when two people "talk a problem to death," going over the same ground again and again without making progress. As one communication book puts it, "More and more negative communication merely leads to more and more negative results."[40] Even when you aren't being critical, too much communication can backfire. Pestering a prospective employer after your job interview or texting too many "call me" messages can generate the opposite reaction from what you're seeking.

Meanings Are Not in Words   The biggest mistake we can make is to assume that *saying* something is the same thing as *communicating* it. As Chapter 4 explains, the words that make perfect sense to you can be perceived and interpreted in entirely different ways by others. Chapter 6 describes the most common types of verbal misunderstandings and suggests ways to minimize them. Chapter 8 introduces listening skills that help ensure that the way you receive messages matches the ideas that a speaker is trying to convey. As the old saying goes, "Words don't mean—*people* mean."

Successful Communication Doesn't Always Involve Shared Understanding   George Bernard Shaw once remarked, "The problem with communication... is the illusion that it has been accomplished." This observation may sound cynical, but research (and most likely your personal experience) demonstrates that misunderstandings are common.[41] In fact, evidence suggests that people who are well acquainted may be more likely to misunderstand one another than relative strangers.[42]

Mutual understanding can be one measure of successful communication,[43] but there are times when success comes from *not* completely understanding one another. For example, we are often deliberately vague in order to spare another's feelings. Imagine how you might reply when a friend asks, "What do you think about my new tattoo?" You might tactfully say, "Wow—that's really unusual," instead of honestly and clearly answering, "I think it's grotesque." In cases like this, we sacrifice clarity for the sake of kindness and to maintain our relationships. Some research suggests that satisfying relationships depend in part on flawed understanding. Couples who *think* their partners understand them are more satisfied with each other than those who *actually* understand what the other says and means.[44] In other words, more satisfying relationships can sometimes come from less-than-perfect understanding. Chapter 3 describes in detail the way we sometimes sacrifice clarity for the sake of maintaining relationships.

Communication Will Not Solve All Problems   Sometimes even the best-planned, best-timed communication won't solve a problem. Imagine, for example, that you ask an instructor to explain why you received a poor grade on a project that you believe deserved top marks. The instructor clearly outlines the reasons why you received the poor grade and sticks to that position after listening thoughtfully to your protests. Has communication solved the problem? Hardly.

Sometimes clear communication is even the *cause* of problems. Suppose, for example, that a friend asks you for an honest opinion of the $200 outfit she has just bought. Your clear and sincere answer, "I think it makes you look fat," might do more harm than good. Deciding when and how to self-disclose isn't always easy. See Chapter 3 for suggestions.

WHAT MAKES AN EFFECTIVE COMMUNICATOR?

It's easy to recognize good communicators and even easier to spot poor ones, but what characteristics distinguish effective communicators from their less successful counterparts?

Communication Competence Defined

Defining **communication competence** isn't as easy as it might seem. Although scholars struggle to agree on a precise definition, most would agree that competent communication involves achieving one's goals in a manner that, in most cases, maintains or enhances the relationship in which it occurs.[45] Put another way, competence seeks to be both *effective* and *appropriate*. You can probably think of people who achieve one of these goals at the expense of the other, such as the high-achieving businessperson who regularly ruffles feathers, or the kind and gracious person who doesn't stand up for herself or himself. Competence is a balancing act that requires looking out both for yourself and for others—sometimes a challenging task.[46]

The following characteristics typify a competent communicator.

There Is No Ideal Way to Communicate Your own experience shows that a variety of communication styles can be effective. Some very successful communicators are serious, whereas others use humor; some are gregarious, whereas others are quieter; and some are more straightforward, whereas others hint diplomatically. Just as there are many kinds of beautiful music or art, there are many kinds of competent communication. It certainly is possible to learn new, effective ways of communicating from observing models, but it would be a mistake to try to copy others in a way that doesn't reflect your own style or values.

Competence Is Situational Even within a culture or relationship, the specific communication that is competent in one setting might be a colossal blunder in another. The joking insults you routinely trade with one friend might offend a sensitive family member, and last Saturday night's romantic approach would most likely be out of place at work on Monday morning.

Because competent behavior varies so much from one situation and person to another, it's a mistake to think that communication competence is a trait that a person either has or does not have. It's more accurate to talk about *degrees* or *areas* of competence.[47] You might deal quite skillfully with peers, for example, but feel clumsy interacting with people much older or younger, wealthier or poorer, or more or less attractive than yourself. In fact, your competence with one person may vary from situation to situation. This means that it's an overgeneralization to say in a moment of distress, "I'm a terrible communicator!" when it's more accurate to say, "I didn't handle this situation very well, even though I'm better in others."

Competence Can Be Learned To some degree, biology is destiny when it comes to communication style.[48] Studies of identical and fraternal twins suggest that traits including sociability, anger, and relaxation seem to be partially

∧ In the TV series *House of Cards*, the communication of conniving politician Frank Underwood (Kevin Spacey) is high in *effectiveness* (he almost always achieves his goals and gets his way) but low on *appropriateness* (he routinely damages others and his relationships with them). How would an impartial observer evaluate the moral dimensions of *your* communication?

NETFLIX/Allstar

a function of our genetic makeup. Some research suggests that certain personality traits predispose people towards particular competence skills.[49] For instance, those who are agreeable and conscientious by nature find it easier to be appropriate, and harder to be (and become) assertive and effective. Chapter 3 will have more to say about the role of neurobiology in communication traits.

Fortunately, biology isn't the only factor that shapes how we communicate. Communication competence is, to a great degree, a set of skills that anyone can learn. Skills training has been shown to help communicators in a variety of professional fields.[50] Research also shows that college students typically become more competent communicators over the course of their undergraduate studies.[51] In other words, your level of competence can improve through education and training, which means that reading this book and taking this course can help you become a more competent communicator.[52]

Characteristics of Competent Communicators

Although competent communication varies from one situation to another, scholars have identified several common denominators that characterize effective communication in most contexts.

A Wide Range of Behaviors   Effective communicators are able to choose their actions from a wide range of behaviors.[53] To understand the importance of having a large communication repertoire, imagine that someone you know repeatedly tells jokes—perhaps racist or sexist ones—that you find offensive. You could respond to these jokes in a number of ways:

- You could decide to say nothing, figuring that the risks of bringing the subject up would be greater than the benefits.

- You could ask a third party to say something to the joke teller about the offensiveness of the jokes.

- You could hint at your discomfort, hoping your friend would get the point.

- You could joke about your friend's insensitivity, counting on humor to soften the blow of your criticism.

- You could express your discomfort in a straightforward way, asking your friend to stop telling the offensive jokes, at least around you.

- You could even demand that your friend stop.

With this choice of responses at your disposal (and you can probably think of others as well), you could pick the one that has the best chance of success. But if you were able to use only one or two of these responses when raising a delicate issue—always keeping quiet or always hinting, for example—your chances of success would be much smaller. Indeed, many poor communicators are easy to spot by their limited range of responses. Some are chronic jokers. Others are always belligerent. Still others are quiet in almost every situation. Like a piano player who knows only one tune or a chef who can prepare only a few dishes, these people are forced to rely on a small range of responses again and again, whether or not they are successful.

Many people with disabilities have learned the value of having a repertoire of options available to manage unwanted offers of help.[54] Some of those options include performing a task quickly, before anyone has the chance to intervene; pretending not to hear the offer; accepting a well-intentioned invitation to avoid seeming rude or ungrateful; using humor to deflect a bid for help; declining a well-intentioned offer with thanks; and assertively refusing help from those who won't take no for an answer.

Ability to Choose the Most Appropriate Behavior   Simply possessing a large range of communication skills is no guarantee of success. It's also necessary to know which of these skills will work best in a particular situation. As the Artificial (un)Intelligence reading shows, a response that works well in one setting can flop miserably in another one.

Although it's impossible to say precisely how to act in every situation, you should consider at least three factors when choosing a response. The first factor is the communication *context*. The time and place will almost always influence how you act. Asking your boss for a raise or your lover for a kiss might produce good results if the time is right, but the identical request might backfire if your timing is poor. Likewise, the joke that would be ideal at a bachelor party would probably be inappropriate at a funeral.

Your *goal* will also shape the approach you take. Inviting a new neighbor over for a cup of coffee or dinner could be just the right approach if you want to encourage a friendship, but if you want to maintain your privacy, it might be wiser to be polite but cool. Likewise, your goal will determine your approach in situations in which you want to help another person. As you will learn in Chapter 8, sometimes offering advice is just what is needed. But when you want to help others develop the ability to solve problems on their own, it's better to withhold your own ideas and function as a sounding board to let them consider alternatives and choose their solutions.

Finally, your *knowledge of the other person* should shape the approach you take. If you're dealing with someone who is very sensitive or insecure, your response might be supportive and cautious. With an old and trusted friend, you might be blunt. The social niche of the other party can also influence how you communicate. For instance, you would probably act differently toward an 80-year-old person than you would toward a teenager. Likewise, there are times when it's appropriate to treat a man differently than a woman, even in this age of gender equity. And one study shows that using casual text language (such as "4" instead of "for") will be less successful when emailing your professor than it might be with your friends.[55]

Skill at Performing Behaviors   After you have chosen the most appropriate way to communicate, it's still necessary to perform the required skills effectively.[56] There is a big difference between knowing *about* a skill and being able to put it into practice. Simply being aware of alternatives isn't much help unless you can skillfully put these alternatives to work.

Just reading about communication skills in the following chapters won't guarantee that you can start using them flawlessly. As with any other skills— playing a musical instrument or learning a sport, for example—the road to competence in communication is not a short one. As you learn and practice the

ARTIFICIAL [UN]INTELLIGENCE AND COMMUNICATION [IN]COMPETENCE

Watson, the name for IBM's supercomputer best known for crushing *"Jeopardy!"* contestants at their own game, briefly went from "smart" to "smart ass" with the help of the Urban Dictionary.

According to Eric Brown, the "brains" behind Watson, he and his 35-person team wanted to get IBM's supercomputer to sound more like a real human. In Brown's mind, what better way to learn the intricacies of informal human communication and conversation than having Watson memorize the Urban Dictionary?

The Urban Dictionary, for those who don't know, is comprised of submissions from everyday people and regulated by volunteer editors, who are given an extremely small set of rules to maintain quality control. But for the most part, even with the help of human editors, the Urban Dictionary still turns out to be a rather profane place on the Web.

Watson may have learned the Urban Dictionary, but it never learned the all-important axiom, "There's a time and a place for everything." Watson simply couldn't distinguish polite discourse from profanity. Watson, unfortunately, learned all of the Urban Dictionary's bad habits, including throwing in overly-crass language at random points in its responses. Watson picked up similarly bad habits from reading Wikipedia.

In the end, Brown and his team were forced to remove the Urban Dictionary from Watson's vocabulary, and additionally developed a smart filter to keep Watson from swearing in the future.

For now, Watson will keep doing what it's great at: Helping hospitals diagnose sick patients based on their records and symptoms, and beating the snot out of game show participants. If Watson's brief stint with the Urban Dictionary teaches us anything, it's that artificial intelligence will take a long time to finally learn the complicated, ever-changing ins and outs of human communication.

Dave Smith

MindTap ENHANCE ...

your understanding by answering the following questions, either here or online.

1. Can you think of times when people have used "Urban Dictionary language" in settings where it wasn't appropriate?

2. On the other hand, can you think of times when people have used overly formal language in a situation that called for something more casual?

3. What kinds of guidelines should you follow when it comes to appropriate language use?

communication skills in the following pages, you can expect to pass through several stages,[57] shown in Figure 1.3.

Cognitive Complexity   Social scientists use the term **cognitive complexity** to describe the ability to construct a variety of frameworks for viewing an issue.[58] To understand how cognitive complexity can increase competence, imagine that a longtime friend seems to be angry with you. One possible explanation is that your friend is offended by something you've done. Another possibility is that something has happened in another part of your friend's life that is upsetting. Or perhaps nothing at all is wrong, and you're just being overly sensitive. Considering the issue from several angles might prevent you from overreacting or misunderstanding the situation, increasing the odds of finding a way to resolve the problem constructively. Chapter 4 discusses cognitive complexity—and ways to improve it—in greater detail.

Empathy   Seeing a situation from multiple points of view is important, but there's another step that goes beyond understanding different perspectives.

SKILL *Builder*

Stages in Learning Communication Skills

Learning any new skill requires moving through several levels of competence:

1. **Beginning Awareness.** This is the point at which you first learn that there is a new and better way of behaving. If you play tennis, for example, awareness might grow when you learn about a new way of serving that can improve your power and accuracy. In the area of communication, *Looking Out Looking In* should bring this sort of awareness to you.

2. **Awkwardness.** Just as you were awkward when you first tried to ride a bicycle or drive a car, your initial attempts at communicating in new ways may also be awkward. As the saying goes, "You have to be willing to look bad in order to get good."

3. **Skillfulness.** If you keep working at overcoming the awkwardness of your initial attempts, you'll be able to handle yourself well, although you will still need to think about what you're doing. As an interpersonal communicator, you can expect the stage of skillfulness to be marked by a great deal of thinking and planning, and also by increasingly good results.

4. **Integration.** Integration occurs when you're able to perform well without thinking about it. The behavior becomes automatic, a part of your repertoire.

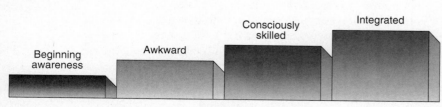

◀ FIGURE 1.3
Stages in Learning Communication Skills

Empathy involves feeling and experiencing another person's situation, almost as they do. This ability is so important that some researchers have labeled empathy the most important aspect of communication competence.[59] Chapters 4 and 8 introduce you to a set of skills that can boost your ability to empathize. For now, it's enough to note that getting a feel for how others view the world is a useful and important way to become a more effective communicator.

Self-Monitoring   Whereas increased cognitive complexity and empathy help you understand others better, self-monitoring is one way to understand yourself better. Psychologists use the term **self-monitoring** to describe the process of paying close attention to one's behavior and using these observations to shape the way one behaves. Self-monitors are able to separate a part of their consciousness and observe their behavior from a detached viewpoint, making observations such as:

"I'm making a fool of myself."

"I'd better speak up now."

"This approach is working well. I'll keep it up."

Although too much self-monitoring can be problematic (see Chapter 3), people who are aware of their behavior and the impression it makes are typically more skillful communicators than people who are low self-monitors.[60] For example, self-monitors are more accurate in judging others' emotional states, better at remembering information about others, less shy, and more assertive. By contrast, low self-monitors aren't able even to recognize their incompetence. One study revealed that poor communicators were blissfully ignorant of their shortcomings and more likely to overestimate their skill than were better communicators.[61] For example, experimental subjects who scored in the lowest quartile on joke-telling skills were more likely than their funnier counterparts to grossly overestimate their sense of humor.

Whereas low self-monitors may blunder through life, succeeding or failing without understanding why, high self-monitors have the detachment to ask themselves the question "How am I doing?" and to change their behavior if the answer isn't positive. This ability can be useful in both personal and professional settings. The President's Council of Economic Advisers maintains that greater "self-awareness, self-monitoring, and self-control" will help students be more successful when they enter the job market.[62]

Commitment   One feature that distinguishes effective communication—at least in qualitatively interpersonal relationships—is commitment. In other words, people who seem to care about relationships communicate better than those who don't.[63] This care shows up in at least two ways. The first is *commitment to the other person*. Concern for the other person is revealed in a variety of ways: a desire to spend time with him or her instead of rushing, a willingness to listen carefully instead of doing all the talking, the use of language that makes sense to the other person, and openness to change after hearing the other person's ideas. Effective communicators also *care about the message*. They appear sincere, seem to know what they are talking about, and demonstrate through words and deeds that they care about what they say.

How do you measure up as a competent communicator? Competence isn't a trait that people either have or do not have. Rather, it's a state that we

SKILL *Builder*

Check Your Competence

MindTap PRACTICE ... your competence as a communicator by answering the following questions, either here or online.

Other people are often the best judges of your competence as a communicator. They can also offer useful information about how to improve your communication. Find out for yourself by following these steps:

1. Choose a person with whom you have an important relationship.

2. In cooperation with this person, identify several contexts in which you communicate. For example, you might choose different situations such as "handling conflicts," "lending support to friends," or "expressing feelings."

3. For each situation, have your friend rate your competence by answering the following questions:

   a. Do you have a wide repertoire of response styles in this situation, or do you always respond in the same way?

   b. Are you able to choose the most effective way of behaving for the situation at hand?

   c. Are you skillful at performing behaviors? (Note that knowing how you want to behave isn't the same as being *able* to behave that way.)

   d. Do you communicate in a way that leaves others satisfied?

4. After reviewing your partner's answers, identify the situations in which your communication is most competent.

5. Choose a situation in which you would like to communicate more competently, and with the help of your partner:

   a. Determine whether your repertoire of behaviors needs to be expanded.

   b. Identify the ways in which you need to communicate more skillfully.

   c. Develop ways to monitor your behavior in the key situation to get feedback on your effectiveness.

achieve more or less frequently. A realistic goal, then, is not to become perfect, but rather to boost the percentage of time when you communicate in ways outlined in this section.

Competence in Intercultural Communication

Throughout history, most people lived and died within a few miles of where they were born. They rarely had much to do with people from different backgrounds. Today is a different story. To use a familiar metaphor, we live in a global village, our lives intertwined with people from very different personal histories and communication styles.

As our world becomes more multicultural, the likelihood of interacting with people from different parts of the world is greater than ever. Given this fact, it's important to realize that what qualifies as competent behavior in one culture might be completely inept, or even offensive, in another.[64] On an obvious level, customs like belching after a meal or appearing nude in public that might be appropriate in some parts of the world would be considered outrageous in others. But there are more subtle differences in competent

Looking at DIVERSITY

Courtesy of Igor Ristic

Igor Ristic: Competent Communication around the World

I was born in Bosnia and spent the first ten years of my life in Eastern Europe. I now live in the United States and have visited more than a dozen countries on five continents. The more of the world I experience, the more I'm inspired to learn how to communicate effectively within and between cultures.

Intercultural communication can be challenging. Take something as simple as customer service in restaurants. Waiters and waitresses in the United States make small talk with their customers, check in with them several times during a meal, and go to great lengths to be friendly and helpful. In contrast, most Eastern European servers quickly take an order, never interrupt diners during a meal, and drop off the bill as inconspicuously as possible. When I first came to the U.S., the friendliness of the wait staffs seemed unusual. Now when I return to Europe, I sometimes perceive their servers as impersonal and curt. Being an effective communicator requires that I remain open-minded and understand the customs of each culture.

This isn't to suggest that Eastern Europeans aren't warm and friendly. In fact, when I talk with family members in Serbia, they often sit right next to me and drape an arm around my shoulder while we chat. After living in the U.S. for more than a decade, I've developed a strong sense of a "personal space bubble"—and I much prefer to sit facing others, at a distance, without touching, while holding a conversation. Those are things I never even thought about while growing up.

What I try to keep in mind is that cultural communication rules aren't "right" or "wrong"—they're simply different. Being a good communicator means I need to be aware of various cultural norms and adapt my communication style as much as possible.

"Competent Communication around the World" by Igor Ristic. Used with permission of author.

communication. For example, qualities like self-disclosing and speaking assertively that are valued in the United States are likely to be considered overly aggressive and insensitive in many Asian cultures, where subtlety and indirectness are considered important.[65]

Even within a single society, members of various co-cultures may have different notions of appropriate behavior. One study revealed that ideas of how good friends should communicate varied from one ethnic group to another.[66] As a group, Latinos valued relational support most highly, whereas African Americans valued respect and acceptance. Asian Americans prized a caring, positive exchange of ideas, and Anglo Americans prized friends who recognized their needs as individuals. Findings like these mean that there can be no surefire list of rules or tips that will guarantee your success as a communicator. They also mean that competent communicators are able to adapt their style to suit the individual and cultural preferences of others.[67]

National and ethnic differences aren't the only dimensions of culture. Within a society **co-cultures** have different communication practices. Consider just a few co-cultures:

- age (e.g., teen, senior citizen)
- occupation (e.g., fashion model, long-distance trucker)

- sexual orientation (e.g., lesbian, gay male)
- physical disability (e.g., wheelchair user, hearing-impaired)
- religion (e.g., evangelical Christian, Muslim)
- activity (e.g., biker, gamer)

Some scholars have even characterized men and women as belonging to different co-cultures, claiming that each gender's style of communication is distinct.[68] We'll have more to say about that topic throughout this book.

Communicating successfully with people from different cultural backgrounds calls for the same elements of competence outlined in what you have just read. But beyond these basic qualities, communication researchers have identified several other especially important ingredients of successful intercultural communication.[69]

Most obviously, it helps to know the rules of a specific culture. For example, the kind of self-deprecating humor that Americans are likely to find amusing may fall flat among Arabs from the Middle East.[70] But beyond knowing the specific rules of an individual culture, there are also attitudes and skills called "culture-general" that help communicators build relationships with people from other backgrounds.[71]

To illustrate the ingredients of culture-general communication competence, imagine you've just been hired to work in a Japanese-owned company in the United States that has manufacturing operations in Mexico and customers around the world. In your new job, you are surrounded by coworkers, supervisors, and clients who come from cultures and co-cultures that are different from your own. You are also required to make occasional trips abroad. How will you handle the communication demands of this position? Ideally, you'll possess the following attributes.

Motivation The desire to communicate successfully with strangers is an important start. For example, people who are high in willingness to communicate with people from other cultures report a greater number of friends from different backgrounds than those who are less willing to reach out.[72] Having the proper motivation is important in all communication, but particularly so in intercultural interactions, because they can be quite challenging.

Tolerance for Ambiguity Communicating with people from different backgrounds can be confusing. A tolerance for ambiguity makes it possible to accept, and even embrace, the often equivocal and sometimes downright incomprehensible messages that characterize intercultural communication.

If you happen to work with colleagues raised in traditional Native American co-cultures, you may find them much quieter and less outgoing than you are used to. Your first reaction might be to chalk up this reticence to a lack of friendliness. However, it may just be a reflection of a co-culture in which quietness is valued more than extraversion, and silence more than loquacity. In cross-cultural situations like this, ambiguity is a fact of life, and a challenge.

Open-Mindedness It's one thing to tolerate ambiguity; it's another to become open-minded about cultural differences. There is a natural tendency to view others' communication choices as "wrong" when they don't match our cultural upbringing. In some parts of the world, you may find that women are not regarded with the same attitude of equality that is common in the West. Likewise, in other cultures, you may be aghast at the casual tolerance of poverty beyond anything at home, or with practices of bribery that don't jibe with homegrown notions of what is ethical. In situations like these, principled communicators aren't likely to compromise deeply held beliefs about what is right. At the same time, competence requires an attitude that recognizes that people who behave differently are most likely following rules that have governed their whole lives. Chapter 4 offers more guidance on the challenges of viewing the world from others' perspectives.

Knowledge and Skill The rules and customs that work with one group might be quite different from those that succeed with another. For example, when traveling in Latin America, you are likely to find that meetings there usually don't begin or end at their scheduled time, and that it takes the participants quite a while to "get down to business." Rather than viewing your hosts as irresponsible and unproductive, you'll want to recognize that the meaning of time is not the same in all cultures. Likewise, the gestures others make, the distance they stand from you, and the eye contact they maintain have ambiguous meanings that you'll need to learn and follow.

Becoming interculturally competent requires *mindfulness*—awareness of your own behavior and that of others.[73] Communicators who lack this quality blunder through intercultural encounters *mindlessly*, oblivious of how their own behavior may confuse or offend others and how behavior that they consider weird may be simply different. When you're in a mindful state, you can use three strategies for moving toward a more competent style of intercultural communication:[74]

1. *Passive observation* involves noticing the behaviors of members of a different culture and using these insights to communicate in ways that are most effective.
2. *Active strategies* include reading, watching films, asking experts and members of the other culture how to behave, and taking academic courses related to intercultural communication and diversity.[75]
3. *Self-disclosure* involves volunteering personal information to people from the other culture with whom you want to communicate.

One type of self-disclosure is to confess your cultural ignorance: "This is very new to me. What's the right thing to do in this situation?" This approach is the riskiest of the three described here, because some cultures may not value candor and self-disclosure as much as others. Nevertheless, most people are pleased when strangers attempt to learn the practices of their culture, and they are usually more than willing to offer information and assistance.

MindTap PRACTICE...
your skill at intercultural communication competence by completing the Concepts in Play activity online.

SUMMARY

Communication is essential on many levels. Besides satisfying practical needs, effective communication can enhance physical health and emotional well-being. Communication also creates our identities and satisfies social needs. The process of communication is not a linear one that people *do* to one another. Rather, communication is a transactional process in which participants create a relationship by simultaneously sending and receiving messages, many of which are distorted by various types of noise.

Interpersonal communication can be viewed quantitatively by the number of people involved, or qualitatively by the nature of interaction between them. In a qualitative sense, interpersonal relationships are unique, irreplaceable, interdependent, and intrinsically rewarding. Both personal and impersonal communication are useful, and most relationships have both elements.

Several principles guide how communication operates. Messages can be intentional or unintentional. It is impossible not to communicate. Communication is irreversible and unrepeatable. Messages have both content and relational dimensions. Some common misconceptions should be avoided when thinking about communication: meanings are not in words, but rather in people; more communication does not always make matters better; communication will not solve all problems; communication—at least effective communication—is not a natural ability.

Communication competence is the ability to get what you are seeking from others in a manner that maintains the relationship. Competence varies from one situation to another. The most competent communicators have a wide repertoire of behaviors, and they are able to choose the best behavior for a given situation and perform it skillfully. They are able to understand others' points of view and respond with empathy. They also monitor their own behavior and are committed to communicating successfully. In intercultural communication, competence involves having the right motivation, a tolerance for ambiguity, open-mindedness, and the knowledge and skill to communicate effectively.

KEY TERMS

channel
co-culture
cognitive complexity
communication competence
content dimension
decode
dyad
encode
environment
impersonal communication

instrumental goals
interpersonal communication
linear communication model
message
noise
receiver
relational dimension
self-monitoring
sender
transactional communication model

CHAPTER ONE

A First Look at Interpersonal Communication

OUTLINE

Use this outline to take notes as you read the chapter in the text and/or as your instructor lectures in class.

I. WHY WE COMMUNICATE	_____
A. Physical Needs	
1. Well-being	_____
B. Identity Needs: Learn Who We Are	
1. Childhood Messages	_____
C. Social Needs	
1. Pleasure	_____
2. Affection	
3. Companionship	_____
4. Escape	
5. Relaxation	_____
6. Control	
D. Practical Goals	
1. Instrumental Goals	_____
a. Influence Other's Behavior	
b. Career Success	_____
2. Maslow's Basic Needs	
a. Physical	_____
b. Safety	
c. Social	_____
d. Self-Esteem	
e. Self-Actualization	_____

II. THE PROCESS OF COMMUNICATION

A. A Linear View

1. Communication Is Something the Sender "Does To" Receiver
2. Linear Elements
   a. Sender
   b. Encodes
   c. Message
   d. Channel
   e. Receiver
   f. Decodes
   g. Noise

B. A Transactional View

1. Communicator Is Simultaneously Sender and Receiver
2. Environments
   a. Physical
   b. Cultural
   c. Experiential
3. Noise
   a. External
   b. Physiological
   c. Psychological

C. Defining Interpersonal Communication

D. Interpersonal and Impersonal Communication

1. Quantitative Approach to Interpersonal Communication
   a. Dyad
   b. Impersonal Communication
2. Qualitative Approach
   a. Uniqueness
   b. Irreplaceability
   c. Interdependence
   d. Disclosure
   e. Intrinsic rewards

III. COMMUNICATION PRINCIPLES AND MISCONCEPTIONS

   A. Communication Principles

      1. Communication Can Be Intentional or Unintentional

      2. It's Impossible Not to Communicate

      3. Communication Is Unrepeatable

      4. Communication Is Irreversible

      5. Communication Has a Content and a Relational Dimension

   B. Communication Misconceptions

      1. More Communication Is Not Always Better

      2. Meanings Are Not in Words

      3. Successful Communication Doesn't Always Involve Shared Understanding

      4. Communication Will Not Solve All Problems

IV. WHAT MAKES AN EFFECTIVE COMMUNICATOR?

   A. Communication Competence Defined

      1. There Is No Ideal Way to Communicate

      2. Competence Is Situational

      3. Competence Is Relational

      4. Competence Can Be Learned

   B. Characteristics of Competent Communicators

      1. Wide Range of Behaviors

      2. Ability to Choose Most Appropriate Behavior

         a. Context

         b. Goal

         c. Knowledge of the Other Person

      3. Skill at Performing Behaviors

         a. Beginning Awareness

         b. Awkwardness

         c. Skillfulness

         d. Integration

4. Cognitive Complexity

5. Empathy

6. Self-Monitoring

7. Commitment

   a. Commitment to the Other Person

   b. Commitment to the Message

C. Competence in Intercultural Communication

1. Co-cultures

2. Learn Specific Cultural Rules

3. Motivation

4. Tolerance for Ambiguity

5. Open-Mindedness

6. Knowledge and Skill

   a. Passive Observation

   b. Active Strategies

   c. Self-Disclosure

KEY TERMS

channel
co-culture
cognitive complexity
communication competence
content dimension
decode
disclosure
disinhibition
dyad

empathy
encode
environment
impersonal communication
instrumental goals
intercultural communication
interpersonal communication
linear communication model
message

noise
receiver
relational dimension
self-monitoring
sender
transactional communication
  model

ACTIVITIES

1.1 COMMUNICATION SKILLS INVENTORY

LEARNING OBJECTIVES

- Identify your communication strengths and weaknesses.
- Create three interpersonal communication goals.

INSTRUCTIONS

1. Below you will find several interpersonal communication situations. As you read each one, think of a similar situation that you have experienced. Take a moment to remember the details of that situation, the outcome, and how you felt about the outcome. If you have never experienced a similar situation, take a moment to imagine yourself in that situation and consider how you might respond, what the outcome would likely be, and how you would feel about that outcome.

2. For each instance, answer the following question: How satisfied am I with the way I would communicate in this situation and ones like it? You can express your answers by placing one of the following numbers in the space by each item:

   5 = Completely satisfied with my probable action
   4 = Generally, though not totally, satisfied with my probable action
   3 = About equally satisfied and dissatisfied with my probable action
   2 = Generally, though not totally, dissatisfied with my probable action
   1 = Totally dissatisfied with my probable action

   1. A new acquaintance has just shared some personal experiences with you that make you think you'd like to develop a closer relationship. You have experienced the same things and are now deciding whether to reveal these personal experiences. (self-disclosure, Chapter 3)

   2. You've become involved in a political discussion with someone whose views are the complete opposite of yours. The other person asks, "Can't you at least understand why I feel as I do?" (empathy, Chapter 4)

   3. You are considered a responsible adult by virtually everyone except one relative who still wants to help you make all your decisions. You value your relationship with this person, but you want to be seen as more independent. (close relationships, Chapter 10)

   4. In a mood of self-improvement a friend asks you to describe the one or two ways you think he or she could behave better. You're willing to do so, but need to express yourself in a clear and helpful way. (improving communication climates, Chapter 11)

   5. A close companion tells you that you've been behaving "differently" lately and asks if you know what he or she means. (perception checking, Chapter 4)

   6. You've grown to appreciate a new friend a great deal lately, and you want to express your feelings to this friend. (close relationships, Chapter 10)

   7. An amateur writer you know has just shown you his or her latest batch of poems and asked your opinion of them. You don't think they are very good. It's time for your reply. (alternatives to self-disclosure, Chapter 3)

8. You've found certain behaviors of an important person in your life have become more and more bothersome to you. It's getting harder to keep your feelings to yourself. (emotions, Chapter 4)

9. You're invited to a party at which everyone except the host will be a stranger to you. Upon hearing about this, a friend says, "Gee, if I were going I'd feel like an outsider. They probably won't have much to do with you." (self-fulfilling prophecy, Chapter 3)

10. A friend comes to you feeling very upset about a recent incident and asks for advice. You suspect that there is more to the problem than just this one incident. You really want to help the friend. (listening to help, Chapter 8)

11. You find yourself defending the behavior of a friend against the criticisms of a third person. The critic accuses you of seeing only what you want to see and ignoring the rest. (improving communication climates, Chapter 11)

12. A boss or instructor asks you to explain a recent assignment to a companion who has been absent. You are cautioned to explain the work clearly so there will be no misunderstandings. (language, Chapter 5)

13. You ask an acquaintance for help with a problem. She says yes, but the way the message is expressed leaves you thinking she'd rather not. You do need the help, but only if it's sincerely offered. (perception checking, Chapter 4)

14. A roommate always seems to be too busy to do the dishes when it's his or her turn, and you've wound up doing them most of the time. You resent the unequal sharing of responsibility and want to do something about it. (managing interpersonal conflicts, Chapter 12)

15. A Facebook friend sent you a message that they'll be visiting in your town and would like to meet you in person. You think this person might be interesting and don't want to hurt their feelings, but you have lots of "real" friends already and aren't sure that you want or need more. (social media, Chapter 2)

By totaling your score for all of the items you can get an idea of how satisfied you are with your overall communication in interpersonal situations. A score of 68–75 suggests high satisfaction, 58–67 indicates moderate satisfaction, while 45–57 shows that you feel dissatisfied with your communication behavior nearly half the time.

Now, identify your three lowest scores. If you have more than three equivalent low scores, choose the three that you feel present you with the greatest challenge. Notice the topic and chapter associated with these items and create three related interpersonal goals. For example, for item 1 you might write, "To improve my interpersonal communication skills, I will pay attention and apply what I learn about self-disclosure in Chapter 3." Or, for item 10 you might write, "To become a more effective listener, I will pay attention and apply what I learn about listening response skills in Chapter 8."

Write your three goals here and review them at the end of the course to check your progress:

1. _____

2. _____

3. _____

1.2 COMMUNICATION PRINCIPLES AND MISCONCEPTIONS

LEARNING OBJECTIVES

- Identify five features of qualitatively interpersonal communication.
- Identify the communication principles expressed in a specific situation.
- Identify the communication misconceptions expressed in a specific situation.
- Reflect on the effects of communication misconception on interpersonal communication.

INSTRUCTIONS

Use the case below and the discussion questions that follow to discuss how communication principles and misconception affect interpersonal communication. Make notes on this page, add other pages on your own, or prepare a group report/analysis based on your discussion. Add your own experiences to individualize the analysis.

CASE

Kristie and Jacob have been dating one another exclusively for four months. They both have part-time jobs and hope to complete their college studies within two years. Jacob thinks they should move in together. Kristie is reluctant to agree until she has more commitment from Jacob. Jacob doesn't want to make promises he can't keep. Kristie thinks that if they just communicate more they will be able to solve the problem, but Jacob thinks that talking about it more won't help.

1. Your text describes five features of qualitatively interpersonal communication. How does Kristie and Jacob's relationship illustrate these features?

    _____

    _____

2. "Communication has a content and a relational dimension" is one of the primary communication principles. Write a conversational dialogue between Kristie and Jacob about their living situation in a way that reflects these two levels of communication—both the content and the relational dimension.

    _____

    _____

3. What communication misconception(s) described in Chapter 1 is expressed in this situation? And how might these misconceptions be affecting their ability to communicate?

    _____

    _____

1.3 ASSESSING COMMUNICATION NEEDS

LEARNING OBJECTIVES

- Assess the needs (physical, identity, social, and practical) that communicators are attempting to satisfy in a given situation or relationship.

INSTRUCTIONS

What's your favorite movie or television show? All dramatic stories are based on characters (even animation with nonhuman characters) trying to get their needs met and running into obstacles.

Remember or re-watch your favorite show and notice how the main characters attempted to meet their social, physical, identity, and practical needs. Include specific examples and comment on the role communication played in their meeting each of the following needs:

Your favorite show: _____

1. Physical needs:

   _____

   _____

   _____

2. Social needs:

   _____

   _____

   _____

3. Identity needs:

   _____

   _____

   _____

4. Practical goals:

   _____

   _____

1.4 UNDERSTANDING THE TRANSACTIONAL COMMUNICATION MODEL

LEARNING OBJECTIVES

- Understand the significance of environments in the transactional communication model.
- Identify the types of noise in a given communication situation.
- Reflect on the effects of noise in a given communication situation.

INSTRUCTIONS

Use the case below and the discussion questions that follow to demonstrate your understanding of the transactional communication model. Make notes on this page, add other pages on your own, or prepare a group report/analysis based on your discussion. Add your own experiences to individualize the analysis.

CASE

Judy and Karen have been friends since childhood, but recently their relationship has been strained. Judy has been attending a local college part time, while she continues to work at a job she's had since high school. Karen left home to go to a college in another state, where she's been having a lot of fun but has been struggling to make ends meet financially. Judy has been dating the same person for 2 years, while Karen has not been on a formal date since she left for college. When Karen comes home on a vacation break, she suggests they meet for dinner and drinks at a busy restaurant. Judy gets delayed at work and arrives half an hour late. Karen is seated and has already finished her first drink. When Judy sits down to join Karen, the conversation does not go well.

1. According to your text, environments are more than just physical places. What role does "environments" have in Judy and Karen's conversation?

   _____

   _____

2. In the transactional communication model, your text refers to three kinds of noise. Explain how each of these three kinds of noise is affecting Judy and Karen's conversation.

   _____

   _____

3. What advice would you give to Judy and Karen to reduce the noise in this specific communication situation and to repair their overall relationship?

   _____

   _____

STUDY GUIDE

CHECK YOUR UNDERSTANDING

TRUE/FALSE

Mark the statements below as true or false. Correct each false statement on the lines below to create a true statement.

_____ 1. Studies show socially connected people live longer than those who are socially isolated.

                   _____

_____ 2. We learn who we are through communication with others and their reactions to us.

                   _____

_____ 3. Communication skills are usually much less important in getting a job than technical competence, work experience, or a degree.

                   _____

_____ 4. Instrumental goals are the same thing as social needs.

                   _____

_____ 5. Psychologist Abraham Maslow claims that basic needs must be satisfied before people concern themselves with higher order needs.

                   _____

_____ 6. The linear view of communication suggests that communication flows in one direction at a time, from sender to receiver or from receiver to sender.

                   _____

_____ 7. Transactional communication is something we "do to" someone else.

                   _____

_____ 8. One feature of qualitatively interpersonal relationships is that a person can be easily replaced with someone else.

                   _____

_____ 9. If we say something we regret, we can always take it back.

                   _____

_____ 10. A quantitative definition of interpersonal communication includes any interaction between two people.

_____

_____ 11. What qualifies as competent behavior in one culture might be completely inept, or even offensive, in another.

_____

_____ 12. Self-monitoring means selfishly paying attention to what everyone else is doing so that you can get your needs met.

_____

_____ 13. Ten minutes per day of socializing improves memory and boosts intellectual function.

_____

_____ 14. Competent communicators are naturally gifted communicators who rarely need to learn new skills.

_____

_____ 15. The term *co-culture* refers to cultures from different countries.

_____

_____ 16. There is no place for impersonal communication in day to day activity.

_____

_____ 17. We can always choose not to communicate if the situation seems too difficult.

_____

COMPLETION

Fill in the blanks with the correct terms chosen from the list below.

instrumental goals	social needs	identity needs	physiological noise
psychological noise	self-monitoring	co-cultures	richness
cognitive complexity	empathy		

1. _____ are the needs we have to define who we are.

2. _____ are the needs we have to link ourselves with others.

3. _____ are the needs we have to get others to behave in ways we want.

4. _____ refers to the forces within a communicator that interfere with the ability to express or understand a message accurately.

5. _____ refers to the biological factors in the receiver or sender that interfere with accurate reception of messages.

6. _____ are groups that shape our perceptions: ethnic, national, religious

7. _____ is the abundance of nonverbal cues that add clarity to a verbal message.

8. _____ is the ability to construct a variety of different frameworks for viewing an issue.

9. _____ is the process of paying close attention to your behavior in order to shape the way you behave.

10. _____ is the ability to imagine how an issue might look from the other's point of view.

Multiple Choice

Choose the letter of the communication process element that is most illustrated by the description found below.

a. encode

b. decode

c. channel

d. message/feedback

e. noise (external, physiological, or psychological)

f. environment

_____ 1. The children make a video of themselves to send to their grandparents instead of writing a letter.

_____ 2. Marjorie tries to decide the best way to tell Martin that she can't go to Hawaii with him.

_____ 3. Martin decides Marjorie means she doesn't love him when she says she can't go to Hawaii.

_____ 4. It's so hot in the room that Brad has a hard time concentrating on what his partner is telling him.

_____ 5. Linda smiles while Larry is talking to her.

_____ 6. Brooke is daydreaming about her date while Allison is talking to her.

_____ 7. Since Jacob has never been married, it's difficult for him to understand why his married friend Brent wants to spend less time with him.

_____ 8. Whitney says, "I'm positive about my vote."

_____   9.   Richard thinks Jon wants to leave when he waves to him.

_____   10. Laura winks when she says she's serious and gestures with her arms.

_____   11. Erin is from a wealthy family, and Kate from a poor one. They have a serious conflict about how to budget their money.

_____   12. Jack has been feeling a cold coming on all day while sitting through the meeting.

Choose the *best* answer for each of the questions below:

13. The concept of co-cultures is closest to the concept of differing
    a. environments.
    b. relational messages.
    c. self-monitoring.
    d. impersonal communication.

14. Martin Buber's concept of communication that is truly interpersonal is called
    a. I-You.
    b. I-They.
    c. I-It.
    d. I-We.

15. Improving intercultural competence involves all of the following except
    a. motivation.
    b. open-mindedness.
    c. knowledge and skill.
    d. avoiding ambiguity.

16. According to the quantitative definition of interpersonal communication, interpersonal communication occurs when
    a. two people interact with one another, usually face to face.
    b. you watch a TV show about relationships.
    c. you read a romance novel.
    d. large numbers of people communicate.

17. All of the following statements are true except
    a. Communication has content and relational dimensions.
    b. Communication is irreversible.
    c. Communication can be unintentional.
    d. Communication is repeatable.

18. All of the following statements are true *except*
    a. Meanings are not in words.
    b. More communication is not always better.
    c. Communication can solve all your problems.
    d. Communication is not a natural ability.

19. Qualitatively interpersonal relationships include all of the following *except*
    a. uniqueness.
    b. intrinsic rewards.
    c. irreplaceability.
    d. dependence.

20. When you are able to perform communication skills without thinking about how you should behave, you have entered the skill stage of
    a. awareness.
    b. awkwardness.
    c. skillfulness.
    d. integration.

21. All of the following are true about communication competence *except*
    a. There is always an ideal way to communicate.
    b. Competence is situational.
    c. Competency can be learned.
    d. Competent communicators are able to choose from a wide range of behaviors.

22. Communication competence seeks to be both
    a. loud and clear.
    b. effective and appropriate.
    c. skillful and concise.
    d. intuitive and cautious.

23. Cognitive complexity is
    a. the ability to solve difficult problems.
    b. the opposite of cognitive simplicity.
    c. the ability to construct a variety of frameworks for viewing an issue.
    d. a way of thinking about complex situations.

24. In becoming a competent intercultural communicator you should
    a. trust the advice of friends.
    b. remain open-minded.
    c. use a linear communication model.
    d. minimize external noise

Class _____   Name _____

CHAPTER ONE STUDY GUIDE ANSWERS

TRUE/FALSE

1. T	4. F	7. F	10. T	13. T	16. F
2. T	5. T	8. F	11. T	14. F	17. F
3. F	6. T	9. F	12. F	15. F	

COMPLETION

1. identity needs
2. social needs
3. instrumental goals
4. psychological noise
5. physiological noise
6. co-cultures
7. richness
8. cognitive complexity
9. self-monitoring
10. empathy

MULTIPLE CHOICE

1. c	5. d	9. b	13. a	17. d	21. a
2. a	6. e	10. c	14. a	18. c	22. b
3. b	7. f	11. f	15. d	19. d	23. c
4. e	8. d	12. e	16. a	20. d	24. b

2

INTERPERSONAL COMMUNICATION AND SOCIAL MEDIA

AFTER STUDYING THE MATERIAL IN THIS CHAPTER, YOU SHOULD BE ABLE TO:

1. Identify the similarities and differences between mediated and face-to-face communication, and identify the relational consequences of choosing each possible channel in a given situation.

2. Describe how the benefits and drawbacks of mediated communication affect a variety of your interpersonal relationships.

3. Comment on how gender and age affect the use of mediated channels, and adapt your use of those channels to best fit a given recipient.

4. Evaluate your online communication competence for ways that you foster positive relationships and protect your own interests.

*T*ake a moment to think about the communication technology you've used recently. Have you logged in to a social networking site such as Facebook or Google +? Posted on Pinterest, Vine, or Instagram? Followed a Twitter feed or updated your own? Read or posted to a blog or message board?

These are all examples of **social media**—forms of electronic communication through which users create online communities.[1] Along with social media, think about the more personal forms of electronic communication that play a role in your interpersonal relationships such as email, mobile phone conversations, and text messaging. All of these channels are forms of **mediated communication**—so named because they all involve connecting through some electronic medium rather than face-to-face interaction.

Imagine how your life would be different without mediated communication channels. How would your relationships suffer? How might they be better?

It wasn't long ago that interpersonal "communication technology" meant using land lines to place phone calls. As little as two decades ago, the most advanced form of technology in most homes was a personal computer. Mobile phones were bulky, expensive, and rare. As a popular tool, email was in its infancy. Social networking sites didn't exist. Today, by contrast, most of us are connected with friends, family, and even strangers in ways that seemed like science fiction a few generations ago.[2] It's not an exaggeration to say that it's a new day and age in interpersonal communication.

This chapter explores the ways that mediated communication shapes interpersonal relationships. We'll discuss how mediated communication is similar to and different from the face-to-face variety. You'll see how electronic communication can help create and sustain interpersonal relationships, and also ways it can create barriers and problems between people. After looking at how gender and age shape the way people interact online, the chapter will conclude with tips on how to communicate more competently when using technology.

Masterfile

∧ Not long ago, "communication technology" meant using a landline telephone. How would your life be different without your everyday electronic devices? In what ways might it be worse? Better?

MEDIATED VERSUS FACE-TO-FACE COMMUNICATION

In today's high-tech world, most people would agree that mediated communication is a valuable—even essential—tool for keeping in touch with coworkers, friends, families, and loved ones. Early theorists didn't share this assumption. In fact, many believed that technology was ill-suited for interpersonal relationships and that mediated communication would replace warm face-to-face interactions with cold electronic exchanges.

When the telephone was introduced in the late 1870s, some experts warned that it would become a poor substitute for face-to-face interaction, and that it would leave behind only a "semblance" of "real world" interaction.[3] Many were afraid of a world where families would be isolated from each other, preferring to communicate electronically, and meeting only occasionally.

Similar fears arose almost a century later when personal computers became popular. Rather than enhancing interpersonal connections, theorists believed that computer-mediated communication would lead to impersonal, task-oriented relationships.[4] They concluded this in part because mediated channels "filter out" nonverbal cues that are available when people communicate in person—eye contact, vocal tone, touch, body posture, and a host of other behaviors described in Chapter 7. This loss of nonverbal and physical cues was expected to render mediated communication emotionless and impersonal—a poor tool for interpersonal relationships.

Several decades of research show that these concerns aren't fully merited—and in some cases, they were downright wrong. As you'll soon read, mediated communication has the potential to both diminish *and* enhance the quality of relationships.

Similarities between Mediated and Face-to-Face Communication

Despite the obvious difference between mediated communication and face-to-face interaction, there are many similarities between the two.

On the JOB

Making Mediated Meetings Productive

The quality may be higher, but the technology for business video chats and conference calls isn't fundamentally different from what you can expect with a decent smartphone: You use voice, and sometimes video, to share ideas, images, and documents with associates.

Don't let the technological similarities confuse you, however. Business meetings—at least among professionals—operate according to a different set of standards than personal conversations. When success is on the line, busy professionals follow some basic but important rules.[a]

- Before the meeting, make sure all participants have the agenda and copies of any documents that will be discussed.

- In phone conversations, parties should identify themselves whenever necessary to avoid confusion. ("Sean talking here with a question for Brenda....")

- Try to avoid interrupting others or leaving out people simply because you can't see them.

- Keep distractions (ringing phones, slamming doors, barking dogs, etc.) to a minimum.

- Use the best equipment possible. Cheap speakers and cameras may make it difficult to understand one another.

You don't have to sound officious or act out of character to meet these standards. The idea is to be a well-organized and efficient version of yourself.

Same Goals   Whether using electronic media or speaking in person, we communicate for the same fundamental reasons described in Chapter 1: to satisfy physical, social, identity, and practical needs. You can appreciate this range of goals by considering the many functions a smartphone serves: calling for help in an emergency, chatting with friends, serving as a status symbol, and connecting you to the Internet from wherever you may be. In many cases, mediated communication is faster and more efficient than face-to-face interaction—but it's still about meeting the same sorts of needs.

Similar Process   All of the components of the transactional model described in Chapter 1 are factors in mediated communication. The process still involves *communicators* sending *messages* through *channels*, and those messages are still affected by *noise* and the communicators' *environment*. And, just like traditional face-to-face communication, mediated channels are capable of supporting *interactivity* through the shared *feedback* between communicators. Of course, the noise in mediated communication might be static on a phone line or unwanted pop-up ads on websites—but these distractions have essentially the same effect on communication as those in face-to-face interactions.

Similar Principles   If you've ever mistakenly clicked "reply all" when sending a confidential message, you know that mediated communication can be unintentional, just like the face-to-face variety. Once the Send button is pushed or a voice message is recorded, the irreversibility of communication comes into play. And if you've ever wondered why someone hasn't returned your text message or isn't responding to your emails, then you know it's impossible not to communicate—because even the absence of a message sends a message. All of these principles outlined in Chapter 1 hold true for mediated communication.

Differences between Mediated and Face-to-Face Communication

Although mediated communication has much in common with face-to-face interaction, there are also some significant differences.

Leaner Messages   Social scientists use the term **richness** to describe the abundance of nonverbal cues that add clarity to a verbal message. Conversely, **leanness** describes messages that are stark from a lack of nonverbal information. Face-to-face communication is rich because it abounds with nonverbal cues that help clarify the meanings of one another's words and offer hints about their feelings. By comparison, most social media offer leaner channels for conveying information.

To appreciate how message richness varies by medium, imagine you haven't heard from a friend in several weeks, and you decide to ask, "Is anything wrong?" Your friend replies, "No, I'm fine." Would that response be more or less descriptive depending on whether you received it via text message, over the phone, or in person? You almost certainly would be able to tell a great deal more from a face-to-face response, because it would contain a richer array of cues: facial expressions, vocal tone, and so on. By contrast, a text message contains only words. The phone message—containing vocal, but no visual cues—would probably fall somewhere in between.

Because most mediated messages are leaner than the face-to-face variety, they can be more difficult to interpret with confidence. Irony and attempts at humor can easily be misunderstood; so as a receiver, it's important to clarify your interpretations before jumping to conclusions. And as a sender, think about how to send unambiguous messages so you aren't misunderstood.

It's important to remember that richer doesn't always mean better. There are times when a lean online message is the best route to take. Maybe you don't want the other person to hear the quiver in your voice, see the sweat on your forehead, or notice the clothing you're wearing, so you send your message via email or text. Moreover, lean messages communicate less information about communicators' personal features. One study found that the text-only format of most online messages can bring people closer by minimizing the perception of differences due to gender, social class, race or ethnicity, and age.[5] When you want people to focus on what you're saying rather than your appearance, leaner communication can be advantageous.

Variable Synchronicity **Synchronicity** is the condition when communicators are all connected in real time.[6] Face-to-face interaction is synchronous, and so are some mediated channels. Phone conversations (via landline, cellular phone, or video-conferencing programs like Skype and Google Talk) match the synchronicity afforded by face-to-face communication.

Other types of mediated communication are **asynchronous**: There's a delay between the time a message is sent and when it's received. Emails, text messages, and social media postings have a lag time ranging from a few seconds to days before they are read. You can also ignore and skim through these sorts of messages—something that's not as easy when you are in the presence of the sender. Asynchrony allows communicators flexibility and choice about when and how to send, receive, and exchange messages. We'll talk about the pros and cons of synchronous and asynchronous communication later in this chapter.

Permanent (and Sometimes Public) Record Sometimes the easy accessibility of old messages is a wonderful thing: you can retrieve important work documents or relive happy times. In other cases, though, you probably wish that the immortal content would disappear, or at least become unavailable to prying eyes.

While some tribunals around the world have propounded a "right to be forgotten,"[7] it's safer to assume that anything you communicate electronically could be available forever. Tweeting about your horrible boss might seem innocuous—until it costs you your job.[8] Postings from Facebook and other social network sites are commonly used as evidence in courts of law—from proving infidelity in divorce cases to arguing that parents are unfit to obtain custody of their children.[9] Although these are extreme examples, they illustrate the importance of carefully considering what you post online, what you allow others to post on your blogs and social network sites, and who has the ability to view and disseminate what you share online.

∧ Concerns about privacy were highlighted when a hacker posted nude photos of film stars including Jennifer Lawrence. Unlike earlier exposés, this time the images were stolen from the private accounts of the victims, suggesting that even "secure" information can become public.

Recent evidence indicates that people are taking notice of the horror stories about people losing their jobs and relationships due to content posted online. For instance, changes in monitoring behavior can be seen on social network sites. Roughly 63 percent of social network site users remove friends, 44 percent delete comments posted by others, and 37 percent un-tag themselves from pictures that others have posted.[10] Although more people are monitoring their online content and restricting profile access to their friends, many still are not. Approximately 40 percent of social network site users do not limit access to their profiles to only friends. It's also worth pointing out that restricting access to *only* hundreds of "friends" is not really the most conservative strategy for privacy management.

With these features of mediated communication in mind, wise communicators realize that the most convenient communication medium may not always be the best one. In a heated face-to-face conversation, the easiest response might be to blurt out something you'll later regret. In such a case, taking the time to compose a thoughtful (and asynchronous) email message could be smart. In other cases, making the effort to share your feelings in person could produce better results than putting them in writing because the face-to-face exchange may be richer with important nonverbal cues. Table 2.1 summarizes the key features of various communication channels. It might be worth consulting when you have choices about the best way to deliver a message.

Consequences of Mediated Communication

At first glance, the differences between mediated and face-to-face communication might not seem especially significant. What does it matter if nonverbal cues are reduced or if messages aren't exchanged in real time? Social

TABLE 2.1 Characteristics of Communication Channels

	SYNCHRONIZATION	RICHNESS/LEANNESS	PERMANENCE
Face-to-Face	Synchronous	Rich	Low
Video Chat	Synchronous	Moderately rich	Low
Telephone	Synchronous	Moderately lean (voice but no visuals)	Low
Voice Mail	Asynchronous	Moderately lean (voice but no visuals)	Moderate (can be stored; typically deleted)
Text Messaging	Asynchronous (but potentially quick)	Lean	Moderate (can be stored; typically deleted)
Email	Asynchronous	Lean	High (often stored; often shared with others)
Social Media Sites	Typically asynchronous	Lean (but can include photos, videos)	High (and very public)

scientists have found that these seemingly small factors can have an impact—sometimes dramatic—on interpersonal communication. We'll look at two such impacts now.

Disinhibition   Research shows that, when online, communicators express themselves more honestly and bluntly with less caution and self-monitoring. Scholars have termed this tendency **disinhibition**.[11] It's easy to understand why people deliver their messages candidly when they don't see, hear, or sometimes even know the target of their remarks. Reduced cues and increased distance can create a sense of "cybercourage" that isn't typical of most face-to-face interaction.

Disinhibition has both pros and cons. On the positive side, communicators often disclose personal emotions more freely through mediated channels. Sociolinguist Deborah Tannen describes how email created a level of disinhibition that transformed the quality of two relationships:

> Email deepened my friendship with Ralph. Though his office was next to mine, we rarely had extended conversations because he is shy. Face to face he mumbled, so I could barely tell he was speaking. But when we both got on email, I started receiving long, self-revealing messages; we poured our hearts out to each other. A friend discovered that email opened up that kind of communication with her father. He would never talk much on the phone (as her mother would), but they have become close since they both got online.[12]

Disinhibition also has a downside. A growing body of research shows that communicators are more direct—often in a critical way—when using mediated channels than in face-to-face contact.[13] Sometimes communicators take disinhibition to the extreme, blasting off angry—even vicious—emails, text messages, and website postings. We'll offer warnings about this kind of behavior later in this chapter.

Hyperpersonal Communication   Leaner messages and asynchronous responses create a climate for what theorists have called **hyperpersonal communication**: an accelerated discussion of personal topics and relational development beyond what normally happens in face-to-face interaction.[14]

VIRTUALLY SEPARATED

Curled up at the foot of my bed, my face inches from the laptop screen, I stared anxiously at the Google chat box. "Will is typing," the box told me, helpfully. Recognizing the stupidity of falling for someone on the Internet does not prevent you from doing it.

With my Skype screen open and my webcam on, I viscerally felt that Will was sitting a foot away on my bed. We started video chatting for hours every night. I learned that he ate take-out for every meal, slept in a series of identical white V-neck T-shirts, and smirked with one side of his mouth when I said something clever.

In the safety of my apartment, I could see Will, but I couldn't touch him. I could summon him when I wanted to talk, but I never knew him in any light other than the one from his bedside lamp. This phenomenon worked in my favor as well. I could call him after a few drinks, when I felt sufficiently talkative and social; I could avoid him if I had videos to edit or blog posts to write. I could say whatever I wanted and risk awkwardness because, at the end of the conversation, one click of the mouse would shut him out of my room.

The irony is that we flock to the Internet for this type of safe, sanitized intimacy, but we want something entirely different. And so—slowly, cautiously—Will and I began circling the question of what it all meant. I wanted to find out. So in early March, I rented a car, begged my professors to let me out of class a day early, and drove 540 miles to spend a long weekend in the midsize city where Will lives.

Will was almost exactly as I expected: thin lips, straight nose, small hazel eyes, glasses. We kissed on the cold, blustery sidewalk as the wind whipped my thoughts around. Mostly, I felt relieved. I thought: "This works in real life. This means something."

But after we kissed and ate pizza and went back to his house, we struggled for things to talk about. In real life, Will stared off at nothing while I talked. In real life, he had no questions about the drive or my work or the stuff that waited for me when I went back to school. He took me out for dinner and read his email while we waited for our food.

In the front hallway, where I stood rubbing my eyes, Will hugged me goodbye and told me to drive safely. He struggled for a closing statement. "It was great to see you," he said at last.

I sat for a long time at his kitchen counter, trying to work out what happened. I didn't like being surrounded by his things. I felt more comfortable in my room, with my things, and with his presence confined to a laptop screen.

Caitlin Dewey

MindTap **ENHANCE** . . .

your understanding by answering the following questions, either here or online.

1 What makes mediated relationships especially appealing?

2 How is communication likely to differ in mediated and face-to-face relationships?

3 In your opinion, what is the best way to transition from mediated to face-to-face communication?

Given time to craft responses, communicators can carefully edit and manage their self-presentation, always putting their best feet forward. (We'll describe the phenomenon of *impression management* in Chapter 3). In a virtual world without bad breath, unsightly blemishes, or stammering responses, relationships often develop at hyperpersonal rates. If you've ever heard stories—or personally experienced—the kinds of intense self-revelations that happen online between people who have never met in person, you understand how mediated communication can be hyperpersonal. Add the dimension of permanence, in which partners can pore over their written exchanges and read deeply into them, and you'll recognize the potentially unique nature of online relationships.

Hyperpersonal communication has both benefits and drawbacks. In one study, researchers found that group members who connected online rated their teammates as more physically and socially attractive, and they reported greater intimacy and affection than did those who communicated face to face.[15] In other words, hyperpersonal communication allowed online groups to quickly form positive relationships to assist in the completion of their tasks.

On the other hand, hyperpersonal communication can be the breeding ground for the kind of relational deception we'll discuss later in this chapter. Healthy relationships usually develop slowly over time, with cautious decisions about personal disclosures. They also typically require some amount of face-to-face interaction. It's no wonder that communicators who create and develop their relationships exclusively online have a difficult time transitioning to face-to-face communication.[16] (For an example, see the "Virtually Separated" reading in this section.)

Clearly there are both benefits and drawbacks to mediated communication, which we'll outline and examine more closely in the following section.

BENEFITS AND DRAWBACKS OF MEDIATED COMMUNICATION

By now you should begin to recognize that mediated communication can be a two-edged sword with both advantages and drawbacks. We'll take time to examine both.

Benefits of Mediated Communication

Steve Jobs, the cofounder of Apple Computer, once suggested that personal computers should be renamed "*inter*personal computers."[17] He had a point: Mediated communication has the potential to bring people together and enhance the quality of their relationships. When it comes to creating and maintaining connections between both strangers and friends, mediated channels offer some distinct advantages.

More Relational Opportunities   In the jargon of scholars, mediated channels offer "low-friction opportunities" to create and maintain close relationships.[18]

Perhaps most notably, social media have revolutionized the world of courtship and dating. Once upon a time, online dating services were viewed as last-ditch options for the romantically challenged. Skeptics questioned how well a computer could match people together and whether relationships started online could be successful in person. Research is putting those concerns to rest. In one survey, over a third of the 19,000 married respondents said their marital relationship began online.[19] When compared with marital relationships that began in person, those that started online had slightly higher satisfaction rates and slightly lower incidences of breakups.

There are good reasons why online dating is so popular.[20] Trying to find a compatible partner outside your own circle can be difficult. Services like Match.com and eHarmony make it easy to meet new people by streamlining the dating process: You can review prospective dates before you invest time and energy in an in-person meeting. As an added benefit, online dating can eliminate some of the initial awkwardness and misunderstandings that often come with courtship.

Social media can also play a role in the startup of nonromantic relationships. Discussion boards, blog sites, and online forums have the potential to create a sense of "virtual community" between strangers.[21] Whether they're fans of a particular sport, backers of a political party, or lovers of Chinese food, like-minded people can find each other on topic-specific websites. Soon the "regulars" recognize and interact with each other, and relationships may form. These virtual community members often provide social support for each other, as we'll explore later in this chapter. The same can occur in distance education, where online students have the potential to connect with each other and their instructors without meeting in person. Educators maintain that creating a sense of community is an important component of successful online classes.[22] Our point here is that mediated communication provides opportunities to initiate relationships beyond those that were available in previous generations.

Communicating online can offer relationship-building opportunities for people who are shy.[23] One study found a positive connection between shyness, Facebook use, and friendship quality.[24] The researchers concluded that social networking services provide "a comfortable environment within which shy individuals can interact with others." Josh Chiles is one such person.[25] In a *Washington Post* article, he explains that when he goes to parties, bars, or restaurants, "I just sit there, hoping someone will talk to me." On social networking sites, however, he's "Mr. Personality." He posts regularly, makes jokes, and registers his likes. He also notes that when he meets digital connections in person, his shyness often disappears. "There is no doubt that Facebook has improved my life in building relationships with other people," Chiles says.

As the Looking at Diversity feature in this section shows, social media can be especially useful for those who find it challenging to get out and about.[26] Mediated friendships can help alleviate lonely feelings.[27] While electronic communication isn't a replacement for the face-to-face variety, it affords relational opportunities beyond the people we meet in person in our daily lives.

Looking at DIVERSITY

Kevin Schomaker

Forging Relationships with Social Media

Building new relationships is tough for me because I have cerebral palsy. I can't move my arms and legs, and I have difficulty speaking. When I'm in face-to-face situations, I usually talk by typing words that get spoken in a computerized voice. This works okay with people who know me, but it isn't an ideal way to start a relationship. People often are so preoccupied with my physical condition that it's hard for them to get beyond that first impression and learn who I am.

Online communication has been great for me because it makes my physical condition almost irrelevant. I met one of my best friends through Facebook. We chatted online for a couple of months before we ever met in person, and later we became suitemates in college because of the relationship we started online. Similarly, I got an email from a student who said she was going to be my Residential Assistant in the fall. I looked her up on Facebook, friended her, and found out we had a lot in common by reading her information page. By the time I arrived at my dorm that year, she and I were already good friends.

For some people, online communication is a nice convenience—but for me, it's been a life-changer. It has increased and enhanced my interpersonal relationships, and for that I'm grateful.

"Forging Relationships with Social Media" by Kevin Schomaker. Used with permission of author.

Sustaining and Enriching Relationships Along with starting new relationships, social media are a powerful way to keep existing relationships strong and to rekindle dormant ones.[28]

Text messaging is the most ubiquitous tool for staying in touch. According to one report, teens between the ages of 12 and 17 text an average of 60 times per day.[29] There are good reasons why texting is so popular. Text messages are discreet and easy to send and receive no matter where you might be. They're also more likely to be read: Over 97 percent of text messages are opened, compared to only 22 percent of emails. And 90 percent of all text messages are read within 3 minutes of their delivery.[30]

As Figure 2.1 shows, texting serves many functions, most of which fall into the category of relational maintenance.[31]

Social networking sites such as Facebook provide another way to maintain relationships. Their asynchronous nature allows friends to stay in touch without having to connect in real time.[32] Of course, there are better and worse ways to do so.

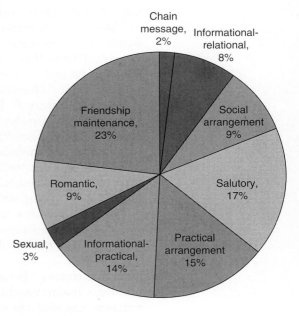

⋏ FIGURE 2.1
Uses of Text Messages in Relational Maintenance

Communication researchers asked hundreds of college students to identify rules specific to Facebook communication.[33] Here are their five most important rules:

- "I should expect a response from this person if I post on his/her profile."

- "I should not say anything disrespectful about this person on Facebook."

- "I should consider how a post might negatively impact this person's relationships."

- "If I post something that this person deletes, I should not repost it."

- "I should communicate with this person outside of Facebook."

Participants said that failure to abide by these rules can jeopardize rather than sustain relationships—and that the closer a relationship is, the more important it is to heed these guidelines.

Blogging is another tool for keeping in touch.[34] One survey found that most bloggers aim their writing at a relatively small audience, and a majority indicated that staying in touch with friends and family is one reason that they publish.[35] This suggests that blogs are often used to maintain existing relationships.

The *masspersonal* quality of blogs—the ability to send personal information to many people at one time—makes it a logical choice for keeping in touch. Imagine that you want to share the news about landing a good job. Delivering the information via phone calls or text messages to your entire network would be cumbersome. Instead, you can inform everyone via a single blog entry. In addition, the interactivity of blogs allows readers to post their own responses (such as congratulations), which creates an environment for further maintenance communication. Toward this end, blogs and other social networking sites provide more maintenance "bang" for the message-sending "buck."[36]

Mediated channels are especially important for sustaining the growing number of long-distance romantic relationships. Some 3 million Americans live apart from their spouses for reasons other than divorce or discord,[37] and between 25 and 50 percent of college students are currently in long-distance relationships.[38] One study demonstrated the value of video chat in maintaining such relationships.[39] For partners who used technologies like Skype and FaceTime, the *number* of daily interactions was lower than those who lived together, but the *quality* of their communication was higher (their exchanges were longer and included more personal disclosures). One researcher explained why: "Seeing someone's face and having those facial expressions really makes a big difference. Sometimes when we're on the telephone, we can be distracted, but if you're sitting down for a video chat, then you're really focused on each other."[40] For reasons such as these, some scholars suggest that interaction via social media can actually be *more* effective than face-to-face interaction in improving the quality of a relationship. [41]

Social Support Before social media existed, getting support for personal problems meant reaching out to friends and family members. Those personal contacts are still important, but today social media provide an alternative source of support for matters ranging from marital problems[42] to substance abuse,[43] suicide prevention,[44] and coping with senseless acts of violence.[45]

Approximately 20 percent of Internet users have gone online to find others with similar health problems.[46] When asked why, a common response is that they feel more comfortable talking with like-minded people with whom they have few formal ties—particularly when the health issues are embarrassing or stigma laden. For example, one study looked at how blogs offer social support for people who are morbidly obese.[47] These sites become interactive communities, where people with similar conditions share their struggles and offer each other affirming feedback. One blogger in the study put it this way: "When I have a bad week on the scale or a problem I don't know how to handle, all I have to do is write up an entry and post it on the blog. My readers are always full of good advice, comments, and support." Because online support groups and blogs are relatively anonymous and the participants are similar, they can offer help in ways that make strangers seem like close friends.

The following reading, *Social Networking, Survival, and Healing*, describes how online social support—some from friends, some from strangers—was a life-saver for one person struggling with substance abuse.

Drawbacks of Mediated Communication

Even at its best, electronic communication isn't a replacement for face-to-face interaction. One study of college students who frequently use text-based messaging concluded that "nothing appears to compare to face-to-face communication in terms of satisfying individuals' communication, information, and social needs."[48] Furthermore, there's an interactive relationship between text-based messages, phone contact, and in-person communication. If you regularly communicate with friends and family online, it is likely that you will also call them and try to see them more often.[49] In other words, few close relationships use mediated channels to the exclusion of in-person communication.

Along with the potential benefits, mediated relationships can have a downside.[50] Understanding the potential drawbacks can help you guard against them.

Superficial Relationships   Social scientists have concluded that most people can only sustain about 150 relationships.[51] (That figure has been termed "Dunbar's number" in recognition of Oxford University anthropologist Robin Dunbar, who established it.) If we're lucky, we have an inner circle of five "core" people and an additional layer of 10 or 15 close friends and family members.[52] Beyond that lies a circle of roughly 35 reasonably strong contacts.[53] That leaves about 100 more people to round out our group of meaningful connections. We simply don't have the time or energy to sustain relationships with many more people.

Dunbar's number is much smaller than the array of "friends" that many people claim on social networking sites. Some Facebook users seem proud to have hundreds or even thousands of social media friends. Dunbar explored the discrepancy between "true" and mediated

"It says no one really knows who he is, but that he's got 400,000 followers on Twitter."

SOCIAL NETWORKING, SURVIVAL, AND HEALING

*T*hroughout 20 years of drinking and drugs, I've always had cyber-friends who, for reasons I can't explain, have stayed up late and saved me more times than I can count.

When I made the decision—or more accurately, when the decision smashed down upon me—to get sober, I was terrified, embarrassed, and angry. I certainly didn't think I needed anyone to help me. Sometime near the end of the third month, the last bits of my sanity were gone. I couldn't function any longer. That's when I turned to the Web. I began to post what I've been told was an ever-increasing series of erratic blurbs.

Those messages started a dialogue that took on a life of its own. I began to get emails, phone calls, text messages, tweets, and other digital notes from people around the world. Some offered kind words. Some offered support. Many people shared their own stories of addiction. In my darkest times, these notes would come. And always, without question, they pulled me back from the brink. Many of these messages were from people I have known for years. Another

handful came from childhood friends and people I'd grown up with. Some I had known well; many I had not. Others came from complete strangers. I have no idea how they found me.

The moment when I knew I'd be okay came one night, during a cross-country drive. The phone rang as I blew through Tennessee, but I didn't recognize the number so I let it go to voice mail. When I pulled into a gas station, I listened to the message. The woman on the phone didn't leave her name, and to this day I have no idea who she was. She told me about her father and his drinking. She told me that she was proud of me for getting sober and that she wanted me to keep trying. Already tenuous with my emotions, I sat on the side of the road crying. I listened to that message dozens of times, over and over.

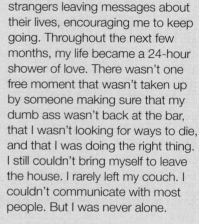

mattjeacock/istockphoto/Getty Images

The encouragement kept coming: strangers leaving messages about their lives, encouraging me to keep going. Throughout the next few months, my life became a 24-hour shower of love. There wasn't one free moment that wasn't taken up by someone making sure that my dumb ass wasn't back at the bar, that I wasn't looking for ways to die, and that I was doing the right thing. I still couldn't bring myself to leave the house. I rarely left my couch. I couldn't communicate with most people. But I was never alone.

AA keeps me sane. But social media got me there. Without that far-reaching network of people—friends and strangers alike—I wouldn't be here today.

Brad K.

Brad K., "Social Networking, Survival, and Healing." Used by permission of the author.

MindTap ENHANCE . . .

your understanding by answering the following questions, either here or online.

1. How often do you give or receive interpersonal support through social media? Consider times when you've exchanged supportive messages via social networking sites, email, texts, or tweets.

2. Can you think of a time when you received social support from someone you didn't know in person—perhaps in an online forum, blog, or support group? Was that support similar to or different from the kind you receive from people you know?

friends by comparing the online exchanges of people with thousands of friends to those who identified smaller numbers of online relationships.[54] He discovered that there was no significant difference between the two groups. Regardless of how many online friends social networkers claimed, they only maintained relationships with the same number of people—roughly 150 people. As Dunbar put it, "People obviously like the kudos of having hundreds of friends, but the reality is that they're unlikely to be bigger than anyone else's."[55]

Besides being superficial, a large number of Facebook "friendships" can actually yield diminishing returns. You may impress others if you list 150 friends in your profile, but research shows that as that number doubles or triples, you're likely to be perceived in less flattering terms.[56] Some scholars have suggested that seeking an unrealistically large number of social media friends might be compensation for low self-esteem.[57]

Keep in mind that superficial relationships aren't all bad. As Chapter 1 explained, some relationships are more impersonal than others, and that's altogether appropriate for acquaintances, many business encounters, or distant relatives. The concern here is when having numerous social media connections is perceived to be a substitute for the kinds of close, interpersonal relationships that human beings need to survive and thrive. Quantity—of friends, of posts, of electronic messages exchanged—is not a replacement for quality.

Social Isolation   There's a correlation between loneliness and what social scientists call a *preference for online social interaction*.[58] The cause-effect relationship isn't always clear, but research shows that lonely people prefer to interact with others online, which can lead to problematic Internet use, which can create a greater sense of loneliness.[59]

Two complementary factors help explain how and why a preference develops for online communication to the exclusion of face-to-face interaction. The first involves social skills—or more accurately, a lack of those skills. People who typically struggle to communicate successfully in person because of nervousness or anxiety can communicate online without facing many challenges. They can edit thoughts and transmit them when and how they want, and they can even construct identities that are more attractive than their in-person presence.

As online interaction proves successful, users' sense of *self-efficacy* (what they believe they are capable of doing) grows. When lonely and socially anxious people who struggle with social interaction offline receive positive feedback from others online, it enhances their self-efficacy. The result? These people begin to feel respected and important online but disconfirmed offline.[60] This leads to an increasing dependence on and desire for online interpersonal interaction.

Unfortunately, the benefits of relying on mediated channels can also come with costs. Research suggests that those who spend excessive time on the Internet may begin to experience problems at school or work and withdraw further from their offline relationships.[61] Retreating further from offline relationships may diminish the already low social skills people had offline to begin with. Although the relationship between problematic Internet use, its negative outcomes, and the preference for online social interaction is well documented, the cause-result relationship is still difficult to determine. Are people socially awkward because they play interactive online games all day— or do people play interactive online games all day because they are socially awkward and can escape a not-so-kind reality?

Relational Deterioration   Social scientists have begun to see a pattern connecting heavy social media usage with relational problems. For instance, one study found a negative relationship between interpersonal intimacy and involvement in online social networking.[62] Other studies have revealed that the mere presence of mobile devices can have a negative effect on closeness, connection, and conversation quality during face-to-face discussions of personal topics.[63] (You can probably think of times when you've heard or said, "Put away that phone and talk to me!"). Some even blame Facebook for relational cheating and breakups.[64] Although holding social media responsible for a relationship's demise may be extreme, it's important to recognize that online affairs are as serious as the in-person variety.[65]

In a broad overview of U.S. demographic data, researchers found a correlation between social network use, marital dissatisfaction, and divorce.[66] Facebook usage in particular emerged as "a significant predictor of divorce rate and spousal troubles." The authors make clear, however, that social media may not be a *cause* as much as a *symptom* of relational problems in that "men and women troubled by their marriage may turn to social media for emotional support." The through line in all of these studies is that time spent online with others can detract from our closest relationships.

∧ Notre Dame football star Manti Te'o won widespread sympathy by talking about the death of his beloved girlfriend. It turned out he had been duped. His romantic partner was actually an elaborate online hoax, orchestrated by a "friend." Have you ever been deceived by social media? How can you protect yourself from future embarrassment and disappointment?

Deception   Nev Schulman, a hip, twentysomething, New York photographer, was flattered and intrigued when a bright, 8-year-old, Michigan girl named Abby began sending him fan mail and paintings based on his work. Nev and Abby struck up an online friendship, and soon he was exchanging increasingly romantic messages with Abby's older sister Megan. Nev was intrigued by the soulful songs Megan claimed to have written and by the beautiful photos of herself she posted online. When Nev and his buddies visited Michigan to meet Megan and her family, they discovered that he had been duped. "Megan" was actually a housewife and mother named Angela. These events were depicted in the movie *Catfish*. Nev parlayed the lessons he learned into *Catfish: The TV Show*, where he tries to help online communicators connect in person. These face-to-face meetings often lead to the uncovering of interpersonal deceit.

Although *Catfish* is an extreme case, misrepresentation occurs frequently in online dating websites.[67] For instance, men and women tend to underreport their weight and overreport their height in online dating profiles. Some online daters rationalize their decision, claiming that it's not really deception since they intend to lose a few pounds in the future. Others explain that identity misrepresentation is a social norm—"everyone else is doing it, so I need to as well." In other cases, online representations are outright lies. People declare

ALONE TOGETHER

We live in a technological universe in which we are always communicating. And yet we have sacrificed conversation for mere connection. We've become accustomed to a new way of being "alone together."

Each of us is in our own bubble, furiously connected to keyboards and tiny touch screens. E-mail, Twitter, Facebook, all of these have their places—in politics, commerce, romance, and friendship. But no matter how valuable, they do not substitute for conversation.

Face-to-face conversation unfolds slowly. It teaches patience. When we communicate on our digital devices, we learn different habits. As we ramp up the volume and velocity of online connections, we start to expect faster answers. To get these, we ask one another simpler questions; we dumb down our communications, even on the most important matters. It is as though we have all put ourselves on cable news.

We expect more from technology and less from one another and seem increasingly drawn to technologies that provide the illusion of companionship without the demands of relationship.

I am a partisan for conversation. To make room for it, I see some first, deliberate steps. At home, we can create sacred spaces: the kitchen, the dining room. We can make our cars "device-free zones." And we can do the same thing at work. Employees asked for casual Fridays; perhaps managers should introduce conversational Thursdays.

Most of all, we need to remember—in between texts and emails and Facebook posts—to listen to one another, even to the boring bits, because it is often in unedited moments, moments in which we hesitate and stutter and go silent, that we reveal ourselves to one another.

Sherry Turkle

MindTap **ENHANCE . . .**

your understanding by answering the following questions, either here or online.

1. To what extent do you prioritize mediated communication when you're in face-to-face encounters with others?

2. How would your important relationships change if you created device-free zones and times?

they are single when they're actually involved in a romantic relationship, and others salt their LinkedIn profiles with jobs they never held. Given the unreliable nature of online self-characterizations, it's probably a good idea to view them with at least a little skepticism.

Along with the moral dimension of deception, research suggests that seriously misrepresenting yourself can damage your reputation, especially with strangers and new acquaintances. In one study, experimenters had college students identify items they thought were misleading on the Facebook profiles of a close friend and an acquaintance.[68] The results of the study indicated that people were more willing to give their close friends "a pass" for their misrepresentations than they were for acquaintances. People were more likely to claim that the misleading information indicated that the acquaintance was a hypocritical and untrustworthy person.

Stalking and Harassment   Have you ever searched the Internet to find out more about someone who you find interesting? Or have you ever used social media to follow the life of a former friend or lover? **Online surveillance** is a discreet way of monitoring the social activities of unknowing targets through social computing spaces.

Although it may seem relatively harmless, research suggests that low-level online surveillance behavior can escalate into unhealthy obsessive behaviors such as "cyber obsessional pursuit" or "obsessive relational pursuit."[69] Taken to its extreme, such behaviors can turn into full-blown **cyberstalking**.[70] One study[71] found that cyberstalkers are typically male, and they're usually monitoring their female ex-partners—but of course, it can happen in any unwanted relationship. Victims who discover they're being cyberstalked suffer the same types of mental and emotional trauma experienced in offline stalking. If you believe you're under unwanted surveillance by someone you know, it's recommended that you alert legal authorities and victim assistance professionals. You also might want to consider getting off the social media grid for a period of time until you feel safe again.[72]

Unhealthy as it may be, cyberstalking isn't as painfully intrusive as **cyberbullying**—a malicious act in which one or more parties aggressively harass a victim online, often in public forums. Cyberbullies can create hateful posts on social networking sites and circulate disparaging texts, emails, and photos about their victims. Cyberbullying has become a widespread phenomenon with some dire consequences.[73] More than 4 out of 10 teens report being the target of online harassment—and the problem is international in scope.[74] Recipients of cyberbullying often feel helpless and scared to such a degree that they are eight times more likely to carry a weapon to school than other students. There are several reported cases in the United States where a victim of cyberbullying committed suicide,[75] which is sobering in light of reports that 81 percent of cyberbullies admit their only reason for bullying is because "it's funny." [76]

Because cyberbullying is a relatively recent phenomenon, researchers are busy compiling data about the process and its outcomes.[77] Here are a few of their findings:

• Although middle school is the peak period for cyberbullying, it can start as early as grade school and continue into the college years and beyond.

- More than a third of contemporary students report being cyberbullied during their school careers.

- Cyberbullying has been linked to a variety of negative consequences, including poor academic performance, depression, withdrawal, psychosomatic pain, drug and alcohol abuse, and even suicide.

A key to stopping cyberbullying is blowing the whistle on the perpetrators. Unfortunately, most adolescents are unwilling to do so for reasons ranging from fear of reprisal to fear of losing their social media privileges. They are far more likely to tell their friends than adults about online harassment, so many school programs encourage peer-led support and intervention.

Cyberbullying will remain a problem as long as it stays a secret. If you're being bullied online, keep copies of the harassing messages—and then contact an appropriate teacher, administrator, or supervisor. Most schools and companies have policies that can help provide protection. And if you know someone who is being victimized—especially if it's a young person—be receptive and help arrange professional intervention. Open communication is vital to bringing cyberbullying out of the shadows.

INFLUENCES ON MEDIATED COMMUNICATION

Who we are determines, in part, the way we use social media and other forms of mediated communication. Two of the strongest influences on personal use are gender and age.

Gender

Men and women communicate differently online.[78] Researchers using word-count programs found that men tend to use more large words, nouns, and swear words than women do. On the other hand, females use more personal pronouns, verbs, and hedge phrases ("I think"). Of course, word count doesn't tell the whole story. For instance, while males and females use the word "we" about equally, they do so in different ways. Closer scrutiny suggests that women are more likely to use what's known as the "warm we" ("We have so much fun together"), while men are more inclined toward the "distant we" ("We need to do something about this"). It's also worth noting that the computer programs used for these analyses aren't foolproof: They can correctly identify the sex of an author about 72 percent of the time (50 percent is chance). In other words, while there are indeed gender tendencies in language usage, they aren't absolute.

Data gathered from social networking sites show even greater distinctions. In one study, researchers analyzed more than 15 million Facebook status

FIGURE 2.2 >
This word cloud depicts distinctive phrases, topics, and words used by women in Facebook statuses.
Source: Schwartz, H. A. et al. (2013). Personality, gender, and age in the language of social media: The open-vocabulary approach. PLoS ONE, 8, e73791.

updates from approximately 75,000 volunteers over a 34-month period.[79] There were marked differences in male and female language usage. Females used more emotion words and first-person singular pronouns. Men made more object references (talking about things rather than people) and swore far more often. Figure 2.2 shows a word cloud identifying some of the topics and terms that were distinctive to women in the study. The corresponding male word cloud—which is quite different—isn't provided because it contains too many swear words to publish here. That finding seems to hold true across every study conducted about male and female word usage: Men swear more than women.

It appears that people are intuitively aware of gender differences in online language. For instance, one study found that online communicators adopt different writing styles depending on their online gender identities.[80] Participants were given randomly selected gendered avatars—some matching their biological sex, some not. Communicators who were assigned feminine avatars expressed more emotion, made more apologies, and used more tentative language than did those with masculine avatars. In other words, participants adapted their language to match linguistic gender stereotypes.

Online language differences between the sexes are more pronounced among adolescents. A study looked at the word choices of teenage boys and girls in chat rooms.[81] The teen males were more active and assertive, initiating interaction and making proposals, while the females were more reactive ("wow," "omg," "lmao"). The boys were also more flirtatious and sexual ("any hotties wanna chat?"). The researchers noted that these accentuated differences were probably due to the age of the participants and that some of the distinctions would likely recede in adulthood.

Age

If you're a *digital native* who was born after the early 1990s, mediated communication probably feels as natural as breathing. It's a different story for many *digital immigrants* who grew up in a world without the technology that we take for granted today.[82] If you have firsthand experience with telegrams, floppy disks, and dial-up modems, you're a digital immigrant. If technologies like these seem almost as remote as the Pony Express, you're probably a digital native.

Age isn't the only factor determining digital natives—socioeconomic status and country of origin also play roles. Nevertheless, there are some clear trends in the preferred communication modes for different generations. It's probably no surprise that texting, emailing, and telephoning form a young-to-old continuum, with teens loving texting and older communicators preferring e-messages and phone conversations.[83] Many young adults strongly favor texting to voice calls,[84] viewing the latter as annoying and even intrusive.[85] Contemporary parent-child arguments often include "Why don't you just call?" followed by "Why don't you just text me back?" It's also not surprising that younger communicators use social networking sites more than older communicators do, although the gap isn't as large as it used to be.[86]

These age distinctions may not hold true in the future. Today's texting teen won't necessarily become an emailer in middle age, and older communicators (sometimes called "silver surfers") are joining the digital revolution at rapid rates.[87] But for now, knowing generational tendencies can be helpful when choosing a communication channel. You might want to consider the age of your message recipient when deciding to text, email, or call. Your choice may have a bearing on when—or even whether—you get a response.

Along with channel preferences, age also shapes what topics people discuss when using mediated communication. The same study that produced the word cloud in Figure 2.2 also analyzed age differences in more than 15 million Facebook posts.[88] Here are some of the findings:

- Not surprisingly, school was a major topic for 13- to 18-year-olds. Typical terms in teens' messages include "homework," "math," and "prom." Abbreviations such as "lol," "jk," and "<3" were also common.

- 19- to 22-year-olds post often about college. Typical terms include "semester," "studying," and "campus." Other lifestyle choices were also prominent: "drunk," "tattoo," and a host of swear words.

- By their mid-20s, the content shifted to more mature topics including "office," "pay/paying," and "wedding." But communication isn't all about obligations and commitments: "beer" was still a common term.

- 30- to 65-year-olds post often about family. Typical terms include "daughter/son," "pray/prayer," "friends," and "country."

The age range of the final category was so broad because there were fewer older Facebook participants in the study—something the researchers believe will change over time. One final result of interest: Beginning at age 22, use of the word "we" in Facebook posts increases in linear fashion, while use of "I" decreases. This suggests the increasing importance of friendships and relationships as people age.

COMPETENCE IN SOCIAL MEDIA

The principles of interpersonal competence described throughout this book apply to online communication. In addition, communicating via social media calls for a unique set of skills.

Fostering Positive Relationships

"Etiquette" may seem like an old-fashioned term—but whatever label you use, mostly unspoken rules of conduct still keep society running smoothly. The unique nature of social media requires its own set of civil behaviors, which some refer to as "netiquette."[89]

Respect Others' Need for Undivided Attention   If you've been texting since you could master a keypad, it might be hard to realize that some people are insulted when you divide your attention between your in-person conversational partner and distant contacts. As one observer put it, "While a quick log-on may seem, to the user, a harmless break, others in the room receive it as a silent dismissal. It announces: 'I'm not interested.'"[90]

Keep Your Tone Civil   If you've ever posted a snide comment on a blog, shot back a nasty reply to a text or instant message, or forwarded an embarrassing email, you know that it's easier to behave badly when the recipient of your message isn't right in front of you. After receiving an abusive, insulting email in response to a piece he had published, one writer noted how and why people tend to be more abusive online than in person:

> The guy couldn't have said this to me on the phone, because I would have hung up and not answered if the phone rang again, and he couldn't have said it to my face, because I wouldn't have let him finish. If this had happened to me in the street, I could have used my status as a physically large male to threaten the person, but in the online world my size didn't matter. I suppose the guy could have written me a nasty letter: he probably wouldn't have used the word "rectum," though, and he probably wouldn't have mailed the letter; he would have thought twice while he was addressing the envelope. But the nature of email is that you don't think twice. You write and send.[91]

One way to behave better in asynchronous situations is to ask yourself a simple question before you send, post, or broadcast: Would you deliver the same message to the recipient in person? If your answer is no, then you might want to think before hitting "send."

Don't Intrude on Bystanders   Everyone has suffered from rude technology use by moviegoers whose screens distract other viewers, restaurant patrons whose phone voices infringe on your conversation, pedestrians who are more focused on their handheld device than on avoiding others, or people in line who are trying to pay the cashier and talk on their cell phone at the same time. If you aren't bothered by this sort of behavior, it can be hard to feel sympathetic with others who are offended by it. Nonetheless, this is another situation where the "Platinum Rule" applies: Consider treating others the way they would like to be treated.

Protecting Yourself

Being considerate of others is an important goal when communicating via social media. However, it's equally important to look out for yourself. Here are some cautions to consider when communicating online.

Think Before You Post   Because the Internet never forgets, personal information posted today can haunt you in the future. A society in which everything is recorded will, as one scholar put it, "forever tether us to all our past actions, making it impossible, in practice, to escape them."[92]

ETHICAL *Challenge*

The Ethics of Online Anonymity

"The promise of the Internet," writes digital reporter Ricardo Bilton, "is the opportunity to have a two-way dialogue. Anyone visiting a publisher's comment section, however, might wonder whether that's a promise or a threat."[a]

Indeed, online comments often devolve into nasty diatribes and vicious arguments, emboldened by the anonymity of the people who post them. As a result, some publishers are doing away with online comment sections. Others require identifying information—for instance, mandating the use of Facebook accounts and real names in order to post. But even when commenters identify themselves, they still tend to be more disinhibited online than they would be in person— often to the detriment of civil dialogue.

Philosopher Hubert Dreyfus acknowledges that the relative anonymity of the Internet "frees people to develop new and exciting selves."[b] However, that can come at the cost of interpersonal commitment.

He notes that when online messages are offered without the risks and consequences inherent in face-to-face dialogue, it compromises genuine identities and relationships.

It's important to remember the potential value of anonymous communication, especially in public affairs. Without fear of reprisal, whistleblowers and witnesses can call out abuses and injustices. But in most social media, the veil of anonymity simply provides cover for insensitive and hurtful comments that few people would make if their identity was known.

MindTap® **APPLY . . .** the ethical principle(s) introduced here by answering the following questions, either here or online.

1 Does the obligation to communicate in a civil, respectful way differ in online posts and face-to-face communication?

2 Are there ever instances in your life when it's justifiable to post anonymously?

Carl Casper/Allstar

∧ In the movie *Chef*, Carl Casper (Jon Favreau) impulsively tweets nasty remarks about a critical reviewer. His rant goes viral and destroys his professional reputation. Have you ever posted something that you later regretted? What steps can you take to prevent that from happening in the future?

Personal information can be especially damaging to your career. According to some surveys, 70 percent of recruiters in the United States have rejected candidates because of information found online—photographs, comments by and about the candidate, and membership in groups.[93] We'll discuss the role of social media in impression management—and "reputation management"—in Chapter 3.

For one cautionary tale about how your digital indiscretions can haunt you, consider the case of Stacy Snyder. The 25-year-old high school teacher in training posted a photo that showed her in costume at a party wearing a pirate hat and drinking from a plastic cup. The caption read "Drunken Pirate." Snyder's supervisor at the high school announced that the photo was "unprofessional," and officials at the university where she was enrolled said she was promoting drinking in virtual view of her underage students. A few days before Snyder's graduation ceremony, the university denied her a teaching degree.

Stories like this abound. A 16-year-old British girl lost her office job for complaining on Facebook, "I'm so totally bored!!" A 66-year-old Canadian psychotherapist was permanently banned from visiting the United States after a border guard's Internet search found that he had written an article in a philosophy journal describing his experiments with LSD thirty years earlier.[94] While you could make a case that such treatment is unfair, the point is that a little discretion could save a lot of trouble.

An especially dangerous kind of indiscretion is the practice of "sexting"— sharing explicit photos of one's self or others via mediated channels. One survey revealed that 10 percent of young adults between the ages of 14 and 24 have texted or emailed a nude or partially nude image of themselves to someone else, and 15 percent have received such pictures or videos of someone else they know.[95] Perhaps even more disturbing, 8 percent reported that they had received a nude or partially nude image of someone they knew from a third party.[96] The impulsive message or post that seems harmless at the time can haunt you for a lifetime.

Verify What You See Online   Because so much information exists on the Internet, it can be difficult to determine what is truthful and what is not. Take, for instance, a Facebook profile. Almost all of that information is selectively self-presented and under control of the profile owner. So is it truthful or a lie? What about information on someone's personal blog? Or Twitter page? One way to discern the veracity of information is to evaluate its *warranting value*—the degree to which information is controllable by the person being described.[97] For instance, a reporter-written newspaper article featuring your achievements has a higher warranting value than if you were to post the same information yourself to your Facebook profile. This is because self-authored information carries the potential for selective self-presentation.

Research has shown that people evaluate the warranting value of information when they form impressions of others.[98] When asked to judge a person's physical attractiveness using information on a Facebook profile, friends' wall posts were crucial pieces of information when determining if someone was "hot or not." When friends posted statements that confirmed the profile-owner's physical attractiveness ("Hey Gorgeous! You're bringing sexy back!"), people rated her as being very pretty. But when friends didn't confirm her beauty, people were less likely to think she was physically attractive. Because the profile-owner had no control over what her friends' posted to her wall, people viewing the profile judged these statements as more truthful than anything the profile-owner posted about herself.

On a more serious level, it's important not to fall victim to the kind of hoaxes described earlier in the "Deception" section. Nev Schulman of *Catfish* fame offers these tips on how not to plunge into the dark side of virtual romance:[99]

- If it seems too good to be true, it probably is. Proceed with caution and make the other person earn your trust before telling too much about yourself.

- Get proof that the other person exists. Ask for photos of the person holding something specific that you've requested.

- Use a webcam and communicate with the other person visually and in real time.

- Be yourself and know what you want. It's easy to get wrapped up in a fairy-tale version of love, but remember real life isn't a fairy tale or a movie. Love takes work.

Balance Mediated and Face Time   Being connected 24/7 can steal time from in-person communication. Research confirms what common sense suggests: "face time" is still important.[100] Overuse of social media can range from slightly abnormal to borderline obsessive. For instance, online gaming—especially intensive role-playing games—can decrease the relational satisfaction of marriage partners.[101] Overuse of online communication (to the exclusion of the in-person variety) can lead to loneliness and other negative consequences.[102]

How much online time is too much? If your loved ones hint—or directly tell you—that they would like more face time with you, it's probably wise to heed their request. And if you find that technological devices are subtracting from, rather than adding to, your interpersonal relationships, it might be time to monitor and limit your use of social media. Beyond those common sense standards, here are some other indicators that you are probably spending too much time online, culled from a diagnostic tool:[103]

- Failure to resist the urge to use the Internet

- Increase in time needed online to achieve satisfaction

- Time of Internet use exceeding the amount anticipated or intended

"I wonder what our phones are doing right now."

- Failure in attempts to reduce Internet use
- Internet use resulting in failure to fulfill responsibilities at work, home, or school
- Important social or recreational activities are given up or reduced

PAUSE *and* REFLECT

How Do You Use Social Media?

MindTap® **REFLECT** . . . on your own communication by answering the following questions, either here or online.

Respond to each of the statements below using a scale from 1 to 6, where 1 = strongly disagree and 6 = strongly agree. Consider inviting someone who knows you well to also rate you on each item.

For this assessment, the term *social media* refers primarily to social networking sites such as Facebook, but also to text messaging, tweeting, instant messaging, and emailing.

_____ 1. I feel disconnected from friends when I am not logged in to social media.

_____ 2. I would like it if everyone used social media to communicate.

_____ 3. I would be disappointed if I could not use social media at all.

_____ 4. I get upset when I can't log in to social media.

_____ 5. I prefer to communicate with others mainly through social media.

_____ 6. Social media play an important role in my social relationships.

Add your responses from 1 through 6. The total is your "Social Integration and Emotional Connection" score—a measure of how social media are integrated into your daily life and the extent to which you have an emotional connection to your use of social media. The average college student scores about 18 on this instrument. Did you score higher or lower? As you consider your score, answer the following questions:

1. Are you more interested in interacting with friends via social media than in person? If you are, what might you be missing?

2. What's a healthy balance of mediated and face-to-face communication in your life?

Adapted from: Jenkins-Guarnieri, M. A., Wright, S. L., & Johnson, B. (2013). Development and validation of a social media use integration scale. *Psychology of Popular Media Culture, 2,* 38–50.

SUMMARY

Social media are forms of electronic communication through which users create online communities. Mediated communication refers to all the channels that connect people through some electronic medium rather than via face-to-face interaction. In today's world, technology plays an important role in most people's interpersonal communication.

Mediated communication is similar to the face-to-face variety in that the goals are the same, as are most of the processes and principles. On the other hand, mediated messages are typically leaner, less synchronous, and more permanent. These factors can lead online communicators to be more disinhibited and hyperpersonal than they would be in person.

Communicating through mediated channels can enhance relational opportunities. Interacting through social media can also help sustain and enrich relationships and provide a means for social support. On the other hand, mediated communication can play a role in more superficial relationships, social isolation, and relational deterioration. The potential for deception and harassment can also be downsides of communicating online.

Gender and age influence how people communicate through mediated channels. A variety of tendencies distinguish male and female interaction online, as well as the patterns of younger and older communicators.

To become a more competent online communicator, it's important to engage in a measure of "netiquette" to foster positive relationships. This includes respecting others' need for undivided attention, keeping your tone civil, and not intruding on bystanders. It's also important to protect yourself by thinking before you post, verifying what you see online, and balancing mediated and face time.

KEY TERMS

asynchronous
cyberbullying
cyberstalking
disinhibition
hyperpersonal communication
leanness

mediated communication
online surveillance
richness
social media
synchronicity

CHAPTER TWO

Interpersonal Communication and Social Media

OUTLINE

Use this outline to take notes as you read the chapter in the text and/or as your instructor lectures in class.

I. MEDIATED VS. FACE-TO-FACE COMMUNICATION

  A. Similarities between Mediated and Face-to-Face Communication

    1. Same Goals

    2. Similar Process

    3. Similar Principles

  B. Differences between Mediated and Face-to-Face Communication

    1. Leaner Messages

    2. Variable Synchronicity

    3. Permanent (and Sometimes Public) Record

  C. Consequences of Mediated Communication

    1. Disinhibition

    2. Hyperpersonal Communication

II. BENEFITS AND DRAWBACKS OF SOCIAL MEDIA

  A. Benefits

    1. More Relational Opportunities

    2. Sustaining and Enriching Relationships

    3. Social Support

  B. Drawbacks

    1. Superficial Relationships

    2. Social Isolation

    3. Relational Deterioration

    4. Deception

    5. Stalking and Harassment

III. INFLUENCES ON MEDIATED COMMUNICATION

A. Gender

B. Age

IV. COMPETENCE IN SOCIAL MEDIA

A. Fostering Positive Relationships

    1. Respect Others' Need for Undivided Attention

    2. Keep Your Tone Civil

    3. Don't Intrude on Bystanders

B. Protecting Yourself

    1. Think Before You Post

    2. Verify What You See Online

    3. Balance Mediated and Face Time

_____

_____

_____

_____

_____

_____

KEY TERMS

asynchronous
cyberbullying
cyberstalking
disinhibition
hyperpersonal communication
leanness

low-friction opportunities
masspersonal
mediated communication
netiquette
online surveillance
richness

self-efficacy
social isolation
social media
synchronicity
warranting value
virtual community

ACTIVITIES

2.1 MEDIATED COMMUNICATION SELF-ASSESSMENT

LEARNING OBJECTIVES

- Assess your use of mediated communication and face-to-face communication.
- Understand the impact of your use of mediated communication in particular situations and relationships.
- Reflect on the overall effects of your use of mediated communication.

INSTRUCTIONS

Answer the questions below. Then, in small- or large-group discussion, compare your experiences with classmates.

1. Observe your communication over the course of an entire day. What percentage of your time do you communicate through mediated channels? What percentage is face-to-face?

    _____

    _____

2. In general, do you prefer email, phone, text-messaging, or other mediated communication or face-to-face communication? Why or why not?

    _____

    _____

3. Specifically, when and why do you choose email, phone, text-messaging, or other mediated communication or face-to-face communication with instructors, family, friends, coworkers, or supervisors? How have those choices affected those relationships?

    _____

    _____

4. Is your use of mediated communication specific to particular situations, such as quick conversations, sharing pictures, or avoiding uncomfortable conversations? What has been the impact of your choices in those types of situations?

    _____

    _____

5. Does your choice of mediated communication or face-to-face communication vary with the person's age, gender, or relational dynamic? How have those choices affected those relationships?

_____

_____

6. In general, how do you think your relationships are affected when you use mediated communication rather than face-to-face communication?

_____

_____

2.2 MESSAGE RICHNESS AND LEANNESS

LEARNING OBJECTIVES

- Create messages reflecting richness and leanness in specific situations.
- Understand the impact of message richness and leanness.
- Choose effective message richness or leanness in specific situations.

INSTRUCTIONS

1. Read the situations below. In the corresponding spaces provided, fill in the messages reflecting richness or leanness, as requested. Then, answer the questions that follow.
2. If you are working in a group, after all have finished, compare the responses of group members.

EXAMPLE

You haven't heard from a close friend in several weeks. You decide to ask if anything is wrong.

Face-to-Face Richness:	Mediated Leanness: Type (text, email, Facebook, etc.):
Your Verbal Message: "Is anything wrong?	Your Verbal Message: "Is anything wrong?"
Your Nonverbal Message: Facial expression of concern, eye contact, sincere tone of voice	No Nonverbal Message:
Friend's Verbal Response: "Thank you for asking. I have been overwhelmed with school and work lately." Friend's Nonverbal Response: Smile, warm eye contact, tone of voice	Friend's Verbal Response: "So now you're pissed off because I haven't been in touch! Like I have time to worry about you too. I have been super busy with school and work lately."

QUESTIONS:

1. In this situation, is face-to-face or mediated communication more effective?
2. What changes could you make to improve the outcomes in this communication situation?

SITUATION

1. You are arranging to meet with a classmate to work on a group project and need to choose a time and place.

Face-to-Face Richness:	Mediated Leanness: Type (text, email, Facebook, etc.):
Your Verbal Message:	Your Verbal Message:
Your Nonverbal Message:	No Nonverbal Message:
Classmate's Verbal Response:	Classmate's Verbal Response:

QUESTIONS:

1. In this situation, is face-to-face or mediated communication more effective?
2. What changes could you make to improve the outcomes in this communication situation?

SITUATION

2. You rely on your car for school and work, and it needs an unexpected repair. You need to ask to borrow money from a family member.

Face-to-Face Richness:	Mediated Leanness: Type (text, email, Facebook, etc.):
Your Verbal Message:	Your Verbal Message:
Your Nonverbal Message:	No Nonverbal Message:
Classmate's Verbal Response:	Classmate's Verbal Response:

QUESTIONS:

1. In this situation, is face-to-face or mediated communication more effective?
2. What changes could you make to improve the outcomes in this communication situation?

SITUATION

3. The last time you saw the person you've been dating, he or she promised to be in touch in a couple of days. It's been a week, you still haven't heard from him or her, and you need to communicate about an upcoming event you had planned to attend together.

Face-to-Face Richness:	Mediated Leanness: Type (text, email, Facebook, etc.):
Your Verbal Message:	Your Verbal Message:
Your Nonverbal Message:	No Nonverbal Message:
Classmate's Verbal Response:	Classmate's Verbal Response:

QUESTIONS:

1. In this situation, is face-to-face or mediated communication more effective?
2. What changes could you make to improve the outcomes in this communication situation?

2.3 VIRTUAL INTIMACY

LEARNING OBJECTIVES

- Understand how disinhibition and hyperpersonal communication contribute to virtual intimacy.
- Relate the Chapter 1 concepts of communication needs and qualitative relationship to mediated communication.
- Understand the relationship developmental differences between face-to-face and mediated communication.

INSTRUCTIONS

Reread Virtually Separated on page 40 of your text. Answer the questions below. Then, in small or large group discussion, compare your experiences with classmates.

1. Describe Caitlin and Will's relationship prior to meeting in person. Did they share more than a face-to-face communication or less? Did they know more about each other than they would have in a face-to-face communication or less?

   _____

   _____

2. Reflecting on what you learned in Chapter 1 about the reasons we communicate (physical needs, social needs, identity needs, instrumental needs), which of Caitlin and Will's communication needs was their relationship fulfilling?

   _____

   _____

3. Reflecting on what you learned in Chapter 1 about the qualitative approach to relationships (relationships which include uniqueness, irreplaceability, interdependence, disclosure, and intrinsic rewards), would you consider Caitlin and Will's relationship prior to meeting *qualitative*? Why or why not?

   _____

   _____

4. Describe Caitlin and Will's meeting. What happened? Why do you think they had difficulty with face-to-face communication?

   _____

   _____

2.4 DEVICE-FREE ZONES

LEARNING OBJECTIVES

- Understand the impact of devices on relationships.
- Analyze the pros and cons of creating device-free zones.
- Engage in active discussion about the pros and cons of device-free zones.

INSTRUCTIONS

Answer the questions below. Then divide the class or a larger class group into three subgroups. One subgroup will argue *for* device-free zones, and the second subgroup will argue *against* device-free zones. The third subgroup will act as judges. The two subgroups who present will support their positions to the judging group, who will then decide which side has presented the best case. The entire group will then have an open discussion about the pros and cons of device-free zones.

1. Give three reasons why you think there SHOULD be device-free zones?

   _____

   _____

2. Give three reasons why you think there SHOULD NOT be device-free zones?

   _____

   _____

3. In addition to places that are already device-free zones (hospitals, jails, etc.), name three places that SHOULD be device-free zones. Name three places that SHOULD NOT be device-free zones.

   _____

   _____

4. Would your life be better or worse if there were more device-free zones? Explain your answer.

   _____

   _____

5. Who should decide whether or not a place is designated a device-free zone?

   _____

   _____

STUDY GUIDE

CHECK YOUR UNDERSTANDING

TRUE/FALSE

Mark the statements below as true or false. Correct each false statement on the lines below to create a true statement.

_____   1. Leaner messages are always less effective than richer messages.

_____

_____   2. Synchronicity is the condition when communicators are all connected in real time.

_____

_____   3. "The right to be forgotten" means you don't have to worry about content that you contribute to social media.

_____

_____   4. Telephone calls are asynchronous.

_____

_____   5. Disinhibition refers to the tendency of online communicators to express themselves with less caution and self-monitoring.

_____

_____   6. Hyperpersonal communication speeds up getting to know another person, which is always beneficial.

_____

_____   7. According to your text, teens text message an average of once a minute for at least 8 hours a day.

_____

_____   8. 97 percent of all text messages are opened.

_____

_____   9. Blogs send personal information to many people at a time, a quality referred to as *masspersonal*.

_____

_____ 10. Social scientists have concluded that most people can only sustain about 1,500 relationships.

_____

_____ 11. Ironically, when isolated communicators' sense of self-efficacy increases due to successful mediated communication, they may increase the amount of time they spend in mediated communication and become more isolated.

_____

_____ 12. Studies indicate that the presence of mobile devices can offer a much needed break from the stress of face-to-face communication.

_____

_____ 13. Online surveillance requires a webcam and security software.

_____

_____ 14. *Cyberstalking* usually occurs between strangers.

_____

_____ 15. In mediated messages, men and women use the word *we* about equally, but in different ways.

_____

_____ 16. In mediated messages, men swear more than women.

_____

_____ 17. *Digital natives* were born in a hospital that had computers.

_____

_____ 18. According to some studies, 70 percent of recruiters in the United States have rejected candidates because of information they found online.

_____

_____ 19. *Warranting value* refers to the degree to which information is controllable by the person being described online.

_____

_____ 20. If the amount of time you spend on the Internet exceeds the amount you anticipated or intended, you're probably spending too much time online.

_____

COMPLETION

Fill in the blanks with the correct terms chosen from the list below:
asynchronous, cyberbullying, disinhibition, hyperpersonal communication, leanness, netiquette, richness, synchronicity, warranting value, virtual community

1. _____ describes messages that are stark from a lack of nonverbal communication.

2. _____ occurs when communicators express themselves will minimal caution and self-monitoring.

3. _____ is a set of civil behaviors that apply to social media.

4. _____ refers to the delay between the time a message is sent and when it is received.

5. _____ is an accelerated discussion of personal topics and relational development beyond what normally happens in face-to-face interaction.

6. _____ is the degree to which online information is controllable by the person being described.

7. _____ are malicious acts that harass victims online.

8. _____ describes the abundance of nonverbal cues that add clarity to a verbal message.

9. _____ are online groups that gather around shared interests.

10. _____ is the condition when communicators are all connected in real time.

MULTIPLE CHOICE

Choose the *best* answer for each of the questions below:

1. A phone message includes which of the cues of a face-to-face conversation:
   a. vocal tone
   b. eye contact
   c. posture
   d. facial expression

2. According to your text, studies have found leaner mediated communication can be advantageous when:
   a. you're too busy to pay attention.
   b. you have no interest in the topic being discussed.
   c. you want people to focus on what you're saying rather than your appearance.
   d. you have a head cold.

3. Synchronicity is the condition when communicators are all
    a. able to dance together.
    b. happy to see each other.
    c. on time for a meeting.
    d. connected in real time.

4. Research shows that, when online, communicators express themselves
    a. less honestly and with more self-monitoring.
    b. more honestly and bluntly, with less caution and self-monitoring.
    c. more honestly and with more caution.
    d. less honestly and with more caution.

5. An accelerated discussion of personal topics and relational development beyond what normally happens in face-to-face interaction is called
    a. personal communication.
    b. impersonal communication.
    c. hyperpersonal communication.
    d. interpersonal communication.

6. When compared with marital relationships that began in person, those that started online had
    a. slightly higher satisfaction rates and slightly lower incidences of breakups.
    b. slightly lower satisfaction rates and slightly higher incidences of breakups.
    c. slightly higher satisfaction rates and slightly higher incidences of breakups.
    d. none of the above.

7. The following reasons why texting is so popular are true *except*:
    a. Text messages are discreet.
    b. Text messages are easy to send and receive no matter where you might be.
    c. Text messages are less expensive than email.
    d. Text messages are more likely to be read.

8. The *masspersonal* quality of blogs is
    a. the ability to share massive amounts of information.
    b. the ability to send personal information to many people at one time.
    c. the ability to accumulate mass amounts of feedback.
    d. none of the above.

9. According to your text, studies have revealed that the mere presence of mobile devices can have a negative effect during face-to-face discussions of personal topics on all of the following *except*:
    a. closeness
    b. connection
    c. conversation topics
    d. conversation quality

10. All of the following factors contribute to determining digital natives *except*:
    a. age
    b. country of origin
    c. digital dexterity
    d. socio-economic status

11. Warranting value is the degree to which information is controllable by the
    a. person editing a publication.
    b. public.
    c. person being described.
    d. employer of the person being described.

12. The text suggests all of the following are indicators that you are probably spending too much time online *except*:
    a. decrease in time needed online to achieve satisfaction
    b. time of Internet use exceeding the amount anticipated or intended
    c. failure in attempts to reduce Internet use
    d. Internet use resulting in failure to fulfill responsibilities at work, home, or school

CHAPTER TWO STUDY GUIDE ANSWERS

TRUE/FALSE

1. F	4. F	7. F	10. F	13. F	16. T	19. T
2. T	5. T	8. T	11. T	14. F	17. F	20. T
3. F	6. F	9. T	12. F	15. T	18. T	

COMPLETION

1. leanness
2. disinhibition
3. netiquette
4. asynchronous
5. hyperpersonal communication
6. warranty value
7. cyberbullying
8. richness
9. virtual community
10. synchronicity

MULTIPLE CHOICE

1. A
2. C
3. D
4. B
5. C
6. B
7. B
8. B
9. C
10. C
11. C
12. A

3

COMMUNICATION AND IDENTITY: CREATING AND PRESENTING THE SELF

AFTER STUDYING THE TOPICS IN THIS CHAPTER, YOU SHOULD BE ABLE TO:

1. Describe the relationship between self-concept, self-esteem, and communication.

2. Explain how self-fulfilling prophecies shape the self-concept and influence communication.

3. Compare and contrast the perceived self and the presenting self as they relate to impression management.

4. Describe the role that impression management plays in both face-to-face and mediated relationships.

5. Use the social penetration and Johari Window models to identify the nature of self-disclosing communication in one of your relationships.

6. Outline the potential benefits and risks of disclosing in a selected situation.

7. Assess the most competent mixture of candor and equivocation in a given situation.

Who are you? Take a moment now to answer this question. You'll need the following list as you read the rest of this chapter, so be sure to complete it now. Try to include all the characteristics that describe you:

Your moods or feelings (e.g., happy, angry, excited)
Your appearance (e.g., attractive, short)
Your social traits (e.g., friendly, shy)
Talents you have or do not have (e.g., musical, nonathletic)
Your intellectual capacity (e.g., smart, slow learner)
Your strong beliefs (e.g., religious, environmentalist)
Your social roles (e.g., parent, girlfriend)
Your physical condition (e.g., healthy, overweight)

Now look at what you've written. How did you define yourself? By career status or social role? Your temperament? Gender or sexual orientation? By your age? Your religion? Your occupation?

There are many ways of identifying yourself. List as many as you can. You'll probably see that the words you've chosen represent a profile of what you view as your most important characteristics. In other words, if you were required to describe the "real you," this list ought to be a good summary.

George Mayer/Bigstock

COMMUNICATION AND THE SELF

You might be wondering how this self-analysis is related to interpersonal communication. The short answer is that who you are both reflects and affects your communication with others. The long answer involves everything from biology to socialization to culture to gender. We'll begin with a look at two terms that are basic to the relationship between the self and communication.

Self-Concept and Self-Esteem

The list you created is at least a partial answer to the question "Who do you think you are?" It's likely that the phrases you chose generated some emotional responses—perhaps terms like "happy" or "sad," "confident" or "nervous." Replies like these show that how you *feel* about yourself is a big part of who you think you are. What we think and feel about ourselves are important components of the self that we'll examine now.

Self-Concept   Who you think you are can be described as your **self-concept**: the relatively stable set of perceptions you hold of yourself. If a special mirror existed that reflected not only your physical features but also other aspects of yourself—emotional states, talents, likes, dislikes, values, roles, and so on—the reflection you'd see would be your self-concept. You probably recognize that the self-concept list you recorded earlier is only a partial one. To make the description complete, you'd have to keep adding items until your list ran into hundreds of words.

For most people this list dramatically illustrates just how fundamental the concept of self is. Even when the item being abandoned is an unpleasant one, it's often hard to give it up. And when asked to let go of their most central feelings or thoughts, most people balk. "I wouldn't be *me* without that," they insist. Of course, this proves our point: The concept of self is perhaps our most fundamental possession. Knowing who we are is essential because without a self-concept it would be impossible to relate to the world.

Self-Esteem   While your self-concept describes who you think you are, **self-esteem** involves evaluations of self-worth. A hypothetical communicator's self-concept might include being quiet, argumentative, or self-controlled. His or her self-esteem would be determined by how he or she *felt* about these qualities. Consider these differing evaluations:

Quiet	"I'm a coward for not speaking up."
	versus
	"I enjoy listening more than talking."
Argumentative	"I'm pushy, and that's obnoxious."
	versus
	"I stand up for my beliefs."
Self-controlled	"I'm too cautious."
	versus
	"I think carefully before I say or do things."

People with high self-esteem tend to think well of others and expect to be accepted by them. On the other hand, those who dislike themselves are likely to believe that others won't like them either. Realistically or not, they imagine that others are constantly viewing them critically, and they accept these imagined or real criticisms as more proof that they are indeed unlikable people. Sometimes this low self-esteem is manifested in hostility toward others because the communicator takes the approach that the only way to look good is to put others down.

High self-esteem has obvious benefits, but it doesn't guarantee interpersonal success.[1] People with exaggerated self-esteem may *think* they make better impressions on others and have better friendships and romantic lives, but neither impartial observers nor objective tests verify these beliefs. It's easy to see how people with an inflated sense of self-worth could irritate others by

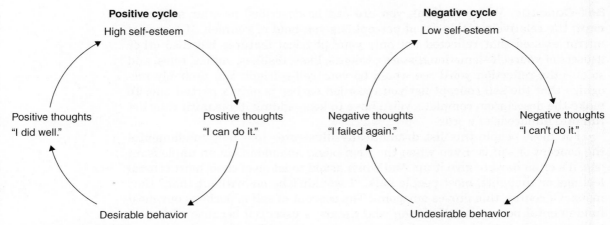

A FIGURE 3.1 The Relationship between Self-Esteem and Communication Behavior

coming across as condescending know-it-alls, especially when their self-worth is challenged.[2]

Despite these cautions, self-esteem *can* be the starting point for positive behaviors and interactions. Figure 3.1 shows the cycles that may begin from both positive and negative self-evaluations. These patterns often become self-fulfilling prophecies, as we'll discuss later in this chapter.

Biological and Social Roots of the Self

How did you become the kind of communicator you are? Were you born that way? Are you a product of your environment? As you'll now see, the correct answer to both of these questions is "yes."

PAUSE *and* REFLECT

Your Self-Esteem

MindTap REFLECT... on your own self-esteem, either here or online.

Take a self-guided tour of your self-esteem provided by the National Association of Self-Esteem. As you explore, consider how the past and present have shaped your current level of self-esteem. Additionally, speculate about how your current level of self-esteem affects your own communication style and interpersonal relationships. You can find the link to this site by visiting CengageBrain.com to access the Speech Communication MindTap for *Looking Out Looking In*. The activity will take about 10 to 15 minutes.

Biology and the Self   Take another look at the "Who am I?" list you developed at the beginning of this chapter. You will almost certainly find some terms that describe your **personality**—characteristic ways that you think and behave across a variety of situations. Your personality tends to be stable throughout your life, and often it grows more pronounced over time.[3]

Research suggests that personality is formed in part by our genetic makeup.[4] For example, people who were judged shy as children still show a distinctive reaction in their brains as adults when they encounter new situations.[5] Some studies show that biology accounts for as much as half of communication-related personality traits such as extraversion,[6] shyness,[7] assertiveness,[8] verbal aggression,[9] and overall willingness to communicate.[10] In other words, to some degree, we come programmed to communicate in characteristic ways.

While you may have a disposition toward traits like shyness or aggressiveness, you can do a great deal to control how you actually communicate. More and more research suggests that personality is flexible, dynamic, and shaped by experiences.[11] Even shy people can learn how to reach out to others, and those with aggressive tendencies can learn to communicate in more sociable ways. One author put it this way: "Experiences can silence genes or activate them. Even shyness is like Silly Putty once life gets hold of it."[12] Throughout this book you will learn about communication skills that, with practice, you can build into your repertoire.

Socialization and the Self-Concept   How important are others in shaping our self-concept? Imagine growing up on a deserted island, with no one to talk to or share activities. How would you know how smart you are—or aren't? How would you gauge your attractiveness? How would you decide if you're short or tall, kind or mean, thin or heavy? Even if you could view your reflection in a mirror, you still wouldn't know how to evaluate your appearance without appraisals from others or people with whom to compare yourself. In fact, the messages we receive from the people in our lives play a central role in shaping how we regard ourselves.

Social scientists use the metaphor of a mirror to identify the process of **reflected appraisal**: the fact that each of us develops a self-concept that reflects the way we believe others see us. In other words, we are likely to feel less valuable, lovable, and capable to the degree that others have communicated ego-busting signals; and we will probably feel good about ourselves to the degree that others affirm our value.[13]

To illustrate this point further, let's start at the beginning. Children aren't born with any sense of identity. They learn to judge themselves only through the way others treat them. As children learn to speak and understand language, verbal messages contribute to a developing self-concept. Every day a child is bombarded with scores of appraisals about himself or herself. Some of these are positive: "You're so cute!" "I love you." "What a big girl." Other messages are negative: "What's the matter with you?" "Can't you do anything

Design Pics/Superstock

right?" "You're a bad boy." "Leave me alone. You're driving me crazy!" Evaluations like these are the mirror by which we know ourselves. Because children are trusting souls who have no other way of viewing themselves, they accept at face value both the positive and negative appraisals of the apparently all-knowing and all-powerful adults around them.

These same principles in the formation of the self-concept continue in later life, especially when messages come from what sociologists term **significant others**—people whose opinions we especially value. A look at the "ego boosters" and "ego busters" you will develop later in this chapter will show that the evaluations of a few especially important people can be powerful. Family members are the most obvious type of significant other, and their ego busters can be particularly hurtful as a result.[14] Others, though, can also be significant others: a special friend, a teacher, someone you dated, or perhaps an acquaintance whose opinion you value can leave an imprint on how you view yourself—sometimes for better, sometimes for worse.[15] To see the importance of significant others, ask yourself how you arrived at your opinion of yourself as a student, as a person attractive to others, as a competent worker, and you'll see that these self-evaluations were probably influenced by the way others regarded you.

The impact of significant others remains strong during adolescence. Inclusion in (or exclusion from) peer groups is a crucial factor in self-concept development for teenagers.[16] The good news is that parents who are understanding of their children's self-concepts during the adolescent years typically have better communication with their teens and can help them create a strong self-concept.[17] The influence of significant others becomes less powerful as people grow older. After most people approach the age of thirty, their self-concepts don't change radically, at least not without a conscious effort.[18]

So far we have looked at the way in which others' messages shape our self-concept. In addition to these messages, each of us forms our self-image by the process of **social comparison**: evaluating ourselves in terms of how we compare with others.

Two types of social comparison need highlighting. In the first type, we decide whether we are *superior* or *inferior* by comparing ourselves to others. Are we attractive or ugly? A success or failure? Intelligent or stupid? It depends on those against whom we measure ourselves.[19] For instance, research shows that young women who regularly compare themselves with ultra-thin media models develop negative appraisals of their own bodies.[20] In one study, young women's perceptions of their bodies changed for the worse after watching just thirty minutes of televised images of the "ideal" female form.[21] Men, too, who compare themselves to media-idealized male physiques evaluate their bodies negatively.[22] People also use others' online profiles as points of comparison, and they may feel less attractive after doing so.[23]

You'll probably never be as beautiful as a Hollywood star, as agile as a professional athlete, or as wealthy as a millionaire. When you consider the matter logically, these facts don't mean you're worthless. Nonetheless, many people judge themselves against unreasonable standards and suffer accordingly.[24] This is particularly true of people with perfectionistic tendencies, whose self-concepts have been shaped by demanding messages from significant others.[25] These distorted self-images can lead to serious behavioral disorders, such as depression, anorexia nervosa, and bulimia.[26] You'll read more about how to avoid placing perfectionistic demands on yourself in Chapter 5.

In addition to feelings of superiority and inferiority, social comparison provides a way to decide if we are the *same as* or *different from* others. A child who is interested in ballet and who lives in a setting where such preferences are regarded as weird will start to accept this label if there is no support from others. When at a dance camp, however, the child will likely flourish. Likewise, adults who want to improve the quality of their relationships but are surrounded by friends and family who don't recognize or acknowledge the importance of these matters may think of themselves as oddballs. Thus, it's easy to recognize that the **reference groups** against which we compare ourselves play an important role in shaping our view of ourselves.

You might argue that not every part of one's self-concept is shaped by others, insisting that certain objective facts are recognizable by self-observation. After all, nobody needs to tell a person that he is taller than others, speaks with an accent, has acne, and so on. These facts are obvious. Though it's true that some features of the self are immediately apparent, the *significance* we attach to them—the rank we assign them in the hierarchy of our list and the interpretation we give them—depends greatly on the opinions of others. After all, many of your features are readily observable, yet you don't find them important at all, because nobody has regarded them as significant.

By now you might be thinking, "It's not my fault that I've always been shy or insecure. Because I developed a picture of myself as a result of the way others have treated me, I can't help being what I am." Though it's true that to a certain extent you are a product of your environment, to believe that you are forever doomed to a poor self-concept would be a big mistake. Having held a poor self-image in the past is no reason for continuing to do so in the future. You *can* change your attitudes and behaviors, as you'll soon read.

⋀ In the film *The Way Way Back*, shy, awkward Duncan (Liam James) endures a host of negative appraisals during his early adolescence, leading to low self-esteem. He then spends a summer working for fun-loving boss Owen (Sam Rockwell) who gives Duncan plenty of affirming messages. Can you think of significant others who have influenced how you think and feel about yourself? How have those messages affected the way you communicate with others?

Fox Searchlight/AllStar

PAUSE *and* REFLECT

"Ego Boosters" and "Ego Busters"

MindTap˙ REFLECT... on your own "ego boosters" and "ego busters" by answering the following questions, either here or online.

1. Recall someone you know or once knew who was an "ego booster"—who helped enhance your self-esteem by acting in a way that made you feel accepted, competent, worthwhile, important, appreciated, or loved.

2. Now recall an "ego buster" from your life—someone who acted in a large or small way to reduce your self-esteem. Recall how you felt after receiving the damaging message.

3. Now that you've thought about how others shape your self-concept, recall a time when *you* were an ego booster to someone else—when you intentionally or unintentionally boosted another's self-esteem. Look for a time when your actions left another person feeling valued, loved, needed, and so on.

4. Finally, recall an instance in which you were an ego buster for someone else. What did you do to diminish another's self-esteem? Were you aware of the effect of your behavior at the time?

After completing the exercise, you should begin to see the role communication plays in shaping the self-concept.

Characteristics of the Self-Concept

Now that you have a better idea of how your self-concept developed, we can look closer at some of its characteristics.

The Self-Concept Is Subjective Although we tend to believe that our self-concept is accurate, in truth it may well be distorted. For example, researchers have found that there is no relationship between the way college students rate their ability as interpersonal communicators, public speakers, or listeners and their true effectiveness.[27] In all cases, the self-reported communication skill is higher than actual performance. In another study, college students were asked to rank themselves on their ability to get along with others.[28] Defying mathematical laws, all subjects—every last one of more than 800,000—put themselves in the top half of the population. Sixty percent rated themselves in the top 10 percent of the population, and an amazing 25 percent believed they were in the top 1 percent. Similarly, online daters often have a "foggy mirror"—that is, they see themselves more positively than others do.[29] This leads to inflated self-descriptions that don't always match what an objective third party might say about them.

Not all distortion of the self-concept is positive. Many people view themselves more harshly than the objective facts warrant. We have all experienced a temporary case of the "uglies," convinced that we look much worse than others assure us we do. Research confirms what common sense suggests: People are more critical of themselves when they are experiencing these negative moods than when they are feeling more positive.[30] Although we all suffer occasional bouts of self-doubt that affect our communication, some people suffer from long-term or even permanent states of excessive self-doubt and criticism.[31] It's easy to understand how this chronic condition can influence the way they approach and respond to others.

Suzanne Tucker/Shutterstock.com

Distorted self-evaluations like these can occur for several reasons:

- *Obsolete information.* The effects of past failures in school or social relations can linger long after they have occurred, even though such events don't predict failure in the future. Likewise, your past successes don't guarantee future success.

- *Distorted feedback.* The remarks of overly critical parents, cruel friends, uncaring teachers, excessively demanding employers, or even memorable strangers can have a lasting effect. Other distorted messages are unrealistically positive. For instance, a child's inflated ego may be based on the praise of doting parents, and a boss's inflated ego may come from the praise of brownnosing subordinates.

- *Perfectionism.* From the time most of us learn to understand language, we are exposed to models who appear to be perfect. The implicit message is "A well-adjusted, successful person has no faults." Given this naive belief that everyone else is perfect and the knowledge that one isn't, it's easy to see how one's self-concept would suffer.

- *Social expectations.* Curiously, the perfectionist society to which we belong rewards those people who downplay the strengths we demand that they possess (or pretend to possess). We consider those who honestly appreciate their strengths to be "braggarts" or "egotists," confusing them with the people who boast about accomplishments they do not possess.[32] This convention leads most of us to talk freely about our shortcomings while downplaying our accomplishments.

After a while we begin to believe the types of statements we repeatedly make. The disparaging remarks are viewed as modesty and become part of our self-concept, and the strengths and accomplishments go unmentioned and are thus forgotten. And in the end, we see ourselves as much worse than we are. One way to avoid falling into the trap of becoming overly critical is to recognize your strengths rather than focusing exclusively on your shortcomings.

Scholars have coined the term *Internet-mediated reflected appraisal* to describe how communicators draw conclusions about themselves by considering how others view them online. [33] You might decide who you think you are (in part) by looking at how you portray yourself on social networking sites. Researchers asked participants to spend time reviewing their own Facebook profiles, then measured the participants' self-esteem. They found that participants felt better about themselves after looking at their Facebook pages.[34] In essence, the participants viewed their well-crafted profiles and thought, "This is how others see me—and I look pretty good!"

Of course, this raises questions about the validity of these self-appraisals. Facebook profiles are edited presentations that usually put a person's best foot forward. As you'll read later in this chapter, managing impressions via social media can lead to less-than-accurate portrayals and perceptions by the self and others. But at the very least, social networking sites can be a tool for helping people view themselves in the best light possible.

The Self-Concept Resists Change   Although we all change, there is a tendency to cling to an existing self-concept, even when evidence shows that it is obsolete. This tendency to seek and attend to information that conforms to an existing self-concept has been labeled **cognitive conservatism**.

This tendency toward cognitive conservatism leads us to seek out people who support our self-concept. For example, both college students and married couples with high self-esteem seek out partners who view them favorably, whereas those with negative self-esteem are more inclined to interact with people who view them unfavorably.[35] It appears that we are less concerned with learning the "truth" about ourselves than with reinforcing a familiar self-concept.

It's understandable why we're reluctant to revise a previously favorable self-concept. A student who did well in earlier years but now has failed to study might be unwilling to admit that the label "good scholar" no longer applies. Likewise, a previously industrious worker might resent a supervisor's mentioning increased absences and low productivity. These people aren't *lying* when they insist that they're doing well despite the facts to the contrary; they honestly believe that the old truths still hold, precisely because their self-concepts are so resistant to change.

Curiously, the tendency to cling to an outmoded self-perception also holds when the new self-perception would be more favorable than the old one. We recall a former student whom almost anyone would have regarded as beautiful, with physical features attractive enough to appear in any glamour magazine. Despite her appearance, in a class exercise, this woman characterized herself as "ordinary" and "unattractive." When questioned by her classmates, she described how as a child her teeth were extremely crooked and how she had worn braces for several years in her teens to correct this problem. During this time she was often teased by her friends, who never let her forget her "metal mouth," as she put it. Even though the braces had been off for two years, our student reported that she still saw herself as ugly and brushed aside our compliments by insisting that we were just saying these things to be nice—she knew how she *really* looked.

Communicators who are presented with information that contradicts their self-perception have two choices: They can either accept the new data and change their perception accordingly, or they can keep their original perception and in some way refute the new information. Because most communicators are reluctant to downgrade a favorable image of themselves, their tendency is to opt for refutation, either by discounting the information and rationalizing it away or by counterattacking the person who transmitted it. The problem of defensiveness is so great that we will examine it in detail in Chapter 11.

There are times when changing a distorted or obsolete self-concept can be a good thing. For example, you may view yourself as a less competent, desirable, and skilled person than the facts would suggest. Here are a few suggestions for embracing a more positive self-image.

1. **Have a realistic perception of yourself**. While some people have inaccurately inflated egos, others are their own worst critic. A periodic session of recognizing your strengths, such as you tried earlier in this chapter, is often a good way to put your strengths and weaknesses into perspective. It's also wise to surround yourself with supportive people who will give you the positive feedback you need and deserve.

2. **Have realistic expectations**. If you demand that you handle every act of communication perfectly, you're bound to be disappointed. And if you constantly compare yourself with gifted people, you're going to come up short. Rather than feel miserable because you're not as talented as an expert, realize that you probably are a better, wiser, or more skillful person than you used to be, and that this is a legitimate source of satisfaction.

3. **Have the will to change**. Often we say we want to change, when in fact we're simply not willing to do what's required (we'll discuss the fallacy of helplessness and ridding yourself of "can't" statements in Chapter 4). You *can* change in many ways, if only you are motivated to do so.

4. **Have the skill to change**. Trying isn't always enough. In some instances you would change if you knew how to do so. Seek out advice from books such as this one, or ask for suggestions from instructors, counselors, and other experts. Observing models can also be a powerful way to master new ways of communicating. Watch what people you admire do and say, not so that you can copy them, but so that you can adapt their behavior to fit your own personal style.

Culture, Gender, and Identity

We have already seen how experiences in the family, especially during childhood, shape our sense of who we are. Along with the messages we receive at home, many other forces mold our identity, and thus our communication, including age, physical ability/disability, sexual orientation, and socioeconomic status. Along with these forces, culture and gender are powerful forces that affect how we view ourselves and others and how we communicate. We will examine each of these forces now.

Culture   Although we seldom recognize the fact, our sense of self is shaped, often in subtle ways, by the culture in which we have been reared.[36] Most Western cultures are highly individualistic, whereas other traditional cultures—most Asian ones, for example—are much more collectivist. When asked to identify themselves, individualists in the United States, Canada, Australia, and Europe would probably respond by giving their first name, surname, street, town, and country. Many Asians do it the other way around.[37] If you ask Hindus for their identity, they will give you their caste and village as well as their name. The Sanskrit formula for identifying one's self begins with lineage and goes on to state family, house, and ends with one's personal name.[38] When members of different cultures were asked to create an "I am" list similar to the one you completed earlier in this chapter, those from collectivist cultures made far more group references than those from individualistic cultures.[39]

The difference between individualism and collectivism shows up in everyday interaction. Communication researcher Stella Ting-Toomey has developed a theory that explains cultural differences in important norms, such as honesty and directness.[40] She suggests that in individualistic Western cultures where there is a strong "I" orientation, the norm of speaking directly is honored, whereas in collectivistic cultures, where the main desire is to build connections between the self and others, indirect approaches that maintain harmony are considered more desirable. "I gotta be me" could be the motto of a Westerner, but "If I hurt you, I hurt myself" is closer to the Asian way of thinking.

You don't need to travel overseas to appreciate the influence of culture on the self. Within societies, co-cultural identity plays an important role in how we see ourselves and others. For example, ethnicity can have a powerful effect on how people think of themselves and how they communicate. Recall how you described yourself in the "Who Am I?" list you created when you began this chapter. If you are a member of a nondominant ethnic group, it's likely that you included your ethnicity in the most important parts of who you are. There's no surprise here: If society keeps reminding you that your ethnicity is important, then you begin to think of yourself in those terms. If you are part of the dominant majority, you probably aren't as conscious of your ethnicity. Nonetheless, it plays an important part in your self-concept. Being part of the majority increases the chances that you have a sense of belonging to the society in which you live and of entitlement to being treated fairly. Members of less privileged ethnic groups often don't have these feelings.

Sex and Gender   One way to appreciate the tremendous importance of gender on your sense of self is to imagine how your identity would be different if you had been born as a member of the other sex. Would you express your emotions in the same way? Deal with conflict? Relate to friends and strangers? The answer is quite likely "no."

From the earliest months of life, being male or female shapes the way others communicate with us, and thus our sense of self. Think about the first questions most people ask when a child is born. One of them is almost always "Is it a boy or a girl?" After most people know what the baby "is," they often behave accordingly.[41] They use different pronouns and often choose gender-related nicknames. With boys, comments often focus on size, strength, and activity; comments about girls more often address beauty, sweetness, and facial responsiveness. It's not surprising that these messages shape a child's sense of identity and how he or she will communicate. The implicit message is that some ways of behaving are masculine and others feminine. Little girls, for example, are more likely to be reinforced for acting "sweet" than are little boys.

Talking with
LITTLE GIRLS

NeonShot/Bigstock

I went to a dinner party at a friend's home last weekend and met her five-year-old daughter for the first time. Little Maya was all curly brown hair, doe-like dark eyes, and adorable in her shiny pink nightgown. I wanted to squeal, "Maya, you're so cute! Look at you! Turn around and model that pretty ruffled gown, you gorgeous thing!"

But I didn't. I always bite my tongue when I meet little girls, restraining myself from my first impulse, which is to tell them how darn cute/pretty/beautiful/well-dressed/well-manicured/well-coiffed they are.

What's wrong with that? It's our culture's standard talking-to-little-girls icebreaker, isn't it? And why not give them a sincere compliment to boost their self-esteem?

15 to 18 percent of girls under 12 now wear mascara, eyeliner, and lipstick regularly; eating disorders are up and self-esteem is down; and 25 percent of young American women would rather win *America's Next Top Model* than the Nobel Peace Prize. Even bright, successful college women say they'd rather be hot than smart.

Teaching girls that their appearance is the first thing you notice tells them that looks are more important than anything. It sets them up for dieting at age 5 and foundation at age 11 and boob jobs at 17 and Botox at 23. That's why I force myself to talk to little girls as follows:

"Maya," I said, crouching down at her level, looking into her eyes, "very nice to meet you. Hey, what are you reading?" I asked. Her eyes got bigger, and the practiced, polite facial expression gave way to genuine excitement over this topic.

"What's your favorite book?" I asked.

"I'll go get it! Can I read it to you?"

Purplicious was Maya's pick and a new one to me, as Maya snuggled next to me on the sofa and proudly read aloud every word. Not once did we discuss clothes or hair or bodies or who was pretty. It's surprising how hard it is to stay away from those topics with little girls.

So, one tiny bit of opposition to a culture that sends all the wrong messages to our girls. One tiny nudge towards valuing female brains. One brief moment of intentional role modeling.

Try this the next time you meet a little girl. Ask her what she's reading. What does she like and dislike, and why? There are no wrong answers. You're just generating an intelligent conversation that respects her brain. For older girls, ask her about current events issues: pollution, wars, school budgets slashed. What bothers her out there in the world? How would she fix it if she had a magic wand?

Here's to changing the world, one little girl at a time.

Lisa Bloom

MindTap ENHANCE... your understanding by answering the following questions, either here or online.

1. Do you think people talk differently to little girls than they talk to little boys? If so, offer examples.

2. What impact does communication with children have on the development of their self-concept and self-esteem?

3. Do you generally agree or disagree with the author's central point about talking to little girls? Explain why or why not.

The same principle operates in adulthood: A man who stands up for his beliefs might get approval for being "tough" or "persistent," whereas a woman who behaves in the same way could be described by critics as a "nag" or "bitch."[42] It's not hard to see how the gender roles and labels like these can have a profound effect on how men and women view themselves and on how they communicate.

Self-esteem is also influenced by gender. In a society that values competitiveness more in men than in women, it isn't surprising that the self-esteem of adolescent young men is closely related to having abilities that are superior in some way to those of their peers, whereas teenage women's self-worth is tied more closely to the success of their social relationships and verbal skills.[43] Research also suggests that young women struggle more with self-esteem issues than do young men. For example, the self-esteem of about two-thirds of the males in one study (ages 14 to 23) increased.[44] The same study revealed that about 57 percent of females in the same age group grew to feel *less* good about themselves.

Don't resign yourself to being a prisoner of expectations about your gender. Research demonstrates that our sense of self is shaped strongly by the people with whom we interact and by the contexts in which we communicate.[45] For example, a nonaggressive young man who might feel unwelcome and inept in a macho environment might gain new self-esteem by finding others who appreciate his style of communicating. A woman whose self-esteem is stifled by the limited expectations of bosses and coworkers can look for more hospitable places to work. Children usually can't choose the reference groups that shape their identities, but adults can.

The Self-Fulfilling Prophecy and Communication

The self-concept is such a powerful force on the personality that it not only determines how you see yourself in the present but also can actually influence your future behavior and that of others. Such occurrences come about through a phenomenon called the self-fulfilling prophecy.

A **self-fulfilling prophecy** occurs when a person's expectations of an event, and his or her subsequent behavior based on those expectations, make the event more likely to occur than would otherwise have been true.[46] A self-fulfilling prophecy involves four stages:

1. Holding an expectation (for yourself or for others)
2. Behaving in accordance with that expectation
3. Coming to pass of the expectation
4. Reinforcing the original expectation

You can see how this process operates by considering an example. Imagine you're scheduled to interview for a job you really want. You are nervous about how you'll do, and not at all sure you are really qualified for the position. You share your concerns with a professor who knows you well and a friend who works for the company. Both assure you that you're perfect for the job and that the firm would be lucky to have you as an employee. Based on these comments, you come to the interview feeling good about yourself. As a result, you speak with authority and sell yourself with confidence. The employers are clearly impressed, and you receive the job offer. Your conclusion: "My friend and professor were right. I'm the kind of person an employer would want!"

This example illustrates the four stages of a self-fulfilling prophecy. Thanks to the assurances of your professor and friend, your expectations about the interview were upbeat (Stage 1). Because of your optimistic attitude, you communicated confidently in the interview (Stage 2). Your confident behavior—along with your other qualifications—led to a job offer (Stage 3). Finally, the positive results reinforced your positive self-assessment, and you'll probably approach future interviews with greater assurance (Stage 4).

It's important to recognize the tremendous influence that self-fulfilling prophecies play in our lives. To a great extent we become what we believe. In this sense, we and those around us constantly create and re-create our self-concepts.

"I don't sing because I am happy. I am happy because I sing."

Types of Self-Fulfilling Prophecies   There are two types of self-fulfilling prophecies. *Self-imposed prophecies* occur when your own expectations influence your behavior. In sports you've probably psyched yourself into playing either better or worse than usual, so that the only explanation for your unusual performance was your attitude. Similarly, you've probably faced an audience at one time or another with a fearful attitude and forgotten your remarks, not because you were unprepared, but because you said to yourself, "I know I'll blow it."

Research has demonstrated the power of self-imposed prophecies.[47] In one study, communicators who believed they were incompetent proved less likely than others to pursue rewarding relationships and more likely to sabotage their existing relationships than did people who were less critical of themselves.[48] On the other hand, students who perceived themselves as capable achieved more academically.[49] In another study, subjects who were sensitive to social rejection tended to expect rejection, perceive it where it might not have existed, and overreact to their exaggerated perceptions in ways that jeopardized the quality of their relationships.[50] Research also suggests that communicators who feel anxious about giving speeches seem to create self-fulfilling prophecies about doing poorly that cause them to perform less effectively.[51]

A second category of self-fulfilling prophecies is imposed by one person on another. A classic example was demonstrated by Robert Rosenthal and Lenore Jacobson in a study described in their book *Pygmalion in the Classroom*.[52] The experimenters told teachers that 20 percent of the children in a certain elementary school showed unusual potential for intellectual growth. The names of these 20 percent were drawn randomly. Eight months later, these "gifted" children showed significantly greater gains in IQ than did the remaining children, who had not been singled out for the teachers' attention. The change in the teachers' behavior toward these allegedly special students led to changes in the intellectual performance of these randomly selected children. Among other things, the teachers gave the "smart" students more

∧ The film *Divergent* depicts a dystopian society where citizens are pigeonholed into categories that shape their adult lives—in essence, an other-imposed prophecy. Sixteen-year-old Tris Prior (Shailene Woodley) doesn't fit those categories, so she sets out to define herself on her own terms. In doing so, she demonstrates the power of self-fulfilling prophecies to help us become the kind of person we choose. What are some other-imposed messages that shaped you in your formative years? Which of those did you accept and which did you reject?

time to answer questions, more feedback, and more praise. In other words, the selected children did better—not because they were any more intelligent than their classmates, but because their teachers held higher expectations for them and treated them accordingly.

This type of self-fulfilling prophecy has been shown to be a powerful force for shaping the self-concept and thus the behavior of people in a wide range of settings outside of schools.[53] In one study, a group of welders with relatively equal aptitudes began training. Everyone, including the trainer, was told that five of the welders had higher scores on an aptitude test—even though they were chosen randomly. All five finished at the top of the class. They had fewer absences and significantly higher final test scores. Most impressively, they learned the skills of their trade twice as quickly as those who weren't identified as being so talented. In another [54] study, military personnel who were randomly labeled as having high potential performed up to the expectations of their superiors. They were also more likely to volunteer for dangerous special duty.[55]

It's important to note that an observer must do more than just *believe* to create a self-fulfilling prophecy for the person who is the target of the expectations. The observer also must *communicate* that belief in order for the prediction to have any effect. If parents have faith in their children, but the kids aren't aware of that confidence, they won't be affected by their parents' expectations. If a boss has concerns about an employee's ability to do a job but keeps those concerns to herself, the employee won't be influenced. In this sense, the self-fulfilling prophecies imposed by one person on another are as much a communication phenomenon as a psychological one.

PRESENTING THE SELF: COMMUNICATION AS IMPRESSION MANAGEMENT

So far we have described how communication shapes the way communicators view themselves. We will now turn the tables and focus on the topic of **impression management**—the communication strategies that people use to influence how others view them.[56] You will see that many of our messages aim at creating a desired impression.

Public and Private Selves

To understand how impression management operates, we have to discuss the notion of self in more detail. So far we have referred to the "self" as if each of us had only one identity. In truth, each of us has several selves, some private and others public. Often these selves are quite different.

The **perceived self** is a reflection of the self-concept. Your perceived self is the person you believe yourself to be in moments of honest self-examination. We can call the perceived self "private," because you are unlikely to reveal all of it to another person. You can verify the private nature of the perceived self by reviewing the self-concept list you developed at the beginning of this chapter. If you were completely forthright when compiling that list, you'll probably find some elements of yourself there that you would not disclose to many people and some that you would not share with anyone. You might, for example, be reluctant to share some feelings about your appearance ("I think I'm rather unattractive"), your intelligence ("I'm smarter than most of my friends"), your goals ("The most important thing to me is becoming rich"), or your motives ("I care more about myself than about others").

In contrast to the perceived self, the **presenting self** is a public image—the way we want others to view us. The presenting self is sometimes called one's **face**. In most cases the presenting self that we seek to create is a socially approved image: diligent student, loving partner, conscientious worker, loyal friend, and so on. Social norms often create a gap between the perceived and presenting selves. In one study of college students, both men and women said their perceived selves included being "friendly" and "responsible." When it came to their public selves, the men wanted to be seen as "wild" and "strong," while the women presented themselves as "active" and "able."[57]

You can recognize the difference between public and private behaviors by recalling a time when you observed a driver, alone in his or her car, acting in ways that would never be acceptable in public. All of us engage in backstage ways of acting that we would never do in public. Just recall how you behave in front of the bathroom mirror when the door is locked, and you will appreciate the difference between public and private behaviors. If you knew that someone was watching, would you act differently?

Characteristics of Impression Management

Now that you have a sense of what impression management is, we can look at some characteristics of this process.

We Strive to Construct Multiple Identities   It is an oversimplification to suggest that each of us uses impression management strategies to create just one identity. In the course of even a single day, most people perform a variety of roles: "respectful student," "joking friend," "friendly neighbor," and "helpful worker," to suggest just a few.

As you grew up you almost certainly changed characters as you interacted with your parents. In one context you acted as responsible adult ("You can trust me with the car!"), and in another context you were the helpless child ("I can't

Kissing   Tongue-Tied   Indifferent   Happy

Laughing   Screaming   Skeptical   Angry

Yawning   Sealed Lips   Confused   Questioning

Gary Blakeley/Fotolia

find my socks!"). At some times—perhaps on birthdays or holidays—you were a dedicated family member, and at other times you may have played the role of rebel. Likewise, in romantic relationships we switch among many ways of behaving, depending on the context: friend, lover, business partner, scolding critic, apologetic child, and so on. And as you read in Chapter 1, the ability to shift styles from setting to setting and culture to culture is a feature of communication competence.

Impression Management Is Collaborative Sociologist Erving Goffman used a dramatistic metaphor to describe impression management.[58] He suggested that each of us is a kind of playwright who creates roles that reflect how we want others to see us, as well as a performer who acts out those roles. But unlike the audience for most forms of acting, our audience is made up of other actors who are trying to create their own characters. Impression-related communication can be viewed as a kind of process theater in which we collaborate with other actors to improvise scenes in which our characters mesh.

You can appreciate the collaborative nature of impression management by thinking about how you might handle a gripe with a friend or family member who has not returned your repeated calls to coordinate important details for a party. Suppose that you decide to raise the issue tactfully in an effort to avoid seeming like a nag (desired role for yourself: "nice person") and also to save the other person from the embarrassment of being confronted (hoping to avoid suggesting that the other person's role is "screw-up"). If your tactful bid is accepted, the dialogue might sound like this:

You: By the way, I've left a couple of messages on your cell. I'm not sure whether you've gotten them. We need to talk about the invitations before they go out tomorrow.

Other: Oh, sorry. I've been meaning to get back with you. It's just that I've been really busy lately with school and work.

You: That's okay. Could we talk about it now?

Other: How about I call you back in an hour?

You: Sure, no problem.

In this upbeat conversation, both you and the other person accepted one another's bids for identity as thoughtful, responsible friends. As a result, the conversation ran smoothly. Imagine, though, how differently the outcome would be if the other person didn't accept your presenting self:

You: By the way, I've left two messages on your cell. I'm not sure whether you've gotten them …

Other: *(Defensively)* Okay, so I forgot. It's not that big a deal. You're not perfect yourself, you know!

PAUSE *and* REFLECT

Your Many Identities

MindTap® **REFLECT...** on your many identities by keeping a record, either here or online.

You can get a sense of the many roles you try to create by keeping a record of the situations in which you communicate over a one- or two-day period. For each situation, identify a dramatic title to represent the image you try to create. A few examples might be "party animal," "helpful housekeeper," "wise older sibling," and "sophisticated film critic."

At this point you have the choice of persisting in trying to play the original role of "nice person": "Hey, I'm not mad at you, and I know I'm not perfect!" Or, you might switch to the new role of "unjustly accused person," responding with aggravation, "I never said I was perfect. But we're not talking about me here …"

As this example illustrates, *collaboration* in impression management doesn't mean the same thing as *agreement*. The small issue of the phone message might mushroom into a fight in which you and the other person both adopt the role of combatants. The point here is that virtually all conversations provide an arena in which communicators construct their identities in response to the behavior of others. As you read in Chapter 1, communication isn't made up of discrete events that can be separated from one another. Instead, what happens at one moment is influenced by what each party brings to the interaction and what happened in their relationship up to that point.

Impression Management Can Be Deliberate or Unconscious   There's no doubt that sometimes we are highly aware of managing impressions. Most job interviews and first dates are clear examples of deliberate impression management. As noted in Chapter 1, high self-monitoring is usually helpful in these situations. But in other cases, we unconsciously act in ways that are really small public performances.[59] For example, experimental subjects expressed facial disgust in reaction to eating sandwiches laced with a supersaturated saltwater solution only when there was another person present. When they were alone, they made no faces while eating the same sandwiches.[60]

Another study showed that communicators engage in facial mimicry (such as smiling or looking sympathetic in response to another's message) in face-to-face settings only when their expressions can be seen by the other person. When they are speaking over the phone, and their reactions cannot be seen, they do not make the same expressions.[61] Studies like these suggest that most of our behavior is aimed at sending messages to others—in other words, impression management.

The experimental subjects described in the preceding paragraphs didn't consciously think, "Somebody is watching me eat this salty sandwich, so I'll make a face" or "Because I'm in a face-to-face conversation, I'll show I'm sympathetic by mimicking the facial expressions of my conversational partner." Decisions like these are often instantaneous and outside of our conscious awareness. In the same way, many of our choices about how to act in the array of daily interactions aren't highly considered strategic decisions. Rather, they rely on "scripts" that we have developed over time.

Despite the pervasiveness of impression management, it seems like an exaggeration to suggest that *all* behavior is aimed at making impressions. Young children certainly aren't strategic communicators. A baby spontaneously laughs when pleased and cries when sad or uncomfortable without any notion of creating an impression in others. Likewise, there are times when we, as adults, act spontaneously. Despite these exceptions, most people consciously or unconsciously communicate in ways that help construct desired identities for themselves and others.

Why Manage Impressions?

Why bother trying to shape others' opinions of you? Social scientists have identified several overlapping reasons.[62]

To Start and Manage Relationships Think about times when you have consciously and carefully managed your approach when meeting someone you would like to know better. You may do your best to appear charming and witty—or perhaps cool and suave. You don't need to be a phony to act this way; you simply are trying to show your best side. Once relationships are up and running, we still manage impressions—perhaps not as much, but often.

To Gain Compliance of Others We often manage our impressions to get others—both those we know and strangers—to act in ways we want. You might, for example, dress up for a visit to traffic court in the hope that your image (responsible citizen) will convince the judge to treat you sympathetically. You might chat sociably with neighbors you don't find especially interesting so that you can exchange favors or solve problems as they come up.

To Save Others' Face We often modify the way we present ourselves to support the way other people want to be seen. For example, able-bodied people often mask their discomfort upon encountering someone who is disabled by acting nonchalant or stressing similarities between themselves and the disabled person.[63] Young children who haven't learned about the importance of face-saving often embarrass their parents by behaving inappropriately ("Mommy, why is that man so fat?"), but by the time they enter school, behavior that might have been excusable or even amusing just isn't acceptable.

To Explore New Selves Sometimes we try on a new self in the same way we try on a different style of clothing: to see if it changes the way others view us and how we think and feel about ourselves. Toward this end, trying on new selves can be a means to self-improvement. For example, one study found that teens—especially lonely ones—who experimented with new identities online wound up reaching out more to people of different ages and cultural backgrounds than they did in their face-to-face lives. As a result, they actually increased their social competence.[64]

Face-to-Face Impression Management

Minerva Studio/Shutterstock.com

In face-to-face interaction, communicators can manage their front in three ways: manner, appearance, and setting.[65] *Manner* consists of a communicator's words and nonverbal actions. Physicians, for example, display a wide variety of manners as they conduct physical examinations. Some are friendly and conversational, whereas others adopt a curt and impersonal approach. Much of a communicator's manner comes from what he or she says. A doctor who remembers details about your interests and hobbies is quite different from one who sticks to clinical questions. One who explains a medical procedure creates a different impression than another who reveals little information to the patient.

Along with the content of speech, nonverbal behaviors play a big role in creating impressions.[66] A doctor who greets you with a smile and a handshake comes across differently from one who gives nothing more than a curt nod. Manner varies widely in other professions and settings—professors, salespeople, hair stylists, and so on—and the impressions they create vary accordingly. The same principle holds in personal relationships. Your manner plays a major role in shaping how others view you. Chapters 6 and 7 will describe in detail how your words and nonverbal behaviors create impressions. Because you have to speak and act, the question isn't *whether* your manner sends a message, but rather *what* message it will send.

A second dimension of impression management is *appearance*—the personal items that people use to shape an image. Sometimes appearance is part of creating a professional image. A physician's white lab coat and a police officer's uniform both set the wearers apart as someone special. A tailored suit or a rumpled outfit creates very different impressions in the business world. Off the job, clothing is just as important. We choose clothing that sends a message about ourselves, sometimes trendy and sometimes traditional. Some people dress in ways that accent their sexuality, whereas others hide it. Clothing can say, "I'm an athlete," "I'm wealthy," or "I'm an environmentalist." Along with dress, other aspects of appearance play a strong role in impression management. Do you wear makeup? What is your hairstyle? Do you make an effort to look friendly and confident?

A final way to manage impressions is through the choice of *setting*— physical items that we use to influence how others view us. In modern Western society, the automobile is a major part of impression management. This explains why many people lust after cars that are far more expensive and powerful than they really need. A sporty convertible or fancy imported sedan doesn't just get drivers from one place to another; it also makes statements about the kind of people they are. The physical setting we choose and the way we arrange it are another important way to manage impressions. What colors do you choose for the place you live? What artwork? What music do you play? Of course, we choose a setting that we enjoy, but in many cases we create an environment that will present the desired front to others.

Online Impression Management

The preceding examples involve face-to-face interaction, but impression management is just as common and important in other types of communication.

At first glance, the technology of mediated communication seems to limit the potential for impression management. Texting, emailing, and blogging, for example, appear to lack the richness of other channels. They don't convey the tone of your voice, postures, gestures, or facial expressions. However, communication scholars recognize that what is missing in online communication can actually be an *advantage* for communicators who want to manage the impressions they make.[67]

Communicating online generally gives us more control over managing impressions than we have in face-to-face communication. As you read in Chapter 2, asynchronous forms of mediated communication like email, blogs, and web pages allow you to edit your messages until you create just the desired impression.[68] With email (and, to a lesser degree, with text messaging), you can compose difficult messages without forcing the receiver to respond immediately, and ignore others' messages rather than give an unpleasant response. Perhaps most important, when communicating via text-based technology, you generally don't have to worry about stammering or blushing, apparel or appearance, or any other unseen factor that might detract from the impression you want to create. (Photos, video, and streaming may be involved in some mediated communication—but you have choices about those as well.)

Of course, communicating via social media also allows strangers to change their age, history, personality, appearance, and other matters that would be impossible to hide in person.[69] A survey of one online dating site's participants found that 86 percent felt others misrepresented their physical appearance in their posted descriptions.[70] Online daters acknowledge the delicate task of balancing an ideal online identity against the "real" self behind their profile. Many admit they sometimes fudge facts about themselves—using outdated photos or "forgetting" information about their age, for instance. But they are less tolerant when prospective dates post inaccurate identities. For example, one date-seeker expressed resentment upon learning that a purported "hiker" hadn't hiked in years.[71] We'll talk about the ethics of such misrepresentations in the following section.

One study asked undergraduate Facebook users how they believe they come across in their profiles.[72] Most acknowledged that their self-presentations are highly positive—but not *too* positive. In general, they believed their profiles portrayed them as better than reality on certain dimensions (e.g., "funny," "adventurous," "outgoing"), accurately on other dimensions (e.g., "physically attractive," "creative"), and worse than reality on yet other dimensions

What I Instagrammed versus What Was Really Happening, Or, My Entire Life Is a Lie

I love Instagram. Whether I'm drinking a coffee, heading to the gym, or simply feeling in the mood for the occasional (okay, a little more than occasional) selfie, I love posting photos and interacting with other users.

Instagram, like all social media, is about presenting the ideal version of yourself. It's not *not* yourself per se.... It's more like, all the best parts of you displayed to the world and ignoring all the worst parts. So I, like most people, post the things that are going to reflect the best aspects of my life and personality.

Anyway, as a sort of confession: here is what I'm really doing in all those Instagrams versus what I presented to the world. Prepare to be shocked.

The Ultimate Selfie

Olivia muenter

What It Looks Like I'm Doing...

I just got back from vacation and thought I'd share my new, totally natural glow with all of you. I AM SO HAPPY BECAUSE MY LIFE IS TOTALLY AND COMPLETELY PERFECT. I took this photo one time. One time. This is how I look all the time. All. The. Time.

What I'm Actually Doing/Thinking...

Do you want to know how many pictures I shot before I actually captured a photo that both accurately (and attractively) displayed how happy I was in this moment? 56. I hope you're judging me, because I am. Also, the entire epidermis of my forehead is peeling off in this photo because I didn't use sunscreen one day by the pool. Ah, cropping.

The Farmers Market Shot

Olivia muenter

What It Looks Like I'm Doing...

AH, PRODUCE! So bright. So fresh. So healthy. Perhaps I will throw some blueberries and spinach in my high-speed blender and create some juice to take to the office today. I only buy locally. And if you don't, I am judging you.

What I'm Actually Doing/Thinking...

I wonder how long that fruit has been sitting there. I'm going to buy a blueberry muffin the size of my head instead.

The "I Am Productive" Shot

Olivia muenter

What It Looks Like I'm Doing...

What? You're not a morning person. How unfortunate. I start my day with green tea and fresh fruit every day, at the crack of dawn. I like to check my emails as the sun rises, right before I head to yoga.

What I'm Actually Doing/Thinking...

I had to wake up at 7 A.M. because I had three assignments that I had quite literally left until the day that they were due. I have no recollection of whether I passed any of those assignments, but my memory is leaning toward no. P.S.: I hate mornings.

Olivia Muenter

MindTap ENHANCE... your understanding by answering the following questions, either here or online.

1. In what ways do you present yourself differently online than you do in person?

2. Have you ever carefully managed social media posts to portray yourself in a particular way, similar to what Olivia Muenter describes here?

3. Are there ethical boundaries that shouldn't be crossed when engaging in online impression management?

On the JOB

Managing Your Professional Identity

According to the *New York Times*, 70 percent of U.S. recruiters have rejected job candidates because of personal information online.[a] It's not hard to imagine how a careless image or post could scuttle your chances with a prospective employer.

To see how your online identity might help or harm your job prospects, start by plugging your name into one or more search engines. If the results might work against you, consider changing privacy settings on your profiles, customizing who can see certain updates and deleting unwanted information about yourself.[b]

Along with discovering unflattering information, you might be surprised to find that another person with the same name and an embarrassing profile pops up.

To minimize the chances of mistaken identity, consider distinguishing your professional self by including your middle name or middle initial on your résumé and all other information you post where online seekers might find it.

If you find potentially damaging information about yourself online and you can't remove it, consider seeking professional help to set the record straight. Services like www.reputation.com will monitor your online identity and take steps to protect your privacy and have damaging information removed.

Once you're on the job, recognize that your mediated messages are a powerful way to create and maintain your identity. Typos, brusque tone, and potentially offensive humor can be career-killers.[c]

("intelligent," "polite," "reliable"). It appears that the participants realized—perhaps intuitively—that their Facebook sites are an exercise in impression management.

Blogs, personal web pages, and profiles on social networking sites all provide opportunities for communicators to construct an identity.[73] Even the simple choice of a screen name ("lovemyporsche," "fun2bewith," "footballdude") says something about you and is likely to lead others to create impressions of you.[74] And interestingly, research shows that regularly viewing your own Facebook page can enhance your self-esteem.[75] This makes sense: Assuming you're carefully managing impressions on that site, it can be an ego-booster to remind yourself what you look like "at your best."

Impression Management and Honesty

After reading this far, you might think that impression management sounds like an academic label for manipulation or phoniness. There certainly are situations where impression management is dishonest. A manipulative date who pretends to be affectionate in order to gain sexual favors is clearly unethical and deceitful. So are job applicants who lie about academic records to get hired or salespeople who pretend to be dedicated to customer service when their real goal is to make a quick buck.

But managing impressions doesn't necessarily make you a liar. In fact, it is almost impossible to imagine how we could communicate effectively without making decisions about which front to present in one situation or another. It would be ludicrous to act the same way with strangers as you do with close friends, and nobody would show the same face to a two-year-old as he or she would to an adult.

Each of us has a repertoire of faces—a cast of characters—and part of being a competent communicator is choosing the best face for the situation. Consider a few examples:

- You offer to teach a friend a new skill: playing the guitar, operating a computer program, or sharpening up a tennis backhand. Your friend is making slow progress with the skill, and you find yourself growing impatient.

- You've been exchanging texts for several weeks with someone you met online, and the relationship is starting to turn romantic. You have a physical trait you haven't mentioned.

- At work you face a belligerent customer. You don't believe anyone has the right to treat you this way.

- A friend or family member makes a joke about your appearance that hurts your feelings. You aren't sure whether to make an issue of the joke or to pretend that it doesn't bother you.

In each of these situations—and in countless others every day—you have a choice about how to act. It is an oversimplification to say that there is only one honest way to behave in each circumstance and that every other response would be insincere and dishonest. Instead, impression management involves deciding which face—which part of yourself—to reveal. For example, when teaching a new skill, you choose to display the "patient" instead of the "impatient" side of yourself. In the same way, at work you have the option of acting defensive or nondefensive in difficult situations. With strangers, friends, or family you can choose whether to disclose your feelings. Which face to show to others is an important decision, but in any case you are sharing a real part of yourself. You may not be revealing everything, but as you will learn in the following section, complete self-disclosure is rarely appropriate.

SELF-DISCLOSURE IN RELATIONSHIPS

One way by which we judge the strength of our relationships is the amount of information we share with others. "We don't have any secrets," some people proudly claim. Opening up certainly is important. As you read in Chapter 1, disclosure is an ingredient in qualitatively interpersonal relationships. Given the obvious importance of self-disclosure, we need to look closer at the subject. Just what is it? When is it desirable? How can it best be done?

The best place to begin is with a definition. **Self-disclosure** is the process of deliberately revealing information about oneself that is significant and would not normally be known by others. Let's look closer at this definition. Self-disclosure must be *deliberate*. If you accidentally mention to a friend

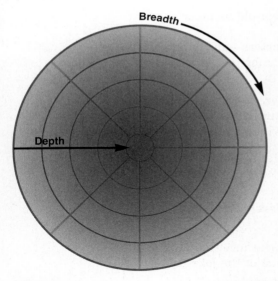

∧ FIGURE 3.2
Social Penetration Model

that you're thinking about quitting a job, or if your facial expression reveals irritation you wanted to hide, that doesn't qualify as self-disclosure. Besides being deliberate, the information must also be *significant*. Volunteering trivial facts, opinions, or feelings—that you like fudge, for example—hardly counts as disclosure. The third requirement is that the information being disclosed is *not known by others*. There's nothing noteworthy about telling others that you are depressed or elated if they already know that.

Models of Self-Disclosure

Although our definition of self-disclosure is helpful, it doesn't reveal the important fact that not all self-disclosure is equally revealing—that some disclosing messages tell more about us than others.

Social psychologists have described two ways in which communication can be more or less disclosing.[76] Their model of **social penetration** is pictured in Figure 3.2. The first dimension of self-disclosure in this model involves the **breadth** of information volunteered—the range of subjects being discussed. For example, the breadth of disclosure in your relationship with a coworker will expand as you begin revealing information about your life away from the job as well as on-the-job information. The second dimension of self-disclosure is the **depth** of information volunteered, the shift from relatively impersonal messages to more personal ones.

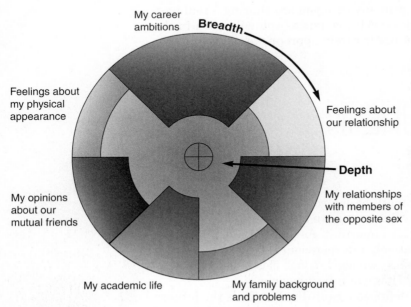

∧ FIGURE 3.3
Sample Model of Social Penetration

Depending on the breadth and depth of information shared, a relationship can be casual or intimate. In a casual relationship, the breadth may be great, but not the depth. A more intimate relationship is likely to have high depth in at least one area. The most intimate relationships are those in which disclosure is great in both breadth and depth. Social psychologists Irwin Altman and Dalmas Taylor see the development of a relationship as a progression from the periphery of their model to its center, a process that typically occurs over time. Each of your personal relationships probably has a different combination of breadth of subjects and depth of disclosure. Figure 3.3 pictures a student's self-disclosure in one relationship.

Looking at DIESITY

Lexie Lopez-Mayo: Culture, Gender, and Self-Disclosure

I was born in Mexico and have lived in the U.S. since I was ten. One of the things I've noticed about my Latin friends and family is that we tend to be more expressive and disclosing than many of my Euro-American friends. Of course there are exceptions to that rule, but overall I think people from my cultural background tend to reveal a lot. If we think it, we say it; if we feel it, we express it.

But culture isn't the only issue. Gender also plays a role. In my experience, Latin men easily express positive emotions, but they often hide negative feelings such as hurt and sadness. There's a strong cultural norm for Latinos to be tough, not admit failure, or show weakness—in other words, to be "macho."

I have other opportunities to see how culture and gender affect communication. My husband, who

is African-American, is generally a laid-back, quiet kind of guy. However, when he's around his African-American buddies, he's much less reserved and much more disclosing. His language, volume, and mannerisms all change, and he becomes a lot more expressive.

And of course, personality plays a role in communication. I know quiet Latinas and disclosing Latinos, so culture doesn't always dictate how people express themselves. In the end, I think the way people communicate is influenced by who they are, where they're from, and whom they're with. In my case, I'm a highly expressive Latina who will tell just about anybody what I think, feel, and want!

"Culture, Gender, and Self-Disclosure" by Lexie Lopez-Mayo. Used with permission of author.

What makes the disclosure in some messages deeper than others? One way to measure depth is by how far it goes on two of the dimensions that define self-disclosure. Some revelations are certainly more *significant* than others. Consider the difference between saying "I love my family" and "I love you." Other revelations qualify as deep disclosure because they are *private*. Sharing a secret that you've told to only a few close friends is certainly a revealing act of self-disclosure, but it's even more revealing to divulge information that you've never told anyone. In general, facts ("I'm new in town") are more disclosing than clichés; opinions ("I really like it here") more than facts; and feelings ("... but I get a little lonely sometimes") more than opinions.

Another way to look at self-disclosure is by means of a device called the **Johari Window**.[77] (The window takes its name from the first names of its creators, Joseph Luft and Harry Ingham.) Imagine a frame like Figure 3.4 that contains everything there is to know about you: your likes and dislikes, your goals, your secrets, your needs—everything. This frame could be divided into information you know about yourself and things you don't know (Figure 3.5). It could also be split into things others know about you and things they don't know (Figure 3.6). Figure 3.7 reflects these divisions and has four parts.

Part 1 represents the information of which both you and the other person are aware. This part is your *open area*. Part 2 represents the *blind area*: information

Everything
about
you

∧ **FIGURE 3.4**

∧ FIGURE 3.5

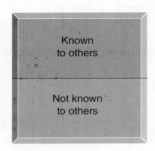

∧ FIGURE 3.6

∧ FIGURE 3.7

of which you are unaware but of which the other person is aware. You learn about information in the blind area primarily through feedback from others. Part 3 represents your *hidden area*: information that you know but aren't willing to reveal to others. Items in this hidden area become public primarily through self-disclosure, which is the focus of this section. Part 4 represents information that is *unknown* to both you and others. At first the unknown area seems impossible to verify. After all, if neither you nor others know what it contains, how can you be sure it exists? We can deduce its existence because we are constantly discovering new things about ourselves. It is not unusual to discover, for example, that you have an unrecognized talent, strength, or weakness.

PAUSE *and* REFLECT

Building a Johari Window

MindTap° **REFLECT…** on your own communication by answering the following questions, either here or online.

You can use the Johari Window model to examine the level of self-disclosure in your own relationships.

1. Use the format described in this section to draw two Johari Windows representing the relationship between you and one other person. Remember to reverse one of the windows so that your open area and that of the other person face each other.

2. Describe which parts of yourself you keep in the hidden area. Explain your reasons for doing so. Describe the advantages or disadvantages or both of not disclosing these parts of yourself.

3. Look at the blind area of your model. Is this area large or small because of the amount of feedback (much or little) that you get from your partner or because of your willingness to receive the feedback that is offered?

4. Explain whether you are satisfied with the results illustrated by your answers. If you are not satisfied, explain what you can do to remedy the problem.

Benefits and Risks of Self-Disclosure

Occasionally we may blurt out a piece of revealing personal information, but most of the time our decision to self-disclose is conscious and deliberate. Communication researchers use the term **privacy management** to describe the choices people make to reveal or conceal information about themselves.[78] Those decisions are often made by weighing the pros and cons of self-disclosing. What are the risks and benefits of opening up?

Benefits of Self-Disclosure   There are several reasons why people choose to share personal information. As you read about each of them, see which apply to you.

Catharsis Sometimes you might disclose information in an effort to "get it off your chest." In a moment of candor, you might, for instance, reveal your regrets about having behaved badly in the past. Catharsis can provide mental and emotional relief—when handled properly.[79] Later in this chapter, you'll read guidelines for disclosing that increase the odds that you can achieve catharsis in a way that helps, instead of harms, relationships.

Reciprocity A well-documented conclusion from research is that one act of self-disclosure begets another.[80] There is no guarantee that your self-disclosures will trigger self-disclosures by others, but your own honesty can create a climate that makes others feel safer and perhaps even obligated to match your level of honesty. It's easy to imagine how telling a partner how you feel about the relationship ("I've been feeling bored lately …") would generate the same degree of candor ("You know, I've felt the same way!"). Reciprocity doesn't always occur on a turn-by-turn basis. Telling a friend today about your job-related problems might help her feel comfortable opening up to you later about her family history, when the time is right for this sort of disclosure.

Self-Clarification Sometimes you can clarify your beliefs, opinions, thoughts, attitudes, and feelings by talking about them with another person. This sort of "talking the problem out" occurs with psychotherapists, but it also goes on with others, all the way from good friends to bartenders or hairdressers.

Self-Validation If you disclose information ("I think I did the right thing …") with the hope of obtaining the listener's agreement, you are seeking validation of your behavior—confirmation of a belief that you hold about yourself. On a deeper level, this sort of self-validating disclosure seeks confirmation of important parts of your self-concept. Self-validation through self-disclosure is an important part of the "coming out" process through which gay people recognize their sexual preference and choose to integrate this knowledge into their personal, family, and social lives.[81]

Building and Maintaining Relationships Getting a relationship started requires some self-disclosure. Consider the role it plays in everything from a first date to a job interview (although the types of disclosures will be very different in these two contexts). Self-disclosure also plays a role in ongoing relational success.[82] For example, there is a strong relationship between the quality of self-disclosure and marital satisfaction.[83] The same principle applies in other personal relationships.

Social Influence Revealing personal information may increase your control over the other person and sometimes over the situation in which you and the other person find yourselves. For example, an employee who tells the boss that another firm has made overtures probably will have an increased chance of getting raises and improvements in working conditions.

Risks of Self-Disclosure While the benefits of disclosing are certainly important, opening up can also involve risks that make the decision to disclose a difficult and sometimes painful one.[84] The risks of self-disclosure fall into several categories.[85]

Rejection John Powell summed up the risks of disclosing in answering the question that forms the title of his book *Why Am I Afraid to Tell You Who I Am?*: "I am afraid to tell you who I am, because, if I tell you who I am, you may not like who I am, and that's all I have."[86] The fear of disapproval is powerful. Sometimes it is exaggerated and illogical, but there are real dangers in revealing personal information:

A: I'm starting to think of you as more than a friend. To tell the truth, I love you.
B: I think we should stop seeing one another.

Negative Impression Even if disclosure doesn't lead to total rejection, it can create a negative impression.
A: I've been thinking that we should get another dog.
B: To tell you the truth, I really don't like dogs. I haven't said so before because I know how much you love them.
A: Really? I can't imagine living with somebody who doesn't love dogs as much as I do.

Decrease in Relational Satisfaction Besides affecting others' opinions of you, disclosure can lead to a decrease in the satisfaction that comes from a relationship.

A: I need to tell you something. I really don't like it when you want to cuddle so much.
B: But I want to be close to you. ...

Loss of Influence Another risk of disclosure is a potential loss of influence in the relationship. Once you confess a secret weakness, your control over how the other person views you can be diminished.

"Since we're both being honest, I should tell you I have fleas."

A: *(Manager to employee)* I'd like to give you the weekend off, but to tell you the truth, I don't get to make any judgment calls around here. My boss makes all the decisions. In fact, he doesn't respect my opinions at all.

B: No kidding. I guess I know who to ask when I want to get anything done around here.

Hurting the Other Person   Even if revealing hidden information leaves you feeling better, it might hurt others—cause them to be upset, for example. It's probably easy to imagine yourself in a situation like this:

A: I'm so ugly! I can't think of anything that will change the way I look.
B: Neither can I.

Guidelines for Self-Disclosure

By now it should be clear that deciding when and how much personal information to disclose is not a simple matter. The following guidelines can help you choose the level of self-disclosure that is appropriate in a given situation.

Is the Other Person Important to You?   There are several ways in which someone might be important to you. Perhaps you have an ongoing relationship deep enough so that sharing significant parts of yourself justifies keeping your present level of togetherness intact. Or perhaps the person to whom you're considering disclosing is someone with whom you've previously related on a less personal level. But now you see a chance to grow closer, and disclosure may be the path toward developing that personal relationship.

Are the Amount and Type of Disclosure Appropriate?   Some people have trouble with what's popularly known as "TMI"—sharing "too much information."[87] Classrooms are one setting where oversharing sometimes occurs. Communication researchers asked college students to report on self-disclosures they had heard in their classes.[88] While participants readily identified disclosures that helped the learning process (such as a student describing her heart condition in a physiology class), they also noted comments that crossed the line. In particular, participants objected to classroom self-disclosures that were too (a) frequent, (b) negative, (c) irrelevant to course materials, and (d) unexpected. (Take a moment and you can probably think of an example from each of these categories that you've encountered during a class.)

In general, it's wise not to divulge personal secrets in classroom discussions, with strangers, or on public Facebook postings, among other settings. Even students who appreciate self-disclosure from their teachers acknowledge that they don't want to hear too much, too often about their instructors' personal lives.[89] Of course, it's also possible to *withhold* too much information—perhaps in a counseling session or at a doctor's appointment, or in intimate relationships where nondisclosure might be regarded as deceit. The key is to recognize that there's a time and a place for engaging in, and refraining from, self-disclosure.

Is the Risk of Disclosing Reasonable?   Take a realistic look at the potential risks of self-disclosure. Even if the probable benefits are great, opening yourself up to almost certain rejection may be asking for trouble. On the other

In Real Life

Appropriate and Inappropriate Self-Disclosure

Ramon has been working in an entry-level sales job for almost a year after graduating from the university. He likes the company, but he is growing frustrated at his lack of advancement. After much thought, he decides to share his concerns with his boss, Julie. Notice that Ramon's self-disclosure has the potential to enhance or jeopardize personal goals and relationships, depending on how well it follows the guidelines in these pages.

© John Harris/Cengage Learning

Ramon: Do you have a few minutes to talk?

Julie: Sure, no problem. Come on in.

Ramon: Do you mind if we close the door?

Julie: *(Looking a bit surprised)* Sure.

Ramon: I'd like to talk to you about the future.

Julie: The future?

Ramon: Well, it's been over a year since I started to work here. One of the things you told me in the interview back then was that people move up fast here …

Julie: Well, …

Ramon: …and I'm confused because I've been doing pretty much the same work since I was hired.

Julie: Well, we do think a lot of your work.

Ramon: I'm glad to hear that. But I'm starting to wonder how much of a chance I'll have to grow with this company. *(Ramon is disclosing his concerns about career advancement—a very appropriate topic to raise with his boss. There is some risk in this sort of disclosure, but given Ramon's apparently good standing with his boss, it seems reasonable.)*

Julie: I can understand that you're anxious about taking on more responsibility. I can tell you that you've got a good shot at advancing, if you can just hang in there for a little while.

Ramon: *(Impatiently)* That sounds good, but I've been waiting—longer than I expected to. I'm starting to wonder if some of the things I've heard around here are true.

hand, knowing that your partner is trustworthy and supportive makes the prospect of disclosing more reasonable.

Revealing personal thoughts and feelings can be especially risky on the job.[90] The politics of the workplace sometimes require communicators to keep feelings to themselves in order to accomplish both personal and organizational goals. You might, for example, find the opinions of a boss or customer personally offensive but decide to bite your tongue rather than risk losing your job or goodwill for the company.

In anticipating risks, be sure that you are realistic. It's sometimes easy to indulge in catastrophic expectations and imagine all sorts of disastrous consequences when in fact such horrors are unlikely to occur.

Will the Effect Be Constructive? Self-disclosure can be a vicious tool if it's not used carefully. Each person has a psychological "beltline." Below-the-belt

Julie: *(Suspiciously)* What kinds of things are you talking about, Ramon?

Ramon: Well, Bill and Latisha were telling me about some people who left here because they didn't get the promotions they were promised. *(Ramon discloses information that was told to him in confidence, jeopardizing the standing of two coworkers with Julie.)*

Julie: *(Firmly)* Ramon, I'm sure you understand that I can't talk about personnel decisions involving former employees. I can tell you that we try to give people all the challenges and rewards they deserve, though it can take a while.

Ramon: A year seems like more than "a while." I'm starting to think this company is more interested in having somebody with a Hispanic name on the payroll than giving me a real shot at promotion. *(Ramon's concern may be legitimate, but the sarcastic tone of his disclosure isn't constructive.)*

Julie: Look, I probably shouldn't be saying this, but I'm as frustrated as you are that it's taking so long to get a promotion arranged for you. I can tell you that there will be some personnel changes soon that will give you a good chance to make the kinds of changes you want. I think you can expect to see some changes in the next six weeks. *(Julie offers two items of self-disclosure that encourage Ramon to reciprocate.)*

Ramon: That's really good to hear! I have to tell you that I've started to think about other career options.

Not because I want to leave here, but because I just can't afford to stand still. I really need to start bringing home more money. I don't want to be one of those losers who still can't afford to buy his own house by the time he's forty. *(Ramon makes a big mistake disclosing his opinion about home ownership—a topic that has no relevance to the discussion at hand.)*

Julie: Gee, I'm still renting …

Ramon: Oh, I didn't mean that the way it sounded … *(But the damage from the inappropriate disclosure is already done.)*

Julie: Anyway, I'm glad you let me know about your concerns. I hope you can hang in there for just a little while longer.

Ramon: Sure. Six weeks, huh? I'll keep an eye on the calendar!

After the conversation, Julie still thinks Ramon is a candidate for promotion, but some of his inappropriate disclosures have left her with doubts about his maturity and good judgment, which she didn't have before they spoke. Julie makes a mental note to keep an eye on Ramon and to reconsider the amount of responsibility she gives him until he has demonstrated the ability to share his personal feelings and concerns more constructively.

MindTap® APPLY… this situation to your life by answering questions online.

jabs are a powerful way to disable another person, though usually at great cost to the relationship. It's important to consider the effects of your candor before opening up to others. Comments such as "I've always thought you were pretty unintelligent" or "Last year I made love to your best friend" can be devastating—to the listener, to the relationship, and to your self-esteem.

Is the Self-Disclosure Reciprocated? The amount of personal information you reveal will usually depend on how much the other person reveals. As a rule, disclosure is a two-way street. For example, couples are happiest when their levels of openness are roughly equal.[91]

There are a few times when one-way disclosure is acceptable. Most of them involve formal, therapeutic relationships in which a client approaches a trained professional with the goal of resolving a problem. For instance, you wouldn't necessarily expect to hear about your doctor's personal ailments during a physical checkup—although it's been known to happen, sometimes to the chagrin of the patient.[92]

Do You Have a Moral Obligation to Disclose?

Sometimes we are morally obliged to disclose personal information. For example, surveys reveal that a majority of HIV-positive patients believe they have a duty to reveal their status to healthcare providers and partners, even when doing so risks their pride and dignity and can lead to being stigmatized.[93] Despite this prevailing belief, two decades of research has shown that 40 percent of persons testing positive for HIV did not reveal this result to their sexual partners.[94]

ALTERNATIVES TO SELF-DISCLOSURE

Although self-disclosure plays an important role in interpersonal relationships, it isn't the only type of communication available. To understand why complete honesty isn't always an easy or ideal choice, consider some familiar dilemmas:

- A new acquaintance is much more interested in becoming friends than you are. She invites you to a party this weekend. You aren't busy, but you don't want to go. What would you say?

- Your boss asks you what you think of his new wardrobe. You think it's cheap and flashy. Would you tell him?

- You're attracted to your best friend's mate, who has confessed that she or he feels the same way about you. You both agreed that you won't act on your feelings and that even bringing up the subject would make your friend feel terribly insecure. Now your friend has asked whether you're attracted at all to the mate. Would you tell the truth?

- You've just been given a large, extremely ugly painting as a gift by a relative who visits your home often. How would you respond to the question "Where will you put it?"

Although total honesty is desirable in principle, it can have potentially unpleasant consequences. It's tempting to avoid situations where self-disclosure would be difficult, but examples like the preceding ones show that evasion isn't always possible. Research and personal experience show that communicators— even those with the best intentions—aren't always completely honest when they find themselves in situations in which honesty would be uncomfortable.[95] Four common alternatives to self-disclosure are silence, lying, equivocating, and hinting. We will look closer at each one.

Silence

One alternative to self-disclosure is to keep your thoughts and feelings to yourself. You can get a sense of how much you rely on silence instead of disclosing by keeping a record of when you do and don't express your opinions. You're likely to find that withholding thoughts and feelings is a common approach for you. Telling the whole truth may be honest, but it can jeopardize you, the other person, and your relationship. Most thoughtful communicators would keep quiet rather than blurt out unsolicited opinions like "You look awful" or "You talk too much." Social scientists have found that people often make distinctions between "lies of omission" and "lies of commission"—and that saying nothing (omission) is usually judged less harshly than telling an outright lie (commission).[96] One study showed that, in the workplace, withholding information is often seen as a better alternative than lying or engaging in intentional deception.[97]

Lying

To most of us, lying appears to be a breach of ethics. Although lying to gain unfair advantage over an unknowing victim seems clearly wrong, another kind of mistruth—the "benevolent lie"—isn't so easy to dismiss as completely unethical. A **benevolent lie** is defined (at least by the teller) as unmalicious, or even helpful, to the person to whom it is told.

Whether or not they are innocent, benevolent lies are quite common, both in face-to-face and online relationships.[98] In research spanning four decades, a significant majority of people acknowledged that, even in their closest relationships, there are times when lying is justified.[99] In one study, 130 subjects were asked to keep track of the truthfulness of their everyday conversational statements.[100] Only 38.5 percent of these statements—slightly more than one-third—proved to be totally honest. In another experiment, subjects recorded their conversations over a two-day period and later counted their own deceptions. The average lie rate: three fibs for every ten minutes of conversation.[101]

Most people think that benevolent lies are told for the benefit of the recipient. In the study cited earlier, the majority of subjects claimed that such lying is "the right thing to do." Other research paints a less flattering picture of who benefits most from lying. One study found that two out of every three lies are told for "selfish reasons."[102] Table 3.1 identifies many of the reasons that people choose to lie—some more self-serving than others.

Research has shown that lying does, in fact, threaten relationships.[103] Not all lies are equally devastating, however. One study suggests that a liar's motives make a significant difference in whether the deception is perceived as acceptable

TABLE 3.1 Some Reasons for Lying

Reason	Example
Save face for others	"Don't worry—I'm sure nobody noticed that stain on your shirt."
Save face for self	"I wasn't looking at the files—I was accidentally in the wrong drawer."
Acquire resources	"Oh, *please* let me add this class. If I don't get in, I'll never graduate on time!"
Protect resources	"I'd like to lend you the money, but I'm short myself."
Initiate interaction	"Excuse me, I'm lost. Do you live around here?"
Be socially gracious	"No, I'm not bored—tell me more about your vacation."
Avoid conflict	"It's not a big deal. We can do it your way. Really."
Avoid interaction	"That sounds like fun, but I'm busy Saturday night."
Leave taking	"Oh, look what time it is! I've got to run!"

© Cengage Learning

by others.[104] If a lie appears to be self-serving and exploitive, it will most likely be treated as a relational transgression. On the other hand, if a mistruth seems aimed at sparing another's feelings, the chances of being forgiven increase.

Feelings like dismay and betrayal are greatest when the relationship is most intense, when the importance of the subject is high, and when there is previous suspicion that the other person isn't being completely honest. Of these three factors, the importance of the information lied about proved to be the key factor in provoking a relational crisis. We may be able to cope with "misdemeanor" lying, but "felonies" are a grave threat. In fact, the discovery of major deception can lead to the end of the relationship. More than two-thirds of the subjects in one study reported that their relationship had ended because they discovered a lie. Furthermore, they attributed the breakup directly to the lie.

The lesson here is clear: Lying about major parts of your relationship can have the gravest consequences. If preserving a relationship is important, honesty—at least about important matters—really does appear to be the best policy.

Equivocating

When faced with the dilemma of either lying or telling an unpleasant truth, communicators typically opt for a third approach—equivocation.[105] When a friend asks what you think of an awful outfit, you could say, "It's really unusual—one of a kind!" Likewise, if you are too angry to accept a friend's apology but don't want to appear petty, you might say, "Don't worry about it." One humorous set of suggestions shows how equivocation can help a reluctant business contact provide ambiguous references for an incompetent job applicant:

For a lazy worker: "You will be lucky to get this person to work for you." For someone with no talent: "I recommend this candidate with no qualifications."

For a candidate who should not be hired under any circumstances: "Waste no time hiring this person."

The value of equivocation becomes clear when you consider the alternatives. Consider the dilemma of what to say when you've been given an unwanted present—an ugly painting, for example—and the giver asks what you think of it. How can you respond? On one hand, you need to choose between telling the truth and lying. On the other hand, you have a choice of whether to make your response clear or vague. Figure 3.8 displays these choices. Among the choices, it's clear that Option 1—an equivocal, true response—is preferable to the others in several respects.

As one team of researchers put it, "equivocation is neither a false message nor a clear truth, but rather an alternative used precisely when both of these are to be avoided."[106]

Most people will usually choose to equivocate rather than tell a lie. In a series of experiments, subjects chose among telling a face-saving lie, telling the truth, and equivocating. Only 6 percent chose the lie, and only between 3 and 4 percent chose the hurtful truth. By contrast, more than 90 percent chose the equivocal response.[107] People *say* they prefer truth telling to equivocating, but given the choice, they prefer to finesse the truth.[108]

Equivocal

OPTION I: (Equivocal, True Message) "What an unusual painting! I've never seen anything like it!"	**OPTION II:** (Equivocal, False Message) "Thanks for the painting. I'll hang it as soon as I can find just the right place."
OPTION III: (Clear, True Message) "It's just not my kind of painting. I don't like the colors, the style, or the subject."	**OPTION IV:** (Clear, False Message) "What a beautiful painting! I love it."

True — False

Clear

▲ FIGURE 3.8
Dimensions of Truthfulness and Equivocation

© Cengage Learning

DILBERT BY SCOTT ADAMS

© 1992 United Feature Syndicate, Inc.

Dilbert, Scott Adams/Universal Uclick

Direct Statement	Face-Saving Hint
I'm too busy to continue with this conversation.	I know you're busy; I better let you go.
Please don't smoke in here because it's bothering me.	I'm pretty sure that smoking isn't permitted here.
I'd like to invite you out for lunch, but I don't want to risk a "no" answer.	Gee, it's almost lunchtime. Have you ever eaten at that new Italian restaurant around the corner?

ETHICAL *Challenge*

Must We Always Tell the Truth?

"Is there really a Santa Claus?"
"Am I talking too much?"
"Isn't this the cutest baby you've ever seen?"
"Was it good for you?"

Questions like these often seem to invite answers that are less than totally honest. The research summarized in the "Alternatives to Self-Disclosure" section reveals that, at one time or another, virtually everyone avoids telling the complete truth. We seem to be caught between the time-honored commandment "Thou shall not lie" and the fact that everybody does seem to bend the truth, if only for altruistic reasons. What, then, are the ethics of honesty?

Philosopher Immanuel Kant had a clear answer: We may be able to evade unpleasant situations by keeping quiet, but we must always tell the complete truth when there is no way to avoid speaking up. He said that "truthfulness in statements which cannot be avoided is the formal duty of an individual ... however great may be the disadvantage accruing to himself or another."[a] Kant's unbending position didn't make any exception for lies or equivocations told in the best interests of the receiver. In his moral code, lying is wrong—period.

Not all ethicists have shared Kant's rigid standards of truth telling. Utilitarian philosophers claim that the way to determine the morality of a behavior is to explore whether it leads to the greatest happiness for the greatest number of people. While encouraging truth-telling whenever possible, philosopher Sissela Bok offers some circumstances in which deception may be justified: doing good, avoiding harm, and protecting a larger truth.[b]

Bok is realistic enough to recognize that liars are prone to self-deceptive justifications. For this reason, she tempers her utilitarian position with a *test of publicity*. She suggests that we ask how others would respond if they knew that we were being untruthful. If most disinterested observers with all the facts supported untruthful speech as the best course, then it passes the test of publicity.

MindTap' **APPLY...** the ethical principles introduced here by answering the following questions, either here or online.

Submit your case for avoiding the truth to a "court of self-disclosure":

1. Recall recent situations in which you have used each of the following evasive approaches: lying, equivocating, and hinting.

2. Write an anonymous description of each situation, including a justification for your behavior, on a separate sheet of paper. Submit the cases to a panel of "judges" (most likely fellow students), who will evaluate the morality of these decisions.

Hinting

Hints are more direct than equivocal statements. Whereas an equivocal statement isn't necessarily aimed at changing others' behavior, a hint does aim to get a desired response from others.[109]

Hinting can spare others discomfort that comes with the undiluted truth. The face-saving value of hints explains why communicators are more likely to be indirect than fully disclosing when they deliver a potentially embarrassing message.[110] The success of a hint depends on the other person's ability to pick up the unexpressed message. Your subtle remarks might go right over the head of an insensitive receiver—or one who chooses not to respond. If this happens, you may decide to be more direct. If the costs of a direct message seem too high, however, you can withdraw without risk.

The Ethics of Evasion

It's easy to see why people choose hints, equivocations, and benevolent lies instead of complete self-disclosure. These strategies provide a way to manage difficult situations that is easier than the alternatives for both the speaker and the receiver of the message. In this sense, successful liars, equivocators, and hinters can be said to possess a certain kind of communicative competence. On the other hand, there are certainly times when honesty is the right approach, even if it's painful. At times like these, evaders could be viewed as lacking the competence or the integrity to handle a situation most effectively.

Are hints, benevolent lies, and equivocations ethical alternatives to self-disclosure? Some of the examples in these pages suggest that the answer is a qualified "yes." Many social scientists and philosophers agree. As the Ethical Challenge in this section shows, some argue that the morality of a speaker's *motives* for lying, not the lie itself, ought to be judged, and others ask whether the *effects* of a lie will be worth the deception.

Perhaps the right questions to ask are whether an indirect message is truly in the interests of the receiver and whether this sort of evasion is the only, or the best, way to behave in a given situation.

SUMMARY

The self-concept is a relatively stable set of perceptions that individuals hold about themselves. Self-esteem has to do with evaluations of self-worth. Some of the characteristics of the self are a result of inherited personality traits. In addition, the self-concept is created through messages from significant others—reflected appraisal—and through social comparison with reference groups. The self-concept is subjective and may vary from the way a person is perceived by others. Although the self evolves over time, the self-concept resists change. Other factors that affect the self-concept are culture and sex/gender. One's self-concept, as well as the self-concepts of others, can be changed through self-fulfilling prophecies.

Impression management consists of strategic communication designed to influence others' perceptions of an individual. Impression management aims at presenting to others one or more faces, which may be different from private, spontaneous behavior that occurs outside of others' presence. Communicators engage in creating an identity by managing their manner, appearance, and the settings in which they interact with others. Impression management occurs both in face-to-face and mediated communication. Because each person has a variety of faces that he or she can reveal, choosing which one to present need not be dishonest.

An important issue in interpersonal relationships is self-disclosure: honest, revealing messages about the self that are intentionally directed toward others. The social penetration model and the Johari Window are tools for describing our self-disclosure with others. Communicators disclose personal information for a variety of reasons and benefits: catharsis, reciprocity, self-clarification, self-validation, impression management, relationship maintenance and enhancement, and social influence. The risks of self-disclosure include the possibility of rejection, making a negative impression, a decline in relational satisfaction, a loss of influence, and hurting the other person. Four alternatives to self-disclosure are silence, lying, equivocating, and hinting. These can be ethical alternatives to self-disclosure; however, whether they are depends on the speaker's motives and the effects of the deception.

KEY TERMS

benevolent lie
breadth
cognitive conservatism
depth
face
impression management
Johari Window
perceived self
personality
presenting self

privacy management
reference groups
reflected appraisal
self-concept
self-disclosure
self-esteem
self-fulfilling prophecy
significant others
social comparison
social penetration

CHAPTER THREE

Communication and Identity: Creating and Presenting the Self

OUTLINE

Use this outline to take notes as you read the chapter in the text and/or as your instructor lectures in class.

I. COMMUNICATION AND THE SELF

  A. Definitions

    1. Self-Concept

    2. Self-Esteem

  B. Biological and Social Roots of the Self

    1. Personality

    2. Traits

    3. Socialization and the Self-Concept

      a. Reflected Appraisals

      b. Significant Others

        i. Ego Booster

        ii. Ego Buster

  C. Characteristics of the Self-Concept

    1. The Self-Concept Is Subjective

      a. Obsolete Information

      b. Distorted Feedback

      c. Emphasis on Perfection

      d. Social Expectations

    2. The Self-Concept Resists Change (cognitive conservatism)

      a. Have a Realistic Perception of Yourself

      b. Have Realistic Expectations

      c. Have the Will to Change

      d. Have the Skill to Change

D. Culture, Gender, and Identity

　　1. Culture

　　　　a. Individualistic

　　　　b. Collectivistic

　　2. Sex and Gender

E. The Self-Fulfilling Prophecy and Communication

　　1. Self-Fulfilling Prophecies

　　　　a. Holding an Expectation

　　　　b. Behaving within Expectations

　　　　c. The Expectation Coming to Pass

　　　　d. Reinforcing the Original Expectation

　　2. Types

　　　　a. Self-Imposed

　　　　b. Imposed by Others

II. PRESENTING THE SELF: COMMUNICATION AS IMPRESSION MANAGEMENT

A. Public and Private Selves

　　1. Perceived Self

　　2. Presenting Self (Face)

B. Characteristics of Identity Management

　　1. We Construct Multiple Identities

　　2. Identity Management Is Collaborative

　　3. Identity Management Can Be Deliberate or Unconscious

C. Why Manage Identities?

　　1. To Start and Manage Relationships

　　2. To Gain Compliance of Others

　　3. To Save Others' Face

　　4. To Explore New Selves

D. Managing Identities in Person and Online

　　1. Face-to-Face Identity Management

　　　　a. Manner

　　　　b. Appearance

　　　　c. Setting

    2. Online Impression Management

E. Identity Management and Honesty

III. SELF-DISCLOSURE IN RELATIONSHIPS

A. Definition

B. Models of Self-Disclosure

    1. Social Penetration Model

      a. Breadth

      b. Depth

    2. Johari Window

      a. Open

      b. Hidden

      c. Blind

      d. Unknown

C. Benefits and Risks of Self-Disclosure

    1. Benefits of Self-Disclosure

      a. Catharsis

      b. Reciprocity

      c. Self-Clarification

      d. Self-Validation

      e. Building and Maintaining
        Relationships

      f. Social Influence

    2. Risks of Self-Disclosure

      a. Rejection

      b. Negative Impression

      c. Decrease in Relational Satisfaction

      d. Loss of Influence

      e. Hurting the Other Person

D. Guidelines for Self-Disclosure

    1. Is the Other Person Important to You?

    2. Are the Amount and Type of Disclosure
      Appropriate?

    3. Is the Risk of Disclosing Reasonable?

    4. Will the Effect Be Constructive?

    5. Is the Self-Disclosure Reciprocated?

    6. Do You Have a Moral Obligation to
      Disclose?

IV. ALTERNATIVES TO SELF-DISCLOSURE

A. Silence

B. Lying

    1. Benevolent Lies

    2. Reasons for Lying

    3. Effects of Lies—Threats to the Relationship

C. Equivocating

D. Hinting

    1. Hints May Prevent Receiver or Sender Embarrassment

    2. Hints May Not be Perceived

E. The Ethics of Evasion

    1. Motives

    2. Effects

_____

_____

_____

_____

_____

_____

KEY TERMS

benevolent lies	identity management	reflected appraisal
breadth	impression management	self-concept
cognitive conservatism	Johari Window	self-disclosure
depth	perceived self	self-esteem
ego booster	personality	self-fulfilling prophecy
ego buster	presenting self	significant others
equivocating	privacy management	social comparison
face	reference groups	social penetration

ACTIVITIES

3.1 WHO DO YOU THINK YOU ARE?

LEARNING OBJECTIVES

- Describe the relationship between self-concept and self-esteem.
- Explain how significant others or reference groups contributed to your self-concept.
- Understand the role cognitive conservatism plays in identity formation.

INSTRUCTIONS

1. First, if possible, take The Jung Typology Test at www.humanmetrics.com/cgi-win/JTypes2.asp. This will get you thinking about the way you describe yourself.
2. For each category below, supply the words or phrases that describe you best.
3. After filling in the spaces within each category, organize your responses so that the most fundamental characteristic is listed first, with the rest of the items following in order of descending importance.

PART A: IDENTIFY THE ELEMENTS OF YOUR SELF-CONCEPT

1. How would you describe your typical social behaviors (friendly, shy, aloof, talkative, etc.)?

   a. _____   b. _____   c. _____

2. How would you describe your dominant personality traits (stable, extraverted, introverted, etc.)?

   a. _____   b. _____   c. _____

3. What beliefs do you hold so strongly that they have come to define who you are (vegetarian, green, Christian, pacifist, etc.)?

   a. _____   b. _____   c. _____

4. What social roles are the most important in your life (brother, student, friend, bank teller, club president, etc.)?

   a. _____   b. _____   c. _____

5. How would you describe your intellectual habits and abilities (curious, poor reader, good mathematician, etc.)?

   a. _____   b. _____   c. _____

6. How would you describe your physical condition and/or your appearance (fit, sedentary, tall, attractive, etc.)?

   a. _____   b. _____   c. _____

7. What talents do you possess or lack (good artist, lousy carpenter, competent swimmer, etc.)?

   a. _____   b. _____   c. _____

8. What other descriptors are important to describe you (cultural, ethnic, gender, sexual orientation, moods, feelings, others)?

   a. _____   b. _____   c. _____

PART B: ARRANGE YOUR SELF-CONCEPT ELEMENTS IN ORDER OF IMPORTANCE

1. _____   11. _____

2. _____   12. _____

3. _____   13. _____

4. _____   14. _____

5. _____   15. _____

6. _____   16. _____

7. _____   17. _____

8. _____   18. _____

9. _____   19. _____

10. _____   20. _____

Which of your self-concept elements contribute to building positive self-esteem? Describe any factors that have contributed in a positive way (significant others, reference groups, personal experience, self-talk) to the formation of those positive self-concept elements.

_____

_____

_____

_____

Which of your self-concept elements contribute to building negative self-esteem? Describe any factors that have contributed in a negative way (significant others, reference groups, personal experience, self-talk) to the formation of those negative self-concept elements.

_____

_____

_____

_____

How much of your self-concept is based on obsolete information, social expectations, distorted feedback, or perfection beliefs? Are there ways you can you bring your self-concept up to date to more accurately reflect your current reality?

_____

_____

_____

_____

NOTE: You will use these descriptors in Activity 3.2.

3.2 SELF-CONCEPT INVENTORY

LEARNING OBJECTIVES

- Describe the relationship between self-concept, self-esteem, and communication.
- Compare and contrast the perceived self and the presenting self as they relate to identity management.

INSTRUCTIONS

1. Transfer the list of up to 20 elements of your self-concept from the previous exercise (3.1) to index cards (or strips of paper).

2. Arrange your cards in a stack, with the one that *best* describes you at the top and the one that *least* describes you at the bottom.

3. Record the order in which you arranged the cards (1 is the most like you) in the Perceived Self column (Column 1). You may leave out some cards or add on to your list.

4. Without revealing your Perceived Self column, ask two other people (a friend, coworker, roommate, family member, classmate) to arrange the descriptors in an order in which they see you. Record these perceptions in Columns 2 and 3. Neither should see Column 1 or the other person's column. Record the name/relationship of your reviewers at the top of the appropriate column.

5. Compare the three tables, circling any descriptors that are exactly the same across the three columns. Highlight any that have similar ranks (no more than three numbers different).

6. Answer the questions at the end of this exercise.

Column 1 Perceived Self	Column 2 Presenting Self to _____ (relationship to you)	Column 3 Presenting Self to _____ (relationship to you)
1. _____	1. _____	1. _____
2. _____	2. _____	2. _____
3. _____	3. _____	3. _____
4. _____	4. _____	4. _____
5. _____	5. _____	5. _____
6. _____	6. _____	6. _____
7. _____	7. _____	7. _____
8. _____	8. _____	8. _____

Class _____   Name _____

9. _____	9. _____	9. _____
10. _____	10. _____	10. _____
11. _____	11. _____	11. _____
12. _____	12. _____	12. _____
13. _____	13. _____	13. _____
14. _____	14. _____	14. _____
15. _____	15. _____	15. _____
16. _____	16. _____	16. _____
17. _____	17. _____	17. _____
18. _____	18. _____	18. _____
19. _____	19. _____	19. _____
20. _____	20. _____	20. _____

Describe any differences between how you perceive your *perceived self* and the ways your reviewers perceive your *presenting self.*

_____

_____

_____

_____

_____

What factors do you think contribute to the differences in perception about who you are? Do you present the same *presenting self* to each reviewer? How does your relationship with each reviewer influence how you present yourself to them? How does the background and personality of each reviewer also influence how they perceive you?

_____

_____

Class _____   Name _____

_____

_____

_____

Whose view do you think most accurately reflects who you are? Why?

_____

_____

_____

_____

Would other people in your life view you like either of the people in this exercise? Give some specific examples with reasons why they would or would not have a similar perception.

_____

_____

_____

_____

In what, if any, ways did the reviewers' perceptions of who you are affect your sense of self?

_____

_____

_____

_____

3.3 EGO BOOSTERS AND EGO BUSTERS

LEARNING OBJECTIVES

- Describe the relationship between self-concept, self-esteem, and communication.
- Demonstrate how the principles in Chapter 3 can be used to change the self-concept, and hence communication.
- Compare and contrast the perceived self and the presenting self as they relate to identity management.

INSTRUCTIONS

1. In the appropriate spaces below describe the actions of several *ego boosters*: significant others who shaped your self-concept in a positive way. Also describe the behavior of *ego busters* who contributed to a more negative self-concept.
2. Next, recall several incidents in which you behaved as an ego booster or ego buster to others. Not all ego boosters and busters are obvious. Include in your description several incidents in which the messages were **subtle** or **nonverbal**.
3. Summarize the lessons you have learned from this experience by answering the questions at the end of this exercise.

EGO BOOSTER MESSAGES YOU HAVE RECEIVED

Example

I perceive(d) *my communication lab partner* **(significant other)** as telling me I am/was *attractive* **(self-concept element)** when he or she kept *sneaking glances at me and smiling during our taping project.*

MESSAGE

1. I perceived _____ (significant other) as telling me I am/was

   _____ (self-concept element) when he/she _____

   _____

   _____

MESSAGE

2. I perceived _____ (significant other) as telling me I am/was

   _____ (self-concept element) when he/she _____

_____

_____

EGO BUSTER MESSAGES YOU HAVE RECEIVED

Example

1. I perceive(d) _my neighbor_ **(significant other)** as telling me I am/was _not an important friend_ **(self-concept element)** when he/she _had a big party last weekend and didn't invite me._

MESSAGE

1. I perceived _____ (significant other) as telling me I am/was

    _____ (self-concept element) when he/she _____

    _____

    _____

MESSAGE

2. I perceived _____ (significant other) as telling me I am/was

    _____ (self-concept element) when he/she _____

    _____

    _____

EGO BOOSTER MESSAGES YOU HAVE SENT

Example

I was an ego booster to _my instructor_ when I _told her I enjoyed last Tuesday's lecture._

MESSAGE

1. I was a booster to _____ when I _____

    _____

    _____

MESSAGE

2.   I was a booster to _____ when I _____

_____

_____

EGO BUSTER MESSAGES YOU HAVE SENT

Example
I was an ego buster to *my sister* when I *forgot to phone her or send even a card on her birthday.*

MESSAGE

1.   I was a buster to _____ when I _____

_____

MESSAGE

2.   I was a buster to _____ when I _____

_____

CONCLUSIONS

Who are the people who have most influenced your self-concept in the past? What messages did each one send to influence you so strongly?

_____

_____

_____

What people are the greatest influences on your self-concept now? Is each person a positive or a negative influence? What messages does each one send to influence your self-concept?

_____

_____

_____

_____

Who are the people whom *you* have influenced greatly? What messages have you sent to each one about his or her self-concept? How have you sent these messages?

_____

_____

_____

What ego booster or ego buster messages do you want to send to the important people in your life? How (with what channels) can you send each one?

_____

_____

_____

GROUP DISCUSSION

After completing the first part of this activity individually, share some of your answers with a small group of classmates. Then, as a group, answer the questions that follow.

1. How have ego boosters been important in your life? Why do you think they took the time to act as a booster to you? When you act as an ego booster to others, what's your motivation?

   _____

   _____

2. What role have ego busters played in your life? Looking back, do you think they were purposefully acting as an ego buster, or were they unconscious about how they were communicating? What advice would you have in order to avoid inadvertently sending ego busters?

   _____

   _____

   _____

3. How has reviewing your experiences affected your understanding of the role you can play as a significant other in the lives of those you have relationships with?

   _____

   _____

   _____

3.4 RE-EVALUATING YOUR "CAN'TS"

LEARNING OBJECTIVES

- Explain how self-fulfilling prophecies shape the self-concept and influence communication.
- Understand how eliminating the word *can't* from your self-talk can improve your self-concept and influence how you communicate.

INSTRUCTIONS

1. Complete the following lists by describing communication-related difficulties you have in the following areas.
2. After filling in each blank space, follow the starred instructions that follow the list (*).

DIFFICULTIES YOU HAVE COMMUNICATING WITH FAMILY MEMBERS

EXAMPLES

I can't *discuss politics with my dad without having an argument* because *he's so set in his ways.*
I can't *tell my brother how much I love him* because *I'll feel foolish.*

1. I can't _____

    because _____

2. I can't _____

    because _____

* Corrections (see instructions at end of exercise)

_____

_____

DIFFICULTIES YOU HAVE COMMUNICATING WITH PEOPLE AT SCHOOL OR AT WORK

EXAMPLES

I can't *say "no" when my boss asks me to work overtime*
because *he'll fire me.*
I can't *participate in class discussions even when I know the answers or have a question*
because *I just freeze up.*

1. I can't _____

    because _____

Class _____   Name _____

2. I can't _____

    because _____

* Corrections (see instructions at end of exercise)

_____

_____

DIFFICULTIES YOU HAVE COMMUNICATING WITH STRANGERS

EXAMPLES

I can't *start a conversation with someone I've never met before*
because *I'll look stupid.*
I can't *ask smokers to move or stop smoking*
because *they'll get mad.*

1. I can't _____

    because _____

2. I can't _____

    because _____

* Corrections (see instructions at end of exercise)

_____

_____

DIFFICULTIES YOU HAVE COMMUNICATING WITH FRIENDS

EXAMPLES
I can't *find the courage to ask my friend to repay the money he owes me*
because *I'm afraid he'll question our friendship.*
I can't *say no when friends ask me to do favors and I'm busy*
because *I'm afraid they'll think I'm not their friend.*

1. I can't _____

    because _____

2. I can't _____

      because _____

* Corrections (see instructions at end of exercise)

_____

_____

DIFFICULTIES YOU HAVE COMMUNICATING WITH YOUR ROMANTIC PARTNER (PAST OR PRESENT)

EXAMPLES

I can't *tell Bill to wear a tie to the party*
because *he'll laugh at me.*
I can't *bring up going to visit my parents*
because *we'll fight.*

1. I can't _____

      because _____

2. I can't _____

      because _____

* Corrections (see instructions at end of exercise)

_____

_____

LIMITING PREDICTIONS MADE BY OTHERS

EXAMPLES

You'll never amount to anything.   You can't expect much with your background.
You're just like your father.   The James children never were too bright.

1. _____

Class _____   Name _____

2. _____

* Corrections (see instructions at end of exercise)

_____

_____

*After you have completed the list, continue as follows:

a.   Read the list you have made. Actually say each item to yourself and note your feelings.
b.   Now read the list again, but with a slight difference. For each "can't," substitute the word "won't" or "until now I've chosen not to." For instance, "I can't say no to friends' requests" becomes "I won't say no" or "Until now I've chosen not to say no." Are any of your statements actually *won'ts* or *choices* rather than *can'ts?* Circle them now.
c.   Read the list for a third time. For this repetition, substitute "I don't know how" or "I haven't yet learned to" for your original "can't." Instead of saying "I can't approach strangers," say, "I don't know how to approach strangers." *Correct* your original list to show which statements are actually truer when you say "don't know how" or "haven't yet learned" rather than "I can't."
d.   For the Limiting predictions made by others' statements, substitute a nonlimiting statement to make the prediction untrue by inserting "I can choose" or "I can learn." (Example: "I am my father's child, but I can choose not to repeat behaviors he has that I don't like.")

After completing this exercise, consider your greater awareness of the power that negative self-fulfilling prophecies have on your self-concept and thus on your communication behavior. Imagine how differently you would behave if you eliminated any incorrect uses of the word *can't* from your thinking.

3.5 MEDIATED MESSAGES—IDENTITY MANAGEMENT

LEARNING OBJECTIVES

- Understand how mediated impression management differs from face-to-face impression management.
- Identify the ways individuals manage identity in mediated contexts.
- Reflect on how impression management in mediated contexts can affect honesty.

INSTRUCTIONS

For each question, take a minute and jot down some notes. Then, discuss each of the questions in your group, letting each person share something. After everyone has had the opportunity to share, have a more extended discussion and, if directed by your instructor, prepare to report your group's conclusions back to the whole class.

1. Identity management is important in mediated contexts. Describe how you manage identity in any mediated contexts you use (online dating services, written notes, email, email address, instant messaging, blogging, personal ads, web pages).

   _____

   _____

2. Do you prefer to meet people online or face-to-face initially? Why? Is your answer the same or different for friendships than for work or career situations? Why?

   _____

   _____

3. Have you ever questioned someone's online representation of who they are? What led you to feel that their presenting self wasn't honest? What were the consequences?

   _____

   _____

4. Have you ever deliberately misrepresented who you are online? What led you to feel that you needed to manage your presenting self in that way? Do you feel you were being dishonest? What were the consequences?

   _____

   _____

3.6 ASSESSING IDENTITY MANAGEMENT

LEARNING OBJECTIVES

- Compare and contrast the ways identities adapt to differing contexts.
- Understand the relationship between the presenting self and identity management.

INSTRUCTIONS

Return to Activity 3.1 Who Do You Think You Are?
From Part B, choose your top three identities and list them below. Then in the context below, describe the communication strategies you use to influence how others view you when you are presenting that identity. If you don't present one of your identities in one of the contexts, explain why.

Identity #1 _____ Identity #2 _____ Identity #3 _____

At school:

IDENTITY #1 _____

IDENTITY #2 _____

IDENTITY #3 _____

With your family:

IDENTITY #1 _____

IDENTITY #2 _____

IDENTITY #3 _____

At work:

IDENTITY #1 _____

IDENTITY #2 _____

IDENTITY #3 _____

Online:

IDENTITY #1 _____

IDENTITY #2 _____

IDENTITY #3 _____

After completing this activity, reflect on what you've learned about the role identity management plays in your everyday life. What's the most surprising thing you learned about how you manage your identity?

_____

_____

3.7 BREADTH AND DEPTH OF RELATIONSHIPS

LEARNING OBJECTIVES

- Identify the dimensions of intimacy that operate and how they are expressed in a specific relationship.
- Explain the need for both intimacy and distance in a given relationship.
- Use the social penetration model to identify the nature of self-disclosing communication in one of your relationships.

INSTRUCTIONS

1. Use the form below to make a social penetration model for a significant relationship you have, indicating the depth and breadth of various areas. See Figure 3.2 in Chapter 3 of *Looking Out / Looking In* for an example of the social penetration model.
2. Answer the questions at the end of the exercise.

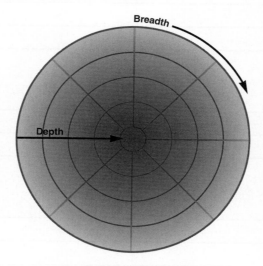

Social Penetration Model

Significant relationship described: _____

Based on the Social Penetration Model:

How deep or shallow (the degree of intimacy in the information that is shared) is your relationship with this person?

_____

_____

Class _____   Name _____

Does the depth vary from one area (area reflecting the breadth information across a range of topics) to another? In what way?

_____

_____

_____

Are you satisfied with the depth and breadth of this relationship? Why or why not?

_____

_____

_____

If you are not satisfied, what could you do to change the relationship? What would you predict the results would be?

_____

_____

_____

_____

_____

_____

_____

_____

3.8 REASONS FOR NONDISCLOSURE

LEARNING OBJECTIVES

- Use the social penetration and Johari Window models to identify the nature of self-disclosing communication in one of your relationships.
- Outline the potential benefits and risks of disclosing in a selected situation.

INSTRUCTIONS

1. Choose a particular individual about whom you want to analyze your self-disclosing behavior.
2. In the column to the left of each item, indicate the extent to which you use each reason to avoid disclosing.

    5 = almost always
    4 = often
    3 = sometimes
    2 = rarely
    1 = never

3. In the column to the right of each item, indicate how reasonable and realistic the reason is.

    5 = totally realistic
    4 = mostly realistic
    3 = partly realistic, partly unrealistic
    2 = mostly unrealistic
    1 = totally unrealistic

How Frequently Do You Use the Reason?		How Realistic and Rational Is the Reason?
_____	1. I can't find the opportunity to self-disclose with this person.	_____
_____	2. If I disclose, I might hurt the other person.	_____
_____	3. If I disclose, I might be evaluating or judging the person.	_____
_____	4. I can't think of topics that I would disclose.	_____
_____	5. Self-disclosure would give information that might be used against me at some time.	_____
_____	6. If I disclose, it might cause me to make personal changes.	_____
_____	7. Self-disclosure might threaten relationships I have with people other than the close acquaintance to whom I disclose.	_____

_____   8. Self-disclosure is a sign of weakness.   _____

_____   9. If I disclose, I might lose control over the other person.   _____

_____   10. If I disclose, I might discover I am less than I wish to be.   _____

_____   11. If I disclose, I might project an image I do not want to project.   _____

_____   12. If I disclose, the other person might not understand what
I was saying.   _____

_____   13. If I disclose, the other person might evaluate me negatively.   _____

_____   14. Self-disclosure is a sign of some emotional disturbance.   _____

_____   15. Self-disclosure might hurt our relationship.   _____

_____   16. I am afraid that self-disclosure might lead to an intimate
relationship with the other person.   _____

_____   17. Self-disclosure might threaten my physical safety.   _____

_____   18. If I disclose, I might give information that makes me appear
inconsistent.   _____

_____   19. Any other reasons: _____

*Based on a survey developed by Lawrence B. Rosenfeld, "Self-Disclosure Avoidance: Why Am I Afraid to Tell You Who I Am?"
Communication Monographs 46 (1979): 63–74.

What does this personal survey tell you about your thoughts and feelings about self-disclosure with
this person?

_____

_____

_____

Do you think your level of self-disclosure is appropriate or inappropriate with this person? Why or
why not?

_____

_____

How would you summarize and categorize the major reasons that you self-disclose using these categories: Catharsis, Reciprocity, Self-clarification, Self-validation, Identity management, Relational maintenance, Social influence?

_____

_____

_____

How different would your survey look if you'd chosen a different relationship? Why?

_____

_____

3.9 DEGREES OF SELF-DISCLOSURE

LEARNING OBJECTIVES

- Use the social penetration and Johari Window models to identify the nature of self-disclosing communication in one of your relationships.
- Identify the qualitative differences inherent in various topics for self-disclosure.

INSTRUCTIONS

For each of the following topics, write two statements for each level of self-disclosure. (See Chapter 3 of *Looking Out / Looking In* for descriptions of each level.)

EXAMPLE

Topic: School

1. Clichés
   a. *Finals are no fun!*
   b. *Textbooks sure are expensive!*

2. Facts
   a. *I'm a psychology major at the university.*
   b. *I'm getting a teaching certificate so I'll be able to teach social studies.*

3. Opinions
   a. *I think people over 18 should be allowed to keep a driver's license if they don't vote.*
   b. *I don't think instructors should count attendance as part of a person's grade.*

4. Feelings
   a. *I feel scared when I think about the future. I'm almost finished with four years of college, and I'm still confused about what to do with my life.*
   b. *I get angry when Professor Autel doesn't prepare adequately for our class.*

TOPIC: MY FAMILY

1. Clichés

   a. _____

   b. _____

2. Facts

   a. _____

   b. _____

3. Opinions

    a. _____

    b. _____

4. Feelings

    a. _____

    b. _____

TOPIC: MY CAREER PLANS

1. Clichés

    a. _____

    b. _____

2. Facts

    a. _____

    b. _____

3. Opinions

    a. _____

    b. _____

4. Feelings

    a. _____

    b. _____

TOPIC: POLITICS

1. Clichés

    a. _____

    b. _____

Class _____   Name _____

2. Facts

    a. _____

    b. _____

3. Opinions

    a. _____

    b. _____

4. Feelings

    a. _____

    b. _____

TOPIC: SPORTS

1. Clichés

    a. _____

    b. _____

2. Facts

    a. _____

    b. _____

3. Opinions

    a. _____

    b. _____

4. Feelings

    a. _____

    b. _____

3.10 DISCLOSURE AND ALTERNATIVES

LEARNING OBJECTIVES

- Understand the range of alternatives to self-disclosure.
- Assess the effectiveness and ethical nature of the range of alternatives to self-disclosure.

INSTRUCTIONS

1. For each situation described below, record responses for the types listed.
2. Evaluate the effectiveness and ethics of your responses.
3. Describe a disclosure situation of your own in the same manner.

EXAMPLE

Your friend asks you if you had a good time when you went out with his cousin last night.
Self-disclosure: *I didn't have a great time, but then we were just getting to know one another. I don't think that we had much in common.*
Silence: *If I don't answer or don't say anything, my friend might think it was worse than I do.*
Lying: *Your cousin was a lot of fun and the movie was great.*
Equivocating: *First dates are really times of discovery, aren't they?*
Hinting: *I don't think I have to have a great time every night.*
Which response is most effective/which most ethical? *I think equivocating is effective.*
While I wasn't exactly self-disclosing with my friend, I just don't want to tell him how boring I think his cousin is. I haven't lied, and both of them can save face, too.

1. After your romantic partner has a bad week at work, his or her boss asks you how he or she is feeling about the company.

   Self-Disclosure _____

   Silence _____

   Lying _____

   Equivocating _____

   Hinting _____

   Which responses are most effective? Which are most ethical? _____

   _____

   _____

2. You are applying to rent an apartment that prohibits animals. You have a cat.

Self-Disclosure _____

Silence _____

Lying _____

Equivocating _____

Hinting _____

Which responses are most effective? Which are most ethical? _____

_____

_____

3. Your siblings ask you about your financial status (which is much better than theirs).

Self-Disclosure _____

Silence _____

Lying _____

Equivocating _____

Hinting _____

Which responses are most effective? Which are most ethical? _____

_____

_____

4. Your roommates ask what you think of the bright posters they've just put up around the living room.

Self-Disclosure _____

Silence _____

Lying _____

Equivocating _____

Hinting _____

Which responses are most effective? Which are most ethical? _____

_____

_____

5. Your romantic partner asks how many other people you've really loved before you met him or her.

Self-Disclosure _____

Silence _____

Lying _____

Equivocating _____

Hinting _____

Which responses are most effective? Which are most ethical? _____

_____

_____

6. Your very opinionated father, whose opinions differ from yours, asks what you think of the person running for governor.

Self-Disclosure _____

Silence _____

Lying _____

Equivocating _____

Hinting _____

Which responses are most effective? Which are most ethical? _____

_____

_____

7. Your boss wants to know what your plans for the future are; you're looking around for a new job.

Self-Disclosure _____

Silence _____

Lying _____

Equivocating _____

Hinting _____

Which responses are most effective? Which are most ethical? _____

_____

_____

8. Your mother asks you about what your brother has been up to lately. You know he is probably moving out of state in a few months, but he doesn't want your mom to know yet.

Self-Disclosure _____

Silence _____

Lying _____

Equivocating _____

Hinting _____

Which responses are most effective? Which are most ethical? _____

_____

_____

9. Your example: _____

Self-Disclosure _____

Silence _____

Lying _____

Equivocating _____

Hinting _____

Which responses are most effective? Which are most ethical? _____

_____

_____

STUDY GUIDE

CHECK YOUR UNDERSTANDING

TRUE/FALSE

Mark the statements below as true or false. Correct each statement that is false on the lines below to create a true statement.

_____ 1. Collaboration in identity management means absolute agreement about each person's role.

_____

_____ 2. Most researchers agree that we are born with a fully formed self-concept.

_____

_____ 3. Some studies show that people strongly influenced by media body images develop more negative self-images.

_____

_____ 4. Obsolete information can contribute to a distorted self-evaluation.

_____

_____ 5. Research has shown that people with high self-esteem seek out partners who view them unfavorably because they are strong enough to take the criticism.

_____

_____ 6. Personality is flexible, dynamic, and shaped by experiences.

_____

_____ 7. Self-concept is objective.

_____

_____ 8. The self-concept is such a powerful force that it not only influences how you see yourself in the present but also can actually influence your future behavior and that of others.

_____

_____ 9. Your presenting self is the person you believe yourself to be in a moment of honest self-examination.

_____

_____ 10. High self-monitors feel less intimacy, satisfaction, and commitment in their romantic relationships because they do not hide what they really feel.

_____

_____ 11. Trying on a "new self" can be a means to self-improvement.

_____

_____ 12. Communication researchers use the term *privacy management* to describe the choices people make to reveal or conceal information about themselves.

_____

COMPLETION

Fill in the blanks with the correct terms chosen from the list below.

distorted feedback	obsolete information	self-delusion
ego booster	ego buster	realistic expectations
realistic perceptions	manner	self-fulfilling prophecy
appearance		

1. _____ is someone who helps enhance your self-esteem by acting in ways that make you feel accepted, important, and loved.

2. _____ is someone who acts to reduce your self-esteem.

3. _____ are messages that others send to you that are unrealistically positive or negative.

4. _____ consists of a communicator's words and nonverbal actions that help create an impression.

5. _____ is information that was once true about you that is no longer true.

6. _____ are the personal items people use to shape an image.

7. _____ is the inability to see a real need for change in the self, due to holding an unrealistically favorable picture of yourself.

8. _____ are reasonable goals to set for self-growth.

9. _____ occurs when expectations of an event influence a person's behavior, which in turn influences the event's outcome.

10. _____ are relatively accurate views of the strengths and weaknesses of the self.

MULTIPLE CHOICE

Identify which principle influences the self-concept in each example.

    a. obsolete information

    b. distorted feedback

    c. emphasis on perfection

    d. social expectations

1. _____ You always scored more points than anyone else on your team in high school. You still think you're the best even though your college teammates are scoring more than you.

2. _____ You keep getting down on yourself because you can't cook as well as Megan, even though you are a great student and a fair athlete.

3. _____ You believe people shouldn't brag or boast, so you tell others that you "blew" the chemistry test and got a C– but you never acknowledge your A's in math.

4. _____ Your parents tell you, their friends, and all your relatives about all your wonderful accomplishments, even though you have only average achievement.

5. _____ Janee says that you are insensitive to her perspective despite your many attempts to listen honestly to her and empathize.

6. _____ You pay a lot of attention to the magazines showing perfectly dressed and groomed individuals and keep wishing you could look as good as they do.

7. _____ You think of yourself as the shy fifth grader despite being at the social hub of at least three clubs on campus.

8. _____ You feel uncomfortable accepting the compliments your friends honestly give you.

9. _____ You're exhausted by trying to get all A's, working 30 hours a week, and being a loving romantic partner at the same time. You don't see how so many other people manage to get it all done.

10. _____ "You're the perfect weight," your father tells you despite your recent gain of twenty pounds over the normal weight for your height.

Choose the *best* answer for each statement below:

11. Deciding which part of your self-concept to reveal to others is termed
    a. prophecy.
    b. impression management.
    c. collectivism.
    d. two-faced syndrome.

12. The most significant part of a person's self-concept is
    a. the social roles the person plays.
    b. his or her appearance.
    c. his or her accomplishments.
    d. different for different people.

13. Self-esteem has to do with evaluations of
    a. self-concept.
    b. self-image.
    c. self-worth.
    d. self-discovery.

14. Which of the following could be an example of a self-fulfilling prophecy?
    a. Sid is born with a very large nose.
    b. Margarita has a very large, extended family.
    c. Serge is a Russian immigrant.
    d. Joy has given up on trying to talk to her unreasonable father.

15. All of the following are benefits of self-disclosure *except*:
    a. building relationships.
    b. self-clarification.
    c. self-indulgence.
    d. self-validation.

16. Which of the following statements about gender and self-concept is correct?
    a. Women struggle with self-esteem issues more than men.
    b. Men's sense of superiority tends to decrease over time.
    c. Men tend to have low appraisals of their leadership and athletic abilities.
    d. Women tend to have high appraisals of their leadership and athletic abilities.

17. The influence of significant others
    a. is the sole determinant of our self-concept.
    b. becomes less powerful as people grow older.
    c. is synonymous with the term reflected appraisal.
    d. only occurs in people with poor self-concepts.

18. Online impression management always
    a. is dishonest.
    b. is an opportunity to effectively manage impressions.
    c. is a disadvantage compared to face-to-face communication.
    d. lessens the amount of interpersonal communication.

19. Which is the fourth stage of a self-fulfilling prophecy?
    a. holding an expectation (for yourself or for others)
    b. behaving in accordance with that expectation
    c. coming to pass of the expectation
    d. reinforcing the original expectation

20. All of the following are alternatives to self-disclosure *except*:
    a. hinting
    b. equivocating
    c. defending your position
    d. lying

CHAPTER THREE STUDY GUIDE ANSWERS

TRUE/FALSE

1. F	5. F	9. F
2. T	6. T	10. F
3. T	7. F	11. T
4. T	8. T	12. T

COMPLETION

1. ego booster	5. obsolete information	9. self-fulfilling prophecy
2. ego buster	6. appearance	10. realistic perceptions
3. distorted feedback	7. self-delusion	
4. manner	8. realistic expectations	

MULTIPLE CHOICE

1. a	5. b	9. c	13. c	17. b
2. c	6. c	10. b	14. d	18. b
3. d	7. a	11. b	15. c	19. d
4. b	8. d	12. d	16. a	20. c

MindTap START ...
Explore this chapter's
topics online.

4

PERCEPTION: WHAT YOU SEE IS WHAT YOU GET

AFTER STUDYING THE TOPICS IN THIS CHAPTER, YOU SHOULD BE ABLE TO:

1. Describe how the processes of selection, organization, interpretation, and negotiation shape communication in a given situation.

2. Explain how influences on perception affect communication in a specific situation.

3. Analyze how common perception tendencies have distorted your appraisals of another person, and hence your communication. Use this information to present a more accurate alternative set of perceptions.

4. Demonstrate how you might use the skill of perception checking in a significant relationship.

5. Enhance your cognitive complexity by applying the "pillow method" in a significant disagreement. Explain how your expanded view of this situation might affect your communication with the other(s) involved.

Study M. C. Escher's drawing *Relativity* seen here. It pictures a strange universe in which the inhabitants of each world exist at right angles, disconnected from one another's experience. This surreal vision provides a useful metaphor for challenges we encounter every day. Each of us experiences a different reality, and failing to understand other people's point of view can lead to problems on both practical and relational levels. But perceptual differences can enhance as well as interfere with relationships. By seeing the world through others' eyes, you can gain insights that are different—and often more valuable—than those arising out of your own experiences.

This chapter will help you deal with the challenge of communicating in the face of perceptual differences. We will begin by looking at some of the reasons why the world appears different to each of us. In our survey we'll explore several areas: how our psychological makeup, personal needs, interests, and biases shape our perceptions; the physiological factors that influence our view of the world; the social roles that affect our image of events; and the role that culture plays in creating our ideas of what behavior is proper. After examining the perceptual factors that can drive us apart, we'll look at two useful skills for bridging the perceptual gap.

THE PERCEPTION PROCESS

Our perception of the world around us is affected by who we are. A simple walk in the park would probably be a different experience for companions with different interests. A botanist might notice the vegetation; a fashion designer might pay attention to the way people are dressed; and an artist might be aware of the colors and forms of the people and surroundings. It's simply impossible to be aware of everything, no matter how attentive we might be. There's just too much going on. Because this ability to organize our perceptions is such a critical factor in our ability to function, we need to begin our study of perception by taking a closer look at this process. We can do so by examining the four steps by which we attach meaning to our experiences: selection, organization, interpretation, and negotiation.

Selection

Since we're exposed to more input than we can possibly manage, the first step in perception is the **selection** of which impressions we will attend to. Several factors cause us to notice some things and ignore others.

Stimuli that are *intense* often attract our attention. Something that is louder, larger, or brighter stands out. This explains why—other things being equal—we're more likely to remember extremely tall or short people, and why someone who laughs or talks loudly at a party attracts more attention (not always favorable) than do quiet guests.

Repetitious stimuli, repetitious stimuli, repetitious stimuli, repetitious stimuli, repetitious stimuli, repetitious stimuli also attract attention.[1] Just as a quiet but steadily dripping faucet can come to dominate our awareness, people to whom we're frequently exposed become noticeable.

ATTENTION IS ALSO FREQUENTLY RELATED TO contrast OR change IN STIMULATION. Put differently, unchanging people or things become less noticeable. This principle gives an explanation (excuse?) for why we take wonderful people for granted when we interact with them frequently. It's only when they stop being so wonderful or go away that we appreciate them.

Motives also determine what information we select from our environment. If you're anxious about being late for a date, you'll notice whatever clocks may be around you; and if you're hungry, you'll become aware of any restaurants, markets, and billboards advertising food in your path. Motives also determine how we perceive people. For example, someone on the lookout for a romantic adventure will be especially aware of attractive potential partners, whereas the same person at a different time might be oblivious to anyone but police or medical personnel in an emergency.

Selection isn't just a matter of attending to some stimuli: It also involves ignoring other cues. If, for example, you decide that someone is a terrific person, you may overlook his or her flaws. If you are focused on examples of unfair male bosses, you might not recognize unfair female bosses. For an interesting example of how we select some stimuli and ignore others, search "perception illusion" online and look for videos related to the work of researcher Daniel Simons.[2]

∧ FIGURE 4.1
© Cengage Learning

Organization

Along with selecting information from the environment, we must arrange it in some meaningful way. You can see how the principle of **organization** works by looking at Figure 4.1. You can view the picture either as one of a vase or as one of two twins, depending on whether you focus on the light or the dark areas. In instances such as this, we make sense of stimuli by noticing some data that stand out as a *figure* against a less striking *ground*. The "vase-face" drawing is interesting, because it allows us to choose between two sets of figure-ground relationships.

This principle of figure-ground organization operates in communication, too. Recall, for instance, how certain speech can suddenly stand out from a babble of voices. Sometimes the words are noticeable because they include your name, whereas at other times they might be spoken by a familiar voice.

Each of us can organize our impressions of other communicators using a number of schemes (called *perceptual schema* by social scientists). Sometimes we classify people according to their *appearance*: male or female, beautiful or ugly, heavy or thin, young or old, and so on. At other times we classify people according to their *social roles*: student, attorney, wife, etc. Another way we classify people is by their *interaction style*: friendly, helpful, aloof, and sarcastic are examples. In other cases we classify people by their *psychological traits* such as curious, nervous, and insecure. Finally, we can use others' *membership*, classifying them according to the group to which they belong: Democrat, immigrant, Christian, and so on.

The perceptual schemas we use shape the way we think about and communicate with others. If you've classified a professor, for example, as "friendly," you'll handle questions or problems one way; if you've classified a professor as "mean," your behavior will probably be quite different. What constructs do you use to classify the people you encounter in your life? Consider how your relationship might change if you used different schemas.

Stereotyping   After we've chosen an organizing scheme to classify people, we use that scheme to make generalizations and predictions about members of the groups who fit the categories we use. For example, if you're especially aware of gender, you might be alert to the differences between the way men and women behave or the way they are treated. If religion plays an important part in your life, you might think of members of your faith differently from others. If ethnicity is an important issue for you, you probably tune in to the differences between members of various ethnic groups. There's nothing wrong with generalizations as long as they are accurate. In fact, it would be impossible to get through life without them.

But when generalizations lose touch with reality, they lead to **stereotyping**— exaggerated generalizations associated with a categorizing system.[3] Stereotypes may be based on a kernel of truth, but they go beyond the facts at hand and make claims that usually have no valid basis.

You can begin to get a sense of your tendency to make generalizations and to stereotype by completing the following sentences:

1. Women are _____
2. Men are _____

3. Republicans are _____
4. Vegetarians are _____
5. Muslims are _____
6. Older people are _____

It's likely that you were able to complete each sentence without much hesitation. Does this mean you were stereotyping? You can answer this question by deciding whether your generalizations fit the three characteristics of stereotypes (we'll use "older people" as an example):

- *You often categorize people on the basis of an easily recognized characteristic.* Age is relatively simple to identify, so if you see someone who appears to be in her eighties, you might quickly categorize her as "elderly."

- *You ascribe a set of characteristics to most or all members of a category.* Based on your (limited) experiences with some elderly relatives, you conclude that older people have trouble hearing and are not mentally alert.

- *You apply the set of characteristics to any member of the group.* When you run into an elderly person at the store, you talk very loudly and slowly. Of course, that can be extremely annoying to energetic and sprightly older people who do not fit your stereotype.[4]

PAUSE *and* REFLECT

Your Perceptual Schema

MindTap **REFLECT . . .** on your perceptual schema by answering the following questions, either here or online.

1. Identify which of the five general types of organizing schema (i.e., appearance, social roles, interaction style, psychological traits, or membership) you would use to classify people in each of the following contexts. After you've selected a primary organizing schema, offer a personal description within each type (e.g., attractive, roughly the same age as me).

   a. Spending time with new acquaintances at a party

   b. Socializing with fellow workers on the job

   c. Choosing teammates for an important class project

   d. Offering help to a stranded motorist

2. For each of the given contexts, consider:

   a. Other schema you might use.

   b. The consequences of using the schema you originally chose and the alternative you identified in the preceding step.

   c. In general, how might your relationships change if you used different constructs?

Allstar Picture library

∧ The comedy *Dear White People* chronicles the challenges faced by the handful of black students at a fictitious Ivy League university. The film shines a humorous spotlight on the juggling act the students of color face retaining their unique identities while being stereotyped by the white majority. When do you stereotype others? How does that affect your relationships with people from different backgrounds?

Once we buy into stereotypes, we often seek out isolated behaviors that support our inaccurate beliefs. For example, men and women in conflict often remember only behaviors of the other sex that fit their gender stereotypes.[5] They then point to these behaviors— which might not be representative of how the other person typically behaves—as "evidence" to suit their stereotypical and inaccurate claims: "Look! There you go criticizing me again. Typical for a woman!"

Stereotypes can plague interracial communication.[6] Surveys of college student attitudes show that many blacks characterize whites as "demanding" and "manipulative," whereas many whites characterize blacks as "loud" and "ostentatious." Stereotypes like these can hamper professional relationships as well as personal ones. For example, doctor–patient communication in the United States—particularly between white physicians and minority patients— can suffer from stereotyping on both sides. Physicians may fail to provide important information because they think their patients won't understand, and patients may not ask important questions because they believe their doctors don't have time for them. These kinds of expectations lead to self-fulfilling spirals and poorer health care.[7]

Stereotyping doesn't always arise from bad intentions. In some cases, careless generalizations can grow from good intentions, and even from a little bit of knowledge. For example, knowing that people raised in collectivistic cultures (see Chapter 3) tend to conform to group norms may lead you to mistakenly assume that anyone you meet from such a background is likely to be a selfless team player. But not all members of a group are equally collectivistic, or individualistic, for that matter. For example, a study of Americans of European and Latin descent showed differences within each group.[8] Some Latinos were more independent than some Euro Americans, and vice versa. Moreover, teens in Japan (a traditionally collectivist culture) say they often feel torn between collectivism and individualism, between time-honored traditions and contemporary trends.[9] As our world's "global village" becomes more connected by technology and media, generalizations about specific cultures are likely to become less accurate.

One way to avoid the kinds of communication problems that come from excessive stereotyping is to decategorize others, giving yourself a chance to treat them as individuals instead of assuming that they possess the same characteristics as every other member of the group to which you assign them. Consider how your communication with others might change if you moved some of their characteristics to the "background" and others to the "foreground" during your interactions.

Punctuation   The process of organizing goes beyond our generalized perceptions of people. We also can sequence our interactions with others in different ways, and this can have a powerful effect on our relationships. Communication theorists use the term **punctuation** to describe the determination of causes and effects in a series of interactions.[10] You can begin to understand how punctuation operates by visualizing a running quarrel between a husband and wife. The husband accuses the wife of being too demanding, whereas she complains that he is withdrawing from her. Notice that the order in which each partner punctuates this cycle affects how the quarrel looks. The husband begins by blaming the wife: "I withdraw because you're so demanding." The wife organizes the situation differently, starting with the husband: "I demand so much because you withdraw." These kinds of demand-withdraw arguments are frequent in intimate relationships.[11] After the cycle gets rolling, it is impossible to say which accusation is accurate. The answer depends on how the sentence is punctuated. Figure 4.2 illustrates how this process operates.

Differing punctuations can lead to a variety of communication problems. Notice how the following situations seem different depending on how they're punctuated:

"I don't like your friend because he never has anything to say."

"He doesn't talk to you because you act like you don't like him."

"I keep talking because you interrupt so much."

"I interrupt because you don't give me a chance to say what's on my mind."

The kind of finger-pointing that goes along with arguing over which punctuation scheme is correct will probably make matters worse. It's far more productive to recognize that a dispute can look different to each party and then move on to the more important question of "What can we do to make things better?"

John Jonik

Interpretation

After we have selected and organized our perceptions, we interpret the information we've collected and sorted. **Interpretation**—attaching meaning to

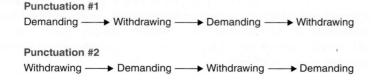

Punctuation #1

Demanding ⟶ Withdrawing ⟶ Demanding ⟶ Withdrawing

Punctuation #2

Withdrawing ⟶ Demanding ⟶ Withdrawing ⟶ Demanding

◄ **FIGURE 4.2**
The Same Event Can Be Punctuated in More Than One Way

SKILL *Builder*

Punctuation Practice

MindTap® **PRACTICE . . .** your skill at different punctuation patterns by answering the following questions either here or online.

You can appreciate how different punctuation patterns can influence attitudes and behavior by following these directions.

1. Use the format pictured in Figure 4.2 to diagram the following situations from the point of view of both people involved. Consider how the differing punctuation patterns would affect the way the two people in each situation respond to one another.

   a. A father and daughter are growing more and more distant. The daughter withdraws because she interprets her father's coolness as rejection. The father views his daughter's aloofness as a rebuff and withdraws further.

   b. The relationship between two friends is becoming strained. One jokes to lighten up the tension, and the other becomes more tense.

   c. A dating couple is on the verge of breaking up. One partner frequently asks the other to show more affection. The other withdraws physical contact.

2. Now identify an ongoing difficult communication issue in your own life. Punctuate it in two ways: how you would punctuate it, and how the other person might punctuate it. Discuss how seeing the issue from the other person's point of view might change the way you communicate as you discuss the issue.

---

sense data—plays a role in virtually every interpersonal act. Is the person who smiles at you across a crowded room interested in romance or simply being polite? Is a friend's kidding a sign of affection or irritation? Should you take an invitation to "drop by any time" literally or not?

Several factors cause us to interpret an event in one way or another:

Degree of involvement with the other person. Two coworkers offer you the same excuse for why they were late to work. One is a close friend; the other is someone you barely know. Chances are good that you'll interpret your friend's excuse far more charitably.

Personal experience. What meanings have similar events held? If, for example, you've been gouged by landlords in the past, you might be skeptical about an apartment manager's assurances that careful housekeeping will assure you the refund of your cleaning deposit.

Assumptions about human behavior. "People generally do as little work as possible to get by." "In spite of their mistakes, people are doing the best they can." Beliefs like these will shape the way we interpret another's actions.

Attitudes. The attitudes we hold shape the way we make sense of others' behaviors. For example, what would you think if you overheard one man say "I love you" to another man? In one study, people with a high degree of homophobia (the fear of or discrimination against homosexuals) were likely to interpret this comment as an indication that the speaker was gay. Those with lower levels of homophobia were more likely to regard the affectionate statement as platonic rather than romantic.[12]

Expectations. Anticipation shapes interpretations.[13] As you read in Chapter 3, teachers who expect their students to do well will regard and treat those pupils differently. The same is true with our interpersonal interactions: Our expectations affect how we perceive and behave around others. We'll talk more about this common tendency later in the chapter.

Knowledge. If you know that a friend has just been jilted by a lover or been fired from a job, you'll interpret his aloof behavior differently than you would if you were unaware of what had happened. If you know that an instructor speaks sarcastically to all students, you won't be as likely to take her remarks personally.

Self-concept. When you're feeling insecure, the world is a very different place from the world you experience when you're feeling secure. For example, the recipient's self-concept is the most significant factor in determining whether people who are being teased interpret the teaser's motives as being friendly or hostile, and whether they respond with comfort or defensiveness.[14] The way we feel about ourselves strongly influences how we interpret others' behavior.

Relational satisfaction. The behavior that seems positive when you are happy with a partner might seem completely different when you are discontent with that person. For example, unsatisfied partners in a couple are more likely than satisfied partners to blame one another when things go wrong.[15] They are also more likely to believe that their partners are selfish and have negative intentions.

Although we have talked about selection, organization, and interpretation separately, the three phases of perception can occur in differing sequences. For example, a parent or babysitter's past interpretations (such as "Jason is a troublemaker") can influence future selections (his behavior becomes especially noticeable) and the organization of events (when there's a fight, the assumption is that Jason started it). As with all communication, perception is an ongoing process in which it is difficult to pin down beginnings and endings.

Negotiation

So far our discussion has focused on the components of perception—selection, organization, and interpretation—that take place in each individual's mind. But perception isn't just a solitary activity. A big part of sense-making occurs between and among people as they influence one another's perceptions and try to achieve a shared perspective. This process is known as **negotiation**.

It's rare to draw a conclusion about something or someone without comparing notes with others. Say for instance that you think a person you just met is attractive. It's likely that you'll ask friends for their opinions. If you hear negative appraisals, you might shift your initial perception—maybe not radically, but at least a bit. In one study that examined this process, college students rated the attractiveness of models in a series of photos.[16] Those who were able to see others' evaluations of the same photos slowly shifted their ratings to match the consensus. This suggests that beauty isn't just in the eye of the (individual) beholder—it's in the eyes of the (negotiating) beholders.

∧ In the film *Enough Said*, Eva (Julia Louis-Dreyfus) changes her positive appraisal of new boyfriend Albert (James Gandolfini) after hearing negative information about him from his ex-wife. Has your narrative opinion of another person shifted after receiving new input from others?

20th Century Fox/Allstar

One way to understand how negotiation operates is to view interpersonal communication as an exchange of stories. Scholars call the stories we use to describe our personal world **narratives**.[17] Virtually every interpersonal situation can be described by more than one narrative. These narratives often differ. Ask two quarreling children why they're fighting, and they'll each describe how the other person is responsible for launching the conflict. Likewise, courtrooms are filled with opponents who tell very different narratives about who is the "villain" and who is the "hero." Conflict management is often a process of negotiating divergent perceptions of the same event.

When our narratives clash with those of others, we can either hang on to our own point of view and refuse to consider anyone else's (usually not productive) or we can try to negotiate a narrative that creates at least some common ground. Shared narratives provide the best chance for smooth communication. For example, romantic partners who celebrate their successful struggles against relational obstacles are happier than those who don't have this shared appreciation.[18] Likewise, couples who agree about the important turning points in their relationships are more satisfied than those who have different views of what incidents were most important.[19]

Shared narratives don't have to be accurate to be powerful. Couples who report being happily married after fifty or more years seem to collude in a relational narrative that doesn't jibe with the facts.[20] They agree that they rarely have conflict, although objective analysis reveals that they have had their share of struggles. Without overtly agreeing to do so, they choose to blame outside forces or unusual circumstances for problems instead of blaming each other. They offer the most charitable interpretations of each other's behavior, believing that their spouse acts with good intentions when things don't go well. They seem willing to forgive, or even forget, transgressions. Communication researcher Judy Pearson evaluates these findings:

> Should we conclude that happy couples have a poor grip on reality? Perhaps they do, but is the reality of one's marriage better known by outside onlookers than by the players themselves? The conclusion is evident. One key to a long happy marriage is to tell yourself and others that you have one and then to behave as though you do![21]

INFLUENCES ON PERCEPTION

Now that we've explored the processes by which we perceive, it's time to look at some of the influences that cause us to select, organize, interpret, and negotiate information.

Access to Information

We can only make sense of what we know, and none of us knows everything about even the closest people in our lives. When new information becomes available, your perceptions of others change. If you see your instructor only when she's teaching in the classroom, your conclusions about her will be based solely on her behaviors in that role. You might change your perception if you observe her in the roles of rush-hour driver, concert-goer, or grocery shopper. (Many of us have memories of running into our grade school teachers at the store and being shocked that they had lives outside of school.)

Dreambridge Films/Allstar

⋀ *The Disappearance of Eleanor Rigby* is the collective title of three separate movies. Writer/director Ned Benson tells the same story from three different perspectives, titled *Him, Her,* and *Them.* How might an interpersonal relationship of yours look and sound different if told from your point of view, your partner's perspective, or your joint retelling of the story?

We often gain access to new information about others when their roles overlap. Consider how that might occur at an office party. A person's "office" and "party" roles are usually quite different— so at an offsite work celebration, you may see behaviors you hadn't expected. Similarly, when your sweetheart takes you home to meet the family, you might get to watch your partner playing "spoiled son" or "princess daughter" roles. If you've ever said, "I saw a whole new side of you tonight," chances are good it's because you gained access to information you didn't have before.

Social media can provide new information that can affect perceptions. That's why job hunters are encouraged to clean up their Internet profiles, being careful to manage the impressions they might make.[22] It's also why children and parents don't always want to be Facebook friends with each other.[23] Some roles are best kept private—or at least played to a select audience.

Physiological Influences

Another set of influences we need to examine involves our physical makeup. Within the wide range of human similarities, each of us perceives the world in a unique way because of physiological factors. In other words, although the same events exist "out there," each of us receives different images because of our unique perceptual hardware. Consider the long list of physiological factors that shapes our views of the world: the senses, age, health and fatigue, hunger, biological cycles, and psychological challenges.

The Senses   The differences in how each of us sees, hears, tastes, touches, and smells stimuli can affect interpersonal relationships. Consider the following everyday situations:

> "Turn down that radio! It's going to make me go deaf."
> "It's not too loud. If I turn it down, it will be impossible to hear it."

> "It's freezing in here."
> "Are you kidding? We'll suffocate if you turn up the heat!"

> "Why don't you pass that truck? The highway is clear for a mile."
> "I can't see that far, and I'm not going to get us killed."

These disputes aren't just over matters of opinion. The sensory data we receive are different. Differences in vision and hearing are the easiest to recognize, but other differences exist as well. There is evidence that identical foods taste differently to different individuals.[24] Scents that please some people repel others. Likewise, temperature variations that leave some of us uncomfortable are inconsequential to others. Recognizing these differences won't eliminate them, but it will make it easier to remember that the other person's preferences aren't crazy, just different.

Psychological Challenges   Some differences in perception are rooted in neurology. For instance, people with AD/HD (attention-deficit/hyperactivity disorder) are easily distracted from tasks and have difficulty delaying gratification. It's easy to imagine how those with AD/HD might find a long lecture boring and tedious, while other audience members are fascinated by the same lecture. People with bipolar disorder experience significant mood swings in which their perceptions of events, friends, and even family members shift dramatically. The National Institute of Mental Health estimates that between five and seven million Americans are affected by these two disorders alone—and many other psychological conditions influence people's perceptions.[25] It's important to remember that when others see and respond to the world differently than we do, there may be causes beyond those we immediately recognize.

Age   We experience the world differently throughout our lifetimes. Besides the obvious physical changes, age also alters perspective. Consider, for instance, how you've viewed your parents through the years. When you were a child, you probably thought they were all-knowing and flawless. As a teen, you may have viewed them as old-fashioned and mean. In adulthood, most people begin to regard their parents as knowledgeable and perhaps even wise.

Health and Fatigue   Recall the last time you came down with a cold, flu, or some other ailment. Do you remember how different you felt? You probably had much less energy. It's likely that you felt less sociable and that your thinking was slower than usual. These kinds of changes have a strong impact on how you relate to others. It's good to realize that someone else may be behaving differently because of illness. In the same way, it's important to let others know when you feel ill so that they can give you the understanding you need.

Just as being ill can affect your relationships, so can being overly tired. Trying to deal with important issues at such a time can get you into trouble. One study found that, when married couples don't sleep well, they have more negative perceptions of each other the following day, leading to more interpersonal discord.[26] Toward that end, a good night's sleep is an invaluable asset for managing interpersonal conflict. [27]

Hunger   People often get grumpy when they haven't eaten and get sleepy after stuffing themselves. Research confirms that lack of nutrition affects how we interact with others. In one study, teenagers who reported that their family did not get enough food to eat were almost three times as likely to have been suspended from school, almost twice as likely to have difficulty getting along with others, and four times as likely to have no friends.[28]

Biological Cycle   Are you a "morning person" or a "night person"? Most of us can answer this question easily, and there's a good physiological reason behind our response. Each of us is in a daily cycle in which all sorts of changes constantly occur, including body temperature, sexual drive, alertness, tolerance to stress, and mood.[29] Most of these changes are caused by hormonal cycles. For instance, adrenal hormones, which affect feelings of stress, are secreted at higher rates during some hours. In the same manner, the male and female sex hormones enter our systems at variable rates. We often aren't conscious of these changes, but they surely influence the way we relate to one another. After we're aware that our own daily cycles and those of others govern our feelings and behavior, it becomes possible to manage our lives so that we deal with important issues at the most effective times.

Cultural Differences

So far you have seen how physical factors can make the world a different place for each of us. But there's another kind of perceptual gap that often blocks communication—the gap between people from different backgrounds. Every culture has its own worldview, its own way of looking at the world. At times it's easy to forget that people everywhere don't see things the way we do.

Looking at DIVERSITY

Courtesy of Christa Kilvington

Christa Kilvington: Socioeconomic Stereotyping

What comes to mind when you hear the description "4.0 college student"? How about when you hear "welfare mom"? Most likely you get two very different mental pictures. Perhaps you imagine those kinds of people as complete opposites. And yet, I am both: A college student with straight-A grades who is also a single mother on public assistance. To some people, the combination doesn't fit. They figure that anyone smart enough to earn a 4.0 GPA shouldn't have ended up on welfare, or that anybody on welfare is probably too dumb and lazy to be in college and have straight-A grades.

The stereotypes people use to classify me shape the way they communicate. Most people who only know me from school and have no idea of my economic situation think of me as intelligent and ambitious—an academic standout. They speak to me formally and respectfully. Those who know me only by my income level—caseworkers, healthcare workers, grocery store clerks—tend to communicate with me in quite a different way. When I go to the welfare office, present my Medicaid card for a prescription, or pay for groceries with food stamps I am often treated as unintelligent, lazy, and dishonest. People speak to me in condescending and disrespectful tones.

Why do some people equate income level with intelligence? Why do they treat me and others differently based on our economic status? Why is it all right to treat people disrespectfully just because they are poor? Stereotypes exist for a reason, but it's important to go beyond them to find out each person's unique story. When you leave your mind open to the possibility that there is more to a person than meets the eye, that is when you grow as a person yourself.

"Socioeconomic Stereotyping" by Christa Kilvington. Used with permission of author.

The range of cultural differences is wide. In Middle Eastern countries, personal scents play an important role in interpersonal relationships. Arabs consistently breathe on people when they talk. As anthropologist Edward Hall explains:

> To smell one's friend is not only nice, but desirable, for to deny him your breath is to act ashamed. Americans, on the other hand, trained as they are not to breathe in people's faces, automatically communicate shame in trying to be polite. Who would expect that when our highest diplomats are putting on their best manners they are also communicating shame? Yet this is what occurs constantly, because diplomacy is not only "eyeball to eyeball" but breath to breath.

Even beliefs about the very value of talk differ from one culture to another.[30] Western cultures view talk as desirable and use it for social purposes as well as for task performance. Silence has a negative value in these cultures. It is likely to be interpreted as lack of interest, unwillingness to communicate, hostility, anxiety, shyness, or a sign of interpersonal incompatibility. Westerners are uncomfortable with silence, which they find embarrassing and awkward.

On the other hand, Asian cultures perceive talk differently. For thousands of years, Asian cultures have discouraged the expression of thoughts and feelings. Silence is valued, as Taoist sayings indicate: "In much talk there is great weariness," or "One who speaks does not know; one who knows does not speak." Unlike most North Americans, who are uncomfortable with silence, Japanese and Chinese believe that remaining quiet is the proper state when there is nothing to be said. In Asian cultures, a talkative person is often considered a show-off or insincere.

It's easy to see how these different views of speech and silence can lead to communication problems when people from different cultures meet. Both the talkative American and the silent Asian are behaving in ways they believe are proper, yet each views the other with disapproval and mistrust. This may require them to recognize and deal with their **ethnocentrism**—the attitude that one's own culture is superior to others. An ethnocentric person thinks—either privately or openly—that anyone who does not belong to his or her in-group is somehow strange, wrong, or even inferior. Travel writer Rick Steves describes how an ethnocentric point of view can interfere with respect for other cultural practices:

> … we [Americans] consider ourselves very clean and commonly criticize other cultures as dirty. In the bathtub we soak, clean, and rinse, all in the same water. (We would never wash our dishes that way.) A Japanese visitor, who uses clean water for each step, might find our way of bathing strange or even disgusting. Many cultures spit in public and blow their nose right onto the street. They couldn't imagine doing that into a small cloth, called a hanky, and storing that in their pocket to be used again and again. Too often we think of the world in terms of a pyramid of "civilized" (us) on the top and "primitive" groups on the bottom. If we measured things differently (maybe according to stress, loneliness, heart attacks, hours spent in traffic jams, or family togetherness) things stack up differently.

It isn't necessary to travel overseas to encounter differing cultural perspectives. Within this country there are many subcultures, and the members of each one have backgrounds that cause them to see things in different ways. Failure to recognize these differences can lead to unfortunate and unnecessary misunderstandings. For example, an uninformed Anglo teacher or police officer might interpret a lack of eye contact by a Latina as a sign of avoidance, or even dishonesty, when in fact this is the proper behavior in her culture for a female being addressed by an older man. To make direct eye contact in such a case would be considered undue brashness or even a sexual come-on.

It's encouraging to know that open-minded communicators can overcome preexisting stereotypes and learn to appreciate people from different backgrounds as individuals. In one study, college students who were introduced to strangers from different cultural backgrounds developed attitudes about their new conversational partners based more on their personal behavior than on preexisting expectations about how people from those backgrounds might behave.[31]

Social Roles

From the time we're born, each of us is indirectly taught a whole set of roles that we'll be expected to play. In one sense this set of prescribed parts is necessary because it enables a society to function smoothly and provides the security that comes from knowing what's expected of you. But in another sense, having roles defined in advance can lead to wide gaps in understanding. When roles become unquestioned and rigid, people tend to see the world from their own viewpoint, having no experiences that show them how other people see it. Let's look at how social roles affect our perception and communication.

lev radin/Shutterstock.com

∧ In the TV series *Orange Is the New Black*, Laverne Cox plays the role of Sophia Burset, a transgender prisoner who has forsaken life as a husband and firefighter to become a woman. While never denying her personal history, the Burset character—and Cox in real life—refuses to be pigeonholed into traditional gender categories. Have gender stereotypes distorted your perception of others?

Gender Roles   Although people use the terms *sex* and *gender* as if they were identical, there is an important difference.[32] *Sex* refers to biological characteristics of a male or female, whereas *gender* refers to the social and psychological dimensions of masculine and feminine behavior. A large body of research shows that males and females do perceive the world differently, for reasons ranging from genes to neurology to hormones.[33] However, even cognitive researchers who focus on biological differences between males and females acknowledge that societal gender roles and stereotypes affect perception dramatically.[34]

Gender roles are socially approved ways that men and women are expected to behave. Children learn the importance of gender roles by watching other people and by being exposed to media, as well as by receiving reinforcement.[35] After members of a society learn these customary roles, they tend to regard violations as unusual—or even undesirable.

Some theorists have suggested that stereotypical masculine and feminine behaviors are not opposite poles of a single continuum, but rather two separate sets of behavior.[36] With this view, an individual can act in a masculine manner or a feminine manner or exhibit both types of characteristics. The male–female

TABLE 4.1 Gender Roles

	MALE	FEMALE
Masculine	Masculine males	Masculine females
Feminine	Feminine males	Feminine females
Androgynous	Androgynous males	Androgynous females
Undifferentiated	Undifferentiated males	Undifferentiated female

dichotomy, then, is replaced with four psychological sex types: masculine, feminine, **androgynous** (combining masculine and feminine traits), and undifferentiated (neither masculine nor feminine traits). Combining the four psychological sex types with the traditional physiological sex types produces the eight categories listed in Table 4.1.

Each of these eight psychological sex types perceives interpersonal relationships differently. For example, masculine males may be likely to see their interpersonal relationships as opportunities for competitive interaction, as opportunities to win something. Feminine females often see their interpersonal relationships as opportunities to be nurturing, to express their feelings and emotions. Androgynous males and females, on the other hand, differ little in their perceptions of their interpersonal relationships.

Occupational Roles   The kind of work we do often influences our view of the world. Imagine five people taking a walk through the park. One, a botanist, is fascinated by the variety of trees and other plants. Another, a zoologist, is looking for interesting animals. The third, a meteorologist, keeps an eye on the sky, noticing changes in the weather. The fourth companion, a psychologist, is totally unaware of nature, instead concentrating on the interaction among the people in the park. The fifth person, a pickpocket, quickly takes advantage of the others' absorption to make some money. There are two lessons in this little scenario. The first, of course, is to watch your wallet carefully. The second is that our occupational roles shape our perceptions.

Even within the same occupational setting, the different roles that participants have can affect their perceptions. Consider a typical college classroom, for example. The experiences of the instructor and students often are dissimilar. Having dedicated a large part of their lives to their work, most instructors see their subject matter—whether French literature, physics, or communication—as vitally important. Students who are taking the course to satisfy a general education requirement may view the subject differently: maybe as one of many obstacles that stand between them and a degree, or perhaps as a chance to meet new people. Another difference centers on the amount of knowledge possessed by the parties. To an instructor who has taught the course many times, the material probably seems extremely simple, but to students encountering it for the first time, it may seem strange and confusing. We don't need to spell out the interpersonal strains and stresses that come from such differing perceptions.

Relational Roles   Think back to the "Who am I?" list you made in the opening of Chapter 3. It's likely your list included roles you play in relation to others: daughter, roommate, husband, friend, and so on. Roles like these don't just define who you are—they also affect your perception.

Take, for example, the role of parent. As most new mothers and fathers will attest, having a child alters the way they see the world. They might perceive their crying baby as a helpless soul in need of comfort, while nearby strangers have a less charitable appraisal. As the child grows, parents often pay more attention to the messages in the child's environment. One father we know said he never noticed how much football fans curse and swear until he took his six-year-old to a game with him. In other words, his role as father affected what he heard and how he interpreted it.

The roles involved in romantic love can also dramatically affect perception. These roles have many labels: partner, spouse, boyfriend/girlfriend, sweetheart, and so on. There are times when your affinity biases the way you perceive the object of your affection. You may see your sweetheart as more attractive than other people do, and perhaps you overlook some faults that others notice.[37] Your romantic role can also change the way you view others. One study found that when people are in love, they view other romantic candidates as less attractive than they normally would.[38]

Perhaps the most telltale sign of the effect of "love goggles" is when they come off. Many people have experienced breaking up with a romantic partner and wondering later, "What did I ever see in that person?" The answer—at least in part—is that you saw what your relational role led you to see.

PAUSE *and* REFLECT

Role Reversal

MindTap REFLECT … on new roles by answering the following questions, either here or online.

Walk a mile in another person's shoes. Find a group that is foreign to you, and try to become a member of it for a while.

1. If you're down on the police, see if your local department has a ride-along program where you can spend several hours on patrol with one or two officers.

2. If you think the present state of education is a mess, become a teacher yourself. Maybe an instructor will give you the chance to plan one or more classes.

3. If you're a political conservative, try getting involved in a liberal organization; if you're a liberal, check out the conservatives.

Whatever group you join, try to become part of it as best you can. Don't just observe. Get into the philosophy of your new role and see how it feels. You may gain a new appreciation for people you didn't understand.

COMMON TENDENCIES IN PERCEPTION

By now it's obvious that many factors affect the way we interpret the world. Social scientists use the term **attribution** to describe the process of explaining people's behavior.[39] We attribute meaning both to our own actions and to the actions of others, but we often use different yardsticks. Research has uncovered several perceptual tendencies that can lead to attribution errors.[40]

"Don't get me wrong, Ted. I like you, but you're not a special person. I'm a special person."

Jack Ziegler/Cartoonbank.com

We Judge Ourselves More Charitably Than We Judge Others

In an attempt to convince ourselves and others that the positive face we show to the world is true, we tend to judge ourselves in the most generous terms possible. Social scientists have labeled this tendency the **self-serving bias**.[41] When others suffer, we often blame the problem on their personal qualities. On the other hand, when we suffer, we blame the problem on forces outside ourselves. Consider a few examples:

When *they* botch a job, we might think they weren't listening well or trying hard enough; when *we* botch a job, the problem was unclear directions or not enough time.

When *he* lashes out angrily, we say he's being moody or too sensitive; when *we* lash out angrily, it's because of the pressure we've been under.

When *she* gets caught speeding, we say she should have been more careful; when *we* get caught speeding, we deny that we were driving too fast or we say, "Everybody does it."

When *she* uses profanity, it's because of a flaw in her character; when *we* swear, it's because the situation called for it.[42]

One study of "honest but hurtful" messages shows how self-serving bias can operate in romantic relationships.[43] Partners who deliver these candid messages tend to perceive them as helpful and constructive. When on the receiving end, however, the same messages are seen as hurtful and mean. In other words, "I'm a good sweetheart when I tell you the painful truth, but you're a bad sweetheart when you do the same to me."

We Cling to First Impressions

Labeling people according to our first impressions is an inevitable part of the perception process. These labels are a way of making quick interpretations:

"She seems cheerful"; "He appears sincere"; "They sound conceited." If such first impressions are accurate, they can be useful ways of deciding how to respond best to people in the future. Problems arise, however, when the labels we attach are inaccurate. After we form an opinion of someone, we tend to hang on to it and make any conflicting information fit our opinion.

Social scientists have coined the term **halo effect** to describe the tendency to form an overall positive impression of a person on the basis of one positive characteristic. One such characteristic is physical attractiveness, which can lead people to attribute all sorts of other virtues to the good-looking person.[44] For example, employment interviewers rate mediocre but attractive job applicants higher than their less attractive candidates.[45] And once employers form positive impressions, they often ask questions that confirm their image of the applicant.[46] For example, when an interviewer forms a positive impression, he might ask leading questions aimed at supporting his positive views ("What lessons did you learn from that setback?"), interpret answers in a positive light ("Ah, taking time away from school to travel was a good idea!"), encourage the applicant ("Good point!"), and sell the company's virtues ("I think you would like working here"). Likewise, applicants who create a negative first impression are operating under a cloud that may be impossible to dispel—a phenomenon sometimes referred to as "the devil effect."[47]

The power of first impressions is also important in personal relationships. A study of college roommates found that those who had positive initial impressions of each other were likely to have positive subsequent interactions, manage their conflicts constructively, and continue living together.[48] The converse was also true: Roommates who got off to a bad start tended to spiral negatively. This reinforces the wisdom and importance of the old adage, "You never get a second chance to make a first impression."

Given the almost unavoidable tendency to form first impressions, the best advice we can give is to keep an open mind and to be willing to change your opinion as events prove it mistaken.

We Assume That Others Are Similar to Us

In Chapter 3 you read one example of this principle: that people with low self-esteem imagine that others view them unfavorably, whereas people with high self-esteem imagine that others view them positively. The frequently mistaken assumption that others' views are similar to our own applies in a wide range of situations:

- You've heard a slightly raunchy joke that you think is pretty funny. You assume that it won't offend a somewhat straitlaced friend. It does.

- You've been bothered by an instructor's tendency to get off the subject during lectures. If you were an instructor, you'd want to know if anything you were doing was creating problems for your students, so you decide that your instructor will probably be grateful for some constructive criticism. Unfortunately, you're wrong.

- You lost your temper with a friend a week ago and said some things you regret. In fact, if someone said those things to you, you'd consider the relationship finished. Imagining that your friend feels the same way, you avoid making contact. In fact, your friend has avoided you because she thinks *you're* the one who wants to end things.

Examples like these show that others don't always think or feel the way we do and that assuming that similarities exist can lead to problems.[49] How can you find out the other person's real position? Sometimes by asking directly, sometimes by checking with others, and sometimes by making an educated guess after you've thought the matter out. All these alternatives are better than simply assuming that everyone would react as you do.

We Are Influenced by Our Expectations

Suppose you took a class and were told in advance that the instructor is terrific. Would this affect the way you perceive the teacher? Research shows that it almost certainly would. In one study, students who read positive comments about instructors on a website viewed those teachers as more credible and attractive than did students who were not exposed to the same comments.[50]

Expectations don't always lead to more positive appraisals. There are times when we raise our expectations so high that we are disappointed with the events that occur. If you are told that someone you are about to meet is extremely attractive, you may create a picture in your mind of a professional model, only to be let down when the person doesn't live up to your unrealistic expectations. What if you had been told that the person isn't very good-looking? In that case, you might have been pleasantly surprised by the person's appearance, and perhaps you would rate the person's attractiveness more positively. The point is, our expectations influence the way we see others, both positively and negatively—and that may lead to self-fulfilling prophecies.[51]

On the JOB

Sexual Harassment and Perception

Almost 50 years after the U.S. Civil Rights Act prohibited it, sexual harassment in the workplace remains a problem. Complaints of unwanted sexual advances and a hostile work environment have cost employers almost $50 million annually in recent years.[a]

Scholars have tried to understand why complaints of harassment persist when the law clearly prohibits behavior that creates a "hostile work environment." They have discovered that, while clear-cut examples of hostile sexism do exist, differing perceptions help explain many other incidents.

Not surprisingly, what constitutes harassment depends on gender: Women are more likely than men to rate a behavior as hostile and/or offensive.[b]

Perhaps more surprisingly, younger people (both men and women) are less likely than older people to regard a scenario as sexual harassment.

Along with age and sex, cultural background helps shape perceptions of harassment.[c] People from cultures with high power distance are less likely to perceive harassment than those from places with low power distance.

Findings like these don't excuse harassment, but they do help explain it. The more members of an organization understand one another's perceptions, the better the odds that unpleasant and unfortunate feelings of harassment will not arise.

We Are Influenced by the Obvious

The error of being influenced by what is most obvious is understandable. As you read at the beginning of this chapter, we select stimuli from our environment that are noticeable: intense, repetitive, unusual, or otherwise attention-grabbing. The problem is that the most obvious factor is not necessarily the only one—or the most significant one—for an event. For example:

- When two children (or adults, for that matter) fight, it may be a mistake to blame the one who lashes out first. Perhaps the other one was at least equally responsible, teasing or refusing to cooperate.

- You might complain about an acquaintance whose malicious gossiping or arguing has become a bother, forgetting that by putting up with such behavior in the past you have been at least partially responsible.

- You might blame an unhappy working situation on the boss, overlooking other factors beyond his or her control, such as a change in the economy, the policy of higher management, or demands of customers or other workers.

∧ On *The Voice*, judges use blind auditions in the opening rounds. On other performance shows, judges view contestants' appearance and sometimes even know their back-stories before making an appraisal. Does that affect the judges' perceptions of the performer and the performance? Are there times when you would be better off knowing *less* about someone when making an evaluation?

PERCEPTION CHECKING

Serious problems can arise when people treat interpretations as if they were matters of fact. Like most people, you probably resent others jumping to conclusions about the reasons for your behavior.

"Why are you mad at me?" (Who said you were?)

"What's the matter with you?" (Who said anything was the matter?)

"Come on now. Tell the truth." (Who said you were lying?)

As you'll learn in Chapter 11, even if your interpretation is correct, a dogmatic, mind-reading statement is likely to generate defensiveness. The skill of **perception checking** provides a better way to handle your interpretations.[52]

Elements of Perception Checking

A complete perception check has three parts:

1. A description of the behavior you noticed
2. At least two possible interpretations of the behavior
3. A request for clarification about how to interpret the behavior

Perception checks for the preceding three examples would look like this:

"When you stomped out of the room and slammed the door," *(behavior)* "I wasn't sure whether you were mad at me" *(first interpretation)* "or just in a hurry." *(second interpretation)* "How *did* you feel?" *(request for clarification)*

"You haven't laughed much in the last couple of days." *(behavior)* "It makes me wonder whether something's bothering you" *(first interpretation)* "or whether you're just feeling quiet." *(second interpretation)* "What's up?" *(request for clarification)*

"You said you really liked the job I did." *(behavior)* "On the other hand, there was something about your voice that made me think you may not like it." *(first interpretation)* "Maybe it's just my imagination, though." *(second interpretation)* "How do you really feel?" *(request for clarification)*

Perception checking is a tool for helping you understand others accurately instead of assuming that your first interpretation is correct. Because its goal is mutual understanding, perception checking is a cooperative approach to communication. Besides leading to more accurate perceptions, it minimizes defensiveness by preserving the other person's face. Instead of saying, in effect, "I know what you're thinking …," a perception check takes the more respectful approach that states or implies, "I know I'm not qualified to judge you without some help."

Perception-Checking Considerations

Like every communication skill outlined in *Looking Out Looking In*, perception checking isn't a mechanical formula that will work in every situation. As you develop the ability to check your perceptions, consider the following factors in deciding when and how to use this approach.

Completeness   Sometimes a perception check won't need all of the parts listed earlier to be effective:

"You haven't dropped by lately. Is anything the matter?" *(single interpretation combined with request for clarification)*

"I can't tell whether you're kidding me about being cheap or if you're serious." *(behavior combined with interpretations)* "Are you mad at me?"

"Are you sure you don't mind driving? I can use a ride if it's no trouble, but I don't want to take you out of your way." *(no need to describe behavior)*

Sometimes even the most skimpy perception check—a simple question like "What's going on?"—will do the job. You might also rely on other people to help you make sense of confusing behavior: "Rachelle has been awfully quiet lately. Do you know what's up?" A complete perception check is most necessary when the risk of sounding judgmental is highest.

Nonverbal Congruency   A perception check can succeed only if your nonverbal behavior reflects the open-mindedness of your words. An accusing tone of voice or a hostile glare will contradict the sincerely worded request for clarification, suggesting that you have already made up your mind about the other person's intentions.

Cultural Rules   The straightforward approach of perception checking has the best chance of working in what Chapter 6 identifies as *low-context cultures*: ones in which members use language as directly as possible. The dominant cultures of

In REAL LIFE

Perception Checking in Everyday Life

Perception checking only works if it is sincere and fits your personal style. The following examples show how perception checking sounds in everyday life and may help you find ways to use it when you are faced with ambiguous messages.

My Boss's Jokes

I get confused by my boss's sense of humor. Sometimes he jokes just to be funny, but other times he uses humor to make a point without coming right out and saying what's on his mind. Last week he was talking about the upcoming work schedule and he said with a laugh, "I own you all weekend!" I have a life besides work, so his comment left me worried.

I used a perception check to figure out what he meant: "Brad, when you told me 'I own you all weekend,' I wasn't sure whether you were kidding or whether you really expect me to work Saturday and Sunday. Were you serious?"

He kind of smiled and said, "No, I was just kidding. You only have to work Saturday and Sunday."

I still couldn't be sure whether or not he was serious, so I checked again: "You're kidding, right?"

My boss replied, "Well, I do need you at least one day, and two would be better." Once I figured out what he really meant, we worked out a schedule that had me work Friday evening and Saturday morning, which gave me the time off I needed.

If I hadn't used the perception check, I would have wound up worrying about being tied up all weekend, and getting mad at my boss for no good reason. I'm glad I spoke up.

My Dad's Affection

My father and I have a great relationship. A while back I picked him up at the airport after a week-long business trip and a long cross-country flight. On the way home, he was quiet—not his usual self. He said he was exhausted, which I understood. When we got home, he brightened up and started joking and playing with my younger brother. This left me feeling unhappy. I thought to myself, "Why is he so happy to see my brother when he hardly said a word to me?" I didn't say anything at the time. The next day I found myself feeling resentful toward my dad, and it showed. He said, "What's up with you?" But I was too embarrassed to say anything.

After learning this approach in class, I tried a perception check. I said, "Dad—when you were quiet on the way home after your business trip and then you perked up when you got home and saw Jaime, I wasn't sure what was up. I thought maybe you were happier to see him than me, or that maybe I'm imagining things. How come you said you were tired with me and then you perked up with Jaime?"

My dad felt awful. He said he was tired in the car, but once he got back to the house he was glad to be home and felt like a new man. I was too wrapped up in my mind to consider this alternative. Because I didn't use a perception check, I was unhappy and I started an unnecessary fight.

MindTap® **APPLY ...** this situation to your life by answering questions online.

North America and Western Europe fit into this category, and members of these groups are most likely to appreciate perception checking. Members of *high-context cultures* (more common in Latin America and Asia), however, value social harmony over directness. High-context communicators are more likely to regard candid approaches like perception checking as potentially embarrassing, instead preferring less-direct ways of understanding one another. Thus, a "let's get this straight" perception check might work well with a Euro American manager who was raised to value directness, but could be a serious mistake with a Mexican American or Asian American boss who has spent most of his or her life in a high-context culture.

SKILL *Builder*

Perception Checking Practice

MindTap° **PRACTICE ...** your perception-checking ability by answering the following questions either here or online.

Practice your perception-checking ability by developing three-part verifications for the following situations:

1. You made what you thought was an excellent suggestion to an instructor. The instructor looked uninterested but said she would check on the matter right away. Three weeks have passed, and nothing has changed.

2. A neighbor and good friend has not responded to your "Good morning" for three days in a row. This person is usually friendly.

3. You haven't received the usual weekly phone call from the folks back home in over a month. The last time you spoke, you had an argument about where to spend the holidays.

4. An old friend with whom you have shared the problems of your love life for years has recently changed behavior when around you. The formerly casual hugs and kisses have become longer and stronger, and the occasions where you "accidentally" brush up against each other have become more frequent.

Face Saving   Along with clarifying meaning, perception checking can sometimes be a face-saving way to raise an issue without directly threatening or attacking the other person. Consider these examples:

> "Are you planning on doing those dishes later, or did you forget that it's your turn?"

> "Am I boring you, or do you have something else on your mind?"

In the first case, you might have been quite confident that the other person had no intention of doing the dishes, and in the second that the other person was bored. Even so, a perception check is a less threatening way of pointing out their behavior than direct confrontation. Remember, one element of competent communication is the ability to choose the best option from a large repertoire, and perception checking can be a useful strategy at times.

EMPATHY, COGNITIVE COMPLEXITY, AND COMMUNICATION

Perception checking is a valuable tool for clarifying ambiguous messages, but ambiguity isn't the only cause of perceptual problems. Sometimes we understand what people mean without understanding why they believe as they do. At times like this, we are short on the vital ability to empathize.

AT FACEBOOK, CREATING EMPATHY

*O*f Facebook's 7,185 employees, Arturo Bejar may have the most difficult job: teaching the site's 1.3 billion users, especially its tens of millions of teenagers, how to be nice and respectful to one another.

Respectful? Online? Ha! That's never going to happen. Everyone knows that social media is an unwinnable game of who can be meaner. If Mr. Bejar thinks he can make Facebook users nice, he is—to borrow a popular Facebook comment—just stupid!

As the director of engineering for the Facebook Protect and Care team, he believes that most users are not trying to be mean and that they will retract a comment (and even feel bad about it) if they realize it has caused someone harm.

In other words, Mr. Bejar is trying to create empathy among Facebook users, in what used to happen in real settings like the playground, through social cues like crying and laughter. The company told me that each week eight million Facebook members use tools that allow users to report a harmful post or photo. Mr. Bejar's team designed these tools to let people know someone had hurt their feelings.

Teenagers are a particular focus, not just as victims of cyberbullying but because they sometimes lack the emotional maturity to handle negative posts. On Facebook, teenagers are presented with more options than just "it's embarrassing" when they want to remove a post. They are asked what's happening in the post, how they feel about it, and how sad they are. In addition, they are given a text box with a polite pre-written response that can be sent to the friend who hurt their feelings.

More often than not, the posts were not meant to hurt, but were jokes lost in digital translation. When Facebook asked people why they shared a post that hurt someone else, around 90 percent of respondents said they thought their friends would like the post or would think it was funny. Only 2 percent of users wanted to provoke or alarm someone else.

Researchers are looking at other ways to help users be more empathetic on social networks. Last year, Facebook borrowed ideas from Charles Darwin's 1872 book *The Expression of the Emotions in Man and Animals* to create stickers with facial expressions.

Next, Mr. Bejar said, his team is experimenting with sounds to help people convey how they feel. (Imagine sending someone the sound of a grunt, sigh, or a giggle to communicate your feelings about a post.)

Maybe this idea isn't that stupid after all.

Nick Bilton

MindTap® **ENHANCE …**
your understanding by answering the following questions, either here or online.

1. Have you ever been the object of a social media post that the creator apparently thought was funny but hurt your feelings? What factors played into the difference in perception?

2. Do you think the empathy tools identified in this reading can help people communicate more effectively on social networking sites? Would you use these tools if given the opportunity?

3. In general, do you think the use of social media enhances or detracts from interpersonal empathy? Offer examples to support your case.

Empathy

Empathy is the ability to re-create another person's perspective, to experience the world from the other's point of view. It may be impossible to ever experience another person's perspective completely, but with enough effort we can certainly gain a better idea of how the world appears to him or her.

As we'll use the term here, *empathy* involves three dimensions.[53] In one dimension, empathy involves *perspective taking*—an attempt to take on the viewpoint of another person. This requires a suspension of judgment so that for the moment you set aside your own opinions and try to understand the other person. Even a narcissist can be nudged to feel empathy for others by engaging in perspective-taking exercises.[54] Empathy also has an *emotional* dimension that helps us get closer to experiencing others' feelings: to gain a sense of their fear, joy, sadness, and so on. A third dimension of empathy is a genuine *concern* for the welfare of the other person. When we empathize, we go beyond just thinking and feeling as others do and genuinely care about their well-being.

Scores of recent studies show that humans are hardwired to empathize with others—it's built into our brains.[55] Best-selling author Daniel Goleman believes that cultivating this natural tendency toward empathy is the essence of "social intelligence."[56] The ability to empathize seems to exist in a rudimentary form in even the youngest children. Research sponsored by the National Institute of Mental Health revealed what many parents know from experience: Virtually from birth, infants become visibly upset when they hear another baby crying, and children who are a few months old cry when they observe another child in tears. Young children have trouble distinguishing others' distress from their own. If, for example, one child hurts his finger, another might put her own finger into her mouth as if she were feeling pain. Researchers report cases in which children who see their parents in tears wipe their own eyes, even though they are not crying.

Although children may have a basic capacity to empathize, studies with twins suggest that the degree to which we are born with the ability to sense how others are feeling seems to vary according to genetic factors.[57] Although some people may have an inborn edge, environmental experiences are the key to developing the ability to understand others. Specifically, the way in which parents communicate with their children seems to affect their ability to understand others' emotional states.[58] When parents point out to children the distress that others feel from their misbehavior ("Look how sad Jessica is because you took her toy. Wouldn't you be sad if someone took away your toys?"), those children gain

"How would you feel if the mouse did that to you?"

a greater appreciation that their acts have emotional consequences than when parents simply label such behavior as inappropriate ("That was a mean thing to do!"). Studies also show that allowing children to experience and manage frustrating events can help increase their empathic concern for others later in life.[59]

Culture plays an important role in our ability to understand the perspectives of others. Research shows that people raised in individualist cultures (which value independence) are often less adept at perspective-taking than those from collectivist cultures (which value interdependence).[60] In one study, Chinese and American players were paired together in a communication game that required the participants to take on the perspective of their partners. In all measures, the collectivist Chinese had greater success in perspective-taking than did their American counterparts. This isn't to suggest that one cultural orientation is better than the other; it only shows that culture shapes the way we perceive, understand, and empathize with others.

It is easy to confuse empathy with **sympathy**, but the concepts are different. With sympathy, you view the other person's situation from *your* point of view. With empathy, you view it from *the other person's* perspective. Consider the difference between sympathizing and empathizing with an unwed mother or a homeless person. When you sympathize, it is the other person's confusion, joy, or pain. When you empathize, the experience becomes your own, at least for the moment. It's one thing to feel bad (or good) *for* someone; it's more profound to feel bad (or good) *with* someone. Nonetheless, empathy doesn't require you to *agree* with the other person. You can empathize with a difficult relative or a rude stranger without endorsing their behavior. Ultimately, all of us can profit from putting ourselves in anothers' shoes to better understand their worlds.

CBS/Photofest

∧ In the television show *Undercover Boss*, high-ranking company officials in disguise take on the duties of lower-level employees in their organizations. The bosses usually gain a new appreciation and empathy for the challenges faced by their employees, both on the job and in their personal lives. Can you think of a supervisor who has forgotten what it's like to be on the bottom rung of a company? How do *you* regard and treat people who supply you with customer service?

Cognitive Complexity

By now you can probably appreciate the value of empathy in boosting understanding and enhancing relationships. But how can we become more empathic? To answer that question, let's return to a feature of communication competence: cognitive complexity.

Cognitive Complexity and Communication

As noted in Chapter 1, cognitive complexity is the ability to construct a variety of frameworks for viewing an issue. Researchers have found that cognitive complexity increases the chances of satisfying communication in a variety of contexts, including marriage,[61] helping others who are feeling distressed,[62] being persuasive,[63] and career advancement.[64]

It was six men of Indostan

To learning much inclined,

Who went to see the elephant

Though all of them were blind

That each by observation

Might satisfy his mind.

The first approached the elephant

And, happening to fall

Against the broad and sturdy side,

At once began to bawl:

"Why, bless me! But the elephant

Is very much like a wall!"

The second, feeling of the tusk,

Cried: "Ho! What have we here

So very round and smooth and sharp?

To me, 'tis very clear,

This wonder of an elephant

Is very like a spear!"

The third approached the animal,

And, happening to take

The squirming trunk within his hands

Thus boldly up he spake:

"I see," quoth he, "the elephant

Is very like a snake!"

The fourth reached out his eager hand

And felt about the knee:

"What most this wondrous beast is like

Is very plain," quoth he:

"'Tis clear enough the elephant

Is very like a tree!"

The fifth who chanced to touch the ear

Said: "E'en the blindest man

Can tell what this resembles most—

Deny the fact who can:

This marvel of an elephant

Is very like a fan!"

The sixth no sooner had begun

About the beast to grope

Than, seizing on the swinging tail

That fell within his scope,

"I see," quoth he, "the elephant

Is very like a rope!"

And so these men of Indostan

Disputed loud and long,

Each in his own opinion

Exceeding stiff and strong;

Though each was partly in the right,

And all were in the wrong.

John G. Saxe

Library of Congress Prints and Photographs Division [LC-USZCA-8703]

Not surprisingly, studies show a connection between cognitive complexity and empathy.[65] The relationship makes sense: The more ways you have to understand others and interpret their behaviors, the greater is the likelihood that you can see the world from their perspective. Cognitive complexity can also help people describe situations more thoroughly and less simplistically.[66] Interestingly, one study showed that cognitively complex people are better able to identify and understand when others are using sarcasm—an abstract form of communication that is sometimes lost on those with less mental acumen.[67] The good news is that cognitive complexity can be enhanced through training.[68] With that in mind, let's look at a skill that can help you achieve that goal.

Increasing Your Cognitive Complexity: The Pillow Method

The skill of perception checking discussed earlier in this chapter is a relatively quick, easy tool for clarifying potential misunderstandings, but some issues are too complex and serious to be handled with this approach. Writer Paul Reps describes a tool for boosting empathy when finding merit in another's position seems impossible.[69]

Developed by a group of Japanese schoolchildren, the **pillow method** gets its name from the fact that a problem has four sides and a middle, just like a pillow (Figure 4.3). As the following examples show, viewing an issue from each of these perspectives almost always leads to valuable insights—and in so doing enhances cognitive complexity.

Position 1: I'm Right, You're Wrong This is the perspective that we usually take when viewing an issue. We immediately see the virtues in our position and find fault with anyone who happens to disagree with us. Detailing this position takes little effort and provides little new information.

Position 2: You're Right, I'm Wrong At this point you switch perspectives and build the strongest possible arguments to explain how another

FIGURE 4.3
The Pillow Method

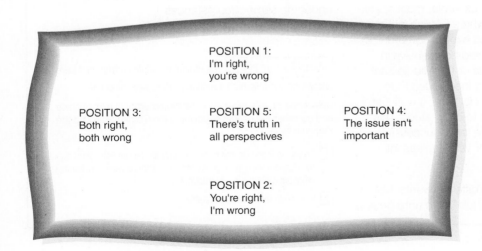

POSITION 1:
I'm right,
you're wrong

POSITION 3:
Both right,
both wrong

POSITION 5:
There's truth in
all perspectives

POSITION 4:
The issue isn't
important

POSITION 2:
You're right,
I'm wrong

person can view the issue differently from you. Besides identifying the strengths in the other's position, this is the time to play the devil's advocate and find flaws in your position. This requires discipline and a certain amount of courage, even though this is only an exercise, and you will soon be able to retreat to position 1 if you choose. But most people learn that switching perspectives reveals there is some merit to the other person's perspective.

ETHICAL *Challenge*

Empathy and the Golden Rule

Virtually everyone is familiar with the Golden Rule, which most of us learned in the form "Do unto others as you would have them do unto you." By obliging us to treat others as well as we would treat ourselves, this maxim seems to offer the foundation for a civil society in which everyone would behave with consideration.

Some ethicists have pointed out that the Golden Rule doesn't work well in situations where others don't want to be treated the same way you would. You may like to blast hip-hop music at top volume at 3 A.M., but appeals to the Golden Rule probably won't placate your neighbors who don't share your musical tastes or late-night hours. Likewise, just because you enjoy teasing banter, you aren't entitled to banter with others who might find this type of humor offensive or hurtful.

The Golden Rule presents special problems in cases of intercultural contacts, where norms for what is desirable vary dramatically. For example, most speakers from low-context cultures where English is the first language value honesty and explicit communication, but this level of candor would be offensive in the high-context cultures of Asia or the Middle East. A naive communicator following the Golden Rule might justify social blunders by claiming, "I was just communicating the way I'd like to be treated." This sort of ethnocentrism is a recipe for unsuccessful communication and perhaps for very unpleasant consequences.

In response to the challenge of differing wants, Milton Bennett proposed a "Platinum Rule": "Do unto others as they themselves would have done unto them." Unlike the Golden Rule, this rule requires us to understand how others think and what they want before we can determine how to act ethically.[a] Put differently, the Platinum Rule implies that empathy is a prerequisite for moral sensitivity.

Despite its initial appeal, the Platinum Rule poses its own problems. There are certainly cases where doing unto others what they want might compromise our own needs or even our ethical principles. It is easy to imagine cases in which the Platinum Rule would oblige us to cheat, steal, or lie on others' behalf.

Even if acting on the Platinum Rule is problematic, the benefit of thinking about it seems clear. An essential requirement for benign behavior is the ability to empathize, helping us recognize that what others want may be different than what we would want under the same circumstances.

MindTap **APPLY …** the ethical principles introduced here by answering the following questions, either here or online.

Select one of your most important interpersonal relationships and consider the effects of applying the Golden Rule and the Platinum Rule.

1. Do you have enough information to apply the Golden Rule? What about the Platinum Rule? What communication might be necessary before you could put each rule into practice?

2. Which rule seems to be preferable?

There are some issues where it seems impossible to call the other position "right." Criminal behavior, deceit, and disloyalty often seem beyond justification. At times like these, it is possible to arrive at position 2 by realizing that the other person's behavior is understandable. For example, without approving, you may be able to understand how someone would resort to violence, tell lies, or cheat. Whatever the particulars, the goal of position 2 is to find some way of comprehending how anyone could behave in a way that you originally found impossible to defend.

Position 3: Both Right, Both Wrong From this position, you acknowledge the strengths and weaknesses of each person's arguments. If you have done a good job with position 2, it should be clear that there is some merit in both points of view, and that each side has its demerits. Taking a more evenhanded look at the issue can lead you to be less critical and more understanding of another's point of view.

Position 3 can also help you find the commonalities between your position and others'. Perhaps you've both been right to care so much about the issue, but both wrong to fail to recognize the other person's concerns. Perhaps there are underlying values that you both share and similar mistakes that you've both made. In any case, the perspective of position 3 should help you see that the issue isn't as much a matter of complete right and wrong as it first appeared to be.

Position 4: The Issue Isn't as Important as It Seems Although it is difficult to consider some issues unimportant, a little thought will show that most aren't as important as we make them out to be. The impact of even the most traumatic events—the death of a loved one or the breakup of a relationship, for example—usually lessens over time. The effects may not disappear, but we learn to accept them and get on with life. The importance of a dispute can also fade when you realize that you've let it overshadow other equally important parts of your relationship. It's easy to become so wrapped up in a dispute about one subject that you forget about the other ways in which you are close to the other person.

Position 5: There Is Truth in All Four Perspectives After completing the first four positions, a final step is to recognize that each of them has some merit. Although logic might suggest that it's impossible for a position to be both right and wrong, both important and unimportant, your own experience will show that there is some truth in each of the positions you have explored. After you have looked at an issue from these five perspectives, it is almost certain that you will gain new insights. These insights may not cause you to change your mind or even solve the problem at hand. Nonetheless, they can increase your understanding of the other person's position and thus improve the communication climate.

In Real Life

The Pillow Method in Action

Planning a Wedding

Background

Who would have thought that planning a wedding would be such a nightmare? My fiancé and I are struggling to decide whether we should have a large, festive wedding or a small, intimate one. I'm in favor of having a big, expensive ceremony and party. He wants a smaller, more affordable one.

Position 1: I'm Right, He's Wrong

I have a big family, and I would feel guilty not inviting everyone. Also, we have lots of friends who would really miss not being present to celebrate our special day. If we invite one friend or relative, I say we have to invite them all to avoid hurting anybody's feelings. Otherwise, where do you draw the line? As far as money goes, I say that you get married only once, and this is no time to scrimp. My parents are willing to help pay the expenses because they want our entire family to be there at the wedding.

Position 2: He's Right, I'm Wrong

My fiancé is right to say that we really don't have the funds to spend on a fancy wedding. Every dollar we spend on a lavish event will be one less dollar we have to buy a house, which we hope to do soon. My fiancé is right to say that a big wedding could postpone our house purchase for a year or two—maybe even longer, if real estate prices go up before we can buy. Even if my parents help pay for the event, our portion would still be more than we can afford. He's also right to say that no matter how many people we invite, someone is always going to be left out. It's just a case of where we draw the line. Finally, he's right to say that planning a big wedding will be a very stressful process.

Position 3: Both of Us Are Right, and Both Are Wrong

Both of us are right, and both are wrong. I'm right to want to include our extended families and friends on this joyous day, and I'm right to say that a special wedding would be a lifetime memory. He's right that doing so could still leave some hurt feelings and that it will postpone our house purchase. He also has a good point when he says that planning a big event could drive us crazy and distract us from the real importance of joining our lives.

Position 4: The Issue Isn't Important

After thinking about it, I've realized that getting married is different from being married. The decision about what kind of ceremony to have is important, but ultimately it won't affect the kind of marriage we have. How we behave after we're married will be much more important. And we are going to face a lot of decisions together—about children and jobs, for example—that will have much bigger consequences than this ceremony.

Position 5: There Is Truth in All Perspectives

Before using the pillow method to think through all sides of this issue, I was focused on getting my way. This attitude was creating some feelings between my fiancé and me that were not what we should be having as we faced this most important event. I've realized that if one or the other of us "wins" but the result is injured feelings, it won't be much of a victory. I don't know what kind of ceremony we will finally decide to have, but I'm determined to keep my focus on the really important goal of keeping our relationship positive and respectful.

MindTap **APPLY** ... this situation to your life by answering questions online.

SKILL *Builder*

Pillow Talk

MindTap® **PRACTICE ...** your skill at applying the pillow method by answering the following questions either here or online.

Try using the pillow method in your life. It isn't easy, but after you begin to understand it, the payoff in increased understanding can be great.

1. Choose a person or viewpoint with whom or which you strongly disagree. If you've chosen a person, it's best to have him or her there with you, but if that's not possible, you can do it alone.

2. What disagreement should you choose? No doubt there are many in your life:

Parent–child	Friend–friend
Teacher–student	Nation–nation
Employer–employee	Republican–Democrat
Brother–sister	

3. For each disagreement you choose, genuinely place yourself in each position on the pillow as you encounter it:

   a. Your position is correct, and your opponent's is wrong.

   b. Your opponent's position is correct, and yours is wrong.

   c. Both your positions are correct, and both are wrong.

   d. It isn't important which position is right or wrong.

   e. Finally, affirm the fact that there is truth in all four positions.

4. The more important the disagreement is to you, the harder it will be to accept positions 2 through 5 as valid, but the exercise will work only if you can suspend your present position and imagine how it would feel to hold the other ones.

5. How can you tell if you've been successful with the pillow method? The answer is simple: If, after going over all the steps, you can understand—not necessarily accept, but just understand—the other person's position, you've done it. After you've reached this *understanding*, do you notice any change in how you feel about the other person?

SUMMARY

There is more to the world "out there" than any person is capable of understanding. We make sense of our environment by the four-step process of selecting certain stimuli from the environment, organizing them into meaningful patterns, interpreting them in a manner that is shaped by a variety of factors, and negotiating them through narratives we share with others.

Many factors affect the way we select, organize, interpret, and negotiate information. Access to information plays an important role. So do physiological factors such as our senses, age, and health. Cultural background also influences the way we view the world, as do social roles. In addition to these factors, some common tendencies affect the way we assign meaning to others' behavior.

Perception checking can be a useful tool for verifying interpretations of others' behavior, instead of assuming that the first hunch is correct. A complete perception check includes a description of the other's behavior, at least two plausible interpretations of its meaning, and a request for clarification about what the behavior does mean.

Empathy is the ability to experience another person's point of view. Empathy differs from sympathy, because it involves seeing the situation from the other person's perspective rather than your own. Cognitive complexity is the ability to construct a variety of frameworks for understanding an issue. One means for boosting both empathy and cognitive complexity is the pillow method, which involves viewing an issue from five different perspectives.

KEY TERMS

androgynous
attribution
empathy
ethnocentrism
gender role
halo effect
interpretation
narrative
negotiation

organization
perception checking
pillow method
punctuation
selection
self-serving bias
stereotyping
sympathy

CHAPTER FOUR

Perception: What You See Is What You Get

OUTLINE

Use this outline to take notes as you read the chapter in the text and/or as your instructor lectures in class.

I. THE PERCEPTION PROCESS	_____
A. Selection Is Influenced by	
1. Intense Stimuli	_____
2. Repetitious Stimuli	
3. Contrast or Change in Stimulation	_____
4. Motives	
B. Organization	
1. Figure–Ground Organization	_____
2. Perceptual Shema	
a. Appearance	
b. Social Roles	_____
c. Interaction Style	
d. Psychological Traits	_____
e. Membership	
3. Stereotyping	_____
4. Punctuation	
C. Interpretation	
1. Degree of Involvement with the Other Person	_____
2. Personal Experience	
3. Assumptions about Human Behavior	_____
4. Attitudes	
5. Expectations	_____
6. Knowledge	
7. Self-Concept	_____
8. Relational Satisfaction	

D. Negotiation

   1. Narratives Tell Our Personal Stories

   2. Narratives May Differ and Cause Conflict

   3. Shared Narratives

II. INFLUENCES ON PERCEPTION

A. Access to Information

   1. Varying Roles

   2. Social Media as Source

B. Physiological Influences

   1. Senses

   2. Psychological Challenges

   3. Age

   4. Health and Fatigue

   5. Hunger

   6. Biological Cycles

C. Cultural Differences

   1. Cultural Worldview

   2. Beliefs about What Has Value

   3. Ethnocentrism

   4. Subcultures

D. Social Roles

   1. Gender Roles (Masculine, Feminine, Androgynous, Undifferentiated)

   2. Occupational Roles

   3. Relational Roles

III. COMMON TENDENCIES IN PERCEPTION

A. We Judge Ourselves More Charitably Than Others

B. We Cling to First Impressions

C. We Assume Others Are Similar to Us

D. We Are Influenced by Our Expectations

E. We Are Influenced by the Obvious

IV. PERCEPTION CHECKING

A. Elements of Perception Checking

1. Describe Behavior
2. Offer Interpretation of the Behavior Two Ways
3. Request Clarification

B. Perception-Checking Considerations

1. Completeness
2. Nonverbal Congruency
3. Cultural Rules
   a. Low-Context Cultures
   b. High-Context Cultures
4. Face Saving

V. EMPATHY, COGNITIVE COMPLEXITY, AND COMMUNICATION

A. Empathy

1. Three Dimensions
   a. Perspective Taking
   b. Experiencing Others' Feelings
   c. Genuine Concern
2. Social Intelligence
3. Cultural Considerations
4. Sympathy

B. Cognitive Complexity

1. Ability to Construct a Number of Frameworks
2. Increasing Cognitive Complexity: The Pillow Method
   a. Position One: I'm Right, You're Wrong
   b. Position Two: You're Right, I'm Wrong
   c. Position Three: Both Right, Both Wrong
   d. Position Four: The Issue Isn't as Important as It Seems
   e. Position Five: There Is Truth in All Four Perspectives

KEY TERMS

androgynous
attribution
empathy
ethnocentrism
expectations
face-saving
gender role
halo effect
interpretation
narrative
negotiation
nonverbal congruency

organization
perception checking
perceptual schema
pillow method
punctuation
selection
self-serving bias
stereotyping
sympathy
undifferentiated

ACTIVITIES

4.1 GUARDING AGAINST PERCEPTUAL ERRORS

LEARNING OBJECTIVES

- Explain how the influences on perception listed in this chapter affect communication in a specific situation.
- Analyze how the tendencies described in this chapter have distorted your perceptions of another person, and hence your communication. Use this information to present a more accurate alternative set of perceptions.

INSTRUCTIONS

1. Identify and describe two people about whom you've formed strong opinions. These opinions can be positive and/or negative.

2. Using the checklist provided, comment on how the five influences on perception affect how you think about each person. See Chapter 4 of *Looking Out/Looking In* for a more detailed description of the five influences. Note: Not every factor may apply to each person.

3. Record your conclusions at the end of the exercise.

4. Compare your examples with those of other classmates.

	EXAMPLE	PERSON A	PERSON B
Identify each person. Describe your opinions.	Joni is my wife's good friend. I don't like her; I think she's boring. Her voice is shrill, and I find her annoying.		
1. We judge ourselves more charitably than others.	When Joni lost her job, I thought it was Joni's fault because she's so annoying. Of course, when I got laid off a few months later, I blamed the economy and mentioned nothing about my performance or personality.		

	EXAMPLE	PERSON A	PERSON B
2. We pay more attention to others' negative characteristics.	Joni is attractive, intelligent, successful, and athletic. I tend to disregard all those positive qualities and focus on her shrill voice.		
3. We are influenced by the obvious.	Because she's my wife's friend, Joni is around a lot, so I probably notice her voice or her calls more than is usual.		
4. We cling to first impressions.	I haven't liked Joni from the beginning. She would call right at our dinner time. Even though she doesn't do this anymore, I still remember it and I'm sure it influences my opinion of her.		
5. We tend to assume that others are similar to us.	I just assume that Joni will know when I don't want her around. I assume she'd be interested in things I'm interested in. Perhaps she finds the topics I talk about boring, too.		

CONCLUSIONS

Based on the observations above, how do you think these influences on perception affect your understanding and attitudes about other people?

_____

_____

_____

_____

Reflecting on your observations, which of the influences on perception are the most apt to provide you with inaccurate perceptions?

_____

_____

_____

_____

What might you do in the future to guard against inaccurate perceptions of people?

_____

_____

_____

_____

4.2 SHIFTING PERSPECTIVES (PILLOW METHOD)

LEARNING OBJECTIVES

- Enhance your cognitive complexity by applying the "pillow method" in a significant disagreement.
- Explain how your expanded view of this situation might affect your communication with the other(s) involved.

INSTRUCTIONS

PART I:

1. Select one disagreement or other issue that is now affecting an interpersonal relationship. This might be an issue such as "I think our children should go to public school; my spouse wants them to go to private school" or a more public disagreement such as "I think voting for a third party helps democracy in our country; my friend thinks it undermines democracy by drawing votes away from the two major parties."

2. In the space below, record enough background information for an outsider to understand your stance on the issue. Who is involved? How long has the disagreement been going on? What are the basic issues involved?

3. Describe the issue from each of the four positions listed below.

Brief Background Information

_____

_____

_____

_____

Position 1: "I'm right, and you're wrong." Explain how you are right and the other person is wrong.

_____

_____

_____

_____

_____

Position 2: "You're right, and I'm wrong." Explain how the other person's position is correct, or at least understandable.

_____

_____

_____

_____

_____

Position 3: "We're both right, and we're both wrong." Show that there are both correct (or understandable) and mistaken (or unreasonable) parts of both positions.

_____

_____

_____

_____

_____

Position 4: "The issue may be less important than it seems; some other things may be more important." Describe at least two ways in which the elements developed in positions 1–3 might affect your relationship. Describe at least one way in which the issue might be seen as less important than it was originally, and describe at least one way in which the issue might be seen as more important than it was originally.

_____

_____

PART II:

1. In class, with a partner, role-play your situation orally for a small group or the entire class.
2. Receive feedback from other class members about how to see the issue from others' point of view.

PART III:

1. Reflect on your experience of perceiving the truth from each of the positions. Was it difficult? How did it feel?

    _____

    _____

    _____

    _____

    _____

    _____

2. Explain how viewing the issue from each of the positions might change your perception of the issue and how it might change your behavior in the future.

    _____

    _____

    _____

    _____

    _____

    _____

3. Explain how viewing the issue from each of the positions might affect your relationship.

    _____

    _____

    _____

    _____

_____

_____

4. Explain the impact of hearing classmates explain how you might view the issue differently.

_____

_____

_____

_____

_____

_____

4.3 PERCEPTION-CHECKING PRACTICE

LEARNING OBJECTIVES

- Describe how the processes of selection, organization, interpretation, and negotiation shape communication in a given situation.
- Explain how the influences on perception listed in this chapter affect communication in a specific situation.
- Demonstrate how you might use the skill of perception checking in a significant relationship.

INSTRUCTIONS

1. Alone or with a partner, write a perception check for each of the situations below. If you're working with a partner, you might also choose to spontaneously create an oral perception check rather than write them down. If you choose to write them first, be sure to practice delivering them aloud to each other.

EXAMPLE

Yesterday your friend Erin laughed at a joke about "dumb blonds." You found it offensive.

Perception-checking statement: *Erin, when Joey cracked the dumb blond joke last night, you laughed. I'm wondering if you disapproved of the joke but laughed just to make Joey feel comfortable, or if you really think that blonds are not as smart as the rest of the population. Can you clarify things for me?*

1. Last night you saw someone you recently had a date with walking on the beach, holding hands with someone else. You'd like to date this person again, but not if a current relationship exists. When you receive a call from this person, asking you to a movie and dinner this weekend, you need to decide what to say.

   _____

   _____

   _____

   _____

2. Ever since the school year began, your father has called weekly, asking how you are doing. His question makes you uncomfortable, and you're not sure that you provide him with the answer he seems to be looking for. He's just called and asked again.

   _____

   _____

_____

_____

3. Your friend was driving you home from a party last night when he began to weave the car between lanes on the highway. You were uncomfortable, but didn't say anything then. Now it is the next morning, and he shows up to take you to a class. You're concerned about driving with him again and have decided to bring up the incident.

_____

_____

_____

_____

4. For the last two weeks, just when you are leaving your house, your roommate has asked for a ride somewhere. Your roommate has a car, but you haven't seen it lately. You are in a hurry now, and your roommate has just asked for another ride.

_____

_____

_____

_____

5. You return home at night to find your roommate reading on the couch. You believe you have a good relationship with your roommate, and it's your habit to engage in a friendly chat when you first come home. On this night, when you walk into the room and greet him, he grunts and turns his face away from you and keeps reading.

_____

_____

_____

_____

6. Last week your instructor returned your exam with a low grade and the comment, "This kind of work paints a bleak picture for the future." You have approached the instructor to discuss the remark.

_____

_____

_____

_____

7. In one of your regular long distance phone conversations, you ask your favorite cousin about his romantic life. He sighs and says, "Oh, it's OK, I guess."

_____

_____

_____

_____

8. Your girlfriend, boyfriend, or spouse announces that she or he plans to spend next Friday night with friends from work. You usually spend Friday nights with each other.

_____

_____

_____

_____

9. Last week your supervisor at work, Ms. Black, gave you a big assignment. Three times since then she has asked you whether you're having any trouble with it.

_____

_____

_____

_____

10. Last weekend your next-door neighbor, Steve, raked a big pile of leaves near your property line, promising to clean them up after work on Monday. It's Wednesday, and the wind is blowing the leaves into your yard.

_____

_____

_____

_____

11. One of your classmates sits by you every day in class, and you've done a lot of homework together. He's called you at home a few times a week, mostly to discuss classwork. You feel there might be romantic chemistry between you, but you're unsure. This time when he calls, he suggests that you meet for dinner this weekend.

_____

_____

_____

_____

12. You've noticed one of your office mates looking over at you a number of times during the past few days. At first she looked away quickly, but now she smiles every time you look up and catch her looking at you. You've been under a lot of pressure at work lately and have been extremely busy. You can't understand why she keeps looking at you. You've decided to ask.

_____

_____

_____

_____

Class _____   Name _____

4.4 PERCEPTION CHECKING

LEARNING OBJECTIVES

- Explain how the influences on perception listed in this chapter affect communication in a specific situation.
- Demonstrate how you might use the skill of perception checking in a significant relationship.

INSTRUCTIONS

PART I:

1. Identify a situation in your life in which a perception check might be appropriate. Possible topics: controversial issues, things that bug you, perceived injustices, personal dilemmas, and misperceptions.
2. Working with a partner, deliver a complete perception check without using notes, following the criteria listed in Chapter 4 of *Looking Out/Looking In* and outlined in the checklist below.
3. Receive feedback from your partner, using the checklist to evaluate your performance.
4. Working with your partner, repeat the process as he or she presents a perception check and you act as evaluator.

PERCEPTION CHECK CHECKLIST

_____ Describes background for a potential perception-checking situation.

_____ Delivers complete perception check.

_____ Reports at least one behavior that describes, without evaluating or judging, what the person has said or done.

_____ States two interpretations that are distinctly different, equally probable, and based on the reported behavior.

_____ Makes a sincere request for feedback, clarifying how to interpret the reported behavior.

_____ Uses verbal and nonverbal behavior.

_____ Reflects sincere desire for clarification of the perception.

_____ Sounds realistic and consistent with style of the speaker.

_____ Uses nonthreatening, nondefensive voice and eye contact.

_____ Realistically and clearly assesses how perception checking and other alternatives can be used in everyday life.

_____ In situation described here

_____ In other situations (be specific)

PART II:

1. Describe how well perception checking might (or might not) work in the situation you have chosen. If you do not think a complete perception check is the best approach for this situation, explain why and describe a more promising alternative.

_____

_____

_____

_____

2. Describe various channels you would choose when perception checking for this situation.

_____

_____

_____

_____

3. Did you find it challenging to have to think of more than one possible interpretation for your situation? Explain your experience.

_____

_____

_____

_____

4. What do you think the impact will be on the person hearing your perception check? How will hearing more than one possible interpretation affect them?

_____

_____

_____

_____

5. What would you predict will be the short term and long term effects on your relationships if you use more perception checks? Consider employee/employer, parent/child, coworkers, friends, partners, etc.

_____

_____

_____

_____

4.5 MEDIATED MESSAGES—PERCEPTION

LEARNING OBJECTIVES

- Describe how the processes of selection, organization, interpretation, and negotiation shape communication in a given situation.
- Explain how the influences on perception affect communication in a specific situation.

INSTRUCTIONS

Discuss each of the questions below in your group. Prepare written answers for your instructor, or be prepared to contribute to a large group discussion, comparing your experiences with those of others in your class.

1. Think of ways in which messages sent through mediated messages may contribute to misperceptions. (Example: I called my grandmother, and she thought my tone of voice sounded like I was irritated with her; she didn't say anything to me at the time, but complained to my mother about me.)

   _____

   _____

   _____

   _____

2. How do the influences on perception (physiological or cultural differences, social roles, self-concept) affect these mediated misperceptions? (Example: Physiological: I was tired when I called my grandmother, and I know she has age-related hearing problems.)

   _____

   _____

   _____

   _____

3. Prepare a perception-checking statement that could be used in a mediated context. Specify the mediated channel and the likelihood of success of the perception-checking attempt. (Example: "When you said in your last email that you were busy on Saturday, I wondered if you had a previous commitment, or if you were irritated with me for some reason I'm not aware of and so don't

want to see me. What did you mean?" I think this perception-checking statement gives my partner a way to bring up anything that might be wrong, so it has a good likelihood of success.)

_____

_____

_____

_____

4. Are there times when using perception checks in mediated contexts might be preferable to using them face-to-face? Explain. Are there times when perception checks in mediated contexts might be less effective or appropriate? Explain.

_____

_____

_____

_____

4.6 PERCEPTION

LEARNING OBJECTIVES

- Explain how the influences on perception listed in this chapter affect communication in a specific situation.

- Analyze how the tendencies described in this chapter have distorted your perceptions of another person, and hence your communication. Use this information to present a more accurate alternative set of perceptions.

- Demonstrate how you might use the skill of perception checking in a significant relationship.

INSTRUCTIONS

Use the following case to explore the variety of communication issues involved in communication and perception.

CASE

Jorge is a registered nurse at a facility that cares for about 80 elderly patients. Jorge has been at the facility longer than any of the other nurses and has his choice of schedule. He believes he deserves this because of his service and seniority. There is now a shortage of nurses. Jorge's supervisor, Marisa, has been trying to hire new nurses, some of whom will only work if they can have Jorge's schedule. Marisa and Jorge are meeting to discuss the situation.

1. What factors are likely to influence Jorge's perception of the situation? What factors are likely to influence Marisa's perception of the situation?

    _____

    _____

    _____

    _____

2. How might their differences in perception affect their ability to communicate effectively?

    _____

    _____

    _____

    _____

3. Prepare a perception-checking statement for Jorge to deliver to Marisa. Then, prepare a perception-checking statement for Marisa to deliver to Jorge.

_____

_____

_____

_____

4. How can Marisa and Jorge communicate competently in order to come to a constructive conclusion to this situation? What specific suggestions would you give Marisa and Jorge based on information in this chapter? Cite information from the text to back up your suggestions.

_____

_____

_____

_____

4.7 ASSESSING OUR PERCEPTION

LEARNING OBJECTIVES

- Explain how the influences on perception listed in this chapter affect communication in a specific situation.

- Analyze how the tendencies described in the text have distorted your perceptions of another person, and hence your communication. Use this information to present a more accurate alternative set of perceptions.

Instructions: Choose three classmates and predict the feelings of each on a current issue such as politics, economy, or pop culture. List the issue below and then list the reason for your prediction.

Classmate #1   Issue: Prediction:

_____

_____

_____

Classmate #2   Issue: Prediction:

_____

_____

_____

Classmate #3   Issue: Prediction:

_____

_____

_____

Class _____   Name _____

Now that you have predicted what your classmates might feel on a certain issue, ask them how they feel on this issue and record their responses below.

Classmate #1   Response:

_____

_____

_____

_____

Classmate #2   Response:

_____

_____

_____

_____

Classmate #3   Response:

_____

_____

_____

_____

Now compare your classmates' responses with your predictions. Were your predictions accurate? What influences on perception affected your initial prediction about each of your classmates? Has your perception on them changed since doing this exercise?

Classmate #1

_____

_____

Class _____   Name _____

_____

_____

Classmate #2

_____

_____

_____

_____

Classmate #3

_____

_____

_____

_____

STUDY GUIDE

CHECK YOUR UNDERSTANDING

TRUE/FALSE

Mark the statements below as true or false. Correct statements that are false on the lines below to create a true statement.

_____ 1. Androgynous males and females are vastly different in their perceptions of interpersonal relationships.

_____

_____ 2. Selection, organization, interpretation, and negotiation comprise the steps of the perception process.

_____

_____ 3. The fact that we pay attention to some things and ignore others illustrates the fact that selection is an objective process.

_____

_____ 4. Self-serving bias is the tendency to judge ourselves more generously than we judge others.

_____

_____ 5. Generalizations and stereotypes of groups are generally accurate for everyone in the group.

_____

_____ 6. The halo effect is the tendency to form an overall positive impression of a person on the basis of one positive characteristic.

_____

_____ 7. Occupational roles have little or no influence on how we view the world.

_____

_____   8.   All cultures view talk as desirable, using it for social purposes as well as to perform
                  tasks.

                  _____

                  _____

                  _____

_____   9.   Societal gender roles refer to the biological characteristics of a male or female.

                  _____

_____ 10.   The way we perceive ourselves influences our opinions of ourselves, but not our opin-
                  ions of others.

                  _____

_____ 11.   When you sympathize with someone, you view the situation from the other person's
                  point of view.

                  _____

_____ 12.   Culture plays an important role in our ability to understand the perspectives of
                  others.

                  _____

                  _____

                  _____

_____ 13.   Recent studies show that humans are "hard-wired" to empathize with one another.

                  _____

_____ 14.   Cognitive complexity is the ability to construct one framework for a variety of issues.

                  _____

                  _____

                  _____

COMPLETION

Fill in the blanks with the correct terms chosen from the list below.

narrative	self-serving bias	sympathy
the pillow method	empathy	stereotypes
punctuation	ethnocentrism	
perceptual schema	androgynous	

1. _____ is the belief that one's culture is superior to others.

2. _____ is the determination of causes and effects in a series of interactions.

3. _____ is a story created by shared perspectives to explain events and behavior.

4. _____ is the tendency to judge ourselves in the most generous terms possible.

5. _____ is the ability to re-create another person's perspective.

6. _____ is one means for boosting empathy and cognitive complexity.

7. _____ are exaggerated generalizations associated with a categorizing system.

8. _____ is an example of a psychological gender type that influences perception.

9. _____ is feeling compassion for another person.

10. _____ shapes the way we think about and communicate with others.

MULTIPLE CHOICE

RECOGNIZING PERCEPTION-CHECKING ELEMENTS

For each of the following statements, identify which element of the perception-checking statement is missing. Place the letter or letters of the most accurate evaluation of the statement on the line before the statement.

a. This statement doesn't describe behavior.
b. This statement doesn't give two distinctly different interpretations.
c. This statement doesn't request clarification of the behavior in an open-ended way.
d. There is nothing missing from this perception-checking statement.

_____ 1. "Why did you send me those flowers? Is this a special occasion or what?"

_____ 2. "When you went straight to bed when you came home, I thought you were sick. Are you all right?"

_____ 3. "You must be either really excited about your grades or anxious to talk about something important. What's going on?"

_____ 4. "When you ran out smiling, I figured you were glad to see me and ready to go, or maybe you were having such a good time here you wanted to stay longer."

_____ 5. "I thought you were angry with me when you didn't come over this afternoon like you'd said you would. But then I thought maybe something came up at work. What is it?"

_____ 6. "When you told me you expected to get an outline with my report, I thought you were trying to trick me into doing more work, or maybe you didn't realize that wasn't part of my job."

_____ 7. "When you told everyone my parents own the company, you must have been indicating I was hired here only because of them. Is that what you think?"

_____ 8. "When you passed the ball to me, I thought you wanted me to shoot. Did you?"

_____ 9. "Why is it that you're so pleased with yourself? Did you win the lottery or accomplish something great? What's up?"

_____ 10. "Dad, when you told my friend Art what a great athlete you think I am, I thought you were either really proud of me and wanted to brag a little, or maybe you wanted to see what Art and I had in common by the way he responded. What were your intentions?"

CHAPTER FOUR STUDY GUIDE ANSWERS

TRUE/FALSE

1. F	4. T	7. F	10. F	13. T
2. T	5. F	8. F	11. F	14. F
3. F	6. T	9. F	12. T	

COMPLETION

1. ethnocentrism
2. punctuation
3. narrative
4. self-serving bias

5. empathy
6. the pillow method
7. stereotypes
8. androgynous

9. sympathy
10. perceptual schema

MULTIPLE CHOICE

1. b	3. a	5. d	7. b, c	9. a
2. b, c	4. c	6. c	8. b	10. d

MindTap® START ...

Explore this chapter's topics online.

5

EMOTIONS: FEELING, THINKING, AND COMMUNICATING

AFTER STUDYING THE TOPICS IN THIS CHAPTER, YOU
SHOULD BE ABLE TO:

1. Describe how the four components of emotions affect
   the way you feel, and hence your communication, in an
   important situation.

2. Describe how the influences on emotional expression
   have affected your communication in an important
   relationship.

3. Apply the guidelines for effectively communicating
   emotions in an important situation.

4. Identify and dispute the fallacies that are creating
   debilitative emotions in an important situation.
   Explain how more rational thinking can lead to more
   constructive communication.

*I*t's impossible to talk about communication without acknowledging the importance of emotions. Think about it: Feeling confident can assist you in everything from giving a speech to asking for a date, whereas feeling insecure can ruin your chances. Feeling angry or defensive can spoil your time with others, whereas feeling and acting calm will help prevent or solve problems. The way you share or withhold your feelings of affection can affect the future of your relationships. On and on goes the list of feelings that influence how we interact with others: appreciation, loneliness, joy, insecurity, curiosity, irritation. The point is clear: Communication shapes our feelings, and feelings shape our communication.

The role of emotions in human affairs is apparent to social scientists and laypeople alike. Researchers coined the term **emotional intelligence (EQ)** to describe the ability to understand and manage one's own emotions and be sensitive to others' feelings.[1] Studies show that EQ is positively linked with self-esteem, life satisfaction, and self-acceptance,[2] as well as with healthy conflict management and relationships.[3] Some employers even use emotional intelligence measures as part of their personnel selection process.[4] Emotional intelligence is unquestionably vital to both personal and interpersonal success.

Stop for a moment and try to identify someone you know who is emotionally intelligent. Perhaps it's a family member who is in touch with a wide range of feelings without being overwhelmed by them, or a boss who makes wise and rational choices even under stress. Now think of a person who might be lacking emotional intelligence. Maybe it's a colleague who is uptight and dismissive about honest human feelings, or a friend who blows up at the smallest inconvenience. And finally, assess your own emotional intelligence. How well do *you* understand and manage your emotions, and how sensitive are you to others' feelings?

Because emotions play such an important role in virtually all types of relationships, this chapter looks closer at analyzing and expressing them. You will learn what feelings are and how to recognize them. You'll read guidelines about when and how to best share your feelings with others. Finally, we will explore how to enhance emotions that make communication more rewarding and decrease ones that interfere with effective relationships. In later chapters we'll discuss how to interpret others' emotional states, but for now we'll focus on identifying and expressing your own emotions.

CBS/Photofest

⋀ In *The Big Bang Theory*, Sheldon Cooper (Jim Parsons) has a keen mind but lacks emotional intelligence. As a result, he often violates social rules and sometimes damages relationships. What is your level of emotional intelligence?

WHAT ARE EMOTIONS?

Suppose that an extraterrestrial visitor asked you to explain emotions. How would you answer? You might start by saying that emotions are things that we feel. But this doesn't say much, because in turn you would probably describe feelings as synonymous with emotions. Social scientists generally agree that there are several components to the phenomena we label as feelings.[5]

Physiological Factors

When a person has strong emotions, many bodily changes occur.[6] For example, the physical components of fear include an increased heart rate, a rise in blood pressure, an increase in adrenaline secretions, an elevated blood sugar level, a slowing of digestion, and a dilation of the pupils. Marriage researcher John Gottman notes that symptoms like these also occur when couples are in intense conflicts.[7] He calls the condition "flooding" and has found that it impedes effective problem-solving. Some physiological changes are recognizable to the person having them: a churning stomach or tense jaw, for example. These cues can offer a significant clue to your emotions after you become aware of them.

Nonverbal Reactions

Not all physical changes that accompany emotions are internal. Feelings are often apparent by observable changes. Some of these changes involve a person's appearance: blushing, sweating, and so on. Other changes involve behavior: a distinctive facial expression, posture, gestures, different vocal tone and rate, and so on. And research confirms what might be guessed: nonverbal expressions of emotions become more pronounced under the influence of alcohol.[8] Alcohol serves as an emotion enhancer—sometimes for better, sometimes for worse.

Although it's reasonably easy to tell when someone is feeling a strong emotion, it's more difficult to be certain exactly what that emotion might be. A slumped posture and sigh may be a sign of sadness, or they may be a sign of fatigue. Likewise, trembling hands might indicate excitement, or they may indicate fear. As you'll learn in Chapter 7, nonverbal behavior is usually ambiguous, and it's dangerous to assume that it can be read with much accuracy.

Although we usually think of nonverbal behavior as the reaction to an emotional state, there may be times when the reverse is true—when nonverbal behavior actually *causes* an emotional state. In one study, subjects who were coached to smile actually reported feeling better, and when they altered their expressions to look unhappy, they felt worse than before.[9] Walking with an upbeat strut can stave off feelings of depression.[10] And "jumping for joy" is more than just an emotional reaction. Research suggests that the act of jumping up and down can actually trigger happiness.[11]

There's also a connection between verbalizing emotions and nonverbal reactions. One study showed that participants who generated words associated with pride and disappointment experienced a change in posture.[12] They unconsciously stood taller when talking about pride and slumped when using words for disappointment. The participants also experienced emotions associated with their words (e.g., feeling sad when speaking about disappointment). This reminds us that verbal and nonverbal expressions of emotion are often interconnected.

INTROVERTS: THOUGHTFUL, NOT SHY

As a card-carrying introvert, I am one of the many people whose personality confers on them a preference for the inner world of their own mind rather than the outer world of sociability. Our psychic opposites, extraverts, prefer schmoozing and social life because such activities boost their mood. They get bored by too much solitude.

Often confused with shyness, introversion does not imply social reticence or discomfort. Rather than being averse to social engagement, introverts become overwhelmed by too much of it, which explains why the introvert is ready to leave a party after an hour and the extravert gains steam as the night goes on. Extraverts are comfortable thinking as they speak. Introverts prefer slow-paced interactions that allow room for thought. Brainstorming does not work for them. Email does.

Like individuals, cultures have different styles. America is a noisy culture, unlike, for example, Finland, which values silence. Individualism, dominant in the United States and Germany, promotes the direct, fast-paced style of communication associated with extraversion. Collectivistic societies, such as those in East Asia, value privacy and restraint, qualities more characteristic of introverts.

"In verbal cultures, remaining silent presents a problem," report Anio Sallinen-Kuparinen, James McCroskey, and Virginia Richmond, who have studied communication styles in the United States and Finland. Perceptions of competence tend to be based on verbal behavior. An introvert who is silent in a group may actually be quite engaged—taking in what is said, thinking about it, waiting for a turn to speak—but will be seen in the United States as a poor communicator.

Introverts are not as mild-mannered as made out to be. They seethe and even will lash out at those who encroach upon or malign their personal comfort zones. Here are a few emotional buttons to avoid with your introverted companions.

- "'Why don't you like parties? Don't you like people?' is a common remark introverts hear," says Marti Laney, a psychologist and the author of *The Introvert Advantage*. "Usually we like people fine," she insists. "We just like them in small doses."

- Don't demand immediate feedback from an introvert. "Extraverts think we have answers but just aren't giving them," Laney says. "They don't understand we need time to formulate them" and often won't talk until a thought is suitably polished.

- Don't interrupt if an introvert does get to talking. Listen closely. "Being overlooked is a really big issue for introverts," Laney says. Introverts are unlikely to repeat themselves; they will not risk making the same mistake twice.

- Above all, "we hate people telling us how we can be more extraverted, as if that's the desired state," says Beth Buelow, a life and leadership coach for introverts. Many introverts are happy with the way they are. And if you're not, that's your problem.

Laurie Helgoe

MindTap ENHANCE …

your understanding by answering the following questions, either here or online.

1. Given the descriptions in this reading, do you generally regard yourself as an introvert or an extravert? How does that affect your interpersonal communication with others?

2. Do you agree that introverts are misunderstood in this culture? If so, can you think of examples from your network of close friends and family?

3. What do you see as the primary differences between shyness and introversion?

Cognitive Interpretations

Although there may be situations in which physical behavior and emotional states are directly connected, in most situations the mind plays an important role in determining emotional states. As you read earlier, some physiological components of fear are a racing heart, perspiration, tense muscles, and elevated blood pressure. Interestingly enough, these symptoms are similar to the physical changes that accompany excitement, joy, and other positive emotions. In other words, if we were to measure the physical condition of someone having a strong emotion, we would have a hard time knowing whether that person was trembling with fear or quivering with excitement.

The recognition that the bodily components of most emotions are similar led some psychologists to conclude that the experience of fright, joy, or anger comes primarily from the label we give to the same physical symptoms at a given time.[13] Psychologist Philip Zimbardo offers a good example of this principle:

> I notice I'm perspiring while lecturing. From that I infer I am nervous. If it occurs often, I might even label myself a "nervous person." Once I have the label, the next question I must answer is "Why am I nervous?" Then I start to search for an appropriate explanation. I might notice some students leaving the room, or being inattentive. I am nervous because I'm not giving a good lecture. That makes me nervous. How do I know it's not good? Because I'm boring my audience. I am nervous because I am a boring lecturer and I want to be a good lecturer. I feel inadequate. Maybe I should open a delicatessen instead. Just then a student says, "It's hot in here, I'm perspiring and it makes it tough to concentrate on your lecture." Instantly, I'm no longer "nervous" or "boring."[14]

Zimbardo found that changing his interpretation of the event affected the way he felt about it. Social scientists refer to this process as **reappraisal**—rethinking the meaning of emotionally charged events in ways that alter their emotional impact.[15] Research shows that reappraisal is vastly superior to suppressing your feelings: It often leads to lower stress, higher self-esteem, and increased productivity.[16] Here are two examples:

- Your self-esteem has been shattered since you lost your job, particularly because some of your less-ambitious coworkers were not fired. You lack confidence as you look for new employment. You could reappraise the event as an opportunity to find a new position (or career) where your hard work and contributions will be better appreciated.

- A friend of yours says some malicious things about you behind your back. Although you are hurt, you decide his actions are a statement about *his* character, not yours—and that you'll demonstrate your character by not speaking poorly about him to others.

Reappraisal also has relational benefits. One study found that couples who regularly step back from their conflicts and reappraise them from a neutral perspective have higher levels of relational satisfaction.[17] In essence, these couples reduce the emotional impact of their disputes by looking at them rationally and dispassionately.

It's important to note that reappraisal is not about denying your feelings. Recognizing and acknowledging emotions such as anger, hurt, and grief (as well as happiness, love, and relief) are vital to psychological and relational health. However, when you're ready to move past difficult emotions, reappraisal can help. We'll take a closer look at using reappraisal to reduce debilitative emotions later in this chapter.

Verbal Expression

As you'll read in Chapter 7, nonverbal behavior is a powerful way of communicating emotion. In fact, nonverbal actions are better at conveying emotions than they are at conveying ideas. But sometimes words are necessary to express feelings. Saying "I'm really angry" is clearer and probably more helpful than stomping out of the room, and "I'm feeling nervous" might help explain a pained expression on your face. Putting emotions into words can help you manage them more effectively,[18] while leaving them unspoken can result in negative mental and even physiological effects.[19]

Some researchers believe there are several basic or primary emotions.[20] However, there isn't much agreement among scholars about what those emotions are, or about what makes them basic.[21] Moreover, emotions that are primary in one culture may not be primary in others, and some emotions have no direct equivalent in other cultures.[22] For example, "shame" is a central emotion in the Chinese experience,[23] whereas it's much less familiar to most people from Western cultures. Despite this debate, most scholars acknowledge that *anger*, *joy*, *fear*, and *sadness* are common and typical human emotions.

We experience most emotions with different degrees of intensity, and it's important to use language that represents these differences. Figure 5.1 illustrates this point clearly. To say you're "annoyed" when a friend breaks an important promise, for example, would probably be an understatement. In other cases, people chronically overstate the strength of their feelings. To them, everything is "wonderful" or "terrible." The problem with this sort of exaggeration is that when a truly intense emotion comes along, they have no words left to describe it adequately. If chocolate chip cookies from the local bakery are "unbelievably fantastic," how does it feel to fall in love?

Researchers have identified a wide range of problems that arise for people who aren't able to talk about emotions constructively, including social isolation, unsatisfying relationships, feelings of anxiety and depression, and misdirected aggression.[24] Furthermore, the way parents talk to their children about emotions has a powerful effect on the children's development. Studies identify two distinct parenting styles: "emotion coaching" and "emotion dismissing."[25] The coaching approach gives children skills for communicating about feelings in later life that lead to much more satisfying relationships. Children who grow up in families where parents dismiss emotions are at higher risk for behavior problems than those who are raised in families that practice emotion coaching.[26] Later in this chapter you will find some guidelines for effectively communicating about emotions.

Annoyed	**Angry**	**Furious**
Pensive	**Sad**	**Grieving**
Content	**Happy**	**Ecstatic**
Anxious	**Afraid**	**Terrified**
Liking	**Loving**	**Adoring**

∧ **FIGURE 5.1**
Intensity of Emotions

PAUSE *and* REFLECT

Recognizing Your Emotions

| MindTap REFLECT ... | on your emotions by answering the following questions, either here or online.

Keep a three-day record of your feelings. You can do this by spending a few minutes each evening recalling what emotions you felt during the day, what other people were involved, and the circumstances in which the emotions occurred. To help make your emotions easier to review and reflect on, create a simple chart of your observations with the following headings: 1. Day, 2. Situation (time/place), 3. Emotion (primary/mixed, mild/intense, physical sensation, thoughts, behaviors), 4. People involved, 5. Show and share feelings (why or why not?), 6. Subject or theme of the conversation.

At the end of the three-day period, you can understand the role that emotions play in your communication by answering the following questions:

1. How did you recognize the emotions you felt: through physiological stimuli, nonverbal behaviors, or cognitive processes?

2. Did you have any difficulty deciding which emotions you were feeling?

3. What emotions do you have most often? Are they primary or mixed? Mild or intense?

4. In what circumstances do you or don't you show your feelings? What factors influence your decision to show or not show your feelings? The type of feeling? The person or persons involved? The situation (time, place)? The subject that the feeling involves (money, sex, and so on)?

5. Consider one of the situations from the above question, during which you decided to show and share your feelings. What were the consequences? Were you satisfied with the outcome? If not, what can you do in the future to become more satisfied?

INFLUENCES ON EMOTIONAL EXPRESSION

Most people are reluctant to express their emotions, at least verbally. People are generally comfortable making statements of fact and often delight in expressing their opinion, but they balk at disclosing how they feel. Why do people hesitate to express their emotions? Let's look at several reasons.

Personality

There is an increasingly clear relationship between personality and the way we experience and communicate emotions.[27] For example, extraverted people—those with a tendency to be upbeat, optimistic, and to enjoy social contact—report more positive emotions in everyday life than less extraverted

Paramount/Allstar

∧ Unlike his hot-headed *Star Trek* colleague James T. Kirk (played here by Chris Pine), the iconic Mr. Spock (Zachary Quinto) suppresses his emotions. Being totally rational both helps and limits Spock's decision making. What are the pros and cons of emotions in your interpersonal encounters?

individuals.[28] Likewise, people with neurotic personalities (those with a tendency to worry, feel anxious, and be apprehensive) report more negative emotions in everyday life than less neurotic individuals. These personality traits are at least partially biological in nature.

Personality can be a powerful force, but it doesn't have to govern your communication satisfaction. For instance, people who are shy by nature can devise comfortable and effective strategies for reaching out. For example, the Internet has proven to be an effective way for reticent communicators to make contact, because it's been found to reduce social anxiety.[29] As described in Chapter 2, social media and computer dating services provide low-threat ways to approach others and get acquainted.[30]

Culture

People around the world generally experience the same emotions, but the same events can generate quite different feelings in different cultures.[31] The notion of eating snails might bring a smile of delight to some residents of France, whereas it would cause many North Americans to grimace in disgust. Culture also has an effect on how emotions are valued. One study found that Asian Americans and Hong Kong Chinese value "low arousal positive affect" (such as "calm") more than do European Americans, who tend to value "high arousal positive affect" (such as "excitement").[32] More specifically, the United States is known internationally as a "culture of cheerfulness." One author from Poland describes U.S. expressiveness this way: "Wow! Great! How nice! That's fantastic! I had a terrific time! It was wonderful! Have a nice day! Americans. So damned cheerful."[33]

There are also differences in the degree to which people in various cultures display their feelings. For example, social scientists have found support for the notion that people from warmer climates are more emotionally expressive than those who live in cooler climates.[34] Nearly 3,000 respondents representing 26 nationalities reported that people from the southern part of their countries were more emotionally expressive than were northerners.

One of the most significant factors that influences emotional expression is the position of a culture on the individualism-collectivism spectrum. Members of collectivistic cultures (such as Japan and India) prize harmony among members of their in-group and discourage expression of negative emotions that might upset relationships among people who belong to it. By contrast, members of highly individualistic cultures (such as the United States and Canada) feel comfortable revealing their emotions to people with whom they are close. It's easy to see how differences in display rules can lead to communication problems. For example, individualistic North Americans might view collectivistic Asians as less than candid, whereas Asians could easily regard North Americans as overly demonstrative.[35]

The phrase "I love you" offers an interesting case study of cultural differences in emotion expression. Researchers found that Americans say

"I love you" more frequently (and to more people) than do members of most other cultures.[36] It's not that love isn't a universal experience; rather, there are significant cultural differences about when, where, how often, and with whom the phrase should be used. For instance, Middle Easterners in the study said that "I love you" should only be expressed between spouses, and they warned that American men who use the phrase cavalierly with Middle Eastern women might be misinterpreted as making a marriage proposal. They were not alone: Study participants from a variety of backgrounds (e.g., Eastern Europe, India, Korea) said that they use the phrase quite sparingly, believing that its power and meaning would be lost if used too often. However, one factor was consistent across cultures: Women tend to say "I love you" more often than men. For more examples of the effect that gender has on emotion expression, read on.

Gender

Even within a culture, biological sex and gender roles often shape the ways in which men and women experience and express their emotions.[37] In fact, biological sex is the best predictor of the ability to detect and interpret emotional expressions—better than academic background, amount of foreign travel, cultural similarity, or ethnicity.[38] For example, research suggests that women are more attuned to emotions than men,[39] both within and across cultures.[40] A team of psychologists tested men's and women's recall of emotional images and found that females were 10 to 15 percent more accurate in remembering them. Furthermore, women's reactions to these emotion-producing stimuli were significantly more intense than men's.

Research on emotional expression suggests that there is at least some truth to the cultural stereotype of the unexpressive male and the more expressive female.[41] In face-to-face communication, one study showed that fathers mask their emotions more than mothers do, which leads their children to have more difficulty reading their fathers' emotional expressions.[42] In online communication, similar differences between male and female emotional expressiveness apply. For example, women are more likely than men to use emoticons, such as the symbol :), to express their feelings.[43] Women also express more affection on Facebook than do men.[44]

The point is that while men and women generally experience the same emotions, there are some significant differences in the ways they express them.[45] These differences are due in large measure to social conventions, which we'll discuss now.

Social Conventions

In mainstream U.S. society, the unwritten rules of communication discourage the direct expression of most emotions.[46] Count the number of genuine emotional expressions that you hear over a two- or three-day period ("I'm angry"; "I feel embarrassed"), and you'll discover that emotional expressions are rare.

Looking at DIVERSITY

Todd Epaloose: A Native American Perspective on Emotional Expression

Todd Epaloose

Todd Epaloose was raised on the Zuñi pueblo in New Mexico. He spent part of his childhood on the reservation and part attending school in the city. He now lives in Albuquerque. As an urbanite who still spends time with his family on the reservation, Todd alternates between two worlds.

Zuñi and Anglo cultures are as different as night and day in the ways they treat communication about emotions. In mainstream U.S. culture, speaking up is accepted, or even approved. This is true from the time you are a child. Parents are proud when their child speaks up. Being quiet gets a child labeled as "shy," and is considered a problem.

In Zuñi culture, emotions are much less public. We are a private people, who consider a public display of feelings embarrassing. Self-control is considered a virtue. I think a lot of our emotional reticence comes from a respect for privacy. Your feelings are your own, and showing them to others is just as wrong as taking off your clothes in public. It's not that traditional Zuñis have fewer or less intense feelings than people in the city: It's just that there is less value placed on showing them in obvious ways.

The way we express affection is a good example of Zuñi attitudes and rules for sharing emotions. Our families are full of love. But someone from the city might not recognize this love, since it isn't displayed very much. There isn't a lot of hugging and kissing, even between children and parents. Also, there isn't a lot of verbal expression: People don't say "I love you" to one another very much. We show our emotions by our actions: by helping one another, by caring for the people we love when they need us. That's enough to keep us happy.

I think some Native American emotional restraint might be helpful for people who are used to Anglo communication styles. Respecting others' privacy can be important: Some feelings are nobody else's business, and prying or demanding that they open up seems pushy and rude. Native American self-control can also add some civility to personal relationships. I'm not sure that "letting it all hang out" is always the best way.

One final word: I believe that in order to really understand the differences between emotional expression in Native American and Anglo cultures you have to live in both. If that isn't possible, at least realize that the familiar one isn't the only good approach. Try to respect what you don't understand.

"A Native American Perspective on Emotional Expression" by Todd Epaloose. Used with permission of author.

Not surprisingly, the emotions that people *do* share directly are usually positive ("I'm happy to say ..."; "I really enjoyed ..."). Communicators are reluctant to send messages that embarrass or threaten the "face" of others.[47] This is particularly true in the early stages of a new relationship, when a high ratio of positive-to-negative emotions is crucial to the relationship's development.[48] But even those in long-term relationships rarely express negative emotions directly. One study of married couples revealed that partners often share complimentary feelings ("I love you") or face-saving ones ("I'm sorry I yelled at you"). They also willingly disclose both positive and negative feelings about absent third parties ("I like Fred," "I'm uncomfortable around Gloria"). On the other hand, husbands and wives rarely verbalize face-threatening feelings ("I'm disappointed in you") or hostility ("I'm mad at you").[49]

Expression of emotions is also shaped by the requirements of many social roles. Researchers use the term **emotion labor** to describe situations in which managing and even suppressing emotions is both appropriate and necessary. Studies show that emotion labor is an important component of many if not most occupations (see the On the Job feature in this section for specific examples).

Social Media

Communicators generally express more emotion online than they do in person.[50] In some cases, that's good news. Those who have trouble sharing feelings face to face may find the freedom to do so behind the safety of a keyboard or touchscreen. Consider how it might be easier to type, rather than say, the words "I'm embarrassed" or "I love you."

Unfortunately, as discussed in Chapter 2, online disinhibition can also encourage emotional outbursts and tirades. This kind of venting can be hazardous to interpersonal relations, and it probably won't make you feel better. In a study of online "rant sites," volunteers who posted complaints felt angrier and less happy after doing so—the opposite of the catharsis the sites hope to provide.[51]

Social media can also feed emotional responses. For instance, regularly checking a romantic partner's Facebook site may spur feelings of jealousy, resulting in relational dissatisfaction.[52] The subtitle of one study asks this question: "Does Facebook Bring Out the Green-Eyed Monster of Jealousy?"[53] The short answer is "yes, it can"—especially when the viewer is already suspicious, and more so for women than men.[54] An unhealthy surveillance of loved ones—or former loved ones[55]—can take an emotional toll. We'll have more to say about jealousy and rumination later in this chapter.

The bottom line is that both senders and receivers experience emotions more intensely

"I'm not in one of my moods. I'm in one of *your* moods."

online. It's wise to keep this in mind before hitting send on emotionally charged messages, and before jumping to conclusions about ambiguous online information.

Emotional Contagion

Our emotions are influenced by the feelings of those around us through **emotional contagion**: the process by which emotions are transferred from one person to another.[56] As one commentator observed, "We catch feelings from one another as though they were some kind of social virus."[57] There is evidence that students catch the mood of their teachers,[58] customers are affected by the emotions of employees who serve them,[59] and husbands and wives directly influence each other's emotions.[60] In fact, studies show that our happiness (or unhappiness) can be affected by neighbors, friends of friends, or even total strangers.[61]

Emotional contagion can take place online as well as in person. In an analysis of millions of status updates on Facebook, researchers found that

On the JOB

Emotion Labor in the Workplace

The rules for expressing emotions on the job are clearly different from those in personal life. In intimate relationships (at least in mainstream Western culture), it's often important to tell friends, family, and loved ones exactly how you feel. In the workplace, however, it can be just as important to *conceal* emotions for the sake of clients, customers, coworkers, and supervisors—and also to protect your job.

Emotion labor—the process of managing and sometimes suppressing emotions—has been studied in a variety of occupational contexts. A few examples:

- If firefighters don't mask their emotions of fear, disgust, and stress, it will impede their ability to help the people whose lives they are trying to save. Emotion-management training is therefore vital for new firefighters.[a]

- Correctional officers at two minimum-security prisons described the tension of needing to be "warm, nurturing, and respectful" to inmates while also being "suspicious, strong, and tough." The officers acknowledged that it's taxing to manage competing emotions and juggle conflicting demands.[b]

- Money is an emotion-laden topic, which means that financial planners often engage in emotion labor. Researchers concluded that "relationships and communication with clients may indeed be more central to the work of financial planners than portfolio performance reports and changes in estate tax laws."[c]

While some of these occupations deal with life-and-death situations, emotion management is equally important in less intensive jobs. For instance, most customer-service positions require working with people who may express their dissatisfaction in angry and inappropriate ways ("I hate this store—I'm never shopping here again!"). In situations like these, it's usually unwise to "fight fire with fire," even if that's your natural impulse. Instead, competent on-the-job communicators can use the listening, defense-reducing, and conflict-management skills described in Chapters 8, 11, and 12.

It's not always easy to manage emotions, especially when you're feeling fearful, stressed, angry, or defensive. Nevertheless, doing the work of emotion labor is often vital for success on the job.

posts about rain—which is typically connected to negative moods—can have a ripple effect on readers.[62] Those exposed to their friends' rainy-day messages began posting more emotionally negative updates, even if it wasn't raining in their area. The good news is that positive posts are contagious too—at even greater rates. The researchers found that every positive status update led to 1.75 more positive posts by one's Facebook followers. It's important to recognize that communicating your emotional state—even online with people who may not know you well—can have an impact on the feelings and moods of others.

Most of us recognize the degree to which emotions are infectious. You can almost certainly recall instances when being around a calm person leaves you feeling more at peace, or when your previously sunny mood was spoiled by contact with a grouch. Researchers have demonstrated that this process occurs quickly and doesn't require much, if any, verbal communication.[63] In one study, two volunteers completed a survey that identified their moods. Then they sat quietly, facing each other for a two-minute period, ostensibly waiting for the researcher to return to the room. At the end of that time, they completed another emotional survey. Time after time, the brief exposure resulted in the less expressive partner's moods coming to resemble the moods of the more expressive one. It's easy to understand how emotions can be even more infectious with prolonged contact. In just a few months, the emotional responses of both dating couples and college roommates become dramatically more similar.[64]

GUIDELINES FOR EXPRESSING EMOTIONS

As you just read, there aren't any universal rules for the best way to communicate emotions. Personality, culture, gender roles, and social conventions all govern what approach will feel right to the people involved and what is most likely to work in a given situation. It's easy to think of times when it's *not* smart to express emotions clearly and directly. You usually can't chew out authority figures like difficult bosses or professors, and it's probably not wise to confront dangerous looking strangers who are bothering you.

Despite all the qualifiers and limitations, there will be times when you can benefit from communicating your feelings clearly and directly—even if you aren't normally an expressive person. When those times come, the following guidelines can help you explain how you feel.

A wide range of research supports the value of expressing emotions appropriately. On one hand, underexpression of feelings can lead to serious ailments. Inexpressive people—those who value rationality and self-control, try to control their feelings and impulses, and deny distress—are more likely to get a host of ailments, including cancer, asthma, and heart disease.[65]

Allstar Picture library

∧ Some might claim that 11-year-old Riley has it easy in the film *Inside Out* because her emotions come with names: Joy (voiced by Amy Poehler), Fear (Bill Hader), Disgust (Mindy Kaling), Anger (Lewis Black), and Sadness (Phyllis Smith). Of course, having these feelings doesn't mean she can always manage them well. Are you able to recognize your emotions when you experience them?

On the other hand, communicators who overexpress their negative feelings also suffer physiologically. When people lash out verbally, their blood pressure jumps an average of twenty points, and in some people it increases by as much as one hundred points.[66] The key to health, then, is to learn how to express emotions *constructively*.

Beyond the physiological benefits, another benefit of expressing emotions effectively is the chance of improving relationships.[67] As Chapter 3 explains, self-disclosure is one path (though not the only one) to intimacy. Even on the job, many managers and organizational researchers are contradicting generations of tradition by suggesting that constructively expressing emotions can lead to career success as well as help workers feel better.[68] Of course, the rules for expressing emotions in the workplace are usually more strict than those in personal relationships, so handle with care.[69]

Despite its benefits, expressing emotions effectively isn't a simple matter. It's obvious that showing every feeling of boredom, fear, anger, or frustration would get you into trouble. Even the indiscriminate sharing of positive feelings—love, affection, and so on—isn't always wise. But withholding emotions can be personally frustrating and can keep relationships from growing and prospering.

The following suggestions can help you decide when and how to express your emotions. Combined with the guidelines for self-disclosure in Chapter 2, they can improve the effectiveness of your emotional expression.

Recognize Your Feelings

Answering the question "How do you feel?" isn't as easy for some people as others. Some people (researchers call them "affectively oriented") are much more aware of their emotional states and use information about those emotional states when making important decisions.[70] By contrast, people with a low affective orientation usually aren't aware of their emotional states and tend to regard feelings as useless and unimportant information.

Beyond being *aware* of one's feelings, research shows that it's valuable to be able to *identify* one's emotions. Researchers have found that college students who can pinpoint the negative emotions they experience (such as "nervous," "angry," "sad," "ashamed," and "guilty") also have the best strategies for managing those emotions.[71] This explains why the ability to distinguish and label emotions is a vital component of emotional intelligence, both within and across cultures.[72]

As you read earlier in this chapter, feelings become recognizable in several ways. Physiological changes can be a clear sign of your feelings. Monitoring nonverbal behaviors is another excellent way to keep in touch with your emotions. You can also recognize your feelings by monitoring your thoughts as well as the verbal messages you send to others. It's not far from the verbal statement "I hate this!" to the realization that you're angry (or bored, nervous, or embarrassed).

Recognize the Difference between Feeling, Talking, and Acting

Just because you feel a certain way doesn't mean you must always talk about it, and talking about a feeling doesn't mean you must act on it. In fact, compelling evidence suggests that people who act out angry feelings—whether by lashing out, or even by hitting an inanimate punching bag—actually feel worse than those who experience anger without lashing out.[73]

Understanding the difference between having feelings and acting them out can help you express yourself constructively in tough situations. If, for instance, you recognize that you are upset with a friend, it becomes possible to explore exactly why you feel so upset. Sharing your feeling ("Sometimes I get so mad at you that I could scream") might open the door to resolving whatever is bothering you. Pretending that nothing is bothering you, or lashing out at the other person, is unlikely to diminish your resentful feelings, which can then go on to contaminate the relationship.

Expand Your Emotional Vocabulary

Most people suffer from impoverished emotional vocabularies. Ask them how they're feeling, and the response will almost always include the same terms: *good* or *bad*, *terrible* or *great*, and so on. Take a moment now to see how many feelings you can write down. After you've done your best, look at Table 5.1 and see which ones you've missed.

Many communicators think they are expressing feelings when, in fact, their statements are emotionally counterfeit. For example, it sounds emotionally revealing to say, "I feel like going to a show" or "I feel we've been seeing too much of each other." But in fact, neither of these statements has any emotional content. In the first sentence the word *feel* really stands for an intention: "I *want* to go to a show." In the second sentence the "feeling" is really a thought: "I *think* we've been seeing too much of each other." You can recognize the absence of emotion in each case by adding a genuine word of feeling to it. For instance, "I'm *bored*, and I want to go to a show" or "I think we've been seeing too much of each other, and I feel *confined*."

Relying on a small vocabulary to describe feelings is as limiting as relying on a small vocabulary to describe colors. To say that the ocean in all its moods, the sky as it varies from day to day, and the color of your true love's eyes are all "blue" tells only a fraction of the story. Likewise, it's overly broad to use a term like *good* or *great* to describe how you feel in situations as different as earning a high grade, finishing a marathon, and hearing the words "I love you" from a special person.

There are several ways to express a feeling verbally:[74]

- By using *single words*: "I'm angry" (or "excited," "depressed," "curious," and so on).

- By describing what's happening *to you*: "My stomach is tied in knots," "I'm on top of the world."

- By describing what you'd like *to do*: "I want to run away," "I'd like to give you a hug."

TABLE 5.1 Common Human Emotions

afraid	concerned	exhausted	hurried	nervous	sexy
aggravated	confident	fearful	hurt	numb	shaky
amazed	confused	fed	hysterical	optimistic	shocked
ambivalent	content	fidgety	impatient	paranoid	shy
angry	crazy	flattered	impressed	passionate	sorry
annoyed	defeated	foolish	inhibited	peaceful	strong
anxious	defensive	forlorn	insecure	pessimistic	subdued
apathetic	delighted	free	interested	playful	surprised
ashamed	depressed	friendly	intimidated	pleased	suspicious
bashful	detached	frustrated	irritable	possessive	tender
befuddled	devastated	furious	jealous	pressured	tense
bewildered	disappointed	glad	joyful	protective	terrified
bitter	disgusted	glum	lazy	puzzled	tired
bored	disturbed	grateful	lonely	refreshed	trapped
brave	ecstatic	happy	loving	regretful	ugly
calm	edgy	harassed	lukewarm	relieved	uneasy
cantankerous	elated	helpless	mad	resentful	up
carefree	embarrassed	high	mean	restless	vulnerable
cheerful	empty	hopeful	miserable	ridiculous	warm
cocky	enthusiastic	horrible	mixed	romantic	weak
cold	envious	hostile	mortified	sad	wonderful
comfortable	excited	humiliated	neglected	sentimental	worried

Sometimes communicators inaccurately minimize the strength of their feelings: "I'm a *little* unhappy" or "I'm *pretty* excited" or "I'm *sort of* confused." Of course, not all feelings are strong ones. We do feel degrees of sadness and joy, for example, but some people have a tendency to discount almost every feeling. Do you?

In other cases, communicators express feelings in a coded manner. This happens most often when the sender is uncomfortable about revealing the feeling in question. Some codes are verbal ones, as when the sender hints more or less subtly at the message.

For example, an indirect way to say "I'm lonesome" might be "I guess there's not much going on this weekend, so if you don't have any plans maybe you could text me and we could hang out." Such a message is so indirect that your real feeling may not be recognized. For this reason, people who send coded messages stand less of a chance of having their feelings understood— and their needs met.

If you do decide to express your feeling, you can be most clear by making sure that both you and your partner understand that your feeling is centered on a specific set of circumstances rather than being indicative of the whole relationship. Instead of saying "I resent you," say "I resent you when you don't keep your promises." Rather than saying "I'm bored with you," say "I'm bored when you talk about your money."

Share Multiple Feelings

The feeling you express often isn't the only one you're experiencing. For example, you might often express your anger but overlook the confusion, disappointment, frustration, sadness, or embarrassment that preceded it. To understand why, consider the following examples. For each one, ask yourself two questions: "How would I feel? What feelings might I express?"

An out-of-town friend has promised to arrive at your place at six o'clock. When he hasn't arrived by nine, you are convinced that a terrible accident has occurred. Just as you pick up the phone to call the police and local hospitals, your friend breezes in the door with an offhand remark about getting a late start.

A photo of you is posted by a friend on Facebook. On the one hand, you're flattered by your friend's display of affection for you. On the other hand, it's a picture that doesn't paint you in the best light. You wish the friend had asked first.

In situations like these, you would probably feel mixed emotions. Consider the case of the overdue friend. Your first reaction to his arrival would probably be relief: "Thank goodness, he's safe!" But you would also be likely to feel anger: "Why didn't he phone to tell me he'd be late?" The second example would probably leave you feeling pleased, embarrassed, and mad—all at the same time.

Despite the commonness of mixed emotions, we often communicate only one feeling—usually the most negative one. In both of the preceding examples, you might show only your anger, leaving the other person with little idea of the full range of your feelings. Consider the different reaction you would get by showing *all* of your emotions in these cases and in others.

Consider When and Where to Express Your Feelings

Often the first flush of a strong feeling is not the best time to speak out. If you're awakened by the racket caused by a noisy neighbor, storming over to complain might result in your saying things you'll regret later. In such a case, it's probably wiser to wait until you have thought out carefully how you might express your feelings in a way that would most likely be heard. Research shows that "imagined interactions" in advance of actual conversations can enhance relationships by allowing communicators to rehearse what they will say and to consider how others might respond.[75]

Even after you've waited for the first wave of strong feeling to subside, it's still important to choose the time that's best suited to the message. Being rushed or tired or disturbed by some other matter is probably a good reason for postponing the expression of your feeling. In the same manner, you ought to be sure that the recipient of your message is ready to hear you out before you begin. Sometimes that means checking the other person's mood before you start sharing emotions. In other cases, it's about calculating whether that person is relationally ready to hear sentiments such as "I love you." And when making personal disclosures, it's often a good idea to ensure a measure of privacy. (YouTube is filled with examples of people being embarrassed by public declarations of affection.)

There are also cases where you may choose to never express your feelings. Even if you're dying to tell an instructor that her lectures leave you bored to a stupor, you might decide it's best to answer her question "How's class going?"

SKILL *Builder*

Feelings and Phrases

MindTap PRACTICE… communicating your feelings by answering the following questions either here or online.

You can try this exercise alone or with a group:

1. Choose a situation from column A and a receiver from column B.

2. Develop an approach for communicating your feelings for this combination.

3. Now create approaches for the same situation with other receivers from column B. How are the statements different?

4. Repeat the process with various combinations, using other situations from column A.

Column A: Situations

a.   You receive a terse text message cancelling a date or appointment. It's the third time the other person has cancelled at the last minute.

b.   The other person posts an inappropriate comment on your Facebook Wall.

c.   The other person compliments you on your appearance, then says, "I hope I haven't embarrassed you."

d.   The other person gives you a hug and says, "It's good to see you."

Column B: Receivers

An instructor

A family member (you decide which one)

A classmate you don't know well

Your best friend

with an innocuous "Okay." And even though you may be irritated by the arrogance of a police officer stopping you for speeding, the smartest approach might be to keep your feelings to yourself. In cases where you experience strong emotions but don't want to share them verbally (for whatever reason), writing your feelings and thoughts has been shown to have mental, physical, and emotional benefits.[76] For instance, one study found that writing about feelings of affection can actually reduce the writer's cholesterol level.[77]

Accept Responsibility for Your Feelings

It's important to make sure that your language reflects the fact that you're responsible for your feelings.[78] Instead of saying "You're making me angry," say "I'm getting angry." Instead of saying "You hurt my feelings," say "I feel

ETHICAL *Challenge*

Aristotle's Golden Mean

Almost two and a half millennia ago, the philosopher Aristotle examined the question of "moral virtue": What constitutes good behavior, and what ways of acting enable us to function effectively in the world? One important part of his examination addresses the management and expression of emotion: what he defines as "passions and actions."

According to Aristotle, an important dimension of virtuous behavior is moderation, which he defines as "an intermediate between excess and deficit … equidistant from the extremes … neither too much nor too little." He acknowledges that it isn't realistic or desirable for a passionate person to strive for the same type of behavior as a dispassionate person. After all, a world in which everyone felt and acted identically would be boring.

Instead of a "one-size-fits-all" approach to emotional expression, Aristotle urges communicators to moderate their own style, to be "intermediate not in the object, but relative to us." Following Aristotle's injunction, a person with a hot temper would strive to cool down, whereas a person who rarely expresses his or her feelings ought to aim at becoming more expressive. The result would still be two people with different styles, but each of whom behaved better than before seeking the golden mean.

According to Aristotle, moderation also means that emotions should be suited to the occasion: We should feel (and express) them "at the right times, with reference to the right objects, towards the right people, with the right motive, and in the right way." We can imagine times when even a normally restrained person could reasonably act with anger and times when a normally voluble person could reasonably behave with restraint. Even then, too much emotion (rage, for example) or too little emotion falls outside the range of virtue. In Aristotle's words, when it comes to "passions and actions … excess is a form of failure and so is deficit."

How would your emotional expression be different if you strived for moderation? Answer this question by identifying which parts of your emotional expression are most extreme, either in their intensity or their absence.

MindTap APPLY ...   the ethical principles introduced here by answering the following questions, either here or online.

1. How might your relationships change if you acted more moderately?

2. Are there any situations in your life when more extreme forms of emotional expression are both moral and effective?

hurt when you do that." As you'll soon read, people don't make us like or dislike them, and believing that they do denies the responsibility that each of us has for our own emotions. Chapter 6 introduces "I" language, which offers a responsible way to express your feelings.

Be Mindful of the Communication Channel

As Chapter 1 explained, the channels we use to communicate make a difference in how others interpret our messages. This is particularly true when expressing emotions.

Communicators today have many more channel choices than they did a few decades ago, and the decision about when to use mediated channels—such as email, instant messaging, cell phones, social media sites, and blogging—call for a level of analysis that wasn't required in the past.[79] For instance, is it appropriate to signal your desire to end a relationship in a voice mail message? When is it acceptable to use CAPITAL LETTERS in a blog post to express displeasure? If you're excited about some good news, should you first tell your family and friends in person before publishing it on Facebook?

Most people intuitively recognize that the selection of a channel depends in part on the kind of message they're sending. In one survey, students identified which channel they would find best for delivering a variety of messages.[80] Most respondents said they would have little trouble expressing positive messages in person, but preferred mediated channels for negative messages.

"Flaming" is an extreme example of how mediated channels lend themselves to expressing negative emotions. The kind of civility that most people honor in other communication channels seems to have less of a hold on the Internet—certainly among strangers, but even among people who belong to the same personal networks. Before saying something you may later regret, it's worth remembering the principle stated in Chapter 1 that communication is irreversible. Once you hit the "Send" button, you can't retract an emotional outburst.

MANAGING EMOTIONS

Although feeling and expressing emotions usually adds to the quality of interpersonal relationships, not all feelings are beneficial. For instance, rage, depression, terror, and jealousy do little to help you feel better or improve your relationships. You will learn about tools to minimize these unproductive emotions. We'll also describe how to maximize the experience of positive emotions.

Facilitative and Debilitative Emotions

First, we need to make a distinction between **facilitative emotions**, which contribute to effective functioning, and **debilitative emotions**, which detract from effective functioning.

One difference between the two types is their *intensity*. For instance, a certain amount of anger or irritation can be constructive because it often provides the stimulus that leads you to improve the unsatisfying conditions. Rage, however, usually makes matters worse—especially when driving, as illustrated by the problems associated with "road rage."[81] The same holds true for fear. A little bit of fear before an important athletic contest or job interview might give you the boost that will improve your performance.[82] (Mellow athletes or employees usually don't do well.) But total terror is something else.

Not surprisingly, debilitative emotions like communication apprehension can lead to a variety of problems in personal, business, educational, and even medical settings.[83] When people become anxious, they generally speak less, which means that their needs aren't met; and when they do manage to speak up, they are less effective at communicating than their more confident counterparts.[84]

A second characteristic that distinguishes debilitative feelings from facilitative ones is their extended *duration*. Feeling depressed for a while after the breakup of a relationship or the loss of a job is natural, but spending the rest of your life grieving over your loss would accomplish nothing. In the same way, staying angry at someone for a wrong inflicted long ago can be just as punishing to you as to the wrongdoer. Social scientists call this **rumination**—dwelling persistently on negative thoughts that, in turn, intensify negative feelings. A substantial body of research confirms that rumination increases feelings of sadness, anxiety, jealousy, and depression[85] and makes them last longer.[86] Just as bad, people who ruminate are more likely to lash out with displaced aggression at innocent bystanders.[87]

∧ In the TV show *Revenge*, Emily Thorne (Emily VanCamp) feels driven to settle scores with people she believes have wronged her. Most observers would agree that while Emily's grievances may be justified, her desire for retribution is debilitating. What emotions typically accompany a desire for vengeance?

Many debilitative emotions involve communication. Here are a few examples, offered by readers of *Looking Out Looking In*:

> When I first came to college, I had to leave my boyfriend. I was living with three girls, and for most of the first semester I was so lonesome and unhappy that I was a pretty terrible roommate.

> I got so frustrated with my overly critical boss that I lost my temper and quit one day. I told him what a horrible manager he was and walked off the job right then and there. Now I'm afraid to list my former boss as a reference, and I'm afraid my temper tantrum will make it harder for me to get a new job.

> I've had ongoing problems with my family, and sometimes I get so upset that I can't concentrate on my work or school, or even sleep well at night.

You will learn a method for dealing with debilitative feelings like these that can improve your effectiveness as a communicator. This method is based on the idea that one way to minimize debilitative feelings is to minimize unproductive thinking.

Sources of Debilitative Emotions

For most people, feelings seem to have a life of their own. You wish you could feel calm when approaching strangers, yet your voice quivers. You try to appear confident when asking for a raise, yet your eye twitches nervously. Where do feelings like these come from?

In REAL LIFE

Guidelines for Emotional Expression

After a long and frustrating search, Logan thinks he has found the ideal job that he wants and needs. The interview went well. As Logan was leaving, the interviewer said he was "very well qualified" and promised "You'll be hearing from us soon." That conversation took place almost two weeks ago, and Logan hasn't heard a word from the company.

The two transcripts below reflect very different ways of responding to this difficult situation. The first one ignores and the second one follows the Guidelines for Expressing Emotions described in this chapter. In each, Logan begins by *ruminating* about the employer's failure to get in touch as promised.

Ignoring Guidelines for Expressing Emotions

Logan doesn't explicitly recognize a single emotion he is experiencing, let alone any mixed emotions. Rather than accepting responsibility for his own feelings, he blames the employer for "driving me crazy."	"I can't believe those inconsiderate idiots! Who do they think they are, promising to call soon and then doing nothing? They're driving me crazy."
Logan jumps to the conclusion that a job offer isn't forthcoming, and lashes out without considering any alternatives.	"I give up. Since they aren't going to hire me, I'm going to call that interviewer and let her know what a screwed-up company they're running. I'll probably get her voice mail, but that's even better: That way I can say what's on my mind without getting nervous or being interrupted. They have no right to jerk me around like this, and I'm going to tell them just that." *(Angrily dials phone)*

Following Guidelines for Expressing Emotions

Logan identifies his mixture of feelings as a starting point for deciding what to do.	"I'm mad at the company for not keeping in touch like they promised. I'm also confused about whether I'm as qualified as I thought I was, and I'm starting to worry that maybe I didn't do as well in the interview as I thought. I'm also sorry I didn't ask her for a more specific time than 'soon.' And I'm really unsure about whether to give up, wait for them to call me, or reach out to the company and ask what's going on."

Physiology   One answer lies in our genetic makeup. As you read in Chapter 3, temperament is, to a large degree, inherited. Communication traits like shyness, verbal aggressiveness, and assertiveness are rooted in biology. Fortunately, biology isn't destiny. As you'll soon read, it is possible to overcome debilitative feelings.

Beyond heredity, cognitive scientists tell us that the cause of some debilitative feelings—especially those involving fight-or-flight responses—lies deep inside the brain, in an almond-sized cluster of interconnected structures

He recognizes the difference between what he would like to do (chew out the interviewer) and what is more appropriate and effective.	"If I'm not going to get the job, I'd like to chew out that interviewer for promising to call. But that would probably be a bad idea—burning my bridges, as my family would say."
Logan uses a perception check and considers sharing his feelings with the employer in a non-blaming way. He deliberately considers when and how to express himself, choosing email as the best channel to achieve his goals.	"Maybe I'll call her and say something like 'I'm confused. You said at the interview that I'd hear from you soon, but it's been almost two weeks now with no word.' I could ask whether I misunderstood (although I doubt that), or whether they need some more information from me. Let me think about that overnight. If the idea still sounds good in the morning, I'll call them."
Having decided to email the employer, Logan could use the face-saving methods described in Chapter 11 to compose his message. He could begin by speaking positively about his continued interest in the company, then raise his concern about not having heard from them, and then close by saying that he's looking forward to hearing back from them.	"Actually, an email would be better. I could edit my words until they're just right, and an email wouldn't put the interviewer on the spot like a phone call would."

MindTap **APPLY ...** this situation to your life by answering questions online.

called the amygdala (pronounced uh-MIG-duh-luh). The amygdala acts as a kind of sentinel that scans every experience, looking for threats. In literally a split second, it can sound an alarm that triggers a flood of physiological reactions: speeding heart rate, elevating blood pressure, heightening the senses, and preparing the muscles to react.[88]

This defense system has obvious value when we are confronted with real physical dangers, but in social situations the amygdala can hijack the brain, triggering emotions like fear and anger when there is no real threat. You might

find yourself feeling uncomfortable when somebody stands too close to you or angry when someone cuts in front of you in line. As you'll soon read, thinking clearly is the way to avoid overreacting to events like these.

Emotional Memory   The source of some threats lies in what neuroscientists have termed our *emotional memory*. Seemingly harmless events can trigger debilitative feelings if they bear even a slight resemblance to troublesome experiences from the past. A few examples illustrate the point:

- Ever since being teased when he moved to a new elementary school, Darnell has been uncomfortable in unfamiliar situations.

- Alicia feels apprehensive around men, especially those with deep, booming voices. As a child, she was mistreated by a family member with a loud baritone voice.

- Miguel feels a wave of insecurity whenever he is around women who use the same perfume worn by a former lover who jilted him.

Self-Talk   Beyond neurobiology, what we think can have a profound effect on how we feel. It's common to say that strangers or your boss make you feel nervous, just as you would say that a bee sting makes you feel pain. The apparent similarities between physical and emotional discomforts become clear if you look at them like this:

EVENT	FEELING
Bee sting	Physical pain
Meeting strangers	Nervous feelings

When looking at your emotions in this way, you seem to have little control over how you feel. However, this apparent similarity between physical pain and emotional discomfort (or pleasure) isn't as great as it seems to be. Cognitive psychologists argue that it is not *events* such as meeting strangers or being jilted by a lover that cause people to feel bad, but rather the *beliefs they hold* about these events. As discussed earlier in the chapter, *reappraisal* involves changing our thoughts to help manage our emotions.

Albert Ellis, who developed an approach to reappraisal called *rational-emotive therapy*, tells a story that makes this point clear. Imagine yourself walking by a friend's house and seeing your friend stick his head out of a window and call you a string of vile names. (You supply the friend and the names.) Under these circumstances, it's likely that you would feel hurt and upset. Now imagine that instead of walking by a house, you are passing a mental institution. The same friend, who is obviously a patient there, shouts the same vile names at you. In this case, your feelings would probably be quite different—most likely sadness and pity.

You can see that in this story the activating event of being called names was the same in both cases, yet the emotional consequences were very different. The reason for your different feelings has to do with your thinking in each case. In the first case, you would most likely think that your friend was very angry with you; further, you might imagine that you must have done something terrible to deserve such a response. In the second case, you would probably assume that your friend had some psychological difficulty, and most likely you would feel sympathetic.

From this example you can start to see that it's the *interpretations* that people make of an event, during the process of **self-talk**, that determine their feelings.[89] Thus, the model for emotions looks like this:

EVENT	THOUGHT (SELF-TALK)	FEELING
Being called names	"I've done something wrong."	Hurt, upset
Being called names	"My friend must be sick."	Concern, sympathy

The same principle applies in more common situations. In job interviews, for example, people who become nervous are likely to use negative self-talk when they think about their performance: "I won't do well," "I don't know why I'm doing this."[90] In romantic relationships, thoughts shape satisfaction. The words "I love you" can be interpreted in a variety of ways. They could be taken at face value as a genuine expression of deep affection:

EVENT	THOUGHT (SELF-TALK)	FEELING
Hearing "I love you"	"This is a genuine statement."	Delight (perhaps)

The same words might be decoded as a sincere but mistaken declaration uttered in a moment of passion, an attempt to make the recipient feel better, or an attempt at manipulation. For example,

EVENT	THOUGHT (SELF-TALK)	FEELING
Hearing "I love you"	"She's just saying this to manipulate me."	Anger

In other words, our emotions are more a result of our thoughts than of the events we encounter. This takes us back to the reappraisal process described earlier in the chapter. It's possible to use self-talk to manage emotional responses. For instance, research shows that telling yourself "I am excited" instead of "Calm down" will generally lead to better performances in public speaking.[91] The words we use—even if they never leave our minds—can have a dramatic effect on how we manage our emotions.

PAUSE *and* REFLECT

Talking to Yourself

MindTap REFLECT . . . on how your thoughts shape your feelings by answering the following questions, either here or online.

You can become better at understanding how your thoughts shape your feelings by completing the following steps:

1. Take a few minutes to listen to the inner voice you use when thinking. Close your eyes now and listen to it. Did you hear the voice? Perhaps it was saying, "What voice? I don't have any voice. . . ." Try again, and pay attention to what the voice is saying.

2. Now think about the following situations and imagine how you would react in each. How would you interpret them with your inner voice? What feelings would follow from each interpretation?

   a. While sitting on a bus, in class, or on the street, you notice an attractive person sneaking glances at you.

   b. During a lecture your professor asks the class "What do you think about this?" and looks toward you.

   c. You are telling friends about your vacation, and one yawns.

   d. You run into a friend on the street and ask how things are going. "Fine," she replies, and rushes off.

3. Now recall three recent times when you felt a strong emotion. For each one, recall the activating event and then the interpretation that led to your emotional reaction.

Irrational Thinking and Debilitative Emotions

Many debilitative emotions come from accepting a number of irrational thoughts—we'll call them *fallacies* here—that lead to illogical conclusions and in turn to debilitative emotions. We usually aren't aware of these thoughts, which makes them especially powerful.[92]

1. The Fallacy of Perfection   People who accept the **fallacy of perfection** believe that a worthwhile communicator should be able to handle every situation with complete confidence and skill.

Nobody is perfect. Given the desire to be valued and appreciated, it's tempting to try to *appear* flawless. But the costs of such deception are high. If others ever find you out, they'll see you as a phony. Even when your act isn't uncovered, it uses up a great deal of psychological energy and thus makes the rewards of approval less enjoyable.

Subscribing to the myth of perfection not only can keep others from liking you, but also can act as a force to diminish your own self-esteem. How can you like yourself when you don't measure up to the way you ought to be? It's liberating to comfortably accept the idea that you are not perfect.

2. The Fallacy of Approval   The **fallacy of approval** is based on the idea that it's not just desirable but vital to get the approval of virtually every person. People who accept this idea seek approval from others, even when they have to sacrifice their own principles and happiness to do so. Accepting this fallacy can lead to some ludicrous situations:

Carol and Mike Werner/Index Stock/Getty Images

> Feeling nervous because people you don't even like seem to disapprove of you
>
> Feeling apologetic when others are at fault
>
> Feeling embarrassed after behaving unnaturally to gain another's approval

The fallacy of approval is irrational because it implies that others will respect and like you more if you go out of your way to please them. Often this simply isn't true. Would *you* respect people who have compromised important values just to gain acceptance? Are you likely to think highly of people who repeatedly deny their own needs as a means of buying approval?

Don't misunderstand: Abandoning the fallacy of approval doesn't mean living a life of selfishness. It's still important to consider the needs of others and to meet them whenever possible. It's also pleasant—we might say even necessary—to strive for the respect of those people you value. The point here is that when you must abandon your own needs and principles in order to seek these goals, the price is too high.

3. The Fallacy of Shoulds   The **fallacy of shoulds** is the inability to distinguish between what is and what should be. You can see the difference by imagining a person who is full of complaints about the world:

> "There should be no rain on weekends."
>
> "People ought to live forever."
>
> "Money should grow on trees."
>
> "We should all be able to fly."

Complaints like these are obviously foolish. Yet many people torture themselves by engaging in this sort of irrational thinking when they confuse preferences with shoulds. They say and think things like this:

> "My friend should be more understanding."
>
> "She shouldn't be so inconsiderate."
>
> "They should be more friendly."
>
> "You should work harder."

The message in each of these cases is that you would *prefer* people to behave differently. Wishing that things were better is legitimate, and trying to change things may be a good idea, but it's unreasonable to *insist* that the world operate just as you want it to or to feel cheated when things aren't ideal.

CRITIC'S MATH

Larry David feels just like me and you when it comes to criticism.

You'd think he wouldn't. He co-created *Seinfeld*, the most successful sitcom of all time. His show *Curb Your Enthusiasm* is a smash success. He's been on the cover of *Rolling Stone* magazine. And yet, he still does the same math you and I do when it comes to critics.

What's critic's math? It's the formula most of us use when it comes to criticism. Here is an example of how it works:

> 1 insult + 1,000 compliments
> = 1 insult.

We need look no further than a story about Larry David in that *Rolling Stone* article to see it in action.

One night during his stay (in New York), David went to Yankee Stadium to see a game. His image went up on the big screen as *Curb Your Enthusiasm's* theme song played over the big speakers. An entire stadium of fans stood and cheered for the hopeless case from Brooklyn. It should have been a life-defining moment, the redemptive final scene in the biopic. But as it

turned out, not so much. As David left the stadium, a guy drove by and yelled, "Larry, you suck!" "That's like, literally all he heard," David's friend says.

David spent the ride back from the Bronx obsessing over that moment. It was as if the other 50,000 people, the ones who loved him, didn't exist. "Who's that guy? What was that?" He asked. "Who would do that? Why would you say something like that?"

That's critic's math. One insult was able to erase an entire stadium of adulation. More than 50,000 people disappeared at the hand of one point of bitterness. Critic's math might be the most powerful magic on the planet.

There are three things you need to know about it:

1. *It doesn't instantly go away with success*. If right now you're thinking "If I sell a certain number of books or get a job promotion, I won't worry so much about what critic's think," you're wrong. Larry David is incredibly successful. If you have a hard time with critic's

math with 10 followers on Twitter, you'll still have a hard time with it with 1 million followers. Don't chase success as a way to beat critic's math.

2. *Every time you believe critic's math, you make it more powerful*. Doubt and fear are like muscles. Every time you believe a lie it gets easier to believe the next time. It took Larry David a lifetime of critic's math to ignore a full stadium of fans.

3. *You're not the only one with a math problem*. You know which Amazon review for my book *Quitter* I think about the most? It's not the 95 5-star reviews the book got. It's the one 1-star review.

It's time you and me, and maybe even Larry David, let it go. Critic's math doesn't add up. In fact, it's all about subtraction. Subtracting compliments. Subtracting happiness. Subtracting joy.

Jon Acuff

MindTap ENHANCE … your understanding by answering the following questions, either here or online.

1. Identify a time when you used "critic's math" in evaluating others' messages about you.

2. Reappraise the situation you identified in question 1, developing a more balanced response to the criticism. How does this reappraisal affect your emotions and your subsequent behavior?

Becoming obsessed with shoulds like these has three troublesome consequences. First, it leads to unnecessary unhappiness because people who are constantly dreaming about the ideal are seldom satisfied with what they have or who they are. Second, merely complaining without acting can keep you from doing anything to change unsatisfying conditions. Third, this sort of complaining can build a defensive climate with others, who will resent being nagged. It's much more effective to tell people about what you'd like than to preach. Say, "I wish you'd be more punctual" instead of "You should be on time." We'll discuss ways of avoiding defensive climates in Chapter 11.

4. The Fallacy of Overgeneralization   The **fallacy of overgeneralization** comprises two types. The first type of overgeneralization occurs when we base a belief on a limited amount of evidence. For instance, how many times have you found yourself saying something like this:

"I'm so stupid! I can't even figure out how to download music on my phone."

"Some friend I am! I forgot my best friend's birthday."

In cases like these, we focus on a limited type of shortcoming as if it represented everything about us. We forget that, along with encountering our difficulties, we have solved tough problems and that, though we're sometimes forgetful, at other times we're caring and thoughtful.

A second type of overgeneralization occurs when we *exaggerate* shortcomings:

"You *never* listen to me."

"You're *always* late."

"I can't think of *anything*."

Absolute statements like these are almost always false and usually lead to discouragement or anger. You'll feel far better when you replace overgeneralizations with more accurate messages to yourself and others:

"You often don't listen to me."

"You've been late three times this week."

"I haven't had any ideas I like today."

5. The Fallacy of Causation   The **fallacy of causation** is based on the irrational belief that emotions are caused by others rather than by your own self-talk.

This fallacy causes trouble in two ways. The first way plagues people who become overly cautious about communicating because they don't want to "cause" any pain or inconvenience for others. This attitude occurs in cases such as:

Visiting friends or family out of a sense of obligation rather than a genuine desire to see them

Keeping quiet when another person's behavior is bothering you

Pretending to be attentive to a speaker when you are already late for an appointment or feeling ill

Praising and reassuring others who ask for your opinion, even when your honest response would be negative

There's certainly no excuse for going out of your way to say things that will result in pain for others, and there will be times when you choose to inconvenience yourself to make life easier for those you care about. It's essential to realize, however, that it's an overstatement to say that you are the one who *causes* others' feelings. It's more accurate to say that they *respond* to your behavior with feelings of their own.

For example, consider how strange it sounds to suggest that you make others fall in love with you. Such a statement simply doesn't make sense. It would be closer to the truth to say that you act in one way or another, and someone might fall in love with you as a result. In the same way, it's incorrect to say that you *make* others angry, upset, or happy, for that matter. It's more accurate to say that others respond to your behavior.

The fallacy of causation also operates when we believe that others cause *our* emotions. Sometimes it certainly seems as if they do, either raising or lowering our spirits by their actions. But think about it for a moment: The same actions that will cause you happiness or unhappiness one day have little effect at other times. The insult or compliment that affected your mood strongly yesterday leaves you unaffected today. You certainly wouldn't feel some emotions without others' behavior, but your reaction, not their actions, determines how you feel.

6. The Fallacy of Helplessness The **fallacy of helplessness** suggests that satisfaction in life is determined by forces beyond your control. People who continuously see themselves as victims make such statements as:

> "There's no way a woman can get ahead in this society. It's a man's world, and the best thing I can do is to accept it."

> "I was born with a shy personality. I'd like to be more outgoing, but there's nothing I can do about that."

> "I can't tell my boss that she is putting too many demands on me. If I do, I might lose my job."

The mistake in statements like these becomes apparent after you realize that you can do many things if you really want to. Most "can't" statements can be more correctly rephrased either as "won't" statements ("I can't tell him what I think" becomes "I won't be honest with him") or as "don't know how" statements ("I can't carry on an interesting conversation" becomes "I don't know what to say"). After you've rephrased these inaccurate "can'ts," it becomes clear that they're either a matter of choice or an area that calls for your action—both quite different from saying that you're helpless.

7. The Fallacy of Catastrophic Expectations Fearful communicators who subscribe to the irrational **fallacy of catastrophic expectations** operate on the assumption that if something bad can possibly happen, it will. Typical catastrophic expectations include:

> "If I invite them to the party, they probably won't want to come."

> "If I speak up in order to try to resolve a conflict, things will probably get worse."

> "If I apply for the job I want, I probably won't be hired."

> "If I tell them how I really feel, they'll probably laugh at me."

After you start expecting catastrophic consequences, a self-fulfilling prophecy can begin to build. One study revealed that people who believed that their romantic partners would not change for the better were likely to behave in ways that contributed to the breakup of the relationship.[93]

Although it's naive to assume that all of your interactions with others will meet with success, it's just as naive to assume that you'll fail. One way to escape from the fallacy of catastrophic expectations is to think about the consequences that would follow even if you don't communicate successfully. Keeping in mind the folly of trying to be perfect and of living only for the approval of others, realize that failing in a given instance usually isn't as bad as it might seem. What if people do laugh at you? Suppose you don't get the job? What if others do get angry at your remarks? Are these matters really *that* serious?

Before moving on, we need to add a few thoughts about thinking and feeling. First, you should realize that thinking rationally won't completely eliminate debilitative emotions. Some debilitative emotions, after all, are very rational: grief over the death of someone you love, euphoria over getting a new job, and apprehension about the future of an important relationship after a serious fight, for example. Thinking rationally can eliminate many debilitative emotions from your life, but not all of them.

Minimizing Debilitative Emotions

How can you overcome irrational thinking? Social scientists and therapists have developed a simple yet effective approach.[94] When practiced conscientiously, it can help you cut down on the self-defeating thinking that leads to many debilitative emotions.

PAUSE *and* REFLECT

How Irrational Are You?

MindTap® **REFLECT...** on your irrational thoughts by answering the following questions, either here or online.

1. Return to the situations described in the Talking to Yourself exercise earlier in this chapter. Examine each one to see whether your self-talk contains any irrational thoughts.

2. Keep a two- or three-day record of your debilitative emotions. Are any of them based on irrational thinking? Examine your conclusions, and see if you repeatedly use any of the fallacies described in the preceding section.

3. Take a class poll to see which fallacies are most popular. Also, discuss what subjects seem to stimulate most of this irrational thinking (e.g., schoolwork, dating, jobs, family).

Monitor Your Emotional Reactions   The first step is to recognize when you're feeling debilitative emotions. (Of course, it's also nice to recognize pleasant emotions when they occur.) As we suggested earlier, one way to recognize emotions is through monitoring physiological responses: butterflies in the stomach, racing heart, hot flashes, and so on. Although such stimuli might be symptoms of food poisoning, more often they are symptoms of a strong emotion. You can also recognize certain ways of behaving that suggest your feelings: stomping instead of walking normally, being unusually quiet, or speaking in a sarcastic tone of voice are some examples.

It may seem strange to suggest that it's necessary to look for emotions—they ought to be immediately apparent. The fact is, however, that we often suffer from debilitative emotions for some time without noticing them. For example, at the end of a trying day you've probably caught yourself frowning and realized that you've been wearing that mask for some time without noticing it.

Note the Activating Event   After you're aware of how you're feeling, the next step is to figure out what activating event triggered your response. Sometimes it is obvious. For instance, a common source of anger is being accused unfairly (or fairly) of foolish behavior; a common source of hurt is being rejected by somebody important to you. In other cases, however, the activating event isn't so apparent.

Sometimes there isn't a single activating event but rather a series of small events that finally builds toward a critical mass and triggers a debilitative emotion. This happens when you're trying to work or sleep and are continually annoyed by a string of interruptions, or when you suffer a series of small disappointments.

The best way to begin tracking down activating events is to notice the circumstances in which you have debilitative emotions. Perhaps they occur when you're around *specific people*. In other cases, you might be bothered by certain *types of individuals* because of their age, role, or background. Or perhaps certain *settings* stimulate unpleasant emotions: parties, work, school. Sometimes the *topic* of conversation is the factor that sets you off, whether it be politics, religion, sex, or some other subject.

"So, when he says, 'What a good boy am I,' Jack is really reinforcing his self-esteem."

Record Your Self-Talk   This is the point at which you analyze the thoughts that are the link between the activating event and your feeling. If you're serious about getting rid of debilitative emotions, it's important to actually write down your self-talk when first learning to use this method. Putting your thoughts on paper will help you see whether they make any sense.

Monitoring your self-talk might be difficult at first. This is a new activity, and any new activity seems awkward. If you persevere, however, you'll

ZITS   BY JERRY SCOTT AND JIM BORGMAN

find that you will be able to identify the thoughts that lead to your debilitative emotions. After you get in the habit of recognizing this internal monologue, you'll be able to identify your thoughts quickly and easily.

Reappraise Your Irrational Beliefs   Reappraising your irrational beliefs is the key to success in the rational-emotive approach. Use the list of irrational fallacies in the preceding section to discover which of your internal statements are based on mistaken thinking.

You can do this most effectively by following three steps. First, decide whether each belief you've recorded is rational or irrational. Next, explain why the belief is rational or irrational. Finally, if the belief is irrational, you should write down an alternative way of thinking that is more rational and that can leave you feeling better when faced with the same activating event in the future.

Replacing self-defeating self-talk with more constructive thinking is an especially effective tool for improving self-confidence and relational communication.[95] Nonetheless, this approach triggers objections from some readers:

"The rational-emotive approach sounds like nothing more than trying to talk yourself out of feeling bad." This accusation is totally correct. After all, because we talk ourselves into feeling bad, what's wrong with talking ourselves out of feeling bad, especially when such feelings are based on irrational thoughts? Rationalizing may be an excuse and a self-deception, but there's nothing wrong with being rational.

"The kind of reappraising we just read sounds phony and unnatural. I don't talk to myself in sentences and paragraphs." There's no need to dispute your irrational beliefs in any special literary style. You can be just as colloquial as you want. The important thing is to clearly understand what thoughts led you

In REAL LIFE

Rational Thinking in Action

The following scenarios demonstrate how the rational thinking method described in this section applies in everyday challenges. Notice that thinking rationally doesn't eliminate debilitative emotions. Instead, it helps keep them in control, making effective communication more possible.

Situation 1: Dealing with Annoying Customers

Activating Event

I work in a shopping mall that swarms with tourists and locals. Our company's reputation is based on service, but lately I've been losing my patience with the customers. The store is busy from the second we open until we close. Many of the customers are rude, pushy, and demanding. Others expect me to be a tour guide, restaurant reviewer, medical consultant, and even a babysitter. I feel like I'm ready to explode.

Beliefs and Self-Talk

1. I'm sick of working with the public. People are really obnoxious!

2. The customers should be more patient and polite instead of treating me like a servant.

3. This work is driving me crazy! If I keep working here, I'm going to become as rude as the customers.

4. I can't quit: I could never find another job that pays this well.

Reappraising Irrational Beliefs

1. It's an overgeneralization to say that *all* people are obnoxious. Actually, most of the customers are fine. Some are even very nice. About 10 percent of them cause most of the trouble. Recognizing that most people are OK leaves me feeling less bitter.

2. It's true that obnoxious customers *should* be more polite, but it's unrealistic to expect that everybody will behave the way they ought to. After all, it's not a perfect world.

3. By saying that the customers are driving me crazy, I suggest that I have no control over the situation. I'm an adult, and I am able to keep a grip on myself.

into your debilitative emotions so that you can clearly reappraise them. While the approach is new to you, it's a good idea to write or talk out your thoughts in order to make them clear. After you've had some practice, you'll be able to do these steps in a quicker, less formal way.

"This approach is too cold and impersonal. It seems to aim at turning people into calculating, emotionless machines." This is simply not true. A rational thinker can still dream, hope, and love. There's nothing necessarily irrational about feelings like these. Basically rational people even indulge in a bit of irrational thinking once in a while, but they usually know what they're doing. Like healthy eaters who occasionally allow themselves a snack of junk food, rational thinkers occasionally indulge in irrational thoughts, knowing that they'll return to their healthy lifestyle soon with no real damage done.

"This technique promises too much. There's no chance I could rid myself of all unpleasant feelings, however nice that might be." We can answer this objection

I may not like the way some people behave, but it's my choice how to respond to them.

4. I'm not helpless. If the job is too unpleasant, I can quit. I probably wouldn't find another job that pays as well as this one, so I have to choose which is more important: money or peace of mind. It's my choice.

Situation 2: Meeting My Girlfriend's Family

Activating Event

Tracy and I are talking about marriage—maybe not soon, but eventually. Her family is very close, and they want to meet me. I'm sure I'll like them, but I am not sure what they will think about me. I was married once before, at a young age. It was a big mistake, and it didn't last. Furthermore, I was laid off two months ago, and I'm between jobs. The family is coming to town next week, and I am very nervous about what they will think of me.

Beliefs and Self-Talk

1. They've *got* to like me! This is a close family, and I'm doomed if they think I'm not right for Tracy.

2. No matter how sensibly I act, all they'll think of is my divorce and unemployment.

3. Maybe the family is right. Tracy deserves the best, and I'm certainly not that!

Reappraising Irrational Beliefs

1. The family's approval is definitely important. Still, my relationship with Tracy doesn't depend on it. She's already said that she's committed to me, no matter what they think. The sensible approach is to say I *want* their approval, but I don't *need* it.

2. I'm expecting the absolute worst if I think that I'm doomed no matter what happens when we meet. There is a chance that they will dislike me, but there's also a chance that things will work out fine. There's no point in dwelling on catastrophes.

3. Just because I've had an imperfect past doesn't mean I'm wrong for Tracy. I've learned from my past mistakes, and I am committed to living a good life. I know I can be the kind of husband she deserves, even though I'm not perfect.

MindTap® **APPLY ...** this situation to your life by answering questions online.

by agreeing that rational-emotive thinking probably won't totally solve your emotional problems. What it can do is reduce their number, intensity, and duration. This method is not the answer to all your problems, but it can make a significant difference—which is not a bad accomplishment.

Maximizing Facilitative Emotions

Reducing debilitative emotions is only part of the emotional health equation. Contemporary scholars maintain that fostering positive emotions is just as important as minimizing negative ones. Whether it's called "learned optimism"[96] or "positivity,"[97] the approach is similar to what we've outlined in this section. If thoughts cause feelings, then positive thoughts can cause positive feelings. Ruminating on the good rather than the bad in life can enhance one's emotional, relational, and even physical health.[98]

SKILL *Builder*

Rational Thinking

1. Return to the diary of irrational thoughts you recorded in the previous Pause and Reflect exercise. Dispute the self-talk in each case, and write a more rational interpretation of the event.

2. Now try out your ability to think rationally on the spot. You can do this by acting out the scenes listed after step 4. You'll need three players for each one: a subject, the subject's "little voice"—his or her thoughts—and a second party.

3. Play out each scene by having the subject and second party interact while the "little voice" stands just behind the subject and says what the subject is probably thinking. For example, in a scene where the subject is asking an instructor to reconsider a low grade, the little voice might say, "I hope I haven't made things worse by bringing this up. Maybe he'll lower the grade after rereading the test. I'm such an idiot! Why didn't I keep quiet?"

4. Whenever the little voice expresses an irrational thought, the observers who are watching the skit should call out, "Foul." At this point the action should stop while the group discusses the irrational thought and suggests a more rational line of self-talk. The players should then replay the scene with the little voice speaking in a more rational way.

Here are some possible scenes (of course, you can invent others as well):

a. Two people are just beginning their first date.

b. A potential employee has just begun a job interview.

c. A teacher or boss is criticizing the subject for showing up late.

d. A student and instructor run across each other in the supermarket.

It's unrealistic to think that you'll have a positive emotional response to every event. The key according to researcher Barbara Fredrickson is to leave plenty of room to enjoy and savor positive emotional experiences.[99] And even though you can't dictate all the events of your life, you have the power to reappraise them. Clichés such as "look on the bright side" and "have an attitude of gratitude" may not be comforting when delivered by others, but they can serve as helpful self-reminders. You can regard challenging situations as growth opportunities. You can focus on what you gained rather than what you lost. You can choose compassion over contempt. The difference between "That really hurt me" and "I found out how strong and capable I really am" is often a matter of mindset—and positive emotions follow positive appraisals.

Many people find it easier to focus on their negative emotional experiences. It often takes mindful effort to pay attention to and express pleasurable feelings in close relationships. Here are ten emotions that Frederickson's research identifies as basic to positivity: *joy, gratitude, serenity, interest, hope, pride, amusement, inspiration, awe*, and *love*. How many have you experienced recently? How often do you express these emotions to people who matter? Is it possible that you felt but can't recall them? Identifying and then talking or writing about your positive emotional experiences can lead to greater personal and interpersonal satisfaction.

SUMMARY

Emotions have several dimensions. They are signaled by internal physiological changes, manifested by nonverbal reactions, and defined in most cases by cognitive interpretations. We can use this information to make choices about whether or not to verbalize our feelings.

There are several reasons why people do not verbalize many of the emotions they feel. Some people have personalities that are less prone toward emotional expression. Culture and gender also have an effect on the emotions we do and don't share with others. Social rules and roles discourage the expression of some feelings, particularly negative ones. Social media may also increase the intensity of emotions for both message senders and receivers. Finally, contagion can lead us to experience emotions that we might not otherwise have had.

Because total expression of emotions is not appropriate, several guidelines help define when and how to express emotions effectively. Expanding your emotional vocabulary, becoming more self-aware, and expressing mixed feelings are important. Recognizing the difference between feeling, thinking, and acting, as well as accepting responsibility for feelings instead of blaming them on others, lead to better reactions. Choosing the proper time and place to share feelings is also important, as is choosing the best channel for expressing emotions.

Whereas some emotions are facilitative, others are debilitative and inhibit effective functioning. Many of these debilitative emotions are biological reactions rooted in the amygdala portion of the brain, but their negative impact can be altered through rational thinking. It is often possible to communicate more confidently and effectively by identifying troublesome emotions, identifying the activating event and self-talk that triggered them, and reappraising any irrational thoughts with a more logical analysis of the situation. It is also important to identify and enjoy facilitative emotions.

KEY TERMS

debilitative emotions
emotional contagion
emotional intelligence (EQ)
emotion labor
facilitative emotions
fallacy of approval
fallacy of catastrophic expectations
fallacy of causation

fallacy of helplessness
fallacy of overgeneralization
fallacy of perfection
fallacy of shoulds
reappraisal
rumination
self-talk

CHAPTER FIVE

Emotions: Feeling, Thinking, and Communicating

OUTLINE

Use this outline to take notes as you read the chapter in the text and/or as your instructor lectures in class.

Outline	Notes

I. EMOTIONAL INTELLIGENCE
  A. Ability to Understand and Manage One's Own Emotions
  B. Ability to Be Sensitive to Others' Feelings	

II. WHAT ARE EMOTIONS?
  A. Physiological Factors
  B. Nonverbal Reactions
  C. Cognitive Interpretations
  D. Verbal Expression	

III. INFLUENCES ON EMOTIONAL EXPRESSION
  A. Personality
  B. Culture
  C. Gender
  D. Social Conventions
  E. Fear of Self-Disclosure
  F. Emotional Contagion	

IV. GUIDELINES FOR EXPRESSING EMOTIONS
  A. Recognize Feelings
  B. Recognize the Difference between Feeling, Talking, and Acting	

C. Expand Your Emotional Vocabulary

   1. Avoid Emotional Counterfeits

     a. Express Verbally

     b. Use Single Words

     c. Describe What's Happening to You

     d. Describe What You'd Like to Do

   2. Avoid Minimizing Feelings

   3. Avoid Coded Feelings

   4. Focus on a Specific Set of Circumstances

D. Share Multiple Feelings

E. Consider When and Where to Express Your Feelings

F. Responsibility for Your Feelings

G. Communication Channel

V. MANAGING DIFFICULT EMOTIONS

  A. Facilitative and Debilitative Emotions

   1. Intensity

   2. Duration

  B. Sources of Debilitative Emotions

   1. Physiology

   2. Emotional Memory

   3. Self-Talk

  C. Irrational Thinking and Debilitative Emotions

   1. Fallacy of Perfection

   2. Fallacy of Approval

   3. Fallacy of Shoulds

   4. Fallacy of Overgeneralization

     a. Limited Amount of Evidence

     b. Exaggerated Shortcomings

5. Fallacy of Causation
   a. Belief: You Cause Emotions in Others
   b. Belief: Others Cause Your Emotions
6. Fallacy of Helplessness
7. Fallacy of Catastrophic Expectations

D. Minimizing Debilitative Emotions
1. Monitor Your Emotional Reactions
2. Note the Activating Event
3. Record Your Self-Talk
4. Reappraise Your Irrational Beliefs

KEY TERMS

debilitative emotions
emotional contagion
emotional intelligence (EQ)
emotion labor
facilitative emotions
fallacy of approval
fallacy of catastrophic expectations
fallacy of causation

fallacy of helplessness
fallacy of overgeneralization
fallacy of perfection
fallacy of shoulds
reappraisal
rumination
self-talk

ACTIVITIES

5.1 THE COMPONENTS OF EMOTION

LEARNING OBJECTIVES

- Describe how the four components listed in this chapter affect your emotions, and hence your communication in an important situation.

INSTRUCTIONS

PART I:

1. Read the situations below and put yourself in the position of the person experiencing the situation. Take a moment to imagine what your experience would be. What physiological changes, nonverbal reactions, cognitive interpretations, and verbal expressions might you use?

2. Describe how the emotions you would experience might manifest themselves in each of the four components listed.

3. If you are working in a group, after all have finished, compare the responses of group members.

PART II:

4. Next, record three examples of your own (include the incident, physiological changes, nonverbal reactions, cognitive interpretations, and verbal expressions). If you wish, share one example with the group.

EXAMPLE

Incident: While rushing to get to class on time, you notice that the flashing blue lights in your rearview mirror are directed at you, indicating you should pull over. _____

Physiological changes: My heart would start racing. _____

Nonverbal reactions: My throat would tighten, changing my vocal tone and volume. _____

Cognitive interpretations: I would immediately start blaming myself, "I'm so stupid. It's all my fault. If only I hadn't wasted time talking to my roommate before I left the house." _____

Verbal expression: I might tell the officer that I was feeling remorse and say, "I'm sorry." _____

1. Incident: Your romantic partner says, "I need to talk to you about something."

   Physiological changes: _____

   Nonverbal reactions: _____

   Cognitive interpretations: _____

   Verbal expression: _____

2. Incident: You run into an "ex" while out with a new partner.

   Physiological changes: _____

   Nonverbal reactions: _____

   Cognitive interpretations: _____

   Verbal expression: _____

3. Incident: As you're telling a story, you notice your listener stifle a yawn.

   Physiological changes: _____

   Nonverbal reactions: _____

   Cognitive interpretations: _____

   Verbal expression: _____

4. Incident: Your professor says, "I'd like to see you in my office after class."

   Physiological changes: _____

   Nonverbal reactions: _____

   Cognitive interpretations: _____

   Verbal expression: _____

YOUR EXAMPLES

1. Incident: _____

   Physiological changes: _____

   Nonverbal reactions: _____

Cognitive interpretations: _____

Verbal expression: _____

2. Incident: _____

Physiological changes: _____

Nonverbal reactions: _____

Cognitive interpretations: _____

Verbal expression: _____

3. Incident: _____

Physiological changes: _____

Nonverbal reactions: _____

Cognitive interpretations: _____

Verbal expression: _____

5.2 EXPRESS THE FEELINGS

LEARNING OBJECTIVES

- Apply the guidelines for effectively communicating emotions in an important situation.

INSTRUCTIONS

I. Analyze the statements below to determine which of the seven guidelines for expressing emotions are followed or ignored. For each statement, there may be more than one guideline.

G (Guideline)1. Recognize Feelings
        G2. Recognize the Difference between Feeling, Talking, and Acting
        G3. Expand Your Emotional Vocabulary
           A. Avoid emotional counterfeits
           B. Express verbally
              1. Use single words
              2. Describe what's happening to you
              3. Describe what you'd like to do
           C. Avoid minimizing feelings
           D. Avoid coded feelings
           E. Focus on a specific set of circumstances
        G4. Share Multiple Feelings
        G5. Consider When and Where to Express Your Feelings
        G6. Accept Responsibility for Your Feelings
        G7. Be Mindful of the Communication Channel

II. Rewrite statements that do not follow the above guidelines to clearly or accurately express the speaker's feelings.

III. Record examples of your own at the end of the exercise.

EXAMPLE

That's the most disgusting thing I've ever heard!

Analysis: *This isn't a satisfactory statement, since the speaker isn't clearly claiming that he or she is disgusted. The speaker doesn't seem to recognize feelings (G1) and doesn't verbally express a feeling (G3) and doesn't accept responsibility by using "I" language (G6).*

Restatement: *I'm upset and angry that those parents left their young children alone overnight.*

1. You're being awfully sensitive about that.

   Analysis _____

   Restatement _____

   _____

2. I can't figure out how to approach him.

   Analysis _____

Restatement _____
_____

3. I'm confused about what you want from me.

Analysis _____

Restatement _____
_____

4. I feel as if you're trying to hurt me.

Analysis _____

Restatement _____
_____

5. You make me so mad when you're late.

Analysis _____

Restatement _____
_____

6. I'm sort of upset with your behavior and a little bit annoyed that you don't apologize.

Analysis _____

Restatement _____
_____

7. I see you're all in there enjoying the game while I clean up the kitchen.

Analysis _____

Restatement _____
_____

8. I feel like the rug's been pulled out from under me.

Analysis _____

Restatement _____
_____

Now record three feeling statements of your own. Analyze and, if necessary, restate.

1. _____.

   Analysis _____

   Restatement _____

   _____

2. _____.

   Analysis _____

   Restatement _____

   _____

3. _____.

   Analysis _____

   Restatement _____

   _____

FEEDBACK TO 5.2 EXPRESS THE FEELINGS

1. The speaker here is labeling another's feelings, but saying nothing about his or her own feelings. Is the speaker concerned, irritated, or indifferent? We don't know. Possible restate: "I worried that I teased you too much about your hair."

2. The emotion here is implied but not stated. The speaker might be frustrated, perplexed, or tired. Possible restate: "I'm nervous about telling him why I was absent."

3. Here is a clear statement of the speaker's emotional state.

4. The statement is emotionally counterfeit. Just because we say "I feel" doesn't mean a feeling is being expressed. This is an interpretation statement because "I feel" can be replaced by "I think." The speaker is expressing that "I think you tried to hurt me" and could then go on to state "I'm anxious about trusting you after you lied to me last week."

5. The speaker doesn't accept responsibility but blames the other person. Possibly there are multiple feelings. Possible restate: "I feel frustrated, hurt, and angry when you're late."

6. The use of minimizing words like "sort of" or "a bit." Possible restate: "I'm upset with your behavior and annoyed that you don't apologize."

7. The statement is coded. Possible restate: "I feel used and taken for granted and would like some help cleaning up so we can all watch the game."

8. Here's a metaphorical statement of feeling, strongly suggesting surprise or shock. This sort of message probably does an adequate job of expressing the emotion here, but it might be too vague for some people to understand. Possible restate: "I feel insecure right now since I didn't get the job I was expecting."

5.3 STATING EMOTIONS EFFECTIVELY

LEARNING OBJECTIVES

- Describe how the four components listed in this chapter affect your emotions, and hence your communication in an important situation.
- Describe how the influences on emotional expression listed in this chapter have affected your communication in an important relationship.
- Apply the guidelines for effectively communicating emotions in an important situation.

INSTRUCTIONS

  I. Identify what's ineffective or unclear about each of the following feeling statements.

 II. Rewrite the feeling statements, making them more effective using the guidelines from your text.

G (Guideline)1. Recognize Feelings
         G2. Recognize the Difference between Feeling, Talking, and Acting
         G3. Expand Your Emotional Vocabulary
             A. Avoid emotional counterfeits
             B. Express verbally
                 1. Use single words
                 2. Describe what's happening to you
                 3. Describe what you'd like to do
             C. Avoid minimizing feelings
             D. Avoid coded feelings
             E. Focus on a specific set of circumstances
         G4. Share Multiple Feelings
         G5. Consider When and Where to Express Your Feelings
         G6. Accept Responsibility for Your Feelings
         G7. Be Mindful of the Communication Channel

FEELING STATEMENT	IDENTIFY INEFFECTIVE, UNCLEAR ELEMENTS/ REWRITE STATEMENT
Example *When you complimented me in front of everyone at the party, I was really embarrassed.*	*I didn't express the mixed emotions I was feeling. I could have expressed this better by saying, "When you complimented me last night at the party, I was glad you were proud of me, but I was embarrassed that so many people heard it."*
1. You should be more sensitive.	
2. I get kind of jealous when you have lunch with colleagues.	

3. I don't hear anyone offering to help with this project.	
4. Well, I guess you don't really care about this—or me.	
5. When you act like that, I don't want to be seen with you.	
6. You make me happy.	
7. Why should I help you now? You never show me any appreciation.	
8. I was a little ticked off when you didn't show up.	
9. You jerk—you forgot to put gas in the car!	
10. It's about time you paid up.	
11. I guess I'm a little attracted to him.	
12. With all that's happened, I feel like I'm in a time warp.	

5.4 EMOTIONAL LANGUAGE—SELF-TALK

LEARNING OBJECTIVES

- Identify and reappraise the fallacies that are creating debilitative emotions in an important situation.
- Explain how more-rational thinking can lead to more constructive communication.

INSTRUCTIONS

PART I:

1. In the statements below, expand the self-talk by using details from your experience and complete the chart as if you were the one having the thoughts.
2. Identify any fallacies contained in the self-talk: approval, overgeneralization, perfection, helplessness, shoulds, catastrophic expectations, causation.
3. Reappraise any irrational self-talk.
4. Complete four additional examples using statements and self-talk you often use.

PART II:

1. As a group, compare and discuss how you analyzed the self-talk, fallacies involved, and reappraisals in the given statements.
2. Continue in your groups, sharing your personal statements and self-talk. Offer feedback and support to each group member to reappraise fallacies to maintain emotional health.

STATEMENT	SELF-TALK	FALLACIES	REAPPRAISE ANY FALLACIES
Example: *She's so critical.*	*She never has anything good to say. She drives me crazy. I can't stand her. I'll never be able to make her happy.*	*Overgeneralization, Causation, Helplessness, Approval*	*I need to focus on the good things she does say, not the criticisms. She doesn't make me crazy; I let her get to me. If I don't like what she is saying at the moment, I can leave. It would be nice to please her, but I don't need her approval to be happy.*
1. No one appreciates me around here.			
2. He's so moody.			

STATEMENT	SELF-TALK	FALLACIES	REAPPRAISE ANY FALLACIES
3. I don't know why I even bother to study for her stupid tests.			
4. Why can't he be more sensitive to my feelings?			
5. She is so embarrassing because she has no manners.			
6. He's a jerk just like his brother.			
7. She's the perfect boss. I'll be completely satisfied in this job.			
8. I'll never get out of here with all her talking.			
9. I can't believe you told me to buy this worthless car.			
10. It's no use talking to him; he's so unreasonable.			

YOUR OWN EXAMPLES: STATEMENT	SELF-TALK	FALLACIES	REAPPRAISE ANY FALLACIES
1.			
2.			
3.			
4.			

5.5 REAPPRAISING IRRATIONAL THOUGHTS

LEARNING OBJECTIVES

- Identify and reappraise the fallacies that are creating debilitative emotions in an important situation.
- Explain how more rational thinking can lead to more constructive communication.

INSTRUCTIONS

PART I:

1. Use the chart provided to record activating events in which you experience communication-related debilitative emotions. The events needn't involve overwhelming, intense, or intimate feelings; consider mildly debilitative emotions as well.

2. For each incident (activating event), record the self-talk that leads to the emotion you experienced.

3. If the self-talk you've identified is based on any of the irrational fallacies described in *Looking Out / Looking In*, identify them.

4. In each case where irrational thinking exists, reappraise the irrational fallacies and provide an alternative, more rational interpretation of the event.

PART II:

1. After completing the examples, record your conclusions in the space provided (or put them on a separate page).

ACTIVATING EVENT	SELF-TALK	IRRATIONAL FALLACIES	EMOTION(S)	REAPPRAISE FALLACIES AND PROVIDE ALTERNATE RATIONAL THINKING
Example: *Getting ready for job interview*	*The employer will ask me questions I can't answer. I'll mess up for sure. I'll never get a good job—it's hopeless!*	*catastrophic failure overgeneralization helplessness*	*apprehension despair*	*I've prepared for the questions and the interview, so if I'm asked something I don't know, I'll say I'll get back to them on that. I have interpersonal skills. I'll find a good job with time and effort.*

ACTIVATING EVENT	SELF-TALK	IRRATIONAL FALLACIES	EMOTION(S)	REAPPRAISE FALLACIES AND PROVIDE ALTER- NATE RATIONAL THINKING
1.				
2.				
3.				
4.				
5.				

CONCLUSIONS

1. What are the situations in which you often experience debilitative emotions?

    _____

    _____

    _____

2. What irrational beliefs do you subscribe to most often? Label them and explain.

    _____

    _____

    _____

3. How can you think more rationally to reduce the number and intensity of debilitative emotions? (Give specific examples related to other aspects of your life, as well as referring to the activating events you have described in this exercise.)

    _____

    _____

    _____

5.6 MEDIATED MESSAGES—EXPRESSING EMOTION

LEARNING OBJECTIVES

- Understand the strengths and weaknesses of expressing emotion through mediated channels of communication.

INSTRUCTIONS

Discuss each of the questions below in your group. Prepare written answers for your instructor, or be prepared to contribute to a large group discussion, comparing your experiences with those of others in your class.

1. Describe, using specific examples, how you recognize and send messages with emotions through mediated channels such as post-it notes, email, and instant messaging.

   _____

   _____

   _____

   _____

2. In some mediated contexts emotional expression can be easier than in person (e.g., write a note upon the death of someone rather than face them). Cite examples from your life where you successfully used mediated contexts to express emotion.

   _____

   _____

   _____

   _____

3. Emotional expression may be more difficult in a mediated context (e.g., lack of touch or facial expression to communicate your empathy, confusion in symbols such as emoticons or written emotional language). Cite examples from your life where the mediated emotional expression you sent or received was misunderstood.

   _____

   _____

_____

_____

4. As a group and based on your discussions, create a set of guidelines for effectively expressing emotion through mediated channels.

_____

_____

_____

_____

5.7 ASSESSING NONVERBAL REACTIONS

LEARNING OBJECTIVES

- Develop emotional intelligence by effectively assessing nonverbal emotional reactions.

INSTRUCTIONS

1. Using a media that you can repeat (such as on-demand TV, DVD, or online streaming), watch a television program or a scene from a movie with the mute button on.

2. Observe four nonverbal reactions and predict the possible emotional meaning behind them without listening to the verbal communication. Describe below.

3. Repeat the television program or scene from a movie with the sound on. Assess how accurately you predicted the emotional meaning in the space below.

Observation 1

_____

_____

Possible Nonverbal Meaning (sound off)

_____

_____

Actual Meaning (sound on)

_____

_____

Observation 2

_____

_____

Class _____   Name _____

Possible Nonverbal Meaning (sound off)

_____

_____

Actual Meaning (sound on)

_____

_____

Observation 3

_____

_____

Possible Nonverbal Meaning (sound off)

_____

_____

Actual Meaning (sound on)

_____

_____

Observation 4

_____

_____

Class _____   Name _____

Possible Nonverbal Meaning (sound off)

_____

_____

Actual Meaning (sound on)

_____

_____

5.8 INTERPRETING EMOTIONAL REACTIONS IN OTHERS

LEARNING OBJECTIVES

- Develop emotional intelligence by effectively assessing others' nonverbal emotional reactions.
- Apply the skill of perception-checking to clarify emotionally-charged communication.

INSTRUCTIONS

PART I:

For the examples outlined below, which reflect confusing emotional expression you observe in another, create a complete perception check, adapting the three steps:

1. Reports the nonverbal behaviors you observe, without evaluating or judging what the person is feeling.

2. States two interpretations that are distinctly different, equally probable, and are based on the reported behavior.

3. Makes a sincere request for feedback clarifying how to interpret the reported behavior.

PART II:

In a group discussion, share and discuss your answers to the group reflection questions.

EXAMPLE

Yesterday your friend Eric laughed and shrugged when you asked him how he was doing. You noticed that his eyes looked sad.

Perception-checking statement: *Eric, when I asked you how you were feeling, you laughed and shrugged. I also noticed that you looked sad. I'm wondering if things are really okay or if there's something that's bothering you. I care about you and would like to hear how you're really feeing.*

4. As pre-arranged, you met a person you've dated a couple of times at a restaurant. You were a few minutes late, and when you arrived he was already seated. As you were walking towards him, you noticed that he didn't smile or stand to greet you. When you sat down, you immediately apologized for being late. He said, "Oh, don't worry," but his facial expression seemed to show displeasure.

_____

_____

_____

_____

5. Though he was always polite, your father never seemed to approve of the person you were dating. When you share the news that you've broken up, he sympathetically said, "That's too bad," but he spontaneously smiled. You're feeling sad, and it appears your father might be happy.

    _____

    _____

    _____

    _____

6. You unexpectedly met a friend at a party last night. He was holding hands with someone who he'd told you he'd broken up with. Previously, the two of you had had a conversation about why she wasn't a good match for him. When he sees you coming towards him, he lets go of her hand, drops his gaze, and looks away. You're concerned that he might be embarrassed, but you're not sure.

    _____

    _____

    _____

    _____

7. At work, a coworker has asked you to help with a project that's usually not part of your job. You said you'd be happy to help, but her vocal tone remained harsh and her expression was stern. You're pretty sure she's angry, and you're concerned this might affect your working relationship.

    _____

    _____

    _____

    _____

8. Your older sister called to ask how you're doing, but instead you find yourself concerned about how she is. Throughout the conversation she sighed a lot, and she didn't laugh at your jokes, like she usually does.

    _____

    _____

    _____

    _____

9. Last week you met with your instructor to get help with an assignment. You noticed balloons and cards in her office, and she seemed to be in a very good mood, smiling and laughing more than usual. You don't want to appear to be nosy, but you do want to offer her congratulations if something important has happened.

    _____

    _____

    _____

STUDY GUIDE

CHECK YOUR UNDERSTANDING

TRUE/FALSE

Mark the statements below as true or false. Correct statements that are false on the lines below to create a true statement.

_____ 1. Marriage researcher John Gottman found that when couples are in intense conflict that bodily changes occur (increased heart rate, a rise in blood pressure, a dilation of pupils) and effective problem solving is impeded.

_____

_____ 2. Emotion labor refers to situations where managing and suppressing emotions is appropriate and necessary.

_____

_____ 3. Because negative emotions overwhelm all others, it's impossible to learn how to be more optimistic.

_____

_____ 4. Children who grow up in families that dismiss emotions are at higher risk for behavioral problems.

_____

_____ 5. All emotions are personal and can't be transferred from one person to another.

_____

_____ 6. Despite the commonness of mixed emotions, we often communicate only one feeling—usually the most negative one.

_____

_____ 7. Because of emotional memory, seemingly harmless events can trigger debilitative emotions.

_____

_____ 8. Reappraisal involves rethinking the meaning of emotionally charged events in ways that alter their emotional impact.

_____

_____ 9. In mediated communication, "flaming" refers to a creative way of expressing positive feelings.

_____

_____ 10. The fallacy of causation exists in two forms: you believe others cause your emotions or you believe you cause others' emotions.

_____

COMPLETION

Fill in the blanks below with the correct terms chosen from the list below.

catastrophic expectations	helplessness	causation
overgeneralization	shoulds	approval
perfection	activating event	reappraisal
rumination		

1. _____ is an irrational fallacy that operates on the assumption that if something bad can possibly happen, it will.

2. _____ is an irrational fallacy that suggests that satisfaction in life is determined by forces beyond your control.

3. _____ is an irrational fallacy based on the belief that emotions are the result of other people and things rather than one's own self-talk.

4. _____ is an irrational fallacy that makes a broad claim based on a limited amount of evidence.

5. _____ is an irrational fallacy based on the inability to distinguish between what is and what ought to be.

6. _____ is an irrational fallacy in which people go to incredible lengths to seek acceptance from virtually everyone.

7. _____ is an irrational fallacy in which people believe that worthwhile communicators should be able to handle every situation with complete confidence and skill.

8. _____ is the single large incident or series of small incidents that lead to thoughts or beliefs about the incident.

9. _____ is the process of rethinking the meaning of emotionally charged events in a way that alters their emotional impact.

10. _____ is dwelling persistently on negative thoughts that, in turn, intensify negative feelings.

MULTIPLE CHOICE

Choose the letter of the irrational fallacy contained in the self-talk found below.

a. perfection
b. approval
c. shoulds
d. overgeneralization

e. causation
f. helplessness
g. catastrophic expectations

_____ 1. "If only I didn't put my foot in my mouth when I ask someone out."

_____ 2. "I just can't initiate conversations—never have been able to, never will be able to."

_____ 3. "He shouldn't be off with his friends on Friday night when he has other responsibilities to take care of."

_____ 4. "If she doesn't like this shirt, I'll be so upset."

_____ 5. "There was a major fire the last time we left; there will probably be an earthquake this time."

_____ 6. "He's never romantic."

_____ 7. "All women are insecure about their looks."

_____ 8. "Other people ought to cut me some slack; they shouldn't be so critical."

_____ 9. "You're going to die or be seriously injured if you go to Mexico at spring break."

_____ 10. "I lost points on the essay part of the exam and only got an A–. Why do I bother?"

_____ 11. "Shaw makes me so mad when he shows off his new car."

_____ 12. "She'll be devastated if I break up with her."

_____ 13. "He's hopeless. It's not even worth trying to reach him."

_____ 14. "I hope they don't notice how much weight I've gained. They won't like it."

Choose the best answer for each of the statements below.

15. Which of the following statements about emotions and culture is true?
    a. The same events will generate the same emotions in all cultures.
    b. Some emotions seem to be experienced by people around the world.
    c. People from different cultures express happiness and sadness with different facial expressions.
    d. Fear of strangers is as strong in Japan as it is in the United States.

16. Which of the following statements about rumination is *not* true?
    a. Rumination increases feelings of sadness.
    b. Rumination increases feelings of anxiety.
    c. Rumination increases feelings of depression.
    d. Rumination lessens aggression towards others.

17. Which of these represents coded emotions?
    a. I feel grateful when you bring soup to me when I'm sick.
    b. I'm upset because you borrowed my white-out.
    c. I feel like a doormat—just used by everyone.
    d. I don't hear any thank-yous. It sure would be nice to hear some appreciation.

18. Which of the following follows the text's guidelines for expressing feelings?
    a. "I feel like watching a movie."
    b. "I feel like you're lonely."
    c. "I'm irritated by the ticking clock."
    d. "I'm totally involved."

19. Which of the following *best* improves the expression of emotion in the statement "I feel like giving up"?
    a. "I'm frustrated after asking him to pay his telephone bill three times."
    b. "I'm going to kill him."
    c. "I am going to tell the landlord about this frustrating situation."
    d. "I feel he's been unreasonable."

20. In which job would emotion labor be needed the most?
    a. firefighter
    b. correctional officer
    c. customer service representative
    d. emotion labor is equally important in all of these jobs

21. Which of the following statements about culture is true?
    a. All cultures are equal in every way.
    b. Emotions are lacking in most collectivistic cultures.
    c. People from different cultures express happiness and sadness with different facial expressions.
    d. The easiest way to understand a culture is to live within it for a period of time.

22. Which of the following statements about emotional intelligence is *not* true?
    a. Emotional intelligence is helpful in the workplace.
    b. Emotional intelligence is a sign of a competent communicator.
    c. Emotional intelligence is as important as cognitive intelligence.
    d. Emotional intelligence refers to how you express emotion and not how you understand the emotions of others.

CHAPTER FIVE STUDY GUIDE ANSWERS

TRUE/FALSE

1. T	3. F	5. F	7. T	9. F
2. T	4. T	6. T	8. T	10. T

COMPLETION

1. catastrophic expectations
2. helplessness
3. causation
4. overgeneralization
5. shoulds
6. approval
7. perfection
8. activating event
9. reappraisal
10. rumination

MULTIPLE CHOICE

1. a	6. d	11. e	16. d	21. d
2. f	7. d	12. e	17. d	22. d
3. c	8. c	13. f	18. c	
4. b	9. g	14. b	19. a	
5. g	10. a	15. b	20. d	

MindTap® START …
Explore this chapter's topics online.

6

LANGUAGE: BARRIER AND BRIDGE

HERE ARE THE TOPICS DISCUSSED IN THIS CHAPTER:

> **Language Is Symbolic**

> **Understandings and Misunderstandings**
  Understanding Words: Semantic Rules
  Understanding Structure: Syntactic Rules
  Understanding Context: Pragmatic Rules

> **The Impact of Language**
  Naming and Identity
  Affiliation
  Power and Politeness
  Disruptive Language
  The Language of Responsibility

> **Gender and Language**
  Content
  Reasons for Communicating
  Conversational Style
  Nongender Variables

> **Culture and Language**
  Verbal Communication Styles
  Language and Worldview

> **Summary**

> **Key Terms**

AFTER STUDYING THE TOPICS IN THIS CHAPTER, YOU SHOULD BE ABLE TO:

1. Analyze a real or potential misunderstanding in terms of semantic or pragmatic rules.

2. Describe how the principles presented in the section of this chapter titled "The Impact of Language" operate in your life.

3. Construct a message at the optimal level of specificity or vagueness for a given situation.

4. Recast "you" statements into "I" or "we" statements to reflect your responsibility for the content of messages.

5. Rephrase disruptive statements in less inflammatory terms.

6. In a given situation, analyze how gender or cultural differences (or both) may affect the quality of interaction.

MindTap® READ AND UNDERSTAND …

the complete chapter text online in a rich interactive platform.

*T*he problems that began with Babel continue today. Sometimes it seems as if none of us speaks the same language. Yet despite its frustrations and challenges, language is clearly a marvelous tool. It is the gift that allows us to communicate in a way that no other animals appear to match. Without language, we would be more ignorant, ineffectual, and isolated.

In this chapter, we explore the nature of language, looking at how to take advantage of its strengths and minimize its weaknesses. After a quick explanation of the symbolic nature of language, we examine the sources of language-based misunderstandings. We then move beyond the challenges of simply understanding one another and explore how the language we use affects the climate of interpersonal relationships. Finally, we broaden our focus even more to look at how linguistic practices shape the attitudes of entire cultures.

Now the whole world had one language and a common speech.

As men moved eastward, they found a plain in Shinar and settled there.

They said to each other, "Come, let's make bricks and bake them thoroughly." They used brick instead of stone, and tar for mortar.

Then they said, "Come, let us build ourselves a city, with a tower that reaches to the heavens, so that we may make a name for ourselves and not be scattered over the face of the whole earth."

But the Lord came down to see the city and the tower that the men were building.

The Lord said, "If as one people speaking the same language they have begun to do this, then nothing they plan to do will be impossible for them.

Come, let us go down and confuse their language so they will not understand each other."

So the Lord scattered them from there over all the earth, and they stopped building the city.

That is why it was called Babel—because there the Lord confused the language of the whole world.

Genesis 11:1–9

LANGUAGE IS SYMBOLIC

In the natural world, signs have a direct connection with the things they represent. For example, smoke is a sign that something's burning, and a high fever is a sign of illness. There's nothing arbitrary about the relationship between natural signs and the things they represent. Nobody made them up, and they exist independently of human opinions.

In human language, the connection between signs and the things they represent isn't so direct. Instead, language is *symbolic*: There's only an arbitrary connection between words and the ideas or things to which they refer. For example, there is nothing particularly fivelike in the number five. The word represents the number of fingers on your hand only because English speakers agree that it does. To a speaker of French, the symbol *cinq* would convey the same meaning; to a computer programmer, the same value would be represented by the coded symbol 101.

Even sign language, as "spoken" by most hearing-impaired people, is symbolic in nature and not the pantomime it might seem. Because this form of communication is symbolic and not literal, hundreds of sign languages around the world have evolved independently whenever significant numbers of hearing-impaired people are in contact.[1] These distinct languages include American Sign Language, British Sign Language, French Sign Language, Danish Sign Language, Chinese Sign Language—even Australian Aboriginal and Mayan Sign Languages.

The symbolic nature of language is a blessing. It enables us to communicate in ways that wouldn't otherwise be possible about ideas, reasons, the past, the future, and things not present. Without symbolic language, none of this would be possible. However, the indirect relationship between symbols and the things they represent leads to communication problems only hinted about in the tower of Babel story.

If everyone used symbols in the same way, then language would be much easier to manage and understand—but your own experience shows that this isn't always the case. Messages that seem perfectly clear to you prove confusing or misleading to others. You tell the hairstylist to "take a little off the top" and are stunned to discover that her definition of "a little" was equivalent to your definition of "a lot." You have a heated argument about the merits of *feminism* without realizing that you and the other person have been using the word to represent entirely

"What part of oil lamp next to double squiggle over ox don't you understand?"

different ideas. Misunderstandings like these remind us that meanings are in people, not in words.

In Washington, DC, an uproar developed when the city's ombudsman, David Howard, used the word *niggardly* to describe an approach to budgeting.[2] Howard, who is white, was accused by some African American critics of uttering an unforgivable racial slur. His defenders pointed out that the word, which means "miserly," is derived from Scandinavian languages and has no link to the racial slur it resembles. Even though the criticisms eventually died away, they illustrate that the meanings that people associate with words—correctly or not—have far more significance than do their dictionary definitions.

UNDERSTANDINGS AND MISUNDERSTANDINGS

Language is rather like plumbing: We pay the most attention to it when something goes wrong. But the problems that arise from misunderstandings aren't always immediately apparent, and they occur more often than we imagine. Most people vastly overestimate how well their explanations get through and how well they understand others.[3] Because misunderstandings are the greatest cause of concern for most people who study language, we'll begin our study by looking at sets of rules we use to understand—and sometimes misunderstand—one another's speech.

Understanding Words: Semantic Rules

Semantic rules reflect the ways in which users of a language assign meaning to a particular linguistic symbol, usually a word. Semantic rules make it possible for us to agree that "bikes" are for riding and "books" are for reading, and they help us know who we will and won't encounter when we use rooms marked "men" or "women." Without semantic rules, communication would be impossible because each of us would use symbols in unique ways, without sharing meaning. Semantic misunderstandings arise when people assign different meanings to the same words. We will look at some of the most common ones.

Equivocation   Equivocal statements can be interpreted in more than one way. As you read in Chapter 3, equivocation can be a strategic alternative to blunt disclosure. It's easier to say "That tattoo is really unusual" than to say "That tattoo is really ugly." Sometimes we use **equivocal language** without realizing that ambiguous statements can be have more than one meaning. Consider a few amusing examples from news headlines:

Family Catches Fire Just in Time

Man Stuck on Toilet; Stool Suspected

20-Year Friendship Ends at the Altar

Trees Can Break Wind

Some equivocal misunderstandings can be embarrassing. As one woman recalls: "In the fourth grade the teacher asked the class what a period was. I raised my hand and shared everything I had learned about girls getting their period. But he was talking about the dot at the end of a sentence. Oops!"[4]

Other equivocal statements can be even more troubling. A nurse gave one of her patients a scare when she told him that he "wouldn't be needing" his robe, books, and shaving materials anymore. The patient became quiet and moody. When the nurse inquired about the odd behavior, she discovered that the poor man had interpreted her statement to mean he was going to die soon. In fact, the nurse meant he would be going home.

"Be honest with me, Roger. By 'mid-course correction' you mean divorce, don't you."

It's difficult to catch every equivocal statement and clarify it while speaking. For this reason, the responsibility for interpreting statements accurately rests in large part with the receiver. Feedback of one sort or another—for example, the kind of perception checking introduced in Chapter 4 and the paraphrasing described in Chapter 8—can help clear up misunderstandings.

Relative Language   **Relative words** gain their meaning by comparison. For example, do you attend a large or small school? This depends on what you compare it to. Alongside a huge state university, your school may not seem big, but compared with a small college, it may seem quite large. Relative words such as *fast* and *slow*, *smart* and *stupid*, *short* and *long* are clearly defined only through comparison.

Some relative terms are so common that we mistakenly assume they have a clear meaning. For instance, if a friend told you it's "likely" she'll show up at your party tonight, what are the chances she's going to come? In one study, students were asked to assign percentages to such terms as *doubtful*, *toss-up*, *likely*, *probable*, *good chance*, and *unlikely*.[5] There was a tremendous variation in the meaning of most of these terms. For example, the responses for *probable* ranged from 0 to 99 percent. *Good chance* fell between 35 percent and 90 percent, whereas *unlikely* fell between 0 and 40 percent.

One way to make words more measurable is to turn them into numbers. Healthcare practitioners have learned that patients often use vague descriptions when describing their pain: "It hurts a little"; "I'm pretty sore." The use of a numeric pain scale can give a more precise response—and lead to a better diagnosis.[6] When patients are asked to rank their pain from 1 to 10, with 10 being the most severe pain they've ever experienced, the number 7 is much more concrete and specific than "It aches a bit." The same technique can be used when asking people to rate anything from the movies they've seen to their job satisfaction.

Static Evaluation   "Mark is a nervous guy." "Mia is short-tempered." "You can always count on Ming." Statements that contain or imply the word *is* lead to the mistaken assumption that people are consistent and unchanging—an incorrect belief known as **static evaluation**. Instead of labeling Mark as permanently and totally nervous, it would be more accurate to outline the particular situations in which he behaves nervously. The same goes for Mia, Ming, and the rest of us: We are more changeable than the way static, everyday language describes us.

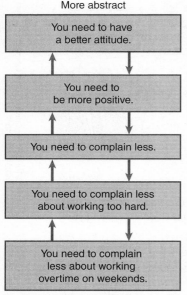

More abstract

You need to have
a better attitude.

You need to
be more positive.

You need to complain less.

You need to complain less
about working too hard.

You need to complain
less about working
overtime on weekends.

More specific

∧ FIGURE 6.1
Abstraction Ladder

Abstraction   When it comes to describing problems, goals, appreciation, and requests, some language is more specific than others. **Abstract language** is vague in nature, whereas **behavioral language**—as its name implies—refers to specific things that people say or do. The **abstraction ladder** in Figure 6.1 illustrates how the same phenomenon can be described at various levels of specificity and abstraction. Notice how the ladder's bottom-rung description is more concrete and behavioral, and thus it is probably clearer than the top rung's abstract injunction to develop a "better attitude."

We use higher-level abstractions all the time. For instance, rather than saying "Thanks for washing the dishes," "Thanks for vacuuming the rug," or "Thanks for making the bed," it's easier to say "Thanks for cleaning up." In such everyday situations, abstractions are a useful kind of verbal shorthand.

Although verbal shorthand like this can be useful, highly abstract language can lead to blanket judgments and stereotyping: "Marriage counselors are worthless," "Skateboarders are delinquents," or "Men are no good." Overly abstract expressions like these can cause people to *think* in generalities, ignoring uniqueness. As you learned in Chapter 4, stereotyping can injure interpersonal relationships because it categorizes and evaluates people in ways that may not be accurate.

You can appreciate the value of behavioral descriptions by looking at the examples in Table 6.1. Notice how much more clearly the behavioral descriptions explain the speaker's thoughts than do the vaguer terms.

TABLE 6.1 Abstract versus Behavioral Descriptions

	Abstract Description	Behavioral Description			Remarks
		Who Is Involved	In What Circumstances	Specific Behaviors	
Problem	I talk too much.	People I find intimidating	When I want them to like me	I talk (mostly about myself) instead of giving them a chance to speak or asking about their lives.	Behavioral description more clearly identifies behaviors to change.
Goal	I want to be more constructive.	My roommate	When we talk about household duties	Instead of finding fault with her ideas, suggest alternatives that might work.	Behavioral description clearly outlines how to act; abstract description doesn't.
Appreciation	"You've really been helpful lately."	Deliver to fellow worker	"When I've had to take time off work because of personal problems …"	"… you took my shifts without complaining."	Give both abstract and behavioral descriptions for best results.
Request	"Clean up your act!"	Deliver to target person	"When we're around my family …"	"… please don't tell jokes that involve sex."	Behavioral description specifies behavior.

SKILL *Builder*

Down-to-Earth Language

MindTap PRACTICE ... your skill at nonabstract language by answering the following questions either here or online.

You can appreciate the value of nonabstract language by translating the following into behavioral terms:

1. An abstract goal for improving your interpersonal communication (e.g., "be more assertive" or "stop being so sarcastic").

2. A complaint you have about another person (e.g., that he or she is "selfish" or "insensitive").

3. A request for someone to change (e.g., "I wish you'd be more punctual" or "Try to be more positive").

4. An appreciation you could share with another person (e.g., "Thanks for being so helpful" or "I appreciate your patience").

In each case, describe the person or persons involved, the circumstances in which the behavior occurs, and the precise behaviors involved. What differences can you expect when you use behavioral descriptions like the ones you have created here?

Understanding Structure: Syntactic Rules

Syntactic rules govern the grammar of a language. You can appreciate how syntax contributes to the meaning of a statement by considering two versions of a letter:

Version 1

Dear John:

I want a man who knows what love is all about. You are generous, kind, thoughtful. People who are not like you admit to being useless and inferior. You have ruined me for other men. I yearn for you. I have no feelings whatsoever when we're apart. I can be forever happy—will you let me be yours?

Mary

Version 2

Dear John:

I want a man who knows what love is. All about you are generous, kind, thoughtful people, who are not like you. Admit to being useless and inferior. You have ruined me. For other men, I yearn. For you, I have no feelings whatsoever. When we're apart, I can be forever happy. Will you let me be?

Yours,
Mary

Semantic rules don't explain why these letters send virtually opposite messages. There's no ambiguity about the meaning of the words they contain: *love, kind, thoughtful,* and so on. The opposite meanings of the letters came from their different syntax.

Although most of us aren't able to describe the syntactic rules that govern our language, it's easy to recognize their existence when they are violated. A humorous example is the way the character Yoda speaks in the *Star Wars* movies. Phrases such as "The dark side are they" or "Your father he is" often elicit a chuckle because they bend syntactical norms. Sometimes, however, apparently ungrammatical speech is simply following a different set of syntactic rules, reflecting regional or co-cultural dialects. Linguists believe it is crucial to view such dialects as *different* rather than *deficient* forms of English.[7]

"I never said 'I love you.' I said 'I love ya.' Big difference!"

Understanding Context: Pragmatic Rules

Semantic and syntactic problems don't account for all misunderstandings.[8] To appreciate a different type of communication challenge, imagine how a young female employee might struggle to make sense of her older male boss's statement, "You look very pretty today." She almost certainly would understand the meaning of the words, and the syntax is perfectly clear. Still, the boss's message could be interpreted in several ways. Was the remark a simple compliment? A come-on? Did it contain the suggestion that she didn't look nice on other days?

If the boss and employee share the same interpretation of the message, their communication would be smooth. But if they bring different perspectives to interpreting it, a problem exists. Table 6.2 shows several ways in which different perspectives of the boss and employee would lead to their attaching different meanings to the same words.

TABLE 6.2 Pragmatic Rules Govern the Use and Meaning of a Statement

	Boss	Employee
Statement	"You look very nice today."	
Self-Concept "Who am I?" "Who is s/he?"	Friendly guy	Woman determined to succeed on own merits
Episode "What's going on in this exchange?"	Casual conversation	Possible come-on by boss?
Relationship "Who are we to one another?"	Boss who treats employees like family members	Subordinate employee, dependent on boss's approval for advancement
Culture "What does my background say about the meaning here?"	Euro-American, raised in United States	Latina, raised in South America

Adapted from Pearce, W. B. & Cronen, V. (1980). Communication, action, and meaning. New York: Praeger; and Griffin, E. (2012). A first look at communication theory (8th ed.). New York: McGraw-Hill.

In situations like this one, we rely on **pragmatic rules** to decide how to interpret messages in a given context. Pragmatic rules govern the way speech operates in everyday interaction. You can't look up pragmatic rules in any dictionary. They are almost always unstated, but they are just as important as semantic and syntactic rules in helping us make sense of one another's messages.

The best way to appreciate how pragmatic rules operate is to think of communication as a kind of cooperative game. Like all games, success depends on all of the players understanding and following the same set of rules. This is why communication scholars use the term *coordination* to describe the way conversation operates when everyone involved uses the same set of pragmatic rules.[9]

Some pragmatic rules are shared by most people in a culture. In North America, for instance, competent communicators understand that the question "How's it going?" usually isn't really a request for information. Anyone familiar with the rules of conversation knows that the proper answer is something like "Pretty good. How's it going with you?" Likewise, most people understand the pragmatic rule that says that "Would you like a drink?" means "Would you like an alcoholic beverage?" whereas "Would you like something to drink?" is a more open-ended question.

Besides following cultural rules, people in individual relationships create their own sets of pragmatic rules. Consider the use of humor: The teasing and jokes you exchange with gusto with one friend might be considered tasteless or offensive in another relationship.[10] For instance, imagine an email message typed in CAPITAL LETTERS and filled with CURSE WORDS, INSULTS, NAME-CALLING, and EXCLAMATION MARKS!!! How would you interpret such a message? An outside observer may consider this an example of "flaming" and be appalled, when in fact the message might be a fun-loving case of "verbal jousting" between buddies.[11] If you have a good friend whom you call by a less-than-tasteful nickname as a term of endearment, then you understand the concept. Keep in mind, however, that those who aren't privy to your relationship's pragmatic rules are likely to misunderstand you, so you'll want to be wise about when and where to use these personal codes.

Allstar Picture library

⋀ In *The Imitation Game*, Alan Turing (Benedict Cumberbatch) is a genius when it comes to breaking Nazi battle codes, but he has trouble understanding the pragmatic rules of everyday speech. He misses the linguistic nuances that are an essential part of jokes, sarcasm, and flirting. Are there times when you misunderstand others' messages because you take them too literally? Have you ever been misunderstood for similar reasons?

THE IMPACT OF LANGUAGE

So far we have focused on language only as a medium for helping communicators understand one another. But along with this important function, language can shape our perceptions of the world around us and reflect the attitudes we hold toward one another.

PAUSE *and* REFLECT

Your Linguistic Rules

MindTap® **REFLECT . . .** on linguistic rules by answering the following questions, either here or online.

To what extent do linguistic rules affect your understanding of and relationships with others? Explore this question by following these steps:

1. Recall a time when you encountered someone whose speech violated the syntactic rules that you are used to. What was your impression of this person? To what degree was this impression influenced by her or his failure to follow familiar linguistic rules? Consider whether this impression was or was not valid.

2. Recall at least one misunderstanding that arose when you and another person followed different semantic rules. Use hindsight to consider whether this misunderstanding (and others like it) could be avoided. If semantic misunderstandings can be minimized, explain what approaches might be useful.

3. Identify at least two pragmatic rules that govern the use of language in one of your relationships. Share these rules with other students. Do they use language in the same way as you and your relational partner?

Naming and Identity

"What's in a name?" Juliet asked rhetorically. If Romeo had been a social scientist, he would have answered "A great deal."

Research has demonstrated that names are more than just a simple means of identification. Names shape the way others think of us, the way we view ourselves, and the way we act. For more than a century, researchers have studied the impact of rare and unique names on the people who bear them.[12] Early studies claimed that people with unusual names suffered everything from psychological and emotional disturbance to failure in college. More recent studies have shown that people often have negative appraisals not only of unusual names but also of unusual name spellings.[13] Of course, what makes a name (and its spelling) unusual changes with time. In 1900, the twenty most popular names for baby girls in the United States included Bertha, Mildred, and Ethel. By 2013, the top twenty names included Madison, Ava, and Isabella—names that would have been highly unusual a century earlier.[14]

Names are one way to shape and reinforce a child's personal identity. Naming a baby after a family member (e.g., "Junior" or "Trey") can create a connection between the youngster and his or her namesake. Name choice can also be a powerful way to make a statement about cultural identity. For example, in recent decades a large percentage of names given to African American babies have been distinctive to that co-culture.[15] In California, more than 40 percent of black girls born in a recent period had names that not a single white baby born in the entire state was given. Researchers suggest that

FINDING THE WORDS
TO TALK ABOUT DISABILITY

DenysKuvaiev/Bigstock

William came home from school a few weeks back and he said, "Mom." He said it as a sentence, the way he does when he has something important to tell me. And then again, "Mom. My friend Ashley is not good at listening. And she screams."

William is three. He attends a local public preschool, and he's in an "integrated" classroom, which is to say, a classroom where typically developing children learn and play alongside children with special needs. Three years ago, William's older sister Penny was in the same classroom. Penny has Trisomy 21, also known as Down syndrome, and that third chromosome impacts nearly every aspect of her development. She wears braces to support her flat feet and weak ankles. When she was in preschool, she relied on sign language in addition to spoken words to communicate.

But just because I have a daughter with a disability doesn't mean that I know how to talk about disabilities with my children. When Penny was first born, I found myself in a maze of words that had never mattered to me before—abnormality, disability, high-risk pregnancy, genetic counseling, special needs. It became easier with time. I started to use "people-first" language, calling her a baby with Down syndrome instead of a Down's baby. I substituted "normal" with "typical" when it came to describing other children. In my subsequent pregnancies, I talked about the "chance" of having another child with Down syndrome instead of the "risk."

And over time, the words became more than politically correct attempts

to support my new identity as the mother of a child with a disability. Over time, the words became reality. I really did see Penny as a child first, with Down syndrome as a descriptive but secondary marker. I really did come to believe that individuals with disabilities were not people to be pitied or people in need of help but rather human beings who were just like me. Our particularities were different, but I came to understand that we all have limitations and places of vulnerability and need, and we all have possibilities for joy and relationships and self-giving.

I was delighted when William was accepted, via lottery, into the integrated preschool class. But I wondered if I would be able to put words to his experience. I wondered if I would be able to talk about disability in a way that was honest and positive, in a way that built bridges instead of creating categories or judgments. So when William told me that Ashley doesn't listen well and screams, I took a deep breath.

I said, "Maybe she hasn't learned how to listen yet." He nodded. And then I asked, "What is Ashley good at?"

He tilted his head. "Playin' games and runnin' around."

"What are you good at?"

"Listening."

"What's hard for you?"

"Coloring."

That was the end of our conversation. William has talked about Ashley since then, but only because he tells me things about his friend—that she takes the bus, that they pretend to do cooking together, that he wanted to have a sticker chart with prizes just like her. As far as William is concerned, Ashley is just another kid in his class. There are some things that are hard for her. There are some things she's good at. Just like him.

Eventually William will realize that many aspects of our culture—from language to legislation—erect walls between kids like him and kids like Ashley. But I hope that growing up with a sister with Down syndrome and going to school alongside boys and girls who have different challenges than he does will open his eyes, and his heart, to understanding our common humanity. I hope he will grow up with an ability to see beyond labels, to trust that he has something to offer to everyone he meets, but that he also has something to receive from them.

Amy Julia Becker

MindTap ENHANCE ... your understanding by answering the following questions, either here or online.

1. What communication principles did the author use when talking with her son William about his friend Ashley? How did they shape William's attitudes and behaviors?

2. What labels have you seen used for people that affect, positively or negatively, the way that others view them and treat them?

3. Are there ways you can adapt your language to reclassify others more constructively?

The high school movie *Mean Girls* captures the role of linguistic convergence in defining and maintaining in-groups. Cady (Linsday Lohan) learns quickly that if she's going to fit in with the popular "Plastics" at her school, she'll have to adopt their language, including terms such as "fetch," "word vomit," and "fugly." Does your language reflect the groups to which you belong?

Paramount/Allstar

distinctive names like these are a symbol of solidarity with the African American community. Conversely, choosing a less distinctive name can be a way of integrating the baby into the majority culture.

Affiliation

Besides shaping an individual's identity, speech can build and demonstrate solidarity with others. Research has demonstrated that communicators are attracted to others whose style of speaking is similar to theirs.[16] Likewise, communicators who want to show affiliation with one another adapt their speech in a variety of ways, including their choice of vocabulary, rate of talking, number and placement of pauses, and level of politeness—a process known as *speech accommodation*.[17] Adolescents who all adopt the same vocabulary of slang words and speech mannerisms illustrate the principle of linguistic solidarity. The same process works among members of other groups ranging from street gangs to military personnel. Communication researchers call the process of adapting one's speech style to match that of others **convergence**. One study even showed that adopting the swearing patterns of bosses and coworkers can help people feel connected on the job (see the On the Job sidebar in this chapter for more about swearing in the workplace).[18]

In one study, the likelihood of mutual romantic interest increased when conversational partners' use of pronouns, articles, conjunctions, prepositions, and negations matched.[19] The same study revealed that when couples used similar language styles while instant messaging, the chances of their relationship continuing increased by almost 50 percent. The researchers speculate that unconscious language-style matching relates to how much each is paying attention to what the other says. Another study found that members of online communities often develop a shared language and conversational style, and their affiliation with each other can be seen in increased uses of the pronoun *we*.[20]

When two or more people feel equally positive about one another, their linguistic convergence will be mutual. But when communicators want or need approval, they often adapt their speech to accommodate the other person's style, trying to say the "right thing" or speak in a way that will help them fit in. We see this process when immigrants who want to gain the rewards of material success in a new culture strive to master the host language. Likewise, employees who seek advancement tend to speak more like their bosses.

The principle of speech accommodation works in reverse, too. Communicators who want to set themselves apart from others adopt the strategy of **divergence**, speaking in a way that emphasizes their differences from others. For example, members of an ethnic group, even though fluent in the dominant language, might use their own dialect as a way of showing solidarity with one another—a sort of "us against them" strategy. The same behavior can occur across ethnic lines, such as teens who adopt the slang of particular subcultures to show divergence with adults and convergence with their peers.[21]

Of course, communicators need to be careful about when—and when not—to converge their language with others. Most of us can remember the embarrassment of hearing a parent using youthful slang and thinking, "You're too old to be saying that—quit trying to sound like us." On a more serious level, using ethnic or racial epithets when you're not a member of that in-group can be inappropriate and even offensive. One of the pragmatic goals of divergence is the creation of norms about who has the "right" to use certain words and who does not.

Power and Politeness

Communication researchers have identified several language patterns that add to or detract from a speaker's power to influence others. Notice the difference between these two statements from an employee to a manager:

> "Excuse me, sir. I hate to say this, but I … uh … I guess I won't be able to finish the project on time. I had a personal emergency, and … well … it was just impossible to finish it by today. I'll have it on your desk on Monday, OK?"

> "I won't be able to finish the project on time. I had a personal emergency, and it was impossible to finish it by today. I'll have it on your desk Monday."

Whether or not the boss finds the excuse acceptable, it's clear that the tone of the second one is more confident, whereas the tone of the first is apologetic and uncertain. Table 6.3 identifies several **powerless speech mannerisms** illustrated in the statements you just read. Some studies have shown that

Table 6.3 Examples of Powerless Language

Hedges	"I'm *kinda* disappointed …" "I *think* we should …" "I *guess* I'd like to …"
Hesitations	"*Uh*, can I have a minute of your time?" "*Well*, we could try this idea …" "I wish you would—*er*—try to be on time."
Intensifiers	"I'm *really* glad to see you." "I'm not *very* hungry."
Polite forms	"Excuse me, *sir* …"
Tag questions	"It's about time we got started, *isn't it*?" "*Don't you think* we should give it another try?"
Disclaimers	"*I probably shouldn't say this, but* …" "*I'm not really sure, but* …"
Rising inflections	See the reading "The Way You Talk Can Hurt You?" in Chapter 7.

speakers whose talk is free of these mannerisms are rated as more competent, dynamic, and attractive than speakers who sound powerless.[22] Powerful speech can help candidates in job interviews. Employers rate applicants who use a powerful style as more competent and employable than candidates who speak less forcefully.[23] One study revealed that even a single type of powerless speech mannerism can make a person appear less authoritative or socially attractive.[24]

A *disclaimer* is a type of powerless speech that attempts to distance a speaker from remarks that might be unwelcome. For example, you might preface a critical message by saying "I don't mean to sound judgmental, but …" and then go on to express your disapproval. One study showed that disclaimers actually *increase* negative judgments.[25] For instance, the phrase "I don't mean to sound arrogant …" followed by a high-handed comment led subjects to regard the speaker as *more* arrogant. Disclaimers involving other negative qualities such as laziness and selfishness produced similar results. It seems that disclaimers backfire because they sensitize listeners to look for—and find—precisely the qualities that the speaker is trying to disavow.

Some scholars question the label "powerless" because tentative and indirect speech styles can sometimes achieve goals better than more assertive approaches.[26] For example, less forceful approaches can be attempts at **politeness**: communicating in ways that save face for both senders and receivers. Politeness is valued is some cultures more than others.[27] In Japan, for instance, saving face for others is an important goal, so communicators there tend to speak in ambiguous terms and use hedge words and qualifiers. Traditional Mexican culture, with its strong emphasis on cooperation, also uses hedging to smooth over interpersonal relationships. By not taking a firm stand with their speech language, Mexicans avoid making others feel ill at ease. The Korean culture represents yet another people who prefer "indirect" speech (e.g., "perhaps," "could be") over "direct" speech.

Even in cultures that value assertiveness, language that is *too* powerful may intimidate or annoy others. Consider these two different approaches to handling a common situation:

> "Excuse me. My baby is having a little trouble getting to sleep. Would you mind turning down the music just a little?"

> "My baby can't sleep because your music is too loud. You need to turn it down."

The more polite, if less powerful, approach would probably produce better results than the stronger statement. How can this fact be reconciled with the research on powerful language? As noted in Chapter 1, interpersonal competence is a balance between effectiveness and appropriateness. If you come across as too powerful, you may get what you're seeking in the short term but alienate the other person in ways that will make your relationship more difficult in the long term. Furthermore, a statement that is *too* powerful can convey relational messages of disrespect and superiority, which are just as likely to antagonize others as to gain their compliance.

In some situations, polite, less apparently powerful forms of speech can even enhance a speaker's effectiveness.[28] For example, a boss might say to an assistant, "Would you mind making copies of this document? In truth, both the boss and secretary know that this is an order and not a request, but the questioning form is more considerate and leaves the assistant feeling better about the boss.[29] The importance of achieving both content and relational goals helps explain why a mixture of powerful speech and polite speech is usually most effective.[30]

Disruptive Language

Not all linguistic problems come from misunderstandings. Sometimes people understand one another perfectly and still wind up in a conflict. Of course, not all disagreements can, or should be, avoided. But eliminating three linguistic habits from your communication repertoire can minimize the kind of disagreements that don't need to happen, allowing you to save your energy for the unavoidable and important disagreements.

Fact–Opinion Confusion Factual statements are claims that can be verified as true or false. By contrast, opinion statements are based on the speaker's beliefs. Unlike factual statements, they can never be proved or disproved. Consider a few examples of the difference between factual and opinion statements:

Fact	Opinion
You forgot my birthday.	You don't care about me.
You keep interrupting me.	You're a control freak.
You tell a lot of ethnic jokes.	You're a bigot.

On the JOB

Swearing in the Workplace

Swearing may offend some people, but it serves a variety of communication functions.[a] It's a way to express emotions and to let others know how strongly you feel. It can be a compliment ("that was #$&@ing terrific!") or a harsh insult. Swearing can even be a term of endearment.

Swearing on the job can be especially problematic.[b] Communication researchers investigated the effects of swearing in work settings. Not surprisingly, their research shows that the more formal the situation, the more negative the appraisal. The chosen swear word also makes a difference: "F-bombs" have been rated as more inappropriate than other less-volatile terms. Relational history also is important: Hearers who are surprised by a speaker's swearing are likely to deem the person as incompetent.

Despite its downside, swearing can have its place at work. Stanford University professor Robert Sutton notes that choosing *not* to swear can actually violate the norms of some organizations.[c] He maintains that swearing on rare occasions can be effective for the shock value. (The fact that Sutton authored a book called *The No Asshole Rule* suggests he practices what he preaches.)

But even Sutton adds a cautionary note about swearing on the job: "If you are not sure, don't do it." The rules of interpersonal competence apply: Analyze and adapt to your audience, and engage in self-monitoring. And when in doubt, err on the side of restraint.

When factual and opinion statements are set side by side like this, the difference is clear. In everyday conversation, however, we often present our opinions as if they were facts, and in doing so we invite an unnecessary argument. For example:

"That was a dumb thing to say!"

"Spending that much on a pair of shoes is a waste of money!"

"You can't get a fair shake in this country unless you're a white male."

Notice how much less antagonistic each statement would be if it were prefaced by a qualifier that takes responsibility for the opinion such as "I believe ...," "In my opinion ...," or "It seems to me...." We'll discuss the importance of responsible "I" language later in this chapter.

Fact–Inference Confusion   Problems also arise when we confuse factual statements with inferential statements—conclusions arrived at from an interpretation of evidence.

Arguments often result when we label our inferences as facts:

A: Why are you mad at me?

B: I'm not mad at you. Why have you been so insecure lately?

A: I'm not insecure. It's just that you've been so critical.

B: What do you mean, "critical"? I haven't been critical....

Instead of trying to read the other person's mind, a far better course is to use the skill of perception checking that you learned in Chapter 4: Identify the observable behaviors (facts) that have caught your attention and describe one or more possible interpretations that you have drawn from them. After describing this train of thought, ask the other person to comment on the accuracy of your interpretation.

"When you didn't return my phone call *(fact)*, I got the idea that you're mad at me *(interpretation)*. Are you?" *(question)*

"You've been asking me whether I still love you a lot lately *(fact)*, and that makes me think you're feeling insecure *(inference)*. Or maybe I'm behaving differently. What's on your mind?" *(question)*

Emotive Language

Comedian George Carlin described how we editorialize when he observed that "anybody driving slower than you is an idiot, and anyone going faster than you is a maniac."

Emotive language seems to describe something but actually announces the speaker's attitude toward it. If you approve of a friend's roundabout approach to a difficult subject, you might call her "tactful"; if you don't approve of it, you might accuse her of "beating around the bush." Whether the approach is good or bad is more a matter of opinion than of fact, although this difference is obscured by emotive language.

You can appreciate how emotive words are really statements of opinion when you consider these examples:

If you approve, say	If you disapprove, say
thrifty	cheap
traditional	old-fashioned
extravert	loudmouth
cautious	cowardly
progressive	radical
information	propaganda
military victory	massacre
eccentric	crazy

The best way to avoid arguments involving emotive words is to describe the person, thing, or idea you are discussing in neutral terms and to label your opinions as such. Instead of saying "Quit making sexist remarks," say "I really don't like it when you call us 'girls' instead of 'women.'" These behavioral statements not only are more accurate but also have a much better chance of being well received by others.

The Language of Responsibility

Besides providing a way to make the content of a message clear or obscure, language reflects the speakers' willingness to take responsibility for their beliefs and feelings. This acceptance or rejection of responsibility says a great deal about the speaker and can shape the tone of a relationship. To see how, read on.

PAUSE *and* REFLECT

Conjugating "Irregular Verbs"

MindTap⁺ **REFLECT ...** on your usage of emotive language by answering the following questions, either here or online.

The technique is simple: Just take an action or personality trait and show how it can be viewed either favorably or unfavorably, according to the label it's given and the person who is engaging in the behavior. For example:

I'm casual. (most favorable)

You're a little careless. (less favorable)

He's a slob. (least favorable)

Or try this one:

I'm thrifty. (most favorable)

You're money conscious. (less favorable)

She's a tightwad. (least favorable)

Notice how these labels display the self-serving bias discussed in Chapter 3, as well as the principle that we're usually less charitable when describing others' behavior than our own.

1. Try a few conjugations yourself, using the following statements:

    a. I'm tactful.

    b. I'm conservative.

    c. I'm quiet.

    d. I'm relaxed.

    e. My child is high-spirited.

    f. I have high self-esteem.

2. Now recall at least two situations in which you used emotive language as if it was a description of fact and not an opinion. A good way to recall these situations is to think of a recent disagreement and imagine how the other people involved might have described it differently than you.

"It" Statements   Notice the difference between the sentences of each set:

"It bothers me when you're late."
"I'm worried when you're late."

"It's nice to see you."
"I'm glad to see you."

"It's a boring class."

"I'm bored in the class."

As the name implies, **"it" statements** replace the personal pronoun *I* with the less immediate word *it*. By contrast, **"I" language** clearly identifies the speaker as the source of a message. Communicators who use "it" statements avoid responsibility for ownership of a message, attributing it instead to some unidentified source. This habit isn't just imprecise—more important, it is an unconscious way to avoid taking a position.

Dreamworks/Allstar

"But" Statements   Statements that take the form "X-but-Y" can be confusing. A closer look at **"but" statements** explains why. In each sentence, the word *but* cancels the thought that precedes it:

> "You're really a great person, but I think we ought to stop seeing each other."

> "You've done good work for us, but we're going to have to let you go."

> "This paper has some good ideas, but I'm giving it a D grade because it's late."

∧ In *The Help*, white 1960s socialites use a positive-sounding title— "The Home Help Sanitation Initiative"—to try to enact a policy that reinforces their prejudices against black housekeepers. Abstract and ambiguous language can sometimes obscure the truth. Can you think of words, labels, or titles that overstate (or understate) the actions of the people involved?

These "buts" often are a strategy for wrapping the speaker's real but unpleasant message between more palatable ideas in a psychological sandwich. This approach can be a face-saving strategy worth using at times. When the goal is to be absolutely clear, however, the most responsible approach is to deliver the positive and negative messages separately so they both get heard.

"I" and "You" Language   We've seen that "I" language is a way of accepting responsibility for a message. In contrast, **"you" language** expresses a judgment of the other person. Positive judgments ("You look great today!") rarely cause problems, but notice how each of the following critical "you" statements implies that the subject of the complaint is doing something wrong:

> "You left this place a mess!"

> "You didn't keep your promise!"

> "You're really crude sometimes!"

It's easy to see why "you" language can arouse defensiveness. A "you" statement implies that the speaker is qualified to judge the target—not an idea that most listeners are willing to accept, even when the judgment is correct.

Fortunately, "I" language provides a more accurate and less provocative way to express a complaint.[31] "I" language shows that the speaker takes responsibility for the complaint by describing his or her reaction to the other's

Silver-John/Bigstock

behavior without making any judgments about its worth. Here are some "I" language alternatives for the examples offered above:

> "I don't want to be responsible for all of the cleaning in the apartment."

> "I'm angry that I was on time and you weren't."

> "I don't like when you tell off-color jokes in front of my parents."

The In Real Life feature in this section shows what "I" language sounds like as part of a conversation.

Despite its obvious advantages, even the best-constructed and delivered "I" message won't always succeed. As author and "I" language advocate Thomas Gordon acknowledges, "Nobody welcomes hearing that his behavior is causing someone a problem, no matter how the message is phrased."[32] Furthermore, "I" language in large doses can start to sound egotistical. Research shows that self-absorbed people, also known as "conversational narcissists," can be identified by their constant use of first-person singular pronouns.[33] For this reason, "I" language works best in moderation. Chapter 11 will discuss how to use "I" language effectively as a central component of the assertive message format.

"We" Language   One way to avoid overuse of "I" language is to consider the pronoun *we*. **"We" language** implies that the issue is the concern and responsibility of both the speaker and receiver of a message. Consider a few examples:

> "We need to figure out a budget that doesn't bankrupt us."

> "I think we have a problem. We can't seem to talk about your friends without fighting."

> "We aren't doing a very good job of keeping the place clean, are we?"

It's easy to see how "we" language can help build a constructive climate. It suggests a kind of "we're in this together" orientation that reflects the transactional nature of communication. People who use first-person plural pronouns signal their closeness, commonality, and cohesiveness with others.[34] For example, couples who use "we" language are more satisfied and manage conflict better than those who rely more heavily on "I" and "you" language.[35] In another study, strangers who were required to use the pronoun "we" instead of the phrase "you and I" in their interactions felt closer to one another.[36]

On the other hand, "we" statements aren't always appropriate. Sometimes using this pronoun sounds presumptuous and demanding because it suggests that you are speaking for the other person as well as yourself.[37] It's easy to imagine someone responding to your statement "We have a problem ..." by saying "Maybe you have a problem, but don't tell me I do!"

Given the pros and cons of both "I" language and "we" language, what advice can we give about the most effective pronouns to use in interpersonal communication? Researchers have found that "I" and "we" combinations (e.g., "I think that we ..." or "I would like to see us ...") have a good chance of being received favorably.[38] Because too much of any pronoun comes across

TABLE 6.4 Pronoun Use and Its Effects

	ADVANTAGES	DISADVANTAGES	TIPS
"I" language	Takes responsibility for personal thoughts, feelings, and wants. Less defense-provoking than evaluative "you" language.	Can be perceived as egotistical, narcissistic, and self-absorbed.	Use "I" messages when the other person doesn't perceive a problem. Combine "I" with "we" language.
"We" language	Signals inclusion, immediacy, cohesiveness, and commitment.	Can speak improperly for others.	Combine with "I" language. Use in group settings to enhance unity. Avoid when expressing personal thoughts, feelings, and wants.
"You" language	Signals other orientation, particularly when the topic is positive.	Can sound evaluative and judgmental, particularly during confrontations.	Use "I" language during confrontations. Use "you" language when praising or including others.

as inappropriate, combining pronouns is generally a good idea. If your "I" language reflects your position without being overly self-absorbed, your "you" language shows concern for others without judging them, and your "we" language includes others without speaking for them, you will probably come as close as possible to the ideal use of pronouns. Table 6.4 summarizes the advantages and disadvantages of each type of language and offers suggestions for approaches that have a good chance of success.

SKILL *Builder*

Practicing "I" Language

MindTap PRACTICE ... your skill at delivering "I" messages by answering the following questions either here or online.

You can develop your skill at delivering "I" messages by following these steps:

1. Visualize situations in your life when you have, or might have, sent each of the following messages:

   You're not telling me the truth!
   You think only of yourself!
   Don't be so touchy!

   Quit fooling around!
   You don't understand a word I'm saying!

2. Write alternatives to each statement using "I" language.

3. Think of three "you" statements you might make to people in your life. Transform each of these statements into "I" language and rehearse them with a classmate.

In REAL LIFE

"I" and "You" Language on the Job

For some time, Rebecca has been frustrated by her fellow worker Tom's frequent absences from the job. She hasn't spoken up because she likes Tom and also because she doesn't want to sound like a complainer. Lately, though, Tom's absences have become longer and more frequent. Today he extended his half-hour lunch an extra 45 minutes. When he returns to the office, Rebecca confronts him with her gripe using "you" language:

© Jason Harris/Cengage Learning

Rebecca: Where have you been? You were due back at 12:30, and it's almost 1:30 now.

Tom: *(Surprised by Rebecca's angry tone, which she has never used before with him)* I had a few errands to run. What's the problem?

Rebecca: We all have errands to run, Tom. But it's not fair for you to do yours on company time.

Tom: *(Feeling defensive after hearing Rebecca's accusation)* I don't see why you have to worry about how I do my job. Beth [their boss] hasn't complained, so why should you worry?

Rebecca: Beth hasn't complained because all of us have been covering for you. You should appreciate what a tight spot we're in, making excuses every time you come in late or leave early. *(Again, Rebecca uses "you" language to tell Tom how he should think and act.)*

Tom: *(Now too defensive to consider Rebecca's concerns)* Hey, I thought we all covered for one another here. What about the time last year when I worked late for a week so you could go to your cousin's wedding in San Antonio?

Rebecca: That's different! Nobody was lying then. When you take off, I have to make up stories about where you are. You're putting me in a very difficult spot, Tom, and it's not fair. You can't count on me to keep covering for you.

GENDER AND LANGUAGE

So far we have discussed language use as if it were identical for both sexes. Some popular writers and researchers believe that men and women speak in distinct ways, as if they are from different cultures.[39] Other scholars suggest that the differences are few and mostly not significant.[40] What are the similarities and differences between male and female language use?

Content

The first research on conversational topics and gender was conducted more than two generations ago. Despite the changes in male and female roles since then, the results of several studies are remarkably similar.[41] In these studies, women and men ranging in age from 17 to 80 described the range of topics each discussed with friends of the same sex. Certain topics were common

Tom: *(Feeling guilty but too angry from Rebecca's judgments and threat to acknowledge his mistakes)* Fine. I'll never ask you for a favor again. Sorry to put you out.

Rebecca may have succeeded in reducing Tom's lateness, but her choice of "you" language left him feeling defensive and angry. The climate in the office is likely to be more strained—hardly the outcome Rebecca was seeking.

Here's how she could have handled the same issue using "I" language to describe her problem instead of blaming Tom.

Rebecca: Tom, I need to talk to you about a problem. *(Notice how Rebecca identifies the problem as hers instead of attacking Tom.)*

Tom: What's up?

Rebecca: You know how you come in late to work sometimes or take long lunch hours?

Tom: *(Sensing trouble ahead and sounding wary)* Yeah?

Rebecca: Well, I need to tell you that it's putting me in a tight spot. *(Rebecca describes the problem in*

behavioral terms and then goes on to express her feeling.)* When Beth asks where you are, I don't want to say you're not here because that might get you in trouble. So sometimes I make excuses or even lie. But Beth is sounding suspicious of my excuses, and I'm worried about that.

Tom: *(Feeling defensive because he knows he's guilty but also sympathetic to Rebecca's position)* I don't want you to get in trouble. It's just that I've got to take care of a lot of personal business.

Rebecca: I know, Tom. I just want you to understand that it's getting impossible for me to cover for you.

Tom: Yeah, OK. Thanks for helping out.

Notice how "I" language made it possible for Rebecca to confront Tom honestly but without blaming or attacking him personally. Even if Tom doesn't change, Rebecca has gotten the problem off her chest, and she can feel proud that she did so in a way that didn't sound ugly or annoying.

MindTap **APPLY ...** this situation to your life by answering questions online.

---

to both men and women: work, movies, and television. Both men and women tended to reserve discussions of sex and sexuality for members of the same sex.

The differences between the men and women in these studies were more striking than the similarities. Female friends spent much more time discussing personal and domestic subjects; relationship problems; family, health and reproductive matters; weight; food and clothing; men; and other women. Men, on the other hand, were more likely to discuss music, current events, sports, business, and other men. Both men and women were equally likely to discuss personal appearance, sex, and dating in same-sex conversations. True to one common stereotype, women were more likely to gossip about close

"Sometimes I think he can understand every word we're saying."

friends and family. By contrast, men spent more time gossiping about sports figures and media personalities. Women's gossip was no more derogatory than men's. Many of these differences still appear in analyses of gender differences in online topics (see "Gender" in Chapter 2).[42]

These differences can lead to frustration when men and women try to converse with one another.[43] Researchers report that *trivial is the word often used by both men and women to describe topics discussed by the opposite sex.* "I want to talk about important things," a woman might say, "like how we're getting along. All he wants to do is talk about the news or what we'll do this weekend." Likewise, some men complain that women ask for and offer more details than necessary and focus too often on feelings and emotions.

Reasons for Communicating

Both men and women, at least in the dominant cultures of North America, use language to build and maintain social relationships. Regardless of the sex of the communicators, the goals of almost all ordinary conversations include making the conversation enjoyable by being friendly, showing interest in what the other person says, and talking about topics that interest the other person.[44] *How* men and women accomplish these goals is often different, though. Although most communicators try to make their interaction enjoyable, men are more likely than women to emphasize making conversation fun. Their discussions involve a greater amount of joking and good-natured teasing.

By contrast, women's discussions tend to involve feelings, relationships, and personal problems.[45] In fact, communication researcher Julia Wood flatly states that "for women, talk *is* the essence of relationships."[46] When members of a group of women were surveyed to find out what kinds of satisfaction they gained from talking with their friends, the most common theme mentioned was a feeling of empathy—"To know you're not alone," as some put it.[47] Whereas men commonly described same-sex conversations as something they *liked*, women described their same-sex conversations as a kind of contact they *needed*. The characteristically female orientation for relational communication is supported by studies of married couples showing that wives spend proportionately more time than husbands communicating in ways that help maintain their relationship.[48]

Conversational Style

Women tend to behave somewhat differently in conversations than do men, although the differences aren't as dramatic as you might imagine.[49] For instance, the popular myth that women are more talkative than men doesn't hold up under scientific scrutiny—researchers have found that men and women speak roughly the same number of words per day.[50]

One way to analyze gender-linked language differences is to observe men and women talking with each other. Communication scholar Anthony Mulac found that in mixed-sex conversations, men are more likely than women to use sentence fragments ("Nice photo"), judgmental adjectives ("Reading can be a drag"), directives ("Think of some more"), and "I" references ("I have a lot to do").[51] Women are more likely to use intensive adverbs ("He's *really* interested"), emotional references ("If he really cared about you …"), uncertainty verbs

Self-Assessment

How Sexist Is Your Language?
To complete two quizzes related to this question, visit CengageBrain.com to access the Speech Communication MindTap for *Looking Out Looking In.*

("It seems to me …"), and relational maintenance questions ("How was your day?"). Differences like these are consistent with studies showing that men's speech is characteristically more direct, succinct, and task-oriented. By contrast, women's speech is more typically indirect, elaborate, and focused on relationships.[52]

Women often use statements showing support for the other person, demonstrations of equality, and efforts to keep the conversation going.[53] With these goals, it's not surprising that traditionally female speech often contains statements of sympathy and empathy: "I've felt just like that myself," "The same thing happened to me!" Women are also inclined to ask questions that invite the other person to share information: "How did you feel about that?" "What did you do next?" The importance of nurturing a relationship also explains why female speech is often somewhat tentative. Saying, "This is just my opinion …" is less likely to put off a conversational partner than a more definite "Here's what I think.…"

An accommodating style isn't always a disadvantage. One study found that female authors often use less-powerful language when writing for a female audience and that this approach is particularly effective in health-focused magazines.[54] Another study revealed that women who spoke tentatively were actually more persuasive with men than those who used more powerful speech.[55]

As you read in Chapter 2, gender differences in language use and conversational topics show up vividly in online communication. The language of social media also shapes the way some people talk in person. For instance, clipped versions of words that are popular in texting and tweeting ("adorb" "presh," "probs") have found their way into face-to-face interactions. Research suggests that women (typically younger ones) are more likely than men to use these jargon shortcuts in conversations.[56]

Nongender Variables

The link between gender and language use isn't as clear-cut as it might seem. Several research reviews have found that the ways women and men communicate are more similar than different. For example, one analysis of more than 1,200 research studies found that only 1 percent of variance in communication behavior resulted from gender difference.[57] According to this review, there is no significant difference between male speech and female speech in areas such as use of qualifiers ("I guess" or "This is just my opinion"), tag questions, and vocal fluency.[58] Another meta-analysis involving more than 3,000 participants found that women were only slightly more likely than men to use tentative speech.[59] Finally, researchers looked for sex differences in adults' talkativeness, affiliative speech, and assertive speech—and found negligible differences in every instance.[60] In essence, these studies found that men's and women's speech is far more similar than different.

Some on-the-job research shows that male and female supervisors in similar positions behave the same way and are equally effective. In light of this research, which shows considerable similarities and relatively minor differences between the sexes, one communication scholar suggests that the "Men are from Mars, women are from Venus" metaphor should be replaced by the notion that "Men are from North Dakota, women are from South Dakota."[61]

A growing body of research explains some of the apparent contradictions between the similarities and differences between male speech and female speech. Research has revealed other factors that influence language use as much or more than does gender.[62] For example, social philosophy plays a role. Feminist wives talk longer than their partners, whereas nonfeminist wives speak less than their partners. In addition, cooperative or competitive orientations of speakers have more influence on how they interact than does their gender.[63] The speaker's occupation also influences speaking style. For example, male day-care teachers' speech to their students resembles the language of female teachers more closely than it resembles the language of fathers at home. And female farm operators working in a male-dominated profession often use more masculine language patterns by swearing and talking "tough as nails."[64]

Another powerful force that influences the way individual men and women speak is their gender role. Recall the gender roles described in Chapter 4: masculine, feminine, and androgynous. Remember that these gender roles don't necessarily line up neatly with biological sex. There are "masculine" females, "feminine" males, and androgynous communicators who combine traditionally masculine and feminine characteristics. These gender roles can influence a communicator's style more than his or her biological sex. For example, one study revealed that masculine subjects used significantly more dominance language than did either feminine or androgynous subjects.[65] Feminine subjects expressed slightly more submissive behaviors and more equivalence behaviors than did the androgynous subjects, and their submissiveness and equivalence were much greater than those of the masculine subjects, regardless of their biological sex. And in gay and lesbian relationships, the conversational styles of partners reflect power differences in the relationship (e.g., who is earning more money) more than the biological sex of the communicators.[66]

While there are differences in male and female speech patterns, they may not be as great as some popular books suggest—and some of them may not result from biological sex at all. In practical terms, the best approach is to recognize that differences in communication style—whether they come from biological sex, gender, culture, or individual factors—present both challenges and opportunities. We need to take different styles into account but not exaggerate or use them to stigmatize one another.

PAUSE *and* REFLECT

Exploring Gender Differences in Communication

MindTap REFLECT ... on exploring gender differences in communication by answering the following questions, either here or online.

As noted, some pop-culture writers claim that the communication styles of men and women are so different that "men are from Mars, women are from Venus." Others say the differences aren't that dramatic, and that a more apt metaphor would be "men are from North Dakota, women are from South Dakota." From your experience, which metaphor seems more accurate? If your answer is "neither," create another geographical metaphor to describe your experience. Be sure to provide examples.

CULTURE AND LANGUAGE

Anyone who has tried to translate ideas from one language to another knows that conveying the same meaning isn't always easy.[67] Sometimes the results of a bungled translation can be amusing. For example, the American manufacturers of Pet milk unknowingly introduced their product in French-speaking markets without realizing that the word *pet* in French means "to break wind."[68] Likewise, the English-speaking representative of a U.S. soft drink manufacturer naively drew laughs from Mexican customers when she offered free samples of Fresca soda pop. In Mexican slang, the word *fresca* means "lesbian."

Even choosing the right words during translation won't guarantee that non-native speakers will use an unfamiliar language correctly. For example, Japanese insurance companies warn their policyholders who are visiting the United States to avoid their cultural tendency to say "Excuse me" or "I'm sorry" if they are involved in a traffic accident.[69] In Japan, apologizing is a traditional way to express goodwill and maintain social harmony, even if the person offering the apology is not at fault. But in the United States an apology can be taken as an admission of fault and result in Japanese tourists being wrongly held responsible for accidents.

Difficult as it may be, translation is only a small part of the differences in communication between members of different cultures. Differences in the way language is used and the worldview that a language creates make communicating across cultures a challenging task.

Verbal Communication Styles

Using language is more than just choosing a particular group of words to convey an idea. Each language has its own unique style that distinguishes it from others. Matters such as the amount of formality or informality, precision or vagueness, and brevity or detail are major ingredients in speaking competently. And when a communicator tries to use the verbal style from one culture in a different one, problems are likely to arise.[70]

One way in which verbal styles vary is in their *directness*. Anthropologist Edward Hall identified two distinct cultural ways of using language.[71] **Low-context cultures** generally value using language to express thoughts, feelings, and ideas as directly as possible. Low-context communicators look for the meaning of a statement in the words spoken. By contrast, **high-context cultures** value using language to maintain social harmony. Rather than upset others by speaking directly, high-context communicators learn to discover meaning from the context in which a message is delivered: the nonverbal behaviors of the speaker, the history of the relationship, and the general social rules that govern interaction between people. Table 6.5 summarizes some key differences between the way low- and high-context cultures use language.

North American culture falls toward the low-context end of the scale. Residents of the United States and Canada value straight talk and grow impatient with "beating around the bush." By contrast, most Asian and Middle Eastern cultures fall toward the high-context end of the scale. In many Asian cultures, for example, maintaining harmony is important, so communicators

TABLE 6.5 Low- and High-Context Communication Styles

LOW CONTEXT	HIGH CONTEXT
Majority of information carried in explicit cues. High reliance on explicit verbal messages.	Important information not always expressed explicitly. Clues carried in the situational context (time, place, relationship).
Self-expression valued. Communicators state opinions and desires directly and strive to persuade others to accept their own viewpoint.	Relational harmony valued and maintained by indirect expression of opinions. Communicators abstain from saying "no" directly.
Clear, eloquent speech considered praiseworthy. Verbal fluency admired.	Communicators talk "around" the point, allowing the other to fill in the missing pieces. Ambiguity and use of silence admired.

Looking at DIVERSITY

Courtesy of Pilar Bernal de Pheils

Pilar Bernal de Pheils: Speaking the Patient's Language

A native of Colombia, Pilar Bernal de Pheils is a clinical professor in the School of Nursing at the University of California San Francisco. She supervises nurse practitioners in training at both San Francisco's Mission Neighborhood Health Center and Women's Community Clinic.

I work in a setting where linguistic and cultural barriers make communication especially challenging. At the Mission Neighborhood Health Center, almost all of our patients are monolingual Spanish speakers from under-served backgrounds. Most were born outside the USA, and very few have received anything beyond a basic education. Many seek help for medical and psychosocial issues that require linguistic and cultural sensitivity.

Everyone on our clinic staff is bilingual, which is important for the population we serve. Serious problems can occur when patients don't have the benefit of a healthcare provider or translator who can understand and speak their language fluently.

It can be especially dangerous to *think* you understand another language when you don't know the nuances. For example, one common phrase Latino patients use to express the sensation of bloating is "Estoy inflamada." The literal translation is "I am inflamed," but that doesn't capture what the patient

is trying to describe. A provider or trainee who lacks a good grasp of the language could misunderstand the patient and misdiagnose the problem.

I remind my trainees to keep humble, both because their linguistic skills may not be as good as they may think, and because overconfidence can cause patients to feel intimidated. I also train my students to ask "Tell me more" as a way of increasing the odds that they will understand what our patients are trying to explain. And because the stakes are so high, it's important to provide a skilled professional translator when a staff member is not fluent in medical Spanish. It's expensive and time consuming, but in the end the results justify the costs.

It's hard enough for both patients and healthcare providers to communicate effectively under any circumstances, but the differences escalate when different languages are involved. Both attitude and skill are essential to bridge the gap.

will avoid speaking directly if that would threaten another person's face. For this reason, Japanese and Koreans are less likely than Americans to offer a clear "no" to an undesirable request. Instead they will probably use roundabout expressions such as "I agree with you in principle, but …" or "I sympathize with you.…"

The same sort of clash between directness and indirectness can aggravate problems between straight-talking, low-context Israelis, who value speaking directly, and Arabs, whose high-context culture stresses smooth interaction. It's easy to imagine how the clash of cultural styles could lead to misunderstandings and conflicts between Israelis and their Palestinian neighbors. Israelis could view the Palestinians as evasive, whereas the Palestinians could view the Israelis as insensitive and blunt.

It's worth noting that even generally straight-talking residents of the United States raised in the low-context Euro-American tradition often rely on context to make their point. When you decline an unwanted invitation by saying, "I can't make it," it's likely that both you and the other person know that the choice of attending isn't really beyond your control. If your goal was to be perfectly clear, you might say, "I don't want to get together." As Chapter 3 explains in detail, we often equivocate precisely because we want to obscure our true thoughts and feelings.

Besides their degrees of clarity and vagueness, language styles can also vary across cultures in being *elaborate* or *succinct*. Speakers of Arabic, for instance, commonly use language that is much richer and more expressive than that of most communicators who use English. Strong assertions and exaggerations that would sound ridiculous in English are a common feature of Arabic. This contrast in linguistic styles can lead to misunderstandings between people from different backgrounds. As one observer put it:

> First, an Arab feels compelled to overassert in almost all types of communication because others expect him [or her] to. If an Arab says exactly what he [or she] means without the expected assertion, other Arabs may still think that he [or she] means the opposite. For example, a simple "no" by a guest to the host's requests to eat more or drink more will not suffice. To convey the meaning that he [or she] is actually full, the guest must keep repeating "no" several times, coupling it with an oath such as "By God" or "I swear to God." Second, an Arab often fails to realize that others, particularly foreigners, may mean exactly what they say even though their language is simple. To the Arabs, a simple "no" may mean the indirectly expressed consent and encouragement of a coquettish woman. On the other hand, a simple consent may mean the rejection of a hypocritical politician.*

Succinctness is most extreme in cultures where silence is valued. In many Native American cultures, for example, the favored way to handle ambiguous social situations is to remain quiet.[72] In contrasting this silent style to the talkativeness that is common in mainstream American cultures when people first meet, it's easy to imagine how the first encounter between an Apache or Navajo and an Anglo might feel uncomfortable to both people.

A third way in which languages differ from one culture to another involves *formality* and *informality*. The informal approach that characterizes relationships in countries such as the United States, Canada, and Australia,

* Almaney, A. & Alwan, A. (1982). Communicating with the Arabs. Prospect Heights, IL: Waveland.

as well as the Scandinavian countries, is quite different from the great concern for using proper speech in many parts of Asia and Africa. Formality isn't so much a matter of using correct grammar as of defining social position. In Korea, for example, the language reflects the Confucian system of relational hierarchies.[73] It has special vocabularies for different sexes, different levels of social status, different degrees of intimacy, and different types of social occasions. For example, there are different degrees of formality for speaking with old friends, nonacquaintances whose background one knows, and complete strangers. When you contrast these sorts of distinctions with the casual friendliness that many North Americans use even when talking with complete strangers, it's easy to see how a Korean might view communicators in the United States as boorish and how an American might view communicators in Korea as stiff and unfriendly.

Language and Worldview

Different linguistic styles are important, but there may be even more-important differences that separate speakers of various languages. For almost 150 years, theorists have put forth the notion of **linguistic relativity**: that the worldview of a culture is shaped and reflected by the language its members speak.[74] The best-known example of linguistic relativity is the notion that Eskimos have a large number of words (estimated at everything from seventeen to one hundred) for what we simply call *snow*. Different terms are used to describe conditions such as a driving blizzard, crusty ice, and light powder. This example suggests how linguistic relativity operates. The need to survive in an Arctic environment led Eskimos to make distinctions that would be unimportant to residents of warmer environments, and after the language makes these distinctions, speakers are more likely to see the world in ways that match the broader vocabulary.

Even though there is some doubt that Eskimos really have so many words for snow,[75] other examples do seem to support the principle of linguistic relativity.[76] For instance, bilingual speakers seem to think differently when they change languages. In one study, French American people were asked to interpret a series of pictures. When they described the pictures in French, their descriptions were far more romantic and emotional than when they described the pictures in English. Likewise, when students in Hong Kong were asked to complete a values test, they expressed more traditional Chinese values when they answered in Cantonese than when they answered in English. In Israel, both Arab and Jewish students saw greater distinctions between their group and "outsiders" when using their native language than when they used English, a neutral tongue for them. Examples like these show the power of language to shape cultural identity—sometimes for better and sometimes for worse.

The best-known declaration of linguistic relativity is the **Sapir-Whorf hypothesis** credited to Edward Sapir and Benjamin Whorf.[77] Following Sapir's theory, Whorf observed that the language spoken by Hopi Native Americans represents a view of reality that is dramatically different from that of more-familiar tongues. For example, the Hopi language makes no distinction between nouns and verbs. Therefore, the people who speak it describe the entire world as being constantly in process. Whereas in English we use nouns to characterize

LANGUAGE AND HERITAGE

"Mi'ja, it's me. Call me when you wake up." It was a message left on my phone machine from a friend. But when I heard that word mi'ja, a pain squeezed my heart. My father was the only one who ever called me this. Because his death is so recent, the word overwhelmed me and filled me with grief.

Mi'ja (MEE-ha) from *mi hija* (me ee-HA). The words translate as "my daughter." Daughter, my daughter, daughter of mine: They're all stiff and clumsy, and have nothing of the intimacy and warmth of the word *mi'ja*—"daughter of my heart," maybe. Perhaps a more accurate translation of *mi'ja* is "I love you." Sometimes a word can be translated into more than a meaning. In it is the translation of a worldview, a way of looking at things, and,

MediaImages/Photodisc/Getty Images

yes, even a way of accepting what others might not perceive as beautiful. *Urraca*, for example, instead of "grackle." Two ways of looking at a black bird. One sings, the other cackles. Or, *tocayola*, your name-twin, and therefore, your friend. Or the beautiful *estrenar*, which means to wear something for the first time.

There is no word in English for the thrill and pride of wearing something new.

Spanish gives me a way of looking at myself and the world in a new way. For those of us living between worlds, our job in the universe is to help others see with more than their eyes during this period of chaotic transition.

Sandra Cisneros

MindTap **ENHANCE ...** your understanding by answering the following questions, either here or online.

1. Can you think of words and names that others use for you that denote their relationship with you, similar to how hearing the word *Mi'ja* led Sandra Cisneros to think of her father?

2. If you know another language, describe how certain concepts are difficult to translate from one language to another. Discuss the role that *culture* plays in this phenomenon.

people or objects as being fixed or constant, Hopi view them more as verbs, constantly changing. In this sense, English represents much of the world rather like a snapshot camera, whereas Hopi language represents the world more like a motion picture.

Some languages contain terms that have no English equivalents.[78] For example, consider a few words in other languages:

nemawashi (Japanese): The process of informally feeling out all of the people involved with an issue before making a decision.

lagniappe (French/Creole): An extra gift given in a transaction that wasn't expected by the terms of a contract.

lao (Mandarin): A respectful term used for older people, showing their importance in the family and in society.

"The Eskimos have eighty-seven words for snow and not one for malpractice."

dharma (Sanskrit): Each person's unique, ideal path in life and knowledge of how to find it.

koyaanisquatsi (Hopi): Nature out of balance; a way of life so crazy it calls for a new way of living.

A premise of linguistic relativity is that our words don't just *reflect* how we see the world; they also *affect* how we see it. The language we use shapes our perception of things, others, and ourselves. Studies examining the effects of "fat talk" demonstrate this principle.[79] People who regularly put concerns about their weight into words ("I'm so fat"; "My butt is huge") reinforce a poor body image. Researchers identified three particular signs that fat talk is doing harm: (1) when it's used routinely and compulsively; (2) when it involves constant comparisons with others; and (3) when it includes guilt words like "should" and "ought" ("I really should drop some weight"). As you read in Chapter 3, a steady diet of negative self-appraisals and social comparison can turn into a destructive cycle of thoughts, words, and behaviors.

The effects of language on a speaker's thoughts and feelings can also be seen in a study conducted at the University of Bristol.[80] Researchers asked participants to speak aloud three types of words: swear words, euphemisms for swear words (such as saying "the F-word" instead the actual term), and neutral words. When swearing, participants had much stronger physiological stress responses than when they used euphemistic or neutral terms. The researchers see this as an example of linguistic relativity: "Taboo words become directly associated with emotional centers in the brain. Accordingly, taboo words can evoke strong emotions even when they are uttered without any desire to offend." In other words, the language we use has an impact on our minds—sometimes in ways we don't even realize.

SUMMARY

Language is both a marvelous communication tool and the source of many interpersonal problems. Every language is a collection of symbols governed by a variety of rules: semantic, syntactic, and pragmatic.

Terms used to name people influence the way the people are regarded. The terms used to name speakers and the language they use reflect the level of affiliation of a speaker toward others. Language patterns also reflect and shape a speaker's perceived power.

Some language habits—such as confusing facts with opinions or inferences and using emotive terms—can lead to unnecessary disharmony in interpersonal relationships. Language also acknowledges or avoids the speaker's acceptance of responsibility for his or her thoughts and feelings.

There are some differences in the ways men and women speak. The content of their conversations varies, as do their reasons for communicating and their conversational styles. However, not all differences in language use can be accounted for by the speaker's biological sex. Gender roles, occupation, social philosophy, and orientation toward problem solving also influence people's use of language.

Different languages often shape and reflect the views of a culture. Some cultures value directness, brevity, and the succinct use of language, whereas others value indirect or elaborate forms of speech. In some societies, formality is important, whereas others value informality. Beyond these differences, there is evidence to support linguistic relativism—the notion that language exerts a strong influence on the worldview of the people who speak it.

KEY TERMS

abstraction ladder
abstract language
behavioral language
"but" statements
convergence
divergence
emotive language
equivocal language
high-context cultures
"I" language
"it" statements
linguistic relativity

low-context cultures
politeness
powerless speech mannerisms
pragmatic rules
relative words
Sapir-Whorf hypothesis
semantic rules
static evaluation
syntactic rules
"we" language
"you" language

CHAPTER SIX

Language: Barrier and Bridge

OUTLINE

Use this outline to take notes as you read the chapter in the text and/or as your instructor lectures in class.

I. LANGUAGE IS SYMBOLIC

  A. Signs

  B. Symbols

    1. Arbitrary

    2. Meanings Are in People, Not Words

II. UNDERSTANDINGS AND MISUNDERSTANDINGS

  A. Understanding Words: Semantic Rules

    1. Equivocation

    2. Relative Language

    3. Static Evaluation

    4. Abstraction vs. Behavioral Language

      a. Advantages

      b. Problems

  B. Understanding Structure: Syntactic Rules

    1. Grammar

    2. Order

    3. Dialects

  C. Understanding Context: Pragmatic Rules

    1. Often Unstated

    2. Relies on Coordination

    3. Personal Codes

III. THE IMPACT OF LANGUAGE

A. Naming and Identity
1. Personal Identity
2. Group Identity

B. Affiliation
1. Convergence
2. Divergence

C. Power and Politeness
1. Powerful Language
2. Powerless Speech Mannerism
    a. Appear Less Socially Attractive
    b. Can Be Attempts at Politeness
3. Culture and Context

D. Disruptive Language
1. Fact-Opinion Confusion
2. Fact-Inference Confusion
3. Emotive Language

E. Language of Responsibility
1. "It" Statements
2. "But" Statements
3. "I" and "You" Language
4. "We" Language
    a. "You" Language Judges
    b. "I" Statements Describe
       1) Your Observations of Others' Behavior
       2) Your Interpretation
       3) Your Feelings
       4) Consequences of the Behavior
    c. Advantages of "I" Language
       1) Accepts Responsibility
       2) Reduces Defensiveness
       3) Is More Accurate
    d. Reservations about "I" Language
       1) Anger Impedes Use
       2) Defensiveness with Poor Nonverbal
       3) Sounds Artificial without Confidence
       4) Too Much Sounds Narcissistic

e. "We" Language

    1) May Signal Inclusion and Commitment

    2) May Speak Improperly for Others

    3) When to Combine "I" and "We"

IV. GENDER AND LANGUAGE

A. Content

1. Some Common Topics
2. Sex Talk Restricted to Same Gender
3. Many Topics Vary by Gender

B. Reasons for Communicating

1. Build and Maintain Social Relationships
   a. Men: More Joking and Good-Natured Teasing
   b. Women: More Feelings and Relationships
2. Women—Nourish Relationships, Build Harmony
3. Men—Task-Oriented, Advice, Status, Independence

C. Conversational Style

1. Men: Judge, Direct, and "I" Language
2. Women: Questions, Intensifiers, Emotion, Uncertainty, Support, Maintain Conversations

D. Nongender Variables

1. Occupation and Social Philosophy
2. Historical and Gender Roles

V. CULTURE AND LANGUAGE

A. Verbal Communication Styles

1. Direct/Indirect (Low-Context and High-Context Cultures)
2. Elaborate/Succinct
3. Formality/Informality

B. Language and World View

1. Linguistic Relativism
2. Sapir-Whorf Hypothesis
   a. Words Shape Perception
   b. Words Trigger Physiological Responses

KEY TERMS

abstraction ladder
abstract language
affiliation
behavioral language
"but" statements
convergence
disclaimers
divergence
emotive language
equivocal language
fact
hedges
high-context cultures
"I" language
inference

"it" statements
linguistic relativity
low-context cultures
opinion
powerless speech mannerisms
pragmatic rules
relative words
Sapir-Whorf hypothesis
semantic rules
static evaluation
symbolism
syntactic rules
"we" language
"you" language

ACTIVITIES

6.1 SYMBOLIC NATURE OF LANGUAGE

LEARNING OBJECTIVES

- Describe the arbitrary and changeable nature of symbols.
- Identify the sources of language-based misunderstanding.
- Understand the impact of their individual relationship with words.

INSTRUCTIONS

PART I:

1. Choose a word that you "like" and write it in the space below. You might like this word because of what it means, your personal associations with the word, or because you like how it sounds. It doesn't matter why you "like" the word, only that you do.

    _____

    _____

    _____

2. In a few sentences, explain why you like this word.

    _____

    _____

    _____

PART II:

1. Look your word up in a reputable dictionary (such as *Merriam-Webster*) and write the definition here. If your word has multiple definitions, write them down too.

    _____

    _____

    _____

2. Visit a library and look up your word in the *Oxford English Dictionary*, which is actually a kind of encyclopedia of words. In the *Oxford English*, you will find the citation for the very first time your word was found in print and what it meant. You will also discover how your word may have changed in usage over time. Write down the oldest citation, what the word originally meant, and any significant events you discover in its history.

_____

_____

_____

PART III:

1. Reflect on what you learned about your word. Did you discover anything that might make your word difficult for others to understand? Do you feel you understand your word more fully now that you know its history? Did you discover any surprises about your word?

_____

_____

2. Share your word and your reflections with your classmates in a group discussion.

_____

_____

6.2 MISUNDERSTOOD LANGUAGE

LEARNING OBJECTIVES

- Analyze a real or potential misunderstanding in terms of semantic or pragmatic rules.
- Construct a message at the optimal level of specificity or vagueness for a given situation.

INSTRUCTIONS

1. Label the language contained in each of the sentences below as relative language, static evaluation, or equivocal language.

2. Rewrite each sentence in more precise language.

3. Write your own examples of each variety of language in the spaces provided.

EXAMPLE 1

I'm trying to diet, so give me a **small** piece of cake.
Language: *Relative language*
Why you categorized it as you did, and how you can best correct it: *It is relative because it can be compared to many other things; the best way to correct it is to use a number.*
Revised statement: *I'm trying to diet, so give me a piece of cake about two inches square.*

EXAMPLE 2

Helen **is** a troublemaker.
Language: *Static evaluation*
Why you categorized it as you did, and how you can best correct it: *It is static because it uses the verb "to be" implying that troublemaker is a permanent condition of Helen. It can best be corrected with behavioral description.*
Revised statement: *Helen told my mother that I was out until 3 A.M. with Jim.*

EXAMPLE 3

There's a new book in the library; you should **check it out.**
Language: *Equivocal language*
Why you categorized it as you did, and how you can best correct it: *It is equivocal because "check it out" can mean to appropriately remove it from the library in your name or to peruse it. Correct it by clarifying the meaning.*
Revised statement: *There's a new book in the library; you should peruse it and see if it is something you'd like to read.*

1. What do you want to know about **our** relationship?

    Language: _____

    Why you categorized it as you did, and how you can best correct it: _____

    _____

Revised statement: _____
_____

2. They **are** real nerds.

   Language: _____

   Why you categorized it as you did, and how you can best correct it: _____
   _____

   Revised statement: _____
   _____

3. She's very **conservative**.

   Language: _____

   Why you categorized it as you did, and how you can best correct it: _____
   _____

   Revised statement: _____
   _____

4. I haven't done my laundry for **a long time**.

   Language: _____

   Why you categorized it as you did, and how you can best correct it: _____
   _____

   Revised statement: _____
   _____

5. Your essay should be brief.

   Language: _____

   Why you categorized it as you did, and how you can best correct it: _____
   _____

   Revised statement: _____
   _____

6. My job isn't taking me anywhere.

   Language: _____

Why you categorized it as you did, and how you can best correct it: _____

_____

Revised statement: _____

_____

7. She **is** such a braggart.

Language: _____

Why you categorized it as you did, and how you can best correct it: _____

_____

Revised statement: _____

_____

8. You've got **especially** poor attendance.

Language: _____

Why you categorized it as you did, and how you can best correct it: _____

_____

Revised statement: _____

_____

Now write your own examples of each type of language and revise the statements to illustrate alternative language.

1. Equivocal language: _____

_____

Revised: _____

_____

2. Relative language: _____

_____

Revised: _____

_____

3. Static evaluation: _____

_____

Revised: _____

_____

6.3 BEHAVIORAL LANGUAGE

LEARNING OBJECTIVES

- Construct a message at the optimal level of specificity or abstraction for a given situation.

INSTRUCTIONS

In each of the situations below, change the language to describe behavior in optimally specific terms. Remember to focus on the behavior (e.g., Bev did "x," rather than Bev is "x"). If you are giving instructions, be specific enough (low abstractions) to clearly get your idea across to someone else so that they can perform the task. On the other hand, don't be inappropriately specific, offering far more detail than is necessary for the situation.

EXAMPLE 1

John's a live wire.
John ran a 5K in the morning, volunteered for two hours at the homeless shelter in the afternoon, and then danced at a party until dawn.

EXAMPLE 2

Go over that way.
Go across the footbridge, turn right, and go up the five large steps to the third building on your left.

1. Will you just wash the car the right way this time?

   _____

   _____

2. Natasha needs to get real.

   _____

   _____

3. You can't rely on Randy.

   _____

   _____

4. That teacher is hard-headed.

   _____

   _____

5. Get organized.

   _____

   _____

6. Josh just blows me off when I have something important to say.

   _____

   _____

7. He acts weird.

   _____

   _____

8. Do the report correctly this time.

   _____

   _____

9. My parents are understanding.

   _____

   _____

10. Get a decent movie this time.

   _____

   _____

11. I like it that your family is emotional.

   _____

   _____

6.4 EFFECTIVE LANGUAGE

LEARNING OBJECTIVES

- Analyze a real or potential misunderstanding in terms of semantic or pragmatic rules.

- Describe how principles presented in the section of this chapter titled "The Impact of Language" operate in your life.

INSTRUCTIONS

1. For each of the situations below, imagine the speaker is talking directly to you. Record the types of language used by the speaker. Focus on high and low abstraction, powerful or powerless speech mannerisms, facts or opinions, inferences, high- and low-context language styles, and language and worldview.

2. Next, imagine that you're responding to the speaker using much the same types of language he or she spoke to you. Record the language you would use in response (as listed above).

3. Evaluate the effectiveness of the speaker's message and of your response.

4. Finally, describe any alternative language you might have used in your response. What might have been its effectiveness?

EXAMPLE

Situation: Your supervisor at work has called you aside three times this week to correct work you have done. Each time she says, "You've messed up on this."

Type of language the speaker used: *My supervisor used "**you**" language and **high abstraction**.*

What you imagined you said in response: *"You're on me all the time about something or other."*

Type of language and effectiveness: *My supervisor's language wasn't very effective with me because I wasn't sure exactly what I'd messed up on, and I got very defensive, thinking she was about to fire me. She was very direct with me, however; she didn't keep silent about what was bothering her (this is consistent with the **low-context culture** in which I live). I used "**you**" language and **high abstraction** in response. This is probably not very effective. My supervisor is likely to get defensive. Actually, my supervisor may think this is "helpful" and "caring" behavior and not realize that I am feeling hassled and threatened.*

Alternative language and effectiveness: *"Ms. Gomez, I'm worried that I'm not doing my job correctly because you've corrected me three times this week. Which part of the report do you want corrected?" This "I" language is more likely to let Ms. Gomez know what specifically is bothering me without raising a good deal of defensiveness. She's likely to appreciate my directness and specific request for help.*

1. Situation: Your romantic partner has been extremely busy with school and work the last two weeks, and you've been feeling left out. When you suggest going out to a party, your partner replies, "You need a personal circus to have fun."

Type of language the speaker used:

_____

_____

What you imagined you said in response:

_____

_____

Type of language and effectiveness:

_____

_____

Alternative language and effectiveness:

_____

_____

2.   Situation: You have a hard time saying "no." Lately your roommate has been asking you to do chores that are not your responsibility. Tonight the roommate says, "You're such a great roommate. You won't mind doing the dishes for me tonight since I've got a date and you're just staying home anyway, will you?"

Type of language the speaker used:

_____

_____

What you imagined you said in response:

_____

_____

Type of language and effectiveness:

_____

_____

Alternative language and effectiveness:

_____

_____

3. Situation: Your cousins are moving to town. They just called, addressing you by your old family nickname, and said, "You lucky person, you get to have the pleasure of our company for a while until we find a place to live. We thought you'd be glad to have us."

Type of language the speaker used:

_____

_____

What you imagined you said in response:

_____

_____

Type of language and effectiveness:

_____

_____

Alternative language and effectiveness:

_____

_____

4. Situation: You're working on a project with a partner from class, and the partner says, "We'll never get this done. You're too meticulous about everything."

Type of language the speaker used:

_____

_____

What you imagined you said in response:

_____

_____

Type of language and effectiveness:

_____

_____

Alternative language and effectiveness:

_____

_____

5. Situation: Your boss's five-year-old is visiting the workplace. The child has broken two items and is now running from door to door, laughing loudly. Two customers look your way. Your boss says, "Isn't he great? Really an energetic kid!"

    Type of language the speaker used:

_____

_____

What you imagined you said in response:

_____

_____

Type of language and effectiveness:

_____

_____

Alternative language and effectiveness:

_____

_____

Class _____   Name _____

Record a situation of your own here:

6. Situation (What the speaker said to you):

_____

_____

Type of language the speaker used:

_____

_____

What you imagined you said in response:

_____

_____

Type of language and effectiveness:

_____

_____

Alternative language and effectiveness:

_____

_____

6.5 MEDIATED MESSAGES—LANGUAGE

LEARNING OBJECTIVES

- Understand the impact of *naming* on identity.

- Analyze a real or potential misunderstanding in mediated messages due to misunderstanding of semantic or pragmatic rules.

- Describe how principles presented in the section of this chapter titled "The Impact of Language" operate in your life.

INSTRUCTIONS

Discuss each of the questions below in your group. Prepare written answers for your instructor, or be prepared to contribute to a large group discussion, comparing your experiences with those of others in your class.

1. Research has shown that names shape the way others think of us, the way we think of ourselves, and the way we act. Think back to a time when you created a name to use in a mediated context. (e.g., *your email address, website identities, or your chat room identity*). What were your reasons for choosing that name?

    _____

    _____

2. Have your self-chosen, mediated names had an impact on your identity? In what ways has the impact been positive? Have you experienced any negative consequences from these names? Do you wish you had chosen differently? Why or why not?

    _____

3. As with everyday speech, the mediated language we use can be very businesslike or very informal. Do you find that you use different degrees of formality or informality on different mediated channels? For example, are you more formal in email and less so when you text? Have you ever sent a mediated message inappropriately by choosing the wrong channel and being either too formal or too informal (for example, texting your employer with abbreviated language to tell him or her you'll be late for work)? Discuss the pros and cons of formal versus informal mediated messages and channels.

    _____

    _____

4. There are other ways people fail to adapt their language style to the medium they are using. For example, they use time inappropriately, leaving a 5-minute voice mail that should have been

summarized in 30 seconds, or they use tone inappropriately, appearing to be cold and indifferent about important issues. Share an example of a time when you created a misunderstanding by failing to adapt your language style effectively.

_____

_____

6.6 LANGUAGE, PERCEPTION, AND CONFLICT

LEARNING OBJECTIVES

- In a given situation, analyze how gender and/or cultural differences may affect the quality of interaction.
- Construct a message at the optimal level of specificity or vagueness for a given situation.
- Recast "you" statements into "I" or "we" statements to reflect your responsibility for the content of messages.

INSTRUCTIONS

Use the case below and the discussion questions that follow to discuss the variety of communication issues involved in effective communication. Make notes on this page, add other pages on your own, or prepare a group report/analysis based on your discussion. Add your own experiences to individualize the analysis.

CASE

Professor Polle paired Matt and Magda as class project partners. After three weeks, both Matt and Magda came to their professor to complain about the other. Matt called Magda a "flake" and said she didn't work hard enough and didn't take the project seriously. Magda said that Matt was "arrogant," wanted the project done only his way, and didn't care about all the commitments Magda had. It was too late in the semester for the professor to give them new partners.

1. Identify the language that Matt and Magda are using about one another. What effect does using this language have on their perception of each other? On the successful completion of their project?

    _____

    _____

2. Rewrite the high level abstractions that Matt and Magda use with specific, concrete language. How could this change their perceptions? Improve their situation?

    _____

    _____

3. Give an example of an "I" language statement from each of the three persons involved that could improve the situation.

    _____

    _____

4. Gender and culture may influence the way language is used. Identify differences mentioned in your text and describe how those differences might apply to this situation.

_____

_____

STUDY GUIDE

CHECK YOUR UNDERSTANDING

TRUE/FALSE

Mark the statements below as true or false. For statements that are false, correct them on the lines below to create a true statement.

_____ 1. Words are not arbitrary symbols; they have meaning in and of themselves.

_____

_____ 2. Language can both *shape* our perceptions of the world and *reflect* our attitudes towards others.

_____

_____ 3. Research has shown that people are rated as more competent when their talk is free of powerless speech mannerisms; therefore, choosing a consistently powerful style of speaking is always the best approach.

_____

_____ 4. The effective direct language of someone from a low-context culture can become ineffective when communicating with someone from a high-context culture.

_____

_____ 5. Linguists believe that we should view varying syntactic rules as deficient forms of English.

_____

_____ 6. Since it includes and connects people, "we" language is always the best choice.

_____

_____ 7. Naming children can be a way to express personal and ethnic identity.

_____

_____ 8. In the research cited in your text, conversational topics used by men and women are remarkably similar.

_____

_____ 9. Swearing patterns of bosses and coworkers can help people feel connected on the job.

_____

_____ 10. Opinion statements express fact because they are based on the speaker's beliefs.

_____

COMPLETION

Fill in the blanks below with the correct terms chosen from the list below.

abstraction ladder	equivocation	convergence	divergence	polite forms
tag questions	elaborateness	hedges	disclaimers	succinctness
formality	informality			

1. _____ is the process of adapting one's speech style to match that of others with whom the communicator wants to identify.

2. _____ in language use involve(s) denying direct responsibility for the statement, such as "I could be wrong, but . . . "

3. _____ of language involve(s) using respectful terms of address, such as "You're welcome, ma'am."

4. _____ involve(s) speaking in a way that emphasizes a person's differences from the other persons with whom he or she is speaking.

5. _____ in language use involve(s) using words that have more than one commonly accepted definition, such as "They eat *healthy* food."

6. _____ in language use involve(s) a negation statement, such as *"Didn't you think that party was boring?"*

7. _____ in language use make(s) less of the feeling or intention statement, such as "I'm *rather* upset."

8. _____ is an illustration of how the same phenomenon can be described at various levels of specificity.

9. _____ involve(s) speaking with few words, and it is usually most extreme in cultures where silence is valued.

10. _____ involve(s) speaking with rich and expressive terms, sometimes involving strong assertions and exaggerations.

11. _____ is a way of using correct grammar as a way of defining social position in some cultures.

12. _____ is a way of using language that is casually friendly and does not reflect a series of relational hierarchies in a particular culture.

MULTIPLE CHOICE

Label the examples of language given below by writing the letter of the language type illustrated on the line in front of the example.

a. inference
b. relative word
c. abstract words

d. emotive word
e. equivocal language
f. fact

_____   1. John didn't call so he must be angry.

_____   2. I have a stomach problem.

_____   3. The first astronaut landed on the moon in 1969.

_____   4. That guy is a real hunk.

_____   5. My car is hot.

_____   6. She left the meeting early; she must have been irritated.

_____   7. When I said I'd always help bail you out, I didn't mean from jail, just that I'd help you pay your bills.

_____   8. As your governor, I'd improve education in the state.

_____   9. He showed up, so he must agree with the protest.

_____   10. He's a real tight-wad.

_____   11. All of the measures I've supported in Congress promote security.

_____   12. Ian gave a long speech.

_____   13. My grandfather was born in 1952.

_____   14. My sister is a pill.

Choose the letter of the *least* abstract alternative to the high abstraction terms.

_____   15. Jo's constantly complaining.
   a. Jo whines a lot.
   b. Jo complains often about the workload.
   c. Jo told me three times this week that she feels overworked.
   d. Every time we meet, Jo complains about all the work she does.

_____   16. He can never do anything because he's always busy.
   a. He couldn't take me to dinner last night because he had to work.
   b. He can never do anything fun because he's always working.
   c. He didn't ever take time off to be with me.
   d. He works too much so we have a boring life.

_____ 17. There are a lot of problems associated with freedom.
         a. Freedom carries with it responsibility.
         b. Since I moved into my own apartment, I have to pay ten bills.
         c. I don't like all the responsibility of living on my own.
         d. My economic responsibilities limit my freedom.

_____ 18. Shannon is worthless as a roommate.
         a. Shannon is always gone, so she's really not part of our house.
         b. Shannon never does her part around here.
         c. Shannon's jobs seldom get done around here.
         d. Shannon has attended only one of our six house meetings.

_____ 19. Carlos is the most wonderful friend.
         a. Carlos has never told anyone about my fear of failing.
         b. Carlos listens to me about everything.
         c. Carlos is the best listener I've ever met.
         d. I can trust Carlos implicitly with all my secrets.

_____ 20. Keiko goes overboard in trying to make people like her.
         a. Keiko gave everyone on the team a valentine.
         b. Keiko is the biggest kiss-up you ever met.
         c. I think Keiko is trying to make my friends like her better than me.
         d. I want Keiko to stop trying to outdo everybody else.

Choose the *best* answer for each of the statements below:

_____ 21. Semantic misunderstandings arise when
         a. people assign the same meaning to the same words.
         b. people assign different meanings to different words.
         c. people assign different meanings to the same words.
         d. people assign the same meaning to different words.

_____ 22. One way to make words more measurable is to
         a. use words such as "doubtful, toss-up, likely, probable, good chance, and unlikely."
         b. use abstract concepts.
         c. use equivocal language.
         d. turn them into numbers.

_____ 23. One way to make words more effective to the listener is to
         a. use words that offend but get your point across.
         b. use abstract concepts.
         c. use equivocal language.
         d. adapt to the listener's language patterns.

_____ 24. Words are
         a. useless and should be avoided.
         b. arbitrary and their meaning is assigned by the receiver.
         c. the most important part of communication.
         d. helpful only if you choose the right ones.

CHAPTER SIX STUDY GUIDE ANSWERS

TRUE/FALSE

1. F	3. F	5. F	7. T	9. T
2. T	4. T	6. F	8. F	10. F

COMPLETION

1. convergence
2. disclaimers
3. polite forms
4. divergence

5. equivocation
6. tag questions
7. hedges
8. abstraction ladder

9. succinctness
10. elaborateness
11. formality
12. informality

MULTIPLE CHOICE

1. a	5. e	9. a	13. f	17. b	21. c
2. c	6. a	10. d	14. d	18. d	22. d
3. f	7. e	11. c	15. c	19. a	23. d
4. d	8. c	12. b	16. a	20. a	24. b

NONVERBAL COMMUNICATION: MESSAGES BEYOND WORDS

AFTER STUDYING THE TOPICS IN THIS CHAPTER, YOU SHOULD BE ABLE TO:

1. Explain the defining characteristics of nonverbal communication.

2. List and offer examples of each type of nonverbal message introduced in this chapter.

3. In a given situation, recognize your own nonverbal behavior and its relational significance.

4. Monitor and manage your nonverbal cues in ways that achieve your goals.

5. Share appropriately your interpretation of another's nonverbal behavior with that person.

What's going on in the photo seen here? You don't need to be a mind reader to recognize that, along with whatever words are being spoken, other messages are being expressed here. Some social scientists have argued that 93 percent of the emotional impact of a message comes from nonverbal cues. Others have reasoned more convincingly that the figure is closer to 65 percent.[1] Whatever the precise figure, the point remains: Nonverbal communication plays an important role in how we make sense of one another's behavior.

Recall a recent exchange in one of your important relationships. What kinds of nonverbal behaviors might an observer notice? What might those behaviors say about your relationship?

Image Source/Alamy

CHARACTERISTICS OF NONVERBAL COMMUNICATION

As you read this chapter, you'll become acquainted with the field of nonverbal communication: the way we express ourselves—not by what we say but rather by what we do.

Nonverbal Communication Defined

We need to begin our study of nonverbal communication by defining that term. At first this might seem like a simple task: If *non* means "not" and *verbal* means "words," then *nonverbal communication* means "communicating without words." In fact, this literal definition isn't completely accurate. For instance, most communication scholars do not define American Sign Language as nonverbal even though the messages are unspoken. On the other hand, you'll soon read that certain aspects of the voice aren't really verbal, although they are vocal. (Can you think of any? Table 7.1 will help.)

For our purposes, we'll define **nonverbal communication** as "messages expressed by nonlinguistic means." This rules out sign languages and written

language

TABLE 7.1 Types of Communication

	VOCAL COMMUNICATION	NONVOCAL COMMUNICATION
Verbal Communication	Spoken words	Written words
Nonverbal Communication	Vocal tone, rate, pitch, volume, etc.	Gestures, movement, appearance, facial expression, touch, etc.

words, but it includes messages transmitted by vocal means that don't involve language—such as sighs, laughs, throat clearing, and other assorted noises. In addition, our definition allows us to explore the nonlinguistic dimensions of the spoken word—volume, rate, pitch, and so on. It also encompasses more abstract factors such as physical appearance, the environment in which we communicate, how close or far we stand from each other, and the way we use time. And, of course, it includes the features most people think of when they consider nonverbal communication: body language, gestures, facial expression, and eye contact.

Nonverbal Skills Are Vital

It's hard to overemphasize the importance of effective nonverbal expression and the ability to read and respond to others' nonverbal behavior.[2] Nonverbal encoding and decoding skills are a strong predictor of popularity, attractiveness, and socioemotional well-being.[3] Good nonverbal communicators are more persuasive than people who are less skilled, and they have a greater chance of success in settings ranging from careers to poker games to romance. Nonverbal sensitivity is a major part of the "emotional intelligence" described in Chapter 5, and researchers have come to recognize that it is impossible to study spoken language without paying attention to its nonverbal dimensions.[4]

All Behavior Has Communicative Value

Suppose you tried not to communicate any messages at all. What would you do? Stop talking? Close your eyes? Curl up into a ball? Leave the room? You can probably see that even these behaviors communicate messages—that you're avoiding contact. One study demonstrated this fact.[5] When communicators were told not to express nonverbal clues, others viewed them as dull, withdrawn, uneasy, aloof, and deceptive. This impossibility of not communicating is extremely important to understand because it means that each of us is a kind of transmitter that cannot be shut off. No matter what we do, we give off information about ourselves.[6]

Stop for a moment and examine yourself as you read this. If someone were observing you now, what nonverbal clues would that person get about how you're feeling? Are you sitting forward or reclining back? Is your posture tense or relaxed? Are your eyes wide open, or do they keep closing? What does your facial expression communicate? Can you make your face expressionless? Don't people with expressionless faces communicate something to you?

Of course, we don't always intend to send nonverbal messages. Unintentional nonverbal behaviors differ from intentional ones.[7] For example, we often stammer, blush, frown, and sweat without meaning to do so. Whether or not our nonverbal behavior is intentional, others recognize it and make

20th Century Fox/Allstar

▲ Simian characters in *The Dawn of the Planet of the Apes* behave in ways that are recognizable to moviegoers. Their emotions are easy to gauge from their facial expressions, gestures, and body language, without a word being said. What nonverbal cues can you use to make informed guesses about how others are feeling?

interpretations about us based on their observations. Some theorists argue that unintentional behavior may provide information but that it shouldn't count as communication.[8] We draw the boundaries of nonverbal communication more broadly, suggesting that even unconscious and unintentional behavior conveys messages and thus is worth studying as communication.

Nonverbal Communication Is Primarily Relational

Some nonverbal messages serve utilitarian functions. For example, a police officer directs the flow of traffic, and a team of street surveyors uses hand motions to coordinate its work. But nonverbal communication more commonly expresses the kinds of relational (rather than content) messages discussed in Chapter 1 and the kinds of identity messages that you read about in Chapter 3.[9]

Consider, for example, the role of nonverbal communication in *impression management*.[10] Chapter 3 discussed how we strive to create an image of ourselves as we want others to view us. Nonverbal communication plays an important role in this process—in many cases more important than verbal communication. For instance, think what happens when you attend a party where you are likely to meet strangers you would like to get to know better. Instead of managing impressions verbally ("Hi! I'm attractive, friendly, and easygoing"), you behave in ways that will present this image. You might smile a lot and perhaps try to strike a relaxed pose. It's also likely that you dress carefully—even if that requires looking as though you hadn't given a lot of attention to your appearance.

Along with impression management, nonverbal communication *reflects and shapes the kinds of relationships we have with others*. Think about the wide range of ways you could behave when greeting another person. You could wave, shake hands, nod, smile, clap the other person on the back, give a hug, or avoid all contact. Each one of these decisions would send a message about the nature of your relationship with the other person. Within romantic relationships, nonverbal behaviors are especially important. For example, displays of affection such as sitting close, holding hands, and giving affectionate gazes are strongly connected to satisfaction and commitment in romantic relationships.[11]

Nonverbal communication performs a third valuable social function: *conveying emotions* that we may be unwilling or unable to express—or ones that we may not even be aware of. In fact, nonverbal communication is much better suited to expressing attitudes and feelings than ideas. You can prove this by imagining how you could express each item on the following list nonverbally:

a. You're tired.
b. You're in favor of capital punishment.
c. You're attracted to another person in the group.
d. You think prayer in the schools should be allowed.
e. You're angry at someone in the room.

This experiment shows that, short of charades, nonverbal messages are much better at expressing attitudes and emotions (a, c, and e) than other sorts of messages (b and d). Among other limitations, nonverbal messages can't convey:

Simple matters of fact ("The book was written in 1997.")

The past or future tenses ("I was happy yesterday"; "I'll be out of town next week.")

An imaginary idea ("What would it be like if ...")

Conditional statements ("If I don't get a job, I'll have to move out.")

Nonverbal Communication Occurs in Mediated Messages

As you read in Chapter 2, face-to-face communication is richer in nonverbal cues than mediated messages. Despite that fact, there is plenty of nonverbal information available when we use technology to communicate. Video calls obviously provide nonverbal information, as do photos on social networking sites. However, even text-based electronic communication has nonverbal features.

The most obvious way to represent nonverbal expressions in type is with *emoticons*, using keyboard characters like these:

- :-) Basic smile

- ;-) Wink and grin

- :-(Frown

- :-@ Screaming, swearing, very angry

- :-/ or :-\ Skeptical

- :-O Surprised, yelling, realization of an error

Many programs now turn these keystroke combinations into graphic icons, known as *emoji*. Emoticons and emoji can clarify the meaning that isn't evident from words alone.[12] For example, see how each graphic below creates a different meaning for the same statement:

- You are driving me crazy 😁

- You are driving me crazy 😠

- You are driving me crazy 😍

Just like their in-person counterparts, emoticons and emoji are ambiguous and can communicate a variety of nonverbal messages.[13] A smiley face could mean "I'm really happy," "I'm only kidding," or "I just zinged you." The same is true of other online communication markers.[14] Exclamation marks (sometimes more than one!!!) can be used at the end of sentences, or even by themselves, to denote a variety of emotional states. Ellipses (...) at the end of a phrase can signal displeasure, thoughtfulness, or bemusement. They can also be turn-taking signals, similar to what might be conveyed nonverbally with your face or with pauses during in-person conversations. And "lexical surrogates" such as "hmmm" or "ooooh" have meanings ranging from delight to disapproval. Paralinguistic markers like these are best understood within their communicative and relational contexts.

Not only does the content of a nonverbal message matter, but when it is sent matters as well.[15] If you've ever been upset by a friend who hasn't responded punctually to one of your texts, then you know the role that timeliness plays in mediated interpersonal communication. We'll talk more about *chronemics* later in this chapter, but here we want to note that time management is a vital feature of online interaction. It's also a good example of the principle that you cannot *not* communicate. Communicators have expectations about when others should reply to their posts, emails, and text messages, and delays can be perceived negatively.

Although nonverbal information can be communicated online, constant use of electronic channels can dull the perception of nonverbal cues. A group of preteens in one study was cut off from all forms of electronic communication for five days at camp.[16] Interaction with their peers during that period took place exclusively in person. When compared with a control group that was free to use electronic devices during that same period, those who were restricted from technology dramatically improved their ability to recognize others' nonverbal cues of emotion. This serves as a reminder that in-person communication offers greater access to important nonverbal cues than is available through most modes of electronic interaction.

Nonverbal Communication Serves Many Functions

Just because this chapter focuses on nonverbal communication, don't get the idea that our words and our actions are unrelated. Quite the opposite is true: Verbal and nonverbal communication are interconnected elements in every act of communication. (See Table 7.2 for a comparison of verbal and nonverbal communication.) Nonverbal behaviors can operate in several relationships with verbal behaviors.

Repeating If someone asked you for directions to the nearest drugstore, you might say, "North of here about two blocks," **repeating** your instructions

TABLE 7.2 Some Differences between Verbal and Nonverbal Communication

	VERBAL COMMUNICATION	NONVERBAL COMMUNICATION
Complexity	One dimension (words only)	Multiple dimensions (voice, posture, gestures, distance, etc.)
Flow	Intermittent (speaking and silence alternate)	Continuous (it's impossible to not communicate nonverbally)
Clarity	Less subject to misinterpretation	More ambiguous
Impact	Has less impact when verbal and nonverbal cues are contradictory	Has stronger impact when verbal and nonverbal cues are contradictory
Intentionality	Usually deliberate	Often unintentional

nonverbally by pointing north. This sort of repetition isn't just decorative: People remember comments accompanied by gestures more than those made with words alone.[17]

Complementing   Even when it doesn't repeat language, nonverbal behavior can reinforce what's been said. **Complementing** nonverbal behaviors match the thoughts and emotions the communicator is expressing linguistically. You can appreciate the value of this function by imagining the difference between saying "Thank you" with a sincere facial expression and tone of voice and saying the same words in a deadpan manner.

Substituting   When a friend asks "What's up?" you might shrug your shoulders instead of answering in words. Many facial expressions operate as substitutes for speech. It's easy to recognize expressions that function like verbal interjections and say "Gosh," "Really?," "Oh, please!," and so on.[18] Nonverbal **substituting** can be useful when communicators are reluctant to express their feelings in words. Faced with a message you find disagreeable, you might sigh, roll your eyes, or yawn when speaking out would not be appropriate. Likewise, a parent who wants a child to stop being disruptive at a party can flash a glare across the room without saying a word (and what child doesn't know the power of "the look" from Mom or Dad?).

Accenting   Just as we use italics to emphasize an idea in print, we use nonverbal devices to emphasize oral messages. Pointing an accusing finger adds emphasis to criticism (as well as probably creating defensiveness in the receiver). **Accenting** certain words with the voice ("It was *your* idea!") is another way to add nonverbal emphasis.

Regulating   Nonverbal behaviors can serve a **regulating** function by influencing the flow of verbal communication.[19] We can regulate conversations nonverbally by nodding (indicating "I understand" or "keep going"), looking away (signaling a lack of attention), or moving toward the door (communicating a desire to end the conversation). Of course, most of us have learned the hard way that nonverbal signals like these don't guarantee that the other party will pay attention to, interpret, or respond to them in the ways we had hoped.

Contradicting   People often express **contradicting** messages in their verbal and nonverbal behaviors. A common example of this sort of **mixed message** is the experience we've all had of hearing someone with a red face and bulging veins yelling, "Angry? No, I'm not angry!" In situations like these, we tend to believe the nonverbal message instead of the words.[20] A humorous illustration of this concept can be seen in the Cingular cell phone commercial "Mother Love" (available on popular video sites). A mother and daughter appear to be having an argument with raised voices, flailing arms, and scowling faces. Careful listening to their words, however, reveals that they're slinging compliments and praise at each other, including the phrases "I really like it!" and "I love you!" What makes the commercial amusing is that their verbal and nonverbal messages don't match—and it's easy to believe they're angry rather than happy, no matter what their words say.

She dresses in flags
comes on
like a mack truck
she paints
her eyelids green
and her mouth
is a loud speaker rasping out
profanity
at cocktail parties
she is everywhere
like a sheep dog
working a flock
nipping at your sleeve
spilling your drink
bestowing
wet sloppy kisses
but i
have received
secret messages
carefully written
from the shy
quiet woman
who hides
in this
bizarre
gaudy castle

Ric Masten

© SuperStock/SuperStock

Nonverbal Communication Offers Deception Clues

When message senders are telling lies, their nonverbal behavior sometimes gives them away. Inadvertent signals of deception—often called **leakage**—can come through a variety of nonverbal channels.

Some of these channels are more revealing than others. Facial expressions offer important information,[21] but deceivers also pay more attention to monitoring these cues in an attempt to maintain a "poker face." More reliable is pupil dilation, a physiological response that can't easily be controlled.[22] Speech patterns also offer a variety of leakage clues.[23] In one experiment, subjects

TABLE 7.3 Leakage of Nonverbal Cues to Deception

Deception Cues Are More Likely When the Deceiver

Wants to hide emotions being felt at the moment
Feels strongly about the information being hidden
Feels apprehensive or guilty about the deception
Gets little enjoyment from being deceptive
Has not had time to rehearse the lie in advance
Knows there are severe punishments for being caught

Based on Ekman, P. (2001). Telling lies. New York: Norton.

who were encouraged to be deceitful made more speech errors, spoke for shorter periods of time, and had a lower rate of speech than did others who were encouraged to express themselves honestly. Another experiment revealed that the pitch of a liar's voice tends to be higher than that of a truth teller. Liars leak nonverbal cues of deception in some situations more than others. Table 7.3 outlines some conditions under which leakage is more likely.

A variety of self-help books and seminars claim that liars can be easily identified by monitoring their nonverbal cues, but scientific research doesn't support that notion. Communication scholars Judee Burgoon and Tim Levine have studied deception detection for years. In their review of decades of research on the subject, they came up with what they call "Deception Detection 101"—three findings that have been repeatedly supported in studies.[24] They are:

- We are accurate in detecting deception only slightly more than half the time—in other words, only a shade better than what we could achieve with a coin flip.

- We overestimate our abilities to detect other's lies—in other words, we're not as good at catching deception as we think we are.

- We have a strong tendency to judge others' messages as truthful—in other words, we want to believe people wouldn't lie to us (which biases our ability to detect deceit).

As one writer put it, "There is no unique telltale signal for a fib. Pinocchio's nose just doesn't exist, and that makes liars difficult to spot."[25] Moreover, some popular prescriptions about liars' nonverbal behaviors simply aren't accurate.

Fx Network/Allstar

⋀ In the TV series *The Americans*, Russian spies Philip (Matthew Rhys) and Elizabeth (Keri Russell) must carefully monitor their nonverbal cues so as not to give away their identities. This means paying close attention to every detail—their apparel, eye contact, proxemics, accents—in an attempt to seem "American" (and happily married). What do your nonverbal cues reveal about where and how you were raised? In what ways do you change those cues depending on the situation?

For instance, conventional wisdom suggests that liars avert their gaze and fidget more than nonliars. Research, however, shows just the opposite: Liars often sustain *more* eye contact and fidget *less*, in part because they believe that to do otherwise might look deceitful.[26] While it's possible to make some generalizations about the nonverbal tendencies of liars, caution should be exercised in making evaluations of others' truth telling based on limited and ambiguous nonverbal cues.[27]

Nonverbal Communication Is Ambiguous

You learned in Chapter 5 that verbal messages are open to multiple interpretations, but nonverbal messages are even more ambiguous. For example, consider the photo seen here. What do you think is the relationship between the people in it? Can you be sure? Or consider the example of a wink: In one study, college students interpreted this nonverbal signal as meaning a variety of things, including an expression of thanks, a sign of friendliness, a measure of insecurity, a sexual come-on, and an eye problem.[28]

Even the most common nonverbal behavior can be ambiguous. A group of Safeway supermarket employees filed grievances over the company's "Superior Service" policy that required workers to smile and make eye contact with customers. The grocery clerks reported that some customers took the friendly greetings as come-ons.[29] Although nonverbal behavior can be very revealing, it can have so many possible meanings that it's impossible to be certain which interpretation is correct. Law-enforcement officials in California discouraged one motorist group from publicizing a set of hand signals drivers

could use to signal one another with messages such as "Danger ahead" or "There's a problem with your car." They warned that hand signs could be misinterpreted as gang signs that would provoke violent reactions.[30]

The ambiguous nature of nonverbal behavior becomes clear in the area of courtship and sexuality. Does a kiss mean "I like you a lot" or "I want to have sex"? Does pulling away from a romantic partner mean "Stop now" or "Keep trying"? Communication researchers explored this question by surveying one hundred college students about sexual consent in twelve dating scenarios in order to discover under what conditions verbal approaches (for example, "Do you want to have sex with me?") were considered preferable to nonverbal indicators (such as kissing as an indicator of a desire to have sex).[31] In every scenario, verbal consent was seen as less ambiguous than nonverbal consent. This doesn't mean that romantic partners don't rely on nonverbal signals; many of the respondents indicated that they interpret nonverbal cues (such as kissing) as signs of sexual willingness. However, nonverbal cues were far less likely to be misunderstood when accompanied by verbal cues.

Some people have more difficulty decoding nonverbal signals than do others. For people with a syndrome called *nonverbal learning disorder* (NVLD), reading facial expressions, tone of voice, and other cues is dramatically more difficult.[32] Because of a processing deficit in the right hemisphere of the brain, people with NVLD have trouble making sense of many nonverbal cues. Humor or sarcasm can be especially difficult to understand for people—especially children—with NVLD. For example, if they learn the right way to introduce themselves to an unfamiliar adult (by shaking hands and saying "Pleased to meet you"), they may attempt the same response in a group of children where it might be viewed as odd or "nerdy." When peers do give them subtle feedback, such as raised eyebrows, they miss the information completely and therefore cannot modify their behavior next time.[33]

Even for those of us who don't suffer from NVLD, the ambiguity of nonverbal behavior can be frustrating. The perception-checking skill you learned in Chapter 4 can be a useful tool for figuring out what meanings you can accurately attach to confusing cues.

PAUSE *and* REFLECT

Body Language

MindTap **REFLECT ...** on body language by answering the following questions, either here or online.

This exercise will both increase your skill in observing nonverbal behavior and show you the dangers of being too sure that you're a perfect reader of body language. Begin by choosing a partner from your class. You can try the exercise either in or out of class, and the period of time over which you do it is flexible—from a single class period to several days. Follow these directions:

1. For the first period of time (however long you decide to make it), observe the way your partner behaves. Notice movements, mannerisms, postures, style of dress, and so on. To remember your observations, jot them down. If you're doing this exercise out of class over an extended period of time, there's no need to let your observations interfere with whatever you'd normally be doing: Your only job here is to compile a list of your partner's behaviors. In this step, you should be careful *not to interpret* your partner's behaviors—just record what you see.

2. At the end of the time period, share what you've seen with your partner, who should do the same with you.

3. For the next period of time, your job not only is to observe your partner's behavior but also to *interpret* it. This time in your conference you should tell your partner what you thought his or her behaviors revealed. For example, does careless dressing suggest oversleeping, loss of interest in appearance, or the desire to feel more comfortable? If you noticed frequent yawning, did you think this meant boredom, fatigue after a late night, or sleepiness after a big meal? Don't feel bad if your guesses weren't all correct. Remember that nonverbal clues tend to be ambiguous. You may be surprised how checking out the nonverbal clues you observe can help build a relationship with another person.

INFLUENCES ON NONVERBAL COMMUNICATION

The way we communicate nonverbally is influenced to a certain degree by biological sex and to a great degree by the way we are socialized. To learn more about these influences, read on.

Gender

It's easy to identify stereotypical differences in male and female styles of nonverbal communication. Just think about exaggerated caricatures of macho men and delicate women that appear from time to time. Many jokes, as well as humorous films and plays, have been created around the results that arise when characters try to act like members of the opposite sex.

Although few of us behave like stereotypically masculine or feminine movie characters, there are recognizable differences in the way men and women look and act. Some of the most obvious differences are physiological: height, depth and volume of the voice, and so on. Other differences are rooted more in socialization. In general, females are usually more nonverbally expressive, and they are better at recognizing others' nonverbal behavior.[34] More specifically, research shows that, compared to men, women smile more; use more facial expression; use more head, hand, and arm gestures (but less expansive gestures); touch others more; stand closer to others; are more vocally expressive; and make more eye contact.[35]

After looking at differences like these, it might seem as if men and women communicate in radically different ways. In fact, men's and women's nonverbal communication is more similar than different in many respects.[36] Differences like the ones described in the preceding paragraph are noticeable, but they are outweighed by the similar rules we follow in areas such as making eye contact, posture, gestures, and so on. You can prove this by imagining what it would be like to use radically different nonverbal rules: standing only an inch away from others, sniffing strangers, or tapping the forehead of someone when you want his or her attention. Moreover, male–female nonverbal differences are less pronounced in conversations involving gay and lesbian participants.[37] Gender certainly has an influence on nonverbal style, but the differences are often a matter of degree rather than kind.

Culture

Cultures have different nonverbal languages as well as verbal ones.[38] Fiorello LaGuardia, legendary mayor of New York from 1933 to 1945, was fluent in English, Italian, and Yiddish. Researchers who watched films of his campaign speeches found that they could tell with the sound turned off which language he was speaking by noticing the changes in his nonverbal behavior.[39]

Some nonverbal behaviors have different meanings from culture to culture. The OK gesture made by joining the tips of thumb and forefinger to form a circle is a cheery affirmation to most Americans, but it has less positive meanings in other parts of the world.[40] In France and Belgium, it means "You're worth zero." In Greece and Turkey, it is a vulgar sexual invitation, usually meant as an insult. Given this sort of cross-cultural ambiguity, it's easy to imagine how an innocent tourist might wind up in serious trouble.

Culture also affects how nonverbal cues are monitored. In Japan, for instance, people tend to look to the eyes for emotional cues, whereas Americans and Europeans focus on the mouth.[41] These differences can be seen in the text-based emoticons used in these cultures. American emoticons focus on mouth expressions, while Japanese emoticons feature the eyes. (Search for "Western and Eastern emoticons" in your browser for examples.)

Even though we recognize that differences exist in the nonverbal rules of different cultures, subtle differences can damage relationships without the parties ever recognizing exactly what has gone wrong. Anthropologist Edward Hall points out that, whereas Americans are comfortable conducting business at a distance of roughly 4 feet, people from the Middle East stand much closer.[42] It is easy to visualize the awkward advance-and-retreat pattern that might occur when two diplomats or businesspeople from these cultures meet. The Middle Easterner would probably keep moving forward to close the gap, whereas the American would continually back away. Both would feel uncomfortable, probably without knowing why.

kosmos11/Shutterstock.com

Like distance, patterns of eye contact vary around the world.[43] A direct gaze is considered appropriate, if not imperative, for speakers seeking power in Latin America, the Arab world, and southern Europe. However, Asians, Indians, Pakistanis, and northern Europeans gaze at a listener peripherally or not at all out of respect rather than a lack of interest.[44] In either case, deviations from the norm are likely to make a listener uncomfortable.

The use of time depends greatly on culture.[45] Some cultures (e.g., North American, German, and Swiss) tend to be **monochronic**, emphasizing punctuality, schedules, and completing one task at a time. Other cultures (e.g., South American, Mediterranean, and Arab) are more **polychronic**, with flexible schedules in which multiple tasks are pursued at the same time.[46] One psychologist discovered the difference between North and South American attitudes when teaching at a university in Brazil.[47] He found that some Brazilian students arrived halfway through a two-hour class and most of them stayed put and kept asking questions when the class was scheduled to end. A half-hour after the official end of the class, the psychologist finally closed off discussion because there was no indication that the students intended to leave. This flexibility of time is quite different from what is common in most North American colleges!

As Table 7.4 shows, differences in cultural rules can lead to misunderstandings. For example, observations have shown that black women in all-black groups are nonverbally more expressive and interrupt one another

TABLE 7.4 Cultural Differences in Nonverbal Communication Can Lead to Misunderstandings

Behaviors that have one meaning for members of the same culture or co-culture can be interpreted differently by members of other groups.

BEHAVIOR	PROBABLE IN-GROUP PERCEPTION	POSSIBLE OUT-GROUP PERCEPTION
Avoidance of direct eye contact (Latino/Latina)	Used to communicate attentiveness or respect	A sign of inattentiveness; direct eye contact is preferred
Aggressively challenging a point with which one disagrees (African American)	Acceptable means of dialogue; not regarded as verbal abuse or a precursor to violence	Arguments are viewed as inappropriate and a sign of potential imminent violence
Use of finger gestures to beckon others (Asian)	Appropriate if used by adults for children, but highly offensive if directed at adults	Appropriate gesture to use with both children and adults
Silence (Native American)	Sign of respect, thoughtfulness, and/or uncertainty/ambiguity	Interpreted as boredom, disagreement, or refusal to participate
Touch (Latino/Latina)	Normal and appropriate for interpersonal interactions	Deemed appropriate for some intimate or friendly interactions; otherwise perceived as a violation of personal space
Public display of intense emotions (African American)	Accepted and valued as measure of expressiveness; appropriate in most settings	Violates expectations for self-controlled public behaviors; inappropriate in most public settings
Touching or holding hands of same-sex friends (Asian)	Acceptable in behavior that signifies closeness in platonic relationships	Perceived as inappropriate, especially for male friends

more than white women in all-white groups. This doesn't mean that black women always feel more intensely than their white counterparts. A more likely explanation is that the two groups follow different cultural rules. One study found that in racially mixed groups both black and white women moved closer to each others' style.[48] This nonverbal convergence shows that skilled communicators can adapt their behavior when interacting with members of other cultures or subcultures in order to make the exchange smoother and more effective.

Despite the many cultural differences, some nonverbal behaviors have the same meanings around the world. Smiles and laughter are universal signals of positive emotions, for example, whereas sour expressions are universal signals of displeasure.[49] Charles Darwin believed that expressions like these are the result of evolution, functioning as survival mechanisms that allowed early humans to convey emotional states before the development of language. The innateness of some facial expressions becomes even clearer when we examine the behavior of children who are born with impaired hearing and sight.[50] Despite a lack of social learning, these children often display a broad range of expression. They smile, laugh, and cry in ways that are similar to those of seeing and hearing children. In other words, nonverbal behavior—like much of our communication—is influenced by both our genetic heritage and our culture.

TYPES OF NONVERBAL COMMUNICATION

Keeping the characteristics of nonverbal communication in mind, let's look at some of the ways we communicate in addition to words.

Body Movement

The first area of nonverbal communication we'll discuss is the broad field of **kinesics**, or body position and motion. In this section, we'll explore the role that body orientation, posture, gestures, facial expressions, and eye contact play in our relationships with one another.

Body Orientation   We'll start with **body orientation**—the degree to which we face toward or away from someone with our body, feet, and head. To understand how this kind of physical positioning communicates nonverbal messages, imagine that you and a friend are in the middle of a conversation when a third person approaches and wants to join you. You're not especially glad to see this person, but you don't want to sound rude by asking him to leave. By turning your body slightly away from the intruder, you can make your feelings very clear. The nonverbal message here is "We're interested in each other right now and don't want to include you in our conversation." The general rule is that facing someone directly signals your interest and facing away signals a desire to avoid involvement.

You can learn a good deal about how people feel by observing the way people position themselves. The next time you're in a crowded place where people can choose whom to face directly, try noticing who seems to be included in the action and who is being subtly shut out. And in the same way, pay attention to your own body orientation. You may be surprised to discover that you're avoiding a certain person without being conscious of it or that at times you're "turning your back" on people altogether. If this is the case, it may be helpful to figure out why.

Posture   Another way we communicate nonverbally is through **posture**. To see if this is true, stop reading for a moment and notice how you're sitting. What does your position say nonverbally about how you feel? Are there any other people near you now? What messages do you get from their current posture? By paying attention to the postures of those around you, as well as your own, you'll find another channel of nonverbal communication that can furnish information about how people feel about themselves and one another.

An indication of how much posture communicates is shown by our language. It's full of expressions that link emotional states with body postures:

I won't take this lying down! (Nor will I stand for it!)

I feel the weight of the world on my shoulders.

He's a real slouch in the office (but he's no slouch on the basketball court).

She's been sitting on that project for weeks.

Posture may be the least ambiguous type of nonverbal behavior. In one study, 176 computer-generated mannequin figures were created, and observers were asked to assign emotions to particular postural configurations. The raters had more than 90-percent agreement on postures that were connected with anger, sadness, and happiness.[51] Some postures seem easier to interpret than others. Disgust was the emotion that was hardest to identify from body posture, and some raters thought that surprise and happiness had similar postural configurations.

Tension and relaxation offer other postural keys to feelings. We take relaxed postures in nonthreatening situations and tighten up in threatening situations.[52] Based on this observation, we can tell a good deal about how others feel simply by watching how tense or loose they seem to be. For example, tenseness is a way of detecting status differences: The lower-status person is generally the more rigid and tense-appearing one, and the higher-status person appears more relaxed. Research shows that adopting a high-status pose—such as putting your feet up on a desk with hands clasped behind your head—can actually lead to increased feelings of power.[53]

Gestures   Movements of the hands and arms—**gestures**—are an important type of nonverbal communication. Some social scientists claim that a language of gestures was the first form of human communication, preceding speech by tens of thousands of years.[54]

The most common forms of gestures are what social scientists call **illustrators**—movements that accompany speech but don't stand on their own.[55] For instance, if someone on a street corner asked you how to get to a restaurant across town, you might offer street names and addresses—but all the while you'd probably point with your fingers and gesture with your hands to illustrate how to get there. Remove the words from your directions and it's unlikely that the other person would ever find the restaurant. Think also of people who like to "talk with their hands," gesturing vigorously even when they're conversing on the phone and can't be seen by the other party. Research shows that North Americans use illustrators more often when they are emotionally aroused—trying to explain ideas that are difficult to put into words when they are furious, horrified, agitated, distressed, or excited.[56] Studies also show that it is easier to comprehend and learn a second language when it is accompanied by illustrators and other nonverbal cues.[57]

A second type of gestures is **emblems**—deliberate nonverbal behaviors that have a precise meaning and are known to virtually everyone within a cultural group. Unlike illustrators, emblems can stand on their own and often function as replacements for words. For example, all North Americans know that a head nod means "Yes," a head shake means "No," a wave means "Hello" or "Goodbye," and a hand to the ear means "I can't hear you." And almost every Westerner over the age of seven knows the meaning of a raised middle finger. It's important to remember, however, that the meanings of emblems like these are not universal. For instance, the "thumbs-up" sign means "good" in the United States but is an obscene gesture in Iraq and several other countries.[58]

A third type of gestures is **adaptors**—unconscious bodily movements in response to the environment. For instance, shivering when it's cold and folding your arms to get warmer are examples of adaptors. Of course, sometimes we cross our arms when we're feeling "cold" toward another person—and thus adaptors can reveal the climate of our relationships. In particular, self-touching behaviors—sometimes called **manipulators**—are often a sign of discomfort, such as fiddling with your hands or rubbing your arms during an interview.[59] But not *all* fidgeting signals uneasiness. People also are likely to engage in self-touching when relaxed. When they let down their guard (either alone or with friends), they will be more likely to fiddle with an earlobe, twirl a strand of hair, or clean their fingernails. Whether or not the fidgeter is hiding something, observers are likely to interpret these behaviors as a signal of dishonesty. Because not all fidgeters are dishonest, it's important not to jump to conclusions about the meaning of adaptors.

Actually, *too few* gestures may be just as significant an indicator of mixed messages as *too many*.[60] Limited gesturing may signal a lack of interest, sadness, boredom, or low enthusiasm. Illustrators also decrease whenever someone is cautious about speaking. For these reasons, a careful observer will look for either an increase or a decrease in the usual level of gestures.

On the JOB

Nonverbal Communication in Job Interviews

The old adage "You never get a second chance to make a first impression" is never truer than in job interviews. The impression you make in the first few minutes of this crucial conversation can define the way a prospective employer views you—and thus the path of your career. Research highlights the vital role that nonverbal communication plays in shaping how interviewers regard job applicants.[a]

Here's a look at three specific behaviors that have been the subject of studies on employment interviewing:

- *Handshaking*. In American culture, most professional interactions begin with a handshake. As simple as this ritual might seem, research shows that the quality of a handshake is related to interviewer hiring recommendations. Handshakes should be firm and energetic without being overpowering—and this holds true for both men and women.[b]

- *Attire and Appearance*. Being well dressed and properly groomed is basic to interview success. A business-appropriate appearance enhances perceptions of a candidate's credibility and social skills. A rule of thumb is that it's better to err on the side of formality than casualness, and conservative colors and fashion are preferable to being flashy.[c]

- *Smiling*. While it may seem obvious, one study found that "authentically smiling interviewees were judged to be more suitable and were more likely to be short-listed and selected for the job."[d] The word *authentically* is important—judges in the study made negative appraisals of plastered-on smiles that didn't seem genuine. The key is to smile naturally and regularly, exhibiting a friendly and pleasant demeanor.

It's easy to imagine how other nonverbal cues discussed in this chapter (e.g., eye contact, posture, tone of voice, etc.) are vital in making a good impression in a job interview. For more information, consult the myriad books and websites devoted to employment interviewing. You can also visit your school's career-development center or perhaps even take a course in interviewing. In every case, you'll be coached that what you do and how you look is as important as what you say in a job interview.

THE EYES HAVE IT

Look inside your kitchen cabinet and odds are you have a collection of old friends gazing back at you—the Quaker Oats man, the Sun-Maid girl, Aunt Jemima, and maybe a Keebler elf or two. The reason they are there may have more do with your subconscious craving for eye contact than the taste of the products.

In a study published in the journal *Environment and Behavior*, researchers at Cornell University manipulated the gaze of the cartoon rabbit on Trix cereal boxes and found that adult subjects were more likely to choose Trix over competing brands if the rabbit was looking at them rather than away.

"Making eye contact even with a character on a cereal box inspires powerful feelings of connection," said Brian Wansink, one of the study's authors.

This follows a flurry of recent research on the magnetic and mesmeric nature of eye contact and its essential role in developing emotional stability and social fluency. Studies show that newborns instinctively lock eyes with their caregivers. Researchers have also found that children and adults who avoid or are denied eye contact are more likely to suffer from depression and feelings of isolation as well as exhibit antisocial traits such as callousness. This is alarming in a society where people increasingly spend more time looking at their mobile devices than at one another.

Eye contact makes us more socially aware and empathetic. It allows us to make sense of our relationships and social orientation. Avoiding eye contact out of fear or insecurity, or breaking eye contact to read a text, check email, or play Candy Crush, degrades your social facility and emotional intelligence.

Researchers at Northwestern University found that patients of doctors who made more eye contact had better health, adhered more to medical advice and were more likely to seek treatment for future problems. Not surprisingly, doctors who brought laptops into the examining room made less eye contact.

"Eye contact is a really good surrogate for where attention is and the level of accord building in a relationship," said Enid Montague, a professor of engineering and medicine at Northwestern who used video recordings of 100 patient visits to a primary care clinic for her analysis. "We found eye contact leads to significantly better patient outcomes."

Which brings us back to the Quaker Oats man and Aunt Jemima gazing out of your kitchen cabinet—not to mention Chef Boyardee, Cap'n Crunch, Uncle Ben, and the Gerber baby. It's probably no accident that these brands have endured while some competing brands with fancy fonts and clever graphics—but no eye contact—have fallen by the wayside.

Kate Murphy

MindTap **ENHANCE …**

your understanding by answering the following questions, either here or online.

1. Observe the degree of eye contact others use when they engage with you. Based on your experience, what is the optimal level of eye contact in varying types of relationships and contexts?

2. Pay attention to your level of eye contact in important personal relationships. How might adjusting this level change the nature of your interactions?

Face and Eyes   The face and eyes are probably the most noticed parts of the body, but this doesn't mean that their nonverbal messages are the easiest to read. The face is a tremendously complicated channel of expression for several reasons.

First, it's difficult to describe the number and kind of expressions we produce with our face and eyes. Researchers have found that there are at least eight distinguishable positions of the eyebrows and forehead, eight of the eyes and lids, and ten for the lower face.[61] When you multiply this complexity by the number of emotions we feel, you can see why it's almost impossible to compile a dictionary of facial expressions and their corresponding emotions.

Second, facial expressions are difficult to understand because of the speed with which they can change. For example, slow-motion films show **microexpressions** fleeting across a subject's face in as short a time as it takes to blink an eye.[62] Without being aware, liars may leak how they genuinely feel through brief furrows of the brow, pursing of the lips, or crinkling around the eyes.[63] Microexpressions like these are more likely to occur during what's known as "high-stakes" lying, such as when there are severe punishments for being caught.[64] Keep in mind that slow-motion recordings and trained professionals are often required to pick up these brief deception cues.

Despite the complex way in which the face shows emotions, you can still pick up clues by watching faces carefully. One of the easiest ways is to look for expressions that seem too exaggerated to be true. For instance, genuine facial expressions usually last no longer than five seconds—anything more and we start to doubt they are real (contestants in pageants with smiles plastered on their faces often come across as "fake" or "plastic").[65] Another way to detect feelings is to watch others' expressions when they aren't likely to be thinking about their appearance. We've all had the experience of glancing into another car while stopped in a traffic jam, or of looking around at a sporting event, and seeing expressions that the wearer would probably never show in more guarded moments.

The eyes can send several kinds of messages. Meeting someone's glance with your eyes is usually a sign of involvement, whereas looking away is often a sign of a desire to avoid contact. This principle has a practical application in commerce: Customers leave larger tips when their servers (male and female) maintain eye contact with them.[66] Research also shows that communicators who make direct eye contact are far more likely to get others to comply with their requests than are those who make evasive glances.[67] We'll see later in this chapter how the same principle holds true with touching others—which is why the term *eye contact* is relevant. A sense of connection leads to compliance.

Another kind of message the eyes communicate is a positive or negative attitude.[68] When someone looks toward us with the proper facial expression, we get a clear message that the looker is interested in us—hence the expression "making eyes." At the same time, when our long glances toward someone else are avoided, we can be pretty sure that the other person isn't as interested in a relationship as we are. (Of course, there are all sorts of courtship games in which the receiver of a glance pretends not to notice any message by glancing away yet signals interest with some other part of the body.) The eyes can also communicate both dominance and submission.[69] We've all played the game of trying to stare down somebody, and there are times when downcast eyes are a sign of giving in.

Looking at DIVERSITY

Photo courtesy of Annie Donnellon

Annie Donnellon: Blindness and Nonverbal Cues

I have been blind since birth, so I've never had access to many of the nonverbal cues that sighted people use. In fact, I think that "sightlings" (a pet name for my friends who are sighted) take for granted how much of their meaning comes through nonverbal channels. When I recently took an interpersonal communication course, the material on nonverbal communication was in some ways a foreign language to me.

For instance, I felt a bit left out when the class discussed things like body movement, eye contact, and facial expressions. I understand how these cues work, but I haven't experienced many of them myself. I have never "stared someone down" or "shot a look" at anyone (at least not intentionally!). While I know that some people "talk with their hands," that's something I've never witnessed and rarely do.

When the subject turned to paralanguage, I was back on familiar territory. I listen very carefully to the way people speak to figure out what they're thinking and feeling. My family and friends tell me I'm more tuned in to these issues than most sightlings are. It's typical for me to ask "Are you okay today?" when friends send messages that seem mixed. They may say everything's fine, but their voice often tells a different story.

I'm a singer and performer, and some of my biggest frustrations have come from well-meaning teachers who coach me on my nonverbals. I remember one acting instructor asking me, "How do you think your character would express herself nonverbally

in this scene?" and I thought to myself "I have no idea." People who are sighted may think that anger cues like clenched fists, rigid posture, or shrugged shoulders are "natural" expressions, but I believe that many of them are learned by watching others.

Let me pass along some keys that can help make communication smoother and more effective. It's important to mention your name when starting a conversation with people who are blind: Don't assume they can figure out who you are from your voice. At the end of a conversation, please say that you're leaving. I often feel embarrassed when I'm talking to someone, only to find out that they walked away mid-sentence.

Most important: Clue in visually-impaired people when something is going on that they can't see. Often at my sorority meetings, something will happen that everyone is laughing about, but I'm left out of the loop because I can't see the nonverbal cues. Over the years my friends and family have learned that whispering a quick description of the events helps me feel more a part of the interaction.

The interpersonal course I took was an enriching experience for me, my professor, and my classmates. I think we learned a lot from each other—especially about the vital and complex role of nonverbal communication in interpersonal relationships.

"Blindness and Nonverbal Cues" by Annie Donnellon. Used with permission of author.

Voice

The voice is another channel of nonverbal communication. Social scientists use the term **paralanguage** to describe nonverbal, vocal messages. The way a message is spoken can give the same word or words many meanings. For example, note how many meanings come from a single sentence just by shifting the emphasis from one word to another:

This is a fantastic communication book. (Not just any book, but *this* one in particular.)

This is a *fantastic* communication book. (This book is superior, exciting.)

This is a fantastic *communication* book. (The book is good as far as communication goes; it may not be so great as literature or drama.)

This is a fantastic communication *book*. (It's not a play or album; it's a book.)

There are many other ways we communicate paralinguistically through tone, rate, pitch, volume—even through pauses. Consider two types of pauses that can lead to communication snags. The first is the *unintentional pause*—those times when people stop to collect their thoughts before deciding how best to continue their verbal message. It's no surprise that liars tend to have more unintentional pauses than truth tellers, as they often make up stories on the fly.[70] When people pause at length after being asked a delicate question ("Did you like the gift I bought you?"), it might mean they're buying time to come up with a face-saving—and perhaps less-than-honest—response.

A second type of pause is the *vocalized pause*. These range from disfluencies such as "um," "er," and "uh" to filler words that are used habitually such as "like," "okay," and "ya know." Research shows that vocalized pauses reduce a person's perceived credibility[71] and negatively affect perceptions of candidates in job interviews.[72] When Caroline Kennedy was considering running for the Senate, her press tour interviews were filled with vocalized pauses. In one case she used "ya know" 142 times in a single interview with *The New York Times*. Although this wasn't the reason she decided not to run for office, many commentators noted that it certainly didn't help her professional image.[73]

Researchers have identified the power of paralanguage through the use of content-free speech—ordinary speech that has been electronically manipulated so that the words are unintelligible but the paralanguage remains unaffected. (Hearing a foreign language that you don't understand has the same effect.) Subjects who hear content-free speech can consistently recognize the emotion being expressed as well as identify its strength.[74] Young children respond to the paralanguage of adults, warming up to those who speak warmly and shying away from those who speak in a less-friendly manner.[75]

Paralanguage can affect behavior in many ways, some of which are rather surprising. Researchers have discovered that communicators are most likely to comply with requests delivered by speakers whose rate was similar to their own: People who spoke rapidly responded most favorably to rapid talkers, whereas slow speakers preferred others whose rate was also slow.[76] Besides complying with same-rate speakers, listeners also feel more positively about people who speak at their own rate.

Sarcasm is one instance in which we use both emphasis and tone of voice to change a statement's meaning to the opposite of its verbal message. Experience this reversal yourself with the following three statements. First say them literally and then sarcastically.

"Thanks a lot!"

"I really had a wonderful time on my blind date."

"There's nothing I like better than lima beans."

As they do with other nonverbal messages, people often ignore or misinterpret the vocal nuances of sarcasm. Members of certain groups—children, people with weak intellectual skills, and poor listeners—are more likely to misunderstand sarcastic messages than others.[77] In one study, children younger than age ten lacked the linguistic sophistication to tell when a message was sarcastic.[78]

The Way You Talk Can Hurt You?

Women have a distinctive style of speaking: "I was shopping last night? And I saw this wonderful dress? It was so black and slinky?" It's hard to convey intonation in print, but the question marks indicate a rise in pitch at the end of the sentence, as in a question. Many women, especially younger women, use this intonation in declarative sentences: "This is Sally Jones? I have an appointment with Dr. Smith? And I'd like to change it to another day?"

I cringe when I hear this. The rising intonation sounds timid and lacking in self-confidence; the speaker seems to be asking for approval or permission to speak when there's no need to. She should make her point straightforwardly, in an assertion that drops in pitch as it ends.

And I worry that rising intonation harms women. It gets them taken less seriously than they should be in public debates; it encourages salesmen and car mechanics to cheat them when they wouldn't try cheating a man.

A woman friend who studies languages says I've got it wrong. Unlike men, who use conversation to fight for status, she tells me, women see it as cooperative. And they use rising pitch to convey this to their audience. Their tone encourages the supportive interjections, such as "Uh-huh," "Exactly," and "I know what you mean," with which women far more than men interlard each other's speech. And it asks listeners to contribute their ideas on the speaker's topic.

At the very least, women's use of rising intonation involves an ambiguity. It uses a sound that in other contexts conveys timidity, for a very different purpose. Given this ambiguity, we shouldn't be surprised if female speakers who are trying to be cooperative are often heard as hesitant.

It's clearly idiotic to treat conversation as a contest, as so many men do. We'd all benefit from a more cooperative approach. But we need a new symbol to express this, one with no connotations of weakness.

If we find this symbol, we can all, men and women, speak in friendly but firm tones. We can tell anecdotes without lecturing but also without seeming to kowtow. When we call the doctor's, we can say: "This is Sally (or Sam) Jones." (No question about it.) "I have an appointment with Dr. Smith." (I'm reminding you of a fact.) "And I'd like to change it to another day." (Now, can you help me?)

Thomas Hurka

MindTap ENHANCE ...

your understanding by answering the following questions, either here or online.

1. Can you identify people in your life who speak the way the author describes in this reading? If so, what is your reaction to them?
2. Describe the role that tone of voice plays in getting you to comply with requests and directives from others.
3. Are there changes you might consider making in your paralanguage to become a more effective communicator?

Some vocal factors are perceived more positively than others. For example, communicators who speak loudly and without hesitations are viewed as more confident than those who pause and speak quietly.[79] People with more-attractive voices are rated more highly than those with less-attractive voices.[80] Just what makes a voice attractive can vary. As Figure 7.1 shows, culture can make a difference. Surveys show that there are both similarities and differences between what Mexicans and Americans view as the ideal voice. Accent plays an important role in shaping perceptions. Generally speaking, accents that identify a speaker's membership in a group lead to more positive evaluations (if the group is high status) or to negative evaluations (if the group is low status).[81]

Touch

Shortly after her husband was elected U.S. president, First Lady Michelle Obama violated diplomatic protocol by returning the hug of Great Britain's Queen Elizabeth II. Some observers were appalled, and others delighted. Regardless of their reaction, everyone would have agreed that touch is a powerful way of communicating.

Social scientists use the word **haptics** to describe the study of touching. Touch can communicate many messages and signal a variety of relationships, such as the following:[82]

Functional and professional (dental exam, haircut)

Social and polite (handshake)

Friendship and warmth (clap on back, Spanish *abrazo*)

Sexual arousal (some kisses, strokes)

Aggression (shoves, slaps)

Some nonverbal behaviors occur in several types of relationships. A kiss, for example, can mean anything from a polite but superficial greeting to the most intense arousal. What makes a given touch more or less intense? Researchers have suggested several factors:

Which part of the body does the touching

Which part of the body is touched

How long the touch lasts

How much pressure is used

Whether there is movement after contact is made

Whether anyone else is present

The situation in which the touch occurs

The relationship between the people involved[83]

From this list you can see that there is, indeed, a complex language of touch. Because nonverbal messages are inherently ambiguous, it's no surprise that this language can often be misunderstood. Is a hug playful or suggestive of stronger feelings? Is a touch on the shoulder a friendly gesture or an

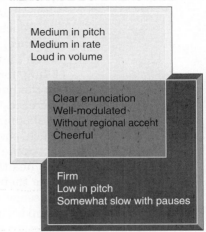

MEXICAN IDEAL SPEAKER'S VOICE

Medium in pitch
Medium in rate
Loud in volume

Clear enunciation
Well-modulated
Without regional accent
Cheerful

Firm
Low in pitch
Somewhat slow with pauses

U.S. IDEAL SPEAKER'S VOICE

∧ **FIGURE 7.1**

A Comparison of the Ideal Speakers' Voice Types in Mexico and the United States

Adapted from "Communicative Power: Gender and Culture as Determinants of the Ideal Voice," in *Women and Communicative Power: Theory, Research and Practice*, edited by Carol A. Valentine and Nancy Hoar. ©1988 by SCA. Reprinted by permission.

attempt at domination? The ambiguity of nonverbal behavior often leads to serious problems.

Touch plays a powerful role in shaping how we respond to others. For instance, in a laboratory task, subjects evaluated partners more positively when they were touched (appropriately, of course) by them.[84] Besides increasing liking, touch also increases compliance. A restaurant server's fleeting touches on the hand and shoulder result in larger tips.[85] Touching customers in a store increases their shopping time, their evaluation of the store, and also the amount of shopping.[86] When an offer to try samples of a product is accompanied by a touch, customers are more likely to try the sample and buy the product.[87]

Some of the most pronounced benefits of touching occur in medicine and the health and helping professions. For example, patients are more likely to take their medicines when physicians give a slight touch while prescribing.[88] Massage can help premature children gain weight, help colicky children to sleep better, improve the mood of depressed adolescents, and boost the immune function of cancer and HIV patients.[89] Research shows that touch between therapists and clients has the potential to encourage a variety of beneficial changes: more self-disclosure, better client self-acceptance, and more positive client–therapist relationships.[90]

Touch also has an impact in school. Students are twice as likely to volunteer and speak up in class if they have received supportive touch on the back or arm from their teacher.[91] Even athletes benefit from touch. One study of National Basketball Association players revealed that the "touchiest" teams had the most successful records while the lowest-scoring teams had the least amount of touch among teammates.[92]

Of course, touch must be culturally appropriate. Furthermore, touching by itself is no guarantee of success, and too much contact can be bothersome, annoying, or even downright creepy. But research confirms that appropriate contact can enhance your success.

PAUSE *and* REFLECT

The Rules of Touch

MindTap REFLECT . . . on the rules that govern touch by answering the following questions, either here or online.

Like most types of nonverbal behavior, touching is governed by cultural and social rules. Imagine that you are writing a guidebook for visitors from another culture. Describe the rules that govern touching in the following relationships. In each case, describe how the gender of the participants also affects the rules.

1. An adult and a five-year-old child
2. An adult and a twelve-year-old
3. Two good friends
4. Boss and employee

Appearance

Whether or not we're aware of the fact, how we look sends messages to others. There are two dimensions to appearance: physical attractiveness and clothing.

Physical Attractiveness   There is little dispute that people who are deemed physically attractive receive many social benefits.[93] For example, females who are perceived as attractive have more dates, receive higher grades in college, persuade males with greater ease, and receive lighter court sentences. Both men and women perceived by others as attractive are rated as being more sensitive, kind, strong, sociable, and interesting than their less-fortunate brothers and sisters.

The influence of physical attractiveness begins early in life.[94] Preschoolers were shown photographs of children their own age and asked to choose potential friends and enemies. The researchers found that children as young as three agreed as to who was attractive and unattractive. Furthermore, the children valued their attractive counterparts—both of the same and the opposite sex—more highly. Teachers also are affected by students' attractiveness. Physically attractive students are usually judged more favorably—as being more intelligent, friendly, and popular—than their less-attractive counterparts.[95] Teacher–student assessments work in both directions—research shows that physically attractive professors receive higher evaluations from their students.[96]

Warren Brothers/Allstar

Physical attractiveness is also an asset in the professional world, affecting hiring, promotion, and performance evaluation decisions.[97] This bias has been referred to as "lookism" and can lead to the same kinds of prejudice as racism and sexism.[98] For instance, research shows that women gain an 8 percent wage bonus for above-average looks; they pay a 4 percent wage penalty for below-average appearance. For men, the attractiveness wage bonus is only 4 percent; however, the penalty for below-average looks is a full 13 percent. Occasionally physical attractiveness has a negative effect: Interviewers may turn down good-looking candidates because they're perceived as threats.[99] While attractiveness generally gets rewarded, glamorous beauty can be intimidating.[100]

Fortunately, attractiveness is something we can control without having to call a plastic surgeon. If you aren't totally gorgeous or handsome, don't despair: Evidence suggests that, as we get to know more about people and like them, we start to regard them as better looking.[101] Moreover, we view others as beautiful or ugly not just on the basis of their "original equipment" but also on the basis of how they use that equipment. Posture, gestures, facial expressions, and other behaviors can increase the physical attractiveness of an otherwise unremarkable person. Finally, the way we dress can make a significant difference in the way others perceive us, as you'll now see.

⋀ When his wife dumps him, Cal Weaver (Steve Carrell) turns to hunky Jacob Palmer (Ryan Gosling) for advice about how to act to attract women in *Crazy, Stupid Love*. Jacob overhauls Cal's appearance: shoes, shirts, suits, jeans, hair. And as happens in the movies, Cal emerges with a new sense of confidence and dating success. How much does your appearance affect how you feel about yourself? Can it change the way you interact with others?

Clothing   Besides being a means of protecting us from the elements, clothing is a means of communicating nonverbally. One writer has suggested that clothing conveys at least ten types of messages to others:[102]

Economic background

Economic level

Educational background

Educational level

Level of sophistication

Level of success

Moral character

Social background

Social position

Trustworthiness

Research shows that we do make assumptions about people based on their clothing.[103] For example, experimenters dressed in uniforms resembling police officers were more successful than those dressed in civilian clothing in requesting pedestrians to pick up litter and in persuading them to lend money to an overparked motorist. Likewise, solicitors wearing sheriff's and nurse's uniforms increased the level of contributions to law-enforcement and healthcare campaigns. We are also more likely to follow the lead of those in more formal attire when it comes to violating social rules. Eighty-three percent of the pedestrians in one study copied the action of a jaywalker dressed in higher-status clothing who violated a "wait" crossing signal, whereas only 48 percent followed a confederate dressed in lower-status clothing.

George Doyle/Stockbyte/Getty Images

Physical Space

Proxemics is the study of the way people and animals use space. There are at least two dimensions of proxemics: distance and territoriality.

Distance   Each of us carries around a sort of invisible bubble of personal space wherever we go. We think of the area inside this bubble as our private territory—almost as much a part of us as our own bodies. To appreciate this, take a moment to complete the "Distance Makes a Difference" exercise in this section. As you move closer to your partner, the distance between your bubbles narrows and at a certain point disappears altogether: Your space has been invaded, and this is the point at which you probably feel uncomfortable. As you move away again, your partner retreats out of your bubble, and you feel more relaxed.

Of course, if you were to try this experiment with someone very close to you—a romantic partner, for example—you might not have felt any discomfort at all, even while touching. The reason is that our willingness to get close to others—physically as well as emotionally—varies according to the person we're with and the situation we're in. And it's precisely the distance that we voluntarily put between ourselves and others that gives a nonverbal clue about our feelings and the nature of the relationship.

As you read earlier in this chapter, appropriate proxemic distances differ from culture to culture. Anthropologist Edward T. Hall has defined four distances that most North Americans use in their everyday lives.[104] He says we choose a particular distance depending on how we feel toward the other person at a given time, the context of the conversation, and our interpersonal goals.

- The first of Hall's four spatial zones begins with skin contact and ranges out to about 18 inches. We usually use **intimate distance** with people who are emotionally the closest to us and then mostly in private situations—making love, caressing, comforting, protecting.

- The second spatial zone, **personal distance**, ranges from 18 inches at its closest point to 4 feet at its farthest. Its closer range is the distance at which most couples stand in public. The far range runs from about 2½ to 4 feet. As Hall puts it, at this distance we can keep someone "at arm's length." This choice of words suggests the type of communication that goes on at this range: The contacts are still reasonably close, but they're much less personal than the ones that occur a foot or so closer.

- The third spatial zone, **social distance**, ranges from 4 to about 12 feet. Within it are the kinds of communication that usually occur in business. Its closer range, from 4 to 7 feet, is the distance at which conversations usually occur between salespeople and customers and between people who work together. We use the far range of social distance—7 to 12 feet—for more formal and impersonal situations. Sitting at this distance signals a far different and less-relaxed type of conversation than would pulling a chair around to the boss's side of the desk and sitting only three or so feet away.

- **Public distance** is Hall's term for the farthest zone, running outward from 12 feet. The closer range of public distance is the one that most teachers use in the classroom. In the farther ranges of public space—25 feet and beyond—two-way communication is almost impossible. In some cases, it's necessary for speakers to use public distance because of the size of their audience, but we can assume that anyone who voluntarily chooses to use it when he or she could be closer is not interested in having a dialogue.

Choosing the optimal distance can have a powerful effect on how we regard others and how we respond to them. For example, students are more satisfied with teachers who reduce the distance between themselves and their classes. They also are more satisfied with a course itself, and they are more likely to follow a teacher's instructions.[105] Likewise, medical patients are more satisfied with physicians who operate at the closer end of the social distance zone.[106]

Territoriality Whereas personal space is the invisible bubble we carry around as an extension of our physical being, **territory** remains stationary.

PAUSE *and* REFLECT

Distance Makes a Difference

MindTap REFLECT ... on how distance makes a difference in communication by answering the following questions, either here or online.

1. Choose a partner, and go to opposite sides of the room and face each other.

2. Very slowly begin walking toward each other while carrying on a conversation. You might simply talk about how you feel as you follow the exercise. As you move closer, try to be aware of any change in your feelings. Continue moving slowly toward each other until you are only an inch or so apart. Remember how you feel at this point.

3. Now, while still facing each other, back up until you're at a comfortable distance for carrying on your conversation.

4. Share your feelings with each other or the whole group.

Any geographical area such as a work area, room, house, or other physical space to which we assume some kind of "rights" is our territory. What's interesting about territoriality is that there is no real basis for the assumption of proprietary rights of "owning" many areas, but the feeling of ownership exists nonetheless. Your room at home probably feels like yours whether you're there or not, unlike personal space, which is carried around with you. In the same way, you may feel proprietary about the seat you always occupy in class, even though you have no illusions about owning that piece of furniture.[107]

The way people use space can communicate a good deal about power and status.[108] Generally, we grant people with higher status more personal territory and greater privacy. We knock before entering the boss's office, whereas she can usually walk into our work area without hesitating. In traditional schools, professors have offices, dining rooms, and even toilets that are private, whereas students, who are presumably less important, have no such sanctuaries. Among the military, greater space and privacy usually come with rank: Privates sleep forty to a barrack, sergeants have their own private rooms, and generals have government-provided houses.

Physical Environment

Physical settings, architecture, and interior design affect our communication. The impressions that home designs communicate can be remarkably revealing. Researchers showed students slides of the insides or outsides of twelve upper-middle-class homes and then asked them to infer the personality of the owners from their impressions.[109] The students were especially accurate after glancing at interior photos. The decorating schemes communicated information about the homeowners' intellectualism, politeness, maturity, optimism, tenseness, willingness to take adventures, and family orientations. The home exteriors also gave viewers accurate perceptions of the owners' artistic interests, graciousness, privacy, and quietness.

Besides communicating information about the designer, an environment can shape the kind of interaction that takes place in it. In one experiment, subjects working in a "beautiful" room were more positive and energetic than those working in "average" or "ugly" spaces.[110] In another experiment, students perceived professors who occupied well-decorated offices as being more credible than those occupying less-attractive offices.[111] Doctors have shaped environments to improve the quality of interaction with their patients. Simply removing a doctor's desk makes patients feel almost five times more at ease during office visits.[112] In another study, redesigning a convalescent ward of a hospital greatly increased the interaction between patients. In the old design, seats were placed shoulder to shoulder around the edges of the ward. By grouping the seats around small tables so that patients faced each other at a comfortable distance, the amount of conversations doubled. And in office cubicles, occupants who face out (rather than in) send the message that they're open to communication—and it also allows them to better protect their work's confidentiality.[113]

Time

Social scientists use the term **chronemics** to describe the study of how humans use and structure time. The way we handle time can express both intentional and unintentional messages.[114] For instance, sending a delayed response—or no response at all—to a work email can create the impression of untrustworthiness, especially from a subordinate or peer.[115]

In a culture that values time highly, waiting can be an indicator of status. "Important" people (whose time is supposedly more valuable than that of others) may be seen by appointment only, whereas it is acceptable to intrude without notice on lesser beings. A related rule is that low-status people must never make high-status people wait. It would be a serious mistake to show up late for a job interview, whereas the interviewer might keep you cooling your heels in the lobby. Important people are often whisked to the head of a restaurant or airport line, while presumably less-exalted masses are forced to wait their turn.

Time can be a marker not only of power and status but also of relationships. Research shows that the amount of time spent with a relational partner sends important messages about valuing that person.[116] In one study analyzing 20 nonverbal behaviors, "spending time together" was the most powerful predictor of both relational satisfaction and perceived interpersonal understanding.[117] Time is also measured and valued in mediated communication. Studies show that the length of time it takes for someone to respond to email messages or to postings in virtual groups has a strong correlation with perceptions of that person.[118] As you might guess, quick responses get positive appraisals, while tardy or neglected replies can have an adverse effect on trust and effectiveness in virtual groups.[119]

In REAL LIFE

Recognizing Nonverbal Cues

You can appreciate how nonverbal cues reflect attitudes by reading the following transcript twice. The first time, imagine that Kim's non-verbal behavior signals that she is glad to meet Stacy and looking forward to getting to know Stacy better. For your second reading, imagine that Kim feels just the opposite: She is put off by Stacy and feels uncomfortable around her.

© John Harris/Cengage Learning

Think about all the ways Kim's nonverbal behaviors might change, depending on her attitude toward Stacy. Even though she speaks the same words, imagine how her posture, gestures, facial expressions, voice, and use of distance might differ and how these nonverbal cues would reflect her feelings about her new neighbor.

Stacy: Hi. I'm new here. Just moved into Unit 14 yesterday. My name's Stacy. (*Extends her hand, ready to shake*)

Kim: Hi! I'm Kim. I'm your next-door neighbor in number 12.

Stacy: Great! This looks like a nice place.

Kim: It is. Everybody's friendly, and we all get along really well.

Stacy: (*Glancing down at a magazine in Kim's mail*) Hmmm. *American Songwriter*. Are you a musician?

Kim: Yeah, I'm a singer-songwriter. Mostly acoustic. I play around town. Nothing too big yet, but I'm hoping …

Stacy: (*Excitedly*) Whoa! I'm a musician too!

Kim: Really!

Stacy: Yeah. I play rhythm guitar with The Festering Sores. Have you heard of us?

Kim: Yeah, I think so.

Stacy: Well, you'll have to come hear us some time. And maybe we could even jam together, since we're both guitarists.

Kim: That would be interesting!

Stacy: Wow! I can already tell I'm going to like it here. Hey … what's the attitude around here about pets?

Kim: They're pretty strict about the "No dogs or cats" policy.

Stacy: No problem! Jezebel isn't either.

Kim: Well, what is Jezebel?

Stacy: (*Proudly*) She's a green iguana. A real beauty.

Kim: You're kidding, right?

Stacy: Nope. You'll probably meet her one of these days. In fact, she's kind of a runaway, so you might find her in your place if you leave the door open. Especially when the weather cools down. (*Semi-kidding*) She really likes to snuggle up to a warm body.

Kim: Well, I'm more of a bird person, so …

Stacy: She makes friends with everybody. You'll love her!

Kim: Look, I've gotta run. I'm already late for a practice session.

Stacy: I'll see you around. Really glad we're gonna be neighbors!

Kim: Me too.

MindTap® **APPLY …** this situation to your life by answering questions online.

SUMMARY

Nonverbal communication consists of messages expressed by nonlinguistic means such as body movement, vocal characteristics, touch, appearance, physical space, physical environment, and time.

Nonverbal skills are vital for competent communicators. Nonverbal communication is pervasive; in fact, it is impossible to not send nonverbal messages. Although many nonverbal behaviors are universal, their use is affected by both culture and gender. Most nonverbal communication reveals attitudes and feelings; in contrast, verbal communication is better suited to expressing ideas. Even mediated messages carry nonverbal cues. Nonverbal communication serves many functions. It can repeat, complement, substitute for, accent, regulate, and contradict verbal communication. When presented with conflicting verbal and nonverbal messages, communicators are more likely to rely on the nonverbal ones. For this reason, nonverbal cues are important in detecting deception. It's necessary to exercise caution in interpreting such cues, however, because nonverbal communication is ambiguous.

KEY TERMS

accenting
adaptors
body orientation
chronemics
complementing
contradicting
emblems
gestures
haptics
illustrators
intimate distance
kinesics
leakage
manipulators
microexpression

mixed message
monochronic
nonverbal communication
paralanguage
personal distance
polychronic
posture
proxemics
public distance
regulating
repeating
social distance
substituting
territory

CHAPTER SEVEN

Nonverbal Communication: Messages beyond Words

OUTLINE

Use this outline to take notes as you read the chapter in the text and/or as your instructor lectures in class.

I. CHARACTERISTICS OF NONVERBAL COMMUNICATION	_____
A. Nonverbal Communication Defined	_____
B. Nonverbal Skills Are Vital	_____
C. All Behavior Has Communicative Value	_____
1. Deliberate	
2. Unintentional	_____
D. Nonverbal Communication Is Primarily Relational	_____
1. Managing Identity	_____
2. Defining Relationships	
3. Conveying Emotion	_____
E. Nonverbal Communication Occurs in Mediated Messages	_____
1. Emoticons	
2. Chromemics	_____
F. Nonverbal Communication Serves Many Functions	_____
1. Repeating	
2. Complementing	_____
3. Substituting	
4. Accenting	_____
5. Regulating	
6. Contradicting	_____

G. Nonverbal Communication Offers Deception Clues

1. Leakage
2. Deception Detection 101
   a. We Are Only Accurate Half the Time
   b. We Overestimate Our Ability to Detect Other's Lies
   c. We Have a Strong Tendency to Judge Other's Messages as Truthful

H. Nonverbal Communication Is Ambiguous

1. Silence
2. Sexual Behavior
3. Nonverbal Learning Disorder

II. INFLUENCES ON NONVERBAL COMMUNICATION

A. Gender

1. Physiological and Sociological Differences
2. Cultural Norms

B. Culture

1. Differing Nonverbal Rules
2. Nonverbal Misunderstandings

III. TYPES OF NONVERBAL COMMUNICATION

A. Body Movement

1. Body Orientation
   a. Facing Toward or Away
   b. Signals Interest or Exclusion
2. Posture
   a. Emotions
   b. Tension/Relaxation
3. Gestures
   a. Illustrators
   b. Emblems
   c. Adaptors (manipulators)

4. Face and Eyes

   a. Face

      1. Large Number and Kind of Expressions

      2. Speed of Change

      3. Microexpressions

   b. Eyes

      1. Involvement

      2. Avoiding Contact

      3. Attitude

      4. Interest

      5. Dominance and Submission

B. Voice (Paralanguage)

   1. Emphasis

   2. Tone, Rate, Pitch, Volume, Pauses (unintentional and vocalized)

   3. Sarcasm

   4. Credibility and Liking

C. Touch (Haptics)

   1. Signals Type of Relationship

   2. Context Matters: Who, Where, When

   3. Shapes Responses: Liking and Compliance

   4. Essential to Development and Health

      a. Physical Health

      b. School Performance

D. Appearance

   1. Physical Attractiveness

      a. Social Benefits

      b. Lookism

   2. Clothing

      a. 10 Types of Messages

      b. Assumptions about People

E. Physical Space (Proxemics)

   1. Distance

      a. Intimate

      b. Personal

      c. Social

      d. Public

   2. Territoriality

F. Physical Environment
  1. Architecture and Design
  2. Shaping Interactions

G. Time (Chronemics)
  1. Status
  2. Culture: Monochromic/Polychronic

_____

_____

_____

KEY TERMS

accenting
adaptors
body orientation
chronemics
complementing
contradicting
emblems
emoticons
gestures
haptics
illustrators
intimate distance
kinesics
leakage
lookism
manipulators
microexpression

mixed message
monochronic
nonlinguistic
nonverbal communication
nonverbal learning disorder
paralanguage
personal distance
polychronic
posture
proxemics
public distance
regulating
repeating
social distance
substituting
territory

ACTIVITIES

7.1 DESCRIBING NONVERBAL STATES

LEARNING OBJECTIVES

- Explain the defining characteristics of nonverbal communication as described in this chapter.
- List and offer examples of each type of nonverbal message introduced in this chapter.

INSTRUCTIONS

PART I.

1. For each of the statements below, imagine someone you know is sharing their experience with you. What nonverbal behaviors would they use to reflect the attitude or emotions expressed in this statement?
2. For each item, describe as many types of nonverbal behavior as you can: body movement (orientation, posture, gestures, face/eyes), voice, touch, appearance, physical space, physical environment, time.
3. Compare your responses with those of others in the class and note the similarities and differences in your responses.

EXAMPLE 1

He says I'm too eager to please.
I respond quickly after a request. I lean toward the person a lot. I smile and keep the smile on my face continuously. I gesture quickly. I stand a bit bowed over. I tilt my head to the side submissively.

EXAMPLE 2

She listens well.
Turns body toward me, leans forward, smiles once or twice, nods, maintains eye contact about 80 percent of the time.

1. My boss is mean.

   _____

   _____

2. My coworkers say I don't treat them well.

   _____

   _____

3. He's not into this project.

_____

_____

4. She can't stop flirting.

_____

_____

5. They tell me I'm too tense.

_____

_____

6. She acts like she's in charge.

_____

_____

7. He makes a big deal of everything.

_____

_____

8. You need to act more sure of yourself.

_____

_____

9. He seems friendly.

_____

_____

10. You're not exactly a ray of sunshine.

_____

_____

11. They tell me I'm too aggressive.

_____

_____

12. She's "hyper."

_____

_____

PART II.

1. Review your answers in 1 to 12 above and identify at least two statements that could be taken in both positive and negative ways (i.e., number 6 could be positive if you are grateful that she's organizing things, but negative if you're resentful of her influence).

_____

_____

_____

_____

2. For those two statements, describe nonverbal behaviors that are associated with the alternate interpretation (the one you didn't record initially).

_____

_____

_____

_____

3. In both cases, share your reaction to describing your intial response and the alternative response (i.e., I can see the positive side of taking charge—assigning seating, standing erect, firm voice, keeping to a schedule, making eye contact with those who should speak to you. There's often a small difference between the nonverbal behaviors I find positive and those I find annoying or bossy).

    _____

    _____

    _____

    _____

4. Once again, compare your responses with those of others in the class and note similarities and differences.

    _____

    _____

    _____

    _____

7.2 DESCRIBING NONVERBAL BEHAVIORS

LEARNING OBJECTIVES

- Explain the defining characteristics of nonverbal communication as described in the text.
- In a given situation, recognize your own nonverbal behavior and its relational significance.

INSTRUCTIONS

1. For each of the social situations below, list the nonverbal behaviors you believe will achieve the stated goal. Use as many categories of nonverbal behavior as you can: body movement (orientation, posture, gestures, face/eyes), voice, touch, appearance, physical space, physical environment, and time.

2. Reflect on the behavior of yourself and others important to you. How might you change some of the nonverbal cues you display to communicate what you desire more effectively?

3. Compare your answers with those of others in your class.

EXAMPLE:

Initiate conversation with a stranger at a party.
Make eye contact, offer hand in greeting, smile, come within four feet of other person, turn body toward other person, nod occasionally when other is talking.

1. Take control or exercise leadership in a class group.

   _____

   _____

2. Come across well in a job interview.

   _____

   _____

3. Tell an interesting joke or story.

   _____

   _____

4. Appear friendly and warm without "coming on too strong."

_____

_____

5. Signal your desire to leave a conversation when the other person keeps on talking.

_____

_____

6. Appear confident when asking boss for a raise.

_____

_____

7. Appear interested in class lecture.

_____

_____

8. Avoid talking with a person on a plane or bus.

_____

_____

9. Show kindness toward an elderly relative.

_____

_____

10. Appear concerned about a friend's dilemma.

_____

_____

11. Why might you want to change them?

_____

_____

_____

_____

_____

7.3 SELF-MONITORING NONVERBAL BEHAVIORS

LEARNING OBJECTIVES

- Identify your own habitual nonverbal behaviors.
- Monitor the impact of your habitual nonverbal behaviors on your communication with others.
- Monitor and manage your nonverbal cues in ways that achieve your goals.

INSTRUCTIONS

1. For at least four times a day for three days, conduct a personal nonverbal behavior assessment. You might set an alarm on your watch or phone to particular times or choose four daily markers, such as purchasing a cup of coffee or going to the library, to act as reminders.
2. At these four previously chosen times, stop what you're doing and pay attention to your nonverbal behavior. Were you leaning or slouching? What was your facial expression? Were you using any gestures? If other people are with you, ask them to comment on the nonverbal behaviors you were exhibiting at that moment.
3. Use the chart below to list those nonverbal behaviors. Use as many categories of nonverbal behavior as you can: body movement (orientation, posture, gestures, face/eyes), voice, touch, appearance, physical space, physical environment, and time.
4. After you've completed your assessment period, reflect on what you've learned about your nonverbal behaviors. Answer the questions provided.

DAY/TIME	SITUATION	NONVERBAL BEHAVIORS YOU OBSERVED	NONVERBAL BEHAVIORS OTHERS OBSERVED

Class _____   Name _____

DAY/TIME	SITUATION	NONVERBAL BEHAVIORS YOU OBSERVED	NONVERBAL BEHAVIORS OTHERS OBSERVED

1. After conducting your nonverbal behavior self-assessment, do you see any patterns or habits in your nonverbal behavior? If yes, describe them.

    _____

    _____

    _____

    _____

2. Could any of these nonverbal patterns or habits be misunderstood by others, affecting your ability to communicate? If yes, describe which ones and how.

    _____

    _____

    _____

    _____

3. Have you identified any nonverbal behaviors that you would like to change? If yes, describe the behavior as you exhibit it now and then describe the behavior as if you have already changed it. How might changing this behavior affect your ability to communicate?

    _____

    _____

    _____

    _____

7.4 AMBIGUITY, CONTRADICTION, AND CONGRUENCE

LEARNING OBJECTIVES

- In a given situation, recognize your own nonverbal behavior and its relational significance.
- Monitor and manage your nonverbal cues in ways that achieve your goals.
- Evaluate the ethical dimension of nonverbal behavior.

INSTRUCTIONS

1. In each of the following situations, describe verbal and nonverbal behaviors likely to occur: body movement (orientation, posture, gestures, face/eyes), voice, touch, appearance, physical space, physical environment, time. Nonverbal behaviors seldom occur alone, so describe clusters of at least three nonverbal behaviors for each situation. Note whether the verbal and nonverbal behaviors are ambiguous, contradictory, or congruent. Finally, evaluate the possible consequences of the ambiguity, contradictions, or congruency.

2. Next, describe situations from your own life and how you would send verbal and nonverbal messages. Include the possible consequences of your congruent or ambiguous behaviors.

3. After you've completed the examples, answer the questions about congruency/ambiguity.

SITUATION	YOUR VERBAL BEHAVIOR	YOUR NONVERBAL BEHAVIOR (USE A CLUSTER OF BEHAVIORS HERE)	ARE BEHAVIORS CONTRADICTORY, AMBIGUOUS, OR CONGRUENT?	POSSIBLE CONSEQUENCES
Example Person I like a lot takes me out to dinner, and I have a good time and enjoy the food.	"I'm really enjoying this; the food is terrific and so is the company."	I look at my partner when I talk, smiling and tilting my head, and leaning slightly forward. I touch my partner lightly on the arm and hand.	My verbal and nonverbal behaviors are congruent, not ambiguous.	I hope my partner will understand how much I care and enjoy our time together. I run the risk of being hurt if my partner's feelings don't match mine, but I'm willing to take that risk.
1. My boss asks me to work late when I've made other plans.				
2. My roommate asks, while I'm doing homework, if I can make dinner.				

SITUATION	YOUR VERBAL BEHAVIOR	YOUR NONVER-BAL BEHAVIOR (USE A CLUSTER OF BEHAVIORS HERE)	ARE BEHAVIORS CONTRADICTORY, AMBIGUOUS, OR CONGRUENT?	POSSIBLE CONSEQUENCES
3. My relative drops in to visit me when other people are over for the evening.				
4. My romantic partner says I act like I'm indifferent when we discuss our future.				
5. Our waiter starts to take my plate and asks if I'm finished while food is still on my plate.				
6. (your example)				
7. (your example)				
8. (your example)				

REFLECTIONS

1. Have you ever found it advantageous to send one message verbally and another one nonverbally? Provide an example (perhaps from one of your examples above).

   _____

   _____

   _____

   _____

2. Describe a situation when you found ambiguity clearly was not desirable (again it might be one of the examples above). How did you make sure that your verbal and nonverbal behaviors matched?

   _____

   _____

   _____

   _____

3. Consider the ethical implications of nonverbal congruence, ambiguity, and contradiction. Does ethics always require that we behave with congruence? Is it always unethical to intentionally be ambiguous or contradictory? Can you think of a situation when choosing NOT to behave in an ambiguous or contradictory manner could be considered unethical?

   _____

   _____

   _____

4. Are there situations in which nonverbal ambiguity or contradiction is unintentional and unavoidable? Explain your answer.

   _____

   _____

   _____

   _____

7.5 NONVERBAL ANALYSIS

LEARNING OBJECTIVES

- Explain the defining characteristics of nonverbal communication as described in the text.
- Identify and understand the difference between intentional and unintentional nonverbal communication.
- Analyze the impact of intentional and unintentional nonverbal communication.

INSTRUCTIONS

Use the case below and the discussion questions that follow to discuss the variety of communication issues involved in effective communication. Make notes on this page, add other pages on your own, or prepare a group report/analysis based on your discussion. Add your own experiences to individualize the analysis.

CASE

Malena and Dolly are coworkers in different departments in a large company. Over coffee one day, Malena tells Dolly that she's been feeling very uneasy lately about her boss's behavior. "I'm not exactly sure how to describe it," Malena says, "but I think he's coming on to me, and I don't know what to do."

1. Malena would communicate more effectively if she could describe her boss's behavior. Imagine a situation like this and describe the possible behavior of Malena's boss.

   _____

   _____

2. Of the descriptions you used for Malena's boss's behavior (listed in question 1), which might be intentional and which might be unintentional? Why?

   _____

   _____

3. Now, describe possible intentional or unintentional nonverbal behaviors of Malena that might be misunderstood.

   _____

   _____

4. Using ideas from this and the previous chapters in the text, describe what could Malena do
    verbally and nonverbally to handle this issue effectively?

    _____

    _____

    _____

    _____

7.6 ASSESSING NONVERBAL BEHAVIOR

LEARNING OBJECTIVES

- List and offer examples of each type of nonverbal message introduced in this chapter.

INSTRUCTIONS:

1. Using a medium that you can repeat (such as on-demand TV, DVD, or online streaming) watch a television program or a scene from a movie with the sound muted.
2. Evaluate how the actor uses nonverbal behavior to convey an emotion. Record your descriptions in the spaces below.
3. Repeat the scene with the sound on. Assess how accurately you predicted the emotional meaning in the space below.

Scene 1 _____

Sound Off: Emotion being conveyed _____

Body movement _____

Posture _____

Gestures _____

Face and eyes _____

Appearance _____

Sound On: Emotion being conveyed _____

How accurately did you predict the emotional meaning? _____

Scene 2 _____

Sound Off: Emotion being conveyed _____

Body movement _____

Class _____   Name _____

Posture _____

Gestures _____

Face and Eyes _____

Appearance _____

Sound On: Emotion being conveyed _____

How accurately did you predict the emotional meaning? _____

STUDY GUIDE

CHECK YOUR UNDERSTANDING

TRUE/FALSE

Mark the statements below as true or false. Correct statements that are false on the lines below to create a true statement.

_____ 1. Not all nonverbal behaviors have communicative value.

_____

_____ 2. Nonverbal communication reflects and shapes the kinds of relationships you have with others.

_____

_____

_____

_____ 3. Emblems are personal nonverbal gestures that differ in meaning among member of a group.

_____

_____ 4. Nonverbal communication is much better suited to expressing attitudes and feelings than it is to expressing concrete ideas.

_____

_____ 5. Research on nonverbal communication and lying shows that individuals who are trying to deceive make less eye contact and fidget more than nonliars.

_____

_____ 6. Because mediated communication is missing visual cues, nonverbal cues are not available.

_____

_____   7. People with NVLD have a hard time reading facial expressions, tone of voice, and other nonverbal cues.

_____

_____   8. Unlike verbal communication that is intermittent (starts and stops), nonverbal communication is continuous and never ending.

_____

_____   9. It's never appropriate to substitute nonverbal behavior for words.

_____

_____ 10. Because paralanguage is expressed nonverbally it doesn't affect the meaning of words.

_____

_____

_____

_____ 11. The concept of leakage is most often associated with deception.

_____

_____ 12. Manipulators are gestures used to control another person's behavior.

_____

_____ 13. Behaviors that have one meaning for members of the same culture or co-culture can be interpreted differently by members of another group.

_____

_____ 14. Haptics is a word used to describe the study of touch.

_____

_____ 15. Lookism is a term used to describe our tendency to feel sympathetic for people who are physically unattractive.

_____

COMPLETION

Fill in the blanks below with the correct terms chosen from the list below.

illustrator	intimate	personal	social	body orientation
relaxation	paralanguage	emblem	adaptor	touch
public	text-based messages			

4. _____ is the distance zone identified by Hall that ranges from four to about twelve feet; within it are the kinds of communication that usually occur in business.

5. _____ is a postural cue such as leaning back or lowering shoulders that a higher status person usually exhibits when not feeling threatened.

6. _____ is a deliberate, nonverbal behavior that has a very precise meaning known to virtually everyone within a cultural group.

7. _____ is the distance zone identified by Hall that ranges from eighteen inches to four feet and includes behavior found in most social conversations.

8. _____ is a gesture that accompanies speech but doesn't stand on its own.

9. _____ is the degree to which we face toward or away from someone with our body, feet, and head.

10. _____ is the distance zone identified by Hall that ranges from skin contact to about eighteen inches; we usually use this distance with people in private who are emotionally very close to us.

11. _____ is the distance zone identified by Hall that ranges from twelve feet outward and includes communication such as that found in a typical classroom.

12. _____ is nonverbal behavior that includes having a foreign accent.

13. _____ is nonverbal behavior that includes brushing up against someone.

14. _____ is an unconscious body movement that helps us adjust to the environment.

15. _____ can use linguistic shortcuts and acronyms to indicate nonverbal messages.

MULTIPLE CHOICE

Choose the letter of the type of nonverbal communication that is illustrated below.

a. environment   b. paralinguistics   c. proxemics   d. territoriality

_____ 1. No one dared to sit in Ralph's chair.

_____ 2. Jeremy put a "NO ENTRANCE" sign on his door.

_____ 3. The students rearranged the chairs in the classroom.

_____ 4. Manuela stepped back three feet from her friend.

_____ 5. The lovers were sitting only inches apart.

_____ 6. Rob's voice softened when he spoke to her.

_____ 7. There was a long pause after the decision was made.

_____ 8. Mitchell sighed audibly.

_____ 9. Gretchen took the third seat down from Yayoi.

_____ 10. Kevin was annoyed that someone was leaning on his car.

a. body orientation   b. gesture   c. touch   d. face and eyes

_____ 11. The children playfully kicked one another.

_____ 12. Professor Jimenez illustrated her lecture with many arm movements.

_____ 13. Leland shifted his shoulders toward the speaker.

_____ 14. Ernie avoided looking at her.

_____ 15. The executive stared at her employee.

_____ 16. Martin turned his body away from his brother.

_____ 17. The officer pointed in the correct direction.

_____ 18. Letoya didn't appreciate the slap on the back.

_____ 19. Blake set his jaw in disgust.

_____ 20. Francesca signaled "OK" across the room.

Choose the best answer for each of the statements below:

_____ 21. Paralanguage describes
      a. nonverbal, silent messages.
      b. vocal messages.
      c. verbal messages.
      d. nonverbal, vocal messages.

_____ 22. According to researchers, women tend to
      a. smile less than men.
      b. use more facial expressions.
      c. use fewer facial expressions.
      d. are less vocally expressive than men.

_____ 23. Deceivers try to maintain a
      a. poker face when communicating.
      b. blank face when communicating.
      c. plain face when communicating.
      d. pleasant face when communicating.

_____ 24. Touch can
      a. increase liking.
      b. increase compliance.
      c. both a and b.
      d. none of the above.

CHAPTER SEVEN STUDY GUIDE ANSWERS

TRUE/FALSE

1. F	4. T	7. T	10. F	13. T
2. F	5. F	8. T	11. T	14. T
3. F	6. F	9. F	12. F	15. F

COMPLETION

1. social	5. illustrator	9. paralanguage
2. relaxation	6. body orientation	10. touch
3. emblem	7. intimate	11. adaptor
4. personal	8. public	12. text-based messages

MULTIPLE CHOICE

1. d	5. c	9. c	13. a	17. b	21. d
2. d	6. b	10. d	14. d	18. c	22. b
3. a	7. b	11. c	15. d	19. d	23. a
4. c	8. b	12. b	16. a	20. b	24. c

MindTap® START ...
Explore this chapter's topics online.

8

LISTENING: MORE THAN MEETS THE EAR

AFTER STUDYING THE TOPICS IN THIS CHAPTER, YOU SHOULD BE ABLE TO:

1. Identify the situations in which you listen mindfully and those when you listen mindlessly and then evaluate the appropriateness of each style in a given situation.

2. Identify the circumstances in which you listen ineffectively and the poor listening habits you use in these circumstances.

3. Identify the response styles you commonly use when listening to others.

4. Demonstrate a combination of listening styles you could use to respond effectively in a given situation.

I have just

wandered back

into our conversation

and find

that you

are still

rattling on

about something

or other

i think i must

have been gone

at least

twenty minutes

and you

never missed me

now this might say

something

about my acting ability

or it might say

something about

your sensitivity

one thing

troubles me tho

when it

is my turn

to rattle on

for twenty minutes

which I

have been known to do

have you

been missing too.

Ric Masten

Poem "Conversations" from *Dragonflies, Codfish & Frogs* by Ric Masten. Copyright © Sunflower Ink, Palo Colorado Road, Carmel, CA 93923. Reprinted with permission.

*R*ic Masten's poem here shows there's more to listening than gazing politely at a speaker and nodding your head. As you will soon learn, listening is a demanding and complex activity—and just as important as speaking in the communication process.

If we use frequency as a measure, then listening easily qualifies as the most important kind of communication. We spend more time listening to others than in any other type of communication. One study (summarized in Figure 8.1) revealed that college students spend about 11 percent of their communicating time writing, 16 percent speaking, and 17 percent reading—but more than 55 percent listening.[1] On the job, listening is just as important. Studies show that most employees of major corporations in North America spend about 60 percent of each workday listening to others.[2]

Besides being the most frequent form of communication, listening is at least as important as speaking in terms of making relationships work. In committed relationships, listening to personal information in everyday conversations is considered a vital ingredient of satisfaction.[3] In one survey, marital counselors identified "failing to take the other's perspective when listening" as one of the most frequent communication problems in the couples with whom they worked.[4]

∧ Figure 8.1
Time Devoted to Communication Activities

- 11.4% Writing
- 16.1% Speaking
- 17.1% Reading
- 27.9% Media listening
- 27.5% Interpersonal listening

When a group of adults was asked what communication skills were most important in family and social settings, listening was ranked first.[5]

The *International Journal of Listening* devoted an entire issue to exploring various contexts in which listening skills are crucial, including education,[6] health care,[7] religion,[8] and the business world.[9] When working adults were asked to name the most common communication behavior they observed in their place of business, "listening" topped the list.[10] The On the Job box in the following section explores in detail the vital role listening plays in the workplace.

This chapter will explore the nature of listening. After defining listening, we will examine the elements that make up the listening process and look at challenges that come with becoming a better listener. Finally, you will read about a variety of listening response styles that you can use to better understand and even help others.

LISTENING DEFINED

So far we've used the term *listening* as if it needs no explanation. Actually, there's more to this concept than you might think. We will define **listening**—at least the interpersonal type—as the process of making sense of others' messages.

Traditional approaches to listening focus on the reception of *spoken* messages. However, we've broadened the definition to include messages of all sorts because much of contemporary listening takes place through mediated channels, some of which involve the written word. Consider times you've said something like, "I was talking with a friend, and she told me … "—and the conversation you recount actually took place via texting, emailing, or instant messaging. Chapter 2 describes how social support can be offered through blogs, Facebook posts, and other social media (for example, see the reading "Texting to Save Lives" later in this chapter). We'll continue to focus on spoken messages in this chapter (beginning with our discussion of "hearing" below), but recognize that "listening" in contemporary society involves more than meets the ear.

Hearing versus Listening

People often think of hearing and listening as the same thing, but they are quite different. *Hearing* is the process in which sound waves strike the eardrum and cause vibrations that are transmitted to the brain. (You'll read more about hearing in the following section.) *Listening* occurs when the brain reconstructs these electrochemical impulses into a representation of the original sound and then gives them meaning. Barring illness, injury, or cotton plugs, you can't stop hearing.[11] Your ears will pick up sound waves and transmit them to your brain whether you want them to or not.

Listening, however, isn't automatic. People hear all the time without listening. Sometimes we automatically and unconsciously block out irritating sounds, such as a neighbor's lawnmower or the roar of nearby traffic. We also stop listening when we find a subject unimportant or uninteresting.

Boring stories, TV commercials, and nagging complaints are common examples of messages we may hear but tune out.

Mindless Listening

When we move beyond hearing and start to listen, researchers note that we process information in two very different ways—sometimes referred to as the *dual-process theory*.[12] Social scientists use the terms *mindless* and *mindful* to describe these different ways of listening.[13] **Mindless listening** occurs when we react to others' messages automatically and routinely, without much mental investment. Words such as *superficial* and *cursory* describe mindless listening better than terms like *ponder* and *contemplate*.

While the term *mindless* may sound negative, this sort of low-level information processing is a potentially valuable type of communication because it frees us to focus our minds on messages that require our careful attention.[14] Given the number of messages to which we're exposed, it's impractical to listen carefully and thoughtfully 100 percent of the time. It's also unrealistic to devote your attention to long-winded stories, idle chatter, or remarks you've heard many times before. The only realistic way to manage the onslaught of messages is to be "lazy" toward many of them. In situations like these, we forgo careful analysis and fall back on the schemas—and sometimes the stereotypes—described in Chapter 4 to make sense of a message. If you stop right now and recall the messages you have heard today, it's likely that you processed most of them mindlessly.

On the JOB

Listening in the Workplace

Being an effective speaker is important in career success, but good listening skills are just as vital. A study examining the link between listening and career success revealed that better listeners rose to higher levels in their organizations.[a] When human resource executives across the country were asked to identify skills of the ideal manager, the ability to listen effectively ranked at the top of the list.[b] In problem-solving groups, effective listeners are judged as having the most leadership skills.[c]

Listening is just as important in careers that involve cold facts as in ones that involve lots of one-on-one interaction. For example, a survey of more than 90,000 accountants identified effective listening as the most important communication skill for professionals entering that field.[d] When a diverse group of senior executives was asked what skills are most important on the job, listening was identified more often than any other skill, including technical competence, computer knowledge, creativity, and administrative talent.[e]

Just because businesspeople believe listening is important doesn't mean they do it well. A survey in which 144 managers were asked to rate their listening skills illustrates this point. Astonishingly, not one of the managers described himself or herself as a "poor" or "very poor" listener, whereas 94 percent rated themselves as "good" or "very good."[f] The favorable self-ratings contrasted sharply with the perceptions of the managers' subordinates, many of whom said their bosses' listening skills were weak. Of course, managers aren't the only people whose listening needs work—all of us could stand to improve our skills.

Mindful Listening

By contrast, **mindful listening** involves giving careful and thoughtful attention and responses to the messages we receive. You tend to listen mindfully when a message is important to you and also when someone you care about is speaking about a matter that is important to him or her. Think of how your ears perk up when someone starts talking about your money ("The repairs will cost me how much?") or how you tune in carefully when a close friend tells you about the loss of a loved one. In situations like these, you want to give the message sender your complete and undivided attention.

Sometimes we respond mindlessly to information that deserves—and even demands—our mindful attention. Ellen Langer's determination to study mindfulness began when her grandmother complained about headaches coming from a "snake crawling around" beneath her skull. The doctors quickly diagnosed the problem as senility—after all, they reasoned, senility comes with old age and makes people talk nonsense. In fact, the grandmother had a brain tumor that eventually took her life. The event made a deep impression on Langer:

> For years afterward I kept thinking about the doctors' reactions to my grand-mother's complaints, and about our reactions to the doctors. They went through the motions of diagnosis, but were not open to what they were hearing. Mindsets about senility interfered. We did not question the doctors; mindsets about experts interfered.[15]

Most of our daily decisions about whether to listen mindfully don't have life-and-death consequences, but the point should be clear: There are times when we need to consciously and carefully listen to what others are telling us. That kind of mindful listening will be the focus of the remainder of this chapter.

ELEMENTS IN THE LISTENING PROCESS

By now, you can begin to see that there is more to listening than sitting quietly while another person speaks. In truth, listening is a process that consists of five elements: hearing, attending, understanding, responding, and remembering.[16]

Hearing

As we have already discussed, **hearing** is the physiological dimension of listening. It occurs when sound waves strike the ear at a certain frequency and loudness. Hearing is influenced by a variety of factors, including background noise. If there are other loud noises, especially at the same frequency as the message we are trying to hear, we find it difficult to sort out the important signals from the background. Hearing is also affected by auditory fatigue, a temporary loss of hearing caused by continuous exposure to the same tone or loudness. If you spend an evening at a loud party, you may have trouble hearing well, even after getting away from the crowd. If you are exposed to loud noise often enough, permanent hearing loss can result—as many rock musicians and fans can attest.

For many communicators, the challenge of hearing is even more difficult as a result of physiological problems. In the United States alone, more than 31 million people communicate with some degree of hearing loss.[17] One study revealed that, on any given day, one-fourth to one-third of the children in a typical classroom do not hear normally.[18] As a competent communicator, you need to recognize when you may be speaking to someone with a hearing loss and adjust your approach accordingly.

Attending

Whereas hearing is a physiological process, **attending** is a psychological one and is part of the process of selection described in Chapter 4. We would go crazy if we attended to every sound we hear, so we filter out some messages and focus on others. Needs, wants, desires, and interests determine what is attended to. It is not surprising that research shows we attend most carefully to messages when there's a payoff for doing so.[19] If you're planning to see a movie, you'll listen to a friend's description more carefully than you would have otherwise. And when you want to get better acquainted with others, you'll pay careful attention to almost anything they say in hopes of improving the relationship.

It is surprising, though, that attending helps more than the listener; it also helps the message sender. Participants in one study viewed brief

"One of my strengths as an employee is my ability to multitask."

movie segments and then described them to listeners who varied in their degree of attentiveness to the speakers. Later on, the researchers tested the speakers' long-term recall of details from the movie segments. Those who had recounted the movie to attentive listeners remembered more details of the film.[20]

Understanding

Understanding occurs when we make sense of a message. It is possible to hear and attend to a message without understanding it at all. And, of course, it's possible to misunderstand a message. Communication researchers use the term **listening fidelity** to describe the degree of congruence between what a listener understands and what the message sender was attempting to communicate.[21] This chapter describes the many reasons why we misunderstand others—and why they misunderstand us. It also outlines skills that will help you improve your understanding of others.

Responding

Responding to a message consists of giving observable feedback to the speaker. Although listeners don't always respond visibly to a speaker, research suggests they should do so more often. One study of 195 critical incidents in banking and medical settings showed that a major difference between effective and ineffective listening was the kind of feedback offered.[22] Good listeners show they are attentive by nonverbal behaviors such as keeping eye contact and reacting with appropriate facial expressions—which was of particular importance to children in one study who were asked to evaluate "good" versus "bad" listeners.[23] Verbal behavior—answering questions and exchanging ideas, for example—also demonstrates attention. [24] It's easy to imagine how other responses would signal less-effective listening. A slumped posture, bored expression, and yawning send a clear message that you are not tuned in to the speaker.

Adding responsiveness to our listening model demonstrates a fact that we discussed in Chapter 1: Communication is *transactional* in nature. Listening isn't just a passive activity. As listeners, we are active participants in a communication transaction. At the same time that we receive messages, we also send them. Responding is such an integral part of good listening that we'll devote an entire section to listening responses in the second half of this chapter.

Remembering

Remembering is the ability to recall information. If we don't remember a message, listening is hardly worth the effort. Research suggests that most people remember only about 50 percent of what they hear immediately after hearing it.[25] Within 8 hours, the 50 percent remembered drops to about 35 percent. After two months, the average recall is only about 25 percent of the original message. Given the amount of information we process every day—from teachers, friends, the radio, TV, cell phones, and other sources—the residual message (what we remember) is a small fraction of what we hear. You can begin to get a sense of how tough it is to listen effectively by trying the following Pause and Reflect "Listening Breakdowns" exercise.

Looking at DIGIVERSITY

Austin Lee

Seungcheol Austin Lee

Culture and Listening Responses

As a researcher who also teaches courses in intercultural communication, I pay close attention to the impact of culture on interpersonal interaction. It's easy to see how culture affects factors such as nonverbal cues and language style. It's not quite as simple to see the role culture plays in people's listening styles. Over the years, however, I've made a few observations.

I was born and raised in South Korea, where power distance is an important ingredient in communication patterns. People in roles of authority—parents, teachers, employers—are treated with great respect and deference. This affects listening styles—and more particularly, listening responses. A person with low power will usually listen silently to a person in authority. To ask questions or offer suggestions might be perceived as an inappropriate challenge. On the other hand, people in high power positions are likely to offer listening responses such as analyzing, advising, and judging. In fact, they would probably view such responses as their obligation.

When I came to the United States as a graduate student, I learned that remaining silent during conversations can create the wrong impression. Some of my professors thought I was passive and uninterested because I was listening silently when I was trying to show respect. They expected me to offer suggestions and feedback. This wasn't easy as it contradicted deep-rooted norms of my culture.

Another cultural difference I have noticed is about interruptions. When I stumble with words, Americans are less likely to help me out by suggesting the word or phrase that I'm searching for, while Koreans are willing to jump in and fill in the blanks, and even complete the sentence for me. In American culture, interruptions may be perceived as an attempt to take over the floor. But in a collectivistic society like Korea, people show their connectedness with good-natured interruptions to help the conversation flow. But again, this only happens when talking to peers or subordinates. Most Koreans wouldn't dare interrupt when a higher-up is talking.

"Culture and Listening Responses" by Austin Lee. Used with permission of author.

PAUSE *and* REFLECT

Listening Breakdowns

MindTap **REFLECT ...** on listening breakdowns by answering the following questions, either here or online.

You can overcome believing in some common myths about listening by recalling specific instances when:

1. You heard another person's message but did not attend to it.

2. You attended to a message but forgot it almost immediately.

3. You attended to and remembered a message but did not understand it accurately.

4. You understood a message but did not respond sufficiently to convey your understanding to the sender.

5. You failed to remember some or all of an important message.

THE CHALLENGE OF LISTENING

It's easy to acknowledge that listening is important and to describe the steps in the listening process. What's difficult is to actually become a better listener. This section will describe the challenges that listeners must face and overcome to become more effective communicators. We'll look at various types of ineffective listening, then we'll explore the many reasons we don't listen better. As you read this material, think to yourself, "How many of these describe *me*?" The first step to becoming a better listener is to recognize areas that need improvement.

Types of Ineffective Listening

Your own experience will probably confirm the fact that poor listening is all too common. Although a certain amount of ineffective listening is inescapable and sometimes even understandable, it's important to be aware of these types of problems so you can avoid them when listening well really counts.

Pseudolistening Whereas mindless listening may be a private matter, **pseudolistening** is an imitation of the real thing—an act put on to fool the speaker. Pseudolisteners give the appearance of being attentive: They look you in the eye; they may even nod and smile. But the show of attention is a polite façade because their minds are somewhere else. Paradoxically, pseudolistening can take more effort than simply tuning out the other person.

Stage-Hogging   Stage-hogs (sometimes called *conversational narcissists*) try to turn the topic of conversations to themselves instead of showing interest in the speaker.[26] One **stage-hogging** strategy is a *shift-response*—changing the focus of the conversation from the speaker to the narcissist: "You think your math class is tough? You ought to try my physics class!" Interruptions are another hallmark of stage-hogging. Besides preventing the listener from learning potentially valuable information, they can damage the relationship between the interrupter and the speaker. For example, applicants who interrupt the questions of employment interviewers are likely to be rated less favorably than applicants who wait until the interviewer has finished speaking before they respond.[27]

Selective Listening   Selective listeners respond only to the parts of your remarks that interest them, rejecting everything else. Sometimes **selective listening** is legitimate, as when we screen out radio commercials and music and keep an ear cocked for a weather report or an announcement of the time. Selective listening is less appropriate in personal settings when obvious inattention can be a slap in the face to the other person. Consider how you feel when listeners perk up only when the topic relates to them.

Insulated Listening   Insulated listeners are almost the opposite of their selective cousins just described. Instead of looking for specific information, these people avoid it. Whenever a topic arises that they'd rather not deal with, those who use **insulated listening** simply fail to hear or acknowledge it. You remind them about a problem, and they'll nod or answer you—and then promptly ignore or forget what you've just said.

Defensive Listening   Defensive listeners take others' remarks as personal attacks. The teenager who perceives her parents' questions about her friends and activities as distrustful snooping uses **defensive listening**, as do touchy parents who view any questioning by their children as a threat to their authority and parental wisdom.

Ambushing   Ambushers listen carefully to you, but only because they're collecting information that they'll use to attack what you say. The technique of a

MY BOSS KEEPS MICROMANAGING ME.

HAVE YOU TRIED DOING GOOD WORK SO SHE DOESN'T FEEL THE NEED?

MAYBE I SHOULD JUST LISTEN.

cross-examining prosecution attorney is a good example of **ambushing**. Needless to say, using this kind of strategy will justifiably initiate defensiveness in the other person.

Insensitive Listening   Those who use **insensitive listening** respond to the superficial content in a message but miss the more important emotional information that may not be expressed directly. "How's it going?" an insensitive listener might ask. When you reply by saying "Oh, okay I guess" in a dejected tone, he or she responds "Well, great!" Insensitive listeners tend to ignore the nonverbal cues described in Chapter 7 and lack the empathy described in Chapter 4.

Why We Don't Listen Better

After thinking about the styles of ineffective listening described previously, most people begin to see that they listen carefully only a small percentage of the time. Sad as it may be, it's impossible to listen well *all* of the time for several reasons that we'll outline here.

Message Overload   It's especially difficult to focus on messages—even important ones—when you are bombarded by information. Face-to-face messages come from friends, family, work, and school. Personal media—text messages, phone calls, emails, and instant messages—demand your attention. Along with these personal channels, we are awash in messages from mass media. This deluge of communication has made the challenge of attending tougher than at any time in human history.[28]

Tristar/Allstar

Preoccupation   Another reason we don't always listen carefully is that we're often wrapped up in personal concerns that seem more important than the messages that others are sending. It's difficult to pay attention to someone else when you're worrying about an upcoming exam or thinking about the great time you plan to have over the next weekend.

Rapid Thought   Listening carefully is also difficult for a physiological reason. Although we're capable of understanding speech at rates of 600 words per minute, the average person only speaks between 100 and 150 words per minute.[29] Thus, we have mental "spare time" while someone is talking. The temptation is to use this time in ways that don't relate to the speaker's ideas: thinking about personal interests, daydreaming, planning a rebuttal, and so on. The trick to effective listening is to use this spare time to understand the speaker's ideas better rather than to let your attention wander.

Effort   Listening effectively is hard work. The physical changes that occur during careful listening show the effort it takes: the heart rate quickens,

∧ In *The Devil Wears Prada*, the domineering boss Miranda Priestly (Meryl Streep) is a model of ineffective listening. She attends only to things that matter to her ("The details of your incompetence do not interest me") and does so insensitively ("Bore someone else with your questions"). She also interrupts, rolls her eyes, and walks out on her subordinates in mid-conversation. Do you know people who "listen" this way? How do you react to them?

Darrin Henry/Bigstock

respiration increases, and body temperature rises.[30] Notice that these changes are similar to the body's reaction to physical effort. This is no coincidence. Listening carefully to a speaker can be just as taxing as a workout—which is why some people choose not to make the effort.[31] If you've come home exhausted after an evening of listening intently to a friend in need, you know how draining the process can be.

External Noise   The physical world in which we live often presents distractions that make it difficult to pay attention to others. Consider, for example, how the efficiency of your listening decreases when you are seated in a crowded, hot, stuffy room surrounded by others talking next to you and traffic noises outside. It's not surprising that noisy classrooms often make learning difficult for students.[32] In such circumstances, even the best intentions aren't enough to ensure clear understanding.

Faulty Assumptions   We often make faulty assumptions that lead us to believe we're listening attentively when quite the opposite is true. When the subject is a familiar one, it's easy to tune out because you think you've heard it all before. A related problem arises when you assume that a speaker's thoughts are too simple or too obvious to deserve careful attention when, in fact, they do. At other times just the opposite occurs. You think that another's comments are too complex to be understood (as in some lectures), so you give up trying to make sense of them.

Lack of Apparent Advantages   It often seems that there's more to gain by speaking than by listening. When business consultant Nancy Kline asked some of her clients why they interrupted their colleagues, these are the reasons she heard:

> My idea is better than theirs.
>
> If I don't interrupt them, I'll never get to say my idea.
>
> I know what they are about to say.
>
> They don't need to finish their thoughts since mine are better.
>
> Nothing about their idea will improve with further development.
>
> It is more important for me to get recognized than it is to hear their idea.
>
> I am more important than they are.[33]

Even if some of these thoughts are true, the egotism behind them is stunning. Furthermore, nonlisteners are likely to find that the people they cut off are less likely to treat their ideas with respect. Like defensiveness, listening is often reciprocal. You get what you give.

Lack of Training   Even if we want to listen well, we're often hampered by a lack of training. A common but mistaken belief is that listening is like breathing—an activity that people do well naturally. "After all," the common belief goes, "I've been listening since I was a child. I don't need to study the subject

TABLE 8.1 Comparison of Communication Activities

	LISTENING	SPEAKING	READING	WRITING
Learned	First	Second	Third	Fourth
Used	Most	Next to most	Next to least	Least
Taught	Least	Next to least	Next to most	Most

in school." The truth is that listening is a skill much like speaking: Virtually everybody does it, though few people do it well. Unfortunately, there is no connection between how competently most communicators *think* they listen and how competent they really are in their ability to understand others.[34] The good news is that listening can be improved through instruction and training.[35] Despite this fact, the amount of time spent teaching listening is far less than that spent on other types of communication. Table 8.1 reflects this upside-down arrangement.

Hearing Problems   Sometimes a person's listening ability suffers from a physiological hearing problem. In such cases, both the person with the problem and others can become frustrated at the ineffective communication that results. One survey explored the feelings of adults who have spouses with hearing loss. Nearly two-thirds of the respondents said they feel annoyed when their partner can't hear them clearly. Almost one-quarter said that beyond just being annoyed, they felt ignored, hurt, or sad. Many of the respondents believe their spouses are in denial about their condition, which makes the problem even more frustrating.[36] If you suspect that you or someone you know suffers from a hearing loss, then it's wise to have a physician or audiologist perform an examination.

Meeting the Challenge of Listening

After reading the previous section, you might decide that listening well is next to impossible. Fortunately, with the right combination of attitude and skill, you can indeed listen better. The following guidelines will show you how.

Talk Less   Zeno of Citium put it most succinctly: "We have been given two ears and but a single mouth, in order that we may hear more and talk less." If your true goal is to understand the speaker, avoid the tendency to hog the stage and shift the conversation to your ideas. Talking less doesn't mean you must remain completely silent. As you'll soon read, giving feedback that clarifies your understanding and seeks new

Auremar/Bigstock

information is an important way to understand a speaker. Nonetheless, most of us talk too much when we're claiming to understand others. Other cultures, including many Native American ones, value listening at least as much as talking.[37] You can appreciate the value of this approach by trying the "Talking Stick" Pause and Reflect exercise.

Get Rid of Distractions   Some distractions are external: ringing telephones, radio or television programs, friends dropping in, and so on. Other distractions are internal: preoccupation with your own problems, an empty stomach, and so on. If the information you're seeking is really important, do everything possible to eliminate the internal and external distractions that interfere with careful listening. This might mean turning off the TV, shutting off your cell phone, or moving to a quiet room where you won't be bothered by the lure of the computer, the work on your desk, or the food on the counter.

PAUSE *and* REFLECT

Speaking and Listening with a "Talking Stick"

MindTap REFLECT ... on using a "talking stick" by completing the activity and answering the following questions, either here or online.

PART I:

Explore the benefits of talking less and listening more by using a "talking stick." This exercise is based on the Native American tradition of "council." Gather a group from your class and join in a circle in a quiet room. Designate a particular object as the talking stick. (Almost any easily held object will do.) Participants will then pass the object around the circle. The rules of the talking stick circle are precise. Each person may speak only:

1. When holding the stick

2. For as long as he or she holds the stick

3. Without interruption from anyone else in the circle

When a member is through speaking, the stick passes to the left, and the speaker surrendering the stick must wait until it has made its way around the circle before speaking again.

PART II:

After each member of the group has had the chance to speak, discuss how this experience differed from more common approaches to listening. What desirable parts of the talking stick circle do you think could be introduced into everyday conversations?

Don't Judge Prematurely   Most people would agree that it's essential to understand a speaker's ideas before judging them. However, all of us are guilty of forming snap judgments, evaluating others before hearing them out. This tendency is greatest when the speaker's ideas conflict with our own. Conversations that ought to be exchanges of ideas turn into verbal battles, with the "opponents" trying to ambush one another in order to win a victory. It's also tempting to judge prematurely when others criticize you, even when those criticisms may contain valuable truths and when understanding them may lead to a change for the better. Even if there is no criticism or disagreement, we tend to evaluate others based on sketchy first impressions, forming snap judgments that aren't at all valid. The lesson contained in these negative examples is clear: Listen first. Make sure you understand. *Then* evaluate.

Look for Key Ideas   It's easy to lose patience with long-winded speakers who never seem to get to the point—or *have* a point, for that matter. Nonetheless, most people do have a central idea. By using your ability to think more quickly than the speaker can talk, you may be able to extract the central idea from the surrounding mass of words you're hearing. If you can't figure out what the speaker is driving at, you can always use a variety of response skills, which we'll examine now.

TYPES OF LISTENING RESPONSES

Of the five components of listening (hearing, attending, understanding, responding, and remembering), *responding* lets us know how well others are tuned in to what we're saying. Think for a moment of someone you consider a good listener. Why did you choose that person? It's probably because of the way she or he responds while you are speaking: making eye contact and nodding when you're talking, staying attentive while you're telling an important story, reacting with an exclamation when you say something startling, expressing empathy and support when you're hurting, and offering another perspective or advice when you ask for it.[38]

The rest of this chapter will describe a variety of response styles. We'll begin by describing responses that are focused on gathering more information to better understand the speaker. By chapter's end, our focus will be on listening responses that offer a speaker our assessment and direction.

Prompting

In some cases, the best response a listener can give is a small nudge to keep the speaker talking. **Prompting** involves using silences and brief statements of encouragement to draw others out. Besides helping you better understand

TEXTING TO SAVE LIVES

Crisis Text Line is the first national, 24/7 crisis-intervention hotline to conduct its conversations exclusively by text message. The majority of their clients are teens, and the range of issues for which they offer help include dating and domestic abuse, eating disorders, self-injury, GLBT challenges, veterans' problems, and suicide.

Counselors have found that adolescents often open up via text messaging in ways they don't through other channels. In this description, note how the counselors use some of the listening response skills described in this chapter—prompting, questioning, paraphrasing, and supporting.

Depression is common among teens, and its consequences are volatile: suicide is the third leading cause of death for Americans between the ages of ten and twenty-four. In that same age group, the use of text messaging is near-universal. The average adolescent sends almost two thousand text messages a month. They contact their friends more by text than by phone or e-mail or instant-message or even face-to-face conversations. For teens, texting isn't a novel form of communication; it's the default.

The act of writing, even if the product consists of only a hundred and forty characters composed with one's thumbs, forces a kind of real-time distillation of emotional chaos. The young people who contact Crisis Text Line might be doing so between classes, while waiting in line for the bus, or before soccer practice. In addition, more than ninety-eight percent of text messages are opened; they are four times more likely to be read by the recipient than e-mails. If you are a distressed teen or a counselor, you know that what you say will be read.

Counselors are trained to put texters at ease and not to jump too quickly into a problem-solving mode. Open-ended questions are good; "why" questions are bad. Also bad: making assumptions about the texter's gender or sexual orientation, sounding like a robot, using language that a young person might not know. Techniques that are encouraged include validation ("What a tough situation"); "tenta-fiers" ("Do you mind if I ask you ..."); strength identification ("You're a great brother for being so worried about him"); and empathetic responses ("It sounds like you're feeling anxious because of all these rumors"). The implicit theory is that in a conversation people are naturally inclined to fill silences.

Often, the conversations are about minor-seeming problems—fights with friends, academic pressure from parents—and the bar for helpfulness is quite low. "A lot of times, when chatting with young people, it's clear that they just need someone to listen to them," one counsellor told me. "Sometimes it's obvious. They'll say, 'Thanks for listening. Nobody ever does that,' and at other times it's less explicit; they just want to get everything out, and they provide you with a very, very detailed account."

The etiquette encouraged for counsellors can be surprising. When an agitated friend texts me bad news (a breakup, a layoff, a sudden rent increase), my instinct is to find a positive response to the predicament ("But you didn't even like him!" "Now you can finally go freelance!" "MOVE!"). But this is precisely what one is not supposed to do when communicating with a teenager in crisis. Instead, counsellors are trained to deploy language that at first seems inflammatory: "You must be devastated" is a common refrain; so is "That sounds like torture." The idea is to validate texters' feelings and respond in a way that doesn't belittle them.

Alice Gregory

MindTap ENHANCE ... your understanding by answering the following questions, either here or online.

1. What advantages might arise from using texting to seek help?

2. Which strategies described in this reading might prove helpful to you if/when you seek help?

3. Which strategies could you use when others seek your help?

the speaker, prompting can also help others clarify their thoughts and feelings. Consider this example:

Pablo: Julie's dad is selling a complete computer system for only $600, but if I want it, I have to buy it now. He's got another interested buyer. It's a great deal, but buying it would wipe out my savings. At the rate I spend money, it would take me a year to save up this much again.
Tim: Uh-huh.
Pablo: I wouldn't be able to take that ski trip over winter break … but I sure could save time with my schoolwork … and do a better job, too.
Tim: That's for sure.
Pablo: Do you think I should buy it?
Tim: I don't know. What do you think?
Pablo: I just can't decide.
Tim: *(Silence)*
Pablo: I'm going to do it. I'll never get a deal like this again.

In cases like this, your prompting can be a catalyst to help others find their own answers. Prompting will work best when it's done sincerely. Your nonverbal behaviors—eye contact, posture, facial expression, tone of voice—have to show that you are concerned with the other person's problem. Mechanical prompting is likely to irritate instead of help.

Questioning

It's easy to understand why **questioning** has been called "the most popular piece of language."[39] Asking for information can help both the person doing the asking and the one providing answers.[40]

Questioning can help you, the asker, in at least three ways. Most obviously, the answers you get can fill in facts and details that will sharpen your understanding ("Did he give you any reasons for doing that?" "What happened next?"). Also, by asking questions you can learn what others are thinking and feeling ("What's on your mind?" "Are you mad at me?") as well as what they might want ("Are you asking me to apologize?").

Besides being useful to the person doing the asking, questions can also be a tool for the one who answers. As people in the helping professions know, questions can encourage self-discovery. You can use questions to encourage others to explore their thoughts and feelings. "So, what do you see as your options?" may prompt an employee to come up with creative problem-solving alternatives. "What would be your ideal solution?" might help a friend get in touch with various wants and needs. Most important is that encouraging discovery rather than dispensing advice indicates you have faith in others' ability to think for themselves. This may be the best message that you can communicate as an effective listener.

Despite their apparent benefits, not all questions are equally helpful. Whereas **sincere questions** are aimed at understanding others, **counterfeit questions** are aimed at sending a message, not receiving one. Counterfeit questions come in several varieties:

* *Questions that trap the speaker*. When your friend says, "You didn't like that movie, did you?," you're being backed into a corner. It's clear that

your friend disapproves, so the question leaves you with two choices: You can disagree and defend your position, or you can devalue your reaction by lying or equivocating—"I guess it wasn't perfect." Consider how much easier it would be to respond to the sincere question, "What did you think of the movie?"

- *A tag question.* Phrases like "did you?" or "isn't that right?" at the end of a question can be a tip-off that the asker is looking for agreement, not information. Although some tag questions are genuine requests for confirmation, counterfeit ones are used to coerce agreement: "You said you'd call at 5 o'clock, but you forgot, didn't you?" Similarly, leading questions that begin with "Don't you," such as "Don't you think he would make a good boss?," direct others toward a desired response. As a simple solution, changing "Don't you?" to "Do you?" makes the question less leading.

- *Questions that make statements.* "Are you *finally* off the phone?" is more of a statement than a question—a fact unlikely to be lost on the targeted person. Emphasizing certain words can also turn a question into a statement: "You lent money to *Tony*?" We also use questions to offer advice. The person who asks "Are you going to stand up to him and give him what he deserves?" clearly has stated an opinion about what should be done.

- *Questions that carry hidden agendas.* "Are you busy Friday night?" is a dangerous question to answer. If you say "No," thinking the person has something fun in mind, you won't like hearing "Good, because I need help moving my piano." Obviously, such questions are not designed to enhance understanding. They are setups for the proposal that follows. Other examples include "Will you do me a favor?" and "If I tell you what happened, will you promise not to get mad?" Wise communicators answer questions that mask hidden agendas cautiously, with responses like "It depends" or "Let me hear what you have in mind before I answer."

- *Questions that seek "correct" answers.* Most of us have been victims of questioners who want to hear only a particular response. "Which shoes do you think I should wear?" can be a sincere question—unless the asker has a predetermined preference. When this happens, the asker isn't interested in listening to contrary opinions, and "incorrect" responses get shot down. Some of these questions may venture into delicate territory. "Honey, do you think I look fat?" can be a request for a "correct" answer.

- *Questions based on unchecked assumptions.* "Why aren't you listening to me?" assumes that the other person isn't paying attention. "What's the matter?" assumes that something is wrong. As Chapter 4 explains, perception checking is a much better way of checking out assumptions. As you recall, a perception check offers a description and interpretations followed by a sincere request for clarification: "When you kept looking over at the TV, I thought you weren't listening to me, but maybe I was wrong. Were you paying attention?"

Paraphrasing

For all its value, questioning won't always help you understand or help others. For example, consider what might happen when you ask for directions to a friend's home. Suppose that you've received these instructions: "Drive about a mile and then turn left at the traffic signal." Now imagine that a few common problems exist in this simple message. First, suppose that your friend's idea of "about a mile" differs from yours: Your mental picture of the distance is actually closer to 2 miles, whereas your friend's is closer to 300 yards. Next, consider that "traffic signal" really means "stop sign"; after all, it's common for us to think one thing and say another. Keeping these problems in mind, suppose that you tried to verify your understanding of the directions by asking, "After I turn at the signal, how far should I go?" to which your friend replies that the house is the third from the corner. Clearly, if you parted after this exchange, you would encounter a lot of frustration before finding the elusive residence.

Because questioning doesn't always provide the information you need, consider another kind of listening response—one that would tell you whether you understood what had already been said before you asked additional questions. This type of feedback involves restating in your own words the message you thought the speaker just sent, without adding anything new. Statements that reword the listener's interpretation of a message are commonly termed **paraphrasing**. If the listener in the preceding scenario had offered this paraphrase—"You're telling me to drive down to the traffic light by the high school and turn toward the mountains, is that it?"—it probably would have led the speaker to clarify the message.

The key to success in paraphrasing is to restate the other person's comments in your own words as a way of cross-checking the information. If you simply repeat the other person's comments verbatim, you will sound foolish—and you still might be misunderstanding what has been said. Notice the difference between simply parroting a statement and true paraphrasing:

Speaker: I'd like to go, but I can't afford it.
Parroting: You'd like to go, but you can't afford it.
Paraphrasing: So if we could find a way to pay for you, you'd be willing to come. Is that right?

Speaker: You look awful!
Parroting: You think I look terrible.
Paraphrasing: Sounds like you think I've put on too much weight.

There are two levels at which you can paraphrase messages. The first involves paraphrasing *factual information* that will help you understand the other person's ideas more clearly. At the most basic level, this sort of reflecting can prevent frustrating mix-ups: "So you want to meet *this* Tuesday, not next week, right?"

You can also paraphrase *personal information*: "So my joking makes you think I don't care about your problem." This sort of nondefensive response

In REAL LIFE

Paraphrasing on the Job

This conversation between two coworkers shows how paraphrasing can help people solve their own problems. Notice how Jill comes to a conclusion without Mark's advice. Notice also how the paraphrasing sounds natural when combined with sincere questions and other helping styles.

© Jason Harris/Cengage Learning

Jill: I've had the strangest feeling about John *(their boss)* lately.

Mark: What's that? *(A simple question invites Jill to go on.)*

Jill: I'm starting to think maybe he has this thing about women—or maybe it's just about me.

Mark: You mean he's coming on to you? *(Mark paraphrases what he thinks Jill has said.)*

Jill Oh, no, not at all! But it seems like he doesn't take women—or at least me—seriously. *(Jill corrects Mark's misunderstanding and explains herself.)*

Mark What do you mean? *(Mark asks another simple question to get more information.)*

Jill Well, whenever we're in a meeting or just talking around the office and he asks for ideas, he always seems to pick men. He gives orders to women—men, too—but he never asks the women to say what they think.

Mark So you think maybe he doesn't take women seriously, is that it? *(Mark paraphrases Jill's last statement.)*

Jill He sure doesn't seem interested in their ideas. But that doesn't mean he's a total woman hater. I know he counts on some women in the office. Teresa has been here forever, and he's always saying he couldn't live without her. And when Brenda got the new computer system up and running last month, I know he appreciated that. He gave her a day off and told everybody how she saved our lives.

Mark Now you sound confused. *(Mark reflects her apparent feeling.)*

Jill I *am* confused. I don't think it's just my imagination. I mean I'm a good producer, but he has never—not once—asked me for my ideas about how to

may be difficult when you are under attack, but it can short-circuit defensive arguments. Chapter 11 will explain in more detail how to use paraphrasing when you're being criticized.

Paraphrasing personal information can also be a tool for helping others, as the In Real Life transcript in this chapter shows.[41] Reflecting the speaker's thoughts and feelings (instead of judging or analyzing, for example) shows your involvement and concern. The nonevaluative nature of paraphrasing encourages the problem holder to discuss the matter further. Reflecting thoughts and feelings allows the problem holder to unload more of the concerns he or she has been carrying around, often leading to the relief that comes from catharsis. Finally, paraphrasing helps the problem holder to sort out the problem. The clarity that comes from this sort of perspective can

improve sales or anything. And I can't remember a time when he's asked any other women. But maybe I'm overreacting.

Mark You're not positive whether you're right, but I can tell that this has you concerned. *(Mark paraphrases both Jill's central theme and her feeling.)*

Jill Yes. But I don't know what to do about it.

Mark Maybe you should … *(Starts to offer advice but catches himself and decides to ask a question instead.)* So what are your choices?

Jill Well, I could just ask him if he's aware that he never asks women's opinions. But that might sound too aggressive and angry.

Mark And you're not angry? *(Tries to clarify how Jill is feeling.)*

Jill Not really. I don't know whether I should be angry because he's not taking ideas seriously, or whether he just doesn't take my ideas seriously, or whether it's nothing at all.

Mark So you're mostly confused. *(Reflects Jill's apparent feeling again.)*

Jill Yes! I don't know where I stand with John, and not being sure is starting to get to me. I wish I knew what he thinks of me. Maybe I could just tell him I'm confused about what is going on here and ask him to clear it up. But what if it's nothing? Then I'll look insecure.

Mark *(Mark thinks Jill should confront the boss, but he isn't positive that this is the best approach, so he paraphrases what Jill seems to be saying.)* And that would make you look bad.

Jill I'm afraid maybe it would. I wonder if I could talk it over with anybody else in the office and get their ideas …

Mark: … see what they think …

Jill Yeah. Maybe I could ask Brenda. She's easy to talk to, and I do respect her judgment. Maybe she could give me some ideas about how to handle this.

Mark Sounds like you're comfortable with talking to Brenda first. *(Paraphrases)*

Jill *(Warming to the idea)* Yes! Then if it's nothing, I can calm down. But if I do need to talk to John, I'll know I'm doing the right thing.

Mark Great. Let me know how it goes.

MindTap **APPLY …** this situation to your life by answering questions online.

make it possible to find solutions that weren't apparent before. These features make paraphrasing a vital skill in the human services professions, leadership training, and even hostage negotiation.[42]

Effective paraphrasing is a skill that takes time to develop. You can make your paraphrasing sound more natural by taking any of three approaches, depending on the situation:

1. Change the speaker's wording:

   Speaker: Bilingual education is just another failed idea of bleeding-heart liberals.

   Paraphrase: Let me see if I've got this right. You're mad because you think bilingual ed sounds good, but it doesn't work?

2. Offer an example of what you think the speaker is talking about:

Speaker: Lee is such a jerk. I can't believe the way he acted last night.

Paraphrase: You think those jokes were pretty offensive, huh?

3. Reflect the underlying theme of the speaker's remarks:

Paraphrase: You keep reminding me to be careful. Sounds like you're worried that something might happen to me. Am I right?

Paraphrasing won't always be accurate. However, expressing your restatement tentatively gives the other person a chance to make a correction. (Note how the examples end with questions in an attempt to confirm if the paraphrase was accurate.)

Because it's an unfamiliar way of responding, paraphrasing may feel awkward at first, but if you start by paraphrasing occasionally and then gradually increase the frequency of such responses, you can begin to learn the benefits. You can begin practicing paraphrasing by trying the Skill Builder in this section.

There are several factors to consider before you decide to paraphrase:

1. **Is the issue complex enough?** If you're fixing dinner, and someone wants to know when it will be ready, it would be exasperating to hear, "You're interested in knowing when we'll be eating."

2. **Do you have the necessary time and concern?** Paraphrasing can take a good deal of time. Therefore, if you're in a hurry, it's wise to avoid starting a conversation you won't be able to finish. Even more important than time is concern. Paraphrasing that comes across as mechanical or insincere reflecting can do more harm than good.[43]

3. **Can you withhold judgment?** Use paraphrasing only if you are willing to focus on the speaker's message without injecting your own judgments. It can be tempting to rephrase others' comments in a way that leads them toward the position you think is best without ever clearly stating your intentions.

4. **Is your paraphrasing in proportion to other responses?** Paraphrasing can become annoying when it's overused. This is especially true if you suddenly add this approach to your style. A far better way to use paraphrasing is to gradually introduce it into your repertoire.

Supporting

There are times when other people want to hear more than a reflection of how *they* feel; they would like to know how *you* feel for and about them. **Supporting** reveals a listener's solidarity with the speaker's situation. One scholar describes supporting as "expressions of care, concern, affection, and interest, especially during times of stress or upset."[44]

There are several types of listening responses that can provide support:

Empathizing   "I can understand why you'd be upset about this."
"Yeah, that class was tough for me, too."

Agreement   "You're right—the landlord is being unfair."
"Sounds like the job is a perfect match for you."

Offers to help	"I'm here if you need me."
	"I'd be happy to study with you for the next test if you'd like."
Praise	"Wow—you did a fantastic job!"
	"You're a terrific person, and if she doesn't recognize it, that's her problem!"
Reassurance	"The worst part seems to be over. It will probably get easier from here."
	"I'm sure you'll do a great job."

SKILL *Builder*

Paraphrasing Practice

MindTap° **PRACTICE ...** your skill at paraphrasing by completing the exercise and answering the following questions, either here or online.

This exercise will help you see that it is possible to understand someone who disagrees with you without arguing or sacrificing your point of view.

1. Work in groups of three. Designate one person as A, another as B, and the third as C, the observer.

2. Find a topic on which person A and person B apparently disagree—a current events topic, a philosophical or moral issue, or perhaps simply a matter of personal taste.

3. Person A begins by making a personal statement on the subject, while person B listens without interruption, and person C observes. If person B responds before person A is done speaking, person C's job is to act as a referee, allowing person A to continue.

4. When person A has completed his or her statement, person B's job is to then paraphrase the statement. Person B should offer a clean paraphrase, in no way indicating agreement or disagreement with A's remarks. If person B offers an opinion within the paraphrase, person C's job is to

act as a referee and remind them about the rules of the exercise.

5. Person A then responds by telling person B whether the response was accurate, sticking with the content of the message rather than criticizing person B's performance. If there was some misunderstanding, person A should clarify the message, and B should offer a revised paraphrase of his or her new understanding of the statement. Again, person C's role is to observe and act as a neutral referee if the conversation diverts from the rules of the exercise. This process should continue until everyone is sure that B understands A's statement.

6. Now it's B's turn to respond to A's statement and for A to help the process of understanding by correcting B. Person C will again perform the role of neutral observer. This process continues until all partners are satisfied that they have explained themselves fully and have been heard by their partners.

7. Now, person C should switch places with person A and have an opportunity to send a message to and receive a message from person B, repeating steps 2, 3, and 4 above.

8. After this exercise is complete, answer reflection questions online.

> Adam (Joseph Gordon-Levitt) receives a variety of listening responses—some more helpful than others—from friends, family, and professionals as he battles cancer in the movie 50/50. These range from nondirective empathizing to highly directive advice. What kinds of listening responses do you offer when someone you know is hurting? What kind of responses do you like to receive when you're the one struggling?

Lionsgate/Allstar

It's easy to identify what effective support *doesn't* sound like. Some scholars have called these messages "cold comfort."[45] As the following examples suggest, you're probably *not* being supportive if you:

- *Deny others the right to their feelings.* Consider the stock remark "Don't worry about it." Although it may be intended as a reassuring comment, the underlying message is that the speaker wants the person to feel differently. The irony is that the suggestion probably won't work—after all, it's unlikely that people can or will stop worrying just because you tell them to do so.[46] Research about such responses is clear: "Messages that explicitly acknowledge, elaborate, and legitimize the feelings and perspective of a distressed person are perceived as more helpful messages than those which only implicitly recognize or deny the feelings and perspective of the other."[47]

- *Minimize the significance of the situation.* Consider the times you've been told, "Hey, it's only ___." You can probably fill in the blank in a variety of ways: "a job," "her opinion," "a test," "puppy love," "a party." To someone who has been the victim of verbal abuse, the hurtful message isn't "just words"; to a child who didn't get an invitation, it isn't "just a party"; to a worker who has been chewed out by the boss, it isn't "just a job."

- *Focus on "then and there" rather than "here and now."* Although it is sometimes true that "you'll feel better tomorrow," it sometimes isn't. Even if the prediction that "ten years from now you won't remember her name" proves correct, it provides little comfort to someone experiencing heartbreak today.

- *Cast judgment.* It usually isn't encouraging to hear "You know, it's your own fault—you really shouldn't have done that" after you've confessed to making a poor decision. As you'll learn in Chapter 11, evaluative and condescending statements are more likely to engender defensiveness than to help people change for the better.

- *Focus on yourself.* It can be tempting to talk at length about a similar experience you've encountered ("I know exactly how you feel. Something like that happened to me…."). While your intent might be to show empathy, research shows that such messages aren't perceived as helpful because they draw attention away from the distressed person.[48]

- *Defend yourself.* When your response to others' concerns is to defend yourself ("Don't blame me; I've done my part"), it's clear that you are more concerned with yourself than with supporting the other person.

How often do people fail to provide appropriate supportive responses? One survey of mourners who had recently suffered from the death of a loved one reported that 80 percent of the statements made to them were unhelpful.[49] Nearly half of the "helpful" statements were advice: "You've got to get out more." "Don't question God's will." Despite their frequency, these suggestions were helpful only 3 percent of the time. Far more helpful were expressions that acknowledged the mourner's feelings, such as "This must be so hard—I know how much she meant to you." Chapter 9 will describe other ways to supply social support to the people in your life.

When handled correctly, supporting responses *can* be helpful. Guidelines for effective support include:

1. **Recognize that you can support another person's struggles without approving of his or her decisions**. Suppose, for instance, that a friend has decided to quit a job that you think she should keep. You could still be supportive by saying, "I know you've given this a lot of thought and that you're doing what you think is best." Responses like this can provide face-saving support without compromising your principles.[50]

2. **Monitor the other person's reaction to your support**. If it doesn't seem to help, consider other types of responses that let him or her explore the issue.

3. **Realize that support may not always be welcome**. In one survey, some people reported occasions when social support wasn't necessary because they felt capable of handling the problem themselves.[51] Many regarded uninvited support as an intrusion, and some said it left them feeling more nervous than before. The majority of respondents expressed a preference for being in control of whether their distressing situation should be discussed with even the most helpful friend.

4. **Make sure you're ready for the consequences.** Talking about a difficult event may reduce distress for the speaker but increase distress for the listener.[52] Recognize that supporting another person is a worthwhile but potentially taxing venture.

MindTap PRACTICE…
Your skill at empathic listening by completing the Concepts in Play activity online.

How to Help ...
and Not Help

*S*usan Silk is a clinical psychologist. Barry Goldman is an arbitrator and mediator and the author of The Science of Settlement: Ideas for Negotiators.

When Susan had breast cancer, we heard a lot of lame remarks, but our favorite came from one of Susan's colleagues. She wanted, she needed, to visit Susan after the surgery, but Susan didn't feel like having visitors, and she said so. Her colleague's response? "This isn't just about you."

"It's not?" Susan wondered. "My breast cancer is not about me? It's about you?"

Susan has since developed a simple technique to help people avoid this mistake. It works for all kinds of crises: medical, legal, financial, romantic, even existential. She calls it the Ring Theory.

Draw a circle. This is the center ring. In it, put the name of the person at the center of the current trauma. Now draw a larger circle around the first one. In that ring, put the name of the person next closest to the trauma. Repeat the process as many times as you need to. In each larger ring, put the next closest people. Parents and children before more distant relatives. Intimate friends in smaller rings, less intimate friends in larger ones.

Here are the rules. The person in the center ring can say anything she wants to anyone, anywhere.

She can kvetch and complain and whine and moan and curse the heavens and say, "Life is unfair" and "Why me?" That's the one payoff for being in the center ring.

Everyone else can say those things too, but only to people in larger rings.

When you are talking to a person in a ring smaller than yours, someone closer to the center of the crisis, the goal is to help. Listening is often more helpful than talking. But if you're going to open your mouth, ask yourself if what you are about to say is likely to provide comfort and support. If it isn't, don't say it.

Don't, for example, give advice. People who are suffering from trauma don't need advice. They need comfort and support. So say "I'm sorry" or "This must really be hard for you" or "Can I bring you a pot roast?" Don't say "You should hear what happened to me" or "Here's what I would do if I were you." And don't say "This is really bringing me down."

If you want to scream or cry or complain, if you want to tell someone how shocked you are or how icky you feel or whine about how it reminds you of all the terrible things that have happened to you lately, that's fine. It's a perfectly normal response. Just do it to someone in a bigger ring.

Comfort IN, dump OUT.

Remember, you can say whatever you want if you just wait until you're talking to someone in a larger ring than yours.

And don't worry. You'll get your turn in the center ring. You can count on that.

Comfort IN / lookie loos / significant other, parent, sis, etc. / the aggrieved or afflicted / true friends / colleagues / dump OUT

Analyzing

When **analyzing**, the listener offers an interpretation of a speaker's message. Analyses like these are probably familiar to you:

"I think what's really bothering you is …"

"She's doing it because …"

"I don't think you really meant that."

"Maybe the problem started when he …"

Interpretations are often effective ways to help people with problems to consider alternative meanings—meanings they would have never thought of without your help. Sometimes an analysis will make a confusing problem suddenly clear, either suggesting a solution or at least providing an understanding of what is occurring.

In other cases, an analysis can create more problems than it solves. There are two potential problems with analyzing. First, your interpretation may not be correct, in which case the speaker may become even more confused by accepting it. Second, even if your analysis is correct, telling it to the problem holder might not be useful. There's a chance that it will arouse defensiveness (because analysis implies superiority). Even if it doesn't, the person may not be able to understand your view of the problem without working it out personally.

How can you know when it's helpful to offer an analysis? There are several guidelines to follow:

- *Offer your interpretation as tentative rather than as absolute fact.* There's a big difference between saying "Maybe the reason is …" or "The way it looks to me …" and insisting "This is the truth."

- *You ought to be sure that the other person will be receptive to your analysis.* Even if you're completely accurate, your thoughts won't help if the problem holder isn't ready to consider them.

- *Be sure that your motive for offering an analysis is truly to help the other person.* It can be tempting to offer an analysis to show how brilliant you are or even to make the other person feel bad for not having thought of the right answer in the first place. Needless to say, an analysis offered under such conditions isn't helpful.

Advising

When we are approached with another's problem, a common tendency is to respond with **advising**: to help by offering a solution.[53] Advice can sometimes be helpful, as long as it's given in a respectful, caring way.[54]

Despite its apparent value, advice has its limits. Research has shown that it is actually *unhelpful* at least as often as it's helpful.[55]

ⱽ If you're looking for a shoulder to cry on when you're in trouble, *Scandal's* Olivia Pope (Kerry Washington) is probably the wrong person. Pope's strength is quickly sizing up a problem and then giving directive solutions. She's far more likely to say "Here's what you need to do" than "I'm sorry to hear that." Are there times when you want advice more than empathy? Is it possible to give some of both?

ABC/Photofest

Studies on advice giving offer the following important considerations when trying to help others:[56]

- *Is the advice needed?* If the person has already taken a course of action, giving advice after the fact ("I can't believe you got back together with him") is rarely appreciated.

- *Is the advice wanted?* People generally don't value unsolicited advice. It's usually best to ask if the speaker is interested in hearing your counsel. Remember that sometimes people just want a listening ear, not solutions to their problems.

- *Is the advice given in the right sequence?* Advice is more likely to be received after the listener first seeks to understand the speaker and the situation. For instance, teachers who ask questions in parent-teacher conversations before launching into problem-solving are perceived as more effective communicators.[57] It helps to know the facts prior to offering advice.

- *Is the advice coming from an expert?* If you want to offer advice about anything from car purchasing to relationship managing, it's important to have experience and success in those matters. If you *don't* have expertise, it's a good idea to offer the speaker supportive responses, then encourage that person to seek out expert counsel.

- *Is the advisor a close and trusted person?* Although sometimes we seek out advice from people we don't know well (perhaps because they have expertise), in most cases we value advice given within the context of a close and ongoing interpersonal relationship.

- *Is the advice offered in a sensitive, face-saving manner?* No one likes to feel bossed or belittled, even if the advice is good. Remember that messages have both content and relational dimensions, and sometimes the unstated relational messages when giving advice ("I'm smarter than you"; "You're not bright enough to figure this out yourself") will keep people from hearing counsel.[58]

To see these recommendations in practice, we can look at how one study categorized and analyzed advice exchanges in an online breast cancer support group site.[59] Nearly 40 percent of the posted messages involved advice seeking or giving, so it's clearly a site where people look for and extend counsel. However, very few posters asked the community to tell them what they "should do." They typically requested "comments" rather than "advice." Recommendations were often couched within personal narratives, using a "here's what worked for me" format. Advice seekers tried to find people who were "in the same boat," preferring to hear from those whose situations matched their own.

These observations reinforce some important principles about communicating advice. People are more willing to listen to advice that's requested, especially when it comes from a credible, empathic source. When giving advice, it's best to offer it as open-handed information rather than as heavy-handed prescriptions.

Judging

A **judging** response evaluates the sender's thoughts or behaviors in some way. The judgment may be favorable—"That's a good idea" or "You're on the right

PAUSE *and* REFLECT

When Advising Does and Doesn't Work

MindTap **REFLECT ...** on your advising skills by answering the following questions, either here or online.

To see why advising can be tricky business, follow these steps:

1. Recall an instance when someone gave you advice that proved helpful. Review the guidelines for offering advice in this section and see if you recognize any that your advice giver followed.

2. Now recall an instance when someone gave you advice that *wasn't* helpful. Again, review the guidelines. Did that person violate any of them? Which ones?

3. Based on your insights here, describe how you can advise (or not advise) others in a way that is truly helpful.

track now"—or unfavorable—"An attitude like that won't get you anywhere." But in either case, it implies that the person doing the judging is in some way qualified to pass judgment on the speaker's thoughts or actions.

Sometimes negative judgments are purely critical. How many times have you heard such responses as "Well, you asked for it!" or "I *told* you so!" or "You're just feeling sorry for yourself"? Although responses like these can sometimes serve as a verbal slap that brings problem holders to their senses, they usually make matters worse.

In other cases, negative judgments are less critical. These involve what we usually call *constructive criticism*, which is intended to help the problem holder improve in the future. This is the sort of response given by friends about everything from the choice of clothing to jobs to friends. Another common setting for constructive criticism occurs in school, where instructors evaluate students' work to help them master concepts and skills. But whether it's justified or not, even constructive criticism runs the risk of arousing defensiveness because it may threaten the self-concept of the person at whom it is directed (we'll discuss this further in Chapter 11).

Judgments have the best chance of being received when two conditions exist:

1. The person with the problem has requested an evaluation from you. Occasionally an unsolicited evaluation may bring someone to his or her senses, but more often an unsolicited evaluation will trigger a defensive response.
2. The intent of your judgment has genuinely constructive and not designed as a put-down. If you are tempted to use judgments as a weapon, don't fool yourself into thinking that you are being helpful. Often the statement "I'm telling you this for your own good ..." simply isn't true.

Now that you're aware of all the possible listening responses, try the following Pause and Reflect exercise in this section to see how you might use them in everyday situations.

PAUSE *and* REFLECT

What Would You Say?

MindTap° **REFLECT . . .** on how you would respond by answering the following questions, either here or online.

1. In each of the following situations, describe what you would say in response to the problem being shared and identify the response type(s) used.

    a. My family doesn't understand me. Everything I like seems to go against their values, and they just won't accept my feelings as being right for me. It's not that they don't love me—they do. But they don't accept me.

    b. I've been pretty discouraged lately. I just can't get a good relationship going with any guys. I've got plenty of male friends, but that's always as far as it goes. I'm tired of being just a pal . . . I want to be more than that.

    c. *(Child to parents)* I hate you! You always go out and leave me with some stupid sitter. Why don't you like me?

    d. I don't know what I want to do with my life. I'm tired of school, but there aren't any good jobs around. I could just drop out for a while, but that doesn't really sound very good, either.

    e. Things really seem to be kind of lousy in my marriage lately. It's not that we fight much, but all the excitement seems to be gone. We're in a rut, and it keeps getting worse. . . .

    f. I keep getting the idea that my boss is angry at me. It seems as if lately he hasn't been joking around very much, and he hasn't said anything at all about my work for about three weeks now. I wonder what I should do.

2. After you've written your response to each of these messages, imagine the probable outcome of the conversation that would have followed. If you've tried this exercise in class, you might have two group members role-play each response. Based on your idea of how the conversation might have gone, decide which responses were likely to be productive and which were unproductive, identify which response skills were likely to be productive and which were unproductive, and reflect on what you've learned from this exercise.

Choosing the Best Response

By now you can see that there are many ways to respond as a listener. Research shows that, in the right circumstances, *all* response styles can help others accept their situation, feel better, and have a sense of control over their problems.[60] But there is enormous variability in which style will work with a given person.[61] This fact explains why communicators who use a wide variety of response styles are usually more effective than those who use just one or two styles.[62] However, there are other factors to consider when choosing how to respond to a speaker.

Gender   Research shows that men and women differ in the ways they listen and respond to others.[63] Women are more likely than men to give supportive responses when presented with another person's problem,[64] are more skillful at composing such messages,[65] and are more likely to seek out such responses from listeners.[66] By contrast, men are less skillful at providing emotional support to those who are distressed,[67] and they're more likely to respond to others' problems by offering advice or by diverting the topic. In a study of helping styles in sororities and fraternities, researchers found that sorority women frequently respond with emotional support when asked to help; also, they rated their sisters as being better at listening nonjudgmentally and on comforting and showing concern for them. Fraternity men, on the other hand, fit the stereotypical pattern of offering help by challenging their brothers to evaluate their attitudes and values.[68]

The temptation when hearing these facts is to conclude that in times of distress, women want support and men want advice—but research doesn't bear that out. Numerous studies show that both men and women prefer and want supportive, endorsing messages in difficult situations.[69] The fact that women are more adept at creating and delivering such messages explains why both males and females tend to seek out women listeners when they want emotional support. When it comes to gender, it's important to remember that while men and women sometimes use different response styles, they all need a listening ear.

The Situation   Sometimes people need your advice. At other times, people need encouragement and support, and, in still other cases, your analysis or judgment will be most helpful. And, as you have seen, sometimes your probes and paraphrasing can help people find their own answers. In other words, a competent communicator needs to analyze the situation and develop an appropriate response.[70] As a rule of thumb, it's often wise to begin with responses that seek understanding and offer a minimum of direction, such as prompting, questioning, paraphrasing, and supporting. Once you've gathered the facts and demonstrated your interest and concern, it's likely that the speaker will be more receptive to (and perhaps even ask for) your analyzing, advising, and evaluating responses.[71]

Creatista/Shutterstock.com

The Other Person   Besides considering the situation, you should also consider the other person when deciding which style to use. Some people are able to consider advice thoughtfully, whereas others use advice to avoid making their own decisions. Many communicators are extremely defensive and aren't capable of receiving analysis or judgments without lashing out. Still others aren't equipped to think through problems clearly enough to profit from paraphrasing and probing. One study found that highly rational people tend to respond more positively to advice than do more emotional people.[72]

Sophisticated listeners choose a style that fits the person. One way to determine the most appropriate response is to ask the speaker what she or he wants from you. A simple question such as "Are you looking for my advice, or do you just want a listening ear right now?" can help you give others the kinds of responses they're looking for.

Your Personal Style   Finally, consider yourself when deciding how to respond. Most of us reflexively use one or two response styles. You may be best at listening quietly, offering a prompt from time to time. Or perhaps you are especially insightful and can offer a truly useful analysis of the problem.

ETHICAL *Challenge*

Unconditional Positive Regard

Carl Rogers was the best-known advocate of paraphrasing as a helping tool. As a psychotherapist, Rogers focused on how professionals can help others, but he and his followers were convinced that the same approach can work in all interpersonal relationships.

Rogers used several terms to describe his approach. Sometimes he labeled it *nondirective*, sometimes *client-centered*, and at other times *person-centered*.[a] All of these terms reflect his belief that the best way to help another is to offer a supportive climate in which the people seeking help can find their own answers. Rogers believed that advising, judging, analyzing, and questioning are not the best ways to help others solve their problems. Instead, Rogers and his followers were convinced that people are basically good and that they can improve without receiving any guidance from others, after they accept and respect themselves.

An essential ingredient for person-centered helping is what Rogers called *unconditional positive regard*. This attitude requires the helper to treat the speaker's ideas respectfully and nonjudgmentally. Unconditional positive regard means accepting others for who they are, even when you don't approve of their posture toward life. Treating a help seeker with unconditional positive regard doesn't oblige you to agree with everything the help seeker thinks, feels, or does, but it does oblige you to suspend judgment about the rightness or wrongness of the help seeker's thoughts and actions.

A person-centered approach to helping places heavy demands on the listener. At the skill level, it demands an ability to reflect the speaker's thoughts and feelings perceptively and accurately. Even more difficult, though, is the challenge of listening and responding without passing judgment on the speaker's ideas or behavior.[b]

Unconditional positive regard is especially hard when we are faced with the challenge of listening and responding to someone whose beliefs, attitudes, and values differ profoundly from our own. This approach requires the helper to follow the familiar prescription of loving the sinner while hating the sin.

Of course, it's also possible to rely on a response style that is unhelpful. You may be overly judgmental or too eager to advise, even when your suggestions aren't invited or productive. As you think about how to respond to another's messages, consider both your strengths and weaknesses and adapt accordingly.

SUMMARY

Listening is the most common—and perhaps the most overlooked—form of communication. There is a difference between hearing and listening, and there is also a difference between mindless and mindful listening. Listening, defined as the process of making sense of others' messages, consists of five elements: hearing, attending, understanding, responding, and remembering.

Several responding styles masquerade as listening but actually are only poor imitations of the real thing. We listen poorly for a variety of reasons. Some reasons have to do with the tremendous number of messages that bombard us daily and with the personal preoccupations, noise, and rapid thoughts that distract us from focusing on the information we are exposed to. Another set of reasons has to do with the considerable effort involved in listening carefully and the mistaken belief that there are more rewards in speaking than in listening. A few listeners fail to receive messages because of physical hearing defects; others listen poorly because of lack of training. Some keys to better listening are to talk less, reduce distractions, avoid making premature judgments, and seek the speaker's key ideas.

Listening responses are the primary way we evaluate whether and how others are paying attention to us. Some listening responses put a premium on gathering information and providing support; these include prompting, questioning, paraphrasing, and supporting. Other listening responses focus more on providing direction and evaluation; these include analyzing, advising, and judging. The most effective communicators use a variety of these styles, taking into consideration factors such as gender, the situation at hand, the person with the problem, and their own personal style.

KEY TERMS

advising
ambushing
analyzing
attending
counterfeit questions
defensive listening
hearing
insensitive listening
insulated listening
judging
listening
listening fidelity
mindful listening

mindless listening
paraphrasing
prompting
pseudolistening
questioning
remembering
responding
selective listening
sincere questions
stage-hogging
supporting
understanding

CHAPTER EIGHT

Listening: More Than Meets the Ear

OUTLINE

Use this outline to take notes as you read the chapter in the text or as your instructor lectures in class.

I. LISTENING DEFINED

    A. Hearing versus Listening

    B. Mindless Listening

    C. Mindful Listening

II. ELEMENTS IN THE LISTENING PROCESS

    A. Hearing

    B. Attending

    C. Understanding

    D. Responding

    E. Remembering

III. THE CHALLENGE OF LISTENING

    A. Types of Ineffective Listening

       1. Pseudolistening

       2. Stage Hogging

       3. Selective Listening

       4. Insulated Listening

       5. Defensive Listening

       6. Ambushing

       7. Insensitive Listening

    B. Why We Don't Listen Better

       1. Message Overload

       2. Preoccupation

       3. Rapid Thought

       4. Effort

       5. External Noise

6. Faulty Assumptions

7. Lack of Apparent Advantages

8. Lack of Training

9. Hearing Problems

C. Meeting the Challenge of Listening Better

1. Talk Less

2. Get Rid of Distractions

3. Don't Judge Prematurely

4. Look for Key Ideas

IV. TYPES OF LISTENING RESPONSES

A. Prompting

B. Questioning

1. Ask Sincere Questions

2. Avoid Counterfeit Questions That

   a. Trap the Speaker

   b. Tag Questions

   c. Make Statements

   d. Carry Hidden Agendas

   e. Seek "Correct" Answers

   f. Are Based on Unchecked Assumptions

C. Paraphrasing

1. Factual Information

2. Personal Information

   a. Rephrase the Speaker's Wording

   b. Offer an Example

   c. Maintain the Underlying Meaning and Theme

3. When to Paraphrase

   a. If the Problem Is Complex Enough

   b. If You Have Necessary Time and Concern

   c. When You Are Able to Withhold Judgment

   d. If It Is Proportional

D. Supporting

1. Types

   a. Empathizing Agreement

   b. Offers to Help

   c. Praise

   d. Reassurance

  2. Cold Comfort
    a. Denying Others the Right to Their Feelings
    b. Minimizing the Significance of the Situation
    c. Focusing on "Then and There" Not "Here and Now"
    d. Casting Judgment
    e. Defending Yourself
  3. Guidelines
    a. Approval Not Necessary
    b. Monitor Reactions
    c. Support May Not Always Be Welcome
    d. Be Ready for the Consequences

E. Analyzing
  1. Be Tentative
  2. Have a Receptive Other
  3. Be Sure Your Motives Are to Help

F. Advising
  1. Is the Advice Needed?
  2. Is the Advice Wanted?
  3. Is the Advice Given in the Right Sequence?
  4. Is the Advice Coming from an Expert?
  5. Is the Advisor a Close and Trusted Person?
  6. Is the Advice Offered in a Sensitive, Face-Saving Manner?

G. Judging
  1. Negative Judgments
  2. Constructive Criticism
    a. The Person Should Have Requested an Evaluation
    b. The Intent of Your Judgment Should Be Genuinely Constructive

H. Choosing the Best Listening Response
  1. Gender
  2. The Situation
  3. The Other Person
  4. Your Personal Style

KEY TERMS

advising	insulated listening	questioning
ambushing	judging	rapid thought
analyzing	listening	remembering
attending	listening fidelity	responding
counterfeit questions	message overload	selective listening
defensive listening	mindful listening	shift-response
dual-process theory	mindless listening	sincere questions
external noise	paraphrasing	stage-hogging
faulty assumptions	preoccupation	supporting
hearing	prompting	tag question
insensitive listening	pseudolistening	understanding

Class _____   Name _____

ACTIVITIES

8.1 LISTENING DIARY

LEARNING OBJECTIVES

- Identify the situations in which you listen mindfully and those when you listen mindlessly, and evaluate the appropriateness of each style in a given situation.
- Identify the circumstances in which you listen ineffectively, and the poor listening habits you use in these circumstances.

BACKGROUND

Looking Out Looking In identifies several styles of effective and ineffective listening that you can use when listening to others, including:

pseudolistening	insensitive listening	supporting
stage-hogging	ambushing	analyzing
selective listening	prompting	advising
insulated listening	questioning	judging
defensive listening	paraphrasing	

INSTRUCTIONS

1. Use the following form to record the listening styles you used in various situations during a period of at least four days.
2. After completing your diary, record your conclusions.

TIME AND PLACE	PEOPLE	SUBJECT	LISTENING STYLE(S)	CONSE-QUENCES
EXAMPLE *Saturday night party*	*My date and several new acquaintances*	*Good backpacking trips*	*Stage-hogging: I steered everybody's remarks around to my own experiences.*	*I guess I was trying to get everyone to like me, but my egotistical attitude probably accomplished the opposite.*
1.				

TIME AND PLACE	PEOPLE	SUBJECT	LISTENING STYLE(S)	CONSE-QUENCES
2.				
3.				
4.				

Based on your observations, what styles of effective listening do you use most often? In what situations do you use each of these styles? (Consider the people involved, the time, subject, and your personal mood when determining situational variables.) What are the consequences of using the listening styles you have just described?

_____

_____

_____

Based on your observations, what styles of ineffective listening do you use most often? In what situations do you use each of these styles? (Consider the people involved, the time, subject, and your personal mood when determining situational variables.) What are the consequences of using the listening styles you have just described?

_____

_____

_____

Overall, how might you increase your listening effectiveness? Which styles should you avoid using? Which styles should you use more often? Explain your answers with examples.

_____

_____

_____

8.2 EFFECTIVE QUESTIONING

LEARNING OBJECTIVES

- Recognize the differences between counterfeit and genuine questions.
- Demonstrate the ability to use effective questioning as a listening response skill.

INSTRUCTIONS

1. For each of the following statements, write three questions to get more information. Create one counterfeit question that is designed to trap the speaker, carry hidden agendas, seek "correct" answers, or is based on unchecked assumptions, and write two questions genuinely designed to get more information.
2. Enter statement examples of your own and two genuine (noncounterfeit) questions to solicit information.

EXAMPLE

"It's not fair that I have to work so much. Other students can get better grades because they have the time to study."
Counterfeit question: Even if you had more time to study, you don't really think that you could get a better grade, do you?
Genuine questions: *How do you feel when others score higher than you?*

How many hours a week do you work?

_____

1. "I guess it's OK for you to use my computer, but you have to understand that I've put a lot of time and money into it."

_____

_____

2. "You'll have the best chance at getting a loan for the new car you want if you give us a complete financial statement and credit history."

_____

_____

3. (Instructor to student) "This paper shows a lot of promise. It could probably earn you an A grade if you just develop the idea about the problems that arise from poor listening a bit more."

_____

_____

4. "I do like the communication course, but it's not at all what I expected. It's much more *personal,* if you know what I mean."

    _____

    _____

5. "We just got started on your car's transmission. I'm pretty sure we can have it ready tonight."

    _____

    _____

6. "I do think it's wrong to take any lives, but sometimes I think certain criminals deserve capital punishment."

    _____

    _____

7. "My son never tells me what's going on in his life. And now he's moving away."

    _____

    _____

8. "My family is so controlling. They make it impossible for me to escape."

    _____

    _____

9. "It was a great game, I guess. I played a lot, but only scored once. The coach put Ryan in ahead of me."

    _____

    _____

10. "We had a great evening last night. The dinner was fantastic; so was the party. We saw lots of people. Erin loves that sort of thing."

    _____

    _____

11. (Your example) _____

_____

_____

12. (Your example) _____

_____

_____

8.3 PARAPHRASING

LEARNING OBJECTIVES

- Understand the process and appropriate use of paraphrasing.
- Apply paraphrasing effectively in a given situation.

BACKGROUND

The most helpful paraphrasing responses reflect both the speaker's thoughts and feelings. In order for this style of helping to be effective, you also have to sound like yourself and not another person or a robot. There are many ways to reflect another's thoughts and feelings:

"It sounds like you're…"   "And so…"
"I hear you saying…"   "Is it that…"
"Let me see if I've got it. You're saying…"   "Are you…"
"So you're telling me…"   "Could you mean…"

Leave your paraphrase open (tentative) by using words that invite the speaker to clarify or correct your paraphrase (ex: "Is that right?")

INSTRUCTIONS

Write a paraphrasing response for each of the statements that follow. Be sure that the response fits your style of speaking, while at the same time it reflects the speaker's *thoughts* and *feelings*.

EXAMPLE

"Stan always wants to tell me about the woman he's currently going out with or the project he's currently working on. He gives me details that take hours, but he rarely asks about who I'm going out with or what I'm interested in."
"It seems like you might be tired (feeling) of hearing about Stan's love life (thoughts) and maybe a little put-out (feeling) that he doesn't solicit information from you about whom you're dating (thoughts)—is that it?"

1. "I hate this instructor. First she told me my paper was too short, so I gave her more information. Now she tells me it's too wordy."

   _____

   _____

   _____

2. "I worked up that whole study—did all the surveying, the compiling, and the writing. It was my idea in the first place. But he turned it in to the head office with his name on it, and he got the credit."

_____

_____

_____

3. "We can't decide whether to put Grandmother in a nursing home. She hates the idea, but she can't take care of herself anymore, and it's just too much for us."

_____

_____

_____

4. "She believed everything he said about me. She wouldn't even listen to my side—just started yelling at me. I thought we were better friends than that."

_____

_____

_____

5. "I'm really starting to hate my job. Every day I do the same boring, mindless work. But if I quit, I might not find any better work."

_____

_____

_____

6. "My girlfriend hasn't called me in forever. I think she must be mad at me."

_____

_____

_____

7. "How can I tell him how I really feel? He might get mad, and then we'd start arguing. He'll think I don't love him if I tell him my real feelings. I'm at a loss."

_____

_____

_____

8. "Why don't you try to be a little less messy around here? This place looks like a dump to all our friends."

_____

_____

_____

9. "There's no reasoning with him. All he cares about is his image—not all the work I have to do to cover for him."

_____

_____

_____

10. "You'd think someone who loves you would take off to be with you now and then, wouldn't you?"

_____

_____

_____

11. "This new software program is supposed to save time? That's a joke."

_____

_____

_____

12. "He acts as if staying home with two children all day is easy. I'm more tired now than when I worked full-time—and I got paid then and had weekends and evenings off!"

_____

_____

_____

13. "My father is so needy since my mother died. I have no life of my own."

_____

_____

_____

14. "Group projects are a nightmare. There should be a warning sign for classes that require them."

_____

_____

_____

8.4 LISTENING CHOICES

LEARNING OBJECTIVES

- Demonstrate an array of listening styles that you might use to respond effectively in a given situation.
- Identify the listening style you believe would be the most effective in that situation.

INSTRUCTIONS

For each of the problem statements below, write a response in each style of helping discussed in *Looking Out/Looking In*. Make your response as realistic as possible. Then indicate which style you believe would be the most effective and the least effective in this situation. To conclude, record a situation of your own, write listening responses for it, and indicate which style you would choose and why.

EXAMPLE

"I don't know what to do. I tried to explain to my professor why the assignment was late, but he wouldn't even listen to me."

Prompting *(Short silence): And so… ? (Look expectantly at partner)*.

Questioning: *What did he say? Can you make up the assignment? How do you feel about this?*

Paraphrasing: *You sound really discouraged, since he didn't even seem to care about your reasons—is that it?*

Supporting: *All of your work has been so good that I'm sure this one assignment won't matter. Don't worry!*

Analyzing: *I think the reason he wasn't sympathetic is because he hears lots of excuses this time of year.*

Advising: *You ought to write him a note. He might be more open if he has time to read it and think about it.*

Judging: *You have to accept these things. Moping won't do any good, so quit feeling sorry for yourself.*

1. My girlfriend says she wants to date other guys this summer while I'm away, working construction. She claims it's just to keep busy and that it won't make any difference with us, but I think she wants to break off permanently, and she's trying to do it gently.

   Prompting _____

   Questioning _____

   _____

   Paraphrasing _____

   _____

   Supporting _____

   _____

Analyzing _____

_____

Advising _____

_____

Judging _____

_____

Which listening styles do you think are most effective in this situation? Why?

_____

_____

Which listening styles do you think are least effective in this situation? Why?

_____

_____

2. My roommate and I can't seem to get along. She's always having her boyfriend over, and he doesn't know when to go home. I don't want to move out, but I can't put up with this much longer. If I bring it up I know my roommate will get defensive, though.

Prompting _____

Questioning _____

_____

Paraphrasing _____

_____

Supporting _____

_____

Analyzing _____

_____

Advising _____

_____

Judging _____

_____

Which listening styles do you think are most effective in this situation? Why?

_____

_____

Which listening styles do you think are least effective in this situation? Why?

_____

_____

3. The pressure of going to school and doing all the other things in my life is really getting to me. I can't go on like this, but I don't know where I can cut back.
    What would be your long- and short-term goals in this situation?

Prompting _____

Questioning _____

_____

Paraphrasing _____

_____

Supporting _____

_____

Analyzing _____

_____

Advising _____

_____

Judging _____

_____

Which listening styles do you think are most effective in this situation? Why?

_____

_____

Which listening styles do you think are least effective in this situation? Why?

_____

_____

_____

4. You think that by the time you become an adult your parents would stop treating you like a child, but not mine! If I wanted their advice about how to live my life, I'd ask.

What would be your long- and short-term goals in this situation?

Prompting _____

Questioning _____

_____

Paraphrasing _____

_____

Supporting _____

_____

Analyzing _____

_____

Advising _____

_____

Judging _____

_____

Which listening styles do you think are most effective in this situation? Why?

_____

_____

Which listening styles do you think are least effective in this situation? Why?

_____

_____

5. (record a situation of your own here) _____

_____

Prompting _____

Questioning _____

_____

Paraphrasing _____

_____

Supporting _____

_____

Analyzing _____

_____

Advising _____

_____

Judging _____

_____

Which listening style would you be most likely to use in this situation? Why?

_____

_____

8.5 LISTENING ANALYSIS

LEARNING OBJECTIVES

- Identify the components of a given listening situation.
- Demonstrate an understanding of an array of listening styles that might be used to respond effectively in a given situation.

INSTRUCTIONS

Use the case below and the discussion questions that follow to discuss the variety of communication issues involved in effective communication. Make notes on this page, add other pages on your own, or prepare a group report/analysis based on your discussion. As appropriate, add your own experiences to individualize the analysis.

CASE

Larry and Sam have been friends since elementary school and are now in their thirties. Larry has been happily married for ten years. Sam has been engaged four times, and each time has broken it off as the marriage date approaches. Sam has just announced another engagement.

1. What are the likely barriers that would prevent Larry from listening effectively?

   _____

   _____

2. What types of ineffective listening are likely to occur if Larry doesn't carefully consider his listening options?

   _____

   _____

3. What listening style(s) could Larry use that would be most helpful to Sam? Why? Construct a response for Larry using that style.

   _____

   _____

4. Imagine that the friends described here are both women. Would your responses to the preceding questions change? How? Be specific.

   _____

   _____

8.6 ASSESSING LISTENING SITUATIONS

LEARNING OBJECTIVES

- Demonstrate effective listening strategies you could use to respond in a given situation.

INSTRUCTIONS

We all face challenges in listening to others. Read the following scenarios below and describe what strategy you would use to maintain effective listening. (*Note:* In these scenarios, your focus is on over-all listening strategies rather than specific response styles.)

1. You are trying to talk to your friend about problems with her parents while you are at a bar with loud music in the background.

   Strategy:

   _____

   _____

   _____

2. Your friend needs to talk to you about her new relationship, but you have a difficult time listening because you have an early morning history test to study for and have a trip to plan. With all this on your mind, how can you maintain effective listening?

   Strategy:

   _____

   _____

   _____

3. You are talking on your cell phone and the reception is bad.

   Strategy:

   _____

   _____

   _____

4. In a face-to-face meeting with your boss you receive a long list of tasks that you need to complete. At the end of the meeting, your boss says, "Have you got all of that?" What can you do to make sure that you've remembered all of the tasks accurately?

    Strategy:

    _____

    _____

    _____

5. During one of your least favorite classes, your teacher asks a difficult question that she wants each student to answer aloud. And she says she expects everyone to remember everyone else's answers. She's going around the room clockwise and you happen to be sitting at the end of the circle. What do you do?

    Strategy:

    _____

    _____

    _____

STUDY GUIDE

CHECK YOUR UNDERSTANDING

TRUE/FALSE

Mark the statements below as true or false. Correct statements that are false on the lines below to create a true statement.

_____ 1. We spend more time listening to others than in any other type of communication.

_____

_____ 2. Speaking is active; listening is passive.

_____

_____ 3. Stage-hogs are sometimes called "conversational narcissists."

_____

_____ 4. It's never appropriate to practice mindless listening.

_____

_____ 5. Listening is a natural ability and, therefore, doesn't require special training.

_____

_____ 6. People speak at about the same rate as others are capable of understanding their speech.

_____

_____ 7. Research suggests that most people remember almost all of what they hear immediately after they hear it.

_____

_____ 8. Responding to a message rarely involves giving observable feedback to the speaker.

_____

_____ 9. Judging as a listening response may be favorable or negative.

_____

_____ 10. A good listener pays attention to paralanguage.

_____

COMPLETION

Fill in the blanks below with the correct terms chosen from the list below.

residual message	attending	listening fidelity
sincere question	counterfeit question	constructive criticism
agreement	understanding	remembering
hearing	selective	insulated

1. _____ is the degree of congruence between what the message sender intended to communicate and what the listener understands.

2. _____ is a genuine request for new information aimed at understanding others.

3. _____ is the information we store (remember) after processing information from teachers, friends, radio, TV, and other sources.

4. _____ is the psychological process of listening.

5. _____ is a query that is a disguised attempt to send a message, not receive one.

6. _____ is a lesser form of negative judgment which is intended to help the problem-holder improve in the future.

7. _____ is the physiological process of listening.

8. _____ is the process of making sense of a message.

9. _____ is the ability to recall information.

10. _____ is a listening response designed to show solidarity with speakers by telling them how right they are.

11. _____ is a nonlistening style that responds only to what the listener cares about.

12. _____ is a nonlistening style that ignores information the listener doesn't want to deal with.

MULTIPLE CHOICE

Match the letter of the listening type with its example found below.

a. advising	c. analyzing	e. supporting	g. paraphrasing
b. judging	d. questioning	f. prompting	

_____ 1. "So what do you mean by that?"

_____ 2. "You're mad at me for postponing the meeting?"

_____   3. "You're probably just more upset than usual because of the stress of exams."

_____   4. "What reason did she give for not attending?"

_____   5. "Well, that was good of him not to complain."

_____   6. "Have you tried praising her?"

_____   7. "Have you tried talking to him about it?"

_____   8. "Are you as excited as you sound about this big meet?"

_____   9. "Jim should not have said that to Amy after you asked him not to."

_____   10. "And then what happened?"

_____   11. "So why did you go to Ellie's in the first place?"

_____   12. "You really are good; they'll recognize that."

_____   13. "It's not fair for you to have to work nights."

_____   14. "Maybe you should give her a taste of her own medicine."

_____   15. "And so you feel like retaliating because you're hurt?"

_____   16. "Maybe you're a little insecure because of the divorce?"

_____   17. "Like what?"

_____   18. "What makes you think that he's cheating?"

_____   19. "You've always pulled out those grades before—I know you can do it again."

_____   20. "She's probably jealous so that's why she's doing that."

Choose the best listening response to each statement below.

21. Boss to employee: "Draft a letter that denies this request for a refund, but make it tactful."
    Identify the best paraphrasing of content response.
    a. "What do you want me to say?"
    b. "How can I say no tactfully?"
    c. "So I should explain nicely why we can't give a refund, right?"
    d. "In other words, you want me to give this customer the brush-off?"

22. Friend says, "How do they expect us to satisfy the course requirements when there aren't enough
    spaces in the classes we're supposed to take?" Identify the best questioning response.
    a. "What class do you need that you can't get into?"
    b. "You think that some of the courses are worthless—is that it?"

    c. "Sounds like you're sorry you chose this major."
    d. "Why don't you write a letter to the chairperson of the department?"

23. Friend says, "Why don't I meet you after class at the student union?" Identify the best questioning response.
    a. "So you want me to pick you up at the student union?"
    b. "You want me to pick you up *again*?"
    c. "What time do you think you'll be there?"
    d. "Why can't you drive yourself? Is your car broken again?"

24. Coworker advises, "When you go in for a job interview, be sure and talk about the internship, your coursework, and your extracurricular activities. Don't expect them to ask you." Identify the best paraphrasing response.
    a. "You think they won't ask about those things?"
    b. "Won't that sound like bragging?"
    c. "Why should I talk about the internship?"
    d. "So you're saying not to be bashful about stressing my experience?"

25. Friend says, "I don't think it's right that they go out and recruit women when there are plenty of good men around." Identify the best supporting response.
    a. "I think you're job-hunting well in spite of the challenges."
    b. "You shouldn't let that bother you."
    c. "That's just the way life is."
    d. "I can see that you're angry. What makes you think women are being given an unfair advantage?"

For each of the statements below, identify which response is the most complete and accurate paraphrasing of the speaker's thoughts and feelings.

26. "Sometimes I think I'd like to drop out of school, but then I start to feel like a quitter."
    a. "Maybe it would be helpful to take a break. You can always come back, you know."
    b. "You're afraid that you might fail if you stay in school now, is that it?"
    c. "I can really relate to what you're saying. I feel awkward here myself sometimes."
    d. "So you'd feel ashamed of yourself if you quit now, even though you'd like to?"

27. "I don't want to go to the party. I won't know anyone there, and I'll wind up sitting by myself all night."
    a. "You're anxious about introducing yourself to people who don't know you."
    b. "You never know; you could have a great time."
    c. "So you really don't want to go, eh?"
    d. "What makes you think it will be that way?"

28. "I get really nervous talking to my professor. I keep thinking that I sound stupid."
    a. "Talking to her is really a frightening experience."
    b. "You're saying that you'd rather not approach her."
    c. "You get the idea that she's evaluating you, so you feel inadequate."
    d. "You think that talking to her might affect your grade for the worse."

29. "I don't know what to do about my kids. Their whining is driving me crazy."
    a. "Even though whining is natural, it's getting to you."
    b. "Sometimes you lose patience and feel irritated when they complain."
    c. "You're getting angry at them."
    d. "Even the best parents get irritated sometimes."

30. "I just blew another test in that class. Why can't I do better?"
    a. "You probably need to study harder. You'll get it!"
    b. "You're feeling sorry for yourself because you can't pull a better grade."
    c. "Where do you think the problem is?"
    d. "You're discouraged and frustrated because you don't know what you're doing wrong."

Choose the best answer for each of the statements below:

_____ 31. A good listener pays attention to
    a. paralanguage.
    b. facial expression.
    c. nonverbal cues.
    d. all of the above.

_____ 32. When we move beyond hearing and start to listen and process information in two
    different ways, we are engaging in
    a. dual process theory.
    b. process theory.
    c. critical listening.
    d. careful listening.

_____ 33. In a survey that questioned adults who had spouses with hearing loss,
    a. many respondents were unfazed when their partner couldn't hear them correctly.
    b. many respondents felt that their spouses are open and upfront about their hearing
       obstacles.
    c. many respondents believed their spouses were in denial about their condition.
    d. less than a quarter of respondents felt annoyed when their partner couldn't hear
       them correctly.

_____ 34. When paraphrasing, it is a good idea to
    a. assume your paraphrase is correct.
    b. end with a question to confirm the paraphrase was accurate.
    c. paraphrase in a variety of ways to ensure accuracy.
    d. avoid paraphrasing if it feels awkward.

CHAPTER EIGHT STUDY GUIDE ANSWERS

TRUE/FALSE

1. T	3. F	5. F	7. F	9. T
2. F	4. F	6. F	8. F	10. T

COMPLETION

1. listening fidelity
2. sincere question
3. residual message
4. attending
5. counterfeit question
6. constructive criticism
7. hearing
8. understanding
9. remembering
10. agreement
11. selective
12. insulated

MULTIPLE CHOICE

1. f	7. a	13. b	19. e	25. a	31. d
2. g	8. g	14. a	20. c	26. d	32. a
3. c	9. b	15. g	21. c	27. a	33. c
4. d	10. f	16. c	22. a	28. c	34. b
5. b	11. d	17. f	23. c	29. b	
6. a	12. e	18. d	24. d	30. d	

MindTap START ...
Explore this chapter's
topics online.

9

COMMUNICATION AND RELATIONAL DYNAMICS

AFTER STUDYING THE TOPICS IN THIS CHAPTER, YOU SHOULD BE ABLE TO:

1. Identify factors that have influenced your choice of relational partners.

2. Use Knapp's model to describe the nature of communication in the various stages of a relationship.

3. Describe the dialectical tensions in a given relationship, how they influence communication, and the most effective strategies for managing them.

4. Explain how change and culture affect communication in interpersonal relationships.

5. Identify the content and relational dimensions of communication in a given transaction.

6. Describe how metacommunication can be used to improve the quality of a given relationship.

7. Describe the steps necessary to maintain, support, and repair interpersonal relationships.

"We have a terrific relationship."

"I'm looking for a better relationship."

"Our relationship has changed a lot."

"We need to talk about our relationship."

Relationship is one of those words that people use all the time but have trouble defining. Take a moment to see if you can explain the term in your own words. It isn't as easy as it might seem. For instance, most would agree that it's important to form relationships with clients and customers—but, of course, those relationships are quite different from those with sweethearts or close friends. You have a relationship with your family members (after all, they're *related* to you)—but those relationships might be strained or even broken. And social media users know that it's a big deal to declare online that they're "in a relationship."

Rather than define (and therefore limit) the concept of "relationship," this chapter will look at relational dynamics and how communication operates as people form, manage, and sometimes end their relationships. You will see that relationships aren't static like a painting or photograph: They change over time like an ongoing dance or drama. Even the most stable and satisfying relationships wax and wane in a variety of ways as communication patterns change. By the time you finish reading this chapter, you will have a better sense of how communication both defines and reflects our important relationships.

WHY WE FORM RELATIONSHIPS

What makes us seek relationships with some people and not with others? Sometimes we don't have a choice. Children can't select their parents, and most workers aren't able to choose their bosses or colleagues. In many other cases, however, we seek out some people and actively avoid others. Social scientists have collected an impressive body of research on interpersonal attraction.[1] The following are some of the factors they have identified that influence our choice of relational partners.

Appearance

Most people claim that we should judge others on the basis of how they act, not how they look. However, as Chapter 7 explains, the reality is quite the opposite.[2] Appearance is especially important in the early stages of a relationship. In one study, a group of more than 700 men and women were matched as blind dates for a social event. After the party was over, they were asked whether they would like to date their partners again. The result? The more physically attractive the person (as judged in advance by independent raters), the more likely he or she was seen as desirable. Other factors—social skills and intelligence, for example—didn't seem to affect the decision.[3]

In a more contemporary example, physical appearance is the primary basis of attraction for speed daters.[4] Perhaps this is why online daters routinely enhance their photographs and information about their height and weight to appear more attractive to potential suitors.[5] Online profile owners are also rated more positively when they have pictures of physically attractive friends on their sites, suggesting that they're known—and found attractive—by the company they keep.[6] The opposite is also true: Attractive faces are seen as less attractive when in the middle of unattractive or average faces.[7]

Even if your appearance isn't beautiful by societal standards, consider the following encouraging facts. First, after initial impressions have passed, ordinary-looking people with kind and pleasant personalities are likely to be judged as attractive.[8] Second, physical factors become less important as a relationship progresses.[9] In fact, as romantic relationships develop, partners create "positive illusions," viewing one another as more attractive over time.[10] As one social scientist put it, "Attractive features may open doors, but apparently it takes more than physical beauty to keep them open."[11]

Similarity

A large body of research confirms the fact that we like people who are similar to us, at least in most cases.[12] For example, the more similar a married couple's personalities are, the more likely they are to report being happy and satisfied in their marriage.[13] Friends in middle school and high school report being similar to one another in many ways, including having mutual friends, enjoying the same sports, liking the same social activities, and using (or not using) alcohol and cigarettes to the same degree.[14] Friendships seem most likely to last decades when the friends are similar to one another.[15] For adults, similarity is more important to relational happiness than even communication ability. Friends who have equally low levels of communication skills are just as satisfied with their relationships as are friends who have high levels of communication skills.[16]

Similarity plays an important role in initial attraction. People are more likely to accept a Facebook friend request from a stranger whom they perceive to be similar.[17] Perception is important here. Research shows that we are more attracted to similarities we *believe* exist ("We *seem* to have a lot in common") than to actual similarities.[18] In fact, perceived similarities often *create* attraction. Deciding you like someone often leads to perceptions of similarity rather than the other way around.[19]

One theory for why we are attracted to similar others is that it provides a measure of ego support. If we judge those who are like us to be attractive, then we must be attractive too (or so goes the theory). One study described the lengths to which this *implicit egotism* can affect perceptions of attractiveness.[20] Results showed that people are disproportionately likely to marry others whose first or last names resemble their own, and they are also attracted to those with similar birthdays or even sports jersey numbers. We're also attracted to those whose language style matches our own.[21] On a more substantive level, similar values about politics and religion were found, in one study, to be the best predictors of mate choice—significantly more than attraction to physical appearance or personality traits.[22]

Tanja Giessler/Getty Images

Attraction is greatest when we are similar to others in a high percentage of important areas. For example, two people who support each other's career goals, enjoy the same friends, and have similar beliefs about human rights can tolerate trivial disagreements about the merits of sushi or rap music. With enough similarity in key areas, they can even survive disputes about more important subjects such as how much time to spend with their families or whether separate vacations are acceptable. But if the number and content of disagreements become too great, then the relationship may be threatened.

Similarity turns from attraction to dislike when we encounter people who are like us in many ways but who behave in a strange or socially offensive manner.[23] For instance, you have probably disliked people others have said were "just like you" but who talked too much, were complainers, or had some other unappealing characteristic. In fact, there is a tendency to have stronger dislike for similar but offensive people than for those who are offensive but different. One likely reason is that such people threaten our self-esteem, causing us to fear that we may be as unappealing as they are. In such circumstances, the reaction is often to put as much distance as possible between ourselves and this threat to our ideal self-image.

Complementarity

The familiar saying that "opposites attract" seems to contradict the principle of similarity we just described. In truth, though, both are valid. Differences strengthen a relationship when they are *complementary*—when each partner's characteristics satisfy the other's needs.

Research suggests that attraction to partners who have complementary temperaments might be rooted in biology.[24] Individuals, for instance, are often likely to be attracted to each other when one partner is dominant and the other passive.[25] Relationships also work well when the partners agree that one will exercise control in certain areas ("You make the final decisions about money") and the other will exercise control in different areas ("I'll decide how we ought to decorate the place"). Strains occur when control issues are disputed. One study shows that "spendthrifts and tightwads" are often attracted to each other, but their differences in financial management often lead to significant conflict over the course of a relationship.[26]

When successful and unsuccessful couples are compared over a twenty-year period, it becomes clear that partners in successful marriages are similar enough to satisfy each other physically and mentally but different enough to meet each other's needs and keep the relationship interesting. Successful couples find ways to keep a balance between their similarities and differences, adjusting to the changes that occur over the years. We'll have more to say about balancing similarities and differences later in this chapter.

Reciprocal Attraction

We like people who like us—usually.[27] The power of reciprocal attraction is especially strong in the early stages of a relationship. At that time we are attracted to people who we believe are attracted to us. Conversely, we will probably not care for people who either attack or seem indifferent toward us.

It's no mystery why reciprocal liking builds attractiveness: People who approve of us bolster our feelings of self-esteem. This approval is rewarding in its own right, and it can also confirm a presenting self-concept that says, "I'm a likable person."

You can probably think of cases where you haven't liked people who seemed to like you. For example, you might think the other person's supposed liking is counterfeit—an insincere device to get something from you. At other times the liking may not fit with your own self-concept. When someone says you're good-looking, intelligent, and kind, but you believe you're ugly, stupid, and mean, you may choose to disregard the flattering information and remain in your familiar state of unhappiness. Groucho Marx summarized this attitude when he said he would never join any club that would consider having him as a member.

Competence

We like to be around talented people, probably because we hope their skills and abilities will rub off on us. We are uncomfortable around those who are *too* competent, however, probably because we look bad by comparison. Given these contrasting attitudes, it's no surprise that people are generally attracted to those who are talented but who have visible flaws that show that they are human, just like us.[28] Moreover, we're attracted to people whose competence is paired with interpersonal warmth. "Competent but cool" is generally not seen as an attractive mix.[29]

Disclosure

As noted in Chapter 3, revealing important information about yourself can help build liking.[30] Sometimes the basis of this liking comes from learning about how we are similar, either in experiences ("I broke off an engagement myself") or in attitudes ("I feel nervous with strangers, too"). Self-disclosure also builds liking because it is a sign of regard. When people share private information with you, it suggests that they respect and trust you—a kind of liking that we've already seen increases attractiveness. Disclosure plays an even more important role as relationships develop beyond their earliest stages. This is the case in both online and face-to-face communication and relationships.[31]

Not all disclosure leads to liking. Research shows that the key to satisfying self-disclosure is *reciprocity*: getting back an amount and kind of information equivalent to that which you reveal.[32] A second important ingredient in successful self-disclosure is *timing*. It's probably unwise to talk about your sexual insecurities with a new acquaintance or express your pet peeves to a friend at your birthday party. Finally, for the sake of self-protection, it's important to reveal personal information only when you are sure the other person is trustworthy.[33]

Proximity

As common sense suggests, we are likely to develop relationships with people we interact with frequently.[34] In many cases, proximity leads to liking. For instance, we're more likely to develop friendships with close neighbors than with distant ones, and chances are good that we'll choose a mate with whom we cross paths often. Facts like these are understandable when we consider that proximity allows us to get more information about other people and benefit from a relationship with them. Also, people in close proximity may be more similar to us than those who are not close; for example, if we live in the same neighborhood, odds are we share the same socioeconomic status. The Internet provides a new means for creating closeness, as users are able to experience "virtual proximity" in cyberspace.[35]

Rewards

Some social scientists believe that all relationships—both impersonal and personal—are based on a semi-economic model called *social exchange theory*.[36] This model suggests that we often seek out people who can give us rewards that are greater than or equal to the costs we encounter in dealing with them. According to social exchange theory, relationships suffer when one partner feels "underbenefited."[37]

Rewards may be tangible (a nice place to live, a high-paying job) or intangible (prestige, emotional support, companionship). Costs are undesirable outcomes (unpleasant work, emotional pain, and so on). A simple formula captures the social exchange theory of why we form and maintain relationships:

$$\text{Rewards} - \text{Costs} = \text{Outcome}$$

According to social exchange theorists, we use this formula (often unconsciously) to decide whether dealing with another person is a "good deal" or "not worth the effort," based on whether the outcome is positive or negative.

At its most blatant level, an exchange approach seems cold and calculating, but in some types of relationships it seems quite appropriate. A healthy business relationship is based on how well the parties help one another. Some friendships are based on an informal kind of barter: "I don't mind listening to the ups and downs of your love life because you rescue me when the house needs repairs." Even close relationships have an element of exchange. Friends and lovers often tolerate each other's quirks because the comfort and enjoyment they get make the less-than-pleasant times worth accepting. In more serious cases, social exchange explains why some people stay in abusive relationships. Sadly, these people often report that they would rather be in a bad relationship than have no relationship at all.

"I'd like to buy everyone a drink. All I ask in return is that you listen patiently to my shallow and simplistic views on a broad range of social and political issues."

At first glance, the social exchange approach seems to present a view of relationships that is very different from one based on the need to seek intimacy. In fact, the two approaches aren't incompatible. Seeking intimacy of any type—whether emotional, physical, or even intellectual—has its costs, and our decision about whether to "pay" those costs is, in great measure, made by considering the likely rewards. If the costs of seeking and maintaining an intimate relationship are too great or the payoffs are not worth the effort, we may decide to withdraw.

MODELS OF RELATIONAL DYNAMICS

Your own experience demonstrates that relational beginnings are a unique time. How does communication change as we spend time with others and get to know them? Communication scholars have different perspectives on this question. We'll look at two approaches—developmental and dialectical—in this section.

A Developmental Perspective

One of the best-known models of relational stages was developed by communication researcher Mark Knapp. It breaks the rise and fall of relationships into ten stages, contained in the two broad phases of "coming together" and "coming apart."[38] Other researchers have suggested that any model of relational communication ought to contain a third phase of *relational maintenance*—communication aimed at keeping relationships operating smoothly and satisfactorily (we'll discuss relational maintenance in detail later in this chapter). Figure 9.1 shows how Knapp's ten stages fit into this three-phase view of relational communication.

This model seems most appropriate for describing communication between romantic partners, but in many respects it works well for other types of close

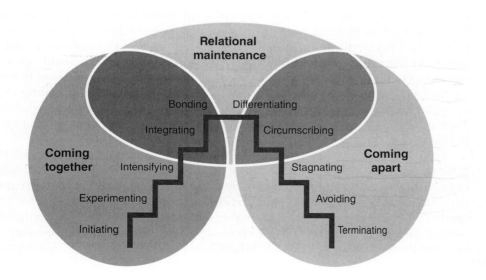

◄ FIGURE 9.1
Stages of Relational Development

Looking at DIVERSITY

Photo by Rakhi Singh

Rakhi Singh and Rajesh Punn: A Modern Arranged Marriage

My husband Raj and I are married because our parents thought we might be right for one another.

The term "arranged marriage" has different meaning for Indians today than it did in previous generations. My grandparents in a rural village were matched by their parents, and married at ages 12 and 13. They had little or no say in the matter. Their children—my parents—were also matched, but not until they were in college. After being introduced, they had a 3-hour meeting before deciding whether to go ahead with their engagement.

It was very different for Raj and me. Our parents back in India published profiles of each of us, and after reviewing possible candidates, they decided together that we might be a good match. They put us in touch, and from there it was up to us to decide whether we were right for one another.

Because we lived in the USA, we were a little resistant to this sort of matchmaking, but we were still willing to give it a try. Thankfully, our parents chose well: We hit it off, and after 18 months we married. Thirteen years and three kids later, we are very happy.

The notion of parents choosing prospective spouses may seem odd at first, but there are some reasons why the approach works as well as it does. Parents match people from similar backgrounds—cultural values, education, and age, for example. That can help insure a good fit. Also, knowing that the family approves takes away a big area of potential stress and conflict.

In some ways, parental matchmaking resembles computer dating. The searchers plug in the qualities they're seeking, and out comes a list of people who fit the profile. I think the key variable is whether the parents are willing to limit their role to finding prospective partners, and to let their children make the final call.

relationships.[39] As you read the following section, consider how the stages could describe a long-term friendship, a couple in love, or even business partners.

Initiating   The goals in the first stage of a relationship are to show that you are interested in making contact and that you are the kind of person worth talking to. Communication during this **initiating** stage is usually brief, and it generally follows conventional formulas: handshakes, remarks about innocuous subjects like the weather, and friendly expressions. These kinds of behavior may seem superficial and meaningless, but they are a way of signaling that we're interested in building some kind of relationship with the other person. They allow us to say without saying, "I'm a friendly person, and I'd like to get to know you."

Initiating relationships—especially romantic ones—can be particularly difficult for people who are shy. Making contact via social media can be helpful in cases like this. One study of an online dating service found that participants who identified themselves as shy expressed a greater appreciation for the system's anonymous, nonthreatening environment than did more outgoing users.[40] The researchers found that many shy users employed the online service specifically to help overcome their inhibitions about initiating relationships in face-to-face settings. This helps explain why many young adults—shy or not—use social media sites such as Facebook to initiate relationships.[41]

Keep in mind that initiating is the opening stage of *all* relationships, not just romantic ones. Friendships start here,[42] and so do business partnerships. In fact, some have compared employment interviews to first dates because they have similar properties.[43] As you read about the stages that follow, consider how the communication involved could be true of landing a job, connecting with a roommate, or joining an organization—as well as forming a romantic relationship.

Experimenting   After we have made contact with a new person, the next stage is to decide whether we are interested in pursuing the relationship further. This involves *uncertainty reduction*—the process of getting to know others by gaining more information about them.[44] A usual part of uncertainty reduction is the search for common ground, and it involves the conversational basics such as "Where are you from?" or "What's your major?" From there we look for other similarities: "You're a runner, too? How many miles do you do a week?"

The hallmark of the **experimenting** stage is small talk. Even though we may dislike it, we tolerate the ordeal of small talk because it serves several functions. First, it is a useful way to find out what interests we share with the other person. It also provides a way to audition the other person—to help us decide whether a relationship is worth pursuing. In addition, small talk is a safe way to ease into a relationship. You haven't risked much as you decide whether to proceed further.

For communicators who are interested in one another, the move from initiating to experimenting seems to occur even more rapidly online than in person. One study found that people who develop relationships via email begin asking questions about attitudes, opinions, and preferences more quickly than those engaged in face-to-face contact.[45] It probably helps that emailers can't see each other's nonverbal reactions; they don't have to worry about blushing, stammering, or looking away if they realize that they asked for too much information too quickly.

Social networking sites may change the nature of this stage of relational development. College students in one study said that experimenting in romantic relationships used to involve securing a person's phone number; now it often involves a Facebook friend request.[46] Once access is given, communicators can look over each other's site, allowing them to "chug" rather than "sip" information about the other person. Photos and mutual friends are also important factors in deciding whether to continue developing a relationship. And of course, gathering this information online is less face-threatening (for both parties) than doing so in person.

Intensifying   In the **intensifying** stage, the kind of truly interpersonal relationship defined in Chapter 1 begins to develop. Several changes in communication patterns occur during intensifying. The expression of feelings toward the other becomes more common. Dating couples use a wide range of communication strategies to describe their feelings of attraction.[47] About one-quarter of the time they express their feelings directly, openly discussing the state of the relationship. More often they use less direct methods of communication:

This remake of the 1986 rom com *About Last Night* traces the rise and decline of the relationship between Danny (Michael Ealy) and Debbie (Joy Bryant). The story illustrates the developmental model from initial attraction through emotional and physical intensifying into integration, and ultimately to the stages of coming apart. How closely have your relationships followed the stages in Knapp's model?

spending an increasing amount of time together, asking for support from one another, doing favors for the partner, giving tokens of affection, hinting and flirting, expressing feelings nonverbally, getting to know the partner's friends and family, and trying to look more physically attractive. In developing friendships, intensifying can include participating in shared activities, hanging out with mutual friends, or taking trips together.[48]

The intensifying stage is usually a time of relational excitement and even euphoria. For romantic partners, it's often filled with starstruck gazes, goosebumps, and daydreaming. As a result, it's a stage that's regularly depicted in movies and romance novels—after all, we love to watch lovers in love.[49] The problem, of course, is that the stage doesn't last forever. Sometimes romantic partners who stop feeling goosebumps begin to question whether they're still in love. Although it's possible that they're not, it's also possible that they've simply moved on to a different, less emotional stage in their relationship—integrating.

Integrating   As a relationship strengthens, the parties begin to take on an identity as a social unit. In romantic relationships, invitations begin to come addressed to the couple. Social circles merge. The partners begin to take on each other's commitments: "Sure, we'll spend Thanksgiving with your family." Common property may begin to be designated—our apartment, our car, our song.[50] Partners develop unique, ritualistic ways of behaving.[51] Close friends may even begin to speak alike, using personal idioms and sentence patterns.[52] In this sense, the **integrating** stage is a time when individuals give up some characteristics of their old selves and develop shared identities.

In contemporary relationships, integrating may include going "Facebook Official" (FBO) by declaring publically that the couple is "in a relationship."[53] Of course, problems can arise when one partner wants to be "FBO" and the other partner doesn't.[54] And the meaning of FBO can be different for each partner. One study found that in heterosexual relationships, women tend to perceive FBO declarations as involving more intensity and commitment than men do.[55] As a result, women may connect FBO status with the rights and restrictions normally associated with bonding—a stage we'll look at now.

Bonding   During the **bonding** stage, the parties make symbolic public gestures to show the world that their relationship exists. What constitutes a bonded, committed relationship isn't always easy to define.[56] Terms such as *common-law, cohabitation,* and *life partners* have been used to describe relationships that don't have the full support of custom and law but still involve an implicit or explicit bond. Nonetheless, given the importance of bonding in validating relationships and taking them to another level, it's not surprising that the gay and lesbian communities have fought hard to have legally sanctioned and recognized marriages.

For our purposes here, we'll define bonded relationships as those involving a significant measure of public commitment. These can include engagement or marriage, sharing a residence, a public ceremony, or a written or verbal pledge. The key is that bonding is the culmination of a developed relationship—the "officializing" of a couple's integration. We'll talk more about the role of commitment in relationships in Chapter 10.

Bonding marks a turning point in a relationship. Up until now the relationship may have developed at a steady pace. Experimenting gradually moved into intensifying and then into integrating. Now, however, there is a spurt of commitment. The public display and declaration of exclusivity make this a distinct stage in the relationship.

Relationships don't have to be romantic to achieve bonding. Consider, for example, the contracts that formalize a business partnership or the initiation ceremony in a fraternity or sorority. As one author notes, even friendships can achieve bonding with acts that "officialize" the relationship:

> Some Western cultures have rituals to mark the progress of a friendship and to give it public legitimacy and form. In Germany, for example, there's a small ceremony called *Duzen*, the name itself signifying the transformation in the relationship. The ritual calls for the two friends, each holding a glass of wine or beer, to entwine arms, thus bringing each other physically close, and to drink up after making a promise of eternal brotherhood with the word *Bruderschaft*. When it's over, the friends will have passed from a relationship that requires the formal *Sie* mode of address to the familiar *du*.[57]

Differentiating   Bonding is the peak of what Knapp calls the "coming together" phase of relational development, but people in even the most committed relationships need to assert their individual identities. This **differentiating** stage is the point where the "we" orientation that has developed shifts, and more "me" messages begin to occur. Instead of talking about "our" weekend plans, differentiating conversations focus on what "I" want to do. Relational issues that were once agreed upon (such as "You'll be the breadwinner and I'll manage the home") may now become points of contention ("Why am *I* stuck at home when I have better career potential than *you*?"). The root of the term *differentiating* is the word *different*, suggesting that change plays an important role in this stage.

Differentiating is likely to occur when a relationship begins to experience the first, inevitable feelings of stress. This need for autonomy and change needn't be a negative experience, however. People need to be individuals as well as parts of a relationship, and differentiation is a necessary step toward autonomy. Think, for instance, of young adults who want to forge their own unique lives and identity, even while maintaining their relationships with their parents.[58] As Figure 9.1 illustrates, differentiating is often a part of normal relational maintenance, in which partners manage the inevitable changes that come their way. The key to successful differentiating is maintaining a commitment to the relationship while creating the space for being an individual as well. (This is a challenge that we will describe in more detail later in this chapter when we discuss dialectical tensions in relationships.)

Circumscribing   In the **circumscribing** stage, communication between members decreases in quantity and quality. Restrictions and restraints characterize this stage. Rather than discuss a disagreement (which requires energy on both sides), members opt for withdrawal—either mental (silence or daydreaming and fantasizing) or physical (people spend less time together). Circumscribing doesn't involve total avoidance, which may come later. Rather, it involves a shrinking of interest and commitment—the opposite of what occurred in the integrating stage.

The word *circumscribe* comes from the Latin meaning "to draw circles around." Distinctions that emerged in the differentiating stage become more clearly marked and labeled: "my friends" and "your friends"; "my bank account" and "your bank account"; "my room" and "your room." As you'll soon read, such distinctions can be markers of a healthy balance between individual and relational identity—between autonomy and connection. They become a problem when there are clearly more areas of separation than integration in a relationship, or when the areas of separation seriously limit interaction, such as "my vacation" and "your vacation."

Stagnating   If circumscribing continues, the relationship enters the **stagnating** stage. The excitement of the intensifying stage is long gone, and the partners behave toward each other in old, familiar ways without much feeling. No growth occurs; relational boredom sets in.[59] The relationship is a hollow shell of its former self. We see stagnation in many workers who have lost enthusiasm for their job, yet continue to go through the motions for years. The same sad event occurs for some couples who unenthusiastically have the same conversations, see the same people, and follow the same routines without any sense of joy or novelty.

Avoiding   When stagnation becomes too unpleasant, parties in a relationship begin to create physical distance between each other. This is the **avoiding** stage. Sometimes they do it indirectly under the guise of excuses ("I've been sick lately and can't see you"); sometimes they do it directly ("Please don't call me; I don't want to see you now"). In either case, by this point the relationship's future is in doubt.

The deterioration of a relationship from bonding through circumscribing, stagnating, and avoiding isn't inevitable. One of the key differences between marriages that end in separation and those that are restored to their former intimacy is the communication that occurs when the partners are unsatisfied.[60] Unsuccessful couples deal with their problems by avoidance, indirectness, and less involvement with each other. By contrast, couples who repair their relationship communicate much more directly. They confront each other with their concerns (sometimes with the assistance of a counselor) and spend time and effort negotiating solutions to their problems.

Terminating   Not all relationships end. Many career partnerships, friendships, and marriages last for a lifetime once they've been established. But many do deteriorate and reach the final stage of **terminating**. Characteristics of this stage include summary dialogues of where the relationship has gone and the desire to dissociate. The relationship may end with a cordial dinner,

a note left on the kitchen table, a phone call, or a legal document. Depending on each person's feelings, this stage can be quite short, or it may be drawn out over time.

Relationships don't always move toward termination in a straight line. Rather, they take a back-and-forth pattern, where the trend is toward dissolution.[61] Regardless of how long it takes, termination doesn't have to be totally negative. Understanding each other's investments in the relationship and needs for personal growth may dilute the hard feelings. In fact, many relationships aren't so much terminated as redefined. A divorced couple, for example, may find new, less intimate ways to relate to each other.

In romantic relationships, the best predictor of whether the parties will be friends after reaching the terminating stage is whether they were friends before their emotional involvement.[62] The way the couple splits up also makes a difference. It's no surprise to find that friendships are most possible when communication during the breakup is positive (expressions that there are no regrets for time spent together, other attempts to minimize hard feelings). When communication during termination is negative (being manipulative, complaining to third parties), friendships are less likely.

After termination, couples often engage in "grave-dressing"—retrospective attempts to explain why the relationship failed.[63] The narrative each partner creates about "what went wrong" has an impact on how the couple will get along after their breakup (imagine the difference between saying and hearing "We just weren't right for each other" versus "He was too selfish and immature for a committed relationship").[64]

Scholars have begun to investigate the role technology can play in relational termination. Thousands of respondents in one survey admitted they had broken up with someone via text message (men were far more likely than women to use this method).[65] Obviously, breaking up this way runs the risk of wounding and infuriating the person being dumped ("He didn't even have the guts to tell me to my face") and lessens the likelihood of post-relationship goodwill. A different study found that those on the receiving end of a breakup via technology tended to have high levels of attachment anxiety—which might explain why their partners didn't want to deliver the news in person.[66]

Once a romantic relationship is over, it may be wise to take a break from being Facebook friends with an ex-partner. Checking up on your former sweetheart may reduce some uncertainty,[67] but surveillance of an ex's Facebook page is associated with greater distress over the breakup, more negative feelings, and lower personal growth.[68]

Limitations of the Developmental Perspective   While Knapp's model offers insights into relational stages, it doesn't describe the ebb and flow of communication in every relationship. For instance, Knapp suggests that movement among stages is generally sequential, so that relationships typically progress from one stage to another in a predictable manner as they develop and deteriorate. One study found that many terminated friendships did follow a pattern similar to the one described by Knapp.[69] However, several other patterns of development and deterioration were also identified.

PAUSE *and* REFLECT

Your Relational Stage

MindTap REFLECT ... on your relational stages by answering the following questions, either here or online.

You can gain a clearer appreciation of the accuracy and value of relational stages by answering the following questions:

1. If you are in a relationship, describe its present stage and the behaviors that characterize your communication in this stage. Give specific examples to support your assessment.

2. Discuss the trend of the communication in terms of the stages described in this section. Are you likely to remain in the present stage, or do you anticipate movement to another stage? Which one? Explain your answer.

3. Describe your level of satisfaction with the answer to question 2. If you are satisfied, describe what you can do to increase the likelihood that the relationship will operate at the stage you described. If you are not satisfied, discuss what you can do to move the relationship toward a more satisfying stage.

4. Because both parties define a relationship, define your partner's perspective. Would she or he say that the relationship is in the same stage as you described? If not, explain how your partner would describe it. What does your partner do to determine the stage at which your relationship operates? (Give specific examples.) How would you like your partner to behave in order to move the relationship to or maintain it at the stage you desire? What can you do to encourage your partner to behave in the way you desire?

5. Now consider a relationship (friendship or romance) you have been in that has terminated. How well does the Knapp model describe the development and decline of that relationship? If the model doesn't match, develop a new model to illustrate your relationship's pattern.

In other words, not all relationships begin, progress, decline, and end in the same linear fashion.

Finally, Knapp's model suggests that a relationship exhibits only the most dominant traits of just one of the ten stages at any given time, but elements of other stages are usually present. For example, two lovers deep in the throes of integrating may still do their share of experimenting ("Wow, I never knew that about you!") and have differentiating disagreements ("Nothing personal, but I need a weekend to myself"). Likewise, family members who spend most of their energy avoiding each other may have an occasional good spell in which their former closeness briefly intensifies. The notion that relationships can experience features of both "coming together" and "coming apart" at the same time is explored in the following section on relational dialectics.

A Dialectical Perspective

Not all theorists agree that stage-related models like the one just described are the best way to explain interaction in relationships. Some suggest that communicators grapple with the same kinds of challenges whether a relationship is brand new or decades old. They argue that communicators seek important but inherently incompatible goals throughout virtually all of their relationships. The struggle to achieve these goals creates **dialectical tensions**: conflicts that arise when two opposing or incompatible forces exist simultaneously. Communication scholars have identified several dialectical forces that make successful communication challenging.[70] They suggest that the struggle to manage these dialectical tensions creates the most powerful dynamics in relational communication. Now, we will discuss three powerful dialectical tensions.

Connection versus Autonomy   No one is an island. Recognizing this fact, we seek out involvement with others. But, at the same time, we are unwilling to sacrifice our entire identity to even the most satisfying relationship. The conflicting desires for both dependence and independence are embodied in the **connection-autonomy dialectic**.

Research on relational breakups demonstrates the consequences for relational partners who can't find a way to manage this dialectical tension.[71] Some of the most common reasons for relational breakups involve failure of partners to satisfy each other's needs for connection: "We barely spent any time together," "She wasn't committed to the relationship," "We had different needs." But other relational complaints involve excessive demands for connection: "I was feeling trapped," "I needed more freedom."[72] Perhaps not surprisingly, some research suggests that men value

Wavebreakmedia Ltd/Istock/Getty images

autonomy in relationships more than women do, whereas women tend to value connection and commitment.[73]

The levels of connection and autonomy that we seek can change over time. In his book *Intimate Behavior*, Desmond Morris suggests that each of us repeatedly goes through three stages: "Hold me tight," "Put me down," and "Leave me alone."[74] This cycle becomes apparent in the first years of life, when children move from the "hold-me-tight" stage that characterizes infancy into a new "put-me-down" stage of exploring the world by crawling, walking, touching, and tasting. The same three-year-old who insists "I can do it myself" in August may cling to parents on the first day of preschool in September. As children grow into adolescents, the "leave-me-alone" orientation becomes apparent. Teenagers who used to happily spend time with their parents now may groan at the thought of a family vacation or even the notion of sitting down at the dinner table each evening. As adolescents move into adulthood, they typically grow closer to their families again.[75]

In adult relationships, the same cycle of intimacy and distance repeats itself. In marriages, for example, the "hold-me-tight" bonds of the first year are often followed by a desire for autonomy. This desire can manifest itself in several ways, such as wanting to make friends or engage in activities that don't include the spouse or the need to make a career move that might disrupt the relationship. As the discussion of relational stages earlier in this chapter explained, this movement from connection to autonomy may lead to the breakup of relationships, but it can also be part of a cycle that redefines the relationship in a new form that can recapture or even surpass the intimacy that existed in the past.

Both men and women in heterosexual romantic pairs cite the connection-autonomy dialectic as one of the most significant factors affecting their relationship.[76] This dialectical tension is crucial in negotiating turning points related to commitment, conflict, disengagement, and reconciliation. On a smaller level, studies have found that satisfied couples negotiate and adhere to rules about cell phone usage as a means to balance connection-autonomy needs.[77] Cell phones allow people to stay connected, but rules help manage expectations about how often couples will (or won't) talk to and text each other. This can help establish a measure of autonomy for partners who want and need it.

Managing the tension between connection and autonomy is also important at the end of a relationship, as partners seek ways to salvage the positive parts of their relationship (if only the good memories) and take steps toward their new independence.[78] Even at the end of life, the connection-autonomy dialectic comes into play. When a loved one is in an extended period of declining health, the partner often feels torn between the desire to stay close and the need to let go. This tension is especially poignant when one partner suffers from a condition like Alzheimer's disease and becomes mentally absent while physically present.[79]

Openness versus Privacy   As Chapter 1 explained, disclosure is one characteristic of interpersonal relationships. Yet, along with the need to disclose, we have an equally important drive to maintain some space between ourselves and others. These conflicting needs create the **openness-privacy dialectic**.

Even the strongest interpersonal relationships require some distance. Lovers may go through periods of much sharing and periods of relative withdrawal. Likewise, they experience periods of passion and then periods of little physical contact. Friends have times of high disclosure when they share almost every feeling and idea and then disengage for days, months, or even longer.

What do you do in an intimate relationship when a person you care about asks an important question that you don't want to answer? As Chapter 3 notes, questions such as "Do you think I'm attractive?" and "Are you having a good time?" can pose self-disclosure dilemmas. Your commitment to honesty may compel you toward a candid response, but your concern for the other person's feelings and a desire for privacy may lead you to be less than completely honest. Partners use a variety of strategies to gain privacy from each other.[80] For example, they may confront the other person directly and explain that they don't want to continue a discussion, or they may be less direct and offer nonverbal cues, change the topic, or leave the room.

Communication via social media adds challenges to privacy management. Facebook, Twitter, blogs, and other mediated outlets make it easy to broadcast personal information. Just because it's easy, however, doesn't mean it's always wise. This is particularly true when the information you're revealing involves someone else. It's important to know how to use privacy controls on social media tools, and also to negotiate what you will and won't share about your relationships with others.[81]

Predictability versus Novelty Stability is an important need in relationships, but too much of it can lead to feelings of staleness. The **predictability-novelty dialectic** reflects this tension. Humorist Dave Barry exaggerates only slightly when he talks about the boredom that can come when husbands and wives know each other too well:

> After a decade or so of marriage, you know *everything* about your spouse, every habit and opinion and twitch and tic and minor skin growth. You could write a seventeen-pound book solely about the way your spouse *eats*. This kind of intimate knowledge can be very handy in certain situations—such as when you're on a TV quiz show where the object is to identify your spouse from the sound of his or her chewing—but it tends to lower the passion level of a relationship.[82]

"And do you, Rebecca, promise to make love only to Richard, month after month, year after year, and decade after decade, until one of you is dead?"

Although too much familiarity can lead to the risk of boredom and stagnation, nobody wants a completely unpredictable relational partner. Too many surprises can threaten the foundations upon which the relationship is based ("You're not the person I married!").

The challenge for communicators is to juggle the desire for predictability with the desire for novelty that keeps the relationship fresh and interesting.

People differ in their desire for predictability and novelty, so there is no optimal mixture of the two. As you will read shortly, people can use several strategies to manage these contradictory drives.

Managing Dialectical Tensions   Although all of the dialectical tensions play an important role in managing relationships, some occur more frequently than others. In one study, young married couples reported that connection-autonomy was the most frequent tension (30.8 percent of all reported contradictions).[83] Predictability-novelty was second (21.7 percent). Least common was openness-privacy (12.7 percent).

Managing the dialectical tensions outlined here presents communication challenges. There are many ways to meet these challenges, and some work better than others.[84]

- *Denial*. In the strategy of denial, communicators respond to one end of the dialectical spectrum and ignore the other. For example, a couple caught between the conflicting desires for predictability and novelty might find their struggle for change too difficult to manage and choose to follow predictable, if unexciting, patterns of relating to each other.

- *Disorientation*. In this strategy, communicators feel so overwhelmed and helpless that they are unable to confront their problems. In the face of dialectical tensions, they might fight, freeze, or even leave the relationship. Two people who discover soon after the honeymoon that a happily-ever-after, conflict-free life isn't realistic might become so terrified that they would come to view their marriage as a mistake.

- *Alternation*. Communicators who use this strategy choose one end of the dialectical spectrum at some times and the other end at other times. Friends, for example, might manage the connection-autonomy dialectic by alternating between times when they spend a large amount of time together and other times when they live independent lives.

- *Segmentation*. Partners who use this tactic compartmentalize different areas of their relationship. For example, a couple might manage the openness-privacy dialectic by sharing almost all their feelings about mutual friends with each other, but keeping certain parts of their past romantic histories private. Segmentation is the most frequently used method for stepchildren to manage openness-privacy tensions with their nonresident parents.[85] In the "Zits" cartoon seen here, Jeremy realizes he has forgotten to use his usual approach of segmentation to manage the openness-privacy dialectic with his inquisitive parents.

- *Balance*. Communicators who try to balance dialectical tensions recognize that both forces are legitimate and try to manage them through compromise. As Chapter 12 points out, compromise is inherently a situation in which everybody loses at least a little of what he or she wants. A couple caught between the conflicting desires for predictability and novelty might seek balance by compromising with a lifestyle that is neither as predictable as one wants nor as surprise-filled as the other wants—not an ideal outcome.

- *Integration*. With this strategy, communicators simultaneously accept opposing forces without trying to diminish them. Communication researcher

Barbara Montgomery describes a couple that accepts the needs for both predictability and novelty by devising a "predictably novel" approach: Once a week they would do something together that they had never done before.[86] In a similar way, some stepfamilies manage the tension between the "old family" and the "new family" by adapting and blending their family rituals.[87]

- *Recalibration.* Communicators can respond to dialectical challenges by reframing them so that the apparent contradiction disappears. For example, a change in thinking can transform your attitude from loving someone *despite* your differences to loving him or her *because* of those differences.[88] Or consider how two people who each felt hurt by each other's unwillingness to share parts of his or her past might redefine the secrets to create an attractive aura of mystery, instead of seeing them as a problem to be solved. The desire for privacy would still remain, but it would no longer compete with a need for openness about every aspect of the past.

- *Reaffirmation.* This strategy acknowledges that dialectical tensions will never disappear. Instead of trying to make them go away, reaffirming communicators accept—or even embrace—the challenges that the tensions present. The metaphorical view of relational life as a kind of roller coaster reflects this strategy, and communicators who use reaffirmation view dialectical tensions as part of the ride.

Which of these strategies do you use to manage the dialectical tensions in your life? How successful is each one? Which strategies might serve your communication better? Generally speaking, the last three options above are seen as the most productive, and researchers suggest it's wise to make use of multiple strategies.[89] For example, broken-up couples report having used denial, alternation, and segmentation less than successfully, and they tended to rely on only one strategy rather than using the variety at their disposal.[90] Since dialectical tensions are a part of life, choosing how to communicate about them can make a tremendous difference in the quality of your relationships.

MindTap® PRACTICE...

your understanding of dialectical tension theory by completing the Concepts in Play activity online.

PAUSE *and* REFLECT

Your Dialectical Tensions

MindTap® **REFLECT ...** on your dialectical tensions by answering the following questions, either here or online.

1. Select one of your significant relationships. Describe how each of the dialectical tensions operate in this relationship.

2. What incompatible goals do you and your relational partner(s) seek?

3. Which of the strategies described in this section do you use to manage these tensions?

4. Are you satisfied with these strategies, or can you suggest better strategies?

CHARACTERISTICS OF RELATIONSHIPS

Whether you analyze a relationship in terms of developmental stages or dialectical tensions, two characteristics are true of every interpersonal relationship. As you read about each, consider how it applies to your own experience.

Relationships Are Constantly Changing

Relationships are certainly not doomed to deteriorate, but even the strongest ones are rarely stable for long periods. In fairy tales a couple may live "happily ever after," but in real life, this sort of equilibrium is less common. Consider a couple that has been married for some time. Although they have formally bonded, their relationship will probably shift from one dimension of a relational dialectic to another, and forward or backward along the spectrum of stages. Sometimes the partners will feel the need to differentiate from each other, and at other times they will need to seek intimacy. Sometimes they will feel secure in the predictable patterns they have established, and at other times one or both will feel hungry for novelty. The relationship may become circumscribed or even stagnant. From this point the marriage may fail, but this fate isn't certain. With effort, the partners may move from the stage of stagnating to experimenting or from circumscribing to intensifying.

Communication theorist Richard Conville describes the constantly changing, evolving nature of relationships as a cycle in which partners move through a series of stages, returning to ones they previously encountered, although at a new level[91] (see Figure 9.2). In this cycle, partners move from security (integration, in Knapp's terminology) to disintegration (differentiating) to alienation (circumscribing) to resynthesis (intensifying, integrating) to a new level of security. This process is constantly repeating.

Relationships Are Affected by Culture

Many of the qualities that shape personal relationships are universal.[92] For example, social scientists have found that communication in all cultures has both the content and relational dimensions described later in this chapter, that the same facial expressions signal the same emotions in all cultures, and that the distribution of power is a factor in every human society. Males in all cultures (in fact, in all species of mammals) are likely to invest less emotionally in sexual relationships, and they are typically more competitive.

Although the general elements of relationships are universal, the particulars often differ from one culture to another. Consider, for example, how the Western notion of romance and marriage is reflected in the model of relational stages described earlier. The notion that bonding only follows after experimenting, intensifying, and integrating doesn't apply everywhere.[93] Indeed, in some cultures, the bride and groom may meet only weeks, days, or even minutes before they become husband and wife. Research shows that these relationships can be both successful and satisfying,[94] as the Looking at Diversity sidebar in this chapter demonstrates.

A variety of differences—profound, but not always apparent—can make relationships between people from different cultures challenging.[95] For example, deciding how much (or how little) to share what's on your mind is a challenge in any relationship. As noted in Chapter 3, this decision can be especially tricky when the cultural rules about self-disclosure vary. Low-context cultures such as the United States value directness, whereas high-context ones like Japan consider tact far more important. The titles of two self-help books offer a revealing peek at the mindset of these approaches. One American self-help book is titled *How to Say No Without Feeling Guilty*,[96] while the Japanese counterpart is titled *16 Ways to Avoid Saying No*.[97] It's easy to see how differing notions of appropriateness could lead to challenges in intercultural relationships.

When challenges arise out of cultural differences, the kinds of intercultural competence described in Chapter 1 become especially important. Motivation, tolerance for ambiguity, open-mindedness, knowledge of others' practices, and skill at adapting to others' communication styles are likely to make communication more smooth and relationships more satisfying.

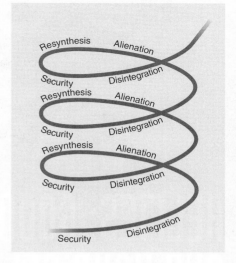

∧ **FIGURE 9.2**
A Helical Model of Relational Cycles

COMMUNICATING ABOUT RELATIONSHIPS

By now you understand that relationships are complex, dynamic, and important. But what kinds of messages do we exchange as we communicate in those relationships?

RELFIES: GOOD FOR YOU AND YOUR RELATIONSHIPS

A relfie is a "relationship selfie" photo, often displayed on social networking sites like Facebook, Twitter, and Tumblr. It shows off you and a relational partner, friend, family member, or someone else with whom you're close. This article describes how relfies communicate important information about their subjects—and help promote healthy relationships.

When a person takes a selfie, *they* are the star of show. Sure, there can be other things in the picture (a cool place you're visiting, something you've accomplished, or basically anything that emphasized your general awesomeness).

With a *relfie*, it is less about the "me" and more about the "we." That is, you take a relfie to emphasize your connection with other people in a way that makes your relationship the picture's main focus. As a result, partners feel more like a couple and less like two distinct individuals. With a selfie, it's all about you. With a relfie, it's all about your relationship.

Now that you know what makes a relfie distinct from a selfie, here are reasons, backed by science, why relfies are important for your relationships.

- Couples who relfie together stay together. Couples who have more of a "we" identity tend to have higher relationship satisfaction, intimacy, and commitment.

- Others see you as having a better romantic relationship. No relfie? People might perceive less of a connection between you and your partner.

- Being in a relfie with your hot partner will make you look more attractive. After all, if you're with an attractive partner, you must be doing something right.

- People take relfies when they are happy and having fun. Emphasizing the good times in relationships benefits your relationships by increasing emotional intimacy, trust, and satisfaction.

- Taking a relfie with a group of your friends? That'll make you appear more attractive as well.

- Couples who feel closer to each other are more likely to display things (perhaps relfies on Twitter) that let the world know they are a couple.

- Did you and your partner do something new, interesting, and/or challenging? (think: skydiving relfie, surfing lessons relfie, tried a new restaurant relfie). Research shows that these types of experiences help you grow as a person and improve the quality of your relationships.

Relfies are not selfies. Whereas selfies may suggest a certain level of narcissism, self-absorption or cry for attention, a relfie may simply say that you value the relationship you share with the other(s) pictured.

Gary Lewandowski

MindTap **ENHANCE ...** your understanding by answering the following questions, either here or online.

1 Which of the research conclusions in this reading rings most true for you? Which does not?

2 Can you think of a social networking page that doesn't accurately reflect a friend's interpersonal relationships? Explain how you arrived at that perception and what changes could be made.

Content and Relational Messages

In Chapter 1, you read that every message has a *content* and a *relational* dimension. The most obvious component of most messages is their content—the subject being discussed. The content of such statements as "It's your turn to do the dishes" or "I'm busy Saturday night" is obvious.

Content messages aren't the only thing being exchanged when two people communicate. In addition, almost every message—both verbal and nonverbal—has a second, relational dimension, which makes statements about how the parties feel toward one another.[98] As you'll read in the following section, these relational messages deal with one or more social needs, most commonly affinity, immediacy, respect, and control. Consider the two examples we just mentioned:

- Imagine two ways of saying "It's your turn to do the dishes": one that is demanding and another that is matter-of-fact. Notice how the different nonverbal messages make statements about how the sender views control in this part of the relationship. The demanding tone says, in effect, "I have a right to tell you what to do around the house," whereas the matter-of-fact tone suggests, "I'm just reminding you of something you might have overlooked."

- You can easily visualize two ways to deliver the statement "I'm busy Saturday night": one with little affinity and the other with warmth and immediacy (in which you sound disappointed and hope for a rescheduling).

Notice that in each of these examples the relational dimension of the message was never discussed. In fact, most of the time we aren't conscious of the many relational messages that bombard us every day. Sometimes we are unaware of relational messages because they match our belief about the amount of respect, control, and affection that is appropriate. For example, you probably wouldn't be offended if your boss told you to do a certain job because you agree that supervisors have the right to direct employees. In other cases, however, conflicts arise over relational messages, even though content is not disputed. If your boss delivered the order in a condescending, sarcastic, or abusive tone of voice, you probably would be offended. Your complaint wouldn't be with the order itself, but rather with the way it was delivered. "I may work for this company," you might think, "but I'm not a slave or an idiot. I deserve to be treated like a human being."

How are relational messages communicated? As the boss–employee example suggests, they are usually communicated nonverbally (which includes tone of voice). To test this fact for yourself, imagine how you could act while saying "Can you help me for a minute?" in a way that communicates each of the following relationships:

Superiority	Friendliness	Sexual desire
Helplessness	Aloofness	Irritation

Although nonverbal behaviors are a good source of relational messages, they are ambiguous. The sharp tone that you receive as a personal insult might be a result of fatigue, and the interruption that you assume is an attempt to ignore your ideas might be a sign of pressure that has nothing to do with you. Before you jump to conclusions about relational clues, it's a good idea to check them out verbally, using the perception-checking skills described in Chapter 4.

Types of Relational Messages

The number and variety of content messages are almost infinite. But unlike the range of content messages, there is a surprisingly narrow range of relational messages. Virtually all of them fit into one of four categories: affinity, immediacy, respect, or control.

Affinity   An important kind of relational communication involves **affinity**— the degree to which people like or appreciate one another.[99] Not surprisingly, affection is the most important ingredient in romantic relationships.[100] Not all affinity messages are positive, though: A glare or an angry word shows the level of (dis)liking just as clearly as a smile or profession of love.

Immediacy   **Immediacy** refers to the degree of interest and attention that we feel toward and communicate to others. Not surprisingly, immediacy is an important element of relationships.[101] A great deal of immediacy comes from nonverbal behavior, such as eye contact, facial expression, tone of voice, and the distance we put between ourselves and others.[102] Immediacy can also come from our language. For example, saying "we have a problem" is more immediate than saying "you have a problem." Chapters 6 and 7 discuss nonverbal and verbal immediacy in more detail.

Immediacy isn't the same thing as affinity: It's possible to like someone without being immediate with them. For instance, you can convey liking with a high degree of immediacy, such as with a big hug and kiss or by shouting "I really like you!" You can also imagine situations where you like someone but operate with a low degree of immediacy. (Picture a quiet, pleasant evening at home where you and another person each read or work comfortably but independently.) You can also imagine communicating dislike in high- and low-immediacy ways.

The most obvious types of immediacy involve positive feelings, but it's possible to express disapproval and disliking with either high or low intensity. Imagine, for instance, the difference between mild and extreme ways—both verbal and nonverbal—of letting a friend know that you are unhappy about something he or she has done.

Highly immediate communication certainly has its value, but there are also times when a low degree of intensity is desirable. It would be exhausting to interact with full intensity all the time.

Juice Images/Alamy

It would also be inappropriate to communicate with high immediacy in cultures that frown upon such behaviors, particularly in public settings. In most cases, the key to relational satisfaction is to create a level of immediacy that works for you and the other person.

Respect   At first glance, respect might seem identical to affinity, but the two attitudes are different.[103] Whereas affinity involves liking, **respect** involves esteem. It's possible to like others without respecting them. For instance, you might like—or even probably love—your two-year-old cousin without respecting her. In the same way, you might have a great deal of affection for some friends, yet not respect the way they behave. The reverse is also true: It's possible to respect people you don't like. You might hold an acquaintance in high esteem for being a hard worker, honest, talented, or clever, yet not particularly enjoy that person's company.

Respect is an extremely important ingredient in good relationships. In fact, it is a better predictor of relational satisfaction than liking, or even loving.[104] Your own experience will show that being respected is sometimes more important than being liked. Think about occasions in school when you were offended because an instructor or fellow students didn't seem to take your comments or questions seriously. The same principle holds on the job, where having your opinions count often means more than being popular. Even in more personal relationships, conflicts often focus on the issue of respect. Being taken seriously is a vital ingredient of self-esteem.

Control   A final dimension of relational communication involves **control**—the degree to which the parties in a relationship have the power to influence one another. Some types of control involve *conversation*: who talks the most, who interrupts whom, and who changes the topic most often.[105] Another dimension of control involves *decisions*: Who has the power to determine what will happen in the relationship? What will we do Saturday night? Shall we use our savings to fix up the house or to take a vacation? How much time should we spend together and how much should we spend apart?

Relational problems arise when the people involved don't have similar ideas about the distribution of control. If you and a friend each push for your own idea, problems are likely to arise. (It can also be difficult when neither person wants to make a decision: "What do you want to do tonight?" "I don't know ... why don't you decide?" "No, *you* decide.")

Most healthy relationships handle the distribution of control in a flexible way. Rather than clinging to the lopsidedness of one-up/one-down relationships or the unrealistic equality of complete shared responsibility, partners shift between one-up, one-down, and straight-across roles. John may handle the decisions about car repairs and menu planning, as well as taking the spotlight at parties with their friends. Mary may manage the finances and make most of the decisions about childcare, as well as controlling the conversation when she and John are alone. When a decision is very important to one partner, the other willingly gives in, knowing that the favor will be returned later. When issues are important to both partners, they try to share power equally. But when an impasse occurs, each will make concessions in a way that keeps the overall balance of power equal.

Metacommunication

Not all relational messages are nonverbal. Social scientists use the term **metacommunication** to describe messages that people exchange, verbally or nonverbally, about their relationship.[106] In other words, metacommunication is communication about communication. Whenever we discuss a relationship with others, we are metacommunicating: "I hate it when you use that tone of voice," or "I appreciate how honest you've been with me." Verbal metacommunication is an essential ingredient in successful relationships. Sooner or later it becomes necessary to talk about what is going on between you and the other person. The ability to focus on the kinds of issues described in this chapter can keep the relationship on track.

Metacommunication isn't just a tool for handling problems. It is also a way to reinforce the satisfying aspects of a relationship: "I really appreciate it when you compliment me about my work in front of the boss." Comments like this serve two functions. First, they let others know that you value their behavior. Second, they boost the odds that others will continue the behavior in the future.

Despite the benefits of metacommunication, bringing relational issues out in the open does have its risks. Your desire to focus on the relationship might look like a bad omen ("Our relationship isn't working if we have to keep talking it over").[107] Furthermore, metacommunication does involve a certain degree of analysis ("It seems like you're angry with me"), and some people resent being analyzed. These cautions don't mean that verbal metacommunication is a bad idea. They do suggest, though, that this tool needs to be used carefully.

MAINTAINING INTERPERSONAL RELATIONSHIPS

Just as gardens need tending, cars need tune-ups, and bodies need exercise, relationships need ongoing attention to keep them successful and satisfying.[108] Social scientists use the term **relational maintenance** to describe communication that keeps relationships running smoothly and satisfactorily.[109]

What kinds of communication help keep relationships satisfying? Researchers have identified five strategies.[110]

1. **Positivity:** Keeping the relational climate polite and upbeat, and also avoiding criticism. (Chapter 11 addresses this topic in detail.)
2. **Openness:** Talking directly about the nature of the relationship and disclosing your personal needs and concerns. (Chapter 3 describes the challenges of finding the optimal amount of self-disclosure.)
3. **Assurances:** Letting the other person know—both verbally and nonverbally—that he or she matters to you and that you are committed to the relationship.
4. **Social networks:** Being invested in each other's friends, family, and loved ones.

5. **Sharing tasks:** Helping one another take care of life's chores and obligations.

These maintenance strategies aren't only for romantic relationships. One study analyzed college students' email to see which maintenance approaches they used.[111] With family and friends, two strategies were used most: openness ("Things have been a little crazy for me lately") and social networks ("How are you and Sam? Hopefully good"). With romantic partners, however, assurances ("This is just a little email to say I love you") were the most-used maintenance device.

The preceding example shows that social media can play an important role in maintaining close relationships.[112] As Chapter 2 notes, tools such as Facebook give loved ones the chance to keep up with each other through status updates and posting comments on each other's walls.[113] Phone calls and emails can help too, with phoning being particularly valuable for more intimate topics.[114] Even swapping photo-messages is a means to maintain a relationship.[115] One study found that women use social media for relational maintenance more often than do men, regardless of the type of relationship maintained.[116] This is consistent with research showing that women expect and receive more maintenance communication with their female friends than men do with other males.[117]

Social media are especially useful for meeting the challenges of long-distance relationships. These relationships are increasingly common; contrary to popular assumptions, they can be as stable or more so than geographically close relationships.[118] This is true not only for romantic and family relationships but also for friendships.[119] The key is a commitment to relational maintenance. In one study, female college students said that openness and mutual problem solving are vital maintenance strategies in long-distance dating relationships.[120] In another study, both men and women reported that openness (self-disclosure) was the most important factor for maintaining closeness with their long-distance friends. (They conceded that sharing tasks and practical help are less viable options in long-distance relationships.)[121]

Social Support

Although relational maintenance is about keeping a relationship thriving, **social support** is about helping loved ones during challenging times by providing emotional, informational, or instrumental resources.[122] Communication plays a central role in giving this aid to those we love.[123] Here's a closer look at those three support resources:

1. **Emotional support:** Few things are more helpful during times of stress, hurt, or grief than a loved one who listens with empathy and responds in caring ways.[124] Chapter 8 describes what supporting does and doesn't sound like when responding to others' emotional needs. It's important to keep your message *person-centered*—that is, focused on the emotions of the speaker ("This must be difficult for you") rather than minimizing those feelings ("It's not the end of the world") or diverting attention ("The sun will come up tomorrow").[125]

20th Century Fox/Allstar

∧ Early in *The Fault in Our Stars*, Gus (Ansel Elgort) provides emotional, informational, and instrumental support to Hazel (Shailene Woodley). Before the story ends, Hazel returns the favor. How have you communicated support to loved ones who were going through challenging times? What kind of support do you most like to receive?

2. **Informational support:** The closest people in our lives can often be our best information sources. They can give us recommendations for shopping, advice about relationships, or observations about our blind spots. You can probably recall times when you've said to a loved one with gratitude, "Thanks for letting me know." Of course, it's important to remember the tips about advice giving in Chapter 8. Information is most likely to be regarded as supportive when it's wanted and requested by the person in need.

3. **Instrumental support:** Sometimes support is best given by rolling up your sleeves and doing a task or favor for a person you love. This can be as simple as a ride to the airport or as involved as caregiving during an illness. We count on romantic partners and family members to offer assistance in times of need, and instrumental support is a primary marker of a close friendship ("A friend in need is a friend indeed").[126]

One study found that partners in romantic relationships generally don't receive as much support from each other as they would like.[127] A small percentage of participants, however, said they sometimes get *too much* support from their partners in the form of unwanted information and advice. It's vital for couples to communicate clearly about the kinds of support they want and need, according to one of the authors of the study: "Your partner shouldn't have to be a mind reader. Couples will be happier if they learn how to say, 'This is how I'm feeling, and this is how you can help me.'"[128]

As a reminder, communicators don't necessarily need to see each other—or in some cases even know each other—to provide social support.[129] See Chapter 2 for a discussion of how support can be provided through social media.

Repairing Damaged Relationships

Sooner or later, even the strongest relationships hit a bumpy patch. Some problems arise from outside forces: work, finances, competing relationships, and so on. At other times, problems arise from differences and disagreements within your relationship. Chapter 12 offers guidelines for dealing with these sorts of challenges.

A third type of relational problem comes from **relational transgressions**: when one partner violates the explicit or implicit terms of the relationship, letting the other one down in some important way.[130]

Types of Relational Transgressions   There are several ways to transgress in a relationship:[131]

- **Lack of Commitment**

  - Failure to honor important obligations (e.g., financial, emotional, task-related)
  - Self-serving dishonesty
  - Unfaithfulness

PAUSE *and* REFLECT

Maintaining Your Relationships

MindTap® **REFLECT ...** on how you maintain your relationships by answering the following questions, either here or online.

1. Choose one relationship that matters to you: with a family member, friend, or a romantic partner. Analyze the degree to which you and the other person use the maintenance strategies listed above to keep the relationship strong and satisfying.

2. Are you satisfied with the way you're maintaining your important relationships through constructive communication?

3. What steps could you take to improve matters?

- **Distance**
  - Physical separation (beyond what is necessary)
  - Psychological separation (avoidance, ignoring)
- **Disrespect**
  - Criticism (especially in front of third parties)
- **Problematic Emotions**
  - Jealousy
  - Unjustified suspicion
  - Rage
- **Aggression**
  - Verbal hostility
  - Physical violence

As you think about transgressions you've experienced, you will recognize that there are several dimensions to each one.

Minor versus Significant Some of the behaviors described above aren't inherently transgressions, and in small doses they can actually aid relationships. For instance, a *little* distance can make the heart grow fonder, a *little* jealousy can be a sign of affection, and a *little* anger can start the process of resolving a gripe. In large and regular doses, however, these acts become serious transgressions that can damage personal relationships.

Social versus Relational Some transgressions violate *social rules* shared by society at large. For example, almost everyone would agree that ridiculing or humiliating a friend or family member in public is a violation of a fundamental social rule regarding saving others' face. Other rules are *relational* in nature—unique norms constructed by the parties involved. For instance, some families have a rule stating "If I'm going to be more than a little bit

On the JOB

How to Repair a Damaged Professional Relationship

Sooner or later the challenges of work will generate damaged relationships. It's tempting to ignore and avoid the problems, but the consequences of doing so can be serious. If you have to work with the other party, the friction can damage effectiveness and make daily life uncomfortable—or downright painful. Also, an aggrieved colleague, boss, subordinate, or customer can sabotage your career.

Writing in the *Harvard Business Review*, business consultant Dorie Clark offers suggestions for making things better:

1. **Propose a reset**. As you read in Chapter 1, you can't undo what's already happened. But you can express your desire for a fresh start. You might say "I feel bad about our past problems. Could we brainstorm ways to make things better in the future?

2. **Acknowledge your own culpability**. It's easy to find fault with the other person, but chances are you have also contributed to the problem in some way. Were you too assertive or too quiet? Too hands-on or too stand-offish? Too demanding or not making your needs known more forcefully? Taking some responsibility makes it easier for the other person to acknowledge his or her role.

3. **Change the communication dynamic**. You may not be able to change the other person, but you can control your own behavior. This book is loaded with strategies you can use to break unproductive patterns. For example, consider perception checking (Chapter 4) to clarify your understanding. Use the strategies in Chapter 5 to manage your problematic emotions. Try behavioral language (Chapter 6) to explain your position more clearly. Do your best to listen more carefully and respectfully (Chapter 8). Use the skills in Chapter 11 to reduce defensiveness, and the strategies in Chapter 12 to manage future conflicts more productively.

late, I'll let you know so you don't worry." Once such a rule exists, failure to honor it feels like a violation, even though outsiders might not view it as such.

Deliberate versus Unintentional Some transgressions are unintentional. You might reveal something about a friend's past without realizing that this disclosure would be embarrassing. Other violations, though, are intentional. In a fit of anger, you might purposely lash out with a cruel comment, knowing that it will hurt the other person's feelings.

One-Time versus Incremental The most obvious transgressions occur in a single episode: an act of betrayal, a verbal assault, or stalking out in anger. But more subtle transgressions can occur over time. Consider emotional withdrawal. Everybody has times when they need isolation, and we usually give one another the space to do just that. But if the withdrawal slowly becomes pervasive, it becomes a violation of the fundamental rule in most relationships that partners should be available to one another.

Strategies for Relational Repair Research confirms the common-sense notion that a first step toward repairing a transgression is to talk about the violation.[132] Chapter 11 offers tips for sending clear, assertive messages when you believe you've been wronged: "I was really embarrassed when you yelled at me in front of everybody last night." In other cases, you might be responsible for the transgression and want to raise it for discussion: "What did I do that you found so hurtful?" "Why was my behavior a problem for you?" Asking questions like these—and listening nondefensively to the answers—can be an enormous challenge. Chapter 8 offers guidelines for listening, and Chapter 11 provides tips about how to manage criticism.

"I said I'm sorry."

It's unrealistic to expect that serious transgressions will be forgotten. When you're the offender, the best chance for righting a wrong is to speak up. It isn't easy to apologize, especially in Western cultures, where saving one's own face is a strong concern.[133] But not expressing regret can be worse than saying "I'm sorry." Participants in one study reported that they had more remorse over apologies they didn't offer than about those they did.[134] There's another benefit of seeking forgiveness: Research shows that transgressors who have been forgiven are less likely to repeat their offenses than those who have not received forgiveness.[135]

There are several ways to make amends:[136]

1. **Expressing regret:** "I'm sorry." "I feel bad about what I did."
2. **Accepting responsibility:** "I was wrong." "It was my fault."
3. **Making restitution:** "What can I do to make it right?"
4. **Genuinely repenting:** "I'll try not to do that again."
5. **Requesting forgiveness:** "Will you please forgive me?"

An apology will only be convincing if the speaker's nonverbal behaviors match his or her words. Even then, it may be unrealistic to expect immediate forgiveness. Sometimes, especially with severe transgressions, expressions of regret and promises of new behavior need to be demonstrated over time before the aggrieved party accepts them as genuine.[137]

Responding to Transgressions   Many people think of forgiveness as a topic for theologians and philosophers. However, social scientists have found that the way we respond to apologies has strong consequences for the future of the relationship. There are three possible ways to respond to an apology:[138]

1. **Acceptance**

   "I'm glad you understand why I was so upset. I sure hope it won't happen again."

   "I can't forget what you did, but I believe your apology and I accept it."

2. **Rejection**

   "I can't let that one go, at least for now. It was too hurtful."

   "Words can't make up for what you did."

PAUSE *and* REFLECT

Your Relational Transgressions

MindTap˙ **REFLECT ...** on your relational transgressions by answering the following questions, either here or online.

1. Describe transgressions you have made in one important relationship. (If you think the relationship can handle it, consider asking the "victim" of your transgressions to describe your behavior and its effects.)

2. Take each transgression listed in the above question separately and identify whether it was minor or significant, social or relational, deliberate or unintentional, and one-time or incremental. Do you think the other person would identify these transgressions in the same way? (You might ask the other person and see how they identify the transgressions.)

3. Consider (or ask the other person) which of the transgressions are necessary to repair and choose the transgression that you (and the other person) determine is the most significant. Then review the five ways for making amends described in this section, and decide how you could put them into action.

4. Which of the five ways for making amends are the hardest for you to say? Which mean the most to you when someone is trying to make amends to you?

3. **Discussion**

"I appreciate the apology, but I don't think you understand why this is such a big deal for me ..."

"How can I be sure you won't do the same thing again?"

While not every apology can be accepted, forgiving others has both personal and relational benefits. On a personal level, forgiveness has been shown to reduce emotional distress and aggression[139] as well as improve cardiovascular functioning.[140] Interpersonally, extending forgiveness to lovers, friends, and family can help restore damaged relationships.[141]

Not surprisingly, some transgressions are harder to forgive than others.[142] One study of dating partners found that sexual infidelity and breaking up with the partner were the two least forgivable offenses.[143] And, as noted earlier, being emotionally unfaithful—as occurs in some online affairs—can be as distressing as sexual infidelity.[144]

Even when a sincere apology is offered, forgiving others can be difficult. Research shows that one way to improve your ability to forgive is to recall times when you have mistreated or hurt others in the past—in other words, to remember that you, too, have wronged others and needed their forgiveness.[145] Knowing that it's in our own best interest to be forgiving, communication researcher Douglas Kelley encourages us to remember these words: "When we have been hurt, we have two alternatives: be destroyed by resentment or forgive. Resentment is death; forgiving leads to healing and life."[146]

SUMMARY

People form interpersonal relationships for a variety of reasons. Attraction can come from physical appearance, perceived similarity, complementarity, reciprocal attraction, perceived competence, disclosure of personal information, proximity, and rewards.

Two models offer somewhat different perspectives on the dynamics of interpersonal relationships. A stage-related model characterizes communication as exhibiting different characteristics as people come together and draw apart. A dialectical model characterizes communicators in every stage as being driven by the need to manage a variety of mutually incompatible needs.

Communication occurs on two levels: content and relational. Relational communication can be both verbal and nonverbal. Relational messages usually refer to one of four dimensions of a relationship: affinity, immediacy, respect, or control. Metacommunication consists of messages that refer to the relationship between the communicators.

Healthy interpersonal relationships require maintenance. They also need emotional, informational, and instrumental support. When relationships become damaged by transgressions, repair strategies and forgiveness become important skills for both parties.

KEY TERMS

affinity
avoiding
bonding
circumscribing
connection-autonomy dialectic
control
dialectical tensions
differentiating
experimenting
immediacy
initiating

integrating
intensifying
metacommunication
openness-privacy dialectic
predictability-novelty dialectic
relational maintenance
relational transgressions
respect
social support
stagnating
terminating

C H A P T E R N I N E

Communication and Relational Dynamics

OUTLINE

Use this outline to take notes as you read the chapter in the text or as your instructor lectures in class.

I. WHY WE FORM RELATIONSHIPS

    A. Appearance

    B. Similarity

    C. Complementarity

    D. Reciprocal Attraction

    E. Competence

    F. Disclosure

    G. Proximity

    H. Rewards

II. MODELS OF RELATIONAL DYNAMICS

    A. Developmental Perspective

       1. Initiating

       2. Experimenting

       3. Intensifying

       4. Integrating

       5. Bonding

       6. Differentiating

       7. Circumscribing

       8. Stagnating

       9. Avoiding

      10. Terminating

    B. A Dialectical Perspective

       1. Connection versus Autonomy

       2. Openness versus Privacy

       3. Predictability versus Novelty

4. Managing Dialectical Tensions
   a. Denial
   b. Disorientation
   c. Alternation
   d. Segmentation
   e. Balance
   f. Integration
   g. Recalibration
   h. Reaffirmation

III. CHARACTERISTICS OF RELATIONSHIPS

A. Relationships Are Constantly Changing
1. Security
2. Disintegration
3. Alienation
4. Resynthesis
5. New Level of Security

B. Relationships Are Affected by Culture
1. Variety of Differences
2. Intercultural Competence

IV. COMMUNICATING ABOUT RELATIONSHIPS

A. Content and Relational Messages
1. Content: Subject Being Discussed
2. Relational: Feelings about Each Other

B. Types of Relational Messages
1. Affinity
2. Immediacy
3. Respect
4. Control
   a. Decisional
   b. Conversational

C. Metacommunication
1. Tool for Handling Problems
2. Way to Reinforce Relationship

V. RELATIONAL MAINTENANCE

A. Positivity

B. Openness

C. Assurances

D. Social Networks

E. Sharing Tasks

F. Social Support
1. Emotional
2. Informational
3. Instrumental

VI. REPAIRING DAMAGED RELATIONSHIPS

A. Types of Relational Transgressions
1. Lack of Commitment
2. Distance
3. Disrespect
4. Problematic Emotions
5. Aggression

B. Dimensions of Transgressions
1. Minor versus Significant
2. Social versus Relational
3. Deliberate versus Unintentional
4. One-Time versus Incremental

C. Strategies for Relational Repair
1. Make Amends
   a. Expressing Regret
   b. Accepting Responsibility
   c. Making Restitution
   d. Genuinely Repenting
   e. Requesting Forgiveness
2. Responding to Transgression
   a. Acceptance
   b. Rejection
   c. Discussion

KEY TERMS

affinity

assurances

avoiding

bonding

circumscribing

complementarity

connection-autonomy dialectic

control

dialectical tension

differentiating

experimenting

immediacy

initiating

integrating

intensifying

metacommunication

openness-privacy dialectic

predictability-novelty dialectic

reaffirmation

recalibration

reciprocal attraction

relational maintenance

relational transgressions

respect

social exchange theory

social support

stagnating

transgression

terminating

ACTIVITIES

9.1 DISCOVERING DIALECTICS

LEARNING OBJECTIVES

- Identify the dialectical tensions in a given relationship.
- Understand how dialectical tensions influence communication within a relationship.
- Analyze the most effective strategies for managing dialectical tensions.

INSTRUCTIONS

1. Identify the dialectical tensions operating between the people in the situations below, taking time to explain the consequences of their conflicting feelings and thoughts: *connection versus autonomy, openness versus privacy, predictability versus novelty.*
2. Identify one or more of the eight strategies for managing dialectical tensions (*denial, disorientation, alternation, segmentation, balance, integration, recalibration,* and *reaffirmation*) that you believe would be most beneficial to the situation and describe how applying this strategy might affect this relationship.
3. Describe dialectical tensions at work in your own relationships and label and explain the strategies that you use to deal with them.

SITUATION	DIALECTICAL TENSION & CONSEQUENCES	STRATEGY FOR MANAGING & LIKELY EFFECT
EXAMPLE: *Sandra, nineteen, and her mother, Tracy, have become good friends over the past few years. Sandra now has a serious boyfriend and spends less time talking to her mother.*	*The open-privacy dialectic is probably at work here. Sandra and Tracy continue to share the intimacy of their mother-daughter relationship, but privacy needs about the boyfriend probably keep them at more distance.*	*Sandra and Tracy are likely to use the segmentation strategy, in which they maintain openness about many areas but keep certain areas of the boyfriend relationship "off limits."*
1. Daryl is new to the software firm where Steve has been for five years. Daryl has asked Steve to play golf this weekend. Steve is uncomfortable about mixing business and pleasure, but still wants to have a good working relationship with Daryl.		

SITUATION	DIALECTICAL TENSION & CONSEQUENCES	STRATEGY FOR MANAGING & LIKELY EFFECT
2. Nesto and Gina have been dating for six months. They continue to enjoy one another's company, but each has begun to notice annoying little habits that the other one has.		
3. Jenner and A. J. are siblings who have always relied on one another completely. Jenner appreciates A. J.'s dependability, but wishes their times together weren't so boring.		
4. Eugenia and Shane have worked at the same business for twenty years. They have collaborated on a number of projects. They've tried to get together socially, but their spouses don't seem to get along.		
5. Christina and Nicole are roommates. Christina wants them to share everything, but Nicole is not proud of a few things she's done and doesn't want to face her friend's judgment.		
6. Your example:		
7. Your example:		

9.2 RELATIONAL STAGES

LEARNING OBJECTIVES

- Identify the developmental stages in Knapp's model as reflected in specified relationship situations.
- Identify the developmental stages in Knapp's model as experience in personal relationship situations.
- Verify your answers with support material from your text.

INSTRUCTIONS

1. Discuss the various situations listed below.
2. Identify the relational stage(s) that many of these behaviors illustrate (e.g., initiating, experimenting, intensifying, integrating, bonding, differentiating, circumscribing, avoiding, stagnating, terminating).
3. Cite a brief passage from Chapter 9 that verifies the stage of the relationship.
4. Record relational situations from your experience that exemplify particular developmental stages. Identify the stages and cite a brief passage for support.

EXAMPLE

Two friends are discussing the effects of divorce in their families.
Relational stage illustrated: *This type of self-disclosure would most likely occur in an intensifying stage of a relationship, where the friends have gone beyond the small talk of experimenting and are beginning to develop more trust, more depth rather than breadth of self-disclosure, and where secrets are told and favors given.*

1. Two friends are telling one another about using/refusing drugs.

   Relational stage illustrated _____

   Cite a brief passage to verify the stage of the relationship

   _____

   _____

   _____

2. Two classmates are comparing the results of their first exam.

   Relational stage illustrated _____

Cite a brief passage to verify the stage of the relationship

_____

_____

3. Two people seated next to each other on an overseas flight begin telling one another about their past romantic involvements.

   Relational stage illustrated _____

   Cite a brief passage to verify the stage of the relationship

   _____

   _____

   _____

4. Two long-time friends are discussing their worries and feelings of responsibility regarding their parents' advancing age.

   Relational stage illustrated _____

   Cite a brief passage to verify the stage of the relationship

   _____

   _____

5. Cousins who practically lived at each other's homes as teenagers five years ago now seem to have nothing to talk about.

   Relational stage illustrated _____

   Cite a brief passage to verify the stage of the relationship

   _____

   _____

6. A divorced couple meets briefly to discuss education and vacation plans for their children.

   Relational stage illustrated _____

Cite a brief passage to verify the stage of the relationship

_____

_____

7. A man and woman who dated for six months during college ten years ago now find themselves working for the same company.

Relational stage illustrated _____

Cite a brief passage to verify the stage of the relationship

_____

_____

8. A manager and employee have agreed to sit down and talk about the problems they are experiencing with each other.

Relational stage illustrated _____

Cite a brief passage to verify the stage of the relationship

_____

_____

9. Your example: _____

Relational stage illustrated _____

Cite a brief passage to verify the stage of the relationship

_____

_____

10. Your example: _____

Relational stage illustrated _____

Cite a brief passage to verify the stage of the relationship

_____

_____

9.3 RECOGNIZING RELATIONAL MESSAGES

LEARNING OBJECTIVES

- Identify the content and relational dimensions of communication in a given transaction.

INSTRUCTIONS

1. Read each message below.
2. Picture in your mind the nonverbal behaviors that accompany each of the statements. Briefly describe the most significant of those nonverbal behaviors.
3. Describe the relational issues that seem to be involved in each of the situations. Use your text to *label and explain* the relational dimensions of **affinity, immediacy, respect,** and **control** shown by the speaker in each example.

MESSAGE CONTENT	NONVERBAL BEHAVIOR	RELATIONAL DIMENSION (affinity, immediacy, respect, control)
EXAMPLE: *You tell your romantic partner, "…Anyhow, that's what I think. What do you think?"*	*You use a sincere vocal tone, strong eye contact, and soft touch.*	*High in immediacy because I invite involvement and show interest by my tone.* *High in affinity as I show liking by my eye contact and touch.*
Example: *Your instructor invites the class to "Tell me what's working and what isn't."*	*Teacher smiles and moves his arms in an open, sweeping gesture.*	*Low in control as the instructor invites influence over how the course is run.* *High in respect by valuing the opinions of students.*
1. You ask a friend to come over and the reply is, "I'm sorry, but I have to work."		
2. Someone you live with complains, "You don't help out enough around the house."		
3. Your roommate says, "You're no fun. I think I'm going to bed."		
4. Your boss asks, "Are your hours working out?"		
5. Your boss says, "You'll need a doctor's note to verify your illness."		

MESSAGE CONTENT	NONVERBAL BEHAVIOR	RELATIONAL DIMENSION (affinity, immediacy, respect, control)
6. Your friend teases, "You can't seem to remember the important stuff."		
7. Your parent says, "I know you'll make the right decision."		
8. Your romantic partner says, "I need you to let me know where you are."		
9. Someone reminds you, "Drive carefully."		
10. A family member says you should spend more time at home and you reply, "I'll do what I please."		
11. The doctor's reception-ist says, "Can you hold, please?" when you call to make an appointment.		
12. You are getting ready to leave and your partner says, "You're going to wear *that*?"		
13. A friend says, "Fine," and hangs up the phone.		
14. When you ask if you can take time off, your boss rolls her eyes and sighs, "Again?"		
15. You tell your friend you don't feel well, and the response is, "Had too good a time last night?"		

9.4 FORMING RELATIONSHIPS

LEARNING OBJECTIVES

- Identify factors that have influenced your choice of relational partners.
- Recognize the effects of these factors on the development of significant relationships.

INSTRUCTIONS

1. In the spaces below, identify three significant relationships, listing the type of relationship (friend, significant relationship, family member, etc.).
2. For each of these relationships, identify three relationship-forming factors (appearance, similarity, complementarity, disclosure, etc.).
3. Describe how these three factors helped you form that relationship.

Relationship type 1: _____

Relationship forming factors:

1. _____

2. _____

3. _____

Describe how these three factors helped you form that relationship:

_____

_____

_____

_____

Relationship type 2: _____

Relationship forming factors:

1. _____

2. _____

3. _____

Describe how these three factors helped you form that relationship:

_____

_____

_____

Relationship type 3: _____

Relationship forming factors:

1. _____

2. _____

3. _____

Describe how these three factors helped you form that relationship:

_____

_____

_____

9.5 APPLYING KNAPP'S MODEL

LEARNING OBJECTIVES:

- Use Knapp's model to describe the nature of communication in the various stages of a relationship.
- Identify the three stages of Knapp's model: coming together, relational maintenance, and coming apart.
- Reflect on how changes in these three stages of the relationship might have caused the relationship to unfold differently.

INSTRUCTIONS:

1. Think of a romantic or close relationship that you had that unfolded through most of the developmental stages, ending in termination. As your text explains, not all relationships move through all of the stages in a linear, predictable order. However, you'll likely find that your significant relationships will reflect most of the stages in some way.
2. In the spaces below, describe a memorable event or conversation that illustrates how your relationship fulfilled that stage of Knapp's model of communication.
3. Answer the reflection questions that follow.

Initiating:

_____

_____

_____

Experimenting:

_____

_____

_____

Intensifying:

_____

_____

_____

Integrating:

_____

_____

Bonding:

_____

_____

Differentiating:

_____

_____

Circumscribing:

_____

_____

Stagnating:

_____

_____

Avoiding:

_____

_____

_____

Terminating:

_____

_____

_____

REFLECT:

1. Review your answers and identify key events that marked the three stages of Knapp's model: coming together, relational maintenance, and coming apart. For example, what happened that led you to move from Differentiating and Circumscribing to Stagnating?

_____

_____

2. Describe how changes in behavior and events in these three stages of the relationship might have caused the relationship to unfold differently.

_____

_____

9.6 SUSTAINING INTERPERSONAL RELATIONSHIPS

LEARNING OBJECTIVES

- Identify and apply strategies that positively contribute to relational maintenance (positivity, openness, assurances, social networks, and sharing tasks).
- Recognize the effects of these strategies on the sustainability of significant relationships.

INSTRUCTIONS

1. For the relationships below, choose two of the five relational maintenance strategies to keep the relationship successful and satisfying (positivity, openness, assurances, social networks, and sharing tasks).
2. Describe in words and actions how each person in this relationship might implement these strategies.
3. Reflect on the possible impact on this relationship if these strategies are implemented.

EXAMPLE

Relationship: mother and teenage daughter
Strategies: *Openness and positivity*
Description: *Mother: I appreciated you calling me last night to let me know you were going to be out later than you'd said. Now that you have your own car, I do worry. When you're thoughtful about my needs, it helps me to relax and trust you more.*
Daughter: My friend Jen was being a jerk and wouldn't leave the party when I asked her to. I didn't want to leave her there without a ride, but I didn't want to stay out later than I said I would. I started getting angry and stressed, so I called. Thanks for understanding.
Effects: The mother will feel better about asking for what she needs and will trust her daughter more the next time. The daughter will trust that her mother won't automatically assume the worst and yell at her. She'll feel more empowered to make mature decisions.

1. Relationship: a newlywed couple

   Strategies:

   _____

   _____

   Description:

   _____

   _____

Effects:

_____

_____

2. Relationship: college roommates

Strategies:

_____

_____

Description:

_____

_____

Effects:

_____

_____

3. Relationship: adult brother and sister

Strategies:

_____

_____

Description:

_____

_____

Effects:

_____

_____

4. Relationship: employee and supervisor

    Strategies:

    _____

    _____

    Description:

    _____

    _____

    Effects:

    _____

    _____

5. Relationship: romantic couple who are experiencing relationship stress

    Strategies:

    _____

    _____

    Description:

    _____

    _____

    Effects:

    _____

    _____

6. Relationship: you and a significant relationship

    Strategies:

    _____

    _____

    Description:

    _____

    _____

    Effects:

    _____

    _____

9.7 REPAIRING DAMAGED RELATIONSHIPS

LEARNING OBJECTIVES

- Identify the types and dimensions of relational transgressions.
- Identify and apply ways to make amends.
- Recognize the possible effects of making amends on relationships.

INSTRUCTIONS

1. For each of the transgressions described in the relationships below, identify the types of transgressions (lack of commitment, distance, disrespect, problematic emotions, aggression).
2. For each of the transgressions described in the relationships below, identify the relative dimensions of that transgression (minor versus significant, social versus relational, deliberate versus unintentional, one-time versus incremental).
3. Identify the ways the person who committed the transgression might make amends (expressing regret, accepting responsibility, making restitution, genuinely repenting, requesting forgiveness).
4. Describe the words and actions that person might use to express her or his amends.
5. Reflect on how this expression of amends might impact this relationship.

EXAMPLE

Relationship: boyfriend and girlfriend
Transgression: *He buys tickets with friends to attend a sporting event that she has no interest in, forgetting that the game is on her birthday.*
Types of transgression: *lack of commitment and distance*
Relative dimensions: *relatively minor, relational, unintentional, one-time*
Amends: *express regret, accepting responsibility, and making restitution*
Description: *I'm so sorry that I forgot your birthday when I made my plans. It was my fault because I didn't add it to the calendar on my new phone. What can I do to make it right? I'm willing to sell my ticket to one of the other guys. Or we maybe could plan a trip on the weekend and have a romantic get-away.*
Effect: She will likely accept his apology and forgive his transgression.

1. Relationship: coworkers

   Transgression: In meetings with their boss, one coworker repeatedly takes credit for work the other person successfully completed and openly criticizes the other person.

   Types:

   _____

   _____

Relative Dimensions:

_____

_____

Amends:

_____

_____

Description:

_____

_____

Effect:

_____

_____

2. Relationship: girlfriends

Transgression: One girlfriend feels left out and jealous of the other's new romantic relationship. She stops responding to her phone calls and texts, deliberately stands her up for a lunch date, and is rude to her when they do talk.

Types:

_____

_____

Relative Dimensions:

_____

_____

Amends:

_____

_____

Description:

_____

_____

Effect:

_____

_____

3. Relationship: student and teacher

Transgression: The student repeatedly fails to submit assignments on time, makes up stories to justify the delays, and doesn't respond to the teacher's email requests.

Types:

_____

_____

Relative Dimensions:

_____

_____

Amends:

_____

_____

Description:

_____

_____

Effect:

_____

_____

4. Relationship: parent and 13-year-old child

    Transgression: A distressed parent displays rage when the child fails to perform a task, calling the child names and slapping them across the face.

    Types:

    _____

    _____

    Relative Dimensions:

    _____

    _____

    Amends:

    _____

    _____

    Description:

    _____

    _____

Effect:

_____

_____

5. Relationship: you and a significant relationship

Transgression: Identify a transgression you committed in one of your significant relationships

_____

_____

Types:

_____

_____

Relative Dimensions:

_____

_____

Amends:

_____

_____

Description:

_____

_____

Effect:

_____

_____

STUDY GUIDE

CHECK YOUR UNDERSTANDING

TRUE/FALSE

Mark the statements below as true or false. Correct statements that are false on the lines below to create a true statement.

_____ 1. Romantic partners create positive illusions of one another and view each other as more attractive over time.

_____

_____ 2. Usually, we like people who like us.

_____

_____ 3. It's possible to respect people you don't like.

_____

_____ 4. It's impossible to like someone without being immediate with them.

_____

_____ 5. Email is not helpful in maintaining interpersonal relationships.

_____

_____ 6. The struggle to achieve important, but seemingly incompatible goals in relationships results in the creation of dialectical tension.

_____

_____ 7. During the integrating stage of a relationships, couples may give up some characteristics of their old selves to gain a shared identity.

_____

_____ 8. "I like the way we don't discuss our political differences in public" is an example of metacommunication.

_____

_____ 9. For a behavior to be considered a transgression, it needs to be deliberate.

_____

_____ 10. Relational partners often go through evolving cycles in which they can repeat a relational stage at a new level.

_____

_____ 11. Research suggests that even when forgiven, transgressors are as likely to repeat their offenses as those who have not received forgiveness.

_____

_____ 12. The key to successful differentiating is maintaining a commitment to the relationship while creating the space for being an individual as well.

_____

COMPLETION

Fill in the blanks below with the correct terms chosen from the list below.

dialectical	positivity	relational transgression
openness	segmentation	metacommunication
forgiveness	immediacy	appearance
complementarity		

1. _____ The messages people exchange about their communication; communication about communication.

2. _____ A relational maintenance strategy of keeping the relational climate upbeat and avoiding disapproval or unconstructive remarks.

3. _____ A strategy to maintain a relationship that involves talking directly about the relationship and disclosing needs and concerns.

4. _____ A strategy used to compartmentalize different areas of their relationship.

5. _____ A violation of the explicit or implicit terms of the relationship.

6. _____ A method of relational repair that promotes physical and emotional health.

7. _____ An attraction variable that is most important at the beginning of relationships, and less important over time.

8. _____ An attraction variable in which people are different in ways that meet each of their needs.

9. _____ A relational message that conveys involvement and interest.

10. _____ is a tension that arises when two incompatible goals exist in a relationship.

MULTIPLE CHOICE

Place the letter of the developmental stage of the relationship on the line before its example found below.

a. initiating
b. experimenting
c. intensifying
d. integrating
e. bonding

f. differentiating
g. circumscribing
h. stagnating
i. avoiding
j. terminating

_____ 1. A public ritual marks this stage.

_____ 2. First glances and "sizing up" each other typifies this stage.

_____ 3. Called the "we" stage, this stage involves increasing self-disclosure.

_____ 4. Lots of "small talk" typifies this stage.

_____ 5. This stage involves much focus on individual rather than dyadic interests.

_____ 6. There's very little growth or experimentation in this stage.

_____ 7. This stage involves much behavior that talks around the relational issues because the partners expect bad feelings.

_____ 8. The partners' social circles merge at this stage, and they make purchases or commitments together.

_____ 9. No attempts are made to contact the other at this stage.

_____ 10. The relationship is redefined or dissolved at this stage.

_____ 11. A marriage ceremony would be typical here.

_____ 12. Roommates who make sure they are never in the same room and who are tolerating one another only until the lease is up might be at this stage.

_____ 13. A couple who avoids talking about future commitment because they are afraid of how the discussion will go is probably at this stage.

Choose the best answer for each of the statements below:

_____ 14. Research suggests attraction to partners who have complementary temperament is rooted in
  a. family history.
  b. socialization.
  c. biology.
  d. communication styles.

Class _____   Name _____

_____ 15. All of the following are important ingredients of satisfying self-disclosure except
         a. reciprocity.
         b. timing.
         c. interesting information.
         d. trustworthiness.

_____ 16. In the early stages of a relationship, _____ is especially important.
         a. metacommunication
         b. a positive illusion
         c. behavior
         d. appearance

CHAPTER NINE STUDY GUIDE ANSWERS

TRUE/FALSE

1. T	4. F	7. T	10. T
2. T	5. F	8. T	11. F
3. T	6. T	9. F	12. T

COMPLETION

1. metacommunication
2. positivity
3. openness
4. segmentation
5. relational transgression
6. forgiveness
7. appearance
8. complementarity
9. immediacy
10. dialectical

MULTIPLE CHOICE

1. e	4. b	7. g	10. j	13. g	16. d
2. a	5. f	8. d	11. e	14. c	
3. c	6. h	9. i	12. i	15. c	

MindTap START ...
Explore this chapter's
topics online.

10

INTERPERSONAL COMMUNICATION IN CLOSE RELATIONSHIPS

AFTER STUDYING THE TOPICS IN THIS CHAPTER, YOU SHOULD BE ABLE TO:

1. Identify the level and types of intimacy in a specific relationship and describe ways in which the quality and extent of intimacy could be improved.

2. For a specific family, explain how family roles are created and perpetuated through communication.

3. Describe the systemic properties of a particular family unit and also describe that family's communication patterns.

4. Identify the various types of friendships in your life and evaluate how effectively they are sustained through communication.

5. Identify the turning points and conflict styles in a specific romantic relationship.

6. Evaluate how effectively the partners in a specific romantic relationship adapt to one another's love languages.

*H*ow important are close, intimate relationships? Empirical studies offer some answers. Researchers asked people who were dying in hospices and hospitals what mattered most in life. Fully 90 percent of these terminally ill patients put intimate relationships at the top of the list. As a fifty-year-old mother of three children who was dying of cancer put it, "You need not wait until you are in my condition to know nothing in life is as important as loving relationships."[1] Another researcher concludes that close relationships "may be the *single most important* source of life satisfaction and emotional well-being, across different ages and cultures."[2]

This chapter will take a close look at close relationships. We'll begin by investigating the role of intimacy in making some relationships more personal and meaningful than others. We'll then look at three contexts—family, friends, and romantic partners—where most of our intimate relationships occur.

INTIMACY IN CLOSE RELATIONSHIPS

Webster's *New Collegiate Dictionary* defines **intimacy** as a state of "close union, contact, association, or acquaintance." Intimacy can occur in a variety of relationships. When researchers asked several hundred college students to identify their "closest, deepest, most involved, and most intimate relationship," the answers were varied.[3] Roughly half (47 percent) identified a romantic partner. About one-third (36 percent) chose a friendship. Most of the rest (14 percent) cited a family member. Let's look at how intimacy operates in these contexts.

Kelvin Murray/Stone/Getty Images

Dimensions of Intimacy

What *kinds* of behavior make a relationship intimate? In fact, intimacy has several dimensions. The first dimension is *physical*. Even before birth, the fetus experiences a physical closeness with its mother that will never happen again, "floating in a warm fluid, curling inside a total embrace, swaying to the undulations of the moving body and hearing the beat of the pulsing heart."[4] As they grow up, fortunate children are continually nourished by physical intimacy: being rocked, fed, hugged, and held. As we grow older, the opportunities for physical intimacy are less regular but still possible and important. Some, but by no means all, physical intimacy is sexual—and it's not always connected with a close relationship. One study revealed that more than half of sexually active teens had partners that they weren't dating, and the majority of the respondents expressed no desire to establish a dating relationship.[5]

A second dimension of intimacy comes from *intellectual* sharing. Not every exchange of ideas counts as intimacy, of course. Talking about next week's midterm with your professor or classmates isn't likely to forge strong relational bonds. But when you engage another person in an exchange of important ideas, a kind of closeness develops that can be powerful and exciting.

A third dimension of intimacy is *emotional*: exchanging important feelings. Sharing personal information can both reflect and create feelings of closeness. Chapter 3 describes the role of self-disclosure in relational development, and Chapter 5 explains how emotions affect interpersonal communication. When you share your feelings with others or tell them personal things about you, a measure of bonding occurs.

If we define intimacy as being close to another person, then *shared activities* is a fourth dimension that can achieve intimacy.[6] Shared activities can include everything from working side by side at a job to meeting regularly for exercise workouts. When partners spend time together, they can develop unique ways of relating that transform the relationship from an impersonal one to an interpersonal one. For example, both friendships and romantic relationships are often characterized by several forms of play. Partners invent private codes, fool around by acting like other people, tease one another, and play games—everything from having punning contests to arm wrestling.[7] Not all shared activities create and express intimacy, but the bond that comes from experiencing significant events with another person is too frequent and significant to ignore. Companions who have endured physical challenges together—in athletics or emergencies, for example—form a bond that can last a lifetime.

Some intimate relationships exhibit all four dimensions: physical, intellectual, emotional, and shared activities. Other intimate relationships exhibit only one or two. Some relationships aren't intimate in any way. Acquaintances, roommates, and coworkers may never become intimate. In some cases, even family members develop smooth but relatively impersonal relationships.

Not even the closest relationships always operate at the highest level of intimacy. At times you might share all of your thoughts or feelings with a friend, family member, or lover; at other times, you might withdraw. You might freely share your feelings about one topic and stay more aloof about another one. The same principle holds for physical intimacy, which waxes and wanes in most relationships.

Although no relationship is *always* intimate, living without *any* sort of intimacy is hardly desirable. For example, people who fear intimacy in dating relationships anticipate less satisfaction in a long-term relationship and report feeling more distant from even longtime dating partners. A great deal of evidence supports the conclusion that fear of intimacy can cause major problems in both creating relationships and sustaining them.[8]

Masculine and Feminine Intimacy Styles

Until recently, most social scientists believed that women are better than men at developing and maintaining intimate relationships.[9] This view grew from the assumption that the disclosure of personal information is the most important ingredient of intimacy. Most research *does* show that women (taken as a group) are somewhat more willing than men to share their thoughts and feelings, although the differences aren't as dramatic as some people might think.[10] In terms of the amount and depth of information exchanged, female–female relationships are at the top of the disclosure list. Male–female relationships come in second, whereas male–male relationships involve less disclosure than any other type. At every age, women disclose more than men, and the information they disclose is more personal and more likely to involve feelings.

A few decades ago, social scientists interpreted the relative lack of male self-disclosure as a sign that men are unwilling or even unable to develop close relationships. Some argued that the female trait of disclosing personal information and feelings makes women more "emotionally mature" and "interpersonally competent" than men. The title of one book captured this attitude of female superiority and male deficiency: *The Inexpressive Male: A Tragedy of American Society*.[11] Personal-growth programs and self-help books urged men to achieve closeness by learning to open up and share their feelings.

More recent scholarship, however, has shown that emotional expression isn't the *only* way to develop close relationships. As you'll read later in this chapter, men often experience and express intimacy through shared activities and by doing things for and with others. The same pattern holds in communication between fathers and their sons. Whereas mothers typically express their love toward sons directly through words and nonverbal behaviors such as hugs and kisses, fathers are less likely to be so direct with their young adult sons.[12] Instead, they often show their sons affection by doing favors and helping the sons with tasks and challenges.

Actually, biological sex isn't most significant in shaping how men express intimacy. Rather, it's the *gender role* that a particular man adopts. Recall that Chapter 4 explained how both men and women can adopt a gender role—masculine, feminine, or androgynous—that may or may not match their biological sex. Applying this range of styles to intimacy reveals that masculine men are most likely to express caring via helping behaviors and shared activities.[13] Men whose communication style includes some stereotypically feminine elements are more likely to express affection more directly, especially to other men.

Bruce Eric Kaplan The New Yorker Collection/Cartoonbank.com

The difference between male and female measures of intimacy helps explain some of the stresses and misunderstandings that can arise between the sexes. For example, a woman who looks for emotional disclosure as a measure of affection may overlook an "inexpressive" man's efforts to show he cares by doing favors or spending time together. Fixing a leaky faucet or taking a hike may look like ways to avoid getting close, but to the man who proposes them, they may be measures of affection and bids for intimacy. Likewise, differing ideas about the timing and meaning of sex can lead to misunderstandings. Whereas many women think of sex as a way to express intimacy that has already developed, men are more likely to see it as a way to *create* that intimacy.[14] In this sense, the man who encourages sex early in a relationship or after a fight may not be just a testosterone-crazed lecher: He may view the shared activity as a way to build closeness. By contrast, the woman who views personal talk as the pathway to intimacy may resist the idea of physical closeness before the emotional side of the relationship has been discussed.

PAUSE *and* REFLECT

Your IQ (Intimacy Quotient)

MindTap® Reflect ... on your intimacy quotient by answering the following questions, either here or online.

What is the level of intimacy in your important relationships? Find out by following these directions.

1. For one of your important relationships, identify the point that best describes that relationship on each dimension of the intimacy scales provided.

   a. Your level of physical intimacy

   1   2   3   4   5
   low _____ high

   b. Your amount of emotional intimacy

   1   2   3   4   5
   low _____ high

   c. The extent of your intellectual intimacy

   1   2   3   4   5
   low _____ high

   d. The degree of shared activities in your relationship

   1   2   3   4   5
   low _____ high

2. For this relationship, which dimensions of intimacy were the easiest to identify on the scale? Why? Which dimensions of intimacy were challenging to identify? Why?

3. What do your responses to each dimension of intimacy reveal about this relationship?

4. Are you satisfied with the intimacy profile outlined by your responses? If you are not satisfied, what steps can you take to change your degree of intimacy?

5. In general, how can understanding your intimacy profile help you to have more satisfying relationships?

As always, it's important to realize that generalizations don't apply to every person. Also, notions of what constitutes appropriate male behavior are changing.[15] For example, one analysis of prime-time television sitcoms revealed that male characters who disclose personal information generally receive favorable responses from other characters.[16] Researchers also note that a cultural shift is occurring in North America in which fathers are becoming more affectionate with their sons than they were in previous generations—although some of that affection is still expressed through shared activities.[17]

Cultural Influences on Intimacy

Historically, the notions of public and private behavior have changed dramatically.[18] What would be considered private behavior in modern terms was quite public at times in the past. For example, in sixteenth-century Germany, a new husband and wife were expected to consummate their marriage upon a bed carried among witnesses who would validate the marriage![19] Conversely, at the same time in England as well as in colonial America, the customary level of communication between spouses was rather formal—not much different from the way acquaintances or neighbors spoke to one another.

Even today, the notion of intimacy varies from one culture to another. In one study, researchers asked residents of Britain, Japan, Hong Kong, and Italy to describe their use of thirty-three rules that governed interaction in social relationships.[20] These included a wide range of communication behaviors: everything from using humor to shaking hands to managing money. The results showed that the greatest differences between Asian and European cultures focused on the rules for dealing with intimacy: showing emotions, expressing affection in public, conducting sexual activity, respecting privacy, and so on.

In some collectivist cultures such as Taiwan and Japan, there is an especially great difference in the way people communicate with members of their in-groups (such as family and close friends) and with their out-groups.[21] They generally do not reach out to outsiders, often waiting until they are properly introduced before entering into a conversation. After they are introduced, they address outsiders with a degree of formality. They go to extremes to hide unfavorable information about in-group members from outsiders on the principle that one doesn't air dirty laundry in public.

By contrast, members of more individualistic cultures such as the United States and Australia make fewer distinctions between personal relationships and casual ones. They act more familiar with strangers and disclose more personal information, making them excellent "cocktail party conversationalists." Social psychologist Kurt Lewin captured the difference nicely when he noted that Americans are easy to meet but difficult to get to know, whereas Germans are difficult to meet but easy to get to know.[22]

Cultural differences in intimacy are becoming less prominent as the world becomes more connected through the media, travel, and technology. For instance, romance and passionate love were once seen as particularly American concepts of intimacy. Recent evidence shows, however, that men and women in a variety of cultures—individualist and collectivist, urban and rural, rich and poverty-stricken—may be every bit as romantic as Americans.[23] These studies suggest that the large differences that once existed between Western and Eastern cultures may be fast disappearing.

Intimacy in Mediated Communication

A few decades ago, it would have been difficult to conceive that the words *computer* and *intimacy* could be positively linked. Electronic devices were viewed as impersonal machines that couldn't transmit important features of human communication such as facial expression, tone of voice, and touch. However, as Chapter 2 describes, researchers now know that mediated communication can be just as personal as face-to-face interaction. In fact, studies show that relational intimacy may develop *more* quickly through mediated channels than in face-to-face communication,[24] and that texting, blogging, Facebooking, and so on enhance verbal, emotional, and social intimacy in interpersonal relationships.[25]

Your own experience probably supports these claims. The relative anonymity of Internet message boards, blogs, and online dating services provides a freedom of expression that might not occur in face-to-face meetings,[26] giving relationships a chance to get started. In addition, emailing, text messaging, videoconferencing, and social networking offer more constant contact with friends, family, and partners than might otherwise be possible.[27] The potential for developing and maintaining intimate relationships via computer is captured well by one user's comment (which has a fun double meaning): "I've never clicked this much with anyone in my life."[28]

Of course, intimate connections in cyberspace can also be problematic. In the digital age, some people are "virtually unfaithful," carrying on romantic relationships online while being in a committed face-to-face relationship. Two different studies found that people regard online infidelity as much as or even more of a betrayal as cheating in person.[29] Although it's tempting to think that a lack of physical intimacy keeps a cyber-relationship "above board," the truth is that most people perceive emotional intimacy—the kind that can be created easily online—as just as important to relational fidelity.

This doesn't mean that all cyber-relationships are (or will become) intimate. Just as in face-to-face relationships, communicators choose varying levels of self-disclosure with their cyberpartners, including the way they manage their privacy settings on social-network sites.[30] Some online relationships are relatively impersonal; others are highly interpersonal. In any case, mediated communication is an important component in creating and maintaining intimacy in contemporary relationships.

Warner Bros/Allstar

∧ In the movie *Her*, Theodore Twombly (Joaquin Phoenix) develops an intimate relationship with an artificially intelligent operating system. The software, who calls herself Samantha (voiced by Scarlett Johansson), draws Theodore out of his self-imposed shell and helps him find joy in everyday life. Whether or not technology can indeed satisfy our interpersonal needs, the movie demonstrates that emotional connection is what humans crave and that they'll go to great lengths to find it. To what degree do you think social media help you meet your intimacy needs? To what degree do they limit interpersonal intimacy?

The Limits of Intimacy

It's impossible to have a close relationship with everyone you know—nor is that necessarily desirable. Social psychologist Roy Baumeister makes a compelling case that, on average, most people want four to six close, important relationships in their lives at any given time.[31] Although fewer than four such relationships can lead to a sense of social deprivation, he argues that more than six leads to diminishing returns: "It is possible that people simply do not have the time or energy to pursue emotional closeness with more than a half dozen people."

Even if we could seek intimacy with everyone we encountered, few of us would want that much closeness. Consider the range of everyday contacts that don't require any sort of intimacy. Some are based on economic transactions (the people at work or the shopkeeper you visit several times a week), some on group membership (church or school), some on physical proximity (neighbors, carpooling), and some grow out of third-party connections (mutual friends, child care). Simply engaging in conversational give-and-take with both strangers and acquaintances can be enjoyable.

Some scholars have pointed out that an obsession with intimacy can actually lead to *less* satisfying relationships.[32] People who consider intimate communication as the only kind worth pursuing place little value on relationships that don't meet this standard. This can lead them to regard interaction with strangers and casual acquaintances as superficial or, at best, as the groundwork for deeper relationships. When you consider the pleasure that can come from polite but distant communication, the limitations of this view become clear. Intimacy is definitely rewarding, but it isn't the only way of relating to others.

On the JOB

Romance in the Workplace

Mixing work with pleasure can be risky business, especially when it comes to romance. As you've read here, proximity often leads to attraction. When coworkers spend many hours interacting with one another, it's no surprise that workplace romances are relatively common. Research on the topic has produced these findings:[a]

- 40 percent of employees in one survey said they had had an office romance at some point in their careers.

- 76 percent of employees in another study said that workplace romances are far more frequent than they were ten years ago.

- 70 percent of human resource professionals said their company had no official verbal or written policy on workplace romance.

Companies that do have policies about office romances discourage them. "Dating on the job is like eating at your desk: Invariably, it's going to get messy," said one researcher. "Workplace romances can seem terrific up front, but if they explode—and they usually do—that shrapnel can land in the workplace and be very distracting."[b]

On a more positive note, 34 percent of people who said they dated a coworker ended up marrying that person. Human resource professionals suggest that if you're going to have a romantic relationship with a coworker, you should know and follow company policies. It's also important to be subtle and discrete about your romance—especially in the office and on company time.

COMMUNICATION IN FAMILIES

When you think of the word *family*, images from your own history may come to mind. Some of your memories probably trigger positive feelings. Others may evoke less-pleasant ones. Popular author Erma Bombeck captured the mixture of struggles and joys that are present in even the happiest families:

> We were a strange little band of characters trudging through life sharing diseases and toothpaste, coveting one another's desserts, hiding shampoo, borrowing money, locking each other out of our rooms, inflicting pain and kissing to heal it in the same instant, loving, laughing, defending, and trying to figure out the common thread that bound us all together. [33]

Today, the meaning of *family* has expanded beyond the traditional set of relationships bound by genetics, legalities, and long-standing customs. You may be from a blended family that includes stepparents and half-siblings. You probably know people in families without biological connections (such as adoptions) or who operate as a family without legal bonds (such as cohabitating couples or foster parents). We'll consider all of these arrangements as we look at the distinctive properties that characterize family communication.

Characteristics of Family Communication

Whatever form families take, their communication has the same fundamental characteristics.

Family Communication Is Formative Messages from family members are the earliest (and among the most important) ones we will ever receive.[34] For example, messages from mothers shape the way daughters view romantic relationships.[35] It's easy to imagine the impact of maternal messages such as "Marriage is the best thing that ever happened to me" or "All men are jerks." Along with attitudes about romance, parental communication shapes attitudes on other subjects. For instance, the messages children hear about academics while growing up influence whether or not they persist or drop out of high school.[36]

Communication in the family of origin can have lifelong effects. *Attachment theory* argues that children develop bonds—either secure or insecure—with family members. Insecure attachment in childhood often leads to adults who are anxious about new relationships, uncomfortable with intimacy, and worried about losing relationships.[37] Romantic partners who fear rejection and abandonment are likely to act in ways that increase the odds of their fears coming to pass.[38] In other words, their dismal expectations create dysfunctional self-fulfilling prophecies.

Fortunately the opposite is also true: When attachment is secure, children grow up to communicate more confidently, develop greater intimacy, and maintain effective relationships with teachers, peers, and others.[39] When both partners in a romantic relationship have secure attachment styles, they tend to communicate constructively, even during conflicts.[40]

Findings like this are likely to help you appreciate the importance of raising secure children. But even if you haven't had the good luck to be nurtured in a positive environment, it's possible to learn ways of communicating that can lead to happier relationships as an adult. This book is loaded with many such skills.

Along with nurturing (and non-nurturing) messages, birth order also plays an important role in shaping how we communicate.[41] For example, first-born siblings are often more extraverted than their younger brothers or sisters. They also are more concerned with control. Middle-borns tend to be closer with their friends but are likely to have more difficult relationships with their family. "Caboose" children who are born last are often more committed and closer to their family members than their older siblings.

Family Communication Is Role-Driven A **role** is a set of expectations about how to communicate. Some roles grow from kinship position. You can probably make a mental list of traditional role norms for a dad, mom, son, and daughter. (Take a moment and do that.) Of course, many of those norms are changing in modern society—and that requires negotiating. When family members communicate according to role expectations, communication is likely to run smoothly. But problems can arise when roles are challenged. (Think about the reaction to a talkative, assertive son or daughter in a family where the rule is "Children should be seen but not heard.")

As children grow, they are labeled (overtly or more subtly) by other family members.[42] Terms such as "the good one," "the black sheep," "the smart kid," and "the screwup" may sound familiar. Once these labels exist, they tend to create the kind of self-fulfilling prophecies described in Chapter 2.[43] If roles are positive, then the expectations can shape good outcomes. But when predictions are negative ("Can't you do *anything* right?") or perhaps even more damaging ("Why can't you be more like your brother?"), the results may include decreased closeness and increased conflict.[44] The effects of this labeling can plague families for decades.[45]

Although labels may persist, family roles can change as both parents and children grow older. During the years of emerging adulthood (typically between ages eighteen and twenty-five), children who once required close supervision from their parents assert their independence.[46] Communication often changes during this period, reflecting transitions in the relationship. In many families, adult children and parents treat one another more as equals. Conflicts arise when children expect to be regarded as adults and parents insist on sticking with roles from earlier years. As parents age, children may take on a caregiving role for parents who are ill or elderly—and thus complete the family circle of life.

Sibling relationships and roles also change over time.[47] During childhood, brothers and sisters consider one another important sources of companionship— and sometimes competition. In adulthood, siblings can often develop a stronger bond as they focus again on communication and companionship with one another, perhaps with less rivalry.[48]

Family Communication Is Involuntary You have the freedom to choose friends and dating partners, but you can't choose your parents, siblings, or other relatives. Even if you take the drastic step of cutting off communication with some relatives, their influence is likely to persist like the phantom pain from a missing limb. Family members may be estranged, but they will always be family.

The web of involuntary family connections grows even more complex in adulthood. The relational partners we choose as adults also come with their own set of relatives. Whether or not they like it, a committed couple is tied to three families: the one they create and the family of origin for each partner.[49] Once children arrive, they are eternally connected to a greater or lesser degree with their kin.[50]

Families as Systems

Before reading on, imagine a family—perhaps *your* family—represented in a mobile. Visualize a photo of each member suspended on its own thread, connected by bars to the hanging images of other members. This family mobile is a simplistic but useful model of a **family system**—a group of interdependent individuals that interact and adapt together as a whole.[51] As you read about the characteristics of family systems, thinking about this mobile will help you understand some important concepts.

Family Systems Are Interdependent   Touch one piece of a mobile and all the other pieces will move. In the same way, one family member's behavior is likely to influence everyone else. If someone in your family is unhappy, your life is likely to be affected. If a member is happy, the atmosphere of the entire family is likely to be more positive. Because of this interdependence, family therapists usually recognize that it's a mistake to give treatment to a single member. It's far more realistic and effective to look at how members affect one another and to treat the entire group.[52]

A recent study illustrates the interdependent nature of family interaction.[53] Spouses reported higher marital quality when they were equally responsible for family tasks. Which shared task best predicted marital satisfaction? Responsibility for child rearing. In other words, if parents want to improve their relationship with each other, one way to do so is to be more invested in the care of their children. A change in one part of the family system (parent-child interaction) affects other parts of the system (spouse-spouse interaction).

∧ The characters in the TV hit *Modern Family* all belong to the same suprasystem, but they also form many subsystems. What systems and subsystems exist within families you know well?

Family Systems Are Manifested through Communication   Just as threads and bars connect the pieces of a mobile, communication connects the members of a family system. Words and symbolic actions jiggle the equilibrium of family life, sometimes for better and sometimes for worse. As you read on in this chapter, you'll see how communication is a potent force that shapes the welfare of families.

Family Systems Are Nested   Within every family system, *subsystems* operate. In a traditional family, the mother and father have their own unique relationship. Siblings form their own systems, and every child's interaction with each parent forms a subsystem (e.g., mother–daughter, father–daughter). The larger the family, the larger the number of subsystems.

Families are also members of larger *suprasystems*. You could illustrate this by expanding your imaginary mobile to include the extended family—grandparents, uncles and aunts, cousins, stepsiblings, in-laws, and so on.

Beyond kinship, families are also part of the society in which they operate. For example, children who grow up in violent environments tend to be more anxious and have weaker social skills in adulthood.[54] They also are more likely to act aggressively themselves.[55] The school environment can also shape the way children communicate, for better or worse.[56]

Families Are More Than the Sum of Their Parts   Just as the mobile you've been visualizing is more than a collection of photos, a family is more than a collection of individuals. Even if you knew each of the members independently, you wouldn't understand the family until you saw them all interact. When those members are together, new ways of communicating emerge.[57] For instance, you may have known friends who turned into very different people when they became a couple. Maybe they became better as individuals—more confident, clever, and happy. Or perhaps they became more aggressive and defensive. Likewise, the nature of a couple's relationship is likely to change when a child arrives, and that family's interaction will change again with the arrival of each subsequent baby.

Communication Patterns within Families

What families talk about is common and unsurprising: reports on activities, logistics, shared events, and so on. But *how* families communicate can vary significantly in two ways: modes of conversation and levels of conformity.[58]

Conversation orientation relates to how open families are to discussing a range of topics. Families with a high conversation orientation interact freely, often, and spontaneously. That's quite different from families with a low conversation orientation, where many topics are taboo and others can only be broached in a restricted way. You can get a sense of the conversation orientation in your family of origin by recalling the rules (probably unstated) about topics including religion, sex, politics, and the personal histories and feelings of each family member.

Families with a high conversation orientation view communicating as a way to express affection and pleasure, and to relax.[59] When conflicts arise, they try to find solutions that work for all members.[60] By contrast, members of families with a low conversation orientation interact less, and there are fewer exchanges of private thoughts. It's no surprise that families with a strong conversation orientation regard communication as rewarding[61] and that children who grow up in these families have a greater number of interpersonal skills in their later relationships.[62]

After reading this far, you might find it easy to conclude that open family communication is good and closed communication is not. But even in families with a high conversation orientation, it's important to recognize that some topical boundaries are necessary and useful.[63] None of us is comfortable or willing to share every bit of our personal history, thoughts, or feelings—even with the people we love the most. And even the most open families have boundaries that protect personal information from the outside world. For example, one study found that adult children who knew about a parent's infidelity kept this information secret from those outside the family as a way to protect the family member, demonstrate loyalty, and keep the family cohesive.[64] This tension between what families share and what they keep private is part of the openness-privacy dialectic discussed in Chapter 9.

Conformity orientation refers to how strongly a family enforces the uniformity of attitudes, values, and beliefs. High-conformity families manage communication in order to seek harmony, avoid conflict, foster interdependence, and gain obedience. They are often hierarchical, with a clear sense that some members have more authority than others. It's not

Looking at DIVERSITY

Courtesy of Scott Johnson

Scott Johnson: Multicultural Families and Communication Challenges

In the decade since adopting our Haitian children and becoming a bi-racial family, we've found the learning curve continues to point steeply upward. At first we didn't understand how simple things like taking photos would change—as our earliest family images show perfectly exposed white parents with their underexposed black children. We didn't understand the importance of hair in the black community—but shopping brought frequent reminders, as black women would politely ask, "Are these your kids? Do you need help with her hair?" We didn't understand how uncertain our whole culture can be when trying to bridge racial differences.

One hot afternoon at a community pool, our then 4-year-old son picked up a younger white admirer who followed him around, playing and chattering happily. As they sat for a time on the edge of the kiddie pool, the younger boy leaned over and licked my son on the shoulder. My wife asked the boy what he was doing, and as if reading from a bad sitcom

script, he said, "I wanted to see if he tasted like chocolate."

A friend and professor of African American Studies once told me my children were growing up without what he called the "warm blanket of acceptance" of the black community that stands against the world's racism. I don't know if he's right about that, and I don't know what other versions (innocent or ill-willed) of "tasting like chocolate" they'll face. I just know our kids have a life they couldn't have dreamed of in their native Haiti. I know they're being raised by white people who are learning a lot about the role of race in our lives. And I know they're feeling the warmest blanket of acceptance we can provide in our home, where we've made family the centerpiece of life. We talk frankly about race and difference and prejudice, and our son and daughter have learned we will face together the challenges of difference that lie ahead.

"Multicultural Families and Communication Challenges" by Scott Johnson. Used with permission of author.

> **Figure 10.1**

Family Communication
Patterns

CONFORMITY ORIENTATION

		HIGH	LOW
CONVERSATION ORIENTATION	HIGH	Consensual families	Pluralistic families
	LOW	Protective families	Laissez-faire families

surprising that conflict in these families is characterized by avoiding and obliging strategies.[65] By contrast, communication in families with a low conformity orientation is characterized by individuality, independence, and equality. The belief in such families is that individual growth should be encouraged and that the interests of each individual member are more important than those of the family as a whole.

Conversation and conformity orientations can combine in four ways, as shown in Figure 10.1. Each of these modes reflects a different **family communication pattern**: consensual, pluralistic, protective, or laissez-faire.

To understand these combinations, imagine four different families. In each, a fifteen-year-old daughter wants to get a very visible and irreverent tattoo that concerns the parents. Now imagine how communication surrounding this issue would differ depending on the various combinations of conversation and conformity orientations.

A family high in both conversation orientation and conformity orientation is *consensual*. Communication reflects the tension between the pressure to agree and preserve the hierarchy of authority and an interest in open communication and exploration. In a consensual family, the daughter would feel comfortable making her case for the tattoo, and the parents would be willing to hear the daughter out. Ultimately, the decision would rest with the mother and father.

Families high in conversation orientation and low in conformity orientation are *pluralistic*. Communication in these families is open and unrestrained, with all family members' contributions evaluated on their own merits. It's easy to visualize an ongoing family discussion about whether the tattoo is a good idea. Older and younger siblings—and maybe even other relatives— would weigh in with their perspectives. In the best of worlds, a consensus would emerge from these discussions.

Families low in conversation orientation and high in conformity orientation are *protective*. Communication in these families emphasizes obedience to authority and the reluctance to share thoughts and feelings. In a protective family, there would be little if any discussion about the tattoo. The parents would decide, and their word would be final.

Families low in both conversation orientation and conformity orientation are *laissez-faire*. Laissez-faire roughly translates from French as "hands off." Communication in these families reflects family members' lack of involvement with each other, and decision making is individual. In this type of family, the daughter might not even bring the tattoo up for discussion before making a decision. If she did, the parents would have little to say about whether their daughter did or didn't decorate her body with permanent art. With the tattoo— and most other matters—their response would be an indifferent "Whatever."

PAUSE *and* REFLECT

Your Family's Communication Patterns

MindTap® REFLECT ... on your family's communication patterns by answering the following questions, either here or online.

1. Use the categories introduced in the text and pictured in Figure 10.1 to describe which communication pattern best describes your family of origin, the family in which you now live, or both.

2. How productive and satisfying is this pattern (are these patterns)? If the communication pattern from your family of origin is different from the family in which you now live, which pattern is more productive and satisfying?

3. If you could change one or both of these patterns, which pattern would you choose? Why?

A growing body of research suggests that some communication patterns are more productive and satisfying than others.[66] For example, young adults from consensual and pluralistic families are more confident listeners and more intellectually flexible than those from protective and laissez-faire backgrounds.[67] Offspring from pluralistic families are less verbally aggressive than those from any other type.[68] By contrast, a protective approach by parents leads to more secrecy by children and lower satisfaction for all members of a family.[69] Fathers tend to be confrontational and pressuring during conflicts in high-conformity families, but they're conciliatory and analytic in pluralistic ones.[70] In other words, open communication and shared decision making produces better results than do power plays and refusal to have open dialogue.

Social Media and Family Communication

Chapter 2 outlines the many effects—both pro and con—of social media on interpersonal relationships. Family communication has been affected by new technologies, often in positive ways.[71] For instance, participants in one study said that texting has given them an increased sense of connection with family members and has had a positive impact on their familial relationships (females expressed this more strongly than males).[72] They also said they could express their feelings to family members more honestly via text than in person. Email provides similar connection opportunities,[73] although that medium is more popular with parents than it is with their children.

Social networking sites such as Facebook provide new challenges for family privacy management. For example, adolescents engage in more online self-disclosure but use fewer privacy settings than adults do.[74] This difference helps explain why many teens are reluctant to accept a parent's friend request. Those who do share online social networks with their parents report stronger relational bonds.[75] Conversely, those who deny parents access tend to have higher levels of aggression and delinquency and lower levels of connectedness.

While the cause-effect relationship isn't clear, it's worth noting that teens who share at least part of their social networks with parents also have better relationships and fewer conflicts.

As teens transition into adulthood, they become less concerned about Facebook privacy with their parents.[76] Young adults who become Facebook friends with their parents are more likely to be female and to come from families with a high conversation orientation.[77] Those from lower conversation orientations are more likely to adjust their privacy settings once they add their parents as friends. Regardless of age or orientation, it's important for family members to communicate social networking expectations. This might include negotiating rules such as "Don't post pictures of me from my childhood" or "If you have something personal to say, please do it through private messaging."

COMMUNICATION IN FRIENDSHIPS

You can't choose the family into which you are born, and you have little say about your neighbors or the people you work with. But friendships are voluntary: We can end them much more easily than we can escape the relational orbit of family, the bonds of marriage, or even the relationships that come with a career. The ease of cutting friendship ties—as well as the hard work of keeping the relationship positive—helps explain why friendships are more likely to end than any other relationship.[78]

Chapter 9 describes some of the ways we form relationships. Whatever the reasons, friendships are created and maintained through communication. We'll look at the nature of friendships and examine how communication operates in this important context.

Types of Friendships

The word *friend* covers a wide variety of relationships—everything from preschoolers who play make-believe games with each other, to teens whose alliances shift in the social currents of high school, to couples who socialize together, to the best friend forever (BFF) for whom you would do anything. As you'll now see, different types of friendships involve different kinds of communication.

Youthful versus Mature Some elements of friendship hold true across the life span. For instance, self-disclosure is typical in close relationships from childhood to old age.[79] But in other ways, the nature of friendships varies as the participants mature.[80]

Preschool children rarely have enduring friendships. Instead, they enjoy time with temporary playmates. As they grow older, children usually form more stable friendships, but primarily to meet their own needs and with little sense of empathy. During adolescence, friendships become a central feature of social life—often more important than family. In these teen years, friends begin to be valued for their personal qualities, not just as playmates or activity companions.

As they move away from familiar environments, young adults expand their circle of friends in ways that often prove highly satisfying.[81] By this point in life, the qualities that are important in a friend become stable and mature: helpfulness, support, trust, commitment, and self-disclosure. As the responsibilities of marriage and family grow, the desire to have strong friendships may stay the same, but the time available to support them can decline.[82] But in older adulthood, friendships become especially valuable as a means of social support. Having strong relationships contributes to both satisfaction and health.[83]

Geom/Bigstock

Long Term versus Short Term Some friendships last for years or even a lifetime, while others fade or end because of life changes (such as finishing high school, moving to a new location, or switching jobs). Although modern technologies decrease the likelihood that a friendship will end because of a long-distance move,[84] some falter or fail without face-to-face contact. Another reason some friendships may be short term is due to a change in values.[85] Perhaps you once had a group of friends with whom you enjoyed parties and nightlife, but as you grew out of that phase of your life, the mutual attraction waned.

Relationship Oriented versus Task Oriented Sometimes we choose friends because of shared activities: teammates in a softball league, coworkers, or fellow movie buffs. These types of friendships are considered task oriented if they primarily revolve around certain activities. On the other hand, relationship-oriented friendships are grounded in mutual liking and social support independently of shared activities. Of course, these categories overlap: Some friendships are based in both joint activities and emotional support.

High-Disclosure versus Low Disclosure How much do you tell your friends about yourself? No doubt your level of disclosure differs from friend to friend. Some only know general information about you, whereas others are privy to your most personal secrets. The social penetration model in Chapter 3 can help you explore the breadth and depth of your disclosure with your various friends.

High Obligation versus Low Obligation There are some friends for whom we would do just about anything—no request is too big. We feel a lower sense of obligation to other friends, both in terms of what we would do for them and how quickly we would do it. Our closest friends usually get fast responses when they ask for a favor, give us a call, or even post on our Facebook Wall.

Frequent Contact versus Occasional Contact   You probably keep in close touch with some friends. Perhaps you work out, travel, socialize, or Skype daily. Other friendships have less frequent contact—maybe an occasional phone call or text message. Of course, infrequent contact doesn't always correlate with levels of disclosure or obligation. Many close friends may see each other only once a year, but they pick right back up in terms of the breadth and depth of their shared information.

After reading this far, you can begin to see that the nature of communication can vary from one friendship to another. Furthermore, communication *within* a friendship can also change over time. Impersonal friendships can have sudden bursts of disclosure. The amount of communication can swing from more to less frequent. Low-obligation friendships can evolve into stronger commitments and vice versa. You'll read about types of communication that are common in virtually all good friendships. But for now it's important to recognize that variety is a good thing.

Sex, Gender, and Friendship

Not all friendships are created equal. Along with the differences previously described, gender plays a role in how we communicate with friends.

Same-Sex Friendships   Communication within same-sex friendships typically differs for men and women. Most women place a somewhat higher value on talking about personal matters as a measure of closeness, whereas men are more likely to create and express closeness through shared activities— what one scholar called "closeness in the doing."[86] In one study, more than 75 percent of the men surveyed said that their most meaningful experiences with friends came from shared activities.[87] They reported that by doing things together they "grew on one another," developed feelings of interdependence, showed appreciation for one another, and demonstrated mutual liking. Likewise, men regarded practical help as a measure of caring. Findings like these show that, for many men, closeness grows from activities that don't always depend heavily on disclosure: A friend is a person who does things *for* you and *with* you.

By contrast, women tend to disclose more personal information than men, both in face-to-face relationships[88] and online.[89] Although both men and women value friends who provide emotional support, women are generally more skilled at doing so and are more likely to seek out female friends when they need this type of support.[90] Of course, findings like these are generalizations that may not apply to specific friendships. The Pause and Reflect questions in this section will help you see how closely they apply to you.

Cross-Sex Friendships   Cross-sex friendships offer benefits that same-sex relationships can't provide.[91] They provide a chance to see things from a different perspective, which can be a welcome contrast to the kinds of interaction that characterize communication with friends of the same sex.[92] For men, this often means a greater chance to share emotions and focus on relationships. For women, it can be a chance to lighten up and enjoy banter and activities without emotional baggage. These friendships also give heterosexual singles access to a broader network of potential romantic partners.[93]

Cross-sex friendships—at least for heterosexuals—present some challenges that don't exist among all-male or all-female companionships. [94] The most obvious is the reality or potential for sexual attraction.[95] As Billy Crystal said to Meg Ryan in the classic film *When Harry Met Sally*, "Men and women can't be friends because the sex part always gets in the way."

Research suggests that Harry was at least partly right. In one survey of 150 working professionals, more than 60 percent noted that sexual tension was a factor in their cross-sex relationships.[96] This seems especially true for men: Research reveals that while it's common for women to view men as platonic friends, men are more likely to feel romantic and physical attraction towards women they know.[97] To make matters worse, males tend to overestimate their female friends' interest in romance.

Although it's possible to have romance-free friendships with people of the other sex, defining that sort of relationship takes work. Some evidence suggests that communicating more online (rather than in person) can help to keep a cross-sex relationship platonic.[98] In face-to-face settings, it can be important for the less-interested partner to communicate "no-go" and "friend zone" messages: less routine contact and activity, less flirtation, and more talk about outside romances.

∧ In a modern "When Harry Met Sally" tale, Wallace (Daniel Radcliffe) and Chantry (Zoe Kazan) attempt to forge a cross-sex friendship while negotiating feelings of romantic attraction in the movie *What If*. Do you think platonic friendships can be maintained when there is the potential for romance in a relationship?

Friends with Benefits   **Friends with benefits (FWB)** is a popular term for nonromantic heterosexual friendships that include sexual activity. These relationships have become increasingly common and come in many varieties.[99] One study claims that nearly 60 percent of university students report having been involved in at least one FWB relationship.[100] Some FWB relationships transition into romances;[101] others are transitioning *out* of romances; still others serve as "placeholders" until better options come along.[102]

Men and women are equally likely to be in FWB relationships. Some surveys suggest that both appreciate the chance to take care of physical needs without the challenges of emotional commitment.[103] Despite this similarity, there are gender differences in the way FWB relationships turn out. Although the majority of men describe their relationships as primarily sexual, women are much more likely to become emotionally involved. From findings like these, some observers have commented that women are typically more focused on being "friends" while men are more likely to be interested in the "benefits."[104]

Given the chance that sexual activity might lead to unreciprocated desires for romantic commitment, it would seem logical that FWB partners would regularly discuss the status of their relationship—but researchers have found that FWBs routinely avoid explicit communication about this important topic.[105] The researchers concluded that "FWB relationships are often problematic for the same reasons that they are attractive."[106]

Gender Considerations   Biological sex isn't the only factor to consider when we examine different sorts of friendships. Another important consideration is gender role (see Chapter 4). For instance, a friendship between a masculine male and a feminine female might have very different properties than a friendship between a masculine female and a feminine male—even though these are both technically cross-sex relationships.[107]

Sexual orientation is another factor that can shape friendships. Most obviously, for gay men and lesbians, the potential for sexual attraction shifts from opposite- to same-sex relationships. But physical attraction aside, sexual orientation can still play a significant role in friendships.[108] For example, many heterosexual women report that they value their friendships with gay

PAUSE *and* REFLECT

Gender and Friendship

MindTap **REFLECT . . .** on gender and friendship by answering the following questions, either here or online.

1. Analyze how gender affects communication in your friendships by keeping logs of communication in two friendship relationships: one same-sex and one cross-sex. Record at least four conversations in the log provided. For each conversation, record both the subject being discussed (e.g., school, finances), the nature of the interaction (e.g., emotional expression, personal information, shared activities), and any comments that you think might be gender related.

DATE/TIME PLACE/CHANNEL	FRIEND	SUBJECT	NATURE OF THE INTERACTION	COMMENTS

2. Based on your findings, do you see a different pattern in the topics you talk about and the nature of the interactions with same- and opposite-sex friendships?

3. Based on your findings, do you see a different pattern in the channel of communication (phone, text, email, face-to-face) you use to talk with same- and opposite-sex friendships?

men because (1) they often share interests, (2) the potential for romantic complications is small or nonexistent,[109] and (3) the women feel more attractive.[110]

Social Media and Friendship

In real life, it's not hard to tell who counts as a friend. The Internet has made friendship more complicated.[111] Consider Facebook, where a "friend" could be someone you met once at a party or on vacation, a former classmate or neighbor whom you haven't seen in years, someone you met online but have never known in person, or even a "publicity whore" who only sought you out to boost the size of his or her friends list.

©KellyPhoto/BigStock

Perhaps the most intriguing scholarship about friendship and social media has to do with the number of friends one has on social networking sites. A survey by the Pew Research Center found that the typical online adult has more than 200 Facebook friends. Younger adults (ages 18–29) have larger Facebook networks, with 27 percent having more than 500 friends.[112] There is a curvilinear relationship between the number of Facebook friends and the perception of those friendships by others.[113] If you have too few Facebook friends, others may regard you (perhaps unfairly) as not very social, attractive, or friendly.[114] On the other hand, if you have too many online friends, people might perceive those relationships as less than genuine. (See Chapter 2's discussion of "Dunbar's number.")

Research is mixed about the connection between number of Facebook friends and well-being. Some scholars suggest "the more the better," finding positive correlations with factors such as perceived social support, reduced stress, and even physical health.[115] Other studies are less positive, finding that large collections of Facebook friends yield diminishing returns and might be compensation for low self-esteem.[116] One thing seems clear: No matter the size of one's online social network, only a small percentage of those friendships qualify as *close*.[117]

While social media have brought new dimensions to communicating with friends, research shows that social-networking sites are used primarily to maintain current friendships or to revive old ones rather than to build new relationships.[118] For example, the highest proportion of Facebook connections is between high school classmates. Even when strangers have met online, it's likely that they will attempt a face-to-face meeting if the relationship becomes close.[119] Findings like these show that social media typically isn't a *replacement* for face-to-face communication, but is a means to support and rekindle friendships that were developed in person.[120]

Of course, social networking sites aren't the only media for communicating with friends. Phoning, texting, emailing, and even blogging are means for keeping up friendships. As noted in Chapter 9, these media can help friends maintain their relationship and provide a measure of social support. But the closest of friends realize that no matter how much they stay in touch with each other electronically, there's no substitute for a night on the town together, a stimulating in-person conversation, or a good hug.

WHEN FRIENDS
GET IN THE WAY

Mike and his date were at the Union Square subway stop, deciding whether to go home together for the first time, when his cell phone suddenly buzzed. The 28-year-old New Yorker cut the evening short and raced to his friend's apartment. The big emergency? A game of Scattergories had begun. "You have to remember the people who are worth your time," he explains. "As opposed to getting some, the Scattergories definitely won."

If Mike sounds as though he's prioritizing his friendships over his love life, he's not alone. Our 24/7 social connectivity means we're swimming in a constant stream of urgent texts from our closest friends, punctuated by Likes and comments from our more casual acquaintances on social media.

Modern friendships take up more time and energy than ever. Mike, who asked that his last name be omitted, says he has three to five friends to whom he sends up to 50 texts a day.

This means that love—and the pursuit of it—can get kicked to the curb. Katie Heaney, the 27-year-old author of *Never Have I Ever*, a memoir of her boyfriend-free life, says she has often refused dates in favor of hanging out with friends. "If I've got a group of people whom I know I love, I don't want to risk time lost from them and given to someone else," she says.

But even as our friendship obsession distracts us from the dating game, some millennials end up hoping their platonic relationships will turn into romantic ones.

[T]he idea of falling in love with a friend feels more genuine than taking up with someone new. "We're spending our time and energy on so many more people that it can get a little scattered," says Jessica Massa, author of *The Gaggle: How to Find Love in the Post-Dating World*. "The idea that there could be someone who knows you through and through and loves all your quirks is becoming even more appealing because it's lacking in the rest of our lives."

Of course, most friendships are platonic and destined to stay that way. That's good, because as much as things have changed, we still need our close friends to help us vet potential partners and get over bad ones. Mike says he

always texts his friends pictures of guys he meets on dating apps so they can weigh in, because "they're like the referees coming in if you're not sure about the play." But his friends will probably have to ditch their own dates to spend five to seven minutes in the bathroom crafting the perfect response.

Charlotte Alter

MindTap® ENHANCE ... your understanding by answering the following questions, either here or online.

1. Have you found that your friendships sometimes sabotage your love life? Or conversely, has your love life intruded on your friendships? What do you think is the ideal balance?

2. What kinds of conversations would you need to have with your friends—or with your romantic partners—to bring about an appropriate balance?

Maksym Poriechkin/Shutterstock.com

COMMUNICATION IN ROMANTIC RELATIONSHIPS

As you read in Chapter 1, research demonstrates that close interpersonal relationships are good for mental, emotional, and physical health. Romantic relationships are especially beneficial.[121] In short, people in loving romantic relationships live longer, happier, healthier lives.

Communication skills are vital to making romantic relationships successful. In a study of more than 2,200 participants recruited by couples therapists and counselors, "communication" was rated the most important competency for ensuring success in romantic relationships—more than sex and romantic passion or any other factor.[122] This section will focus on communication in romantic relationships, which we'll broadly define as longer-term, loving connections between partners. These relationships can include couples who are dating exclusively, partners who live together, and spouses who have been married for years. The crucial issue is whether the people involved identify themselves as being romantically connected.

Characteristics of Romantic Relationships

"Are we 'just friends' or something more?" It's not unusual for couples to ask questions like this to determine if they're moving into a romantic relationship. While the lines aren't always clear, we'll look now at three characteristics that typify most romantic relationships: love, commitment, and affection. As you'll see, these concepts overlap (for instance, Sternberg identifies commitment as a component of love). We break them into three categories as a way to focus on the research about each of these related topics.

Love   More than two millennia ago, Aristotle maintained that "Love is composed of a single soul inhabiting two bodies." His mentor Plato was a bit more cynical: "Love is a serious mental disease." Philosophers and artists through the years have waxed eloquently about love, with mixed conclusions about its joys and sorrows.

If you ask a dozen scholars for a definition of love, you'll get a dozen different responses. For our purposes, we'll turn to the work of Robert Sternberg and his well-known **triangular theory of love**.[123] He maintains that love has three components:

- Intimacy: This is the closeness and connectedness one feels in a relationship. We've already discussed how intimacy can be found and expressed in all the relational contexts described in this chapter. Using temperature as an analogy, Sternberg regards intimacy as the "warm" component of love.

- Passion: This involves physical attraction and emotional arousal, often including sexuality. This is the "hot" component of love.

- Commitment: This is the rational side of love, involving decisions to maintain a relationship over time (more on this later). This is love's "cool" component.

> **FIGURE 10.2**
Three Components of Love

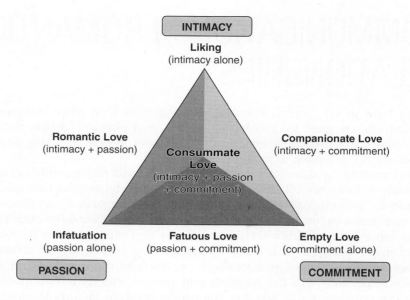

Figure 10.2 depicts these three components as corners of a triangle and identifies seven possible combinations resulting from their intersection. It's easy to imagine the communication patterns that accompany each form of love represented in the model. For instance, couples experiencing *romantic love* might exchange highly emotional messages ("I adore you" in a clutched embrace), with many displays of affection. *Companionate love* would be more verbally and nonverbally subdued, with phrases like "I enjoy your company" more typical. And *empty love* would be a shell of a relationship, void of most if not all affectionate messages. We'll talk more about the communication of affection later in this section.

Sternberg acknowledges that *consummate love*—the combination of intimacy, passion, and commitment—is an ideal that's rare to achieve and challenging to maintain. Typically, love's components wax and wane over the course of a relationship. There can be rushes of passion on occasion; at other times, love is more a cool decision than a warm feeling. Maturity is also a factor in the experience of love. For instance, adolescents don't identify with the triangle components as well as adults do.[124] As couples age, they tend to value commitment more than the other components—although long-term partners experience more passion and intimacy than some stereotypes suggest.[125]

If you consider romantic partnerships you've been in or observed, you can probably think of examples of all the types of love depicted in the triangular model. You can also likely see how the factors ebb and flow over time. Similar to the models of relational stages and dialectics described in Chapter 9, it's healthy to regard love as a dynamic and changing process rather than a static property.

Commitment   How important is the role of commitment in romantic relationships? Sentiments like the following suggest an answer: "I'm looking for a committed relationship." "I'm just not ready for commitment." "I'm committed to making this relationship work."

Relational commitment involves a promise—sometimes implied and sometimes explicit—to remain in a relationship and to make that relationship

---

TABLE 10.1 Major Indicators of a Committed Romantic Relationship

- Providing affection
- Providing support
- Maintaining integrity
- Sharing companionship
- Making an effort to communicate regularly
- Showing respect
- Creating a relational future
- Creating a positive relational atmosphere
- Working on relationship problems together
- Reassuring one's commitment

Source: Weigel, D. J. (2008). Mutuality and the communication of commitment in romantic relationships. Southern Communication Journal, *73,* 24–41.

successful. Commitment is both formed and reinforced through communication. Table 10.1 spells out commitment indicators in romantic relationships. Research shows that couples who regularly communicate their commitment have more positive feelings about their relationship and experience less relational uncertainty.[126]

As Table 10.1 indicates, words alone aren't a surefire measure of true commitment. Deeds are also important. Simply saying "You can count on me" doesn't guarantee loyalty. But without language, commitment may not be clear. For this reason, ceremonies formalizing relationships are an important way to recognize and cement commitment (see Chapter 9's discussion of "Bonding").

A cultural note about commitment: It's a decidedly Western approach to view commitment as a culmination of romantic love (as the familiar chant goes, "First comes love, then comes marriage"). Many of the world's marriages are arranged, and their axiom is "first comes marriage, then comes love." In a study of satisfied couples in arranged marriages, "commitment" was identified as the most important factor that helped their love flourish over time.[127] The second most important factor was "communication," with a strong emphasis on self-disclosure as a means to learn to love one's mate. Regardless of the order, there is a strong relationship between commitment and communication in successful romantic relationships. (See the Looking at Diversity sidebar in Chapter 9 for an example of a successful arranged marriage.)

Affection Expressions of affection—both verbal and nonverbal—are typical in romantic relationships. These can range from holding hands to saying "I love you" to sexual activity. Romantic affection is often communicated privately; sometimes it's expressed publically. In fact, the phrase "public displays of affection" has its own acronym (PDA) and social rules.[128]

Communicating affection is beneficial for romantic partners in a variety of ways. In one study,[129] married and cohabiting couples were asked to increase their amount of romantic kissing over a six-week period. In comparison with a control group, the frequent kissers experienced improvements not only in their stress levels and relational satisfaction, but also in their cholesterol counts (you probably want to know how to sign up for studies like these). Other research shows similar physiological benefits of expressing affection verbally, both in person and in writing.[130] In terms of relational benefits, received affection works like a bank account—when a loved one has made plenty of deposits, the partner is more willing to overlook a transgression than when the affection account is depleted.[131]

There can be discrepancies between feelings and expressions of affection. Perhaps you can recall times when you said "Love ya" at the end of a phone call, despite not feeling very charitable toward your partner. Maybe you gave your partner a hug or a kiss in the midst of a disagreement, even though it didn't match your emotional state. Communication researchers call these acts of "deceptive affection" and say they're common in romantic relationships.[132] Rather than being negative, deceptions of this sort can be a normal part of relational maintenance and support. And of course, while you're busy "deceiving" your partner with these words and behaviors, you might just be convincing yourself. Research shows that engaging in romantic actions, such as gazing into a lover's eyes, sitting at intimate distances, or sharing personal secrets, can often lead to romantic feelings rather than the other way around.[133]

Sexual activity is an important means of expressing and receiving affection in most romantic relationships. One research review notes that the strongest and most reliable predictor of sexual satisfaction is relational satisfaction.[134] In other words, sex is best enjoyed as part of a healthy romantic relationship. Communication also plays an important role: There is a strong correlation between a couple's communication skills and their sexual satisfaction.[135] And contrary to some media depictions of passionate sex occurring in wordless vacuums, research shows that sexual activity is more satisfying when accompanied by direct verbal communication ("Here's how I feel"; "This is what I want"), both before and after the encounter.[136] When those conversations are uncomfortable, satisfied lovers often use face-saving communication and even humor to express themselves.[137]

Romantic Turning Points

If you ask couples when their romantic relationship began, chances are good they can identify a particular marker. Maybe it was a specific date, a special embrace, or the first time a partner uttered the words "I love you." Communication researchers call these **relational turning points**—transformative events that alter the relationship in a fundamental way.[138]

Although other close relationships can have turning points,[139] these events are especially important in romantic relationships. Consider a couple on the verge of moving from "just friends" to "something more." It's easy to imagine a transitional moment ("and then we kissed") when the relationship becomes romantic.[140]

Relational turning points often mark movement among the stages discussed in Chapter 9. They can involve everything from Facebook declarations[141] to physical intimacy[142] to the "first big fight"[143] to breakups and makeups.[144] From this list, it's easy to see that not all turning points are positive. It is not surprising that couples who can identify more negative turning points than positive ones have lower levels of relational satisfaction.[145]

Turning points can provide clues about the status of the relationship: "I think you've been avoiding me since we visited your family" or "I feel much more connected after our big talk last week." Toward that end, they are useful tools for communicating—and metacommunicating—about the status of a romantic relationship.

HOW TO FALL IN LOVE

More than 20 years ago, the psychologist Arthur Aron succeeded in making two strangers fall in love in his laboratory. Last summer, I applied his technique in my own life.

He was a university acquaintance I occasionally ran into at the climbing gym and had thought, "What if?" I had gotten a glimpse into his days on Instagram. But this was the first time we had hung out one-on-one.

"Psychologists have tried making people fall in love," I said, remembering Dr. Aron's study. "It's fascinating. I've always wanted to try it."

I explained the study. A heterosexual man and woman enter the lab through separate doors. They sit face to face and answer a series of increasingly personal questions. Then they stare silently into each other's eyes for four minutes. "Let's try it," he said.

I Googled Aron's questions; there are 36. We spent the next two hours passing my iPhone across the table, alternately posing each question. They began innocuously: "Would you like to be famous? In what way?" And "When did you last sing to yourself? To someone else?" But they quickly became probing. In response to the prompt, "Name three things you and your partner appear to have in common," he looked at me and said, "I think we're both interested in each other."

We exchanged stories about the last time we each cried, and confessed the one thing we'd like to ask a fortuneteller. We explained our relationships with our mothers.

We finished at midnight. Looking around the bar, I felt as if I had just woken up. "That wasn't so bad," I said. "Definitely less uncomfortable than the staring into each other's eyes part would be." He hesitated and asked. "Do you think we should do that, too? We could stand on the bridge," he said, turning toward the window.

The night was warm and I was wide-awake. We walked to the highest point, then turned to face each other. I've skied steep slopes and hung from a rock face by a short length of rope, but staring into someone's eyes for four silent minutes was one of the more thrilling and terrifying experiences of my life. I spent the first couple of minutes just trying to breathe properly.

Most of us think about love as something that happens to us. But what I like about this study is how it assumes that love is an action. It's possible—simple, even—to generate trust and intimacy, the feelings love needs to thrive.

You're probably wondering if he and I fell in love. Well, we did. Although it's hard to credit the study entirely (it may have happened anyway), the study did give us a way into a relationship that feels deliberate. Love didn't happen to us. We're in love because we each made the choice to be.

Mandy Len Catron

MindTap Enhance …

your understanding by answering the following questions, either here or online.

1. What is your initial response to the exercise described in this piece? Do you find it sweet and charming or silly and unrealistic?

2. Would you be willing to engage in this exercise—including the four-minute eye stare—with someone you already know?

3. Explain the communication principles at work in this exercise. Do you think the verbal or the nonverbal exchanges play a more important role?

Couples' Conflict Styles

The fact that "the first big fight" is a common romantic turning point suggests that conflict is a normal part of couples' communication. And for most partners, the first disagreement is rarely the last. John Gottman has spent years studying romantic relationships and finds that couples tend to fall into one of the three following conflict styles.[146]

1. **Volatile:** These couples have intense, heated arguments—sometimes over small issues. They raise their voices, compete to hold the floor, and make their cases passionately. Conflicts for these couples are often seen as contests to be won.
2. **Avoidant:** Couples who use this style prefer to ignore issues rather than confront them. They minimize disagreements and steer clear of sensitive topics. The partners acknowledge that they have conflicts, but they handle them quickly and dispassionately.
3. **Validating:** These couples openly and cooperatively manage conflicts. When they have differences of opinion, they talk them through in civil ways without denying their feelings. They listen carefully to each other and look for collaborative solutions to their problems.

The validating style matches the approach advocated in this book, and it appears to be the ideal way of communicating.[147] Nonetheless, Gottman has come to acknowledge that the other two styles can be successful in some cases. Here's what he learned about happily married volatile couples:

> It turns out that these couples' volcanic arguments are just a small part of an otherwise warm and loving marriage. The passion and relish with which they fight seems to fuel their positive interactions even more. Not only do they express more anger but they laugh and are more affectionate than the average validating couple.[148]

And this is what Gottman discovered about satisfied couples who use an avoidant style:

> Rather than resolve conflicts, avoidant couples appeal to their basic shared philosophy of marriage. They reaffirm what they love and value in the marriage, accentuate the positive, and accept the rest. In this way, they often end an unresolved discussion still feeling good about one another.[149]

So if conflict style isn't the crucial factor in successful romantic relationships, then what is? Gottman maintains it's the number of positive to negative communicative acts. He calls 5:1 "the magic ratio" and says that as long as couples have five times as many positive interactions—touching, smiling, paying compliments, laughing, kind words, and so on—as negative ones, they are likely to have happy and successful relationships. It's easy for avoidant couples to keep the negative number low, as it is for volatile couples to keep the positive number high. The key for all couples, including validating partners, is to maintain the appropriate ratio.

Languages of Love

"If you love me, please listen."

"If you love me, say so."

"If you love me, show me."

PAUSE *and* REFLECT

Relational Turning Points

MindTap REFLECT ... on relational turning points by answering the following questions, either here or online.

1. Begin by identifying at least six turning points, transformative events that altered one of your romantic relationships, either past or present, in a fundamental way. (If you prefer not to analyze a personal relationship, then use one from a film or book.)

2. Describe if and how the turning points you identified mark the transition from one relational stage to another, using the relational stages described in Chapter 9, "Models of Relational Dynamics."

3. Reflect on the distribution of your turning points throughout the ten relational stages. Do they appear across the ten stages or are they clustered in one or two stages? What does your recollection of your turning points reveal about your romantic relationship?

The underlying message in statements like these is "Here is what love means to me." Author Gary Chapman argues that each of us has our own notion of what counts as love. He calls these notions **love languages** and suggests that we get into trouble when we fail to recognize that our way of expressing love may not match our partner's.[150]

Chapman identifies the following five love languages in romantic relationships, and research offers support for these categories.[151]

1. **Words of affirmation:** These include compliments, words of praise, verbal support, written notes or letters, or other ways of saying that a person is valued and appreciated. People who use this love language are easily hurt by insults or ridicule or when their efforts aren't verbally acknowledged.

2. **Quality time:** This is about being present and available for your partner and giving that person your complete, undivided attention for a significant period of time. Being inattentive or distracted takes the "quality" out of time spent together.

Allstar Picture Library

⋀ *Before Midnight* is the third installment of a movie trilogy that tracks the evolving relationship between Jesse (Ethan Hawke) and Celine (Julie Delpy). While on a getaway in the Greek Isles, the couple spends much of the evening arguing. In the end, the film shows that loving couples can have passionate conflict, and also passionate love for one another. When is conflict good for a relationship, and when is it merely destructive? What kinds of communication boundaries should couples follow when they argue?

3. **Gifts:** People who measure love in terms of gifts believe "it's the thought that counts." A gift needn't be expensive to be meaningful. The best ones are the type that the recipient will appreciate. To gift-oriented partners, neglecting to honor an important event is a transgression.

4. **Acts of service:** Taking out the trash, filling the car with gas, doing laundry—the list of chores that can be acts of service is endless. Similar to gifts, the key to service is knowing which acts would be most appreciated by your partner. (*Hint:* It's probably the chore that your partner hates most.)

5. **Physical touch:** Although this might include sexual activity, meaningful touch can also include other expressions of affection: an arm around the shoulder, a held hand, a brush of the cheek, or a neck rub.

Partners understandably but mistakenly can assume that the love language they prefer is also the one that their mate will appreciate. For example, if your primary love language is "gifts," then you probably expect presents from loved ones on special occasions—and perhaps even on ordinary ones. You're also likely to give gifts regularly and assume that they'll be received appreciatively.

As you can imagine, the assumption that your partner speaks the same love language as you can be a setup for disappointment. Chapman says this is often the case in marriages:

> We tend to speak our primary love language, and we become confused when our spouse does not understand what we are communicating. We are expressing our love, but the message does not come through because we are speaking what, to them, is a foreign language.

Most people learn love languages in their family of origin. To a degree then, we're imprinted with ways to give and receive affection from an early age. The good news is that we can learn to communicate love in different ways—especially with help from our romantic partners. Take a look at the types of love languages in the list above and see if you can identify your primary style. You can then ask your partner to do the same and compare notes. The "Languages of Love" reading offers a narrative from someone who engaged in such a self-appraisal.

Social Media and Romantic Relationships

As Chapter 2 notes, it's no longer unusual for romantic relationships to begin online.[152] But even couples who initiate their romance in person need to manage their use of social media. A recent study found that 27 percent of online adults in romantic partnerships say the Internet has had an impact on their relationships.[153] Not all of that impact is positive. About a quarter of cell phone owners in the study said the phone distracts their romantic partners when they are alone together (the percentage is even higher for young adults, ages 18 to 29).

One indicator of romantic commitment is "making an effort to communicate regularly" (see Table 10.1). An easy way to do this is through calling and texting. One study shows a positive relationship between mobile device use and feelings of commitment and love in romantic relationships.[154] Keep in

LEARNING THE LANGUAGES OF LOVE

I used to be in a relationship in which my significant other liked to lavish me with gifts on special occasions. He also never hesitated to help solve any problem I, or any member of my family, had.

I, on the other hand, was physically affectionate. I also liked doing activities together. We were together for a long time, but our relationship eventually fell apart because we each felt unloved by the other. Had we known each other's love language, we might still be together.

I recently read *The 5 Love Languages* by Dr. Gary Chapman. According to him, if we don't learn our partner's love language, we might as well be speaking in Russian to them.

In my past relationship, I would accuse my partner of not loving me because he didn't spend quality time with me or show enough affection. He'd point at the beautiful jewelry around my neck and ask, "How do you like your necklace?"

That would infuriate me. I always thought he was just trying to be a jerk and avoid the conversation. What he was doing was showing me a physical symbol of how much he did love me. Apparently, his love language was "gifting," but mine was not.

He, in turn, would accuse me of not caring for him, because I didn't help him by taking his clothes to the cleaners when he was busy at work. Apparently, his other love language was "acts of service." So, round and round we went, accusing each other of withholding love.

After reading Chapman's book, I've learned that my love languages are physical touch and quality time. I had been loving my partner the way I wanted to be loved, and he had been expressing his love in the ways he wanted to be loved.

My favorite passage in the book is this one: "People tend to criticize their spouse most loudly in the area where they themselves have the deepest emotional need. Their criticism is an ineffective way of pleading for love. If we understand that, it may help us process their criticism in a more productive manner."

Chapman says the beginning of a relationship is the "in-love" stage. During this period of euphoria, your partner can do no wrong, has no flaws, and everything is possible. Once that phase is over, long-lasting emotional love becomes a choice. We have to choose to love our partners for who they are, and love them in the way they need to be loved—in their own love language.

Edie Vaughan

MindTap ENHANCE ...

your understanding by answering the following questions, either here or online.

1. Based on the descriptions in this section and this piece, which of the five love languages is most appealing to you? What do you think are the primary love languages of the people closest to you?

2. Which is the most challenging love language for you to communicate?

3. What changes do you think you could make in the way you communicate love in your close relationships?

mind, however, that it's possible to have too much of good thing. There's a difference between regular contact with loved ones and keeping anxious tabs on them.[155] And while expressing affection via texting can indeed enhance a romantic relationship, it's not a good medium for addressing serious issues.[156]

A couple's use of social networking sites both reflects and affects how the partners feel about each other. Individuals who post profile pictures that include their partners report being more satisfied with their relationships than those who post solo photos.[157] (See the "Relfies" sidebar in Chapter 9.) Moreover, on days when people feel more satisfied in their relationship, they're more likely to share relationship-related information online. But there's a downside to the use of these sites. For instance, one study found a negative relationship between relational intimacy and involvement in online social networking.[158] Closely monitoring others on Facebook can be relationally intrusive and provoke jealousy,[159] particularly for those with low self-esteem.[160] And as you read in Chapter 2 ("Relational Deterioration"), there appears to be a correlation between social network overuse, marital dissatisfaction, and divorce.[161]

This returns us to a familiar maxim in this book: all things in moderation. When overused and abused, social media can negatively impact a romantic relationship. When employed with care and awareness, these tools can help maintain and strengthen loving partnerships.

SUMMARY

Intimacy in interpersonal relationships has four dimensions: physical, intellectual, emotional, and shared activities. Both gender and culture affect the way intimacy is expressed. Intimacy can occur through mediated communication as well as in face-to-face interaction. Not all relationships are intimate; communicators must make choices about when, where, and with whom they will be intimate.

Family relationships are formative, role driven, and generally involuntary. Families operate as systems and develop communication patterns that involve the merging of particular conversation and conformity orientations. Generational differences in the use of social media can present challenges for family communication, so negotiating a shared understanding of such use is important.

Communication in friendships often varies according to the age of the participants, relational history and frequency of contact, level of obligation, task or relational foundations, level of disclosure and obligation, and gender of the friends. Social media play an important role in contemporary relationships.

Relational messages in romantic relationships have three dimensions: love, commitment, and affection. Romantic partnerships often begin, continue, and end based on relational turning points. Couples typically use one of three conflict styles: volatile, avoidant, or validating. Each partner in a romantic relationship favors one of five love languages, and it's helpful for both to become fluent in the other's language. Because social media play an important role in most romantic relationships, it's important to use mediated channels mindfully to maximize their beneficial effects and minimize harmful ones.

KEY TERMS

conformity orientation
conversation orientation
family communication pattern
family system
friends with benefits (FWB)
intimacy

love languages
relational commitment
relational turning point
role
triangular theory of love

C H A P T E R T E N

Interpersonal Communication in Close Relationships

OUTLINE

Use this outline to take notes as you read the chapter in the text or as your instructor lectures in class.

I. INTIMACY IN CLOSE RELATIONSHIPS   _____

  A. The Dimensions of Intimacy

    1. Physical   _____

    2. Intellectual

    3. Emotional

    4. Shared Activities   _____

  B. Masculine and Feminine Intimacy Styles

    1. Women Tend to Value Talk to Develop   _____
       Intimacy

    2. Men Tend to Value Activities to Develop
       Intimacy   _____

    3. Gender Role, Not Biological Sex, Influences
       Intimacy Styles

    4. Differences Can Be Cause of Stress and   _____
       Misunderstandings

  C. Cultural Influences on Intimacy   _____

    1. Historical Perceptions

    2. National/Regional Cultures   _____

      a. Individualist

      b. Collectivist

    3. Globalization of Culture   _____

  D. Intimacy in Mediated Communication

    1. Speed of Intimacy Development   _____

    2. Problems from Being "Virtually Unfaithful"

  E. Limits of Intimacy   _____

    1. Diminishing Returns

    2. Necessity of Nonintimate Relationships

II. COMMUNICATION IN FAMILIES

A. Characteristics of Family Communication

1. Family Communication Is Formative
   a. Attachment Theory
   b. Birth Order
2. Family Communication Is Role-Driven
3. Family Communication Is Involuntary

B. Families as Systems

1. Family Systems Are Interdependent
2. Family Systems Are Manifested through Communication
3. Family Systems Are Nested
4. Families Are More Than the Sum of Their Parts

C. Communication Patterns Within Families

1. Conversation Orientation
   a. High Conversation Orientation
   b. Low Conversation Orientation
2. Conformity Orientation
3. Family Communication Pattern
   a. Consensual
   b. Pluralistic
   c. Protective
   d. Laissez-faire
4. Social Media
   a. Family Privacy Management
   b. Need to Communicate Social Media Expectations

III. COMMUNICATION IN FRIENDSHIPS

A. Types of Friendships

1. Youthful versus Mature
2. Long Term versus Short Term
3. Relationship Oriented versus Task Oriented
4. High Disclosure versus Low Disclosure
5. High Obligation versus Low Obligation
6. Frequent Contact versus Occasional Contact

B. Sex, Gender, and Friendship

    1. Same-Sex Friendships

    2. Cross-Sex Friendships

    3. Friends with Benefits

    4. Gender Considerations

C. Friendship and Social Media

    1. Curvilinear Perception of Number of Friends

    2. Not a Replacement for Face-to-Face Communication

IV. COMMUNICATION IN ROMANTIC RELATIONSHIPS

A. Characteristics of Romantic Relationships

    1. Love

        a. Triangular Theory of Love

        b. Seven Possible Combinations

    2. Commitment

        a. Involves a Promise

        b. Formed and Reinforced through Communication

    3. Affection

        a. Benefits of Affectionate Verbal and Nonverbal Communication

        b. Relational Bank Account

B. Romantic Turning Points

C. Couples Conflict Styles

    1. Volatile

    2. Avoidant

    3. Validating

D. Languages of Love

    1. Words of Affirmation

    2. Quality Time

    3. Gifts

    4. Acts of Service

    5. Physical Touch

KEY TERMS

attachment theory
conformity orientation
consensual pluralistic
conversation orientation
cyber-relationships
family communication pattern
family system

friends with benefits (FWB)
intimacy
laissez-faire
love languages
protective
relational commitment
relational turning point

role
role-driven
social support
subsystems
suprasystems
triangular theory of love

ACTIVITIES

10.1 ASSESSING INFLUENCES ON DIMENSIONS OF INTIMACY IN SAME-GENDER FRIENDSHIPS

LEARNING OBJECTIVES

- Identify the dimensions of intimacy that operate and how they are expressed in same-gender friendships.
- Assess how gender and culture influence intimacy in same-gender friendships.
- Reflect on how social media may impact intimacy in same-gender friendships.

INSTRUCTIONS

PART I: Interview an opposite-gender classmate, asking the following questions about how the dimensions of intimacy influence one of his or her same-gender friendships. Record answers to the following questions on the lines below. Then, ask yourself the same questions about one of your same-gender friendships and record your own answers.

QUESTIONS FOR CLASSMATE

Same-gender friendship description: _____

What role does physical intimacy play in your relationship?

_____

_____

What role does intellectual intimacy play in your relationship?

_____

_____

What role does emotional intimacy play in your relationship?

_____

_____

What role do shared activities play in your relationship?

_____

_____

For this friendship, are these levels of relational intimacy satisfying? Would you prefer more or less intimacy in any of the dimensions?

_____

_____

Does mediated communication help or hurt your ability to maintain intimacy in this friendship?

_____

_____

QUESTIONS FOR YOU

Your same-gender friendship description: _____

What role does physical intimacy play in your relationship?

_____

_____

What role does intellectual intimacy play in your relationship?

_____

_____

What role does emotional intimacy play in your relationship?

_____

_____

What role do shared activities play in your relationship?

_____

_____

For this friendship, are these levels of relational intimacy satisfying? Would you prefer more or less intimacy in any of the dimensions?

_____

_____

Does mediated communication help or hurt your ability to maintain intimacy in this friendship?

_____

_____

PART II: Now that you have interviewed your classmate on the dimensions of intimacy in her or his relationship, compare your answers on the worksheet below. Indicate how gender or culture may have contributed to any differences. Reflect on the impact of social media on intimacy in friendships.

SIMILARITIES	DIFFERENCES	HOW GENDER OR CULTURE MIGHT CONTRIBUTE	IMPACT OF SOCIAL MEDIA
Physical:	Physical:		
Intellectual:	Intellectual:		
Emotional:	Emotional:		
Shared activities:	Shared activities:		
Need for intimacy:	Need for intimacy:		
Need for distance:	Need for distance:		

PART III: Discuss your assessments, first with the classmate you interviewed and then as part of a larger group. When comparing same-gender friendships, did others in your group reach conclusions that were similar to or different from yours? What influences might account for those similarities and/or differences? How do others in your group feel about the impact of social media on intimacy in friendship relationships?

10.2 ASSESSING FORMATIVE EFFECTS
OF FAMILY COMMUNICATION

LEARNING OBJECTIVES

- Identify the formative effects of family communication on your self-concept and self-esteem.
- Reflect on how your early family experience contributed to your self-concept and self-esteem.

INSTRUCTIONS

The formative effects of family communication play an important role in developing our self-concept and self-esteem. Answer the following questions about your family. Reflect on how your early family experience contributed to your self-concept and self-esteem.

1. What are some of the formative messages about life that you received from your family? For example, "If it seems too good to be true, beware" or "People are essentially good."

    _____

    _____

2. Did you grow up in a home with stable caregivers who offered you feelings of security and worthiness? Or did you grow up in an unstable home where you experienced fears of abandonment?

    _____

    _____

3. What is your family birth order? Are you the oldest, middle, youngest, or only child? Did you grow up in a blended family that caused your order in the family to change? How did your birth order affect your role in the family and sense of self?

    _____

    _____

4. What kinship roles did you play in your family, such as sister, brother, son, or daughter? What "label" roles did you receive from others, such as "the athletic one" or "the clumsy one"?

    _____

    _____

5. Review your answers to the previous four questions and reflect on how formative communication in your family may have influenced your self-concept and self-esteem, in the past and in the present. If some of the effects of your family communication had negative results, what steps might you take to reduce the impact on your self-concept and self-esteem in the future?

_____

_____

10.3 SOCIAL MEDIA AND FRIENDSHIP

LEARNING OBJECTIVES

- Assess the quantity and quality of your social media friendships.
- Reflect on how social media may impact friendship development and maintenance.

INSTRUCTIONS

(Note: This activity assumes participation in Facebook, Instagram, Twitter, or another form of social media with "friends" or "followers." If you don't participate in social media, this exercise won't be relevant.)

Your textbook suggests the typical online adult has 200 Facebook "friends," while younger adults may have significantly more. But what kinds of friendships are these?

PART I: Answer the following questions to assess the quantity and quality of your social media friendships.

1. On your favorite social media platform, how many "friends" or "followers" do you have?

   _____

   _____

2. Do you ever wish you had more social media "friends" or "followers"? How many would you like to have? How many would feel like enough?

   _____

   _____

3. Do you know people who have many more social media friends than you? How do you feel about that? Do you envy them or does that make you suspicious? Are you comfortable telling them how many friends you have?

   _____

   _____

4. How many of your social media friends did you first know from face-to-face friendships? How many of those face-to-face friendships did you have for at least five years before they became social media friends?

   _____

   _____

5. How many of your social media friends were originally "friends" of other friends? With how many of your social media friends did you have no previous connection?

_____

_____

6. Do you have any friends who began as friends on social media and subsequently became face-to-face friends?

_____

_____

7. If all social media were to end tomorrow, how many of your virtual friends would remain face-to-face friends?

_____

_____

8. Review your answers and reflect on what you've learned from this assessment about your social media friendships.

_____

_____

PART II: In a class small-group discussion, share and compare what you've learned about the quantity and quality of your social media friendships.

10.4 ASSESSING YOUR ROMANTIC RELATIONSHIP ACCORDING TO THE TRIANGULAR THEORY OF LOVE

LEARNING OBJECTIVES

- Assess a significant romantic relationship according to the triangular theory of love.
- Understand the role the three components of intimacy, passion, and commitment play in romantic relationships.

INSTRUCTIONS

PART I: Select a personal significant romantic relationship to assess (or select a romantic relationship from a movie or book) and answer the questions below.

Intimacy
1. My relationship reflects emotional, physical, intellectual, and shared activity intimacy. Yes, No

Passion
2. My relationship reflects physical attraction and sexual passion. Yes, No

Commitment
1. My relationship reflects commitment as expressed through clearly communicated and shared promise. Yes, No

PART II: Based on your answers in Part I, place your relationship on the Love Triangle (see graphic below). Review what your textbook says about the seven types. Does your result reflect what you feel is true about your relationship? If not, why not? Are you satisfied with your result, or would you like to develop your triangle further? If so, what specific steps could you take?

INTIMACY	PASSION	COMMITMENT	TYPE
Yes	Yes	Yes	Consummate Love
Yes	No	No	Liking
Yes	Yes	No	Romantic Love
No	Yes	No	Infatuation
No	Yes	Yes	Fatuous Love
No	No	Yes	Empty Love
Yes	No	Yes	Companionate

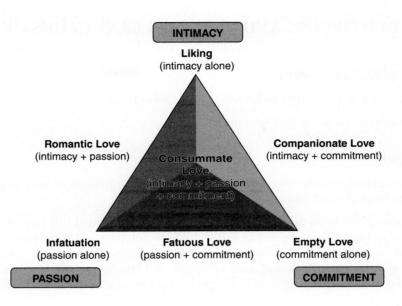

10.5 IDENTIFYING AND APPLYING LANGUAGES OF LOVE

LEARNING OBJECTIVES

- Identify and apply the languages of love in specific situations.
- Reflect on the impact of using love languages.

INSTRUCTIONS

For each of the situations below, offer examples of how the languages of love might be applied and reflect on what the impact might be of using love languages.

1. John and Daphne have been married for six months. He's in school full time during the day and works full time at night. Daphne works full time days and commutes an hour each way to her job. On the weekends, they're both extremely tired and John needs time to study. Lately they've been fighting about little things and John is afraid that the "honeymoon" is truly over. He could express his love to Daphne by (give specific examples for each of the love languages):

   Words of affection: _____

   Quality time: _____

   Gifts: _____

   Acts of service: _____

   Physical touch: _____

   Which love language or combination of love languages do you think would be the most effective for John to use? _____

   Why? _____

2. Cecilia and Jerry have been in a dating relationship for three years. Jerry is divorced and has two young children that he takes care of every other weekend. Jerry has expressed feelings of love for Cecilia, but he's nervous about making another long-term commitment. After three years, Cecilia is ready for a commitment. She would like to have children of her own and is anxious about "wasting her time" with a man who doesn't want what she wants. Cecilia has been showing her discontent by picking lots of fights about small things. But she does love him and still has hopes for the future. She would like to express her love to Jerry and see if they can deepen their commitment by (give specific examples for each of the love languages):

   Words of affection: _____

   Quality time: _____

   Gifts: _____

   Acts of service: _____

   Physical touch: _____

   Which love language or combination of love languages do you think would be the most effective for Cecilia to use? _____

   Why? _____

3. Jane and Samantha have been in a committed romantic relationship for more than 10 years. The state in which they live has recently passed a law making it legal for them to marry. They happily set a date for their wedding, but since that time Jane and Samantha have had many arguments. Jane has been feeling very depressed because many of her family members are against her getting married and have told her that they will not attend. Samantha's family has been very supportive and are actively participating in planning the big event. Jane has withdrawn from participating in the preparations. Instead of fighting, Samantha would like to reconnect with Jane and engage her in their wedding plans in a positive way by (give specific examples for each of the love languages):

    Words of affection: _____

    Quality time: _____

    Gifts: _____

    Acts of service: _____

    Physical touch: _____

    Which love language or combination of love languages do you think would be the most effective for Samantha to use? _____

    Why? _____

4. Using your romantic relationship or the romantic relationship of someone close to you, share expressions of love (give specific examples for each of the love languages):

    Words of affection: _____

    Quality time: _____

    Gifts: _____

    Acts of service: _____

    Physical touch: _____

    Which love language or combination of love languages do you think would be the most effective to use? _____

    Why? _____

STUDY GUIDE

CHECK YOUR UNDERSTANDING

TRUE/FALSE

Mark the statements below as true or false. Correct statements that are false on the lines below to create a true statement.

_____ 1. According to research, intimacy may be the single most important source of life satisfaction and emotional well-being, across different ages and cultures.

_____

_____ 2. Because it requires sharing feelings, emotional intimacy is more important than intellectual intimacy.

_____

_____ 3. Research shows that male-male relationships involve less disclosure than male-female or female-female relationships.

_____

_____ 4. Because online relationships are not face to face, it's impossible to be "virtually unfaithful" to your romantic partner.

_____

_____ 5. Relational intimacy may develop more quickly through mediated channels than face-to-face communication.

_____

_____ 6. It's possible to have a close relationship with everyone you know.

_____

_____ 7. Middle-born siblings tend to be closer with their friends but more likely to have difficult relationships with their family.

_____

_____ 8. Families with a high conversation orientation rarely exchange private thoughts.

_____

_____ 9. Physical intimacy is sexual and is always connected with a close interpersonal relationship.

_____

_____ 10. Conformity orientation refers to how strongly a family enforces uniformity of attitudes, values, and beliefs.

_____

_____ 11. Relational turning points are memorable events, but rarely do they alter the relationship in any meaningful way.

_____

COMPLETION

Fill in the blanks below with the correct terms chosen from the list below.

suprasystem	role	attachment theory	intellectual
physical	emotional	relational turning point	validating

1. _____ is the type of intimacy that comes from an exchange of important ideas.
2. _____ is the type of intimacy that comes from touching, struggling, or sex.
3. _____ is the type of intimacy that comes from exchanging important feelings.
4. _____ is a conflict style where couples openly and cooperatively manage conflict.
5. _____ argues that children develop bonds either secure or insecure with family members.
6. A _____ is a set of expectations about how to communicate.
7. Families are also members of larger _____.
8. _____ is a transformative event that alters the relationship in a fundamental way.

MULTIPLE CHOICE

1. Which of these is *not* a dimension of intimacy in interpersonal relationships?
   a. physical
   b. shared activities
   c. chronological
   d. emotional

2. Researchers have found that in a "friends with benefits" situation people
    a. always form romantic relationships.
    b. never form romantic relationships.
    c. are afraid to develop feelings for the other person because they might be unreciprocated.
    d. have no feelings for the other person.

3. Family is all of these except
    a. formative
    b. role-driven
    c. voluntary
    d. a system

4. A family high in both conversation orientation and conformity orientation is
    a. pluralistic
    b. consensual
    c. protective
    d. laissez-faire

5. "Friends with benefits" deals specifically with friends who also
    a. engage in physical intimacy.
    b. dislike one another without saying.
    c. are part of a family dynamic.
    d. engage in significant emotional and intellectual intimacy.

6. Which of these is a dimension of intimacy in interpersonal relationships?
    a. ignoring the other person
    b. shared activities
    c. shutting down when your partner begins to self-disclose
    d. using the word "feel" as much as possible

7. Fear of intimacy can cause major problems in
    a. creating relationships.
    b. sustaining relationships.
    c. a and b.
    d. none of the above.

8. All of the following are different types of friendships except
    a. youthful vs. mature
    b. long term vs. short term
    c. high disclosure vs. low disclosure
    d. high conformity vs. low conformity

9. According to the text, people want
    a. ten to twelve close relationships in their lives.
    b. one to two close relationships in their lives.
    c. four to six close relationships in their lives.
    d. two to three close relationships in their lives.

10. All of the following are major indicators of a committed romantic relationship except
    a. providing affection
    b. providing affection
    c. avoiding working on problems
    d. reassuring one's commitment

CHAPTER TEN STUDY GUIDE ANSWERS

TRUE/FALSE

1. T	4. F	7. T	10. T
2. F	5. T	8. F	11. F
3. T	6. F	9. F	

COMPLETION

1. intellectual
2. physical
3. emotional
4. validating
5. attachment theory
6. role
7. suprasystem
8. relational turning point

MULTIPLE CHOICE

1. c	4. b	7. c	10. c
2. c	5. a	8. d	
3. c	6. b	9. c	

11

IMPROVING COMMUNICATION CLIMATES

AFTER STUDYING THE TOPICS IN THIS CHAPTER,
YOU SHOULD BE ABLE TO:

1. Identify confirming, disagreeing, and disconfirming messages and patterns in your own important relationships and describe their consequences.

2. Describe how the messages you identified in the previous objective either threaten or honor the self (face) of the communicators involved.

3. Use Gibb's categories and the assertive message format to create messages that are likely to build supportive rather than defensive communication climates.

4. Create appropriate nondefensive responses to real or hypothetical criticisms.

*P*ersonal relationships are a lot like the weather. Some are fair and warm, whereas others are stormy and cold; some are polluted and others healthy. Some relationships have stable climates, whereas others change dramatically—calm one moment and turbulent the next. You can't measure the interpersonal climate by looking at a thermometer or glancing at the sky, but it's there nonetheless. Every relationship has a feeling, a pervasive mood that colors the interactions of the participants. What meteorological terms would you use to describe the prevailing communication climate in your most important relationships? How do the same events and activities feel different when the climate is better? Worse?

Although we can't change the external weather, we *can* change an interpersonal climate. This chapter will explain the forces that make some relationships pleasant and others unpleasant. You will learn what kinds of behavior contribute to defensiveness and hostility and what kinds lead to more positive feelings. After reading this chapter, you will have a better idea of the climate in each of your important relationships and—even more important—how to improve it.

COMMUNICATION CLIMATE AND CONFIRMING MESSAGES

The term **communication climate** refers to the emotional tone of a relationship. A climate doesn't involve specific activities as much as the way people feel about and treat each other as they carry out those activities. Consider two interpersonal communication classes, for example. Both meet for the same length of time and follow the same syllabus. It's easy to imagine how one of these classes might be a friendly, comfortable place to learn, whereas the other could be cold and tense—even hostile.

The same principle holds in close relationships. A large body of research confirms what intuition suggests: Couples who create and maintain emotionally healthy, positive climates have happy, enduring relationships.[1] By contrast, couples who are unsupportive—whether straight or gay, rich or poor, parents or childless—are likely to break up or endure joyless lives together.[2] The communication climate that parents create for their children affects the way they interact.[3] Children who lack confirmation suffer a broad range of emotional and behavioral problems, whereas those who feel confirmed have more open communication with their parents, higher self-esteem, and lower levels of stress.[4] The satisfaction that siblings feel with one another drops sharply as aggressive, disconfirming messages increase.[5]

A healthy communication climate is just as important on the job as it is in personal relationships. Positive communication climates lead to increased job satisfaction.[6] Two factors are consistently connected to supportive workplace environments.[7] The first is praise and encouragement: Employees feel valued when their work is recognized. Acknowledgment doesn't require promotions, raises, or awards, although those are always welcome. As researcher Daniel Goleman notes, "Small exchanges—a compliment on work well done, a word of support after a setback—add up to how we feel on the job."[8] The second climate-boosting practice is open communication. Employees appreciate managers and coworkers with open-door policies, allowing them opportunities to get and give feedback, make suggestions, and voice concerns.

Like their meteorological counterparts, communication climates are shared by everyone involved. It's rare to find one person describing a relationship as open and positive while another describes it as cold and hostile. Also, just like the weather, communication climates can change. A relationship can be overcast at one time and sunny at another. Carrying the analogy to its conclusion, we need to acknowledge that communication climate forecasting is not a perfect science. Unlike the weather, however, people can change the communication climates in their relationships.

∧ Despite some quirky characters and eccentric personalities, the office climate for the employees of *Parks and Recreation* is generally sunny and warm. The leadership of Leslie Knope (Amy Poehler) goes a long way toward creating their positive workplace environment. What has the communication climate been like at places where you've worked? What role did supervisors have in setting and maintaining that climate?

Levels of Message Confirmation

What makes a communication climate positive or negative? In large part, the answer is surprisingly simple. The climate of a relationship is shaped by the degree to which the people believe themselves to be *valued* by one another.

Social scientists use the term **confirming communication** to describe messages that convey valuing and **disconfirming communication** to describe those that show a lack of regard. In one form or another, confirming messages say "You exist," "You matter," "You're important." By contrast, disconfirming communication signals a lack of value. In one form or another, disconfirming messages say "I don't care about you," "I don't like you," "You're not important to me."

Like beauty, the decision about whether a message is confirming or disconfirming is determined by the beholder.[9] Consider, for example, times when you took a comment that might have sounded unsupportive to an outsider ("You turkey!") as a sign of affection within the context of your personal relationship. Likewise, a comment that the sender might have meant to be helpful ("I'm telling you this for your own good …") could easily be regarded as a disconfirming attack.

What makes some messages more confirming than others? Table 11.1 outlines the levels of message confirmation that are described.

Disconfirming Messages Disconfirming communication shows a lack of value for the other person, either by disregarding or ignoring some important part of that person's message.[10] Communication researchers have identified seven types of disconfirming messages.[11]

TABLE 11.1 Levels of Message Confirmation and Disconfirmation

DISCONFIRMING	DISAGREEING	CONFIRMING
Impervious	Aggressiveness	
Interrupting	Complaining	
Irrelevant	Argumentativeness	
Tangential		Recognition
Impersonal		Acknowledgment
Ambiguous		Endorsement
Incongruous		
Least Valuing		**Most Valuing**

Impervious Responses An **impervious response** doesn't acknowledge the other person's message. Whether it's accidental or intentional, few things are more disconcerting than getting no reaction from the person with whom you're attempting to communicate.

As you read in the opening of Chapter 1, being ignored can be more disconfirming than being dismissed or attacked. In the working world, research shows that employees sometimes nudge unwanted coworkers to quit their jobs by avoiding interaction with them, creating a chilling communication climate.[12] In marriage, ignoring a partner (sometimes called *stonewalling*) has been identified as a strong predictor of divorce.[13] On a less-deliberate level, people who tune out others while texting may communicate imperviousness.

Interrupting Beginning to speak before the other person has finished talking can show a lack of concern about what the other person has to say. The occasional **interrupting response** is not likely to be taken as a disconfirmation, but repeatedly interrupting a speaker can be both discouraging and irritating.

Irrelevant Responses A comment unrelated to what the other person has just said is an **irrelevant response**.

A: What a day! I thought it would never end. First the car overheated, and I had to call a tow truck, and then the computer broke down at work.

B: Listen, we have to talk about a present for Ann's birthday. The party is on Saturday, and I have only tomorrow to shop for it.

A: I'm really beat. Could we talk about it in a few minutes? I've never seen a day like this one.

B: I just can't figure out what would suit Ann. She's got everything. ...

Tangential Responses Conversational "takeaways" are called **tangential responses**. Instead of ignoring the speaker's remarks completely, the other party uses them as a starting point for a shift to a different topic.

A: I'd like to know for sure whether you want to go skiing during vacation. If we don't decide whether to go soon, it'll be impossible to get reservations anywhere.

B: Yeah, and if I don't pass my botany class, I won't be in the mood to go anywhere. Could you give me some help with this homework?

Lassedesignen/Fotolia

Impersonal Responses **Impersonal responses** are loaded with clichés and other statements that never truly respond to the speaker.

A: I've been having some personal problems lately, and I'd like to take off work early a couple of afternoons to clear them up.

B: Ah, yes. We all have personal problems. It seems to be a sign of the times.

Ambiguous Responses **Ambiguous responses** contain messages with more than one meaning, leaving the other party unsure of the responder's position.

A: I'd like to get together with you soon. How about Tuesday?
B: Uh, maybe so.
A: Well, how about it? Can we talk Tuesday?
B: Oh, probably. See you later.

Incongruous Responses An **incongruous response** contains two messages that seem to deny or contradict each other. Often at least one of these messages is nonverbal.

A: Darling, I love you.
B: I love you, too. (*said in a monotone while watching TV*)

Disagreeing Messages Between disconfirming and confirming communication lie disagreeing messages. As their name implies, **disagreeing messages** say "You're wrong" in one way or another. As you'll read here, some disagreements are quite hostile. But others aren't so disconfirming as they might first seem. Because there are better and worse ways to disagree with others, disagreeing messages need to be put on a negative-to-positive scale. We will do just that in this section as we discuss three types of disagreement: aggressiveness, complaining, and argumentativeness.

Aggressiveness The most destructive way to disagree with another person is through **aggressiveness**. Researchers define verbal aggressiveness as the tendency to attack the self-concepts of other people in order to inflict psychological pain.[14] Unlike argumentativeness (described later), aggressiveness demeans the worth of others. Name-calling, put-downs, sarcasm, taunting, yelling, badgering—all are methods of "winning" disagreements at others' expense.

One form of aggressiveness—bullying—has received a good deal of attention in the media and from scholars in recent years. The word "bully" often

Ron Elkman/Sports Imagery/Getty Images Sport/Getty Images

^ Professional football tackle Jonathan Martin walked away from the Miami Dolphins team, saying he was bullied and harassed by teammates. The story brought new light to the notion that aggressive taunting and name-calling causes pain in adult relationships, not just among children. Have you encountered bullying in the workplace?

conjures up images of a tough kid on the school playground, but bullying can occur in a variety of contexts. For instance, studies show that it can take place in families, with sibling bullying having long-lasting psychological effects.[15] And as the photo in this section shows, bullying can happen among adults in the workplace.

Aggressiveness isn't limited to face-to-face encounters. Cyberbullying is disturbingly common: About 15 percent of students report abusing someone else online, and twice as many report having been victims.[16] The consequences of cyberbullying can be devastating. Online abuse leaves victims feeling angry, frustrated, sad, frightened, and embarrassed. Targets often respond with apathy and cheating in school, substance abuse, violence, and self-destructive behaviors— and suicide in the most severe cases. And cyberbullying isn't limited to one's school years. Fully 73 percent of adult Internet users have seen someone be harassed online and 40 percent have personally experienced it.[17] See Chapter 2 for more on cyberbullying.

It's no surprise that aggressiveness has such serious consequences. Chapter 12 describes how win–win approaches to conflict are healthier and more productive than the win–lose tactics of aggression.

Complaining When communicators aren't prepared to argue but still want to register dissatisfaction, they often complain. As is true of all disagreeing messages, some ways of **complaining** are better than others. Satisfied couples tend to offer behavioral complaints ("You always throw your socks on the floor"), whereas unsatisfied couples make more complaints aimed at personal characteristics ("You're a slob").[18] Personal complaints are more likely to result in an escalated conflict episode.[19] The reason should be obvious: Complaints about personal characteristics attack a more fundamental part of the presenting self. Talking about socks deals with a habit that can be changed; calling someone a slob is a character assault that is unlikely to be forgotten when the conflict is over. Marriage researcher John Gottman has found that complaining isn't necessarily a sign of a troubled relationship. In fact, it's usually healthy for spouses to get their concerns out in the open as long as the complaint is a behavioral description rather than a personal criticism.[20]

Argumentativeness Normally, when we call a person *argumentative*, we're making an unfavorable evaluation. However, the ability to create and deliver a sound argument is something we admire in lawyers, talk-show participants, letters to the editor, and political debates. Taking a positive approach to the term, communication researchers define **argumentativeness** as presenting and defending positions on issues while attacking positions taken by others.[21] Rather than being a negative trait, argumentativeness is associated with several positive attributes such as enhanced self-concept, communicative competence, and positive climate in the workplace.

The key for maintaining a positive climate while arguing a point is the *way* you present your ideas. It is crucial to attack issues, not people. In addition, a sound argument is better received when it's delivered in an affirming manner.[22] The supportive kinds of messages outlined later in this chapter show how it is possible to argue in a respectful, constructive way.

Confirming Messages   Research shows that three increasingly positive types of messages have the best chance of being confirming: recognition, acknowledgment, and endorsement.[23]

Recognition The most fundamental act of confirmation is to recognize the other person. Recognition seems easy and obvious, and yet there are many times when we don't respond to others on this basic level. Failure to return an email or phone message are common examples. So is a sales clerk who fails to signal awareness that you're waiting for service. Of course, this lack of recognition may simply be an oversight. Nonetheless, if the other person *perceives* you as avoiding contact, then the message has the effect of being disconfirming.

Acknowledgment Acknowledging the ideas and feelings of others is a stronger form of confirmation. Listening is probably the most common form of acknowledgment. Of course, counterfeit listening—ambushing, stage hogging, pseudolistening, and so on—has the opposite effect of acknowledgment. More active acknowledgment includes asking questions, paraphrasing, and reflecting. It is not surprising that employees highly rate managers who solicit their opinions—even when the managers don't accept every opinion.[24] As you read in Chapter 8, reflecting the speaker's thoughts and feelings can be a powerful way to offer support when others have problems.

Endorsement Whereas acknowledgment means that you are interested in another's ideas, endorsement means that you agree with them or otherwise find them important. It's easy to see why endorsement is the strongest type of confirming message: It communicates the highest form of valuing. The most obvious form of endorsement is agreeing. Fortunately, it isn't necessary to agree completely with another person in order to endorse her or his message. You can probably find something in the message that you endorse. "I can see why you were so angry," you might reply to a friend, even if you don't approve of his outburst. Of course, outright praise is a strong form of endorsement and one that you can use surprisingly often after you look for opportunities to compliment others.

How Communication Climates Develop

As soon as two people start to communicate, a relational climate begins to develop. If their messages are confirming, then the climate is likely to be a positive one. If their messages are disconfirming, then the relationship is likely to be hostile, cold, or defensive.

Verbal messages certainly contribute to the climate of a relationship, but many climate-shaping messages are nonverbal.[25] The very act of approaching others is confirming—and avoiding them can be disconfirming. Smiles or frowns, the presence or absence of eye contact, tone of voice, the use of personal space—all these and other cues send messages about how the parties feel toward one another.

AN UNLIKELY FRIENDSHIP

I am coming out in a new way, as a friend of Chick-fil-A's president and COO, Dan Cathy, and I am nervous about it.

For many this news of friendship might be shocking. I am an out, 40-year-old gay man and a lifelong activist for equality. For nearly a decade, my organization, Campus Pride, has been protesting Chick-fil-A. I had researched Chick-fil-A's nearly $5 million in funding to anti-LGBT groups. And the whole nation was aware that Dan was "guilty as charged" in his support of a "biblical definition" of marriage. What more was there to know?

In the heat of the controversy, I got a surprise call from Dan Cathy. I took the call with great caution. He was going to tear me apart, right? Give me a piece of his mind? Turn his lawyers on me?

The first call lasted over an hour. His questions and a series of deeper conversations ultimately led to a number of in-person meetings. It is not often that people with deeply held and completely opposing viewpoints actually risk sitting down and listening to one another.

Dan and I shared respectful, enduring communication and built trust. Even when I continued to question his public actions and the funding decisions, Dan embraced the opportunity to have dialogue and hear my perspective. He and I were committed to a better understanding of one another. We see this failure to listen and learn in our government, in our communities and in our own families. Dan Cathy and I would, together, try to do better than each of us had experienced before.

Throughout the conversations Dan expressed a sincere interest in my life. He wanted to know about where I grew up, my faith, my family, even my husband. In return, I learned about his wife and kids and gained an appreciation for his commitment to being "a follower of Christ" more than a "Christian." Dan expressed regret and genuine

Andrew Baker/Getty Images

sadness when he heard of people being treated unkindly in the name of Chick-fil-A—but he offered no apologies for his genuine beliefs about marriage.

And in that we had great commonality: We were each entirely ourselves. We both wanted to be respected and for others to understand our views. We were different but in dialogue. That was progress.

In the end, it is not about eating a certain chicken sandwich. It is about sitting down at a table together and sharing our views as human beings, engaged in real, respectful, civil dialogue. Dan would probably call this act the biblical definition of hospitality. I would call it human decency. So long as we are all at the same table and talking, does it matter what we call it or what we eat?

Shane L. Windmeyer

After a climate is formed, it can take on a life of its own and grow in a self-perpetuating **spiral**: a reciprocating communication pattern in which each person's message reinforces the other's.[26] In positive spirals, one partner's confirming message leads to a similar message from the other person. This positive reaction leads the first person to be even more confirming. Negative spirals are just as powerful, although they leave the partners feeling worse about themselves and each other.

Research shows how spirals operate in relationships to reinforce the principle that "what goes around comes around." In one study of married couples, each spouse's response in conflict situations was similar to the other's statement.[27] Conciliatory statements (e.g., supporting, accepting responsibilities, agreeing) were likely to be followed by conciliatory responses. Confrontational acts (such as criticism, hostile questions, and fault finding) were likely to trigger equally confrontational responses. The same pattern held for other kinds of messages: Avoidance begets avoidance, analysis begets analysis, and so on. Table 11.2 illustrates reciprocal communication patterns that have the potential to create positive and negative spirals.

Escalatory conflict spirals are the most visible way that disconfirming messages reinforce one another.[28] One attack leads to another until a skirmish escalates into a full-fledged battle:

A: (*Mildly irritated*) Where were you? I thought we agreed to meet here a half-hour ago.

B: (*Defensively*) I'm sorry. I got hung up at the library. I don't have as much free time as you do, you know.

A: I wasn't blaming you, so don't get so touchy. I do resent what you just said, though. I'm plenty busy. And I've got lots of better things to do than wait around for you!

B: Who's getting touchy? I just made a simple comment. You've sure been defensive lately. What's the matter with you?

Although they are less obvious, **de-escalatory conflict spirals** can also be destructive.[29] Rather than fighting, the parties slowly lessen their dependence on each other, withdraw, and become less invested in the relationship. The good news is that spirals can also be positive. A word of praise can lead to a *returned compliment* that can lead to an act of kindness, which can result in an improved relational climate.

Spirals—whether positive or negative—rarely go on indefinitely. Most relationships pass through cycles of progression and regression. If the spiral is negative, partners may find the exchange growing so unpleasant that they switch from negative to positive messages without discussing the matter. In

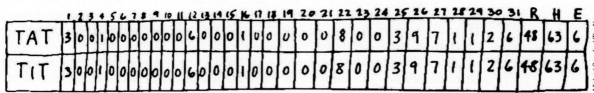

Game called on account of infinity.

TABLE 11.2 Positive and Negative Reciprocal Communication Patterns

NEGATIVE RECIPROCAL PATTERN

Pattern	Example
Complaint–countercomplaint	A: I wish you weren't so self-centered. B: Well, I wish you weren't so critical.
Disagreement–disagreement	A: Why are you so hard on Marta? She's a great boss. B: Are you kidding? She's the biggest phony I've ever seen. A: You wouldn't know a good boss if you saw one. B: Neither would you.
Mutual indifference	A: I don't care if you want to stay. I'm exhausted, and I'm getting out of here. B: Go ahead if you want, but find your own way home.
Arguments involving punctuation	A: How can I talk when you won't listen? B: How can I listen when you won't talk?

POSITIVE RECIPROCAL PATTERNS

Pattern	Example
Validation of other's perspective	A: This assignment is really confusing. Nobody can figure out what we're supposed to do. B: I can understand how it might be unclear. Let me try to explain …
Recognizing similarities	A: I can't believe you want to take an expensive vacation! We should be saving money, not spending more! B: I agree we should be saving. But I think we can take this trip and still save some money. Let me show you what I've figured out …
Supportiveness	A: I'm going crazy with this job. It was supposed to be temporary. I have to do something different, and soon. B: I can see how much you hate it. Let's figure out how we can get the project finished soon, so you can get back to your regular work.

Adapted from *Competence and Interpersonal Conflict*, by W. Cupach and D. Canary. Reproduced by permission of William Cupach and Daniel Canary.

other cases, they may engage in *metacommunication*. "Hold on," one might say. "This is getting us nowhere." This ability to rebound from negative spirals and turn them in a positive direction is a hallmark of successful relationships.[30] However, if the partners pass the "point of no return" and continue spiraling downward, their relationship may end.

Positive spirals also have their limit. Even the best relationships go through periods of conflict and withdrawal, although a combination of time and communication skills can eventually bring the partners back into greater harmony.

PAUSE *and* REFLECT

Evaluating Communication Climates

MindTap® **REFLECT...** on communication climates by answering the following questions, either here or online.

You can probably recognize the communication climate in each of your relationships without much analysis. But taking the following steps will help explain why these climates exist. Taking these steps may also suggest ways in which to improve negative climates:

1. Identify the communication climate of an important interpersonal relationship.

2. List the confirming and/or disconfirming communications that created and now maintain this climate. Be sure to list both verbal and nonverbal messages.

3. Describe what you can do either to maintain and enhance the existing climate (if primarily positive) or to improve it (if primarily negative). Again, list both verbal and nonverbal messages.

DEFENSIVENESS: CAUSES AND REMEDIES

The word ***defensiveness*** suggests guarding oneself from attack, but what kind of attack? Surely, few if any of the times you become defensive involve a physical threat. If you're not threatened by bodily injury, then *what* are you guarding against? To answer this question, we need to talk more about the notions of the *presenting self* and *face* introduced in Chapter 3. Next, we'll look at ways to reduce defensiveness in others.

Face-Threatening Acts

Recall that a person's face consists of the physical traits, personality characteristics, attitudes, aptitudes, and all the other parts of the image that he or she wants to present to the world. Actually, it is a mistake to talk about a single face; we try to project different faces to different people. You might, for instance, try to impress a potential employer with your seriousness but want your friends to see you as a joker.

When others are willing to accept and acknowledge important parts of our presenting image, there is no need to feel defensive. On the other hand, when others confront us with **face-threatening acts**—messages that seem to challenge the image we want to project—we are likely to resist their messages.[31] Defensiveness, then, is the process of protecting our presenting

Photodisc/Getty Images

self, our face. While responding defensively to a face-threatening attack may seem logical, over time defensiveness erodes relationship stability.[32]

You can understand how defensiveness operates by imagining what might happen if an important part of your presenting self were attacked. Suppose, for instance, that your boss criticized you for making a stupid mistake. Or consider how you would feel if a friend called you self-centered or your sweetheart called you lazy. You would probably feel threatened if these attacks were unjustified. But notice that you might very well react defensively even if you knew deep inside that the attacks were justified. For instance, you have probably responded defensively at times when you *did* make a mistake, acted selfishly, or cut corners on your work. In fact, we often feel most defensive when criticism is right on target.[33] The drive to defend a presenting image—even when it is false—leads some people to act in destructive ways such as being sarcastic or verbally abusive.[34]

So far, we have talked about defensiveness as if it is the responsibility of only the person who feels threatened. If this were the case, then the prescription would be simple: Grow a thick skin, admit your flaws, and stop trying to manage impressions. This prescription isn't just unrealistic; it also ignores the role played by those who send face-threatening messages. In fact, competent communicators protect others' face needs as well as their own.[35] For instance, skilled instructors try to support their students' presenting faces, especially when offering constructive criticism. This facework leads to less-defensive responses from their students.[36] Likewise, effective supervisors use face-saving statements such as "You're on the right track, and your work has potential" to buffer corrections.[37] We'll talk more about the importance of sending face-saving messages later in this chapter.

Preventing Defensiveness in Others

The influential work of researcher Jack Gibb offers some useful tools for reducing defensiveness.[38] After observing groups for several years, Gibb was able to isolate six types of defense-arousing communication and six contrasting behaviors that lessen the level of threat and defensiveness by conveying face-honoring relational messages of respect. The **Gibb categories** are listed in Table 11.3 and summarized here.

Evaluation versus Description   The first type of defense-arousing behavior that Gibb noted is **evaluation**. Most people become irritated at judgmental statements, which they are likely to interpret as indicating a lack of regard. One form of evaluation is "you" language, which is described in Chapter 6.

Unlike evaluative "you" language, **description** focuses on the *speaker's* thoughts and feelings instead of judging the other person. Descriptive

TABLE 11.3 The Gibb Categories of Defensive and Supportive Behaviors

DEFENSIVE BEHAVIORS	SUPPORTIVE BEHAVIORS
1. Evaluation	1. Description
2. Control	2. Problem Orientation
3. Strategy	3. Spontaneity
4. Neutrality	4. Empathy
5. Superiority	5. Equality
6. Certainty	6. Provisionalism

Source: Jack Gibb

messages often are expressed in "I" language, which tends to provoke less defensiveness than "you" language.[39] Contrast the following evaluative "you" claims with their descriptive "I" counterparts:

Evaluation: "You don't know what you're talking about!"
Description: "I don't understand how you came up with that idea."

Evaluation: "This place is a mess!"
Description: "When you don't clean up, I have to either do it or live with your mess. That's why I'm mad!"

Evaluation: "Those jokes are disgusting!"
Description: "When you tell those off-color jokes, I get really embarrassed."

Note how each of the descriptive statements focuses on the speaker's thoughts and feelings without judging the other person. Despite its value, descriptive language isn't the only element necessary for success. Its effectiveness depends in part on when, where, and how the language is used. You can imagine how each of the preceding descriptive statements would go over if said in front of a room full of bystanders or in a whining tone of voice. Even the best timing and delivery of a descriptive message won't guarantee success. Some people will react defensively to anything you say or do. Nonetheless, it's easy to see that describing how the other person's behavior affects you is likely to produce better results than judgmentally attacking the other person.

Control versus Problem Orientation A second defense-provoking message involves some attempt to control another. **Controlling communication** occurs when a sender seems to be imposing a solution on the receiver with little regard for the receiver's needs or interests. The object of control can involve almost anything: where to eat dinner, what TV program to watch, whether to remain in a relationship, or how to spend a large sum of money. Whatever the situation, people who act in controlling ways create a defensive climate. Whether it is done through words, gestures, tone of voice, or some other channel, the controller generates hostility wherever he or she goes. The unspoken message that such behavior communicates is "I know what's best for you, and if you do as I say, we'll get along."

By contrast, communicators with a **problem orientation** focus on finding a solution that satisfies both their needs and those of the others involved. The goal here isn't to win at the expense of your partner, but rather to work out some arrangement in which everybody feels like a winner. Problem orientation is often typified by "we" language (see Chapter 6), which suggests the speaker is making decisions *with* rather than *for* other people.[40] University chairpersons found to be most effective by members of their departments were best characterized as using few control communications and adopting a problem orientation.[41] Chapter 12 has a great deal to say about win–win problem-solving as a way to find problem-oriented solutions.

Here are some examples of how some controlling and problem-orientation messages might sound.

Controlling:	"You need to stick around for the next two hours."
Problem orientation:	"I'm expecting an important package to arrive soon. Can you cover the office while I go on a sales call?"
Controlling:	"There's only one way to handle this problem …"
Problem orientation:	"Looks like we have a problem. Let's work out a solution we can both live with."

Strategy versus Spontaneity Gibb uses the word *strategy* to characterize defense-arousing messages in which speakers hide their ulterior motives. The words *dishonesty* and *manipulation* capture the essence of strategy. Even if the motives of strategic communication are honorable, the victim of such deception who discovers the attempt to deceive is likely to feel offended at being played for a naïve sucker.

Spontaneity is the behavior that contrasts with strategy. Spontaneity simply means being honest with others rather than manipulating them. What it doesn't mean is blurting out what you're thinking as soon as an idea comes to you. As we discussed in Chapter 3, there are appropriate (and inappropriate) times for self-disclosure. You would undoubtedly threaten others' presenting selves if you were "spontaneous" about every opinion that crossed your mind. Gibb's notion of spontaneity involves setting aside hidden agendas that others both sense and resist. These examples illustrate the difference.

Strategy:	"What are you doing Friday after work?"
Spontaneity:	"I have a piano I need to move Friday after work. Can you give me a hand?"
Strategy:	"Jermaine and Brianna go out to dinner every week."
Spontaneity:	"I'd like to go out to dinner more often."

Spontaneity doesn't mean indiscriminately saying whatever you're thinking and feeling. That's called *blurting*—and research shows that it's detrimental to interpersonal relationships.[42] Blurters tend to be high in verbal aggressiveness and neuroticism; they rate low in empathy and perspective-taking. They are also relatively unconcerned about the harm their comments might do to others and to their relationships.

Paradoxically, spontaneity can be a strategy, too. Sometimes you'll see people using honesty in a calculating way, being just frank enough to win someone's trust or sympathy. This "leveling" is probably the most defense-arousing strategy of all, because once you have learned someone is using frankness as a manipulation, you are less likely to trust that person in the future.

Neutrality versus Empathy Gibb uses the term **neutrality** to describe a fourth behavior that arouses defensiveness. Probably a better descriptive word would be *indifference*. A neutral attitude is disconfirming because it communicates a lack of concern and implies that the welfare of the other person isn't very important to you. This perceived indifference is likely to promote defensiveness, because people do not like to think of themselves as worthless, and they'll protect a self-concept that regards them as worthwhile.

Notice the following differences between neutral and empathic statements.

Neutral: "That's what happens when you don't plan properly."
Empathic: "Ouch—looks like this didn't turn out the way you expected."

Neutral: "Sometimes things just don't work out. That's the way it goes."
Empathic: "I know you put a lot of time and effort into this project."

The negative effects of neutrality become apparent when you consider the hostility that most people have for the large, impersonal organizations with which they have to deal: "They think of me as a number instead of a person"; "I felt as if I were being handled by computers and not human beings." These two common statements reflect reactions to being handled in an indifferent way. Gibb found that empathy helps rid communication of the quality of indifference. **Empathy** means accepting another's feelings and putting yourself in another's place. This doesn't mean that you need to agree with that person. By simply letting that person know of your care and respect, you'll be acting in a supportive way.

Superiority versus Equality A fifth behavior that arouses defensiveness is **superiority**. Any message that suggests "I'm better than you" is likely to arouse feelings of defensiveness in the recipients. A body of research confirms that patronizing messages irritate recipients ranging from young students to senior citizens, at least in Western cultures.[43] Some superiority comes from the content of messages. In other cases, the *way* we deliver messages suggests a one-up approach. Consider, for example, how using simplified grammar and vocabulary, talking loudly and slowly, not listening, and varying speaking pitch convey a patronizing attitude.

Here are two examples of the difference between superiority and equality.

Superior: "You don't know what you're talking about."
Equal: "I see it a different way."

Superior: "No, that's not the right way to do it!"
Equal: "If you want, I can show you a way that has worked for me."

Andersen Ross/Blend Images/Jupiter Images

On the JOB

Intellectual Humility at Google

Google has been notorious for job interview brainteasers like "How many times a day do a clock's hands overlap?" More recently the company has declared oddball questions useless in hiring. According to Laszlo Bock, that company's head of people operations, pedigrees from elite colleges and even high GPAs are also poor at predicting job performance.[a]

Bock explained that Google now looks for "the ability to step back and embrace other people's ideas when they're better."[b] This "intellectual humility," as Bock calls it, is fundamental to learning. It's expressed as an ability to process information on the fly and to absorb the lessons of failure. Google interviewers screen for it by asking how applicants handled tough situations.

Being intellectually humble does not mean being wishy-washy. As Bock describes it, employees who possess this quality will "fight like hell" for their position. But if a new fact is introduced, they are unafraid to say, "That changes things. You are right."

How could embracing another point of view make you more successful? What difference would it make to work in an organization that values provisionalism compared to one characterized by certainty?

There are certainly times when we communicate with others who possess talents or knowledge lesser than ours, but even then it isn't necessary to communicate an attitude of superiority. Gibb found ample evidence that many people who have superior skills and talents are capable of projecting feelings of **equality** rather than superiority. Such people convey the attitude that, although they may have greater talent in certain areas, they see others as having just as much worth as human beings.

"I understand completely. I like good movies, and you like bad movies."

Certainty versus Provisionalism Have you ever run into people who are positive they're right, who know that theirs is the only or proper way of doing something, who insist that they have all the facts and need no additional information? If you have, then you've met individuals who project the defense-arousing behavior that Gibb calls **certainty**. Communicators who regard their own opinions with certainty while disregarding the ideas of others demonstrate a lack of regard and respect. It's likely that the receiver will take the certainty as a personal affront and react defensively.

In contrast to certainty is **provisionalism**, in which people may have strong opinions but are willing to acknowledge that they don't have a corner on the truth and will change their stance if another position seems more reasonable. Consider these examples that contrast certain and provisional approaches.

Certain:	"That will never work!"
Provisional:	"I think you'll run into problems with that approach."
Certain:	"You don't know what you're talking about!"
Provisional:	"I've never heard anything like that before. Where did you hear it?"

As these examples suggest, provisionalism often surfaces in word choices. While dogmatic communicators use words like *can't, never, always, must,* and *have to,* more provisional speakers say *perhaps, maybe, possibly, might,* and *could*. It's not that provisional people are spineless; they simply recognize what research confirms: People respond better to open-minded messages.[44]

There is no guarantee that using Gibb's supportive, confirming approach to communication will build a positive climate. First, Gibb's emphasis on being direct is better suited for a low-context culture such as the United States, which values self-assertion, than for high-context cultures. Even in a culture that values directness, your appeals may not always be well received. But the chances for a constructive relationship will be greatest when communication consists of the supportive approach described here. Besides boosting the odds of getting a positive response from others, supportive communication can leave you feeling better in a variety of ways: more in control of your relationships, more comfortable, and more positive toward others.

Looking at DIVERSITY

Courtesy of Russel Proctor

Abdel Jalil Elayyadi: Promoting Understanding

I grew up in Morocco and moved to the United States when I was 19. I love the U.S. and have many wonderful friends here—but communicating with strangers is often tense because I'm an Arab Muslim. Many Americans equate Arabs and Muslims with terrorism, and that creates a defensive communication climate.

I feel as if I'm easily stereotyped and misunderstood by people who prejudge me because of my religion and nationality. When I encounter people who think that all Muslims are terrorists who hate Americans, I try to do three things to change the defensive climate.

First, I quickly explain that Muslims are peace-loving people who abhor the taking of innocent life. I want them to know that I completely agree with their disdain for the terrorists. That builds a bridge of trust that allows us to keep talking.

Second, I try to use examples to help them understand how terrorists don't represent most Muslims

or Arabs. I ask them how they would feel if Arabs judged Americans by the acts of Oklahoma City bomber Timothy McVeigh, or Christians by the acts of the Ku Klux Klan. This usually helps them view Muslims in a different and more accurate light.

Finally, the more we talk, the more we focus on things we have in common and beliefs we share. The goal is to discover that we are not enemies simply because we have different religions or nationalities—and in fact, there is no reason we can't be friends.

What do these conversations accomplish? In some cases, not a lot—because there are a few people who prefer to keep their prejudices rather than change them. But in other cases, I think I've made a difference, however small, in promoting peace and understanding in the world.

"Promoting Understanding" by Abdel Jalil Elayyadi. Used with permission of author.

SAVING FACE

Gibb's categories of supportive communication offer useful guidelines for reducing defensiveness. You will learn some specific ways to use these approaches when you need to deliver challenging messages.

The Assertive Message Format

As you've already seen, an essential ingredient in building a supportive climate is to avoid attacking others—to preserve their face. At the same time, you need to share your legitimate concerns when problems arise in a relationship.

The following will describe a method for speaking your mind in a clear, direct, yet nonthreatening assertive way that expresses your needs, thoughts, and feelings clearly and directly without judging or dictating to others. This **assertive message format** builds on the perception-checking skill you learned in Chapter 4 and the "I" language approach you learned in Chapter 6. This new skill works for a variety of messages: your hopes, problems, complaints, and appreciations.[45] We'll examine each part one by one and then discuss how to combine them in your everyday communication.

Behavior   As you read in Chapter 6, a behavioral description describes the raw material to which you react. A behavioral description should be *objective*, describing an event without interpreting it. Two examples of behavioral descriptions might look like this:

Example 1

"One week ago John promised me that he would ask my permission before smoking in the same room with me. Just a moment ago he lit up a cigarette without asking for my OK."

Example 2

"Chris has acted differently over the last week. I can't remember her laughing once since the holiday weekend. She hasn't dropped by my place like she usually does, hasn't suggested we play tennis, and hasn't returned my phone calls."

Notice that both statements describe only facts. The observer hasn't attached any meaning.

Interpretation   An **interpretation statement** describes the meaning you've attached to the other person's behavior. The important thing to realize about interpretations is that they are *subjective*. As you learned via the skill of perception checking (see Chapter 4), we can attach more than one interpretation to any behavior. For example, look at these two different interpretations of each of the preceding descriptions:

Example 1

Interpretation A: "John must have forgotten about our agreement that he wouldn't smoke without asking me first. I'm sure he's too considerate to go back on his word on something he knows I feel strongly about."

Interpretation B: "John is a rude, inconsiderate person. After promising not to smoke around me without asking, he's just deliberately done so. This shows that he cares only about himself. In fact, I bet he's deliberately doing this to drive me crazy!"

Example 2

Interpretation A: "Something must be bothering Chris. It's probably her family. She'll probably just feel worse if I keep pestering her."

Interpretation B: "Chris is probably mad at me. It's probably because I kidded her about losing so often at tennis. I'd better leave her alone until she cools off."

After you become aware of the difference between observable behavior and interpretation, some of the reasons for communication difficulties become clear. Many problems occur when a sender fails to describe the behavior on which an interpretation is based. For instance, imagine the difference between hearing a friend say

"You are a tightwad!" (*No behavioral description*)

versus explaining

"When you never offer to pay me back for the coffee and snacks I often buy you, I think you're a tightwad." *(Behavior plus interpretation)*

Feeling   Reporting behavior and sharing your interpretations are important, but **feeling statements** add a new dimension to a message. For example, consider the difference between saying

"When you laugh at me *(behavior)*, I think you find my comments foolish *(interpretation)*, and *I feel embarrassed.*"

And

"When you laugh at me, I think you find my comments foolish, and *I feel angry.*"

SKILL *Builder*

Behaviors and Interpretations

MindTap **PRACTICE ...** your skill at interpreting behaviors by answering the following questions online.

1. Think of two situations when you recently made interpretations about other people in your life. For each interpretation, describe the behavior on which you based your interpretations.

2. Next, consider some alternate interpretations of the behavior that might be as plausible as your original one.

3. After considering the alternate interpretations, decide

   a. which one was most reasonable and

   b. how you might share that interpretation (along with the behavior) with the other person involved in a tentative, provisional way.

SKILL *Builder*

Name the Feeling

MindTap® **PRACTICE ...** your skill at identifying feelings by answering the following questions online.

Add a feeling that you would be likely to have to each of the following messages:

1. I felt ___ when I found out you didn't invite me on the camping trip. You said you thought I wouldn't want to go, but I have a hard time accepting that.

2. I felt ___ when you offered to help me move. I know how busy you are.

3. When you tell me you still want to be a friend but you want to "lighten up a little," I get the idea you're tired of me, and I feel ___.

4. You told me you wanted my honest opinion about your paintings, and then when I tell you what I think, you say I don't understand them. I'm ___.

How would the impact of each message be different if it didn't include a feeling statement?

It's important to recognize that some statements *seem* as if they're expressing feelings but are actually interpretations or statements of intention. For instance, it's not accurate to say "I feel like leaving" (really an intention) or "I feel you're wrong" (an interpretation). Statements like these obscure the true expression of feelings.

Consequence   A **consequence statement** explains what happens as a result of the situation you've described so far. There are three types of consequences:

- What happens to you, the speaker

   "When you didn't tell me that the landlord came by to ask about last month's rent *(behavior)*, I didn't know that my check had bounced *(consequences)*. It seems to me that you don't care about my credit record or appreciate what it takes for me to handle our rent for the apartment *(interpretation)*, and that's why I'm so mad *(feeling)*."

- What happens to the person you're addressing

   "When you have four or five drinks at a party after I've warned you to slow down *(behavior)*, you start to act strange: You make crude jokes that offend everybody, and on the way home you drive poorly *(consequences)*. For instance, last night you almost hit a telephone pole while you were backing out of the driveway *(more behavior)*. I don't think you realize how differently you act *(interpretation)*, and I'm worried *(feeling)* about what will happen if you don't drink less."

- What happens to others

   "You probably don't know because you couldn't hear her cry *(interpretation)*, but when you rehearse your lines for the play without closing the doors *(behavior)*, the baby can't sleep *(consequence)*. I'm especially concerned *(feeling)* about her because she's had a cold lately."

Consequence statements are valuable for two reasons. First, they help you understand more clearly why you are bothered or pleased by another's behavior. Just as important, telling others about the consequences of their actions can clarify for them the results of their behavior. As with interpretations, we often think that others should be aware of consequences without being told, but the fact is that they often aren't. By explicitly stating consequences, you can be sure that you or your message leaves nothing to the listener's imagination.

Intention   **Intention statements** are the final element of the assertive message format. They can communicate three kinds of messages:

- Where you stand on an issue

    "When you call us 'girls' after I've told you we want to be called 'women' *(behavior)*, I get the idea you don't appreciate how important the difference is to us *(interpretation)* and how demeaning it feels *(feeling)*. Now I'm in an awkward spot: Either I have to keep bringing the subject up or else drop it and feel bad *(consequence)*. I want you to know how much this bothers me *(intention)*."

- Requests of others

    "When I didn't hear from you last night *(behavior)*, I thought you were mad at me *(interpretation)*. I've been thinking about it ever since *(consequence)*, and I'm still worried *(feeling)*. I'd like to know whether you are angry *(intention)*."

- Descriptions of how you plan to act in the future

    "I've asked you to repay the twenty-five dollars I lent you three times now *(behavior)*. I'm getting the idea that you've been avoiding me *(interpretation)*, and I'm pretty angry about it *(feeling)*. I want you to know that unless we clear this up now, you shouldn't expect me ever to lend you anything again *(intention)*."

As in the preceding cases, we are often motivated by one single intention. Sometimes, however, we act from a combination of intentions, which may even be in conflict with each other. When this happens, our conflicting intentions often make it difficult for us to reach decisions:

"I want to be truthful with you, but I don't want to violate my friend's privacy."

"I want to continue to enjoy your friendship and company, but I don't want to get too attached right now."

"I want to have time to study and get good grades, but I also want to have a job with some money coming in."

Using the Assertive Message Format   Before you try to deliver messages by using the clear message format, there are a few points to remember.

1. **The elements may be delivered in mixed order**. As the previous examples show, it's sometimes best to begin by stating your feelings. At other times you can start by sharing your intentions or interpretations or by describing consequences.

In REAL LIFE

The Assertive Message Format

While the elements of the assertive message format don't vary, the way they sound will depend on the situation and your personal style. Here are a few examples to show how this approach can operate in real life.

You can appreciate the value of the assertive approach by imagining how different the likely outcome would be if each message had been delivered in a blaming, aggressive way … or not at all.

To a Neighbor

I had an awful scare just now *(feeling)*. I was backing out of the driveway, and Angela *(neighbor's toddler)* wandered right behind my car *(behavior)*. Thank God I saw her, but she is so small, and it would have been easy to miss her. I can't bear to think what might have happened if I hadn't seen her *(consequences for others)*. I know how hard it is to keep an eye on little kids *(interpretation)*, but I really hope you can keep her inside unless you're watching her *(intention)*.

To a Friend

I just checked my Facebook account and saw that you tagged me in your photos from the party last weekend *(behavior)*. I told you before that I'm trying to get a good job, and I'm afraid those kinds of pictures could blow my chance *(consequence for you)*. I know you like to post lots of pictures, and you probably think I'm overreacting *(interpretations)*. Anyway,

this is a big deal for me. So I need you to remember not to post any pictures that you think would embarrass me. If you aren't sure about a photo, just ask me *(intention)*.

To a Boss

I've got a favor to ask *(intention)*. Last month I told you I wanted to work extra hours, and I know you're doing me a favor by giving me more shifts *(interpretation)*. But it would really help if you could give me a couple of days' advance notice instead of telling me the night before you want me to work *(clarifies intention)*. That way I can say "yes" to the extra shifts *(consequence for boss)*. It would also cause a lot less stress for me *(feeling)*.

To an Auto Mechanic

I need to tell you that I'm pretty unhappy *(feeling)*. When I dropped the car off yesterday, you told me it would definitely be ready today by noon. Now it's 12:30 and it isn't done *(behavior)*. I'm going to be late for an important meeting *(consequence for you)*. I know you aim to please *(interpretation)*, but you have to understand that I can't bring my car to you unless I can count on it being ready when you promise *(consequence for others)*.

MindTap APPLY … the Assertive Message Format to a situation in your life online.

2. **Word the message to suit your personal style**. Instead of saying, "I interpret your behavior to mean …" you might choose to say "I think …" or "It seems to me …" or perhaps "I get the idea. …"

   In the same way, you can express your intentions by saying, "I hope you'll understand (or do) …" or perhaps, "I wish you would. …" The words that you choose should sound authentic in order to reinforce the genuineness of your statement.

3. **When appropriate, combine two elements in a single phrase**. The statement "… and ever since then I've been wanting to talk to you" expresses both a consequence and an intention. In the same way, saying "… and after you said that, I felt confused" expresses a consequence and

SKILL *Builder*

Putting Your Message Together

1. Join with two other class members. Each person in turn should share a message that he or she might want to send to another person, being sure to include behavior, interpretation, feeling, consequence, and intention statements in the message.

2. The others in the group should help the speaker by offering feedback about how the message could be made clearer if there is any question about the meaning.

3. After the speaker has composed a satisfactory message, he or she should practice actually delivering it by having another group member play the role of the intended receiver. Continue this practice until the speaker is confident that he or she can deliver the message effectively.

4. Repeat this process until each group member has had a chance to practice delivering a message.

a feeling. Whether you combine elements or state them separately, the important point is to be sure that each one is present in your statement.

4. **Take your time delivering the message**. It isn't always possible to deliver messages such as the ones here all at one time, wrapped up in neat paragraphs. It will often be necessary to repeat or restate one part before the other person understands what you're saying. As you've already read, there are many types of psychological and physical noise that make it difficult for us to understand each other. In communication, as in many other activities, patience and persistence are essential.

Now try your hand at combining all these elements in the Skill Builder "Putting Your Message Together."

Responding Nondefensively to Criticism

The world would be a happier place if everyone communicated supportively and assertively. But how can you respond nondefensively when others send aggressive messages that don't match the prescriptions outlined in this chapter? Despite your best intentions, it's difficult to be reasonable when you're being attacked. Being attacked is hard enough when the criticism is clearly unfair, but it's often even harder when the criticism is on target. Despite the accuracy of your critic, the tendency is either to counterattack aggressively with a barrage of verbal aggression or to withdraw nonassertively.

Because neither of these counterattacks is likely to resolve a dispute, we need alternative ways of behaving. There are two such ways. Despite their apparent simplicity, they have proven to be among the most valuable skills many communicators have learned.[46]

Otto Greule Jr/Getty Images Sport/Getty Images

Seek More Information

The response of seeking more information makes good sense when you realize that it's foolish to respond to a critical attack until you understand what the other person has said. Even attacks that on first consideration appear to be totally unjustified or foolish often prove to contain at least a grain of truth and sometimes much more.

Many readers object to the idea of asking for details when they are criticized. Their resistance stems from confusing the act of *listening open-mindedly* to a speaker's comments with *accepting* the comments. After you realize that you can listen to, understand, and even acknowledge the most hostile comments without necessarily accepting them, it becomes much easier to hear another person out. If you disagree with a person's criticism, you will be in a much better position to explain yourself after you understand the criticism. On the other hand, after carefully listening to the person's criticism, you might just see that it is valid, in which case you have learned some valuable information about yourself. In either case, you have everything to gain and nothing to lose by paying attention to the critic.

Of course, after one has spent years instinctively resisting criticism, learning to listen to the other person will take some practice. To make matters clearer, here are several ways in which you can seek additional information from your critics.

Ask for Specifics   Often the vague attack of a critic is virtually useless even if you sincerely want to change. Abstract attacks such as "You're being unfair" or "You never help out" can be difficult to understand. In such cases it is a good idea to request more specific information from the sender. "What do I *do* that's unfair?" is an important question to ask before you can judge whether the attack is correct. "When haven't I helped out?" you might ask before agreeing with or disagreeing with the attack.

If you have already asked for specifics and are still accused of reacting defensively, the problem may be in the *way* you ask. Your tone of voice and facial expression, posture, and other nonverbal clues can give the same words radically different connotations. For example, think of how you could use the words "Exactly what are you talking about?" to communicate either a genuine desire to know or your belief that the speaker is crazy. It's important to request specific information only when you genuinely want to learn more from the speaker because asking under any other circumstances will only make matters worse.

Guess about Specifics   On some occasions even your sincere and well-phrased requests for specific information won't meet with success. Sometimes your critics won't be able to define precisely the behavior they find offensive. At these times, you'll hear such comments as "I can't tell you exactly what's wrong with your sense of humor—all I can say is that I don't like it." At other times, your critics may know the exact behaviors they don't like, but for some reason seem to get a perverse satisfaction out of making you struggle to figure it out. At times like this, you hear such comments as, "Well, if you don't know what you did to hurt my feelings, I'm certainly not going to tell you!"

Needless to say, failing to learn the specifics of another's criticism when you genuinely want to know can be frustrating. In instances like these, you can often learn more clearly what is bothering your critic by *guessing* at the specifics of a criticism. In a sense you become both detective and suspect, the goal being to figure out exactly what "crime" you have committed. Like the technique of asking for specifics, guessing must be done with goodwill if it's to produce satisfying results. You need to convey to the critic that for both your sakes you're truly interested in finding out what is the matter. After you have communicated this intention, the emotional climate generally becomes more comfortable because, in effect, both you and the critic are seeking the same goal.

Here are some typical questions you might hear from someone guessing about the specifics of another's criticism:

"When will he be able to sit up and take criticism?"

"So you object to the language I used in writing the paper. Was my language too formal?"

"Okay, I understand that you think the outfit looks funny. What's so bad? Is it the color? Does it have something to do with the fit? The fabric?"

"When you say that I'm not doing my share around the house, do you mean that I haven't been helping enough with the cleaning?"

Paraphrase the Speaker's Ideas Another strategy is to draw out confused or reluctant speakers by paraphrasing their thoughts and feelings and using the active listening skills described in Chapter 8. Paraphrasing is especially good in helping others solve their problems. Because people generally criticize you because your behavior creates some problem for them, the strategy is especially appropriate at such times.

One advantage of paraphrasing is that you don't have to guess about the specifics of your behavior that might be offensive. By clarifying or amplifying what you understand critics to be saying, you'll learn more about their objections. A brief dialogue between a disgruntled customer and an especially talented store manager using paraphrasing might sound like the following.

Customer: The way you people run this store is disgusting! I just want to tell you that I'll never shop here again.

Manager: (*Reflecting the customer's feeling*) It seems that you're quite upset. Can you tell me your problem?

Customer: It isn't *my* problem; it's the problem your salespeople have. They seem to think it's a great inconvenience to help a customer find anything around here.

Manager: So you didn't get enough help locating the items you were looking for, is that it?

Customer: Help? I spent twenty minutes looking around in here before I even talked to a clerk. All I can say is that it's a hell of a way to run a store.

Manager: So what you're saying is that the clerks seemed to be ignoring the customers?

Customer:	No. They were all busy with other people. It just seems to me that you ought to have enough help around to handle the crowds that come in at this hour.
Manager:	I understand now. What frustrated you most was the fact that we didn't have enough staff to serve you promptly.
Customer:	That's right. I have no complaint with the service I get after I'm waited on, and I've always thought you had a good selection here. It's just that I'm too busy to wait so long for help.
Manager:	Well, I'm glad you brought this to my attention. We certainly don't want loyal customers going away mad. I'll try to see that it doesn't happen again.

This conversation illustrates two advantages of paraphrasing. First, the critic often reduces the intensity of the attack after he or she realizes that the complaint is being heard. As soon as the manager genuinely demonstrated interest in the customer's plight, the customer began to feel better and was able to leave the store relatively calm. Of course, this sort of reflective listening won't always mollify your critic, but even when it doesn't, there's still another benefit that makes the strategy worthwhile. In the sample conversation, for instance, the manager learned some valuable information by taking time to understand the customer. The manager discovered that there were certain times when the number of employees was insufficient to help the crowd of shoppers and also that the delays at these times seriously annoyed at least some shoppers, thus threatening a loss in business. This knowledge is certainly important, and by reacting defensively to the customer's complaint, the manager would not have learned from it.

Ask What the Critic Wants Sometimes your critic's demand will be obvious:

"Turn down that music!"

"I wish you'd remember to tell me about phone messages."

"Would you clean up your dirty dishes now?"

At other times, however, you'll need to do some investigating to find out what the critic wants from you:

Abel:	I can't believe you invited all those people over without asking me first!
Brenda:	Are you saying you want me to cancel the party?
Abel:	No, I just wish you'd ask me before you make plans.
Chen:	You're so critical! It sounds like you don't like anything about this paper.
Deven:	But you asked for my opinion. What do you expect me to do when you ask?
Chen:	I want to know what's wrong, but I don't just want to hear criticisms. If you think there's anything good about my work, I wish you'd tell me that, too.

This last example illustrates the importance of accompanying your questions with the right nonverbal behavior. It's easy to imagine two ways in which Deven could have nonverbally supported her response, "What do you expect me to do when you ask?" One would show a genuine desire to clarify what Chen wanted, whereas the other would have been clearly hostile and defensive. As with all the styles in this section, your responses to criticism have to be sincere to work.

Ask about the Consequences of Your Behavior As a rule, people criticize your behavior only when some need of theirs is not being met. One way to respond to this kind of criticism is to find out exactly what troublesome consequences your behavior has for them. You'll often find that behaviors that seem perfectly legitimate to you cause some difficulty for your critic. After you have understood this, criticisms that previously sounded foolish take on a new meaning.

Neighbor A: You say that I ought to have my cat neutered. Why is that important to you?

Neighbor B: Because at night he picks fights with my cat, and I'm tired of paying the vet's bills.

Worker A: Why do you care whether I'm late to work?

Worker B: Because when the boss asks, I feel obligated to make up some story so you won't get in trouble, and I don't like to lie.

Husband: Why does it bother you when I lose money at poker? You know I never gamble more than I can afford.

Wife: It's not the cash itself. It's that when you lose, you're in a grumpy mood for two or three days, and that's no fun for me.

Ask What Else Is Wrong It might seem crazy to invite more criticism, but sometimes asking about other complaints can uncover the real problem:

Raul: Are you mad at me?

Tina: No. Why are you asking?

Raul: Because the whole time we were at the picnic you hardly spent any time talking to me. In fact, it seemed like whenever I came over to where you were, you went off somewhere else.

Tina: Is anything else wrong?

Raul: Well, I've been wondering lately if you're tired of me.

This example shows that asking if anything else bothers your critic isn't just an exercise in masochism. If you can keep your defensiveness in check, probing further can lead the conversation to issues that are the source of the critic's real dissatisfaction.

Sometimes soliciting more information from a critic isn't enough. What do you do, for instance, when you fully understand the other person's criticism and still feel a defensive response on the tip of your tongue? You know that if you try to defend yourself, you'll wind up in an argument. On the other hand, you simply can't accept what the other person is saying about you. The solution to such a dilemma is outrageously simple and is discussed in the following section.

Agree with the Critic

But, you protest, how can you honestly agree with criticisms that you don't believe are true? The following will answer this question by showing that in virtually every situation you can honestly accept the other person's point of view while still maintaining your own position. To see how this can be so, you need to realize that there are two different types of agreement you can use in almost any situation.

Agree with the Facts This is the easiest type of agreement to understand, though not always to practice. Research suggests that it is also highly effective in restoring a damaged reputation with a critic.[47] You agree with your critic when the accusation is factually correct:

"You're right, I am angry."

"I suppose I *was* being defensive."

"Now that you mention it, I did get pretty sarcastic."

Agreeing with the facts seems sensible when you realize that certain facts are indisputable. If you agree to be somewhere at four o'clock and don't show up until five o'clock, you are tardy, no matter how good your explanation for tardiness. If you've broken a borrowed object, run out of gas, or failed to finish

ETHICAL *Challenge*

Nonviolence: A Legacy of Principled Effectiveness

Among the most familiar and challenging biblical injunctions is Christ's mandate, "If someone strikes you on one cheek, turn to him the other. …"

The notion of meeting aggression with nonviolence is an ancient one. The Taoist doctrine of *wu-wei*, promulgated more than 2,400 years ago in China, advocates nonaction in the face of an attack. In ancient India, the principle of *ahimsa*—nonharming—was shared by Buddhists, Jains, and many Hindus. In the West, some Greek stoics advocated nonaction in the face of threats.

Pacifism has a moral foundation, but by the nineteenth century it was used as a potent strategy for achieving political goals. In the United States, abolitionist William Lloyd Garrison advocated the use of nonviolence to protest slavery. On both sides of the Atlantic, the suffragette movement used nonviolent resistance as a tool to secure rights for women. In

czarist Russia, Count Leo Tolstoy led a pacifist movement rejecting war and advocating civil disobedience as a tool for inhibiting violence.

In the twentieth century, nonviolence proved to be a powerful tool for political change. Mahatma Gandhi was demonstrably the most successful practitioner of this tool, first in South Africa and later in India, where his approach of *satyagraha* (truth-force) played a decisive role in the 1947 withdrawal of imperial Britain from India. In the 1950s and 1960s, Martin Luther King, Jr., and his followers used nonviolence to demonstrate against the evils of racial segregation, contributing to the passage of groundbreaking civil rights laws.

The effectiveness of nonviolence in achieving social change can also be effective in interpersonal situations. Nonconfrontational strategies provide communicators with an approach that is both principled and pragmatic.

SKILL *Builder*

Coping with Criticism

MindTap° **PRACTICE ...** coping with criticism by answering the following questions, either here or online.

Take turns practicing nondefensive responses with a partner:

1. Choose one of the following criticisms that feels "familiar" to you. Give your partner some examples of how they might direct this criticism at you as part of a larger story.

   a. You're so selfish sometimes. You think only of yourself.

   b. Don't be so touchy!

   c. You say you understand me, but you don't really.

   d. I wish you'd do your share around here.

   e. You're so critical!

2. As your partner criticizes you, answer with the appropriate response from this section. As you do so, try to adopt an attitude of genuinely wanting to understand the criticism and finding parts with which you can sincerely agree.

3. Ask your partner to evaluate your response. Does it follow the forms described in this section? Does it sound sincere?

4. Replay the same scene, trying to improve your response.

---

a job you started, there's no point in denying it. In the same way, if you're honest, you may have to agree with many interpretations of your behavior even when they're not flattering. You do get angry, act foolishly, fail to listen, and behave inconsiderately. After you rid yourself of the myth of perfection, it's much easier to acknowledge these truths.

If many criticisms aimed at you are accurate, why is it so difficult to accept them without being defensive? The answer to this question lies in a confusion between agreeing with the *facts* and accepting the *judgment* that so often accompanies them. Most critics don't merely describe the action that offends them; they also evaluate it, and it's this evaluation that we resist:

"It's silly to be angry."

"You have no reason for being defensive."

"You were wrong to be so sarcastic."

It's evaluations like these that we resent. By realizing that you can agree with—and even learn from—the descriptive part of many criticisms and still not accept the accompanying evaluations, you'll often have a response that is both honest and nondefensive.

Of course, to reduce defensiveness, your agreements with the facts must be honest ones admitted without malice. It's humiliating to accept descriptions that aren't accurate, and manipulatively pretending to accept these leads only to trouble. You can imagine how unproductive the conversation given earlier would have been if the store manager had spoken the same words in a

In REAL LIFE

Responding Nondefensively to Criticism

Defending yourself—even when you're right—isn't always the best approach. This dialogue shows the importance of using self-control and thinking before responding when you are being criticized. The employee realizes that arguing won't change her boss's mind, so she decides to reply as honestly as she can without becoming defensive.

© Jason Harris/Cengage Learning

Boss: How'd things go while I was out?

Employee: Pretty well, except for one thing. Mr. Macintosh—he said you knew him—came in and wanted to buy about $200 worth of stuff. He wanted me to charge him wholesale, and I asked him for his tax resale number, just like you told me. He said he didn't have it, so I told him he'd have to pay retail. He got pretty mad.

Boss: He's a good customer. I hope you gave him the discount.

Employee: *(Beginning to sound defensive)* Well, I didn't. You told me last week that the law said we had to charge full price and sales tax unless the customer had a resale number.

Boss: Oh, my gosh! Didn't Macintosh tell you he had a number?

Employee: *(Becoming more defensive)* He did, but he didn't have it with him. I didn't want to get you mad at me for breaking the law.

Boss: *(Barely concealing her exasperation)* Well, customers don't always have their resale numbers memorized. Macintosh has been coming here for years, and we just fill in his number on the records later.

Employee: *(Deciding to respond nondefensively instead of getting into an argument that she knows she can't win)* I can see why it looks like I gave Mr. Macintosh a hard time. You don't ask him for the number, and I insisted on having it. *(Agrees with the boss's perception)*

Boss: Yes! There's a lot of competition in this business, and we have to keep our customers happy—especially the good ones—or we'll lose them. Macintosh drives across town to do business with us. There are places right near him. If we jerk him around, he'll go there, and we'll lose a good customer.

Employee: That's true. *(Agrees with the fact that it is important to keep customers happy)* And I want to know how to treat customers right. But I'm confused about how to handle people who want a discount and

sarcastic tone. Agree with the facts only when you can do so sincerely. Though this won't always be possible, you'll be surprised at how often you can use this simple response.

Agree with the Critic's Perception Agreeing with your critics may be fine when you acknowledge that the criticisms are justified, but how can you agree when they seem to be completely unjustified? You've listened carefully and asked questions to make sure you understand the criticisms, but the more you listen,

don't have resale numbers. What should I do? *(Asks what the boss wants)*

Boss: Well, you need to be a little flexible with good customers.

Employee: How should I do that? *(Asks for specifics)*

Boss: Well, it's OK to trust people who are regulars.

Employee: So I don't need to ask regular customers for their resale numbers. I should look them up later? *(Paraphrases to clarify boss's ambiguous directions to "trust" regular customers)*

Boss: That's right. You've got to use your head in business!

Employee: *(Ignores the indirect accusation about not "using her head," recognizing that there's no point in defending herself)* OK, so when regular customers come in, I won't even ask them for their resale numbers … right? *(Paraphrases again to be sure she has the message correct; the employee has no desire to get criticized again about this matter)*

Boss: No, go ahead and ask for the number. If they have it, we won't have to look it up later. But if they don't have the number, just say OK and give them the discount.

Employee: Got it. I only have one question: How can I know who the regular customers are? Should I take their word for it? *(Asks for specifics)*

Boss: Well, you'll get to know most of them after you've been here awhile. But it's OK to trust them until

then. If they say they're regulars, just take their word for it. You've got to trust people sometimes, you know!

Employee: *(Ignores the fact that the boss originally told her not to trust people but rather to insist on getting their number; decides instead to agree with the boss)* I can see how important it is to trust good customers.

Boss: Right.

Employee: Thanks for clearing up how to handle the resale numbers. Is there anything else I ought to know so things will run smoothly when you're not in the store? *(Asks if anything else is wrong)*

Boss: I don't think so. *(Patronizingly)* Don't get discouraged; you'll catch on. It took me twenty years to build this business. Stick with it, and some day you could be running a place like this.

Employee: *(Trying to agree with her boss without sounding sarcastic)* That would be great.

The employee's refusal to act defensively turned what might have been a scolding into a discussion about how to handle a business challenge in the future. The employee might not like the boss's patronizing attitude and contradictory directions, but her communication skill kept the communication climate positive—probably the best possible outcome for this situation.

MindTap **APPLY …** this situation to your life by answering questions online.

the more positive you are that the critics are totally out of line. Even in these cases there is a way of agreeing—this time not with the critics' conclusions but with their right to see things their way.

A: I don't believe that you've been all the places you were just describing. You're probably just making all this up to impress us.

B: Well, I can see how you might think that. I've known people who lie to get approval.

C: I want to let you know right from the start that I was against hiring you for the job. I think you got it because you're a woman.

D: I can understand why you'd believe that with all the antidiscrimination laws on the books. I hope that after I've been here for awhile, you'll change your mind.

E: I don't think you're being totally honest about your reason for wanting to stay home. You say it's because you have a headache, but I think you're avoiding Mary.

F: I can see why that would make sense to you because Mary and I got into an argument the last time we were together. All I can say is that I do have a headache.

One key to feeling comfortable with acknowledging accurate criticism is to understand that *agreeing* with a critic doesn't necessarily oblige you to *apologize*. Sometimes you aren't responsible for the behavior that your critic finds objectionable, in which case an explanation might be more appropriate than an apology:

"I know I'm late. There was an accident downtown, and the streets are jammed." *(Spoken in an explanatory, nondefensive tone)*

In other cases, your behavior might be understandable, if not perfect. When this happens, you can acknowledge the validity of the criticism without apologizing:

"You're right. I *did* lose my temper. I've had to remind you three or four times, and I guess I finally used up all my patience." *(Again, delivered as an explanation, not a defense or counterattack)*

In still other cases, you can acknowledge your critic's right to see things differently than you without backing off from your position.

"I can understand why you think I'm overreacting. I know this doesn't seem as important to you as it does to me. I hope you can understand why I think this is such a big deal."

Apologizing is fine if you can do so sincerely, but you will be able to agree with critics more often if you understand that doing so doesn't require you to grovel.

Some critics don't seem to deserve the kinds of respectful responses outlined here. They seem more interested in attacking you than explaining themselves. Before you counterattack these hostile critics, ask yourself whether a defensive response will be worth the consequences.

SUMMARY

Every relationship has a communication climate. Positive climates are charac-terized by confirming messages, which make it clear that the parties value one another. Negative climates are usually disconfirming. In one way or another, messages in disconfirming relationships convey indifference or hostility. Dis-agreeing messages have some combination of confirmation and disconfirma-tion. Communication climates develop early in a relationship from both verbal and nonverbal messages. After they are created, reciprocal messages create either positive or negative spirals in which the frequency and intensity of either positive or negative messages are likely to grow.

Defensiveness hinders effective communication. Most defensiveness occurs when people try to protect key parts of a presenting self-image that they believe is under attack. Using the supportive behaviors defined by Jack Gibb when expressing potentially threatening messages can reduce the likelihood of triggering defensive reactions in others. In addition, we can share our thoughts and feelings with others in face-saving ways by using the assertive message format. A complete, clear message describes the behavior in question, at least one interpretation, the speaker's feelings, the consequences of the situation, and the speaker's intentions in making the statement.

When faced with criticism by others, it is possible to respond nondefen-sively by attempting to understand the criticism and by agreeing with either the facts or the critic's perception.

KEY TERMS

aggressiveness
ambiguous response
argumentativeness
assertive message format
certainty
communication climate
complaining
confirming communication
consequence statement
controlling communication
de-escalatory conflict spiral
defensiveness
description
disagreeing messages
disconfirming communication
empathy
equality
escalatory conflict spiral
evaluation

face-threatening act
feeling statement
Gibb categories
impersonal response
impervious response
incongruous response
intention statement
interpretation statement
interrupting response
irrelevant response
neutrality
problem orientation
provisionalism
spiral
spontaneity
strategy
superiority
tangential response

C H A P T E R   E L E V E N

Improving Communication Climates

OUTLINE

Use this outline to take notes as you read the chapter in the text and/or as your instructor lectures in class.

I. COMMUNICATION CLIMATE AND CONFIRM-ING MESSAGES

  A. Communication Climate Definition

    1. How People Feel About Each Other

    2. How People Treat Each Other

  B. Levels of Message Confirmation

    1. Confirming Communication

      a. Recognition

      b. Acknowledgment

      c. Endorsement

    2. Disconfirming Communication

      a. Impervious Responses

      b. Interrupting

      c. Irrelevant Responses

      d. Tangential Responses

      e. Impersonal Responses

      f. Ambiguous Responses

      g. Incongruous Responses

    3. Disagreeing Messages

      a. Aggressiveness

      b. Complaining

      c. Argumentativeness

    4. Confirming Messages

      a. Recognition

      b. Acknowledgment

      c. Endorsement

C. How Communication Climates Develop

    1. Escalatory Conflict Spirals

    2. De-escalatory Conflict Spirals

II. DEFENSIVENESS: CAUSES AND REMEDIES

A. Face-Threatening Acts

B. Preventing Defensiveness in Others

    1. Evaluation versus Description

    2. Control versus Problem Orientation

    3. Strategy versus Spontaneity

    4. Neutrality versus Empathy

    5. Superiority versus Equality

    6. Certainty versus Provisionalism

III. SAVING FACE: THE ASSERTIVE MESSAGE FORMAT

A. Behavior

B. Interpretation

    1. Based on Experience, Assumptions

    2. Subjective

C. Feeling

D. Consequence

    1. What Happens to You, the Speaker

    2. What Happens to the Person You're Addressing

    3. What Happens to Others

E. Intention

    1. Where You Stand on an Issue

    2. Requests of Others

    3. How You Plan to Act in the Future

F. Using the Assertive Message Format

    1. Order May Vary

    2. Use Personal Style

    3. Combine Elements

    4. Take Your Time

Class _____   Name _____

G. Responding Nondefensively to Criticism   _____
   1. Seek More Information
   2. Ask for Specifics   _____
   3. Guess about Specifics
   4. Paraphrase the Speaker's Ideas
   5. Ask What the Critic Wants   _____
   6. Ask about the Consequences
   7. Ask if Anything Else Is Wrong   _____
H. Agree with the Critic
   1. Agree with the Facts   _____
   2. Agree with the Critic's Perception
   3. Agreeing versus Apologizing   _____

KEY TERMS

acknowledgment
aggressiveness
ambiguous response
argumentativeness
assertive message format
certainty
communication climate
complaining
confirming communication
consequence statement
controlling communication
de-escalatory conflict spiral
defensiveness
description

disagreeing messages
disconfirming communication
empathy
endorsement
equality
escalatory conflict spiral
evaluation
face-threatening act
feeling statement
Gibb categories
impersonal response
impervious response
incongruous response
intention statement

interpretation statement
interrupting response
irrelevant response
neutrality
problem orientation
provisionalism
recognition
spiral
spontaneity
strategy
superiority
tangential response

ACTIVITIES

11.1 UNDERSTANDING DEFENSIVE RESPONSES

LEARNING OBJECTIVES

- Identify confirming, disagreeing, and disconfirming messages and patterns in your own important relationships, and describe their consequences.
- Describe how the messages you identified in the previous objective the self (face) of the communicators involved.
- Assess the probable consequences of your defense responses.

INSTRUCTIONS

1. Identify the person or people who would be most likely to deliver each of the following critical messages to you. If you are unlikely to hear one or more of the following messages, substitute a defensiveness-arousing topic of your own.

2. For each situation, describe
   a. the person likely to deliver the message.
   b. the typical content of the message.
   c. the general type of response(s) you make: attacking, distorting, or avoiding.
   d. your typical verbal response(s).
   e. your typical nonverbal response(s).
   f. the part of your presenting self being defended.
   g. the probable consequences of these response(s).

EXAMPLE

A negative comment about your use of time.

Person likely to deliver this message: *my parents*
Typical content of the message: *wasting my time watching TV instead of studying*
General type(s) of response: *attacking, distorting*
Your typical verbal response(s): *"Get off my back! I work hard! I need time to relax." "I'll study later; I've got plenty of time."*
Your typical nonverbal response(s): *harsh tone of voice, sullen silence for an hour or two*
Part of presenting self being defended: *good student, not lazy*

Probable consequences of your response(s): *uncomfortable silence, more criticism from parents in the future*

1. Negative comment about your managing money.

    Person likely to deliver this message _____

    Typical content of the message _____

    _____

    General type(s) of response _____

    Your typical verbal response(s) _____

    _____

    Your typical nonverbal response(s) _____

    _____

    Part(s) of presenting self being defended _____

    Probable consequences of your response(s) _____

    _____

2. Criticism about your choice of friends.

    Person likely to deliver this message _____

    Typical content of the message _____

    _____

    General type(s) of response _____

    Your typical verbal response(s) _____

    _____

    Your typical nonverbal response(s) _____

    _____

Class _____   Name _____

    Part(s) of presenting self being defended _____

    Probable consequences of your response(s) _____

    _____

    _____

3. Criticism of a job you've just completed.

    Person likely to deliver this message _____

    Typical content of the message _____

    _____

    General type(s) of response _____

    Your typical verbal response(s) _____

    _____

    Your typical nonverbal response(s) _____

    _____

    Part(s) of presenting self being defended _____

    Probable consequences of your response(s) _____

    _____

    _____

4. Criticism of your schoolwork.

    Person likely to deliver this message _____

    Typical content of the message _____

    _____

    General type(s) of response _____

Your typical verbal response(s) _____

_____

Your typical nonverbal response(s) _____

_____

Part(s) of presenting self being defended _____

Probable consequences of your response(s) _____

_____

_____

5. Criticism of your politics, political action, or lack of political involvement.

Person likely to deliver this message _____

Typical content of the message _____

_____

General type(s) of response _____

Your typical verbal response(s) _____

_____

Your typical nonverbal response(s) _____

_____

Part(s) of presenting self being defended _____

Probable consequences of your response(s) _____

_____

_____

6. A negative comment about your exercise (or lack of it).

Person likely to deliver this message _____

Typical content of the message _____

_____

General type(s) of response _____

Your typical verbal response(s) _____

_____

Your typical nonverbal response(s) _____

_____

Part(s) of presenting self being defended _____

Probable consequences of your response(s) _____

_____

_____

11.2 DEFENSIVE AND SUPPORTIVE LANGUAGE

LEARNING OBJECTIVES

- Use Gibb's categories and the assertive message format to create messages that are likely to build supportive rather than defensive communication climates.

- Use the guidelines in the text to present critical messages in a constructive manner.

- Create appropriate nondefensive responses to real or hypothetical criticisms.

INSTRUCTIONS

1. For each of the situations below, write one statement likely to arouse defensiveness and one statement likely to promote a support climate.
2. Label the Gibb category of language that each statement represents (evaluation, description, control, problem-orientation, strategy, spontaneity, neutrality, empathy, superiority, equality, certainty, or provisionalism).

EXAMPLE

A neighbor's late-night stereo music playing is disrupting your sleep.
Defense-arousing statement: *Why don't you show a little consideration and turn that damn thing down? If I hear any more noise I'm going to call the police!*
Type(s) of defensive language: *evaluation, control*
Supportive statement: *When I hear your stereo music late at night I can't sleep, which leaves me more and more tired. I'd like to figure out some way you can listen and I can sleep.*
Type(s) of supportive language: *description, problem orientation*

1. You're an adult child who moves back in with your parents. They say they expect you to follow the "rules of the house."

   Defense-arousing statement _____

   _____

   Type(s) of defensive language _____

   Supportive statement_____

   _____

   Type(s) of supportive language _____

2. Your roommate tells you you're trying to be "somebody you're not."

Defense-arousing statement _____

_____

Type(s) of defensive language _____

Supportive statement _____

_____

Type(s) of supportive language _____

3. A friend asks you what you see in your new romantic partner.

Defense-arousing statement _____

_____

Type(s) of defensive language _____

Supportive statement _____

_____

Type(s) of supportive language _____

4. Your boss says, "You call that finished?"

Defense-arousing statement _____

_____

Type(s) of defensive language _____

Supportive statement _____

_____

Type(s) of supportive language _____

5. Your friend buys the same thing you did after you bragged about the deal you got.

    Defense-arousing statement _____

    _____

    Type(s) of defensive language _____

    Supportive statement _____

    _____

    Type(s) of supportive language _____

6. On many occasions a friend drops by your place without calling first. Since you often have other plans, this behavior puts you in an uncomfortable position.

    Defense-arousing statement _____

    _____

    Type(s) of defensive language _____

    Supportive statement _____

    _____

    Type(s) of supportive language _____

7. Your roommate says, "You left the lights on *again*."

    Defense-arousing statement _____

    _____

    Type(s) of defensive language _____

    Supportive statement _____

    _____

    Type(s) of supportive language _____

8. Your parent praises your sibling for something without mentioning you.

   Defense-arousing statement _____

   _____

   Type(s) of defensive language _____

   Supportive statement _____

   _____

   Type(s) of supportive language _____

   _____

9. Your situation: _____

   Defense-arousing statement _____

   _____

   Type(s) of defensive language _____

   Supportive statement _____

   _____

   Type(s) of supportive language _____

11.3 WRITING ASSERTIVE MESSAGES

LEARNING OBJECTIVES

- Use the assertive message guidelines in the text to present critical messages in a constructive manner.
- Demonstrate a knowledge of the components of assertive messages.

INSTRUCTIONS

Imagine a situation in which you might have said each of the statements below. Rewrite the messages in the assertive message format, being sure to include each of the five elements described in your text.

EXAMPLE

Unclear message: "It's awful when you can't trust a friend."
Assertive message:
Lena, when I gave you the keys to my house so you could borrow those clothes, I
came back and found the house unlocked.   (behavior)
I figured you'd know to lock up again when you left.   (interpretation)
I was worried and scared.   (feeling)
I thought there was a break-in and was nervous about going in.   (consequence)
I want to know if you left the house unlocked and let you know how upset I am. (intention)

1. "Just get off my case; you're not my warden."

   _____ (behavior)

   _____ (interpretation)

   _____ (feeling)

   _____ (consequence)

   _____ (intention)

2. "I wish you'd pay more attention to me."

   _____ (behavior)

   _____ (interpretation)

   _____ (feeling)

   _____ (consequence)

   _____ (intention)

3. "You've sure been thoughtful lately."

_____ (behavior)

_____ (interpretation)

_____ (feeling)

_____ (consequence)

_____ (intention)

4. "You're the greatest!"

_____ (behavior)

_____ (interpretation)

_____ (feeling)

_____ (consequence)

_____ (intention)

5. "Matt, you're such a slob!"

_____ (behavior)

_____ (interpretation)

_____ (feeling)

_____ (consequence)

_____ (intention)

6. "Let's just forget it; forget I ever asked for a favor."

_____ (behavior)

_____ (interpretation)

_____ (feeling)

_____ (consequence)

_____ (intention)

Class _____   Name _____

Now list three significant messages that you could send to important people in your life: one complaint, one request, and one expression of appreciation. Write them in assertive message format.

7. _____ (behavior)

   _____ (interpretation)

   _____ (feeling)

   _____ (consequence)

   _____ (intention)

8. _____ (behavior)

   _____ (interpretation)

   _____ (feeling)

   _____ (consequence)

   _____ (intention)

9. _____ (behavior)

   _____ (interpretation)

   _____ (feeling)

   _____ (consequence)

   _____ (intention)

11.4 MEDIATED MESSAGES—CLIMATE

LEARNING OBJECTIVES

- Assess the impact of mediated communication on communication climate.
- Identify ways that mediated communication can contribute to building negative and positive communication climates.

INSTRUCTIONS

Discuss each of the questions below in your group. Prepare written answers for your instructor, or be prepared to contribute to a large group discussion, comparing your experiences with those of others in your class.

1. Describe how the use of mediated forms of communication channels (e.g., telephone, email) contributes to the communication climate (emotional tone) of your relationships.

   _____

   _____

2. Compile a list of the ways that you currently use or could begin to use mediated messages to recognize, acknowledge, and endorse others.

   _____

   _____

3. Give examples of how mediated messages have contributed to defensive spirals (negative, ineffective patterns of communication) in your relationships.

   _____

   _____

   _____

4. Give examples of how mediated messages have helped minimize defensive spirals (negative, ineffective patterns of communication) in your relationships.

   _____

   _____

   _____

5. Your text describes ways we can respond nondefensively to criticism. In which mediated contexts could you most effectively use these skills?

_____

_____

11.5 CLIMATE ANALYSIS

LEARNING OBJECTIVES

- Identify defensive messages and patterns in your own important relationships, and describe their consequences.

- Demonstrate understanding of Gibb's theory as it apply to a particular situation.

- Apply "coping with criticism" strategies to a particular situation.

INSTRUCTIONS

Use the case below and the discussion questions that follow to discuss the variety of communication issues involved in effective communication. Make notes on this page, add other pages on your own, or prepare a group report/analysis based on your discussion. Add your own experiences to individualize the analysis.

CASE

Gil and Lydia are brother and sister. They love one another and feel close. Their mother often tells Gil how wonderful Lydia is to call her so often, how smart Lydia is, what a good athlete she is, and how much she enjoys Lydia bringing home her friends to visit. Mom tells Lydia how generous Gil is, how hard he works, how many interesting things he does, and how well he manages money. The overall climate of the relationship between Gil and Lydia and their mother is good, but both Gil and Lydia find themselves getting defensive when their mom spends so much time praising the other.

1. Use aspects of Gibb's theory to explain why Gil and Lydia get defensive about these positive statements about the other.

   _____

   _____

   _____

   _____

2. Discuss situations similar to the one above in which people get defensive about statements that, on the surface, are positive and supportive.

   _____

   _____

   _____

   _____

3. Write coping with criticism responses for Gil or Lydia to use the next time their mother praises their sibling.

_____

_____

_____

4. How could Gil and Lydia's mother change the comments she makes about each sibling to reduce defensive reactions?

_____

_____

_____

11.6 APPLYING THE "SANDWICH METHOD"

LEARNING OBJECTIVES

- Use Gibb's categories and the assertive message format to create messages that are likely to build supportive rather than defensive communication climates.
- Use the guidelines in the text to present critical messages in a constructive manner.
- Create appropriate nondefensive responses to real or hypothetical criticisms.

INSTRUCTIONS

Read the first three scenarios below and apply the "sandwich method" to turn a possible defensive situation into a nondefensive one. Then describe two situations where you can apply the sandwich method in your own life and describe how you will apply this method.

1. You are working on a project for one of your classes with a partner. While your partner is friendly and contributes good ideas to the project, she always arrives late to your project meetings and spends the first 30 minutes of your work time talking about her new boyfriend. You wish the two of you could get to work sooner so you could complete the project and have more free time. Use the sandwich method to offer constructive criticism to your partner.

   Positive Comment:

   _____

   _____

   Concern:

   _____

   _____

   Positive Comment:

   _____

   _____

2. Your new college roommate constantly returns to your dorm late at night and makes a lot of noise when saying good night to her friends. This noise wakes you up at night and you start to struggle to get up for your 7:30 a.m. class. Use the sandwich method to offer constructive criticism to your roommate.

Positive Comment:

_____

_____

Concern:

_____

_____

Positive Comment:

_____

_____

3. One of your coworkers has a tendency to tell inappropriate jokes that you find offensive. Use the sandwich method to offer your coworker some constructive criticism.

Positive Comment:

_____

_____

Concern:

_____

_____

Positive Comment:

_____

_____

Now apply the sandwich method to a situation in your own life.

Situation 1 Description _____

Class _____   Name _____

Positive Comment:

_____

_____

Concern:

_____

_____

Positive Comment:

_____

_____

Situation 2 Description _____

Positive Comment:

_____

_____

Concern:

_____

_____

Positive Comment:

_____

STUDY GUIDE

CHECK YOUR UNDERSTANDING

TRUE/FALSE

Mark the statements below as true or false. Correct false statements on the lines below to create true statements.

_____ 1. The tone or climate of a relationship is shaped by the way people feel about and treat each other.

_____

_____ 2. Disconfirming communication messages convey a lack of value from one person to another.

_____

_____ 3. The occasional interrupting response is just as damaging to a relationship as repeated interruptions.

_____

_____ 4. Both positive and negative communication spirals have their limits; they rarely go on indefinitely.

_____

_____ 5. In a marriage, ignoring or "stone walling" a partner is a strong predictor of divorce.

_____

_____ 6. Because cyberbullying doesn't occur face to face, it isn't considered aggressive.

_____

_____ 7. Using Jack Gibb's supportive behaviors will eliminate defensiveness in your receivers.

_____

_____ 8. Constructive criticism can increase odds of successful confrontation, and rarely requires future acknowledgment.

_____

_____   9. The assertive message format works for a variety of messages: hopes, problems, complaints, and appreciations.

_____

_____   10. Descriptive messages use "you" language to clearly describe what someone else has done.

_____

_____   11. Controlling communication occurs when a sender seems to be imposing a solution on the receiver with little regard for the receiver's needs or interests.

_____

_____   12. Failure to return an email is one example of lack of recognition.

_____

COMPLETION

The Gibb categories of defensive and supportive behavior are six sets of contrasting styles of verbal and nonverbal behavior. Each set describes a communication style that is likely to arouse defensiveness and a contrasting style that is likely to prevent or reduce it. Fill in the blanks with the Gibb behavior described chosen from the list below.

evaluation	description	control	problem orientation	strategy
spontaneity	neutrality	empathy	superiority	equality
certainty	provisionalism			

1. _____ is the attitude behind messages that dogmatically imply that the speaker's position is correct and that the other person's ideas are not worth considering.

2. _____ is communication behavior involving messages that describe the speaker's position without evaluating others.

3. _____ is a supportive style of communication in which the communicators focus on working together to solve their problems instead of trying to impose their own solutions on one another.

4. _____ is a defense-arousing style of communication in which the sender tries to manipulate or deceive a receiver.

5. _____ is a supportive style of communication in which the sender expresses a willingness to consider the other person's position.

6. _____ is a defense-arousing style of communication in which the sender states or implies that the receiver is not worthy of respect.

7. _____ is a supportive communication behavior in which the sender expresses a message openly and honestly without any attempt to manipulate the receiver.

8. _____ is a defense-arousing behavior in which the sender expresses indifference toward a receiver.

9. _____ is a defense-arousing message in which the sender tries to impose some sort of outcome on the receiver.

10. _____ is a type of supportive communication that suggests that the sender regards the receiver as worthy of respect.

11. _____ is a defense-arousing message in which the sender passes some type of judgment on the receiver.

12. _____ is a type of supportive communication in which the sender accepts the other's feelings as valid and avoids sounding indifferent.

MULTIPLE CHOICE

Choose the letter of the defensive or supportive category that is best illustrated by each of the situations below.

a. evaluation
b. control
c. strategy
d. neutrality
e. superiority
f. certainty

g. description
h. problem orientation
i. spontaneity
j. empathy
k. equality
l. provisionalism

_____ 1. Gerry insists he has all the facts and needs to hear no more information.

_____ 2. Richard has a strong opinion but will listen to another position.

_____ 3. Lina kept looking at the clock as she was listening to Nan, so Nan thought Lina didn't consider her comments very important.

_____ 4. "I know Janice doesn't agree with me," Mary said, "but she knows how strongly I feel about this, and I think she understands my position."

_____ 5. "Even though my professor has a Ph.D.," Rosa pointed out, "she doesn't act like she's the only one who knows something; she is really interested in me as a person."

_____ 6. "When I found out that Bob had tricked me into thinking his proposal was my idea so I'd support it, I was really angry."

_____ 7. "Even though we *all* wait tables here, Evanne thinks she's better than any of us—just look at the way she prances around!"

_____ 8. Clara sincerely and honestly told Georgia about her reservations concerning Georgia's planned party.

_____   9. The coworkers attempted to find a solution to the scheduling issue that would satisfy both of their needs.

_____   10. "It seems as though my father's favorite phrase is 'I know what's best for you,' and that really gripes me."

_____   11. "You drink too much."

_____   12. "I was embarrassed when you slurred your speech in front of my boss."

_____   13. "The flowers and presents are just an attempt to get me to go to bed with him."

_____   14. "She looked down her nose at me when I told her I didn't exercise regularly."

_____   15. "Well, if you need more money and I need more help around here, what could we do to make us both happy?"

Choose the letter of the type of coping with criticism that is best illustrated by each of the situations below.

a.   ask for specific details of criticism
b.   guess about specific details
c.   paraphrase to clarify criticism
d.   ask what the critic wants
e.   ask what else is wrong
f.   agree with true facts
g.   agree with critic's right to perceive differently
h.   ask about the consequences

Criticism: "You never seem to care about much."

_____   16. "Are you referring to my not going to the office party?"

_____   17. "You're right that I didn't call you back within 24 hours."

_____   18. "What do you want me to care more about?"

_____   19. "I can see why you'd be upset with me for not coming to the party because you've told me you want me to be more involved with your work's social events."

_____   20. "When I didn't come to the party, were you embarrassed or something?"

_____   21. "So not calling you back right away was a problem. Have I upset you any other way?"

_____   22. "So you're upset that I'm not visiting you every week, and you think that shows a lack of affection on my part—is that it?"

_____   23. "What do you mean?"

_____   24. "You're correct in that I couldn't visit this week because of finals."

_____   25. "Because I wasn't at the party, it reflected badly on you."

Identify which element of an assertive message is being used in each statement according to the following key:

a. behavioral description
b. interpretation
c. feeling
d. consequence
e. intention

_____   26. That's a good idea.

_____   27. I'm worried about this course.

_____   28. Jim looked angry today.

_____   29. I want to talk to you about the $20 you borrowed.

_____   30. I notice that you haven't been smiling much lately.

_____   31. I don't know whether you're serious or not.

_____   32. I'm glad you invited me.

_____   33. Ever since then I've found myself avoiding you.

_____   34. I'm sorry you didn't like my work.

_____   35. I want you to know how important this is to me.

_____   36. It looks to me like you meant to embarrass me.

_____   37. After the party at Art's, you seemed to withdraw.

_____   38. I see you're wearing my ring again.

_____   39. From now on you can count on me.

_____   40. I've never heard you say a curse word before.

_____   41. …and since then I've been sleeping at my dad's house.

_____   42. Because that occurred, they won't work overtime.

_____   43. Dave sighed and looked out the window.

_____   44. I'm excited about the possibility.

_____   45. I'll get another place to live.

CHAPTER ELEVEN STUDY GUIDE ANSWERS

TRUE/FALSE

1. T	3. F	5. T	7. F	9. T	11. T
2. T	4. T	6. F	8. F	10. F	12. T

COMPLETION

1. certainty	5. provisionalism	9. control
2. description	6. superiority	10. equality
3. problem orientation	7. spontaneity	11. evaluation
4. strategy	8. neutrality	12. empathy

MULTIPLE CHOICE

1. f	10. b	19. g	28. b	37. b
2. l	11. a	20. b	29. e	38. a
3. d	12. g	21. e	30. a	39. e
4. j	13. c	22. c	31. b	40. a
5. k	14. e	23. a	32. c	41. d
6. c	15. h	24. f	33. d	42. d
7. e	16. b	25. b	34. c	43. a
8. i	17. f	26. b	35. e	44. c
9. h	18. d	27. c	36. b	45. e

12

MANAGING INTERPERSONAL CONFLICTS

AFTER STUDYING THE TOPICS IN THIS CHAPTER, YOU SHOULD BE ABLE TO:

1. Identify the conflicts in your important relationships and how satisfied you are with the way they have been handled.

2. Describe your personal conflict styles, evaluate their effectiveness, and suggest alternatives as appropriate.

3. Identify the relational conflict styles, patterns of behavior, and conflict rituals that define a given relationship.

4. Demonstrate how you could use the win–win approach in a given conflict.

*F*or most people, conflict has about the same appeal as a trip to the dentist. A quick look at a thesaurus offers a clue about the distasteful nature of conflict. Synonyms for the term include *battle, brawl, clash, competition, discord, disharmony, duel, fight, strife, struggle, trouble*, and *violence*.

Even the metaphors we use to describe our conflicts show that we view conflict as something to be avoided.[1] We often talk about conflict as a kind of war: "He shot down my arguments." "Okay, fire away." "Don't try to defend yourself!" Other metaphors suggest that conflict is explosive: "Don't blow up!" "I needed to let off steam." "You've got a short fuse." Sometimes conflict seems like a kind of trial in which one party accuses another: "Come on, admit you're guilty." "Stop accusing me!" "Just listen to my case." Language suggesting that conflict is a mess is also common: "Let's not open this can of worms." "That's a sticky situation." "Don't make such a stink!" Even the metaphor of a game implies that one side has to defeat the other: "That was out of bounds." "You're not playing fair." "I give up; you win!"

Despite images like these, the truth is that conflict *can* be constructive. With the right set of communication skills, conflict can be less like a struggle and more like a kind of dance in which partners work together to create something that would be impossible without their cooperation. You may have to persuade the other person to become your partner rather than your adversary, and you may be clumsy at first, but with enough practice and goodwill, you can work together instead of at cross-purposes.

The attitude you bring to your conflicts can make a tremendous difference between success and failure. One study revealed that college students in close romantic relationships who believed that conflicts are destructive were most likely to neglect or quit the relationship and less likely to seek a solution than couples who had less-negative attitudes.[2] Of course, attitudes alone won't always guarantee satisfying solutions to conflicts—but the kinds of skills you will learn in this chapter can help well-intentioned partners handle their disagreements constructively.

THE NATURE OF CONFLICT

Before focusing on how to solve interpersonal problems constructively, we need to look briefly at the nature of conflict. What is it? Why is it an inevitable part of life? How can it be beneficial?

Conflict Defined

Before reading further, make a list of the interpersonal conflicts in your life. They probably involve many different people, revolve around very different subjects, and take many different forms. Some become loud, angry arguments. Others may be expressed in calm, rational discussions. Still others might simmer along most of the time with brief but bitter flare-ups.

Whatever form they may take, all interpersonal conflicts share certain characteristics. William Wilmot and Joyce Hocker provide a thorough definition when they define **conflict** as "an expressed struggle between at least two interdependent parties who perceive incompatible goals, scarce resources, and interference from the other party in achieving their goals."[3] A closer look at the key parts of this definition will help you recognize how conflict operates in your life.

Expressed Struggle A conflict can exist only when both parties are aware of a disagreement. For instance, you may be upset for months because a neighbor's loud stereo keeps you awake at night, but no conflict exists between the two of you until the neighbor learns of your problem. Of course, the expressed struggle doesn't have to be verbal. A dirty look, the silent treatment, and avoiding the other person are all ways of expressing yourself. One way or another, both parties must know that a problem exists before they're in conflict.

▲ In *The Hunger Games* trilogy, Katniss Everdeen (Jennifer Lawrence) faces conflicts with life-or-death consequences. Even when resources are scarce and goals seem incompatible, she learns that interdependence and collaboration are keys to survival. What lessons for managing interpersonal conflict can you learn from stories like these?

Perceived Incompatible Goals All conflicts look as if one party's gain would be another's loss. For instance, consider the neighbor whose stereo keeps you awake at night. Doesn't somebody have to lose? If the neighbor turns down the noise, she loses the enjoyment of hearing the music at full volume, but if the neighbor keeps the volume up, you're still awake and unhappy.

The goals in this situation really aren't completely incompatible; there are solutions that allow both parties to get what they want. For instance, you could achieve peace and quiet by closing your windows or getting the neighbor to close hers. You might use a pair of earplugs, or perhaps the neighbor could get a set of earphones, allowing the music to be played at full volume without bothering anyone. If any of these solutions prove workable, then the conflict disappears. Unfortunately, people often fail to see mutually satisfying solutions to their problems. As long as they *perceive* their goals to be mutually exclusive, a conflict exists.

Perceived Scarce Resources Conflicts also exist when people believe there isn't enough of something to go around. The most obvious example of a scarce resource is money—a cause of many conflicts. If a worker asks for a raise in pay and the boss would rather keep the money or use it to expand the business, then the two parties are in conflict.

Time is another scarce commodity. Many people struggle to meet the competing demands of school, work, family, and friends. "If there were only more hours in a day" is a common refrain, and making time for the people in your life—and for yourself—is a constant source of conflict.

Interdependence However antagonistic they might feel, the parties in conflict are usually dependent on each other. The welfare and satisfaction of one depend on the actions of another. If not, then even in the face of scarce resources and incompatible goals, there would be no need for conflict. Interdependence exists between conflicting nations, social groups, organizations, friends, and lovers. In each case, if the two parties didn't need each other to solve the problem, they would go their separate ways. One of the first steps toward resolving a conflict is to take the attitude that "we're all in this together."

Interference from the Other Party   No matter how much one person's position may differ from another's, a full-fledged conflict won't occur until the participants act in ways that prevent one another from reaching their goals. For example, you might let some friends know that you object to their driving after drinking alcohol, but the conflict won't escalate until you act in ways that prevent them from getting behind the wheel. Likewise, a parent–child dispute about what clothing and music are appropriate will blossom into a conflict when the parents try to impose their position on the child.

Conflict Is Natural

Every relationship of any depth at all has conflict.[4] No matter how close, how understanding, how compatible you and other people are, there will be times when your ideas or actions or needs or goals won't match. You like rap music, but your companion likes classical; you want to date other people, but your partner wants to keep the relationship exclusive; you think a paper that you've written is fine, but your instructor wants it changed; you like to sleep late on Sunday mornings, but your housemate likes to get up early and exercise loudly. There's no end to the number and kinds of disagreements possible.

College students who have kept diaries of their relationships report that they take part in about seven arguments per week. Most have argued with the other person before, often about the same topic.[5] In another survey, 81 percent of the respondents acknowledged that they had conflicts with friends.[6] Even the 19 percent who claimed that their friendships were conflict free used phrases such as "push and pull" and "little disagreements" to describe the tensions that inevitably occurred. Among families, conflict can be even more frequent. Researchers recorded dinner conversations for fifty-two families and found an average of 3.3 "conflict episodes" per meal.[7]

At first this might seem depressing. If problems are inevitable in even the best relationships, does this mean that you're doomed to relive the same arguments, the same hurt feelings, over and over? Fortunately, the answer to this question is a definite "no." Even though conflict is part of a meaningful relationship, you can change the way you deal with it.

Conflict Can Be Beneficial

Because it is impossible to avoid conflicts, the challenge is to handle them well when they do arise. Effective communication during conflicts can actually keep good relationships strong. People who use the constructive skills described in this chapter are more satisfied with their relationships[8] and with the outcomes of their conflicts.[9]

Perhaps the best evidence of how constructive conflict skills can benefit a relationship focuses on communication between husbands and wives. More than twenty years of research shows that couples in both happy and unhappy marriages have conflicts, but that they manage conflict in very different ways.[10] One nine-year study revealed that unhappy couples argue in ways that we have catalogued in this book as destructive.[11] They are more concerned with defending themselves than with being problem oriented; they fail to listen carefully to each other, have little or no empathy for their partners, use evaluative "you" language, and ignore each other's nonverbal relational messages.

Many satisfied couples think and communicate differently when they disagree. They view disagreements as healthy and recognize that conflicts need to be faced.[12] Although they may argue vigorously, they use skills such as perception checking to find out what the other person is thinking, and they let each other know that they understand the other side of the argument.[13] They are willing to admit their mistakes, which contributes not only to a harmonious relationship but also to solving the problem at hand.

We'll review communication skills that can make conflicts constructive and introduce still more skills that you can use to resolve the inevitable conflicts you face. Before doing so, however, we need to examine how individuals behave when faced with a dispute.

CONFLICT STYLES

Most people have default styles of handling conflict. (See Figure 12.1.) These habitual styles work sometimes, but they may not be effective in all situations. What styles do you typically use to deal with conflict? Find out by thinking about how two hypothetical characters—Paul and Lucia—manage a problem.

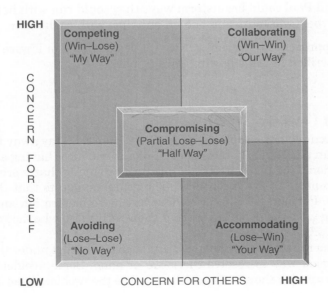

◀ FIGURE 12.1
Conflict Styles

Paul and Lucia have been running partners for more than a year. Three times every week, they spend an hour or more together working out. The two runners are equally matched, and they enjoy challenging one another to cover longer distances at a quicker pace. During their time on the road, the friends have grown quite close. Now they often talk about personal matters that they don't share with anyone else.

Recently, Lucia has started to invite some of her friends along on the runs. Paul likes Lucia's friends, but they aren't strong athletes, so the outings become a much less-satisfying workout. Also, Paul fears losing the special one-on-one time that he and Lucia have had. Paul shared his concerns with Lucia, but she dismissed them. "I don't see what the problem is," she replied. "We still get plenty of time on the road, and you said you like my friends." "But it isn't the same," replied Paul.

This situation has all the elements of a conflict: expressed struggle (their differences are in the open, and they still disagree), seemingly incompatible goals and interference (Lucia wants to run with her friends; Paul wants to run with just Lucia), apparently scarce resources (they only have so much time for running), and interdependence (they enjoy one another's company and run better together than separately).

Here are five ways Paul and Lucia could handle the matter. Each represents a particular approach to managing conflict:

- They could say "Let's just forget it" and stop running together.

- Paul could give in, sacrificing his desire for one-on-one conversations and challenging runs. Or Lucia could give in, sacrificing her other friendships to maintain her friendship with Paul.

- One or the other could issue an ultimatum: "Either we do it my way, or we stop running together."

- They could compromise, inviting friends along on some runs but excluding them on other days.

- Lucia and Paul could brainstorm ways they could run with her friends and still get their workouts and one-on-one time with each other.

These approaches represent the five styles depicted in Figure 12.1, each of which is described in the following paragraphs.

Avoiding (Lose–Lose)

Avoiding occurs when people nonassertively ignore or stay away from conflict. Avoidance can be physical (steering clear of a friend after having an argument) or conversational (changing the topic, joking, or denying that a problem exists). It can be tempting to avoid conflict, but research suggests that this approach has its costs: Partners of *self-silencers* report more frustration and discomfort when dealing with the avoiding partner than with those who face conflict more constructively.[14]

Avoidance reflects a pessimistic attitude about conflict under the belief that there is no good way to resolve the issue at hand. Some avoiders believe it's easier to put up with the status quo than to face the problem head-on and try to solve it. Other avoiders believe it's better to quit (on either the topic or the relationship) than to keep facing the same issues without hope of solution. In either case, avoiding often results in *lose–lose* outcomes in which no party gets what it wants.

In the case of Paul and Lucia, avoiding means that, rather than struggling with their disagreement, they just stop running together. Although it means they'll no longer be fighting, it also means they'll both lose a running partner and an important component of their friendship (and maybe their friendship altogether). This solution illustrates how avoiding can produce lose–lose results.

Although avoiding may keep the peace temporarily, it typically leads to unsatisfying relationships.[15] Chronic misunderstandings, resentments, and disappointments pile up and contaminate the emotional climate. For this reason, we can say that avoiders have a low concern both for their own needs and for the interests of the other person, who is also likely to suffer from unaddressed issues (see Figure 12.1).

Despite its obvious shortcomings, avoiding isn't always a bad idea.[16] You might choose to avoid certain topics or situations if the risk of speaking up is too great, such as triggering an embarrassing fight in public or even risking physical harm. You might also avoid a conflict if the relationship it involves isn't worth the effort. Even in close relationships, though, avoidance has its logic. If the issue is temporary or minor, then you might let it pass. These reasons help explain why the communication of many happily married couples is characterized by "selectively ignoring" the other person's minor flaws.[17] This doesn't mean that a key to successful relationships is avoiding *all* conflicts. Instead, it suggests that it's smart to save energy for the truly important ones.

Accommodating (Lose–Win)

Accommodating occurs when you allow others to have their way rather than asserting your own point of view. Figure 12.1 depicts accommodators as having low concern for themselves and high concern for others, which results in *lose–win*, "we'll do it your way" outcomes. In our hypothetical scenario, Paul could accommodate Lucia by letting her friends join in on their runs, even though it means less of a physical challenge and quality time with Lucia—or Lucia could accommodate Paul by running with just him.

The motivation of an accommodator plays a significant role in this style's effectiveness. If accommodation is a genuine act of kindness, generosity, or love, then chances are good that it will enhance the relationship. Most people appreciate those who "take one for the team," "treat others as they want to be treated," or "lose the battle to win the war." However, people are far less appreciative of those who habitually use this style to play the role of "martyr, bitter complainer, whiner, or saboteur."[18]

On the JOB

Picking Your Workplace Battles

Conflicts are a fact of life, even in the best job. Issues are bound to arise with your boss, coworkers, subordinates, and people outside the organization. Your career success and peace of mind will depend on when and how you deal with those conflicts—and when you choose to keep quiet.

Deciding when to speak up is the first step in managing conflicts successfully. Staying silent about important issues can damage your career and leave you feeling like a doormat. But asserting yourself too often or in the wrong way can earn you a reputation as a whiner or hothead.

Management consultants offer guidelines to help you choose when to speak up and when to let go of an issue.[a]

Consider a retreat when

- The issue isn't important to your organization or your ability to work.

- You can't offer a constructive approach to a solution.

- The issue is outside your area of responsibility.

- The others involved are much more powerful than you.

Before speaking up, be prepared to

1. Test support for your position informally with trusted colleagues.

2. Speak with the person who has the power to do something about the problem.

3. Describe the problem clearly and objectively.

4. Control your emotions during discussions.

5. Be prepared to deal with criticisms that may be directed back at you.

We should pause here to mention the important role that culture plays in perceptions of conflict styles. People from high-context, collectivist backgrounds (such as many Asian cultures) are likely to regard avoidance and accommodation as face-saving and noble ways to handle conflict.[19] In low-context, individualist cultures (such as the United States), avoidance and accommodation are often viewed less positively. For instance, think of the many unflattering terms that Americans use for people who give up or give in during conflicts ("pushover," "yes-man," "doormat," "spineless"). As you will read later in this chapter, collectivist cultures have virtuous words and phrases to describe these same traits. The point here is that all conflict styles have value in certain situations and that culture plays a significant role in determining how each style is valued.

Competing (Win–Lose)

The flip side of accommodating is **competing**. This *win–lose* approach to conflict involves high concern for self and low concern for others. As Figure 12.1 shows, competition seeks to resolve conflicts "my way." If Lucia and Paul each tried to force the other to concede, one of them might prevail, but at the other's expense.

People resort to competing when they perceive a situation as being an either–or one: Either I get what I want, or you get what you want. The most clear-cut examples of win–lose situations are certain games such as baseball or poker in which the rules require a winner and a loser. Some interpersonal issues seem to fit into this win–lose framework: two coworkers seeking a promotion to the same job, or a couple who disagree on how to spend their limited money.

There are cases when competing can enhance a relationship. One study revealed that some men and women in satisfying dating relationships use competition to enrich their interaction.[20] For example, some found satisfaction by competing in play (who's the better racquetball player?), in achievement (who gets the better job offer?), and in altruism (who's more romantic?). These satisfied couples developed a shared narrative (see Chapter 4) that defined competition as a measure of regard, quite different from conflict that signaled a lack of appreciation and respect. Of course, it's easy to see how these arrangements could backfire if one partner became a gloating winner or a sore loser. Feeling like you've been defeated can leave you wanting to get even, creating a downward competitive spiral that degrades to a *lose–lose* relationship.[21]

Power is the distinguishing characteristic in win–lose problem solving because it is necessary to defeat an opponent to get what one wants. The most obvious kind of power is physical. Some parents threaten their children with warnings such as "Stop misbehaving or I'll send you to your room." Adults who use physical power to deal with each other usually aren't so blunt, but the legal system is the implied threat: "Follow the rules or we'll lock you up."

Real or implied force isn't the only kind of power used in conflicts. People who rely on authority of many types engage in win–lose methods without ever threatening physical coercion. In most jobs, supervisors have the authority to assign working hours, job promotions, and desirable or undesirable tasks— and, of course, to fire an unsatisfactory employee. Teachers can use the power of grades to coerce students to act in desired ways. Even the usually admired democratic system of majority rule is a win–lose method of resolving conflicts. However fair it may seem, with this system one group is satisfied and the other is defeated.

The dark side of competition is that it often breeds aggression.[22] Sometimes aggression is obvious, but at other times it can be more subtle. To understand how, read on.

Direct Aggression **Direct aggression** occurs when a communicator expresses a criticism or demand that threatens the face of the person at whom it is directed. Communication researcher Dominic Infante identified several types of direct aggression: character attacks, competence attacks, physical appearance attacks, maledictions (wishing the other ill fortune), teasing, ridicule, threats, swearing, and nonverbal emblems.[23]

Direct aggression can severely affect the target. Recipients can feel embarrassed, inadequate, humiliated, hopeless, desperate, or depressed.[24] These results can lead to decreased effectiveness in personal relationships, on the job, and in families.[25] There is a significant connection between verbal aggression and physical aggression,[26] but even if the attacks never lead to blows, the psychological effects can be devastating. For example, siblings who were teased by a brother or sister report less satisfaction and trust than those whose relationships were relatively free of this sort of aggression,[27] and high school teams with aggressive coaches lose more games than those whose coaches are less aggressive.[28]

Passive Aggression **Passive aggression** occurs when a communicator expresses hostility in an obscure or manipulative way. As the Ethical Challenge in this section explains, this behavior has been termed **crazymaking**. It occurs when people have feelings of resentment, anger, or rage that they are unable or unwilling to express directly. Instead of keeping these feelings to themselves, a crazymaker sends aggressive messages in subtle, indirect ways, thus maintaining the front of kindness. This amiable façade eventually crumbles, leaving the crazymaker's victim confused and angry at having been fooled. The targets of the crazymaker can either react with aggressive behavior of their own or retreat to nurse their hurt feelings. In either case, passive aggression seldom has anything but harmful effects on a relationship.[29] In our scenario, Lucia could take a passive-aggressive approach to Paul's desire to keep their workouts exclusive by showing up late to run just to annoy him. Paul could become passive aggressive by agreeing to include Lucia's friends, then pouring on the speed and leaving them behind.

Compromising (Partial Lose–Lose)

Compromising gives both people at least some of what they want, although both sacrifice part of their goals. People usually settle for a compromise when it seems that partial satisfaction is the best they can hope for. In the case of Paul and Lucia, they could strike a deal by alternating workouts with and without her friends. Unlike avoidance, where both parties lose because they don't address their problem, compromisers actually negotiate a solution that gives them some of what they want, but it also leaves everybody losing something.

Compromise may be better than losing everything, but there are times when this approach hardly seems ideal. One observer has asked why it is that if someone says, "I will compromise my values," we view the action unfavorably, yet we have favorable views of parties in a conflict who compromise to reach a solution.[30] Although compromises may be the best obtainable result in some conflicts, it's important to realize that both people in a conflict can often work together to find much better solutions. In such cases, *compromise* is a negative word.

Most of us are surrounded by the results of bad compromises. Consider a common example: the conflict between one person's desire to smoke cigarettes and another's need for clean air. The win–lose outcomes of this issue are obvious: Either the smoker abstains, or the nonsmoker gets polluted lungs—neither option is very satisfying. But a compromise in which the smoker gets to enjoy only a rare cigarette or must retreat outdoors and in which the nonsmoker still must inhale some fumes or feel like an ogre is hardly better. Both sides have lost a considerable amount of both comfort and goodwill. Of course, the costs involved in other compromises are even greater. For example, if a divorced couple compromises on child care by haggling over custody and then grudgingly agrees to split the time with their children, it's hard to say that anybody has won.

Some compromises do leave both parties satisfied. You and the seller might settle on a price for a used car that is between what the seller was asking and what you wanted to pay. Although neither of you got everything you wanted, the outcome would still leave both of you satisfied. Likewise, you and your companion might agree to see a film that is the second choice for both of you in order to spend an evening together. As long as everyone

ETHICAL *Challenge*

Dirty Fighting with Crazymakers

Psychologist George Bach uses the term *crazymakers* to describe passive-aggressive behavior. His term reflects the insidious nature of indirect aggression, which can confuse and anger a victim who may not even be aware of being victimized. Although a case can be made for using all of the other approaches to conflict described in this chapter, it is difficult to find a justification for passive-aggressive crazymaking.

The following categories represent a nonexhaustive list of crazymaking. They are presented here as a warning for potential victims, who might choose to use perception checking, "I" language, assertion, or other communication strategies to explore whether the user has a complaint that can be addressed in a more constructive manner.

The Avoider. Avoiders refuse to fight. When a conflict arises, they leave, fall asleep, pretend to be busy at work, or keep from facing the problem in some other way. Because avoiders won't fight back, this strategy can frustrate the person who wants to address an issue.

The Pseudoaccommodator. Pseudoaccommodators pretend to give in and then continue to act in the same way.

The Guiltmaker. Instead of expressing dissatisfaction directly, guiltmakers try to make others feel responsible for causing pain. A guiltmaker's favorite line is "It's okay; don't worry about me . . ." accompanied by a big sigh.

The Mind Reader. Instead of allowing their partners to express feelings honestly, mind readers go into character analysis, explaining what the partner really means or what's wrong with the partner. By behaving this way, mind readers refuse to handle their own feelings and leave no room for their partners to express themselves.

The Trapper. Trappers play an especially dirty trick by setting up a desired behavior for their partners and then, when it's met, attacking the very behavior they requested. An example of this technique is for the trapper to say, "Let's be totally honest with each other" and then attack the partner's self-disclosure.

The Crisis Tickler. Crisis ticklers almost bring what's bothering them to the surface but never quite come out and express themselves. Instead of admitting concern about the finances, they innocently ask, "Gee, how much did that cost?," dropping a rather obvious hint but never really dealing with the crisis.

The Gunnysacker. These people don't share complaints as they arise. Instead, they put their resentments into a psychological gunnysack, which bulges after awhile with both large and small gripes. Then, when the sack is about to burst, the gunnysacker pours out all the pent-up aggressions on the overwhelmed and unsuspecting victim.

The Trivial Tyrannizer. Instead of honestly sharing their resentments, trivial tyrannizers do things they know will get their partners' goat—leaving dirty dishes in the sink, clipping fingernails in bed, belching out loud, turning up the television too loud, and so on.

The Beltliner. Everyone has a psychological "beltline," and below it are subjects too sensitive to be approached without damaging the relationship. Beltlines may have to do with physical characteristics, intelligence, past behavior, or deeply ingrained personality traits that a person is trying to overcome. In an attempt to "get even" or hurt their partners, beltliners will use intimate knowledge to hit below the belt, knowing it will hurt.

The Joker. Because they are afraid to face conflicts squarely, jokers kid around when their partners want to be serious, thus blocking the expression of important feelings.

The Withholder. Instead of expressing their anger honestly and directly, withholders punish their partners by keeping back something—courtesy, affection, good cooking, humor, sex. As you can imagine, this is likely to build up even greater resentments in the relationship.

The Benedict Arnold. These characters get back at their partners by sabotage, by failing to defend them from attackers, and even by encouraging ridicule or disregard from outside the relationship.

SOFTWARE TACKLES ROOMMATE CONFLICTS

Roompact, a Chicago start-up, hopes that its digital tools will tackle college-roommate conflicts. The company has developed an online, customizable roommate agreement for incoming students, according to Matt Unger, chief executive. Using the site, roommates can agree on parameters for room cleanliness, when the lights go out, expectations for inviting guests, and other issues.

The Roompact system also sends each student a weekly or bi-weekly text message asking for a roommate-relationship rating—what the company calls "micro-surveys." Students may also respond to the text message with more detailed complaints, which would trigger suggestions by Roompact.

Shawn McQuillan, associate director of residential life at University of Hartford, thinks Roompact's notification system will benefit the university in dealing with disagreements between students who do not seek out help from staff members.

"[Students] either ignore the problem, think it will go away or live with it. Often when they do this, they let it build up until it has a negative impact on their overall experience and student success," he says. "Our hope is with the micro-surveys we can take an even more proactive approach to resolving roommate disputes, especially among those students who struggle with coming to a staff member for help."

McQuillan also believes Roompact's online system will appeal to Millennials. "In this day and age, our students are beyond a doubt tech savvy," he says. "They want to have more resources available to them electronically and in many cases are more likely to complete something that is online and that can be accessed by a click of a button."

Karen Erlandson, professor of communication studies at Albion College, developed Roompact's student-diagnostic survey. "The diagnostic improves communication," she says. "Roompact's system helps students identify areas of conflict that are specific to them and urges them to include these potential 'hot spots' in their roommate contract."

"One component of the Roompact system is to provide students with methods to constructively confront and solve conflict when it first occurs," Erlandson says. "When potential problems are detected by Roompact, students are provided a set of guidelines for initiating and engaging in productive, rational conflict."

Echoing Erlandson, Unger says that Roompact is not meant to encourage students to replace real dialogue with a technology-based solution. "We try to use technology to help students to learn how to interact face-to-face and interact with people who are not like them," he says.

Jonathan Swartz

MindTap **Enhance ...** your understanding by answering the following questions, either here or online.

1. Identify pros and cons of the approach described in this reading. In what ways do you think this technology could help or hurt conflict management between roommates?

2. Describe the conflict management principles you could adopt from this program, even if you didn't use the software.

is satisfied with an outcome, compromise can be an effective way to resolve conflicts. When compromises are satisfying and successful, it might be more accurate to categorize them as the final style we'll discuss: collaborating.

Collaborating (Win–Win)

Collaborating seeks *win–win* solutions to conflict. Collaborators show a high degree of concern for both themselves and others. Rather than trying to solve problems "my way" or "your way," their focus is on "our way." In the best case, collaborating can lead to a win–win outcome: Everybody gets what they want.

If Lucia and Paul were to collaborate, they might determine that the best way for both of them to get what they want is to continue their one-on-one workouts but invite Lucia's friends to join in for a few miles at the end of each run. They might schedule other, less-challenging workouts that include the friends. Or they might find other ways to get together with Lucia's friends that are fun for both of them.

The goal of collaboration is to find a solution that satisfies the needs of everyone involved. Not only do the partners avoid trying to win at the other's expense, but they also believe that by working together it is possible to find a solution that goes beyond a mere compromise and allows all parties to reach their goals. Consider a few examples.

- A newly married husband and wife find themselves arguing frequently over their budget. The husband enjoys buying impractical and enjoyable items for himself and for the house, whereas the wife fears that such purchases will ruin their carefully constructed budget. Their solution is to set aside a small amount of money each month for "fun purchases." The amount is small enough to be affordable yet gives the husband a chance to escape from their spartan lifestyle. The wife is satisfied with the arrangement because the luxury money is now a budget category by itself, which gets rid of the out-of-control feeling that comes when her husband makes unexpected purchases. The plan works so well that the couple continues to use it even after their income rises, increasing the amount devoted to luxuries.

- Marta, a store manager, hates the task of rescheduling employee work shifts to accommodate their social and family needs. She and her staff develop an arrangement in which employees arrange schedule-swaps on their own and notify her in writing after they are made.

- Wendy and Kathy are roommates who have different study habits. Wendy likes to do her work in the evenings, which leaves her days free for other things, but Kathy feels that nighttime is party time. The solution they worked out is that Monday through Wednesday evenings Wendy studies at her boyfriend's place while Kathy does anything she wants; Thursday through Sunday, Kathy agrees to keep things quiet around the house.

The point here isn't that these solutions are the correct ones for everybody with similar problems. The win–win method doesn't work that way. Different people might have found other solutions that suit them better. Collaboration gives you a way of creatively finding just the right answer for your unique problem—and that answer might be one that neither party thought of or expected before collaborating. By generating win–win solutions, you can create a way of resolving your conflicts that everyone can live with comfortably. Later in this chapter, you'll learn a specific process for arriving at collaborative solutions to problems.

Which Style to Use?

Collaborating might seem like the ideal approach to solving problems, but it's an oversimplification to imagine that there is a single "best" way.[31] Generally speaking, win–win approaches are preferable to win–lose and lose–lose solutions. But we've already seen that there are times when avoiding, accommodating, competing, and compromising are appropriate. Table 12.1 lists some of the issues to consider when deciding which style to use when facing a conflict. As you decide which approach to use, consider the following factors.

1. **The relationship.** When someone else clearly has more power than you, accommodating may be the best approach. If the boss tells you to fill that order "Now!," it may be smart to do so without comment. A more assertive response ("I'm still tied up with the job you gave me yesterday") might be reasonable, but it could also cost you your job.

TABLE 12.1 Factors to Consider When Choosing the Most Appropriate Conflict Style

AVOIDING (LOSE–LOSE)	ACCOMMODATING (LOSE–WIN)	COMPETING (WIN–LOSE)	COMPROMISING (PARTIAL LOSE–LOSE)	COLLABORATING (WIN–WIN)
When the issue is of little importance	When you discover you are wrong	When there is not enough time to seek a win–win outcome	To achieve quick, temporary solutions to complex problems	When the issue is too important for a compromise
When the costs of confrontation outweigh the benefits	When the issue is more important to the other person than it is to you	When the issue is not important enough to negotiate at length	When opponents are strongly committed to mutually exclusive goals	When a long-term relationship between you and the other person is important
To cool down and gain perspective	When the long-term cost of winning isn't worth the short-term gain	When the other person is not willing to cooperate	When the issues are moderately important but not enough for a stalemate	To merge insights with someone who has a different perspective on the problem
	To build up credits for later conflicts	When you are convinced that your position is right and necessary	As a backup mode when collaboration doesn't work	To develop a relationship by showing commitment to the concerns of both parties
	To let others learn by making their own mistakes	To protect yourself against a person who takes advantage of noncompetitive people	To come up with creative and unique solutions to problems	

2. **The situation**. Different situations call for different conflict styles. After haggling over the price of a car for hours, it might be best to compromise by simply splitting the difference. In other cases, though, it may be a matter of principle for you to "stick to your guns" and attempt to get what you believe is right.

3. **The other person.** Win–win is a fine ideal, but sometimes the other person isn't willing or able to collaborate. You probably know communicators who are so competitive that they put winning on even minor issues ahead of the well-being of your relationship. In such cases, your efforts to collaborate may have a low chance of success.

4. **Your goals.** Sometimes your overriding concern may be to calm down an enraged or upset person. Accommodating an outburst from your crotchety and sick neighbor, for example, is probably better than standing up for yourself and triggering a stroke. In still other cases, your moral principles might compel an aggressive statement even though it might not get you what you originally sought: "I've had enough of your racist jokes. I've tried to explain why they're so offensive, but you obviously haven't listened. I'm leaving!"

MindTap PRACTICE... your understanding of conflict styles by completing the Concepts in Play activity online.

CONFLICT IN RELATIONAL SYSTEMS

So far we have focused on individual conflict styles. Even though the style you choose in a conflict is important, your style isn't the only factor that will determine how a conflict unfolds. In reality, conflict is relational: Its character usually is determined by the way the parties interact with each other.[32] You might, for example, be determined to handle a conflict with your neighbor assertively only to be driven to aggression by his uncooperative nature—or even to avoidance by his physical threats. Likewise, you might plan to hint to a professor that you are bothered by her apparent indifference but wind up discussing the matter in an open, assertive way in reaction to her constructive response.

Examples like these suggest that conflict doesn't depend on just individual choice. Rather, it depends on how the partners interact. When two or more people are in a long-term relationship, they develop their own **relational conflict style**—a pattern of managing disagreements. The mutual influence that parties have on each other is so powerful that it can overcome the disposition to handle conflicts in the manner that comes most easily to one or the other.[33] As we will soon see, some relational conflict styles are constructive, whereas others can make life miserable and threaten relationships.

Complementary, Symmetrical, and Parallel Styles

Partners in interpersonal relationships—and impersonal ones, too—can use one of three styles to manage their conflicts. In relationships with a **complementary conflict style**, the partners use different but mutually reinforcing behaviors. In a **symmetrical conflict style**, both partners use the same behaviors. In a **parallel conflict style**, both partners shift between complementary and symmetrical patterns from one issue to another. Table 12.2 illustrates how the same conflict can unfold in very different ways, depending on whether the partners' communication is symmetrical or complementary. A parallel style would alternate between these two patterns, depending on the situation.

Research shows that a complementary *fight–flight* style is common in many unhappy marriages. One partner—most commonly the wife—addresses the conflict directly, whereas the other—usually the husband—withdraws.[34] It's easy to see how this pattern can lead to a cycle of increasing hostility and isolation because each partner punctuates the conflict differently, blaming the other for making matters worse. "I withdraw because she's so critical," a husband might say. The wife wouldn't organize the sequence in the same way, however. "I criticize because he withdraws" would be her perception.

Complementary styles aren't the only ones that can lead to problems. Some distressed marriages suffer from destructively symmetrical communication. If both partners treat each other with matching hostility, one threat or insult leads to another in an escalatory spiral. If the partners both withdraw from each other instead of facing their problems, a de-escalatory spiral results in which the satisfaction and vitality ebb from the relationship, leaving it a shell of its former self.

As Table 12.2 shows, complementary and symmetrical behaviors can produce both "good" and "bad" results. If the complementary behaviors are positive, then a positive spiral results and the conflict stands a good chance of being resolved. This is the case in Example 2 in Table 12.2, where the boss is open to hearing the employee's concerns, listening willingly as the employee talks. Here, a complementary talk–listen pattern works well.

TABLE 12.2 Complementary and Symmetrical Conflict Styles

SITUATION	COMPLEMENTARY STYLES	SYMMETRICAL STYLES
Example 1: Wife is upset because husband is spending little time at home.	Wife complains. Husband withdraws, spending even less time at home. *(Destructive)*	Wife complains. Husband responds angrily and defensively. *(Destructive)*
Example 2: Female employee is offended when a male boss calls her "sweetie."	Employee objects to boss, explaining her reasons for being offended. Boss apologizes for his unintentional insult. *(Constructive)*	Employee maliciously "jokes" about boss at company party. *(Destructive)*
Example 3: Parents are uncomfortable with teenager's new friends.	Parents express concerns. Teen dismisses them, saying "There's nothing to worry about." *(Destructive)*	Teen expresses discomfort with parents' protectiveness. Parents and teen negotiate a mutually agreeable solution. *(Constructive)*

PAUSE *and* REFLECT

Understanding Conflict Styles

MindTap® **REFLECT ...** on conflict styles by answering the following questions, either here or online.

You can gain a clearer idea of how conflict styles differ by completing the following exercise.

1. Join a partner and choose one of the following conflicts to work on. If you prefer, you may substitute a conflict of your own.

    a. Roommates disagree about the noise level in their apartment.

    b. Parents want their college sophomore son or daughter to stay home for the winter vacation. The son or daughter wants to travel with friends.

    c. One person in a couple wants to spend free time socializing with friends. The other wants to stay at home together.

2. Role play the conflict four times, reflecting each of the following styles:

    a. Complementary (constructive)

    b. Complementary (destructive)

    c. Symmetrical (constructive)

    d. Symmetrical (destructive)

3. After experiencing each style with your partner, reflect on which of the conflict styles characterizes the way conflict is managed in one of your interpersonal relationships. Are you satisfied with this approach? If not, describe what style would be more appropriate.

Symmetrical styles can also be beneficial. The clearest example of constructive symmetry occurs when both parties communicate assertively, listening to each other's concerns and working together to resolve them. The potential for this sort of solution occurs in Example 3, in the parent–teenager conflict. With enough mutual respect and careful listening, both the parents and their teenager can understand one another's concerns and very possibly find a way to give both parties what they want.

Destructive Conflict Patterns: The Four Horsemen

Some conflict styles are so destructive that they are almost guaranteed to wreak havoc on relationships. These toxic forms of communication include what John Gottman calls "The Four Horsemen of the Apocalypse."[35]

Gottman has gathered decades of data about newlywed couples and their communication patterns. By observing their interactions, he has been able to predict with more than 90 percent accuracy whether the newlyweds will end up divorcing. Here are the four destructive signs he looks for:

1. **Criticism**. These are attacks on a person's character. As you read in Chapters 6 and 11, there's a significant difference between legitimate complaints about behavior phrased in descriptive "I" language ("I wish you had been on time—we're going to be late to the movie") and critical character assaults stated as evaluative "you" messages ("You're so thoughtless—you never think of anyone but yourself").

2. **Defensiveness**. As Chapter 11 explained, defensiveness is a reaction that aims to protect one's presenting self by denying responsibility ("You're crazy—I never do that") and counterattacking ("You're worse about that than I am"). Although some self-protection is understandable, problems arise when a person refuses to listen to or even acknowledge another's concerns.

3. **Contempt**. A contemptuous comment belittles and demeans. It can take the form of name-calling putdowns ("You're a real jerk") or sarcastic barbs ("Oh, *that* was brilliant"). Contempt can also be communicated nonverbally through dramatic eye rolls or disgusted sighs. (Try doing both of those at the same time and imagine how dismissive they can be.)

4. **Stonewalling**. Stonewalling occurs when one person in a relationship withdraws from the interaction, shutting down dialogue—and any chance of resolving the problem in a mutually satisfactory way. It sends a disconfirming "You don't matter" message to the other person.

Here's a brief exchange illustrating how the "four horsemen" can lead to a destructive spiral of aggression:

"You overdrew our account again—can't you do *anything* right?" *(Criticism)*

"Hey, don't blame me—you're the one who spends most of the money." *(Defensiveness)*

"At least I have better math skills than a first grader. Way to go, Einstein." *(Contempt)*

"Whatever." *(said while walking out of the room) (Stonewalling)*

It's easy to see how this kind of communication can be destructive in any relationship, not just a marriage. It's also easy to see how these kinds of comments can feed off each other and develop into destructive conflict rituals, as we'll discuss now.

Conflict Rituals

When people have been in a relationship for some time, their communication often develops into **conflict rituals**—usually unacknowledged but very real patterns of interlocking behavior.[36] Consider the following common rituals.

- A young child interrupts her parents, demanding to be included in their conversation. At first the parents tell the child to wait, but she whines and cries until the parents find it easier to listen than to ignore the fussing.

- A couple fights. One partner leaves. The other accepts the blame for the problem and begs forgiveness. The first partner returns, and a happy reunion takes place. Soon they fight again.

- A boss flies into rage when the pressure builds at work. Recognizing this, the employees avoid him as much as possible. When the crisis is over, the boss compensates for his outbursts by being especially receptive to employee requests.

- Roommates have a blowout over housekeeping responsibilities. One roommate gives the other the "silent treatment" for several days, then begins picking up around the house without admitting being wrong.

There's nothing inherently wrong with the interaction in many rituals, especially when everybody involved accepts them as ways of managing conflict.[37] Consider the preceding examples. In the first, the little girl's whining may be the only way she can get the parents' attention. In the second, both partners might use the fighting as a way to blow off steam, and both might find that the joy of a reunion is worth the grief of the separation. In the third, the ritual might work well for the boss (as a way of releasing pressure) and for employees (as a way of getting their requests met). And in the fourth, at least the house gets cleaned—eventually.

Rituals can cause problems, though, when they become the *only* way relational partners handle their conflicts. As you learned in Chapter 1, competent communicators have a large repertoire of behaviors, and they are able to choose the most effective response for a given situation. Relying on one ritual pattern to handle all conflicts is no more effective than using a screwdriver to handle every home repair or putting the same seasoning on every dish you cook. Conflict rituals may be familiar and comfortable, but they aren't always the best way to resolve the various conflicts that are part of any relationship.

"I'm not yelling *at* you, I'm yelling *with* you."

PAUSE *and* REFLECT

Your Conflict Rituals

MindTap **REFLECT ...** on your conflict rituals by answering the following questions, either here or online.

Describe two conflict rituals in one of your important relationships. One of your examples should consist of a positive ritual and the other of a negative ritual. For each example, explain:

1. a subject that is likely to trigger the conflict (such as money, leisure time, affection)

2. the behavior of one partner that initiates the ritual

3. the series of responses by both partners that follows the initiating event

4. how the ritual ends

Based on your description, explain an alternative to the unsatisfying ritual, and describe how you might be able to manage the conflict in a more satisfying way.

VARIABLES IN CONFLICT STYLES

By now you can see that every relational system is unique. The communication patterns in one family, business, or classroom are likely to be very different from those in any other. But along with the differences that arise in individual relationships, two powerful variables affect the way people manage conflict: gender and culture. We will now look at each variable and see how it affects how conflict is managed.

Gender

Men and women often approach conflicts differently. Even in childhood, males are more likely to be aggressive, demanding, and competitive, whereas females are more likely to be cooperative. Studies of children from preschool to early adolescence have shown that boys try to get their way by ordering one another around: "Lie down." "Get off my steps." "Gimme your arm." By contrast, girls are more likely to make proposals for action, beginning with the verb *let's*: "Let's go find some." "Let's ask her, 'Do you have any bottles?'" "Let's move these out first."[38] Whereas boys tell each other what role to take in pretend play ("Come on, be a doctor"), girls more commonly ask each other what role they want ("Will you be the patient for a few minutes?") or make a joint proposal ("We can both be doctors"). Furthermore, boys often make demands without offering an explanation ("Look, man. I want the wire cutters right now"). By contrast, girls often give reasons for their suggestions ("We gotta clean 'em first ... 'cause they got germs").[39]

Adolescent girls use aggression in conflicts, but their methods are usually more indirect than those of boys. Whereas teenage boys often engage in verbal showdowns and may even engage in physical fights, teenage girls typically use gossip, backbiting, and social exclusion.[40] This is not to suggest that girls' aggression is any less destructive than boys'. The film *Mean Girls* (based on the book *Queen Bees and Wannabes*[41]) offers a vivid depiction of just how injurious these indirect assaults can be on the self-concepts and relationships of young women.

Gender differences in dealing with conflict often persist into adulthood. One survey of college students revealed that men and women viewed conflicts in contrasting ways.[42] Regardless of their cultural background, female students described men as being concerned with power and more interested in content than relational issues. Phrases used to describe male conflict styles included: "The most important thing to males in conflict is their egos." "Men don't worry about feelings." "Men are more direct." By contrast, women were described as being more concerned with maintaining the relationship during a

Bill Sykes Images/The Image Bank/Getty Images

conflict. Phrases used to describe female conflict styles included: "Women are better listeners." "Women try to solve problems without controlling the other person." "Females are more concerned with others' feelings."

These sorts of differences don't mean that men are incapable of forming good relationships. Instead, their notions of what makes a good relationship are different. For some men, friendship and aggression aren't mutually exclusive. In fact, many strong male relationships are built around competition (e.g., at work or in athletics). Women can be competitive, too, but they also are more likely to use logical reasoning and bargaining than aggression.[43] And when it comes to avoidance, women tend to view withdrawal from conflict as more injurious to a relationship than do men (which is why women are more likely to say, "We *have* to talk about this").[44]

A look at the entire body of research on gender and conflict suggests that the differences in how the two sexes handle conflict are relatively small and sometimes different from the stereotypical picture of aggressive men and passive women.[45] It would appear that people may *think* there are greater differences in male and female ways of handling conflicts than there actually are.[46] People who assume that men are aggressive and women are accommodating may notice behavior that fits these stereotypes ("See how much he bosses her around. A typical man!"). On the other hand, behavior that doesn't fit these stereotypes (accommodating men, pushy women) goes unnoticed.

While men and women do have characteristically different conflict styles, the reasons may have little to do with gender. The situation at hand has a greater influence on shaping the way a person handles conflict.[47] For example, both men and women are more likely to respond aggressively when attacked by the other person. (Recall the discussion of defensive spirals in Chapter 11.) In fact, researchers exploring how married couples handle disagreements found that the importance of gender in determining conflict style is "dwarfed" by the behavior of the other person.[48]

What, then, can we conclude about the influence of gender on conflict? Research has demonstrated that there are, indeed, some small but measurable differences in the two sexes. But, although men and women may have characteristically different conflict styles, the individual style of each communicator—regardless of gender—and the nature of the relationship are more important than gender in shaping the way he or she handles conflict.

Culture

The way in which people manage conflict varies tremendously depending on their cultural background. The straight-talking, assertive approach that characterizes many North Americans is not the universal norm.[49]

Perhaps the most important cultural factor in shaping attitudes toward conflict is an orientation toward individualism or collectivism.[50] In individualistic cultures like the United States, the goals, rights, and needs of each person are considered important, and most people would agree that it is an individual's right to stand up for him- or herself. By contrast, collectivist cultures (more common in Latin America and Asia) consider the concerns of the group to be more important than those of any individual. In these cultures, the kind of assertive behavior

ABC/Photofest

∧ Culture plays a role in conflict management on the TV show *Blackish*. Andre "Dre" (Anthony Anderson) and Rainbow "Bow" (Tracee Ellis Ross) Johnson are professionals living in an upper-middle-class environment that is different from their upbringings. They and their children struggle to accommodate their cultural heritage with their unique aspirations and personalities. How do culture and social class affect your personal and professional relationships? Are these factors sometimes a source of conflict—and if so, how do you manage them?

that might seem perfectly appropriate to a North American would be regarded as rude and insensitive.

Another factor that affects conflict is the difference between high- and low-context cultural styles.[51] Recall from our discussion in Chapter 6 that low-context cultures like the United States place a premium on being direct and literal. By contrast, high-context cultures like Japan value self-restraint and avoiding confrontation. For this reason, what seems like "beating around the bush" to an American would seem polite to an Asian. In Japan, for example, even a simple request like "Close the door" would be too straightforward.[52] A more indirect statement such as "It is somewhat cold today" would be more appropriate. Perhaps more important, Japanese are reluctant to say "No" to a request. A more likely answer would be "Let me think about it for a while," which anyone familiar with Japanese culture would recognize as a refusal.

When indirect communication is a cultural norm, it is unreasonable to expect more straightforward approaches to succeed. When people from different cultures face a conflict, their habitual communication patterns may not mesh smoothly. The challenge faced by an American husband and his Taiwanese wife illustrates this sort of problem. The husband would try to confront his wife verbally and directly (as is typical in the United States), leading her to either become defensive or withdraw completely from the discussion. She, on the other hand, would attempt to indicate her displeasure by changes in mood and eye contact (typical of Chinese culture) that were either not noticed or were uninterpretable by her husband. Thus, neither "his way" nor "her way" was working, and they could not see any realistic way to "compromise."[53]

It isn't necessary to look only at Asia to encounter cultural differences in conflict. Americans visiting Greece, for example, often think they are witnessing an argument when they are overhearing a friendly conversation.[54] A comparative study of American and Italian nursery-school children showed that one of the Italian childrens' favorite pastimes was a kind of heated debating that Italians call *discussione* but that Americans would call *arguing*. Likewise, research has shown that the conversations of working-class Jewish people of eastern European origin used arguments as a means of being sociable.

Even within the United States, the ethnic background of communicators plays a role in their ideas about conflict. When members of a group of Mexican American and Anglo American college students were asked about their views regarding conflict, some important differences emerged.[55] For example, Anglo Americans seemed more willing to accept conflict as a natural part of relationships, whereas Mexican Americans were more concerned about the short- and long-term dangers of conflict. It's not surprising that people from collectivist, high-context cultures emphasizing harmony tend to handle conflicts in less-direct ways. With differences like these, it's easy to imagine how two friends, lovers, or fellow workers from different cultural backgrounds might have trouble finding a conflict style that is comfortable for them both.

Despite these differences, it's important to realize that culture isn't the only factor that influences the way people approach conflict or how they

Looking at DIVERSITY

Mandel Ngan/Getty Images

James Comey: Searching for Accord in Troubled Times

Even as some African Americans achieved the highest positions of respect and accomplishment, others died at the hands of white police officers in a series of high profile cases that outraged many citizens. At this difficult time, FBI director James Comey delivered a speech that is excerpted here. His remarks emphasize the importance of reaching across the divide of race and personal experience to regard one another as individuals. Note how he asks parties to move past win–lose conflict approaches and seek more collaborative solutions.

We are at a crossroads. As a society, we can choose to live our everyday lives, raising our families and going to work, hoping that someone, somewhere, will do something to ease the tension—to smooth over the conflict. We can roll up our car windows, turn up the radio, and drive around these problems, or we can choose to have an open and honest discussion about what our relationship is today—what it should be, what it could be, and what it needs to be—if we took more time to better understand one another.

Let me start by sharing some of my own hard truths:

First, all of us in law enforcement must be honest enough to acknowledge that much of our history is not pretty. At many points in American history, law enforcement enforced the status quo, a status quo that was often brutally unfair to disfavored groups. I am descended from Irish immigrants. A century ago, the Irish knew well how American society—and law enforcement—viewed them: as drunks, ruffians, and criminals. The Irish had tough times, but little compares to the experience on our soil of black Americans. That experience should be part of every American's consciousness, and law enforcement's role in that experience—including in recent times—must be remembered. It is our cultural inheritance.

A second hard truth: Much research points to the widespread existence of unconscious bias. Many people in our white-majority culture have unconscious racial biases and react differently to a white face than a black face. In fact, we all, white and black, carry various biases around with us. I am reminded of the song from the Broadway hit, *Avenue Q*: "Everyone's a Little Bit Racist." But if we can't help our latent biases, we can help our behavior in response to those instinctive reactions. Although the research may be unsettling, it is what we do next that matters most.

I believe law enforcement overwhelmingly attracts people who want to do good for a living—people who risk their lives because they want to help other people. They don't sign up to be cops in New York or Chicago or L.A. to help white people or black people or Hispanic people or Asian people. They sign up because they want to help all people. And they do some of the hardest, most dangerous policing to protect people of color.

But that leads me to my third hard truth: something happens to people in law enforcement. Many of us develop different flavors of cynicism that we work hard to resist because they can be lazy mental shortcuts. For example, criminal suspects routinely lie about their guilt, and nearly everybody we charge is guilty. That makes it easy for some folks in law enforcement to assume that everybody is lying and that no suspect, regardless of their race, could be innocent. Easy, but wrong.

Let me be transparent about my affection for cops. When you dial 911, whether you are white or black, the cops come, and they come quickly, and they come quickly whether they are white or black. That's what cops do.

Those of us in law enforcement must redouble our efforts to resist bias and prejudice. We must better understand the people we serve and protect—by trying to know, deep in our gut, what it feels like to be a law-abiding young black man walking on the street and encountering law enforcement. We must understand how that young man may see us. We must resist the lazy shortcuts of cynicism and approach him with respect and decency.

But the "seeing" needs to flow in both directions. Citizens also need to really see the men and women of law enforcement. They need to see the risks and dangers law enforcement officers encounter on a typical late-night shift. They need to understand the difficult and frightening work they do to keep us safe. They need to give them the space and respect to do their work, well and properly. If they take the time to do that, what they will see are officers who are human, who are overwhelmingly doing the right thing for the right reasons, and who are too often operating in communities—and facing challenges—most of us choose to drive around.

In the words of Dr. King, "We must learn to live together as brothers or we will all perish together as fools." Relationships are hard. Relationships require work. So let's begin that work.

behave when they disagree. Some research suggests that our approach to conflict may be part of our biological makeup.[56] Furthermore, scholarship suggests that a person's self-concept is more powerful than his or her culture in determining conflict style.[57] For example, an assertive person raised in an environment that downplays conflict is still likely to be more aggressive than an unassertive person who grew up in a culture where conflicts are common. You might handle conflicts calmly in a job where rationality and civility are the norm but shriek like a banshee at home if that's the way you and a relational partner handle conflicts. Finally, the way each of us deals with conflict is a matter of personal choice. We can choose to follow unproductive patterns or we can choose more constructive approaches.

CONSTRUCTIVE CONFLICT SKILLS

The collaborative, win–win conflict style described earlier in this chapter has many advantages over win–lose and lose–lose approaches. Why, then, is it so rarely used? There are three reasons. The first is lack of awareness. Some people are so used to competition that they mistakenly think that winning requires them to defeat their "opponent."

Even when they know better, there is another factor that prevents many people from seeking win–win solutions. Conflicts are often emotional affairs in which people react combatively without stopping to think of better alternatives. Because this kind of emotional reflex prevents constructive solutions, it's often necessary to stop yourself from speaking out aggressively during a conflict and starting an escalating spiral of defensiveness. The time-honored advice of "stopping and counting to ten" applies here. After you've thought about the matter a bit, you'll be able to *act* constructively instead of *reacting* in a way that's likely to produce a lose–lose outcome.

A third reason win–win solutions are rare is that they require the other person's cooperation. It's difficult to negotiate constructively with someone who insists on trying to defeat you. In this case, use your best persuasive skills to explain that by working together you can find a solution that satisfies both of you.

Collaborative Problem Solving

Despite these challenges, it is definitely possible to become better at resolving conflicts. We will outline a method to increase your chances of being able to handle your conflicts in a collaborative, win–win manner. In a longitudinal study following one hundred couples who had conflict skills training, researchers found that the method works for couples willing to focus on improving their relationships.[58] As you read the following steps, try to imagine yourself applying them to a problem that's bothering you now.

Identify Your Problem and Unmet Needs   Before you speak out, it's important to realize that the problem that is causing conflict is yours. Whether you want to return an unsatisfactory piece of merchandise, complain to noisy neighbors because your sleep is being disturbed by their barking dog, or request a change in working conditions from your employer, the problem is yours. Why? Because in each case you are the person who "owns" the problem— the one who is dissatisfied. You are the one who has paid for the unsatisfactory merchandise; the merchant who sold it to you has the use of your good money. You are the one who is losing sleep as a result of your neighbors' dog; they are content to go on as before. You are the one who is unhappy with your working conditions, not your employer.

Realizing that the problem is yours will make a big difference when the time comes to approach the other party. Instead of feeling and acting in an evaluative way, you'll be more likely to state your problem in a descriptive way, which will not only be more accurate but also reduce the chance of a defensive reaction.

After you realize that the problem is yours, the next step is to identify the unmet needs that make you dissatisfied. For instance, in the barking dog example, your need may be to get some sleep or to study without interruptions. In the case of a friend who teases you in public, your need would probably be to avoid embarrassment.

Sometimes the task of identifying your needs isn't as simple as it first seems. Behind the apparent content of an issue is often a relational need. Consider this example: A friend hasn't returned some money you lent long ago. Your apparent need in this situation might be to get the money back. But a little thought will probably show that this isn't the only, or even the main, thing you want. Even if you were rolling in money, you'd probably want the loan repaid because of a more important need: *to avoid feeling victimized by your friend's taking advantage of you*.

As you'll soon see, the ability to identify your real needs plays a key role in solving interpersonal problems. For now, the point to remember is that before you voice your problem to your partner, you ought to be clear about which of your needs aren't being met.

Make a Date   Destructive fights often start because the initiator confronts a partner who isn't ready. There are many times when a person isn't in the right frame of mind to face a conflict, perhaps owing to fatigue, being in too much of a hurry to take the necessary time, being upset over another problem, or not feeling well. At times like these, it's unfair to "jump" a person without notice and expect to get full attention for your problem. If you do persist, you'll probably have an ugly fight on your hands.

After you have a clear idea of the problem, approach your partner with a request to try to solve it. For example, "Something's been bothering me. Can we talk about it?" If the answer is "Yes," then you're ready to go further. If it isn't the right time to confront your partner, then find a time that's agreeable to both of you.

"Is this a good time to have a big fight?"

Describe Your Problem and Needs   Your partner can't possibly meet your needs without knowing why you're upset and what you want. Therefore, it's up to you to describe your problem as specifically as possible. The best way to deliver a complete, accurate message is to use the assertive message format discussed in Chapter 11. Notice how well this approach works in the following examples:

Example 1

"I have a problem. It's about your leaving dirty clothes around the house after I've told you how much it bothers me *(behavior)*. It's a problem because I have to run around like crazy and pick things up whenever guests come, which is no fun at all *(consequence)*. I'm starting to think that either you're not paying attention to my requests or you're trying to drive me crazy *(thoughts)*, and either way, I'm getting more and more resentful *(feeling)*. I'd like to find some way to have a neat place without my having to be a maid or a nag."

Example 2

"I have a problem. When you drop by without calling ahead, and I'm studying *(behavior)*, I don't know whether to visit or ask you to leave *(thought)*. Either way, I get uncomfortable *(feeling)*, and it seems like whatever I do, I lose: Either I have to put you off or get behind in my work *(consequences)*. I'd like to find a way to get my studying done and still socialize with you *(intention)*."

Example 3

"Something is bothering me. When you tell me you love me and yet spend almost all your free time with your other friends *(behavior)*, I wonder whether you mean it *(thought)*. I get insecure *(feeling)*, and then I start acting moody *(consequence)*. I need some way of finding out for sure how you feel about me *(intention)*."

After stating your problem and describing what you need, it's important to make sure that your partner has understood what you've said. As you can remember from the discussion of listening in Chapter 8, there's a good chance—especially in a stressful conflict—that your words will be misinterpreted.

It's usually unrealistic to insist that your partner paraphrase your statement, and fortunately there are more tactful and subtle ways to make sure that you've been understood. For instance, you might try saying, "I'm not sure I expressed myself very well just now—maybe you should tell me what you heard me say so I can be sure I got it right." In any case, be absolutely sure that your partner understands your whole message before going any further. Legitimate agreements are tough enough without getting upset about a conflict that doesn't even exist.

Consider Your Partner's Point of View After you have made your position clear, it's time to find out what your partner needs to feel satisfied about this issue. There are two reasons why it's important to discover your partner's needs. First, it's fair: Your partner has just as much right as you to feel satisfied, and if you expect help in meeting your needs, then it's reasonable that you behave in the same way. But in addition to fairness, there's another practical reason for concerning yourself with what your partner wants. Just as an unhappy partner will make it hard for you to become satisfied, a happy partner will be more likely to cooperate in letting you reach your goals. Thus, it's in your own self-interest to discover and meet your partner's needs.

You can learn about your partner's needs simply by asking about them: "Now I've told you what I want and why. Tell me what you need to feel okay about this." After your partner begins to talk, your job is to use the listening skills discussed earlier in this book to make sure that you understand.

Negotiate a Solution Now that you and your partner understand each other's needs, the goal becomes finding a way to meet them. This is done by developing as many potential solutions as possible and then evaluating them to decide which one best meets everyone's needs. Probably the best description of the win–win approach was written by Thomas Gordon in his book *Parent Effectiveness Training*.[59] The following steps are a modification of this approach.

1. Identify and define the conflict. We've previously discussed identifying and defining the conflict. These consist of discovering each person's problem and needs and then setting the stage for meeting all of them.
2. Generate a number of possible solutions. In this step, the partners work together to think of as many means as possible to reach their stated ends. The key concept here is quantity: It's important to generate as many ideas as you can think of without worrying about which ones are good or bad. Write down every thought that comes up, no matter how unworkable. Sometimes a far-fetched idea will lead to a more workable one.

3. Evaluate the alternative solutions. This is the time to talk about which solutions will work and which ones won't. It's important for all parties to be honest about their willingness to accept an idea. If a solution is going to work, everyone involved has to support it.
4. Decide on the best solution. Now that you've looked at all the alternatives, pick the one that looks best to everyone. It's important to be sure that everybody understands the solution and is willing to try it out. Remember that your decision doesn't have to be final, but it should look potentially successful.

Follow Up the Solution   You can't be sure that the solution will work until you try it. After you've tested it for a while, it's a good idea to set aside some time to talk over its progress. You may find that you need to make some changes or even rethink the whole problem. The idea is to keep on top of the problem, and to keep using creativity to solve it.

You can expect and prepare for a certain amount of resistance from the other person. When a step doesn't meet with success, simply move back and repeat the preceding ones as necessary.

Win–win solutions aren't always possible. There will be times when even the best-intentioned people simply won't be able to find a way of meeting all their needs. In times like these, the process of negotiation has to include some compromises, but even then the preceding steps haven't been wasted. The genuine desire to learn what the other person wants and to try to satisfy those wants will build a climate of goodwill that can help you find the best solution to the present problem and also improve your relationship in the future.

Constructive Conflict: Questions and Answers

After learning about win–win negotiating, people often express doubts about how well it can work. "It sounds like a good idea," they say, "but … ." Four questions arise more than any others, and they deserve answers.

Isn't the Win–Win Approach Too Good to Be True?   Research shows that seeking mutual benefit is not just a good idea—it actually works. In fact, the win–win approach produces better results than a win–lose approach. In a series of experiments, researchers presented subjects with a bargaining situation called "the prisoner's dilemma," in which they could choose either to cooperate or betray a confederate.[60] There are three types of outcomes in the prisoner's dilemma: One partner can win big by betraying a confederate, both can win by cooperating, or both can lose by betraying each other. Although cynics might assume that the most effective strategy is to betray a partner (a win–lose approach), researchers found that cooperation is actually the best hard-nosed strategy. Players who demonstrated their willingness to support the other person and not hold grudges did better than those using a more competitive approach.

Isn't the Win–Win Approach Too Elaborate?

The win–win approach is detailed and highly structured. In everyday life, you may rarely use every step. Sometimes the problem at hand won't justify the effort, and at other times you and your partner might not need to be so deliberate to take care of the problem. Nonetheless, while learning to use the approach, try to follow all of the steps carefully. After you have become familiar with and skillful at using them all, you will be able to use whichever ones prove necessary in a given situation. For important issues, you are likely to find that every step of the win–win approach is important. If this process seems time consuming, just consider the time and energy that will likely be required if you don't resolve the issue at hand.

Isn't Win–Win Negotiating Too Rational?

Frustrated readers often complain that the win–win approach is so sensible that only a saint could use it successfully. "Sometimes I'm so angry that I don't care about being supportive or empathetic or anything else," they say. "I just want to blow my top!"

At times like this, you might need to temporarily remove yourself from the situation so you don't say or do something you'll later regret. You might feel better confiding in a third party. Or you might blow off steam with physical exercise. There are even cases when an understanding partner might allow you to have what has been called a "Vesuvius"—an uncontrolled, spontaneous explosion. Before you blow your top, though, be sure that your partner understands what you're doing and realizes that whatever you say doesn't call for a response. Your partner should let you rant and rave for as long as you want without getting defensive or "tying in." Then when your eruption subsides, you can take steps to work through whatever still troubles you.

Is It Possible to Change Others?

Readers often agree that win–win problem solving would be terrific—if everyone had read *Looking Out Looking In* and understood the method. "How can I get the other person to cooperate?" the question goes. Though you won't always be able to gain your partner's cooperation, a good job of selling can do the trick most of the time. The key lies in showing that it's in your partner's self-interest to work together with you: "Look, if we can't settle this, we'll both feel miserable. But if we can find an answer, think how much better off we'll be." Notice that this sort of explanation projects both the favorable consequences of cooperating and the unfavorable consequences of competing.

You can also boost the odds of getting your partner's cooperation by modeling the communication skills described in this book. You've read that defense-arousing behavior is reciprocal, but so is supportive communication. If you can listen sincerely, avoid evaluative attacks, and empathize with your partner's concerns, for example, there's a good chance that you'll get the same kind of behavior in return. And even if your cooperative attitude doesn't succeed, you'll gain self-respect from knowing that at least you behaved honorably and constructively.

In REAL LIFE

Win–Win Problem Solving

It is 7:15 A.M. on a typical school day. Chris enters the kitchen and finds the sink full of dirty dishes. It was her roommate Terry's turn to do them. She sighs in disgust and begins to clean up, slamming pots and pans.

Terry: Can't you be a little more quiet? I don't have a class till 10:00, and I want to catch up on sleep.

Chris: *(Expressing her aggression indirectly in a sarcastic tone of voice)* Sorry to bother you. I was cleaning up last night's dinner dishes.

Terry: *(Misses the message)* Well, I wish you'd do it a little more quietly. I was up late studying last night, and I'm beat.

Chris: *(Decides to communicate her irritation more directly, if aggressively)* Well, if you'd done the dishes last night, I wouldn't have had to wash them now.

Terry: *(Finally realizes that Chris is mad at her, responds defensively)* I was going to do them when I got up. I've got two midterms this week, and I was studying until midnight last night. What's more important—grades or a spotless kitchen?

Chris: *(Perpetuating the growing defensive spiral)* I've got classes, too, you know. But that doesn't mean we have to live like pigs!

Terry: *(Angrily)* Forget it. If it's such a big deal, I'll never leave another dirty dish!

Chris and Terry avoid each other as they get ready for school. During the day, Chris realizes that attacking Terry will only make matters worse. She decides on a more constructive approach that evening.

Chris: That wasn't much fun this morning. Want to talk about it?

Terry: I suppose so. But I'm going out to study with Kim and Alisa in a few minutes.

Chris: *(Realizing that it's important to talk at a good time)* If you have to leave soon, let's not get into it now. How about talking when you get back?

Terry: Okay, if I'm not too tired.

Chris: Or we could talk tomorrow before class.

Terry: Okay.

Later that evening Terry and Chris continue their conversation.

Chris: *(Defines the issue as her problem by using the assertive message format)* I hated to start the day with a fight. But I also hate having to do the dishes when it's not my turn *(behavior)*. It doesn't seem fair for me to do my job and yours *(interpretation)*, and that's why I got so mad *(feeling)* and nagged at you *(consequence)*.

Terry: But I was studying! You know how much I have to do. It's not like I was partying.

Chris: *(Avoids attacking Terry by sincerely agreeing with the facts and explaining further why she was upset)* I know. It wasn't just doing the dishes that got me upset. It seems like there have been a lot of times when I've done your jobs and mine, too.

Terry: *(Defensively)* Like when?

Chris: *(Gives specific descriptions of Terry's behavior)* Well, this was the third time this week that I've done the dishes when it's your turn, and I can think of a couple of times lately when I've had to clean up your stuff before people came over.

Terry: I don't see why it's such a big deal. If you just leave the stuff there, I'll clean it up.

Chris: *(Still trying to explain herself, she continues to use "I" language)* I know you would. I guess it's harder for me to put up with a messy place than it is for you.

Terry: Yeah. If you'd just relax, living together would be a lot easier!

Chris: *(Resenting Terry's judgmental accusation that the problem is all hers)* Hey, wait a second! Don't blame the whole thing on me. It's just that we have different standards. It looks to you like I'm too hung up on keeping the place clean …

Terry: Right.

Chris: ... and if we do it your way, then I'd be giving up. I'd have to either live with the place messier than I like it or clean everything up myself. Then I'd get mad at you, and things would be pretty tense around here. *(Describes the unpleasant consequences of not solving the problem in a mutually satisfactory way)*

Terry: I suppose so.

Chris: We need to figure out how to take care of the apartment in a way that we can both live with. *(Describes the broad outline of a win–win solution)*

Terry: Yeah.

Chris: So what could we do?

Terry: *(Sounding resigned)* Look, from now on I'll just do the dishes right away. It isn't worth arguing about.

Chris: Sure it is. If you're sore, the apartment may be clean, but it won't be worth it.

Terry: *(Skeptically)* Okay, what do you suggest?

Chris: Well, I'm not sure. You don't want the pressure of having to clean up right away, and I don't want to have to do my jobs and yours, too. Right?

Terry: Yeah. *(Still sounding skeptical)* So what are we going to do—hire a housekeeper to clean up?

Chris: *(Refusing to let Terry sidetrack the discussion)* That would be great if we could afford it. How about using paper plates? That would make cleaning up from meals easier.

Terry: Yeah, but there would still be pots and pans.

Chris: Well, it's not a perfect fix, but it might help a little. *(Goes on to suggest other ideas)* How about cooking meals that don't take a lot of work to clean up—maybe more salads and less fried stuff that sticks to pans? That would be a better diet, too.

Terry: Yeah. I do hate to scrub crusty frying pans. But that doesn't do anything about your wanting the living room picked up all the time, and I bet I still wouldn't keep the kitchen as clean as you like it. Keeping the place super clean just isn't as big a deal to me as it is for you.

Chris: That's true, and I don't want to have to nag you! *(Clarifies the end she's seeking)* You know, it's not really cleaning up that bothers me. It's doing more than my share of work. I wonder if there's a way I could be responsible for keeping the kitchen clean and picking up if you could do something else to keep the workload even.

Terry: Are you serious? I'd love to get out of doing the dishes! You mean you'd do them ... and keep the place picked up ... if I did something else?

Chris: As long as the work was equal and you really did your jobs without me having to remind you.

Terry: What kind of work would you want me to do?

Chris: How about cleaning up the bathroom?

Terry: Forget it. That's worse than doing the dishes.

Chris: Okay. How about cooking?

Terry: That might work, but then we'd have to eat together all the time. It's nice to do our own cooking when we want to. It's more flexible that way.

Chris: Okay. But what about shopping? I hate the time it takes, and you don't mind it that much, do you?

Terry: You mean shop for groceries? You'd trade that for cleaning the kitchen?

Chris: Sure. And picking up the living room. It takes an hour each time we shop, and we make two trips every week. Doing the dishes would be much quicker.

Terry: All right!

The plan didn't work perfectly. At first Terry put off shopping until all the food was gone, and Chris took advantage by asking Terry to run other errands during her shopping trips. But their new arrangement proved much more successful than the old arrangement. The apartment was cleaner and the workload more even, which satisfied Chris. Terry was less frequently the object of Chris's nagging, and she had no kitchen chores, which made her happier. Just as important, the relationship between Chris and Terry was more comfortable—thanks to win–win problem solving.

MindTap **APPLY ...** this situation to your life by answering questions online.

SUMMARY

Conflict is a fact of life in every interpersonal relationship. The way in which conflicts are handled plays a major role in the quality of a relationship. When managed constructively, conflicts can lead to stronger and more satisfying interaction; but when they are handled poorly, relationships will suffer.

Communicators can respond to conflicts in a variety of ways: avoiding, accommodating, competing, compromising, or collaborating. Each approach can be justified in certain circumstances. The way a conflict is handled is not always the choice of a single person: The parties influence each other as they develop a relational conflict style. This style may be complementary, symmetrical, or parallel, and it can involve constructive or destructive rituals. The "four horsemen" of criticism, defensiveness, contempt, and stonewalling are counterproductive ways to communicate during conflict.

Besides being shaped by the relationship, a conflict style is also shaped by a person's gender and cultural background. In most circumstances a collaborative, win–win outcome is the ideal, and it can be achieved by following the constructive conflict skills discussed.

KEY TERMS

accommodating
avoiding
collaborating
competing
complementary conflict style
compromising
conflict

conflict ritual
crazymaking
direct aggression
parallel conflict style
passive aggression
relational conflict style
symmetrical conflict style

CHAPTER TWELVE

Managing Interpersonal Conflicts

OUTLINE

Use this outline to take notes as you read the chapter in the text and/or as your instructor lectures in class.

I. THE NATURE OF CONFLICT   _____

A. Conflict Defined
1. Expressed Struggle   _____
2. Perceived Incompatible Goals
3. Perceived Scarce Resources   _____
4. Interdependence
5. Interference from the Other Party

B. Conflict Is Natural   _____

C. Conflict Can Be Beneficial

II. CONFLICT STYLES   _____

A. Avoiding (Lose–Lose)

B. Accommodating (Lose–Win)   _____

**C. Competing (Win–Lose May Degenerate
    to Lose–Lose)**   _____
1. Direct Aggression
   a. Connection Between Verbal and Physical   _____
      Aggression
   b. Psychologically Harmful
2. Passive Aggression   _____
   a. Crazymaking
   b. Seldom Has Positive Effects

D. Compromising (Partial Lose–Lose)

E. Collaborating (Win–Win)   _____

F. Which Style to Use?
1. Relationship
2. Situation
3. Other Person
4. Your Goals

III. CONFLICT IN RELATIONAL SYSTEMS

A. Complementary, Symmetrical, and Parallel Styles
1. Complementary
2. Symmetrical
3. Parallel

B. Destructive Conflict Patterns: The Four Horsemen
1. Criticism
2. Defensiveness
3. Contempt
4. Stonewalling

C. Conflict Rituals
1. Patterns of Behavior
2. Problematic if the *Only* Pattern

IV. VARIABLES IN CONFLICT STYLES

A. Gender
1. Socialization
2. Situation

B. Culture
1. Individualism versus Collectivism
2. Low-Context versus High-Context
3. Indirect and Direct
4. Ethnic Background
5. Personal Choice

V. CONSTRUCTIVE CONFLICT SKILLS

A. Collaborative Problem Solving
1. Identify Your Unmet Needs
2. Make a Date

3. Describe Your Problem and Needs

    a. Clear Messages

    b. Listening and Paraphrasing

4. Consider Your Partner's Point of View

5. Negotiate a Solution

    a. Identify and Define the Conflict

    b. Generate a Number of Possible Solutions

    c. Evaluate the Alternative Solutions

    d. Decide on the Best Solution

6. Follow Up the Solution

B. Constructive Conflict: Questions and Answers

1. Isn't Win–Win Too Good to Be True?

2. Isn't Win–Win Too Elaborate?

3. Isn't Win–Win Negotiating Too Rational?

4. Is It Possible to Change Others?

KEY TERMS

accommodating

avoiding

collaborating

competing

complementary conflict style

compromising

conflict

conflict ritual

crazymaking

direct aggression

interdependence

parallel conflict style

passive aggression

relational conflict style

stonewalling

symmetrical conflict style

ACTIVITIES

12.1 UNDERSTANDING CONFLICT STYLES

LEARNING OBJECTIVES

- Identify the relational conflict styles, patterns of behavior, and conflict rituals that define a given relationship.
- Construct responses expressing a particular conflict style.
- Assess probable consequences of a particular conflict style.

INSTRUCTIONS

1. For each of the conflicts described below, write responses illustrating the five types of conflict styles.
2. Describe the probable consequences of each style.

---

1. Your dad wants and expects you to spend every Thanksgiving with his whole extended family. You and some close friends who don't have large families want to get away for those four days and do something different. Your dad already arranged your transportation home.

Avoiding (lose–lose) response _____

_____

Probable consequences _____

_____

Accommodating (lose–win) response _____

_____

Probable consequences _____

_____

Competing response _____

_____

Probable consequences _____

_____

Compromising (partial lose–lose) _____

_____

Probable consequences _____

_____

Collaborating (win–win) _____

_____

Probable consequences _____

_____

2. A fan behind you at a ballgame toots a loud air horn every time the home team makes any progress. The noise is spoiling your enjoyment of the game.

Avoiding (lose–lose) response _____

_____

Probable consequences _____

_____

Accommodating (lose–win) response _____

_____

Probable consequences _____

_____

Competing response _____

_____

Probable consequences _____

_____

Compromising (partial lose–lose) _____

_____

Probable consequences _____

_____

Collaborating (win–win) _____

_____

Probable consequences _____

_____

3. Earlier in the day you asked your roommate to stop by the store and pick up snacks for a party you are both hosting this evening. Your roommate arrives home without the food.

Avoiding (lose–lose) response _____

_____

Probable consequences _____

_____

Accommodating (lose–win) response _____

_____

Probable consequences _____

_____

Competing response _____

_____

Probable consequences _____

_____

Compromising (partial lose–lose) _____

_____

Probable consequences _____

_____

Collaborating (win–win) _____

_____

Probable consequences _____

_____

4. You and Marc share a cubicle and a computer at work and you are both responsible for the same amount and type of work. Marc arrives a few minutes earlier than you and stays on the computer for several hours, then begins his non-computer work. You would be able to work more efficiently if you had some time on the computer early in the day.

Avoiding (lose–lose) response _____

_____

Probable consequences _____

_____

Accommodating (lose–win) response _____

_____

Probable consequences _____

_____

Competing response _____

_____

Probable consequences _____

_____

Compromising (partial lose–lose) _____

_____

Probable consequences _____

_____

Collaborating (win–win) _____

_____

Probable consequences _____

_____

5. You and your spouse have to make a decision about your five-year-olds' schooling. You believe strongly in supporting public schools and having children attend the neighborhood school. Your husband believes he didn't get a good education in public school and since you can afford to, you should send your child to private school.

Avoiding (lose–lose) response _____

_____

Probable consequences _____

_____

Accommodating (lose–win) response _____

_____

Probable consequences _____

_____

Competing response _____

_____

Class _____   Name _____

Probable consequences _____

_____

Compromising (partial lose–lose) _____

_____

Probable consequences _____

_____

Collaborating (win–win) _____

_____

Probable consequences _____

_____

_____

What styles are easiest to use with family? With friends? At work? With strangers? Why?

_____

_____

_____

12.2 YOUR CONFLICT STYLES

LEARNING OBJECTIVES

- Identify the conflicts in your important relationships and how satisfied you are with the way they have been handled.
- Describe your personal conflict styles, evaluate their effectiveness, and suggest alternatives as appropriate.

INSTRUCTIONS

1. Use the following form to record three conflicts that occur in your life that you are comfortable analyzing.
2. For each, describe your behavior, show how it fits the definition of conflict, classify your conflict style, and describe the consequences of your behaviors.
3. Summarize your findings in the space provided.

INCIDENT	YOUR BEHAVIOR	HOW IT MEETS THE DEFINITION OF CONFLICT	YOUR CONFLICT STYLE	CONSEQUENCES
		Expressed struggle Perceived compatible goals Perceived scarce resources Interdependence Interference of other party	Avoid Accommodate Compete Compromise Collaborate	
EXAMPLE *My friend accused me of being too negative about the possibility of finding rewarding, well-paying work.*	*I became defensive and angrily denied his claim. In turn I accused him of being too critical.*	*This was clearly an expressed struggle, and I perceived interference in my choice of jobs. Possibly we both perceived scarcity of the reward of feeling good about ourselves.*	*Competing*	*After arguing for some time, we left each other, both feeling upset. I'm sure we'll both feel awkward around each other for a while.*

1.				
2.				
3.				

CONCLUSIONS

1. Are there any individuals or issues that repeatedly arouse conflicts?

   _____

   _____

2. What conflict style(s) do you most commonly use? Do you use different styles with different people or in different situations? Why or why not?

   _____

   _____

   _____

3. Choose one or more of the conflicts you described in which you did not use a collaborative style and explain how you could have used a collaborative style. Predict what would have happened.

   _____

   _____

   _____

   _____

4. Are you satisfied with your usual way(s) of approaching conflict? Why or why not?

    _____

    _____

12.3 ANIMAL ANOLOGIES OF CONFLICT STYLES

LEARNING OBJECTIVES

- Assess your personal conflict style.
- Compare animal analogy conflict types to your text's labels for conflict styles.

INSTRUCTIONS

1. Go online to http://jeffcoweb.jeffco.k12.co.us/high/wotc/confli1.htm and take a brief quiz about your approaches to conflict (are you a turtle, shark, bear, fox, or owl?).
2. Answer the questions below.

Describe your results of the Animal Analogy quiz.

_____

_____

_____

How do these animals compare to the conflict style labels used in the text (Avoid, Accommodate, Compete, Compromise, and Collaborate)?

_____

_____

_____

What insights did comparing your results of the Animal Analogy quiz to the corresponding conflict styles from your text provide?

_____

_____

_____

12.4 THE END VERSUS THE MEANS

LEARNING OBJECTIVES

- Analyze given conflict situations to determine shared and individual ends and possible means.
- Describe a personal conflict situation and determine shared and individual ends and possible means.

INSTRUCTIONS

1. In each of the conflict situations that follow, identify the <u>ends</u> each party seems to be seeking. There may be ends that the relationship shares as well as individual ends for each of the parties involved. *Ends* in a conflict are the overall, general (often relational) goals that the dyad has.
2. Brainstorm a series of possible <u>means</u> that could achieve each person's (and the relationship's) ends. *Means* are the many possible ways to reach the end state.
3. Record conflict situations of your own, identifying ends and means.

CONFLICT SITUATION	SHARED ENDS	SPEAKER'S ENDS	OTHER'S ENDS	POSSIBLE MEANS
EXAMPLE *My friend wants me to visit her in Washington and meet her family. I'd like to visit, but it would cost a lot, and I'd rather save the money for something else.*	*We both want to maintain the affection in the relationship. We both want one another to know we are important to one another and that we care about one another and our families.*	*I want to spend as little money as possible while still letting my friend know how important she is to me. I don't want to lose her friendship.*	*She wants to show her family what a good friend I am and have some companionship while she has to stay in Washington.*	*She / her family sends me money to go to Washington. We share the cost. I combine whatever else I want to do with a short trip to Washington. We arrange for the family to meet me when they next come to our city. My friend comes back with her sister or mother to spend time with me.*

CONFLICT SITUATION	SHARED ENDS	SPEAKER'S ENDS	OTHER'S ENDS	POSSIBLE MEANS
1. My roommate wants a friend (whom I dislike) to sublease a room in our apartment.				
2. I'm dating a person who's of a different race than I am, and my family thinks this is a mistake.				
3. My older sister thinks that I'll turn into an alcoholic when I have a few beers (there are a few alcohol problems in our family). I tell her not to worry, but she won't get off my case.				
4. My mom keeps asking me about my grades and nagging me on the issue of my boyfriend. She thinks I'm going to make the same mistakes as she did.				

CONFLICT SITUATION	SHARED ENDS	SPEAKER'S ENDS	OTHER'S ENDS	POSSIBLE MEANS
5. Some people in my office listen to country music all day. I've got nothing against it, but it gets old. I'd like more variety.				
6. Your example:				

12.5 WIN–WIN PROBLEM SOLVING

LEARNING OBJECTIVES

- Identify the relational conflict styles, patterns of behavior, and conflict rituals that define a given relationship.
- Demonstrate how you could use the win–win approach in a given conflict.
- Assess the effectiveness and appropriateness of using the win-win approach.

INSTRUCTIONS

1. Follow the instructions below as a guide to dealing with an interpersonal conflict facing you now.
2. After completing the win–win steps, record your conclusions in the space provided.

Step 1: Identify your unmet needs (i.e., the situation, the person(s) involved, the history, etc.).

_____

_____

Step 2: Make a date. (Choose a time and place that will make it easiest for both parties to work constructively on the issue.)

_____

Step 3: Describe your problem and needs (behavior, interpretation, feeling, consequence, intention). Avoid proposing specific means or solutions at this point.

_____

_____

Step 3A: Ask your partner to show that she or he understands you (paraphrase or perception-check).

_____

_____

Step 3B: Solicit your partner's point of view/clear message (behavior, interpretation, feeling, consequence, intention).

_____

_____

Class _____   Name _____

_____

_____

Step 4: Clarify your partner's point of view (paraphrase or perception-check as necessary).

_____

_____

Step 5: Negotiate a solution.

a. Restate the needs of both parties (what both have in common).

_____

_____

b. Work together to generate a number of possible solutions that might satisfy these needs. Don't criticize any suggestions here!

_____

_____

_____

_____

_____

c. Evaluate the solutions you just listed, considering the advantages and problems of each. If you think of any new solutions, record them above.

_____

_____

_____

d. Decide on the best solution, listing it here.

_____

Step 6: Follow up the solution. Set a trial period, and then plan to meet with your partner and see if your agreement is satisfying both your needs. If not, return to step 3 and use this procedure to refine your solution.

_____

_____

CONCLUSIONS

In what ways is this procedure similar to or different from the way in which you usually deal with interpersonal conflicts?

_____

_____

_____

Was the outcome of your problem-solving session different from what it might have been if you had communicated in your usual style? How?

_____

_____

_____

In what ways can you use the no-lose methods in your interpersonal conflicts? With whom? On what issues? What kinds of behavior will be especially important?

_____

_____

_____

What concerns or hesitations do you have about using the win–win approach? Why?

_____

_____

_____

12.6 MEDIATED MESSAGES—CONFLICT MANAGEMENT

LEARNING OBJECTIVES

- Identify the conflicts in your important relationships and how satisfied you are with the way they have been handled.
- Assess the effectiveness of conflict management in mediated contexts.

INSTRUCTIONS

Discuss each of the questions below in your group. Prepare written answers for your instructor or be prepared to contribute to a large group discussion, comparing your experiences with those of others in your class.

1. In your experience, does conflict occur more rapidly or less rapidly in mediated contexts (e.g., email, instant messaging/chat, telephone).

   _____

   _____

   _____

2. Describe how mediated communication channels might help or hinder the brainstorming process (an important aspect of win–win problem-solving). Would the level of emotion involved make a difference? Why or why not?

   _____

   _____

   _____

3. Describe gender and/or cultural differences in conflict management that might occur in mediated contexts.

   _____

   _____

   _____

4. Describe whether in your experience certain mediated contexts tend to promote the use of particular conflict styles and whether or not conflict is easier or harder to manage using particular mediated channels.

_____

_____

_____

12.7 CONFLICT MANAGEMENT

LEARNING OBJECTIVES

- Identify the relational conflict styles, patterns of behavior, and conflict rituals that define a given relationship.
- Evaluate the potential of the win-win problem-solving method to solve this situation.

INSTRUCTIONS

Use the case below and the discussion questions that follow to discuss the variety of communication issues involved in effective communication. Make notes on this page, add other pages on your own, or prepare a group report/analysis based on your discussion. Add your own experiences to individualize the analysis.

CASE

Klaus and Drew have been roommates for two years, and they have had very few problems. But this term Klaus has a difficult and early class schedule, and he has taken on more hours at work to make ends meet. Drew's parents support him completely and he has a very light schedule this term. Klaus and Drew's friends continue to come to their house to party, and Drew is very irritated with Klaus because he's always studying and is a big bore all of a sudden. Klaus thinks Drew is a spoiled brat and insensitive to his needs. Neither Klaus nor Drew has said anything at this point.

1. Should Klaus and Drew bring this conflict out in the open? Would airing their differences be beneficial or harmful to the relationship?

   _____

   _____

2. What are the unmet needs of Klaus and Drew in this situation? Should they keep those unmet needs to themselves and use an avoidance style, or should they use one of the other personal conflict styles?

   _____

   _____

   _____

3. Evaluate the potential of the win–win problem-solving method to solve this situation.

   _____

   _____

12.8 ASSESSING YOUR CONFLICT STYLE

LEARNING OBJECTIVES

- Identify the conflicts in your important relationships and how satisfied you are with the way they have been handled.
- Describe your personal conflict styles, evaluate their effectiveness, and suggest alternatives as appropriate.

INSTRUCTIONS

Describe three conflicts that you have been in that did not have a successful resolution for you. Identify your conflict style in each and then describe what you could have done differently in this conflict.

Conflict 1 Description:

_____

_____

_____

Conflict Style _____

What would you have done differently?

_____

_____

_____

Conflict 2 Description:

_____

_____

_____

Conflict Style _____

_____

Class _____   Name _____

What would you have done differently?

_____

_____

_____

Conflict 3 Description:

_____

_____

_____

Conflict Style _____

What would you have done differently?

_____

_____

_____

STUDY GUIDE

CHECK YOUR UNDERSTANDING

TRUE/FALSE

Mark the statements below as true or false. Correct statements that are false on the lines below to create a true statement.

_____ 1. Gender and culture rarely have an impact on the types and styles of conflict.

_____

_____ 2. A conflict can exist even if both parties aren't aware of the disagreement.

_____

_____ 3. Every relationship of any depth at all has conflict.

_____

_____ 4. Many satisfied couples think and communicate differently when they disagree.

_____

_____ 5. Conflicts can never be constructive.

_____

_____ 6. Because of its indirect approach, passive aggression is a good choice for dealing with conflict.

_____

_____ 7. Competing is clearly superior to other conflict styles to get what you want.

_____

_____ 8. Compromising is never a satisfying way to resolve a conflict.

_____

_____ 9. "It takes two to tango"—in conflict, as in dancing, men and women behave in totally similar ways.

_____

_____ 10. The first step in win–win problem solving is to make a follow-up plan.

_____

COMPLETION

Fill in the blanks with the crazymaker term described below.

avoiders   pseudoaccommodators   guiltmakers   subject changers   distracters
mind readers   trivial tyrannizers   gunnysackers   beltliners   trappers

1. _____ don't respond immediately when they get angry. Instead, they let conflicts build up until they all pour out at once.

2. _____ do things they know will irritate their conflict partner rather than honestly sharing their resentments.

3. _____ engage in character analyses, explaining what the other person *really* means, instead of allowing their partners to express feelings honestly.

4. _____ set up a desired behavior for their partners and then when the behavior is met, they attack the very thing they requested.

5. _____ refuse to fight by leaving, falling asleep, or pretending to be busy.

6. _____ try to make their partners feel responsible for causing their pain even though they won't come right out and say what they feel or want.

7. _____ refuse to face up to a conflict either by giving in or by pretending that there's nothing at all wrong.

8. _____ use intimate knowledge of their partners to get them "where it hurts."

9. _____ attack other parts of their partner's life rather than express their feelings about the object of their dissatisfaction.

10. _____ escape facing up to aggression by shifting the conversation whenever it approaches an area of conflict.

MULTIPLE CHOICE

Match the terms below with their definitions.

a. an indirect expression of aggression, delivered in a way that allows the sender to maintain a façade of kindness
b. an oblique way of expressing wants or needs in order to save face for the recipient
c. an uncontrolled, spontaneous explosion involved in conflict
d. an approach to conflict resolution in which one party reaches its goal at the expense of the other
e. a pattern of managing disagreements that repeats itself over time in a relationship

_____ 1. win–lose

_____ 2. indirect communication

_____ 3. "Vesuvius"

_____ 4. conflict style

_____ 5. passive aggression

Choose the letter of the personal conflict style that is best illustrated by the behavior found below.

a. avoidance
b. accommodation
c. compete/direct aggression
d. compete/passive aggression
e. compromise
f. collaborate/win–win

_____ 6. Stan keeps joking around to keep us from talking about commitment.

_____ 7. "I can't believe you were so stupid as to have deleted the report."

_____ 8. Even though he wanted to go to the party, Allen stayed home with Sara rather than hear her complain.

_____ 9. Alternating bicycling and using a car, roommates are able to share expenses for only one car.

_____ 10. A smoker and nonsmoker agree that smoking on the balcony meets both their needs.

_____ 11. Rather than tell Nick about his frustration over Nick's not meeting the deadline, Howard complained to others about Nick's unreliability while maintaining a smiling front to Nick.

_____ 12. Carol wouldn't answer the phone after their disagreement because she was afraid it would be Nancy on the other end.

_____ 13. Seeing John's obvious distress, Terrell put aside his work to listen to John for a half-hour. This didn't totally meet either's needs, but did partially meet each person's needs.

_____ 14. Even though Sage could see Kham's distress, she told him she had a deadline to meet in one hour and asked if they could talk then.

_____ 15. (Sarcastically) "Oh, sure, I *loved* having dinner with your parents instead of going to the party Saturday night."

Choose the best answer for each statement below.

16. When partners use different but mutually reinforcing behaviors, they illustrate a
    a. complementary conflict style.
    b. symmetrical conflict style.
    c. parallel conflict style.
    d. supportive conflict style.

17. Research suggests that partners of "self-silencers" (people who avoid conflict) often feel
    a. relieved that they never fight.
    b. encouraged to be more honest.
    c. frustrated and uncomfortable.
    d. none of the above.

18. All of the following are The Four Horseman except:
    a. criticism
    b. defensiveness
    c. cowardlyness
    d. stonewalling

19. All of the following are steps for collaborative problem solving except:
    a. identify your problem and unmet needs
    b. set a date
    c. describe your problem and needs
    d. demand a fair solution

20. All of the following are steps for collaborative problem solving except:
    a. consider your partner's point of view
    b. negotiate a solution
    c. monitor and correct your partner's behavior
    d. follow up on the solution

CHAPTER TWELVE STUDY GUIDE ANSWERS

TRUE/FALSE

1. F	3. T	5. F	7. F	9. F
2. F	4. T	6. F	8. F	10. F

COMPLETION

1. gunnysackers
2. trivial tyrannizers
3. mind readers
4. trappers
5. avoiders
6. guiltmakers
7. pseudoaccommodators
8. beltliners
9. distractors
10. subject changers

MULTIPLE CHOICE

1. d	5. a	9. f	13. e	17. c
2. b	6. a	10. f	14. f	18. c
3. c	7. d	11. d	15. c	19. d
4. e	8. b	12. a	16. a	20. c

END NOTES

CHAPTER ONE

1. Williams, K. D. (2001). *Ostracism: The power of silence* (pp. 7–11). New York, NY: Guilford.
2. O'Reilly, J., Robinson, S. L., Berdahl, J. L., & Banki, S. (2014). Is negative attention better than no attention? The comparative effects of ostracism and harassment at work. *Organization Science*.
3. Ross, J. B., & McLaughlin, M. M. (Eds.). (1949). A portable medieval reader. New York, NY: Viking.
4. Schachter, S. (1959). *The psychology of affiliation* (pp. 9–10). Stanford, CA: Stanford University Press.
5. Jackson, W. C. (1978, September 7). Lonely dean finishes "excruciating" voyage. *Wisconsin State Journal*.
6. McCain, J. (1999). *Faith of my fathers* (p. 212). New York, NY: Random House.
7. Gawande, A. (2009, March 30). Hellhole. *The New Yorker*, 36–45.
8. Holt-Lunstad, J., Smith, T. B., & Layton, J. B. (2010). Social relationships and mortality risk: A meta-analytic review. *PLoS Med*, 7(7), e1000316.
9. Three articles in the *Journal of the American Medical Association (JAMA)* 267 (January 22/29, 1992) discuss the link between psychosocial influences and coronary heart disease: Case, R. B., Moss, A. J., Case, N., McDermott, M., & Eberly, S. (1992, January 22/29). Living alone after myocardial infarction. *JAMA, 267*, 515–519; Williams, R. B., Barefoot, J. C., Califf, R. M., Haney, T. L., Saunders, W. B., Pryon, D. B., … & Mark, D. B. (1992, January 22/29). Prognostic importance of social and economic resources among medically treated patients with angiographically documented coronary artery disease. *JAMA, 267*, 520–524; and Ruberman, R. (1992, January 22/29). Psychosocial influences on mortality of patients with coronary heart disease. *JAMA, 267*, 559–560; Cacioppo, J. T., Ernst, J. M., Burleson, M. H., McClintock, M. K., Malarkey, W. B., Hawkley, L. C., … & Berntson G. G. (2000). Lonely traits and concomitant physiological processes: The MacArthur social neuroscience studies. *International Journal of Psychophysiology, 35*, 143–154.
10. Cohen, S., Doyle, W. J., Skoner, D. P., Rabin, B. S., & Gwaltney, J. M. (1997). Social ties and susceptibility to the common cold. *Journal of the American Medical Association, 277*, 1940–1944.
11. Parker-Pope, T. (2010). *For better: The science of a good marriage*. New York, NY: Dutton.
12. Ybarra, O., Burnstein, O. E., Winkielman, P., Keller, M. C., Manis, M., Chan, E., & Rodriguez, J. (2008). Mental exercising through simple socializing: Social interaction promotes general cognitive functioning. *Personality and Social Psychology Bulletin, 34*, 248–259.
13. Bell, R. A. (2010). Conversational involvement and loneliness. In M. L. Knapp & J. A. Daly (Eds.), *Interpersonal communication* (pp. 99–120). Thousand Oaks, CA: Sage.
14. Floyd, K. & Riforgiate, S. (2006). Human affection exchange: XII. Affectionate communication is related to diurnal variation in salivary free cortisol. *Western Journal of Communication, 75*, 351–368.
15. Shattuck, R. (1980). *The forbidden experiment: The story of the wild boy of Aveyron* (p. 37). New York, NY: Farrar, Straus & Giroux.
16. Rubin, R. B., Perse, E. M., & Barbato, C. A. (1988). Conceptualization and measurement of interpersonal communication motives. *Human Communication Research, 14*, 602–628.
17. Diener, E. & Seligman, M. E. P. (2002). Very happy people. *Psychological Science, 13*, 81–84.
18. Kahneman, D., Krueger, A. B., Schkade, D. A., Schwartz, N., & Stone, A. A. (2004). A daily measure. *Science, 306*, 1645.
19. Rehman, U. S. & Holtzworth-Munroe, A. (2007). A cross-cultural examination of the relation of marital communication behavior to marital satisfaction. *Journal of Family Psychology, 21*, 759–763.
20. Rochmis, J. (February 16, 2000). Study: Humans do many things. *Wired*.
21. McPherson, M., Smith-Lovin, L., & Brashears, M. E. (2006). Social isolation in America: Changes in core discussion networks over two decades. *American Sociological Review, 71*, 353–375; McPherson, M., Smith-Lovin, L., & Brashears, M. E. (2008). The ties that bind are fraying. *Contexts, 7*, 32–36.
22. Reis, H. T. & Gable, S. L. (2003). Toward a positive psychology of relationships. In C. L. Keyes & J. Haidt (Eds.), *Flourishing: The positive person and the good life* (pp. 129–159). Washington, DC: American Psychological Association.
23. Harper's index. (1994, December). *Harper's*, 13.
24. Mauksch, L. B., Dugdale, D. C., Dodsonb, S., & Epstein, R. (2007). Relationship, communication, and efficiency in the medical encounter. *Archives of Internal Medicine, 168*, 1387–1395; Holmes, F. (2007). If you listen, the patient will tell you the diagnosis. *International Journal of Listening, 21*, 156–161.
25. Joint Commission on the Accreditation of Healthcare Organizations. (2008). *Sentinel event statistics*. Oakbrook Terrace, IL: Author.
26. Levinson, W., Roter, D., & Mullooly J. P. (1997). Physician-patient communication: The relationship with malpractice claims among primary care physicians and surgeons. *Journal of the American Medical Association, 277*, 553–59; Rodriguez, H. P., Rodday, A. C., Marshall, R. E., Nelson, K. L., Rogers, W. H., & Safran, D. G. (2008). Relation of patients' experiences with individual physicians to malpractice risk. *International Journal for Quality in Health Care, 20*, 5–12.
27. Maslow, A. H. (1968). *Toward a psychology of being*. New York, NY: Van Nostrand Reinhold.
28. Korn, C. J., Morreale, S. P., &Boileau, D. M. (2000). Defining the field: Revisiting the ACA 1995 definition of communication studies. *Journal of the Association for Communication Administration, 29*, 40–52.
29. Ledbetter, A. M. (2014). The past and future of technology in interpersonal communication theory and research. *Communication Studies, 65*, 456–459; Berger, J. & Iyengar, R. (2013). Communication channels and word of mouth: How the medium shapes the message. *Journal of Consumer Research, 40*, 567–579.
30. Shelly, R. K. (1997). Sequences and cycles in social interaction. *Small Group Research, 28*, 333–356.
31. Redmond, M. V. (1995). Interpersonal communication: Definitions and conceptual approaches. In M. V. Redmond (Ed.), *Interpersonal communication: Readings in theory and research* (pp. 4–11). Fort Worth, TX: Harcourt Brace.
32. Miller, G. R. & Steinberg, M. (1975). *Between people: A new analysis of interpersonal communication*. Chicago, IL: SRA; and Stewart, J. & Logan, C. (1998). *Together: Communicating interpersonally* (5th ed.). New York, NY: McGraw-Hill.
33. Bochner, A. P. (1984). The functions of human communication in interpersonal bonding. In C. C. Arnold & J. W. Bowers (Eds.), *Handbook of rhetorical and communication theory* (p. 550). Boston, MA: Allyn and Bacon; Trenholm, S. &

Jensen, A. (1992). *Interpersonal communication* (2nd ed., pp. 27–33). Belmont, CA: Wadsworth; and Stewart, J. & D'Angelo, G. (1998). *Together: Communicating interpersonally* (5th ed., p. 5). New York, NY: McGraw-Hill.

34. Farrell, L. C., DiTunnariello, N., & Pearson, J. C. (2014). Exploring relational cultures: Rituals, privacy disclosure, and relational satisfaction. *Communication Studies, 65,* 314–329.

35. Gergen, K. J. (1991). *The saturated self: Dilemmas of identity in contemporary life* (p. 158). New York, NY: Basic Books.

36. Buck, R. & VanLear, C. A. (2002). Verbal and nonverbal communication: Distinguishing symbolic, spontaneous, and pseudo-spontaneous nonverbal behavior. *Journal of Communication, 52,* 522–541; and Clevenger, T., Jr. (1991). Can one not communicate? A conflict of models. *Communication Studies, 42,* 340–353; Stamp, G. H. & Knapp, M. L. (1990). The construct of intent in interpersonal communication. *Quarterly Journal of Speech, 76,* 282–299.

37. Coupland, N., Giles, H., & Wiemann, J. M. (Eds.). (1991). *Miscommunication and problematic talk.* Newbury Park, CA: Sage.

38. Dillard, J. P., Solomon, D. H., & Palmer, M. T. (1999). Structuring the concept of relational communication. *Communication Monographs, 66,* 49–65; and Watzlawick, P., Beavin, J., & Jackson, D. (1967). *Pragmatics of human communication.* New York, NY: Norton.

39. McCroskey, J. C. & Richmond, V. P. (1996). *Fundamentals of human communication: An interpersonal perspective.* Prospect Heights, IL: Waveland.

40. Sillars, A. (1998). (Mis)Understanding. In B. H. Spitzberg & W. R. Cupach (Eds.), *The dark side of close relationships* (pp. 73–102). Mahwah, NJ: Erlbaum.

41. Keysar, B. & Henley, A. S. (2002). Speakers' overestimation of their effectiveness. *Psychological Science, 13,* 207–212.

42. Wu, S. & Keysar, B. (2007). The effect of information overlap on communication effectiveness. *Cognitive Science, 31,* 169–181.

43. Powers, W. G. & Witt, P. L. (2008). Expanding the framework of communication fidelity theory. *Communication Quarterly, 56,* 247–267.

44. McCroskey, J. C. & Wheeless, L. (1976). *Introduction to human communication* (p. 5). Boston, MA: Allyn and Bacon; Cloven, D. H. & Roloff, M. E. (1991). Sense-making activities and interpersonal conflict: communicative cures for the mulling blues. *Western Journal of Speech Communication, 55,* 134–158; and Stiebel, D. (1997). *When talking makes things worse! Resolving problems when communication fails.* Kansas City, MO: Andrews McMeel.

45. Spitzberg, B. H. (2010). Communication competence as knowledge, skill, and impressions. In M. L. Knapp & J. A. Daly (Eds.), *Interpersonal communication* (pp. 203–210). Thousand Oaks, CA: Sage; and Wilson, S. R. & Sabee, C. M. (2003). Explicating communicative competence as a theoretical term. In J. O. Greene & B. R. Burleson (Eds.), *Handbook of communication and social interaction skills.* Mahwah, NJ: Erlbaum.

46. Ames, D. R. & Flynn, F. J. (2007). What breaks a leader: The curvilinear relation between assertiveness and leadership. *Journal of Personality and Social Psychology, 92,* 307–324.

47. Spitzberg, B. H. (1991). An examination of trait measures of interpersonal competence. *Communication Reports, 4,* 22–29.

48. Teven, J. J., Richmond, V. P., McCroskey, J. C., & McCroskey, L. L. (2010). Updating relationships between communication traits and communication competence. *Communication Research Reports, 27,* 263–270.

49. Hullman, G. A., Planisek, A., McNally, J. S., & Rubin, R. B. (2010). Competence, personality, and self-efficacy: Relationships in an undergraduate interpersonal course. *Atlantic Journal of Communication, 18,* 36–49.

50. Hynes, G. E. (2012). Improving employees' interpersonal communication competencies: A qualitative study. *Business Communication Quarterly, 75,* 466–475; Brown, R. F., Bylund, C. L., Gueguen, J. A., Diamond, C., Eddington, J., & Kissane, D. (2010). Developing patient-centered communication skills training for oncologists: Describing the content and efficacy of training. *Communication Education, 59,* 235–248; Hyvarinen, L., Tanskanen, P., Katajavuori, N., & Isotalus, P. (2010). A method for teaching communication in pharmacy in authentic work situations. *Communication Education, 59,* 124–145.

51. Rubin, R. B., Perse, E. M., & Barbato, C. A. (1988). Conceptualization and measurement of interpersonal communication motives. *Human Communication Research, 14,* 602–628.

52. Morreale, S. P. & Pearson, J. C. (2008). Why communication education is important: The centrality of the discipline in the 21st century. *Communication Education, 57,* 224–240.

53. Hample, D. (2005). Invitational capacity. In F. van Emeren & P. Houtlosser, *The practice of argumentation* (pp. 337–348). Amsterdam, The Netherlands: John Benjamins.

54. Braithwaite, D. O. & Eckstein, N. (2003). Reconceptualizing supportive interactions: How persons with disabilities communicatively manage assistance. *Journal of Applied Communication Research, 31,* 1–26.

55. Stephens, K. K., Houser, M. L., & Cowan, R. L. (2009). R U able to meat me: The impact of students' overly casual email messages to instructors. *Communication Education, 58,* 303–326.

56. Burleson, B. R. (2007). Constructivism: A general theory of communication skill. In B. B. Whaley & W. Samter (Eds.), *Explaining communication: Contemporary theories and exemplars* (pp. 105–128). Mahwah, NJ: Erlbaum.

57. Wackman, D. B., Miller, S., & Nunnally, E. W. (1976). *Student workbook: Increasing awareness and communication skills* (p. 6). Minneapolis, MN: Interpersonal Communication Programs.

58. Burleson, B. R. & Caplan, S. E. (1998). Cognitive complexity. In J. C. McCroskey, J. A. Daly, M. M. Martin, & M. J. Beatty (Eds.), *Communication and personality: Trait perspectives* (pp. 233–286). Creskill, NJ: Hampton Press; Burleson, B. R. (2011). A constructivist approach to listening. *International Journal of Listening, 25,* 27–46.

59. Wiemann, J. M. & Backlund, P. M. (1980). Current theory and research in communication competence. *Review of Educational Research, 50,* 185–199; and Lakey, S. G. & Canary, D. J. (2002). Actor goal achievement and sensitivity to partner as critical factors in understanding interpersonal communication competence and conflict strategies. *Communication Monographs, 69,* 217–235.

60. Hamachek, D. E. (1987). *Encounters with the self* (2nd ed., p. 8). Fort Worth, TX: Holt, Rinehart and Winston; Daly, J. A., Vangelisti, A. L., & Daughton, S. M. (1995). The nature and correlates of conversational sensitivity. In M. V. Redmond (Ed.), *Interpersonal communication: Readings in theory and research.* Fort Worth, TX: Harcourt Brace.

61. Dunning, D. A. & Kruger, J. (1999, December). Unskilled and unaware of it: How difficulties in recognizing one's own incompetence lead to inflated self-assessments. *Journal of Personality and Social Psychology, 77,* 1121–1134.

62. Executive Office of the President, Council of Economic Advisers. (2009, July). *Preparing the workers of today for the jobs of tomorrow* (p. 10).

63. Hart, R. P., as reported by Knapp, M. L. (1984). In *Interpersonal communication and human relationships* (pp. 342–344). Boston, MA: Allyn and Bacon; Hart, R. P. & Burks, D. M. (1972). Rhetorical sensitivity and social interaction. *Speech Monographs, 39,* 75–91; and Hart, R. P., Carlson, R. E., & Eadie, W. F. (1980). Attitudes toward communication and the assessment of rhetorical sensitivity. *Communication Monographs, 47,* 1–22.

64. Kim, Y. Y. (1991). Intercultural communication competence: A systems-theoretic view. In S. Ting-Toomey & F. Korzenny (Eds.), *Cross-cultural interpersonal communication*. Newbury Park, CA: Sage; and Chen, G. M. & Sarosta, W. J. (1996). Intercultural communication competence: A synthesis. In B. R. Burleson & A. W. Kunkel (Eds.), *Communication yearbook 19*. Thousand Oaks, CA: Sage.

65. Yum, J. O. (2012). Communication competence: A Korean perspective. *China Media Report Overseas, 8*, 1–7.

66. Collier, M. J. (1996). Communication competence problematics in ethnic relationships. *Communication Monographs, 63*, 314–336.

67. Chen, L. (1997). Verbal adaptive strategies in U.S. American dyadic interactions with U.S. American or East-Asian partners. *Communication Monographs, 64*, 302–323.

68. Mulac, A., Bradac, J., & Gibbons, P. (2001). Empirical support for the gender-as-culture hypothesis. *Human Communication Research, 27*, 121–152.

69. Hajek, C. & Giles, H. (2003). New directions in intercultural communication competence: The process model. In B. R. Burleson & J. O. Greene (Eds.), *Handbook of communication and social interaction skills*. Mahwah, NJ: Erlbaum; and Ting-Toomey, S. & Chung, L. C. (2005). *Understanding intercultural communication*. Los Angeles, CA: Roxbury.

70. Kalliny, M., Cruthirds, K., & Minor, M. (2006). Differences between American, Egyptian and Lebanese humor styles: Implications for international management. *International Journal of Cross-Cultural Management, 6*, 121–134.

71. Samovar, L. A., & Porter, R. E. (2004). *Communication between cultures* (5th ed.). Belmont, CA: Wadsworth.

72. Kassing, J. W. (1997). Development of the intercultural willingness to communicate scale. *Communication Research Reports, 14*, 399–407;

73. Burgoon, J. K., Berger, C. R., & Waldron, V. R. (2000). Mindfulness and interpersonal communication. *Journal of Social Issues, 56*, 105–128.

74. Berger, C. R. (1979). Beyond initial interactions: Uncertainty, understanding, and the development of interpersonal relationships. In H. Giles & R. St. Clair (Eds.), *Language and social psychology* (pp. 122–144). Oxford, England: Blackwell.

75. Carrell, L. J. (1997). Diversity in the communication curriculum: Impact on student empathy. *Communication Education, 46*, 234–244.

CHAPTER TWO

1. *http://www.merriam-webster.com/dictionary/social%20media*

2. Park, C. (November, 2011). *Yesterday's sci-fi is today's reality*. ThinkWithGoogle.com.

3. Fischer, C. S. (1992). *America calling: A social history of the telephone to 1940*. Berkeley: University of California.

4. Culnan, M. J. & Markus, M. L. (1987). Information technologies. In F. M. Jablin, L. L. Putnam, K. H. Roberts, & L. W. Porter (Eds.), *Handbook of organizational communication: An interdisciplinary perspective* (pp. 420–443). Newbury Park, CA: Sage; Kiesler, S., Siegel, J., & McGuire, T. W. (1984). Social psychological aspects of computer-mediated communication. *American Psychologist, 39*, 1123–1134; Sproull, L. & Kiesler, S. (1986). Reducing social context cues: Electronic mail in organizational communication. *Management Science, 32*, 1492–1512.

5. Hampton, K. (November 4, 2009). *Social isolation and new technology*. Pew Internet & American Life Project.

6. Carlson, J .R. & George, J. F. (2004). Media appropriateness in the conduct and discovery of deceptive communication: The relative influence of richness and synchronicity. *Group Decision and Negotiation, 13*, 191–210.

7. Mantelero, A. (2013). The EU proposal for a general data protection regulation and the roots of the "right to be forgotten." *Computer Law & Security Review, 29*, 229–235.

8. Barnett, E. (2012, February 18). Tweeting about a bad day could lose you your job. *The Telegraph*.

9. Goldwert, L. (2012, May 24). Facebook named in a third of divorce filings in 2011. *New York Daily News*.

10. Madden, M. (2012, February 24). *Privacy management on social media sites*. Pew Internet & American Life Project.

11. Hollenbaugh, E. E. & Everett, M. K. (2013). The effects of anonymity on self-disclosure in blogs: An application of the online disinhibition effect. *Journal of Computer-Mediated Communication, 18*, 283–302; Joinson, A. N. (2011). Disinhibition and the Internet. In J. Gackenbach (Ed.), *Psychology and the Internet: Intrapersonal, interpersonal, and transpersonal implications* (2nd ed.). San Diego, CA: Academic Press; Lapidot-Lefler, N. & Barak, A. (2012). Effects of anonymity, invisibility, and lack of eye contact on toxic online disinhibition. *Computers in Human Behavior, 28*, 434–443.

12. Tannen, D. (1994, May 16). Gender gap in cyberspace. *Newsweek*.

13. Udris, R. (2014). Cyberbullying among high school students in Japan: Development and validation of the Online Disinhibition Scale. *Computers in Human Behavior, 41*, 253–261; Lapidot-Lefler, N. & Barak, A. (2012). Effects of anonymity, invisibility, and lack of eye-contact on toxic online disinhibition. *Computers in Human Behavior, 22*, 434–443.

14. Walther, J. B. (1996). Computer-mediated communication: Impersonal, interpersonal, and hyperpersonal interaction. *Communication Research, 23*, 3–43; Walther, J. B. (2007). Selective self-presentation in computer-mediated communication: Hyperpersonal dimensions of technology, language, and cognition. *Computers in Human Behavior, 23*, 2538–2557.

15. Walther, J. B. (1997). Group and interpersonal effects in international computer-mediated collaboration. *Human Communication Research, 23*, 342–369.

16. Ramirez, A. & Zhang, S. (2007). When online meets offline: The effect of modality switching on relational communication. *Communication Monographs, 74*, 287–310.

17. Kirkpatrick, D. (1992, March 23). Here comes the payoff from PCs. *Fortune*.

18. Anderson, J. Q. & Rainie, L. (2010, July 2). *The future of social relations*. Pew Internet & American Life Project.

19. Cacioppo, J. T., Cacioppo, S., Gonzaga, G. C., Ogburn, E. L., & VanderWeele, T. J. (2013). Marital satisfaction and break-ups differ across on-line and off-line meeting venues. *PNAS, 110*, 10135–10140.

20. Smith, A. & Duggan, M. (October 21, 2013). *Online dating & relationships*. Pew Internet & American Life Project.

21. Porter, C. E. (2006). A typology of virtual communities: A multi-disciplinary foundation for future research. *Journal of Computer-Mediated Communication, 10*, Article 3; Schwammlein, E. & Wodzicki, K. (2012). What to tell about me? Self-presentation in online communities. *Journal of Computer-Mediated Communication, 17*, 387–407.

22. Baturay, M. H. Relationships among sense of classroom community, perceived cognitive learning and satisfaction of students at an e-learning course. *Interactive Learning Environments, 19*, 563–575; Palloff, R. M. & Pratt, K. (2007). *Building online learning communities: Effective strategies for the virtual classroom*. San Francisco, CA: Jossey-Bass.

23. Orr, E. S., Sisic, M., Ross, C., Simmering, M. G., Arseneault, J. M., & Orr, R. R. (2009). The influence of shyness on the use of Facebook in an undergraduate sample. *Cyberpsychology Behavior, 12*, 337–340.

24. Baker, L. R. & Oswald, D. L. (2010). Shyness and online social networking services. *Journal of Social and Personal Relationships, 27*, 873–889.

25. Rosenwald, M. S. (February 12, 2011). Can Facebook help overcome shyness? *Washington Post*.

26. Cotten, S. R., Anderson, W. A., & McCullough, B. M. (2013). Impact of internet use on loneliness and contact with others among older adults: Cross-sectional analysis. *Journal of Medical Internet Research, 15*, e39.

27. Lee, K., Noh, M., & Koo, D. (2013). Lonely people are no longer lonely on social networking sites: The mediating role of self-disclosure and social support. *Cyberpsychology, Behavior, and Social Networking, 16*, 413–418.

28. Tong, S. T. & Walther, J. B. (2011). Relational maintenance and computer-mediated communication. In K. B. Wright & L. M. Webb (Eds.), *Computer mediated communication and personal relationships* (pp. 98–118). New York: Peter Lang; Ledbetter, A. M. (2010). Assessing the measurement invariance of relational maintenance behavior when face-to-face and online. *Communication Research Reports, 27*, 30–37.

29. Lenhart, A. (2012, March 19). *Teens, smartphones & texting*. Pew Internet & American Life Project.

30. Connectmogul (2013, March 22). *Texting statistics*. Connectmogul.com.

31. Thurlow, C. (2003). Generation Txt? The sociolinguistics of young people's text-messaging.

32. Craig, E. & Wright, B. (2012). Computer-mediated relational development and maintenance on Facebook. *Communication Research Reports, 29*, 119–129; Dainton, M. (2013). Relationship maintenance on Facebook: Development of a measure, relationship to general maintenance, and relationship satisfaction. *College Student Journal, 47*, 112–121.

33. Bryant, E. M. & Marmo, J. (2012). The rules of Facebook friendship: A two-stage examination of interaction rules in close, casual, and acquaintance friendships. *Journal of Social and Personal Relationships, 29*, 1013–1035.

34. Nardi, B. A., Schiano, D. J., & Gumbrecht, M. (2004). Blogging as social activity, or, would you let 900 million people read your diary? *Proceedings of CSCW 2004*, Chicago, IL.

35. Lenhart, A. & Fox, S. (2006, Jul 19). *Bloggers*. Pew Internet & American Life Project.

36. Tong, S. T. & Walther, J. B. (2011.) Relational maintenance and computer-mediated communication. In K. Wright & L. Webb (Eds.) *Computer-mediated communication and personal relationships* (pp. 98–118), Cresskill, NJ: Hampton Press.

37. Bergen, K. M., Kirby, E., & McBride, M. C. (2007). "How do you get two houses cleaned?": Accomplishing family caregiving in commuter marriages. *Journal of Family Communication, 7*, 287–307.

38. Stafford, L. (2005). Maintaining long-distance and cross-residential relationships. Mahwah, NJ: Erlbaum.

39. Jiang, C. & Hancock, J. T. (2013). Absence makes the communication grow fonder: Geographic separation, interpersonal media, and intimacy in dating relationships. *Journal of Communication, 63*, 566–577.

40. Pearson, C. (August 12, 2013). Long distance relationship benefits include greater intimacy, study says. *Huffington Post*.

41. Vitak, J. (2014). Facebook makes the heart grow fonder: Relationship maintenance strategies among geographically dispersed and communication-restricted connections. In Proceedings of the 17th ACM Conference on Computer Supported Cooperative Work and Social Computing. New York: ACM; Walther, J. B. & Ramirez, A., Jr. (2010). New technologies and new directions in online relating. In S. W. Smith & S. R. Wilson (Eds.), *New directions in interpersonal communication research* (pp. 264–284). Thousand Oaks, CA: Sage.

42. Valenzuela, S., Halpern, D., & Katz, J. E. (2014). Social network sites, marriage well-being and divorce: Survey and state-level evidence from the United States. *Computers in Human Behavior, 36*. 94–101.

43. McClure, E. A., Acquavita, S. P., Dunn, K. E., Stoller, K. B., & Sitzer, M. L. (2014). Characterizing smoking, cessation services, and quit interest across outpatient substance abuse treatment modalities. *Journal of Substance Abuse Treatment, 46*, 194–201.

44. Luxton, D. D., June, J. D., & Kinn, J. T. (2011). Technology-based suicide prevention: Current applications and future directions. *Telemedicine and e-Health, 17*, 50–54.

45. Hawdon, J. & Ryan, R. (2012). Well-being after the Virginia Tech mass murder: The relative effectiveness of face-to-face and virtual interactions in providing support to survivors. *Traumatology, 18*, 3–12.

46. Fox, S. (2011, June). *Peer-to-peer healthcare*. Pew Internet & American Life Project; Rains, S. A. & Keating, D. M. (2011). The social dimension of blogging about health: Health blogging, social support, and well-being. *Communication Monographs, 78*, 511–553.

47. Sanford, A. A. (2010). "I can air my feelings instead of eating them": Blogging as social support for the morbidly obese. *Communication Studies, 61*, 567–584.

48. Flanagin, A. J. (2005). IM online: Instant messaging use among college students. *Communication Research Reports, 22*, 175–187.

49. Boase, J., Horrigan, J. B., Wellman, B., & Rainie, L. (2006, January 25). *The strength of Internet ties*. Pew Internet & American Life Project.

50. DeAndrea, D. C., Tong, S. T., & Walther, J. B. (2010). Dark sides of computer-mediated communication. In W. R. Cupach & B. H. Spitzberg (Eds.), *The dark side of close relationships II* (pp. 95–118). New York, NY: Routledge.

51. Dunbar, R. (2010). How many friends does one person need? Dunbar's number and other evolutionary quirks. Cambridge, MA: Harvard University Press.

52. Bryant, E. M., & Marmo, J. (2012). The rules of Facebook friendship: A two-stage examination of interaction rules in close, casual, and acquaintance friendships. *Journal of Social and Personal Relationships, 29*, 1013–1035.

53. Parks, M. R. (2007). *Personal networks and personal relationships*. Mahwah, NJ: Lawrence Erlbaum.

54. Dunbar, R. (2012). Social cognition on the Internet: Testing constraints on social network size. *Philosophical Transactions of the Royal Society, 367*, 2192–2201.

55. Loveys, K. (January 24, 2010). 5,000 friends on Facebook? Scientists prove 150 is the most we can cope with. *Mail Online*.

56. Tong, S. T., Van Der Heide, B., Langwell, L., & Walther, J. B. (2008). Too much of a good thing? The relationship between number of friends and interpersonal impressions on Facebook. *Journal of Computer-Mediated Communication, 13*, 531–549.

57. Lee, J. R., Moore, D. C., Park, E., & Park, S. G. (2012). Who wants to be "friend rich"? Social compensatory friending on Facebook and the moderating role of public self-consciousness. *Computers in Human Behavior, 28*, 1036–1043; Kim, J. & Lee, J. R. (2011). The Facebook paths to happiness: Effects of the number of Facebook friends and self-presentation on subjective well-being. *Cyberpsychology, Behavior, and Social Networking, 14*, 359–364.

58. Caplan, S. E. (2003). Preference for online social interaction: A theory of problematic Internet use and psychosocial well-being. *Communication Research, 30*, 625–648.

59. Kim, J., LaRose, R., & Peng, W. (2009). Loneliness as the cause and effect of problematic Internet use: The relationship between Internet use and psychological well-being. *CyberPsychology & Behavior, 12*, 451–455; Yao, M. Z. & Zhong, Z. (2014). Loneliness, social contacts, and Internet addiction: A cross-lagged panel study. *Computers in Human Behavior, 30*, 164–170.

60. Walther, J. B., Van Der Heide, B., Hamel, L., & Shulman, H. (2009). Self-generated versus other-generated statements and impressions in computer-mediated communication: A test of warranting theory using Facebook. *Communication Research, 36*, 229–253

61. Caplan, S. E. (2005). A social skill account of problematic Internet use. *Journal of Communication, 55*, 721–736.

62. Hand, M. M., Thomas, D. B., Walter, C., Deemer, E. D., & Buyanjargal, M. (2013). Facebook and romantic relationships: Intimacy and couple satisfaction associated with online social network use. *Cyberpsychology, Behavior, and Social Networking, 16*, 8–13.

63. Mirsa, S., Cheng, L., Genevie, J., &Yuan, M. (2014). The iPhone effect: The quality of in-person social interactions in the presence of mobile devices. *Environment & Behavior*; Przybylski, A. K. & Weinstein, N. (2013). Can you connect with me now? How the presence of mobile communication technology influences face-to-face conversation quality. *Journal of Social and Personal Relationships, 30*, 237–246.

64. Clayton, R. B., Nagumey, A., & Smith, J. R. (2013). Cheating, breakup, and divorce: Is Facebook to blame? *CyberPsychology, Behavior & Social Networking, 16*, 717–720.

65. Cravens, J. D., Leckie, K. R., & Whiting, J. B. (2013). Facebook infidelity: When poking becomes problematic. *Contemporary Family Therapy, 35*, 74–90; Schneider, J. P., Weiss, R., & Samenow, C. (2012). Is it really cheating? Understanding the emotional reactions and clinical treatment of spouses and partners affected by cybersex infidelity. *Sexual Addiction & Compulsivity, 19*, 123–39.

66. Valenzuela, S., Halpern, D., & Katz, J. E. (2014). Social network sites, marriage well-being and divorce: Survey and state-level evidence from the United States. *Computers in Human Behavior, 36*, 94–101.

67. Toma, C. L., Hancock, J. T., & Ellison, N. B. (2008). Separating fact from fiction: An examination of deceptive self-presentation in online dating profiles. *Personality and Social Psychology Bulletin, 34*, 1023–1036.

68. DeAndrea, D. C. & Walther, J. B. (2011). Attributions for inconsistencies between online and offline self-presentations. *Communication Research,38*, 805–825.

69. Lyndon, A., Bonds-Raacke, J., & Cratty, A. D. (2011). College students' Facebook stalking of ex-partners. *Cyberpsychology, Behavior, & Social Networking, 14*, 711–716.

70. Reyns, B. W., Henson, B., & Fisher, B. S. (2012). Stalking in the twilight zone: Extent of cyberstalking victimization and offending among college students. *Deviant Behavior, 33*, 1–25.

71. DreBing, H., Bailer, J., Anders, A., Wagner, H., & Gallas, C. (2014). Cyberstalking in a large sample of social network users: Prevalence, characteristics, and impact upon victims. *Cyberpsychology, Behavior, and Social Networking, 17*, 61–67.

72. Shahani, A. (September 15, 2014). *Smartphones are used to stalk, control domestic abuse victims*. All Tech Considered.

73. Bauman, S. (2011). *Cyberbullying: What counselors need to know*. Alexandria, VA: American Counseling Association; Holfeld, B. & Grabe, M. (2012). An examination of the history, prevalence, characteristics, and reporting of cyberbullying in the United States. In Q. Li, D. Cross, & P. K. Smith (Eds.), *Cyberbullying in the global playground: Research from international perspectives* (pp. 117–142). San Francisco, CA: Wiley-Blackwell.

74. Huang, Y.-Y. & Chou, C. (2010). An analysis of multiple factors of cyberbullying among junior high school students in Taiwan. *Computers in Human Behavior, 26*, 1581–1590.

75. Bauman, S., Toomey, R. B., & Walker, J. L. (2013). Associations among bullying, cyberbullying, and suicide in high school students. *Journal of Adolescence, 36*, 341–350; Huang, Y.-Y. & Chou, C. (2010). An analysis of multiple factors of cyberbullying among junior high school students in Taiwan. *Computers in Human Behavior, 26*, 1581–1590.

76. National Crime Prevention Council (2007, February 28). *Teens and cyberbullying*. National Crime Prevention Council.

77. Cassidy, W., Faucher, C., & Jackson, M. (2013). Cyberbullying among youth: A comprehensive review of current international research and its implications and application to policy and practice. *School Psychology International, 34*,

575–612; Roberto, A. J., Eden, J., Savage, M. W., Ramos-Salazar, L., & Deiss, D. M. (2014). Prevalence and predictors of cyberbullying perpetration by high school seniors. *Communication Quarterly, 62*, 97–114.

78. Pennebaker, J. W. (2011). *The secret lives of pronouns: What our words say about us*. New York: Bloomsbury.

79. Schwartz, H. A., Eichstaedt, J. C., Kern, M. L., Dziurzynski, L., Ramones, S. M., Agrawal, M., ... Ungar, L. H. (2013). Personality, gender, and age in the language of social media: The open-vocabulary approach. *PLoS ONE, 8*, e73791.

80. Palomares, N. A., & Lee, E. (2010). Virtual gender identity: The linguistic assimilation to gendered avatars in computer-mediated communication. *Journal of Language and Social Psychology, 29*, 5–23.

81. Kapidzic, S. & Herring, S. C. (2011). Gender, communication, and self-presentation in teen chatrooms revisited: Have patterns changed? *Journal of Computer-Mediated Communication, 17*, 39–59.

82. Prensky, M. (2001). Digital natives, digital immigrants. *On the Horizon, 9*, 1–6; Rainie, L. (October 27, 2006). *Digital natives: How today's youth are different from their "digital immigrant" elders and what that means for libraries*. Pew Research Internet Project.

83. Hyman, I. (January 26, 2014). Cell phones are changing social interaction. *Psychology Today*.

84. Smith, A. (September 19, 2011). *Americans and text messaging*. Pew Internet & American Life Project.

85. Kluger, J. (August 16, 2012). We never talk anymore: The problem with text messaging. *Time*.

86. Brenner, J. & Smith, A. (August 5, 2013). *72% of online adults are social networking site users*. Pew Internet & American Life Project.

87. Smith, A. (April 3, 2014). *Older adults and technology use*. Pew Research Internet Project.

88. Schwartz, H. A., Eichstaedt, J. C., Kern, M. L., Dziurzynski, L., Ramones, S. M., Agrawal, M., ... Ungar, L. H. (2013). Personality, gender, and age in the language of social media: The open-vocabulary approach. *PLoS ONE, 8*, e73791.

89. Helsper, E. J. & Whitty, M. T. (2010). Netiquette in married couples: Agreement about acceptable online behavior and surveillance between partners. *Computers in Human Behavior, 26*, 916–926.

90. Bauerlein, M. (2009, September 4). Why Gen-Y Johnny can't read nonverbal cues. *Wall Street Journal*.

91. Seabrook, J. (1994, June 6). My first flame. *The New Yorker*, pp. 70–79.

92. Mayer-Schönberger, V. (2011). *Delete: The virtue of forgetting in the digital age*. Princeton, NJ: Princeton University Press.

93. Preston, J. (2011, July 20). Social media history becomes a new job hurdle. *The New York Times*.

94. Rosen, J. (2010, July 25). The web means the end of forgetting. *New York Times Magazine*, 30–35.

95. Lenhart, A. (December 15, 2009). *Teens and sexting*. Pew Internet & American Life Project; Lenhart, A. & Duggan, M. (2014, February 11). *Couples, the internet, and social media*. Pew Internet & American Life Project.

96. MTV. (2009). *A thin line*. AP Digital Abuse Study.

97. Walther, J. B. & Parks, M. R. (2002). Cues filtered out, cues filtered in: Computer-mediated communication and relationships. In M. L. Knapp & J. A. Daly (Eds.) *Handbook of interpersonal communication* (3rd ed., pp. 529–563). Thousand Oaks, CA: Sage.

98. Walther, J. B., Van Der Heide, B., Hamel, L., & Shulman, H. (2009). Self-generated versus other-generated statements and impressions in computer-mediated communication: A test of warranting theory using Facebook. *Communication Research, 36*, 229–253.

99. ABC News (2012, November 30). *"Catfish" stars Nev Schulman, Max Joseph's advice for online dating*. Yahoo News.

100. Vitak, J., Ellison, N., & Steinfield, C. (2011). The ties that bond: Re-examining the relationship between Facebook use and bonding social capital. In *Proceedings of the 44th Annual Hawaii International Conference on System Sciences.* Computer Society Press.

101. Ahlstrom, M, Lundberg, N., Zabriskie, R., Eggett, D., & Lindsay, G. (2012). Me, my spouse, and my avatar: The relationship between marital satisfaction and playing massively multiplayer online role-playing games (MMORPG's). *Journal of Leisure Research, 44,* 1–22.

102. Kuss, D. J., Rooij, A. J., Shorter, G. W., Griffiths, M. D., & van de Mheen, D. (2013). Internet addiction in adolescents: Prevalence and risk factors. *Computers in Human Behavior, 29,* 1987–1996.

103. Ko, C., Yen, J., Chen, C., Chen, S., Yen, C. (2005). Proposed diagnostic criteria of Internet addiction for adolescents. *The Journal of Nervous and Mental Disease, 11,* 728–733.

CHAPTER THREE

1. Baumeister, R. F. (2005). *The cultural animal: Human nature, meaning, and social life.* New York, NY: Oxford University Press; Baumeister, R. F., Campbell, J. D., Krueger, J. I., & Vohs, K. D. (2003). Does high self-esteem cause better performance, interpersonal success, happiness, or healthier lifestyles? *Psychological Science in the Public Interest, 4,* 1–44.

2. Vohs, K. D. & Heatherton, T. F. (2004). Ego threats elicits different social comparison process among high and low self-esteem people: Implications for interpersonal perceptions. *Social Cognition, 22,* 168–191.

3. Daly, J. A. (2010). Personality and interpersonal communication. In M. L. Knapp & J. A. Daly (Eds.), *Interpersonal communication* (Vol. I, pp. 41–98). Thousand Oaks, CA: Sage; Soldz, W. & Vaillant, G. E. (1999). The big five personality traits and the life course: A 45-year longitudinal study. *Journal of Research in Personality, 33,* 208–232.

4. Wright, W. (1998). *Born that way: Genes, behavior, personality.* New York, NY: Knopf.

5. Schwartz, C. E., Wright, C. I., Shin, L. M., Kagan, J., & Rauch, S. L. (2003, June 20). Inhibited and uninhibited infants 'grown up': Adult amygdalar response to novelty. *Science,* 1952–1953.

6. Cole, J. G. & McCroskey, J. C. (2000). Temperament and socio-communicative orientation. *Communication Research Reports, 17,* 105–114.

7. Heisel, A. D., McCroskey, J. C., & Richmond, V. P. (1999). Testing theoretical relationships and non-relationships of genetically-based predictors: Getting started with communibiology. *Communication Research Reports, 16,* 1–9.

8. Cole, J. G. & McCroskey, J. C. (2000). Temperament and socio-communicative orientation. *Communication Research Reports, 17,* 105–114.

9. Wigley, C. J. (1998). Verbal aggressiveness. In J. C. McCroskey, J. A. Daly, M. M. Martin, & M. J. Beatty (Eds.), *Personality and communication: Trait perspectives.* New York, NY: Hampton.

10. McCroskey, J. C., Heisel, A. D., & Richmond, V. P. (2001). Eysenck's big three and communication traits: Three correlational studies. *Communication Monographs, 68,* 360–366.

11. Dweck, C. (2008). Can personality be changed? The role of beliefs in personality and change. *Current Directions in Psychological Science, 6,* 391–394.

12. Begney, S. (2008, December 1). When DNA is not destiny. *Newsweek, 152,* 14.

13. Jaret, C., Reitzes, D., & Shapkina, N. (2005). Reflected appraisals and self-esteem. *Sociological Perspectives, 48,* 403–419.

14. Salimi, S., Mirzamani, S., & Shahiri-Tabarestani, M. (2005). Association of parental self-esteem and expectations with adolescents' anxiety about career and education. *Psychological Reports, 96,* 569–578; Vangelisti, A. L. & Crumley, L. P. (1998). Reactions to messages that hurt: The influence of relational contexts. *Communication Monographs, 65,* 173–196.

15. Rill, L., Baiocchi, E., Hopper, M., Denker, K., & Olson, L. N. (2009). Exploration of the relationship between self-esteem, commitment, and verbal aggressiveness in romantic dating relationships. *Communication Reports, 22,* 102–113.

16. Leets, L. & Sunwolf. (2004). Being left out: Rejecting outsiders and communicating group boundaries in childhood and adolescent peer groups. *Journal of Applied Communication Research, 32,* 195–223.

17. Sillars, A., Koerner, A., & Fitzpatrick, M. A. (2005). Communication and understanding in parent-adolescent relationships. *Human Communication Research, 31,* 107–128.

18. Adler, T. (1992, October). Personality, like plaster, is pretty stable over time. *APA Monitor,* 18.

19. Brown, J. D., Novick, N. J., Lord, K. A., & Richards, J. M. (1992). When Gulliver travels: Social context, psychological closeness, and self-appraisals. *Journal of Personality and Social Psychology, 62,* 717–734.

20. Krcmar, M., Giles, S., & Helme, D. (2008). Understanding the process: How mediated and peer norms affect young women's body esteem. *Communication Quarterly, 56,* 111–130.

21. Myers, P. N. & Biocca, F. A. (1992). The elastic body image: The effect of television advertising and programming on body image distortions in young women. *Journal of Communication, 42,* 108–134.

22. Cho, A. & Lee, J. (2013). Body dissatisfaction levels and gender differences in attentional biases toward idealized bodies. *Body Image, 10,* 95–102.

23. Cho, H. G. & Edge, N. (2012). "They are happier and having better lives than I am": The impact of using Facebook on perceptions of others' lives. *Cyberpsychology, Behavior, & Social Networking, 15,* 117–121; Haferkamp, N. & Kramer, N. C. (2011). Social comparison 2.0: Examining the effects of online profiles on social-networking sites. *Cyberpsychology, Behavior, and Social Networking, 14,* 309–314.

24. Grodin, D. & Lindolf, T. R. (1995). *Constructing the self in a mediated world.* Newbury Park, CA: Sage.

25. Sheldon, P. (2010). Pressure to be perfect: Influences on college students' body esteem. *Southern Communication Journal, 75,* 277–298.

26. Han, M. (2003). Body image dissatisfaction and eating disturbance among Korean college female students: Relationships to media exposure, upward comparison, and perceived reality. *Communication Studies, 34,* 65–78; Harrison, K. & Cantor, J. (1997). The relationship between media consumption and eating disorders. *Journal of Communication, 47,* 40–67.

27. Carrell, L. J. & Willmington, S. C. (1996). A comparison of self-report and performance data in assessing speaking and listening competence. *Communication Reports, 9,* 185–191.

28. Meyers, D. (1980, May). The inflated self. *Psychology Today, 14,* 16.

29. Ellison, N., Heino, R., & Gibbs, J. (2006). Managing impressions online: Self-presentation processes in the online dating environment. *Journal of Computer-Mediated Communication 11:* Article 2.

30. Sturman, E. D. & Mongrain, M. (2008). The role of personality in defeat: A revised social rank model. *European Journal of Personality, 22,* 55–79; Brown, J. D. & Mankowski, T. A. (1993). Self-esteem, mood, and self-evaluation: Changes in mood and the way you see you. *Journal of Personality and Social Psychology, 64,* 421–430.

31. Gara, M. A., Woolfolk, R. L., Cohen, B. D., & Goldston, R. B. (1993). Perception of self and other in major depression. *Journal of Abnormal Psychology, 102*, 93–100.

32. Miller, L. C., Cooke, L. L., Tsang, J., & Morgan, F. (1992). Should I brag? Nature and impact of positive and boastful disclosures for women and men. *Human Communication Research, 18*, 364–399.

33. Wallace, H. M. & Tice, D. M. (2012). Reflected appraisal through a 21st-century looking glass. In M. R. Leary & J. P. Tangney (Eds.), *Handbook of self and identity* (2nd ed., pp. 124–140). New York, NY: Guilford.

34. Gonzales, A. L. & Hancock, J. T. (2011). Mirror, mirror on my Facebook wall: Effects of exposure to Facebook on self-esteem. *Cyberpsychology, Behavior, and Social Networking, 41*, 79–83.

35. Bower, B. (1992, August 15). Truth aches: People who view themselves poorly may seek the 'truth' and find despair. *Science News*, 110–111; Swann, W. B. (2005). The self and identity negotiation. *Interaction Studies, 6*, 69–83.

36. Wilmot, W. W. (1995). *Relational communication* (pp. 35–54). New York, NY: McGraw-Hill.

37. Servaes, J. (1989). Cultural identity and modes of communication. In J. A. Anderson (Ed.), *Communication yearbook 12* (p. 396). Newbury Park, CA: Sage.

38. Bharti, A. (1985). The self in Hindu thought and action. In A. J. Marsella, G. Devos, & F. Hsu (Eds.), *Culture and self: Asian and Western perspectives* (pp. 185–230). New York, NY: Tavistock.

39. Bochner, S. (1994). Cross-cultural differences in the self-concept: A test of Hofstede's individualism/collectivism distinction. *Journal of Cross-Cultural Psychology, 25*, 273–283.

40. Ting-Toomey, S. (1988). A face-negotiation theory. In Y. Kim & W. Gudykunst (Eds.), *Theory in interpersonal communication*. Newbury Park, CA: Sage.

41. Lederman, L. C. (1993). Gender and the self. In L. P. Arliss & D. J. Borisoff (Eds.), *Women and men communicating: Challenges and changes* (pp. 41–42). Fort Worth, TX: Harcourt Brace.

42. Wittels, A. (1978). *I wonder ... A satirical study of sexist semantics*. Los Angeles, CA: Price Stern Sloan.

43. Knox, M., Funk, J., Elliott, R., & Bush, E. G. (2000). Gender differences in adolescents' possible selves. *Youth and Society, 31*, 287–309.

44. Robins, J. & Robins, R. W. (1993). A longitudinal study of consistency and change in self-esteem from early adolescence to early childhood. *Child Development, 64*, 909–923.

45. Smith, C. J., Noll, J. A., & Bryant, J. B. (1999). The effect of social context on gender self-concept. *Sex Roles, 40*, 499–512.

46. Rosenthal, R. & Rubin, D. B. (2010). Interpersonal expectancy effects: The first 345 studies. In M. L. Knapp & J. A. Daly (Eds.), *Interpersonal communication* (Vol. II, pp. 75–98). Thousand Oaks, CA: Sage.

47. Dweck, C. S. (2006). *Mindset: The new psychology of success*. New York, NY: Random House.

48. Kolligan, J., Jr. (1990). Perceived fraudulence as a dimension of perceived incompetence. In R. J. Sternberg & J. Kolligen, Jr. (Eds.), *Competence considered* (pp. 261–285). New Haven, CT: Yale University Press; Vangelisti, A. L., Corbin, S. D., Lucchetti, A. E., & Sprague, R. J. (1999). Couples' concurrent cognitions: The influence of relational satisfaction on the thoughts couples have as they converse. *Human Communication Research, 25*, 370–398.

49. Zimmerman, B., Bandura, A., & Martinez-Pons, M. (1992). Self-motivation for academic attainment: The role of self-efficacy beliefs and personal goal setting. *American Educational Research Journal, 29*, 663–676.

50. Downey, G. & Feldman, S. I. (1996). Implications of rejection sensitivity for intimate relationships. *Journal of Personality and Social Psychology, 70*, 1327–1343.

51. MacIntyre, P. D. & Thivierge, K. A. (1995). The effects of speaker personality on anticipated reactions to public speaking. *Communication Research Reports, 12*, 125–133.

52. Rosenthal, R. & Jacobson, L. (1968). *Pygmalion in the classroom*. New York, NY: Holt, Rinehart and Winston.

53. Blank, P. D. (Ed.). (1993). *Interpersonal expectations: Theory, research, and applications*. Cambridge, England: Cambridge University Press.

54. Turk, W. (2009). Let's go for self-fulfilling prophecies. *Defense AT&L, 38*, 56–59.

55. Johnson, E. (2006). *Ethics in the workplace: Tools and tactics for organizational transformation*. Thousand Oaks, CA: Sage.

56. Schlenker, B. R. & Weigold, M. F. (2010). Interpersonal processes involving impression regulation and management. In M. L. Knapp & J. A. Daly (Eds.), *Interpersonal communication* (Vol. II, pp. 160–194). Thousand Oaks, CA: Sage.

57. Shaw, C. M. & Edwards, R. (1997). Self-concepts and self-presentations of males and females: Similarities and differences. *Communication Reports, 10*, 55–62.

58. Goffman, E. (1959). *The presentation of self in everyday life*. Garden City, NY: Doubleday; Goffman, E. (1971). *Relations in public*. New York, NY: Basic Books.

59. Leary, M. R. & Kowalski, R. M. (1990). Impression management: A literature review and two-component model. *Psychological Bulletin, 107*, 34–47.

60. Brightman, V., Segal, A., Werther, P., & Steiner, J. (1975). Ethological study of facial expression in response to taste stimuli. *Journal of Dental Research, 54*, 141.

61. Chovil, N. (1991). Social determinants of facial displays. *Journal of Nonverbal Behavior, 15*, 141–154.

62. Metts, S. & Grohskopf, E. (2003). Impression management: Goals, strategies, and skills. In J. O. Greene and B. R. Burleson (Eds.), *Handbook of communication and social skills* (pp. 357–399). Mahwah, NJ: Erlbaum.

63. Coleman, L. M. & DePaulo, B. M. (1991). Uncovering the human spirit: Moving beyond disability and "missed" communications. In N. Coupland, H. Giles, & J. M. Wiemann (Eds.), *"Miscommunication" and problematic talk* (pp. 61–84). Newbury Park, CA: Sage.

64. Valkenburg, P. M. & Peter, J. (2008). Adolescents' identity experiments on the Internet: Consequences for social competence and self-concept unity. *Communication Research, 35*, 208–231.

65. Vander Zanden, J. W. (1984). *Social psychology* (3rd ed., pp. 235–237). New York, NY: Random House.

66. DePaulo, B. M. (2010). Nonverbal behavior and self-presentation. In M. L. Knapp & J. A. Daly (Eds.), *Interpersonal communication* (Vol. II, pp. 251–336). Thousand Oaks, CA: Sage.

67. O'Sullivan, P. B. (2000). What you don't know won't hurt me: Impression management functions of communication channels in relationships. *Communication Monographs, 26*, 403–432; Barnes, S. B. (2003). *Computer-mediated communication: Human-to-human communication across the Internet* (pp. 136–162). Boston, MA: Allyn and Bacon.

68. Sanderson, J. (2008). The blog is serving its purpose: Self-presentation strategies on 38Pitches.com. *Journal of Computer-Mediated Communication, 13*, 912–936.

69. Suler, J. R. (2002). Identity management in cyberspace. *Journal of Applied Psychoanalytic Studies, 4*, 455–459.

70. Gibbs, J. L., Ellison, N. B., & Heino, R. D. (2006). Self-presentation in online personals: The role of anticipated future interaction, self-disclosure, and perceived success in Internet dating. *Communication Research, 33*, 1–26.

71. Toma, C. L., Hancock, J. T., & Ellison, N. B. (2008). Separating fact from fiction: An examination of deceptive self-presentation in online dating profiles. *Personality and Social Psychology Bulletin, 34*, 1023–1036.

72. Toma, C. L. & Carlson, C. L. (2015). How do Facebook users believe they come across in their profiles? A meta-perception approach to investigating Facebook self-presentation. *Communication Research Reports, 32*, 93–101.

73. Salimkhan, G., Manago, A., & Greenfield, P. (2010). The construction of the virtual self on MySpace. *Cyberpsychology: Journal of Psychosocial Research on Cyberspace, 4*, article 1.

74. Bennett, R. (2008, April 4). Revealed: Secrets of choosing an online dating name. *Times Online.*

75. Gonzales, A. L. & Hancock, J. T. (2011). Mirror, mirror on my Facebook wall: Effects of exposure to Facebook on self-esteem. *Cyberpsychology, Behavior, and Social Networking, 14*, 79–83. See also Toma, C. L. & Hancock, J. T. (2013). Self-affirmation underlies Facebook use. *Personality and Social Psychology Bulletin, 39*, 321–331

76. Altman, I. & Taylor, D. A. (1973). *Social penetration: The development of interpersonal relationships.* New York, NY: Holt, Rinehart and Winston; Taylor, D. A. & Altman, I. (1987). Communication in interpersonal relationships: Social penetration processes. In M. E. Roloff & G. R. Miller (Eds.), *Interpersonal processes: New directions in communication research* (pp. 257–277). Newbury Park, CA: Sage.

77. Luft, J. (1969). *Of human interaction.* Palo Alto, CA: National Press Books.

78. Petronio, S. (2007). Translational research endeavors and the practices of communication privacy management. *Journal of Applied Communication Research, 35*, 218–22.

79. Afifi, T. D. & Steuber, K. (2009). The revelation risk model (RRM): Factors that predict the revelation of secrets and the strategies used to reveal them. *Communication Monographs, 76*, 144–176; Afifi, T. D. & Steuber, K. (2009). Keeping and revealing secrets. *Communication Currents, 4*, 1–2.

80. Dindia, K. (2002). Self-disclosure research: Advances through meta-analysis. In M. Allen & R. W. Preiss (Eds.), *Interpersonal communication research: Advances through meta-analysis* (pp. 169–185). Mahwah, NJ: Erlbaum; Derlega, V. J. & Chaikin, A. L. (1975). *Sharing intimacy: What we reveal to others and why.* Englewood Cliffs, NJ: Prentice-Hall.

81. Savin-Williams, R. C. (2001). *Mom, Dad. I'm gay: How families negotiate coming out.* Washington, DC: American Psychological Association.

82. Hess, J. A., Fannin, A. D., & Pollom, L. H. (2007). Creating closeness: Discerning and measuring strategies for fostering closer relationships. *Personal Relationships, 14*, 25–44; Mitchell, A. E. et al. (2008). Predictors of intimacy in couples' discussions of relationship injuries: An observational study. *Journal of Family Psychology, 22*, 21–29.

83. MacNeil, S. & Byers, E. S. (2009). Role of sexual self-disclosure in the sexual satisfaction of long-term heterosexual couples. *Journal of Sex Research, 46*, 3–14; Fincham, F. D. & Bradbury, T. N. (1989). The impact of attributions in marriage: An individual difference analysis. *Journal of Social and Personal Relationships, 6*, 69–85.

84. Derlega, V., Winstead, B. A., Mathews, A., & Braitman, A. L. (2008). Why does someone reveal highly personal information? Attributions for and against self-disclosure in close relationships. *Communication Research Reports, 25*, 115–130; Niederhoffer, K. G. & Pennebaker, J. W. (2002). Sharing one's story: On the benefits of writing or talking about emotional experience. In C. R. Snyder & S. J. Lopez (Eds.), *Handbook of positive psychology* (pp. 573–583). London, England: Oxford University Press.

85. Greene, K., Derlega, V. J., & Mathews, A. (2006). Self-disclosure in personal relationships. In A. Vangelisti & D. Perlman (Eds.), *The Cambridge handbook of personal relationships* (pp. 409–427). New York, NY: Cambridge University Press; Rosenfeld, L. B. (2000). Overview of the ways privacy, secrecy, and disclosure are balanced in today's society. In S. Petronio (Ed.), *Balancing the secrets of private disclosures* (pp. 3–17). Mahwah, NJ: Erlbaum.

86. Powell, J. (1969). *Why am I afraid to tell you who I am?* Niles, IL: Argus Communications.

87. Alter, A. L. & Oppenheimer, D. M. (2009). Suppressing secrecy through metacognitive ease: Cognitive fluency encourages self-disclosure. *Psychological Science, 20*, 1414–1420.

88. Frisby, B. N. & Sidelinger, R. J. (2013). Violating student expectations: Student disclosures and student reactions in the college classroom. *Communication Studies, 64*, 241–258.

89. Myers, S. & Brann, M. (2009). College students' perceptions of how instructors establish and enhance credibility through self-disclosure. *Qualitative Research Reports in Communication, 10*, 9–16.

90. Rosenfeld, L. B. & Gilbert, J. R. (1989). The measurement of cohesion and its relationship to dimensions of self-disclosure in classroom settings. *Small Group Behavior, 20*, 291–301.

91. Rosenfeld, L. B. & Bowen, G. I. (1991). Marital disclosure and marital satisfaction: Direct-effect versus interaction-effect models. *Western Journal of Speech Communication, 55*, 69–84.

92. McDaniel, S. H. et al. (2007). Physician self-disclosure in primary care visits: Enough about you, what about me? *Archives of Internal Medicine, 167*, 1321–1326.

93. Agne, R., Thompson, T. L., & Cusella, L. P. (2000). Stigma in the line of face: Self-disclosure of patients' HIV status to health care providers. *Journal of Applied Communication Research, 28*, 235–261; Derlega, V. J., Winstead, B. A., & Folk-Barron, L. (2000). Reasons for and against disclosing HIV-seropositive test results to an intimate partner: A functional perspective. In S. Petronio (Ed.), *Balancing the secrets of private disclosures* (pp. 71–82). Mahwah, NJ: Erlbaum; Caughlin, J. P. et al. (2009). Do message features influence reactions to HIV disclosures? A multiple-goals perspective. *Health Communication, 24*, 270–283.

94. Allen, M. et al. (2008). Persons living with HIV: Disclosure to sexual partners. *Communication Research Reports, 25*, 192–199.

95. O'Hair, D. & Cody, M. J. (1993). Interpersonal deception: The dark side of interpersonal communication? In B. H. Spitzberg & W. R. Cupach (Eds.), *The dark side of interpersonal communication* (pp. 181–213). Hillsdale, NJ: Erlbaum.

96. Spranca, M., Minsk, E., & Baron, J. (1991). Omission and commission in judgement and choice. *Journal of Experimental Social Psychology, 27*, 76–105.

97. Dunleavy, K. N., Chory, R. M., & Goodboy, A. K. (2010). Responses to deception in the workplace: Perceptions of credibility, power, and trustworthiness. *Communication Studies, 61*, 239–255.

98. George, J. F. & Robb, A. (2008). Deception and computer-mediated communication in daily life. *Communication Reports, 21*, 92–103.

99. Knapp, M. L. (2006). Lying and deception in close relationships. In A. Vangelisti & D. Perlman (Eds.), *The Cambridge handbook of personal relationships* (pp. 517–532). New York, NY: Cambridge University Press.

100. Turner, R. E., Edgely, C., & Olmstead, G. (1975). Information control in conversation: Honesty is not always the best policy. *Kansas Journal of Sociology, 11*, 69–89.

101. Feldman, R. S., Forrest, J. A., & Happ, B. R. (2002). Self-presentation and verbal deception: Do self-presenters lie more? *Basic and Applied Social Psychology, 24*, 163–170.

102. Hample, D. (1980). Purposes and effects of lying. *Southern Speech Communication Journal, 46*, 33–47.

103. McCornack, S. A. & Levine, T. R. (1990). When lies are uncovered: Emotional and relational outcomes of discovered deception. *Communication Monographs, 57*, 119–138.

104. Seiter, J. S., Bruschke, J., & Bai, C. (2002). The acceptability of deception as a function of perceivers' culture, deceiver's intention, and deceiver-deceived relationship. *Western Journal of Communication, 66*, 158–181.

105. Bavelas, J. B., Black, A., Chovil, N., & Mullett, J. (2010). Truths, lies, and equivocations: The effects of conflicting goals on discourse. In M. L. Knapp & J. A. Daly (Eds.), *Interpersonal communication* (Vol. II, pp. 379–408). Thousand Oaks, CA: Sage.

106.   Bavelas, J. B., Black, A., Chovil, N., & Mullett, J. (1990). *Equivocal communication* (p. 171). Newbury Park, CA: Sage.

107.   Bavelas, J. B., Black, A., Chovil, N., & Mullett, J. (1990). *Equivocal communication* (p. 171). Newbury Park, CA: Sage.

108.   Robinson, W. P., Shepherd, A., & Heywood, J. (1998). Truth, equivocation/concealment, and lies in job applications & doctor-patient communication. *Journal of Language & Social Psychology, 17*, 149–164.

109.   Motley, M. T. (1992). Mindfulness in solving communicators' dilemmas. *Communication Monographs, 59*, 306–314.

110.   Shimanoff, S. B. (1988). Degree of emotional expressiveness as a function of face-needs, gender, and interpersonal relationship. *Communication Reports, 1*(2), 1–8.

CHAPTER FOUR

1.   The graphic demonstrations of factors influencing perception in this and the following paragraph are borrowed from Coon, D. & Mitterer, J. (2013). *Introduction to psychology* (13th ed.). Belmont, CA: Cengage Wadsworth.

2.   Simons, D. J. (2011). *The invisible gorilla: How our intuitions deceive us.* New York, NY: Broadway.

3.   Nelson, T. D. (2009). *Handbook of prejudice, stereotyping, and discrimination.* London, England: Psychology Press.

4.   Giles, H. & Gasiorek, J. (2011). Intergenerational communication practices. In K. Schaie & S. L. Willis (Eds.), *Handbook of the psychology of aging* (7th ed., pp. 233–247). San Diego, CA: Elsevier Academic Press; Harwood, J. (2007). Understanding communication and aging: Developing knowledge and awareness. Newbury Park, CA: Sage.

5.   Allen, M. (1998). Methodological considerations when examining a gendered world. In D. Canary and K. Dindia (Eds.), *Handbook of sex differences and similarities in communication* (pp. 427–444). Mahwah, NJ: Erlbaum.

6.   Allen, B. (1995). Diversity and organizational communication. *Journal of Applied Communication Research, 23*, 143–155; Buttny, R. (1997). Reported speech in talking race on campus. *Human Communication Research, 23*, 477–506; Hughes, P. C. & Baldwin, J. R. (2002). Communication and stereotypical impressions. *Howard Journal of Communications, 13*, 113–128.

7.   Perloff, R. M., Bonder, B., Ray, G. B., Ray, E. B., & Siminoff, L. A. (2006). Doctor-patient communication, cultural competence, and minority health: Theoretical and empirical perspectives. *American Behavioral Scientist, 49*, 835–852; Oliver, M. N., Goodwin, M. A., Gotler, R. S., & Strange, K. C. (2001). Time use in clinical encounters: Are African-American patients treated differently? *Journal of the National Medical Association, 93*, 380–385.

8.   Oetzel, J. (1998). The effects of self-construals and ethnicity on self-reported conflict styles. *Communication Reports, 11*, 133–144.

9.   Nishizawa, N. (2004). The 'self' of Japanese teenagers: Growing up in the flux of a changing culture and society. *Dissertation Abstracts International, 65*, 2642.

10.   Watzlawick, P., Beavin, J., & Jackson, D. D. (1967). *Pragmatics of human communication* (p. 65). New York, NY: Norton.

11.   Schrodt, P., Witt, P. L., & Shimkowski, J. R. (2014). A meta-analytical review of the demand/withdraw pattern of interaction and its associations with individual, relational, and communicative outcomes. *Communication Monographs, 81*, 28–58; Reznick, R. M. & Roloff, M. E. (2011). Getting off to a bad start: The relationship between communication during an initial episode of a serial argument and argument frequency. *Communication Studies, 62*, 291–306.

12.   Floyd, K. & Morman, M. T. (2000). Reacting to the verbal expression of affection in same-sex interaction. *Southern Communication Journal, 65*, 287–299.

13.   Rosenthal, R. & Rubin, D. B. (2010). Interpersonal expectancy effects: The first 345 studies. In M. L. Knapp & J. A. Daly (Eds.), *Interpersonal communication* (pp. 297–338). Thousand Oaks, CA: Sage.

14.   Alberts, J. K., Kellar-Guenther, U., & Corman, S. R. (1996). That's not funny: Understanding recipients' responses to teasing. *Western Journal of Communication, 60*, 337–357; Edwards, R., Bello, R., Brandau-Brown, F., & Hollems, D. (2001). The effects of loneliness and verbal aggressiveness on message interpretation. *Southern Communication Journal, 66*, 139–150.

15.   Bradbury, T. N. & Fincham, F. D. (1990). Attributions in marriage: Review and critique. *Psychological Bulletin, 107*, 3–33; Manusov, V. (1990). An application of attribution principles to nonverbal behavior in romantic dyads. *Communication Monographs, 57*, 104–118.

16.   Yang, H. & Lee, L. (2014). Instantaneously hotter: The dynamic revision of beauty assessment standards. *Advances in Consumer Research, 42*, 744–745.

17.   Reissmann, C. K. (2008). *Narrative methods for the human sciences.* Thousand Oaks, CA: Sage; Bromberg, J. B. (2012). Uses of conversational narrative: Exchanging personal experience in everyday life. *Narrative Inquiry, 22*, 165–172.

18.   Flora, J. & Segrin, C. (2000). Relationship development in dating couples: Implications for relational satisfaction and loneliness. *Journal of Social and Personal Relationships, 17*, 811–825.

19.   Baxter, L. A. & Pittman, G. (2001). Communicatively remembering turning points of relational development in heterosexual romantic relationships. *Communication Reports, 14*, 1–17.

20.   Murray, S. L., Holmes, J. G., & Griffin D. W. (2004). The benefits of positive illusions: Idealization and the construction of satisfaction in close relationships. In H. T. Reis & C. E. Rusbult, *Close relationships: Key readings* (pp. 317–338). Philadelphia, PA: Taylor & Francis; Martz, J. M., Verette, J., Arriaga, X. B., Slovik, L. F., Cox, C. L., & Rosbult, C. E. (1998). Positive illusion in close relationships. *Personal Relationships, 5*, 159–181.

21.   Pearson, J. C. (1996). Positive distortion: "The most beautiful woman in the world." In K. M. Galvin & P. Cooper (Eds.), *Making connections: Readings in interpersonal communication* (p. 177). Beverly Hills, CA: Roxbury.

22.   Kluemper, D. H., Rosen, P. A., Mossholder, K. W. (2012). Social networking websites, personality ratings, and the organizational context: More than meets the eye? *Journal of Applied Social Psychology, 42*, 1143–1172.

23.   Child, J. T. & Westermann, D. A. (2013). Let's be Facebook friends: Exploring parental Facebook friend requests from a Communication Privacy Management (CPM) perspective. *Journal of Family Communication, 13*, 46–59.

24.   For a detailed description of how the senses affect perception, see Ackerman, N. (1990). *A natural history of the senses.* New York, NY: Random House.

25.   For descriptions of various psychological disorders and their treatments, visit the National Institute of Mental Health website at http://www.nimh.nih.gov/.

26.   Seidman, B. (2011, June 25). *Do not operate this marriage while drowsy.* PBS.org.

27.   Gordon, A. M. & Chen, S. (2014). The role of sleep in interpersonal conflict: Do sleepless nights mean worse fights? *Social Psychological and Personality Science, 5*, 168–175.

28.   Alaimo, K., Olson, C. M., & Frongillo, E. A. (2001). Food insufficiency and American school-aged children's cognitive, academic, and psychosocial development. *Pediatrics, 108*, 44–53.

29. Maguire, M. (2005). Biological cycles and cognitive performance. In A. Esgate et al., *An introduction to applied cognitive psychology* (pp. 137–161). New York, NY: Psychology Press; Cooper, C. & McConville, C. (1990). Interpreting mood scores: Clinical implications of individual differences in mood variability. *British Journal of Medical Psychology, 63,* 215–225.

30. Giles, H., Coupland, N., & Wiemann, J. M. (1992). Talk is cheap ... but 'my word is my bond': Beliefs about talk. In K. Bolton & H. Kwok (Eds.), *Sociolinguistics today: International perspectives* (pp. 218–243). London, England: Routledge & Kegan Paul.

31. Manusov, V., Winchatz, M. R., & Manning, L. M. (1997). Acting out of our minds: Incorporating behavior into models of stereotype-based expectancies for cross-cultural interactions. *Communication Monographs, 64,* 119–139.

32. Katz-Wise, S. L. & Hyde, J. S. (2014). Sexuality and gender: The interplay. In D. L. Tolman, L. M. Diamond, J. A. Bauermeister, W. H. George, J. G. Pfaus, & L. Ward (Eds.), *APA handbook of sexuality and psychology, Vol. 1: Person-based approaches* (pp. 29–62). Washington, DC: American Psychological Association.

33. Becker, J. B., Berkley, K. J., Geary, N., Hampson, E., Herman, J. P., & Young, E. (2007). *Sex differences in the brain: From genes to behavior.* New York, NY: Oxford University Press; Schroeder, J. A. (2010). Sex and gender in sensation and perception. In J.C. Chrisler & D. R. McCreary (Eds.), *Handbook of gender research in psychology* (Vol. 1, pp. 235–257). New York: Springer; LaFrance, A. (January 8, 2015). What happens to a woman's brain when she becomes a mother. *The Atlantic.*

34. Halpern, D. F. (2000). *Sex differences in cognitive abilities* (3rd ed.). Mahwah, NJ: Erlbaum.

35. Rathus, S. A. (1993). *Psychology* (5th ed.; pp. 640–643). Fort Worth, TX: Harcourt Brace Jovanovich; Wade, C. & Tavris, C. (1987). *Psychology* (pp. 488–490). New York, NY: Harper & Row.

36. Bem, S. L. (1985). Androgyny and gender schema theory: A conceptual and empirical integration. In T. B. Sonderegger (Ed.), *Nebraska symposium on motivation: Psychology and gender* (pp. 179–226). Lincoln: University of Nebraska Press.

37. Swami, V. & Furnham, A. (2008). Is love really so blind? *The Psychologist, 21,* 108–111.

38. Gonzaga, G. C., Haselton, M. G., Smurda, J., Davies, M., & Poore, J. C. (2008). Love, desire, and the suppression of thoughts of romantic alternatives. *Evolution and Human Behavior, 29,* 119–126.

39. Seibold, D. R. & Spitzberg, B. H. (2010). Attribution theory and research: Review and implications for communication. In M. L. Knapp & J. A. Daly (Eds.), *Interpersonal communication* (pp. 297–338). Thousand Oaks, CA: Sage.

40. Hamachek, D. (1992). *Encounters with the self* (3rd ed.). Fort Worth, TX: Harcourt Brace Jovanovich.

41. For a review of these perceptual biases, see Hamachek, D. (1992). *Encounters with the self* (3rd ed.). Fort Worth, TX: Harcourt Brace Jovanovich.; Bradbury, T. N. & Fincham, F. D. (1990). Attributions in marriage: Review and critique. *Psychological Bulletin, 107,* 3–33. For an example of the self-serving bias in action, see Buttny, R. (1997). Reported speech in talking race on campus. *Human Communication Research, 23,* 477–506.

42. Young, S. L. (2004). What the ___ is your problem?: Attribution theory and perceived reasons for profanity usage during conflict. *Communication Research Reports, 21,* 338–347.

43. Zhang, S. (2009). Sender-recipient perspectives of honest but hurtful evaluative messages in romantic relationships. *Communication Reports, 22,* 89–101.

44. Dion, K., Berscheid, E., & Walster, E. (1972). What is beautiful is good. *Journal of Personality and Social Psychology, 24,* 285–290.

45. Watkins, L. & Johnston, L. (2000). Screening job applicants: The impact of physical attractiveness and application quality. *International Journal of Selection and Assessment, 8,* 76–84.

46. Dougherty, T., Turban, D., & Collander, J. (1994). Confirming first impressions in the employment interview. *Journal of Applied Psychology, 79,* 659–665.

47. Cook, G. I., Marsh, R. L., & Hicks, J. L. (2003). Halo and devil effects demonstrate valence-based influences on source-mentoring decisions. *Consciousness and Cognition, 12,* 257–278.

48. Marek, C. I., Wanzer, M. B., & Knapp, J. L. (2004). An exploratory investigation of the relationship between roommates' first impressions and subsequent communication patterns. *Communication Research Reports, 21,* 210–220.

49. Keysar, B. (2007). Communication and miscommunication: The role of egocentric processes. *Intercultural Pragmatics, 4,* 71–84.

50. Edwards, C., Edwards, A., Qingmei, Q., & Wahl, S. T. (2007). The influence of computer-mediated word-of-mouth communication on student perceptions of instructors and attitudes toward learning course content. *Communication Education, 56,* 255–277; Edwards, A. & Edwards, C. (2013). Computer-mediated word-of-mouth communication: The influence of mixed reviews on student perceptions of instructors and courses. *Communication Education, 62,* 412–424.

51. DiPaola, B. M., Roloff, M. E., & Peters, K. M. (2010). College students' expectations of conflict intensity: A self-fulfilling prophecy. *Communication Quarterly, 58,* 59–76.

52. Sillars, A., Shellen, W., McIntosh, A., & Pomegranate, M. (1997). Relational characteristics of language: Elaboration and differentiation in marital conversations. *Western Journal of Communication, 61,* 403–422.

53. Stiff, J. B., Dillard, J. P., Somera, L., Kim, H., & Sleight, C. (1988). Empathy, communication, and prosocial behavior. *Communication Monographs, 55,* 198–213.

54. Hepper, E. G., Hart, C. M., & Sedikides, C. (2014). Moving Narcissus: Can narcissists be empathic? *Personality and Social Psychology Bulletin, 40,* 1079–1091.

55. Goleman, D. (2006). *Social intelligence.* New York, NY: Bantam; Decety, J., Michalska, K., & Aktsuki, Y. (2008). Who caused the pain? An fMRI investigation of empathy and intentionality in children. *Neuropsychologia, 46,* 2607–2614.

56. Goleman, D. (2006). *Social intelligence.* New York, NY: Bantam.

57. Davis, M. (1994). The heritability of characteristics associated with dispositional empathy. *Journal of Personality, 62,* 369–391.

58. Burleson, B., Delia, J., & Applegate, J. (1995). The socialization of person-centered communication: Parental contributions to the social-cognitive and communication skills of their children. In M. A. Fitzpatrick & A. Vangelisti (Eds.), *Perspectives in family communication* (pp. 34–76). Thousand Oaks, CA: Sage.

59. Tucker, D. M., Luu, P., & Derryberry, D. (2005). Love hurts: The evolution of empathic concern through the encephalization of nociceptive capacity. *Development and Psychopathology, 17,* 699–713.

60. Wu, S. & Keysar, B. (2007). Cultural effects on perspective taking. *Psychological Science, 18,* 600–606.

61. Martin, R. (1992). Relational cognition complexity and relational communication in personal relationships. *Communication Monographs, 59,* 150–163; Burleson, B. R. & Caplan, S. E. (1998). Cognitive complexity. In J. C. McCroskey, J. A. Daly, M. M. Martin, & M. J. Beatty (Eds.), *Communication and personality: Trait perspectives* (pp. 233–286). Creskill, NY: Hampton Press.

62. Burleson, B. R. & Caplan, S. E. (1998). Cognitive complexity. In J. C. McCroskey, J. A. Daly, M. M. Martin, & M. J. Beatty (Eds.), *Communication and personality: Trait perspectives* (p. 22). Creskill, NY: Hampton Press.

63. Burleson, B. R. (1989). The constructivist approach to person-centered communication: Analysis of a research exemplar. In B. Dervin, L. Grossberg, B. J. O'Keefe, & E. Wartella (Eds.), *Rethinking communication: Paradigm exemplars* (pp. 33–72). Newbury Park, CA: Sage.

64. Sypher, B. D. & Zorn, T. (1986). Communication-related abilities and upward mobility: A longitudinal investigation. *Human Communication Research, 12*, 420–431.

65. Joireman, J. (2004). Relationships between attributional complexity and empathy. *Individual Differences Research, 2*, 197–202.

66. Medvene, L., Grosch, K., & Swink, N. (2006). Interpersonal complexity: A cognitive component of person-centered care. *The Gerontologist, 46*, 220–226.

67. Rockwell, P. (2007). The effects of cognitive complexity and communication apprehension on the expression and recognition of sarcasm. In A. M. Columbus (Ed.), *Advances in psychology research* (pp. 185–196). Hauppauge, NY: Nova Science Publishers.

68. Little, C., Packman, J., Smaby, M. H., & Maddux, C. D. (2005). The skilled counselor training model: Skills acquisition, self-assessment, and cognitive complexity. *Counselor Education & Supervision, 44*, 189–200.

69. Reps, P. (1967). Pillow education in rural Japan. In *Square sun, square moon* (pp. 17–19). New York, NY: Tuttle.

CHAPTER FIVE

1. Goleman, D. (1995). *Emotional intelligence: Why it can matter more than I.Q.* New York, NY: Bantam; Goleman, D. (2006). *Social intelligence: The new science of human relationships.* New York, NY: Bantam.

2. Carmeli, A., Yitzhak-Halevy, M., & Weisberg, J. (2009). The relationship between emotional intelligence and psychological wellbeing. *Journal of Managerial Psychology, 24*, 66–78.

3. Smith, L., Heaven, P. C., & Ciarrochi, J. (2008). Trait emotional intelligence, conflict communication patterns, and relationship satisfaction. *Personality and Individual Differences, 44*, 1314–1325.

4. Iliescu, D., Ilie, A., Ispas, D., & Ion, A. (2012). Emotional intelligence in personnel selection: Applicant reactions, criterion, and incremental validity. *International Journal of Selection and Assessment, 20*, 347–358.

5. Planalp, S., Fitness, J., & Fehr, B. (2006). Emotion in theories of close relationships. In A. L. Vangelisti & D. Perlman (Eds.), *The Cambridge handbook of personal relationships* (pp. 369–384). New York, NY: Cambridge University Press; Baumeister, R. F. (2005). *The human animal.* New York, NY: Oxford University Press.

6. Rochman, G. M. & Diamond, G. M. (2008). From unresolved anger to sadness: Identifying physiological correlates. *Journal of Counseling Psychology, 55*, 96–105.

7. Gottman, J. M. & Silver, N. (1999). *The seven principles for making marriages work.* New York, NY: Three Rivers Press.

8. Samp, J. A. & Monahan, J. L. (2009). Alcohol-influenced nonverbal behaviors during discussions about a relationship problem. *Journal of Nonverbal Behavior, 33*, 193–211.

9. Kleinke, C. L., Peterson, T. R., & Rutledge, T. R. (1998). Effects of self-generated facial expressions on mood. *Journal of Personality and Social Psychology, 74*, 272–279.

10. Michalak, J., Rohde, K., & Troje, N. F. (2015). How we walk affects what we remember: Gait modifications through biofeedback change negative affective memory bias. *Journal of Behavior Therapy and Experimental Psychiatry, 46*, 121–125.

11. Shafir, T., Taylor, S. F., Atkinson, A. P., Langenecker, S. A., & Zubieta, J. (2013). Emotion regulation through execution, observation, and imagery of emotional movements. *Brain and Cognition, 82*, 219–227.

12. Oosterwijk, S., Rotteveel, M., Fischer, A. H., & Hess, U. (2009). Embodied emotion concepts: How generating words about pride and disappointment influences posture. *European Journal of Social Psychology, 39*, 457–466.

13. Valins, S. (1966). Cognitive effects of false heart-rate feedback. *Journal of Personality and Social Psychology, 4*, 400–408.

14. Zimbardo, P. (1977). Shyness: What it is, what to do about it (p. 53). Reading, MA: Addison-Wesley.

15. Berger, C. R. & Lee, K. J. (2011). Second thoughts, second feelings: Attenuating the impact of threatening narratives through rational reappraisal. *Communication Research, 38*, 3–26.

16. Wallace, J. C., Edwards, B. D., Shull, A., & Finch, D. M. (2009). Examining the consequences in the tendency to suppress and reappraise emotions on task-related job performance. *Human Performance, 22*, 23–43; Moore, S. A., Zoellner, L. A., & Mollenholt, N. (2008). Are expressive suppression and cognitive reappraisal associated with stress-related symptoms? *Behaviour Research and Therapy, 46*, 993–1000; Nezlek, J. B. & Kuppens, P. (2008). Regulating positive and negative emotions in daily life. *Journal of Personality, 76*, 561–580.

17. Finkel, E. J., Slotter, E. B., Luchies, L. B., Walton, G. M., & Gross, J. J. (2013). A brief intervention to promote conflict-reappraisal preserves marital quality over time. *Psychological Science, 24*, 1595–1601.

18. Lieberman, M. D., Eisenberger, N. I., Crockett, M. J., Tom, S., Pfeifer, J. H., & Way, B. M. (2007). Putting feelings into words: Affect labeling disrupts amygdala activity to affective stimuli. *Psychological Science, 18*, 421–428.

19. Eaker, E. D., Sullivan, L. M., Kelly-Hayes, M., D'Agostino, R. B., & Benjamin, E. J. (2007). Marital status, marital strain and the risk of coronary heart disease or total mortality: The Framingham Offspring Study. *Psychosomatic Medicine, 69*, 509–513.

20. Plutchik, R. (1980). *Emotion: A psychoevolutionary synthesis.* New York, NY: Harper & Row; Shaver, P. R., Wu, S., & Schwartz, J. C. (1992). Cross-cultural similarities and differences in emotion and its representation: A prototype approach. In M. S. Clark (Ed.), *Emotion* (pp. 175–212). Newbury Park, CA: Sage.

21. Ekman, P. (1999). Basic emotions. In T. Dalgleish & T. Power (Eds.), *The handbook of cognition and emotion* (pp. 45–60). Sussex, England: Wiley; Ortony, A. & Turner, T. J. (1990). What's basic about basic emotions? *Psychological Review, 97*, 315–331.

22. Ferrari, M. & Koyama, E. (2002). Meta-emotions about anger and amae: A cross-cultural comparison. *Consciousness and Emotion, 3*, 197–211.

23. Shaver, P. R., Wu, S., & Schwartz, J. C. (1992). Cross-cultural similarities and differences in emotion and its representation: A prototype approach. In M. S. Clark (Ed.), *Emotion* (pp. 175–212). Newbury Park, CA: Sage.

24. Goleman, D. (1995). *Emotional intelligence: Why it can matter more than I.Q.* New York, NY: Bantam.

25. Gottman, J. M., Katz, L. F., & Hooven, C. (1997). *Meta-emotion: How families communicate emotionally.* Mahwah, NJ: Erlbaum; Young, S. L. (2009). The function of parental communication patterns: Reflection-enhancing and reflection-discouraging approaches. *Communication Quarterly, 57*, 379–394.

26. Lunkenheimer, E. S., Shields, A. M., & Kortina, K. S. (2007). Parental emotion coaching and dismissing in family interaction. *Social Development, 16*, 232–248.

27. McCroskey, J. C., Richmond, V. P., Heisel, A. D., & Hayhurst, J. L. (2004). Eysenck's big three and communication traits: Communication traits as manifestations of temperament. *Communication Research Reports, 21*, 404–410; Gross, J. J., Sutton, S. K., & Ketelaar, T. V. (1998). Relations between

affect and personality: Support for the affect-level and affective-reactivity views. *Personality and Social Psychology Bulletin, 24,* 279–288.

28. Costa, P. T. & McCrae, R. R. (1980). Influence of extraversion and neuroticism on subjective well-being: Happy and unhappy people. *Journal of Personality and Social Psychology, 38,* 668–678.

29. Yen, J., Yen, C., Chen, C., Wang, P., Chang, Y., & Ko, C. (2012). Social anxiety in online and real-life interaction and their associated factors. *Cyberpsychology, Behavior, and Social Networking, 15,* 7–12.

30. Kelly, L., Duran, R. L., & Zolten, J. J. (2001). The effect of reticence on college students' use of electronic mail to communicate with faculty. *Communication Education, 50,* 170–176; Scharlott, B. W. & Christ, W. G. (2001). Overcoming relationship-initiation barriers: The impact of a computer-dating system on sex role, shyness, and appearance inhibitions. *Computers in Human Behavior, 11,* 191–204.

31. Goddard, C. (2002). Explicating emotions across languages and cultures: A semantic approach. In S. R. Fussell (Ed.), *The verbal communication of emotions* (pp. 18–49). Mahwah, NJ: Erlbaum.

32. Tsai, J. L., Knutson, B., & Fung, H. H. (2006). Cultural variation in affect valuation. *Journal of Personality and Social Psychology, 90,* 288–307.

33. Kotchemidova, C. (2010). Emotion culture and cognitive constructions of reality. *Communication Quarterly, 58,* 207–234.

34. Pennebaker, J. W., Rime, B., & Blankenship, V. E. (1996). Stereotypes of emotional expressiveness of northerners and southerners: A cross-cultural test of Montesquieu's hypothesis. *Journal of Personality and Social Psychology, 70,* 372–380.

35. Mortenson, S. T. (2009). Interpersonal trust and social skill in seeking social support among Chinese and Americans. *Communication Research, 36,* 32–53.

36. Wilkins, R. & Gareis, E. (2006). Emotion expression and the locution 'I love you': A cross-cultural study. *International Journal of Intercultural Relations, 30,* 51–75.

37. Guerrero, L. K., Jones, S. M., & Boburka, R. R. (2006). Sex differences in emotional communication. In K. Dindia & D. J. Canary (Eds.), *Sex differences and similarities in communication* (2nd ed., pp. 242–261). Mahwah, NJ: Erlbaum; Wester, S. R., Vogel, D. L., Pressly, P. K., & Heesacker M. (2002). Sex differences in emotion: A critical review of the literature and implications for counseling psychology. *Counseling Psychologist, 30,* 630–652.

38. Swenson, J. & Casmir, F. L. (1998). The impact of culture-sameness, gender, foreign travel, and academic background on the ability to interpret facial expression of emotion in others. *Communication Quarterly, 46,* 214–230.

39. Canli, T., Desmond, J. E., Zhao, Z., & Gabrieli, J. D. E. (2002). Sex differences in the neural basis of emotional memories. *Proceedings of the National Academy of Sciences, 10,* 10789–10794.

40. Merten, J. (2005). Culture, gender and the recognition of the basic emotions. *Psychologia: An International Journal of Psychology in the Orient, 48,* 306–316.

41. Kunkel, A. W. & Burleson, B. R. (1999). Assessing explanations for sex differences in emotional support: A test of the different cultures and skill specialization accounts. *Human Communication Research, 25,* 307–340.

42. Dunsmore, J., Her, P., Halberstadt, A., & Perez-Rivera, M. (2009). Parents' beliefs about emotions and children's recognition of parents' emotions. *Journal of Nonverbal Behavior, 33,* 121–140.

43. Witmer, D. F. & Katzman, S. L. (1999). On-line smiles: Does gender make a difference in the use of graphic accents? *Journal of Computer-Mediated Communication, 2* (online, domain name expired).

44. Mansson, D. H. & Myers, S. A. (2011). An initial examination of college students' expressions of affection through Facebook. *Southern Communication Journal, 76,* 155–168.

45. Brody, L. R. & Hall, J. A. (2008). Gender and emotion in context. In M. Lewis, J. M. Haviland-Jones, & L. F. Barrett (Eds.), *Handbook of emotions* (3rd ed., pp. 395–408). New York, NY: Guilford.

46. Shimanoff, S. B. (1984). Commonly named emotions in everyday conversations. *Perceptual and Motor Skills, 58,* 514; Gottman, J. M. (1982). Emotional responsiveness in marital conversations. *Journal of Communication, 32,* 108–120.

47. Haybe, J. G. & Metts, S. (2008). Managing the expression of emotion. *Western Journal of Communication, 72,* 374–396; Shimanoff, S. B. (1988). Degree of emotional expressiveness as a function of face-needs, gender, and interpersonal relationship. *Communication Reports, 1,* 43–53.

48. Waugh, C. E. & Fredericson, B. L. (2006). Nice to know you: Positive emotions, self-other overlap, and complex understanding in the formation of a new relationship. *The Journal of Positive Psychology, 1,* 93–106.

49. Shimanoff, S. B. (1985). Rules governing the verbal expression of emotions between married couples. *Western Journal of Speech Communication, 49,* 149–165.

50. Derks, D., Fischer, A. H., & Bos, A. E. R. (2008). The role of emotion in computer-mediated communication: A review. *Computers in Human Behavior, 24,* 766–785.

51. Martin, R. C., Coyier, K. R., VanSistine, L. M., & Schroeder, K. L. (2013). Anger on the Internet: The perceived value of rant-sites. *Cyberpsychology, Behavior, and Social Networking, 16,* 119–122.

52. Elphinston, R. A. & Noller, P. (2011). Time to face It! Facebook intrusion and the implications for romantic jealousy and relationship satisfaction. *Cyberpsychology, Behavior, and Social Networking, 14,* 631–635; Locatelli, S. M., Kluwe, K., & Bryant, F. B. (2012). Facebook use and the tendency to ruminate among college students: Testing meditational hypotheses. *Journal of Educational Computing Research, 46,* 377–394.

53. Muise, A., Christofides, E., & Desmarais, S. (2009). More information than you ever wanted: Does Facebook bring out the green-eyed monster of jealousy? *CyberPsychology & Behavior, 12,* 441–444.

54. Muise, A., Christofides, E., & Desmarais, S. (2014). "Creeping" or just information seeking? Gender differences in partner monitoring in response to jealousy on Facebook. *Personal Relationships, 21,* 35–50.

55. Marshall, T. (2012). Facebook surveillance of former romantic partners: Associations with postbreakup recovery and personal growth. *Cyberpsychology, Behavior, and Social Networking. 15,* 521–526.

56. Hatfield, E., Cacioppo, J. T., Rapson, R. L., & Oatley, K. (1984). *Emotional contagion.* Cambridge, England: Cambridge University Press; Colino, S. (2006, May 30). That look—It's catching. *The Washington Post,* HE01.

57. Goleman, D. (2006). *Social intelligence: The new science of human relationships* (p. 115). New York, NY: Bantam.

58. Bakker, A. B. (2005). Flow among music teachers and their students: The crossover of peak experiences. *Journal of Vocational Behavior, 66,* 822–833.

59. Jiangang, D., Xiucheng, F., & Tianjun, F. (2011). Multiple emotional contagions in service encounters. *Journal of the Academy of Marketing Science, 39,* 449–466.

60. Goodman C. R. & Shippy, R. A. (2002). Is it contagious? Affect similarity among spouses. *Aging and Mental Health, 6,* 266–274.

61. Belluck, P. (2008, December 5). Strangers may cheer you up, study says. *The New York Times,* A12.

62. Coviello, L., Sohn, Y., Kramer, A. D. I., Marlow, C., Franceschetti, M., et al. (2014). Detecting emotional contagion in massive social networks. *PLoS ONE, 9,* e90315.

63. Sullins, E. S. (1991). Emotional contagion revisited: Effects of social comparison and expressive style on mood convergence. *Personality and Social Psychology Bulletin, 17*, 166–174.

64. Anderson, C., Keltner, D., & John, O. P. (2003, May). Emotional convergence between people over time. *Journal of Personality and Social Psychology, 84*, 1054–1068.

65. DeAngelis, T. (1992). Illness linked with repressive style of coping. *APA Monitor, 23*(12), 14–15.

66. Seigman, A. W. & Smith, T. W. (1994). *Anger, hostility, and the heart*. Hillsdale, NJ: Erlbaum.

67. Graham, S., Huang, J. Y., Clark, M. S., & Helgeson, V. S. (2008). The positives of negative emotions: Willingness to express negative emotions promotes relationships. *Personality and Social Psychology Bulletin, 34*, 394–406; Kennedy-Moore, E. & Watson, J. C. (1999). *Expressing emotion: Myths, realities, and therapeutic strategies*. New York, NY: Guilford.

68. Nelton, S. (1996, February). Emotions in the workplace. *Nation's Business*, 25–30.

69. Kramer, M. W. & Hess, J. A. (2002). Communication rules for the display of emotions in organizational settings. *Management Communication Quarterly, 16*, 66–80.

70. Booth-Butterfield, M. & Booth-Butterfield, S. (1998). Emotionality and affective orientation. In J. C. McCroskey, J. A. Daly, M. M. Martin, & M. J. Beatty (Eds.), *Communication and personality: Trait perspectives* (pp. 171–189). Creskill, NY: Hampton.

71. Barrett, L. F., Gross, J., Christensen, T., & Benvenuto, M. (2001). Knowing what you're feeling and knowing what to do about it: Mapping the relation between emotion differentiation and emotion regulation. *Cognition and Emotion, 15*, 713–724.

72. Grewal, D. & Salovey, P. (2005). Feeling smart: The science of emotional intelligence. *American Scientist, 93*, 330–339; Yoo, S. H., Matsumoto, D., & LeRoux, J. (2006). The influence of emotion recognition and emotion regulation on intercultural adjustment. *International Journal of Intercultural Relations, 30*, 345–363.

73. Bushman, B. J., Baumeister, R. F., & Stack, A. D. (1999). Catharsis, aggression, and persuasive influence: Self-fulfilling or self-defeating prophecies? *Journal of Personality and Social Psychology, 76*, 367–376.

74. For an extensive discussion of ways to express emotions, see Fussell, S. R. (2002). *The verbal communication of emotions*. Mahwah, NJ: Erlbaum.

75. Honeycutt, J. M. (2003). *Imagined interactions: Daydreaming about communication*. Cresskill, NJ: Hampton Press; Honeycutt, J. M. & Ford, S. G. (2001). Mental imagery and intrapersonal communication: A review of research on imagined interactions (IIs) and current developments. *Communication Yearbook 25* (pp. 315–338). Thousand Oaks, CA: Sage.

76. Pennebaker, J. (2004). *Writing to heal: A guided journal for recovering from trauma and emotional upheaval*. Oakland, CA: Harbinger.

77. Floyd, K., Mikkelson, A. C., Hesse, C., & Pauley, P. M. (2007). Affectionate writing reduces total cholesterol: Two randomized, controlled studies. *Human Communication Research, 33*, 119–142.

78. Metts, S. & Wood, B. (2008). Interpersonal emotional competence. In M. T. Motley (Ed.), *Studies in applied interpersonal communication* (pp. 267–285). Thousand Oaks, CA: Sage.

79. Spitzberg, B. H. (2006). Preliminary development of a model and measure of computer-mediated communication (CMC) competence. *Journal of Computer-Mediated Communication, 11*, article 12. Retrieved from http://jcmc.indiana.edu/vol11/issue2/spitzberg.html

80. O'Sullivan, P. B. (2000). What you don't know won't hurt me: Impression management functions of communication channels in relationships. *Human Communication Research, 26*, 403–431.

81. Galovski, T. E., Malta, L. S., & Blanchard, E. B. (2005). *Road rage: Assessment and treatment of the angry, aggressive driver*. Washington, DC: American Psychological Association.

82. Mallalieu, S. D., Hanton, S., & Jones, G. (2003). Emotional labeling and competitive anxiety in preparation and competition. *The Sports Psychologist, 17*, 157–174.

83. Bourhis, J. & Allen, M. (1992). Meta-analysis of the relationship between communication apprehension and cognitive performance. *Communication Education, 41*, 68–76.

84. Patterson, M. L. & Ritts, V. (1997). Social and communicative anxiety: A review and meta-analysis. In B. R. Burleson (Ed.), *Communication yearbook 20*. Thousand Oaks, CA: Sage.

85. Smith, J. M. & Alloy, L. B. (2009). A roadmap to rumination: A review of the definition, assessment, and conceptualization of this multifaceted construct. *Clinical Psychology Review, 29*, 116–128; Elphinston, R. A., Feeney, J. A., Noller, P., Connor, J. P., & Fitzgerald, J. (2013). Romantic jealousy and relationship satisfaction: The costs of rumination. *Western Journal of Communication, 77*, 293–304.

86. Verduyn, P. & Lavrijsen, S. (2015). Which emotions last longest and why: The role of event importance and rumination. *Motivation and Emotion, 39*, 119–127.

87. Bushman, B. J., Bonacci, A. M., Pedersen, W. C., Vasquez, E. A., & Miller, N. (2005). Chewing on it can chew you up: Effects of rumination on triggered displaced aggression. *Journal of Personality and Social Psychology, 88*, 969–983.

88. For a thorough discussion of how neurobiology shapes feelings, see LeDoux, J. E. (1996). *The emotional brain*. New York, NY: Simon and Schuster.

89. Vocate, D. R. (1994). Self-talk and inner speech. In D. R. Vocate (Ed.), *Intrapersonal communication: Different voices, different minds* (pp. 3–32). Hillsdale, NJ: Erlbaum.

90. Ayers, J., Keereetaweep, T., Chen, P., & Edwards, P. A. (1998). Communication apprehension and employment interviews. *Communication Education, 47*, 1–17.

91. Brooks, A. W. (2013). Get excited: Reappraising pre-performance anxiety as excitement. *Journal of Psychology: General, 143*, 1144–1158.

92. Bargh, J. A. (1988). Automatic information processing: Implications for communication and affect. In H. E. Sypher & E. T. Higgins (Eds.), *Communication, social cognition, and affect* (pp. 9–32). Hillsdale, NJ: Erlbaum.

93. Metts, S. & Cupach, W. R. (1990). The influence of relationship beliefs and problem-solving relationships on satisfaction in romantic relationships. *Human Communication Research, 17*, 170–185.

94. Meichenbaum, A. (1977). *Cognitive behavior modification*. New York, NY: Plenum; Ellis, A. & Greiger, R. (1977). *Handbook for rational-emotive therapy*. New York, NY: Springer; Wirga, M. & DeBernardi, M. (2002, March). The ABCs of cognition, emotion, and action. *Archives of Psychiatry and Psychotherapy, 1*, 5–16.

95. Chatham-Carpenter, A. & DeFrancisco, V. (1997). Pulling yourself up again: Women's choices and strategies for recovering and maintaining self-esteem. *Western Journal of Communication, 61*, 164–187.

96. Seligman, M. E. P. (2006). *Learned optimism*. New York: Vintage.

97. Fredrickson, B. L. (2009). *Positivity*. New York: Three Rivers.

98. Peterson, C. (2006). *A primer in positive psychology*. New York: Oxford University Press; Rius-Ottenheim, N., Mast, R., Zitman, F. G., & Giltay, E. J. (2013). The role of dispositional optimism in physical and mental well-being. In A. Efklides & D. Moraitou (Eds.), *A positive psychology perspective on quality of life* (pp. 149–173). New York: Springer.

99. Fredrickson, B. L. (2009). *Positivity*. New York: Three Rivers.

CHAPTER SIX

1. Sacks, O. W. (1989). *Seeing voices: A journey into the world of the deaf* (p. 17). Berkeley: University of California Press.
2. Henneberger, M. (1999, January 29). Misunderstanding of word embarrasses Washington's new mayor. *The New York Times* online. Retrieved from http://www.nyt.com
3. Keysar, B. & Henly, A. S. (2002). Speakers' overestimation of their effectiveness. *Psychological Science, 13*, 207–212; Wyer, R. S. & Adava, R. (2003). Message reception skills in social communication. In J. O. Greene & B. R. Burleson (Eds.), *Handbook of communication and social interaction skills* (pp. 291–355). Mahwah, NJ: Erlbaum.
4. Scott, T. L. (2000, November 27). Teens before their time. *Time*, 22.
5. Wallsten, T. (1986). Measuring the vague meanings of probability terms. *Journal of Experimental Psychology, 115*, 348–365.
6. Prentice, W. E. (2005). *Therapeutic modalities in rehabilitation*. New York: McGraw-Hill.
7. Wolfram, W. & Schilling-Estes, N. (2005). *American English: Dialects and variation* (2nd ed.). Malden, MA: Blackwell.
8. Coupland, N., Wiemann, J. M., & Giles, H. (1991). Talk as "problem" and communication as "miscommunication": An integrative analysis. In N. Coupland, J. M. Wiemann, & H. Giles (Eds.), *"Miscommunication" and problematic talk* (pp. 1–17). Newbury Park, CA: Sage.
9. Pearce, W. B. & Cronen, V. (1980). *Communication, action, and meaning*. New York: Praeger; Cronen, V., Chen, V., & Pearce, W. B. (1988). Coordinated management of meaning: A critical theory. In Y. Y. Kim & W. B. Gudykunst (Eds.), *Theories in intercultural communication* (pp. 66–98). Newbury Park, CA: Sage.
10. Graham, E. K. E., Papa, M., & Brooks, G. P. (1992). Functions of humor in conversation: Conceptualization and measurement. *Western Journal of Communication, 56*, 161–183.
11. O'Sullivan, P. B. & Flanagin, A. (2003). Reconceptualizing "flaming" and other problematic communication. *New Media and Society, 5*, 67–93.
12. Christenfeld, N. & Larsen, B. (2008). The name game. *The Psychologist, 21*, 210–213.
13. Mehrabian, A. (2001). Characteristics attributed to individuals on the basis of their first names. *Genetic, Social, and General Psychology Monographs, 127*, 59–88.
14. Social Security Administration. (2013). *Popular baby names*. Retrieved from http://www.ssa.gov/OACT /babynames/
15. Fryer, R. G. & Levitt, S. D. (2004). The causes and consequences of distinctively black names. *Quarterly Journal of Economics, 119*, 767–805.
16. Aune, R. K. & Kikuchi, T. (1993). Effects of language intensity similarity on perceptions of credibility, relational attributions, and persuasion. *Journal of Language and Social Psychology, 12*, 224–238.
17. Giles, H., Mulac, A., Bradac, J. J., & Johnson, P. (2010). Speech accommodation theory: The first decade and beyond. In M. L. Knapp & J. A. Daly (Eds.), *Interpersonal communication* (pp. 39–74). Thousand Oaks, CA: Sage.
18. Baruch, Y. & Jenkins, S. (2006). Swearing at work and permissive leadership culture: When anti-social becomes social and incivility is acceptable. *Leadership & Organization Development Journal, 28*, 492–507.
19. Ireland, M. E., Slatcher, R. B., Eastwick, P. W., Scissors, L. E., Finkel, E. J., & Pennebaker, J. W. (2011). Language style matching predicts relationship initiation and stability. *Psychological Science, 22*, 39–44.
20. Cassell, J. & Tversky, D. (2005). The language of online intercultural community formation. *Journal of Computer-Mediated Communication, 10*, article 2.
21. Reyes, A. (2005). Appropriation of African American slang by Asian American youth. *Journal of Sociolinguistics, 9*, 509–532.
22. Ng, S. H. & Bradac, J. J. (1993). *Power in language: Verbal communication and social influence* (p. 27). Newbury Park, CA: Sage.
23. Parton, S., Siltanen, S. A., Hosman, L. A., & Langenderfer, J. (2002). Employment interview outcomes and speech style effects. *Journal of Language and Social Psychology, 21*, 144–161.
24. Hosman, L. A. (1989). The evaluative consequences of hedges, hesitations, and intensifiers: Powerful and powerless speech styles. *Human Communication Research, 15*, 383–406.
25. El-Alayli, A., Myers, C. J., Petersen, T. L., & Lystad, A. L. (2008). "I don't mean to sound arrogant, but …": The effects of using disclaimers on person perception. *Personality and Social Psychology Bulletin, 34*, 130–143.
26. Lee, J. J. & Pinker, S. (2010). Rationales for indirect speech: The theory of the strategic speaker. *Psychological Review, 117*, 785–807.
27. Dunn, C. D. (2013). Speaking politely, kindly, and beautifully: Ideologies of politeness in Japanese business etiquette training. *Multilingua, 32*, 225–245.
28. Bradac, J. & Mulac, A. (1984). Attributional consequences of powerful and powerless speech styles in a crisis-intervention context. *Journal of Language and Social Psychology, 3*, 1–19.
29. Bradac, J. J. (1983). The language of lovers, flovers [sic], and friends: Communicating in social and personal relationships. *Journal of Language and Social Psychology, 2*, 141–162.
30. Geddes, D. (1992). Sex roles in management: The impact of varying power of speech style on union members' perception of satisfaction and effectiveness. *Journal of Psychology, 126*, 589–607.
31. Kubany, E. S., Richard, D. C., Bauer, G. B., & Muraoka, M. Y. (1992). Impact of assertive and accusatory communication of distress and anger: A verbal component analysis. *Aggressive Behavior, 18*, 337–347.
32. Gordon, T. (1974). *T.E.T.: Teacher Effectiveness Training* (p. 74). New York: Wyden.
33. Vangelisti, A. L., Knapp, M. L., & Daly, J. A. (1990). Conversational narcissism. *Communication Monographs, 57*, 251–274; Zimmermann, J., Wolf, M., Bock, A., Peham, D., & Benecke, C. (2013). The way we refer to ourselves reflects how we relate to others: Associations between first-person pronoun use and interpersonal problems. *Journal of Research in Personality, 47*, 218–225.
34. Dreyer, A. S., Dreyer, C. A., & Davis, J. E. (1987). Individuality and mutuality in the language of families of field-dependent and field-independent children. *Journal of Genetic Psychology, 148*, 105–117.
35. Seider, B. H., Hirschberger, G., Nelson, K. L., & Levenson, R. W. (2009). We can work it out: Age differences in relational pronouns, physiology, and behavior in marital conflict. *Psychology and Aging, 24*, 604–613; Honeycutt, J. M. (1999). Typological differences in predicting marital happiness from oral history behaviors and imagined interactions. *Communication Monographs, 66*, 276–291.
36. Fitzsimons, G. & Kay, A. C. (2004). Language and interpersonal cognition: Causal effects of variations in pronoun usage on perceptions of closeness. *Personality and Social Psychology Bulletin, 30*, 547–557.
37. Rentscher, K. E., Rohrbaugh, M. J., Shoham, V., & Mehl, M. R. (2013). Asymmetric partner pronoun use and demand-withdraw interaction in couples coping with health problems. *Journal of Family Psychology, 27*, 691–701.
38. Slatcher, R. B., Vazire, S., & Pennebaker, J. W. (2008). Am "I" more important than "we"? Couples' word use in instant messages. *Personal Relationships, 15*, 407–424; Proctor, R. F. & Wilcox, J. R. (1993). An exploratory

analysis of responses to owned messages in inter-personal communication. *ETC: A Review of General Semantics, 50,* 201–220; Gustafsson Sendén, M., Lindholm, T., & Sikström, S. (2014). Selection bias in choice of words: Evaluations of "I" and "we" differ between contexts, but "they" are always worse. *Journal of Language & Social Psychology, 33,* 49–67.

39. Tannen, D. (1990). *You just don't understand: Women and men in conversation.* New York: William Morrow; Gray, J. (1992). *Men are from Mars, women are from Venus.* New York: HarperCollins.

40. Dindia, K. (2006). Men are from North Dakota, women are from South Dakota. In K. Dindia & D. J. Canary (Eds.), *Sex differences and similarities in communication: Critical essays and empirical investigations of sex and gender in interaction* (2nd ed., pp. 3–18). Mahwah, NJ: Erlbaum; Goldsmith, D. J. & Fulfs, P. A. (1999). "You just don't have the evidence": An analysis of claims and evidence in Deborah Tannen's *You just don't understand.* In M. E. Roloff (Ed.), *Communication yearbook 22* (pp. 1–49). Thousand Oaks, CA: Sage.

41. Haas, A. & Sherman, M. A. (1982). Conversational topic as a function of role and gender. *Psychological Reports, 51,* 453–454; Fehr, B. (1996). *Friendship processes.* Thousand Oaks, CA: Sage.

42. Schwartz, H. A., Eichstaedt, J. C., Kern, M. L., Dziurzynski, L., Ramones, S. M., Agrawal, M., ... Ungar, L. H. (2013). Personality, gender, and age in the language of social media: The open-vocabulary approach. *PLoS ONE, 8,* e73791.

43. Wood, J. T. (2011). He says/she says: Misunderstandings in communication between women and men. In D. O. Braithwaite & J. T. Wood (Eds.), *Casing interpersonal communication* (pp. 197–202). Dubuque, IA: Kendall-Hunt.

44. Clark, R. A. (1998). A comparison of topics and objectives in a cross section of young men's and women's everyday conversations. In D. J. Canary & K. Dindia (Eds.), *Sex differences and similarities in communication: Critical essays and empirical investigations of sex and gender in interaction* (pp. 303–319). Mahwah, NJ: Erlbaum.

45. DeCapua, A., Berkowitz, D., & Boxer, D. (2006). Women talk revisited: Personal disclosures and alignment development. *Multilingua, 25,* 393–412.

46. Wood, J. T. (2015). *Gendered lives: Communication, gender, & culture* (11th ed.). Stamford, CT: Cengage.

47. Sherman, M. A. & Haas, A. (1984, June). Man to man, woman to woman. *Psychology Today, 17,* 72–73.

48. Ragsdale, J. D. (1996). Gender, satisfaction level, and the use of relational maintenance strategies in marriage. *Communication Monographs, 63,* 354–371.

49. Giles, H. & Street, R. L., Jr. (1985). Communication characteristics and behavior. In M. L. Knapp & G. R. Miller (Eds.), *Handbook of interpersonal communication* (pp. 205–261). Beverly Hills, CA: Sage; Kohn, A. (1988, February). Girl talk, guy talk. *Psychology Today, 22,* 65–66.

50. Mehl, M. R., Vazire, S., Ramírez-Esparza, N., Slatcher, R. B., & Pennebaker, J. W. (2007). Are women really more talkative than men? *Science, 317,* 82.

51. Mulac, A. (2006). The gender-linked language effect: Do language differences really make a difference? In K. Dindia & D. J. Canary (Eds.), *Sex differences and similarities in communication: Critical essays and empirical investigations of sex and gender in interaction* (2nd ed., pp. 127–153). Mahwah, NJ: Erlbaum.

52. Summarized in Wood, J. T. (2015). *Gendered lives: Communication, gender, & culture* (11th ed.). Stamford, CT: Cengage. See also Newman, M. L., Groom, C. J., Handleman, L. D., & Pennebaker, J. W. (2008). Gender differences in language use: An analysis of 14,000 text samples. *Discourse Processes, 45,* 211–236.

53. Clark, R. A. (1998). A comparison of topics and objectives in a cross section of young men's and women's everyday conversations. In D. J. Canary & K. Dindia (Eds.), *Sex*

differences and similarities in communication: Critical essays and empirical investigations of sex and gender in interaction (pp. 303–319). Mahwah, NJ: Erlbaum.

54. Fandrich, A. M. & Beck, S. J. (2012). Powerless language in health media: The influence of biological sex and magazine type on health language. *Communication Studies, 63,* 36–53.

55. Carli, L. L. (1990). Gender, language, and influence. *Journal of Personality and Social Psychology, 59,* 941–951.

56. Reddy, S., Stanford, J., & Zhong, J. (2014). A Twitter-based study of newly formed clippings in American English. *Annual Meeting of the American Dialect Society* (ADS).

57. Canary, D. J. & Hause, K. S. (1993). Is there any reason to research sex differences in communication? *Communication Quarterly, 41,* 129–144.

58. See also Hancock, A. B. & Rubin, B. A. (2015). Influence of communication partner's gender on language. *Journal of Language & Social Psychology, 34,* 46–64; Zahn, C. J. (1989). The bases for differing evaluations of male and female speech: Evidence from ratings of transcribed conversation. *Communication Monographs, 56,* 59–74; Grob, L. M., Meyers, R. A., & Schuh, R. (1997). Powerful/powerless language use in group interactions: Sex differences or similarities? *Communication Quarterly, 45,* 282–303.

59. Leaper, C. & Robnett, R. D. (2011). Women are more likely than men to use tentative language, aren't they? A meta-analysis testing for gender differences and moderators. *Psychology of Women Quarterly, 35,* 129–142.

60. Leaper, C. & Ayres, M. M. (2007). A meta-analytic review of gender variations in adults' language use: Talkativeness, affiliative speech, and assertive speech. *Personality and Social Psychology Review, 11,* 328–363.

61. Dindia, K. (2006). Men are from North Dakota, women are from South Dakota. In K. Dindia & D. J. Canary (Eds.), *Sex differences and similarities in communication: Critical essays and empirical investigations of sex and gender in interaction* (2nd ed., pp. 3–20). Mahwah, NJ: Erlbaum.

62. Zahn, C. J. (1989). The bases for differing evaluations of male and female speech: Evidence from ratings of transcribed conversation. *Communication Monographs, 56,* 59–74.

63. Fisher, B. A. (1983). Differential effects of sexual composition and interactional content on interaction patterns in dyads. *Human Communication Research, 9,* 225–238.

64. Pilgeram, R. (2007). "Ass-kicking" women: Doing and undoing gender in a US livestock auction. *Gender, Work and Organization, 14,* 572–595.

65. Ellis, D. G. & McCallister, L. (1980). Relational control sequences in sex-typed and androgynous groups. *Western Journal of Speech Communication, 44,* 35–49.

66. Steen, S. & Schwarz, P. (1995). Communication, gender, and power: Homosexual couples as a case study. In M. A. Fitzpatrick & A. L. Vangelisti (Eds.), *Explaining family interactions* (pp. 310–343). Thousand Oaks, CA: Sage.

67. Samovar, L. A. & Porter, R. E. (1991). *Communication between cultures* (pp. 165–169). Dubuque, IA: W. C. Brown.

68. Ricks, D. (1983). *Big business blunders: Mistakes in international marketing* (p. 41). Homewood, IL: Dow Jones-Irwin.

69. Sugimoto, N. (1991, March). *"Excuse me" and "I'm sorry": Apologetic behaviors of Americans and Japanese.* Paper presented at the Conference on Communication in Japan and the United States, California State University, Fullerton.

70. Gudykunst, W. B. & Ting-Toomey, S. (1988). *Culture and interpersonal communication.* Newbury Park, CA: Sage.

71. Hall, E. (1959). *Beyond culture.* New York: Doubleday.

72. Basso, K. (1970). To give up on words: Silence in Western Apache culture. *Southern Journal of Anthropology, 26,* 213–230.

73. Yum, J. (1987). The practice of Uye-ri in interpersonal relationships in Korea. In D. Kincaid (Ed.), *Communication theory from Eastern and Western perspectives* (pp. 87–100). New York: Academic Press.

74. Everett, C. (2013). *Linguistic relativity: Evidence across languages and cognitive domains*. Berlin/Boston: Walter de Gruyter; Deutscher, G. (2010). *Through the language glass: Why the world looks different in other languages*. New York: Metropolitan Books.

75. Martin, L. & Pullum, G. (1991). *The great Eskimo vocabulary hoax*. Chicago: University of Chicago Press.

76. Giles, H. & Franklyn-Stokes, A. (1989). Communicator characteristics. In M. K. Asante & W. B. Gudykunst (Eds.), *Handbook of international and intercultural communication* (pp. 117–144). Newbury Park, CA: Sage.

77. Whorf, B. (1956). The relation of habitual thought and behavior to language. In J. B. Carroll (Ed.), *Language, thought, and reality* (pp. 134–159). Cambridge, MA: MIT Press.

78. Rheingold, H. (1988). *They have a word for it*. Los Angeles: Jeremy P. Tarcher.

79. Arroyo, A. (2013). "I'm so fat!" The negative outcomes of fat talk. *Communication Currents, 7*, 1–2; Arroyo, A. & Harwood, J. (2012). Exploring the causes and consequences of fat talk. *Journal of Applied Communication Research, 40*, 167–187.

80. Bowers, J. S. & Pleydell-Pearce, C. W. (2011). Swearing, euphemisms, and linguistic relativity. *PLoS ONE, 6*, e22341. doi:10.1371/journal.pone.0022341

CHAPTER SEVEN

1. Burgoon, J. K. (1994). Nonverbal signals. In M. L. Knapp & G. R. Miller (Eds.), *Handbook of interpersonal communication* (p. 235). Newbury Park, CA: Sage.

2. Riggio, R. E. (2006). Nonverbal skills and abilities. In V. Manusov & M. L. Patterson (Eds.), *The Sage handbook of nonverbal communication* (pp. 79–86). Thousand Oaks, CA: Sage.

3. Burgoon, J. K., Guerrero, L., & Manusov, V. (2011). Nonverbal signals. In M. L. Knapp & J. A. Daly (Eds.), *The Sage handbook of interpersonal communication* (4th ed., pp. 239–282). Thousand Oaks, CA: Sage.

4. Jones, S. E. & LeBaron, C. D. (2002). Research on the relationship between verbal and nonverbal communication: Emerging interactions. *Journal of Communication, 52*, 499–521.

5. DePaulo, B. M. (1994). Spotting lies: Can humans learn to do better? *Current Directions in Psychological Science, 3*, 83–86.

6. Burgoon, J. K. (1994). Nonverbal signals. In M. L. Knapp & G. R. Miller (Eds.), *Handbook of interpersonal communication* (pp. 229–232). Newbury Park, CA: Sage.

7. Manusov, F. (1991, Summer). Perceiving nonverbal messages: Effects of immediacy and encoded intent on receiver judgments. *Western Journal of Speech Communication, 55*, 235–253; Buck, R. & VanLear, C. A. (2002). Verbal and nonverbal communication: Distinguishing symbolic, spontaneous, and pseudo-spontaneous nonverbal behavior. *Journal of Communication, 52*, 522–541.

8. Clevenger, T., Jr. (1991). Can one not communicate? A conflict of models. *Communication Studies, 42*, 340–353.

9. Burgoon, J. K. & LePoire, B. A. (1999). Nonverbal cues and interpersonal judgments: Participant and observer perceptions of intimacy, dominance, composure, and formality. *Communication Monographs, 66*, 105–124.

10. Keating, C. F. (2006). Why and how the silent self speak volumes: Functional approaches to nonverbal impression management. In V. Manusov & M. L. Patterson (Eds.), *The Sage handbook of nonverbal communication* (pp. 321–340). Thousand Oaks, CA: Sage.

11. Horan, S. M. & Booth-Butterfield, M. (2010). Investing in affection: An investigation of affection exchange theory and relational qualities. *Communication Quarterly, 58*, 394–413.

12. Skovholt, K., Gronning, A., & Kankaanranta, A. (2014). The communicative functions of emoticons in workplace e-mails. *Journal of Computer-Mediated Communication, 19*, 780–797; Derks, D., Bos, A. E. R., & von Grumbkow, J. (2007). Emoticons and social interaction on the Internet: The importance of social context. *Computers in Human Behavior, 23*, 442–879.

13. Dresner, E. & Herring, S. C. (2010). Functions of the nonverbal in CMC: Emoticons and illocutionary force. *Communication Theory, 20*, 249–268.

14. Vandergriff, I. (2013). Emotive communication online: A contextual analysis of computer-mediated communication cues. *Journal of Pragmatics, 51*, 1–12

15. Ledbetter, A. M. (2008). Chronemic cues and sex differences in relational e-mail: Perceiving immediacy and supportive message quality. *Social Science Computer Review, 26*, 466–482; Walther, J. B. (2009). Nonverbal dynamics in computer-mediated communication or :(and the net :('s with you, :) and you :) alone. In V. Manusov & M. L. Patterson (Eds.), *The Sage handbook of nonverbal communication* (pp. 461–479). Thousand Oaks, CA: Sage.

16. Uhls, Y. T., Michikyan, M., Morris, J., Garcia, D., Small, G. W., Zgourou, E., & Greenfield, P. M. (2014). Five days at outdoor education camp without screens improves preteen skills with nonverbal emotion cues. *Computers in Human Behavior, 39*, 387–392.

17. Cross, E. S. & Franz, E. A. (2003, April). *Talking hands: Observation of bimanual gestures as a facilitative working memory mechanism*. Paper presented at the Cognitive Neuroscience Society 10th Annual Meeting, New York.

18. Motley, M. T. (1993). Facial affect and verbal context in conversation: Facial expression as interjection. *Human Communication Research, 20*, 3–40.

19. Capella, J. N. & Schreiber, D. M. (2006). The interaction management function of nonverbal cues. In V. Manusov & M. L. Patterson (Eds.), *The Sage handbook of nonverbal communication* (pp. 361–379). Thousand Oaks, CA: Sage.

20. Giles, H. & LePoire, B. A. (2006). The ubiquity of social meaningfulness of nonverbal communication. In V. Manusov & M. L. Patterson (Eds.), *The Sage handbook of nonverbal communication* (pp. xv–xxvii). Thousand Oaks, CA: Sage.

21. Ekman, P. (2003). *Emotions revealed: Recognizing faces and feelings to improve communication and emotional life*. New York: Holt.

22. Vrig, A. (2006). Nonverbal communication and deception. In V. Manusov & M. L. Patterson (Eds.), *The Sage handbook of nonverbal communication* (pp. 341–360). Thousand Oaks, CA: Sage.

23. Guerrero, L. K. & Floyd, K. (2006). *Nonverbal communication in close relationships*. Mahwah, NJ: Erlbaum; DePaulo, B. M. (1980). Detecting deception modality effects. In L. Wheeler (Ed.), *Review of personality and social psychology* (Vol. 1, pp. 125–162). Beverly Hills, CA: Sage; Greene, J., O'Hair, D., Cody, M., & Yen, C. (1985). Planning and control of behavior during deception. *Human Communication Research, 11*, 335–364.

24. Burgoon, J. K. & Levine, T. R. (2010). Advances in deception detection. In S. W. Smith & S. R. Wilson (Eds.), *New directions in interpersonal communication research* (pp. 201–220). Thousand Oaks, CA: Sage.

25. Lock, C. (2004). Deception detection: Psychologists try to learn how to spot a liar. *Science News Online, 166*, 72.

26. Mann, S., Ewens, S., Shaw, D., Vrij, A., Leal, S., & Hillman, J. (2013). Lying eyes: Why liars seek deliberate eye contact. *Psychiatry, Psychology and Law, 20*, 452–461.

27. Harwig, M. & Bond, C. F. (2011). Why do lie-catchers fail? A lens model meta-analysis of human lie judgments. *Psychological Bulletin, 137*, 643–659.

28. Lindsey, A. E. & Vigil, V. (1999). The interpretation and evaluation of winking in stranger dyads. *Communication Research Reports, 16*, 256–265.

29. Smiling through the artichokes. (1998, September 9). *San Francisco Examiner*.

30. Simon, R. (1995, March 20). Proceed with caution if using hand signals. *Los Angeles Times*.

31. Lim, G. Y. & Roloff, M. E. (1999). Attributing sexual consent. *Journal of Applied Communication Research, 27*, 1–23.

32. Rourke, B. P. (1989). *Nonverbal learning disabilities: The syndrome and the model*. New York: Guilford.

33. Fudge, E. S. (n.d.). *Nonverbal learning disorder syndrome?* Retrieved from http://www.nldontheweb.org/fudge.htm

34. Rosip, J. C. & Hall, J. A. (2004). Knowledge of nonverbal cues, gender, and nonverbal decoding accuracy. *Journal of Nonverbal Behavior, 28*, 267–286; Hall, J. A. (1985). Male and female nonverbal behavior. In A. W. Siegman & S. Feldstein (Eds.), *Multichannel integrations of nonverbal behavior* (pp. 69–103). Hillsdale, NJ: Erlbaum.

35. Hall, J. A. (2006). Women and men's nonverbal communication. In V. Manusov & M. L. Patterson (Eds.), *The Sage handbook of nonverbal communication* (pp. 201–218). Thousand Oaks, CA: Sage.

36. Canary, D. J. & Emmers-Sommer, T. M. (1997). *Sex and gender differences in personal relationships*. New York: Guilford.

37. Knofler, T. & Imhof, M. (2007). Does sexual orientation have an impact on nonverbal behavior in interpersonal communication? *Journal of Nonverbal Behavior, 31*, 189–204.

38. Matsumoto, D. & Yoo, S. H. (2005). Culture and applied nonverbal communication. In R. S. Feldman & R. E. Riggio (Eds.), *Applications of nonverbal communication* (pp. 255–277). Mahwah, NJ: Erlbaum.

39. Birdwhistell, R. (1970). *Kinesics and context*. Philadelphia: University of Pennsylvania Press.

40. Ekman, P., Friesen, W. V., & Baer, J. (1984, May). The international language of gestures. *Psychology Today, 18*, 64–69.

41. Yuki, M., Maddux, W. W., & Masuda, T. (2007). Are the windows to the soul the same in the East and West? Cultural differences in using the eyes and mouth as cues to recognize emotions in Japan and the United States. *Journal of Experimental Social Psychology, 43*, 303–311.

42. Hall, E. (1969). *The hidden dimension*. Garden City, NY: Anchor Books.

43. Matsumoto, D. (2006). Culture and nonverbal behavior. In V. Manusov & M. L. Patterson (Eds.), *The Sage handbook of nonverbal communication* (pp. 219–235). Thousand Oaks, CA: Sage.

44. Akechi, H., Senju, A., Uibo, H., Kikuchi, Y., Hasegawa, T., & Hietanen, J. K. (2013). Attention to eye contact in the West and East: Autonomic responses and evaluative ratings. *PLoS ONE, 8*, e59312; Bavelas, J. B., Coates, L., & Johnson, T. (2002). Listener responses as a collaborative process: The role of gaze. *Journal of Communication, 52*, 566–579.

45. Levine, R. (1988). The pace of life across cultures. In J. E. McGrath (Ed.), *The social psychology of time* (pp. 39–60). Newbury Park, CA: Sage.

46. Hall, E. T. & Hall, M. R. (1987). *Hidden differences: Doing business with the Japanese*. Garden City, NY: Anchor Press.

47. Levine, R. & Wolff, E. (1985, March). Social time: The heartbeat of culture. *Psychology Today, 19*, 28–35.

48. Booth-Butterfield, M. & Jordan, F. (1998). *"Act like us": Communication adaptation among racially homogeneous and heterogeneous groups*. Paper presented at the Speech Communication Association meeting, New Orleans.

49. Ekman, P. (2003). *Emotions revealed*. New York: Holt.

50. Eibl-Eibesfeldt, J. (1972). Universals and cultural differences in facial expressions of emotions. In J. Cole (Ed.), *Nebraska symposium on motivation* (pp. 297–314). Lincoln: University of Nebraska Press.

51. Coulson, M. (2004). Attributing emotion to static body postures: Recognition accuracy, confusions, and viewpoint dependence. *Journal of Nonverbal Behavior, 28*, 117–139.

52. Mehrabian, A. (1981). *Silent messages* (2nd ed., pp. 47–48, 61–62). Belmont, CA: Wadsworth.

53. Carney, D. R., Cuddy, A. J., & Yap, A. J. (2010). Power posing: Brief nonverbal displays affect neuroendrocrine levels and risk tolerance. *Psychological Science, 21*, 1363–1368.

54. Corballis, M. C. (2002). *From hand to mouth: The origins of language*. Princeton, NJ: Princeton University Press.

55. Andersen, P. A. (2008). *Nonverbal communication: Forms and functions* (2nd ed., p. 37). Long Grove, IL: Waveland Press.

56. Ekman, P. & Friesen, W. V. (1969). The repertoire of nonverbal behavior: Categories, origins, usage, and coding. *Semiotica, 1*, 49–98.

57. Sueyoshi, A. & Hardison, D. M. (2005). The role of gestures and facial cues in second language listening comprehension. *Language Learning, 55*, 661–699.

58. Koerner, B. I. (2003, March 28). What does a "thumbs up" mean in Iraq? *Slate*. Retrieved from http://www.slate.com/id/2080812

59. Ekman, P. & Friesen, W. V. (1974). Nonverbal behavior and psychopathology. In R. J. Friedman & M. N. Katz (Eds.), *The psychology of depression: Contemporary theory and research* (pp. 3–31). Washington, DC: J. Winston.

60. Ekman, P. (2009). *Telling lies: Clues to deceit in the marketplace, politics, and marriage* (4th ed.). New York: W. W. Norton.

61. Ekman, P. & Friesen, W. V. (1975). *Unmasking the face: A guide to recognizing emotions from facial clues*. Englewood Cliffs, NJ: Prentice-Hall.

62. Yan, W., Wu, Q., Liang, J., Chen, Y., & Fu, X. (2013). How fast are the leaked facial expressions: The duration of microexpressions. *Journal of Nonverbal Behavior, 37*, 217–230.

63. Porter, S., Brinke, L., & Wallace, B. (2012). Secrets and lies: Involuntary leakage in deceptive facial expressions as a function of emotional intensity. *Journal of Nonverbal Behavior, 36*, 23–37.

64. Ekman, P. (2009). *Telling lies: Clues to deceit in the marketplace, politics, and marriage* (4th ed.). New York: W. W. Norton.

65. Krumhuber, E. & Kappas, A. (2005). Moving smiles: The role of dynamic components for the perception of the genuineness of smiles. *Journal of Nonverbal Behavior, 29*, 3–24.

66. Davis, S. F. & Kieffer, J. C. (1998). Restaurant servers influence tipping behavior. *Psychological Reports, 83*, 223–226.

67. Gueguen, N. & Jacob, C. (2002). Direct look versus evasive glance and compliance with a request. *Journal of Social Psychology, 142*, 393–396.

68. Andersen, P. A., Guerrero, L. K., & Jones, S. M. (2006). Nonverbal behavior in intimate interactions and intimate relationships. In V. Manusov & M. L. Patterson (Eds.), *The Sage handbook of nonverbal communication* (pp. 259–278). Thousand Oaks, CA: Sage.

69. Burgoon, J. K. & Dunbar, N. E. (2006). Nonverbal skills and abilities. In V. Manusov & M. L. Patterson (Eds.), *The Sage handbook of nonverbal communication* (pp. 279–298). Thousand Oaks, CA: Sage.

70. Guerrero, L. K. & Floyd, K. (2006). *Nonverbal communication in close relationships*. Mahwah, NJ: Erlbaum.

71. Davis, M., Markus, K. A., & Walters, S. B. (2006). Judging the credibility of criminal suspect statements: Does mode of presentation matter? *Journal of Nonverbal Behavior, 30*, 181–198.

72. Einhorn, L. J. (1981). An inner view of the job interview: An investigation of successful communicative behaviors. *Communication Education, 30*, 217–228.

73. Bone, J. (2009, January 23). Caroline Kennedy says no to Senate but may become London envoy. *London Times*. Retrieved from http://www.timesonline.co.uk

74. Knapp, M. L. & Hall, J. A. (2010). *Nonverbal communication in human interaction* (7th ed., pp. 344–346). Boston: Wadsworth.

75. Trees, A. R. (2000). Nonverbal communication and the support process: Interactional sensitivity in interactions between mothers and young adult children. *Communication Monographs, 67*, 239–261.

76. Buller, D. & Aune, K. (1992). The effects of speech rate similarity on compliance: Application of communication accommodation theory. *Western Journal of Communication, 56*, 37–53; Buller, D., LePoire, B. A., Aune, K., & Eloy, S. V. (1992). Social perceptions as mediators of the effect of speech rate similarity on compliance. *Human Communication Research, 19*, 286–311; Buller, D. B. & Aune, R. K. (1988). The effects of vocalics and nonverbal sensitivity on compliance: A speech accommodation theory explanation. *Human Communication Research, 14*, 301–332.

77. Andersen, P. A. (1984). Nonverbal communication in the small group. In R. S. Cathcart & L. A. Samovar (Eds.), *Small group communication: A reader* (4th ed., pp. 258–270). Dubuque, IA: W. C. Brown.

78. Harris, M., Ivanko, S., Jungen, S., Hala, S., & Pexman, P. (2001, October). *You're really nice: Children's understanding of sarcasm and personality traits*. Poster presented at 2nd Biennial Meeting of the Cognitive Development Society, Virginia Beach.

79. Tusing, K. J. & Dillard, J. P. (2000). The sounds of dominance: Vocal precursors of perceived dominance during interpersonal influence. *Human Communication Research, 26*, 148–171.

80. Zuckerman, M., & Driver, R. E. (1989). What sounds beautiful is good: The vocal attractiveness stereotype. *Journal of Nonverbal Behavior, 13*, 67–82.

81. Ng, S. H. & Bradac, J. J. (1993). *Power in language: Verbal communication and social influence* (p. 40). Newbury Park, CA: Sage.

82. Heslin, R. & Alper, T. (1983). Touch: A bonding gesture. In J. M. Wiemann & R. P. Harrison (Eds.), *Nonverbal interaction* (pp. 47–75). Beverly Hills, CA: Sage.

83. Heslin, R. & Alper, T. (1983). Touch: A bonding gesture. In J. M. Wiemann & R. P. Harrison (Eds.), *Nonverbal interaction* (pp. 47–75). Beverly Hills, CA: Sage.

84. Burgoon, J., Walther, J., & Baesler, E. (1992). Interpretations, evaluations, and consequences of interpersonal touch. *Human Communication Research, 19*, 237–263.

85. Crusco, A. H., & Wetzel, C. G. (1984). The Midas touch: Effects of interpersonal touch on restaurant tipping. *Personality and Social Psychology Bulletin, 10*, 512–517.

86. Hornik, J. (1992). Effects of physical contact on customers' shopping time and behavior. *Marketing Letters, 3*, 49–55.

87. Smith, D. E., Gier, J. A., & Willis, F. N. (1982). Interpersonal touch and compliance with a marketing request. *Basic and Applied Social Psychology, 3*, 35–38.

88. Gueguen, N. & Vion, M. (2009). The effect of a practitioner's touch on a patient's medication compliance. *Psychology, Health & Medicine, 14*, 689–694.

89. Adler, T. (1993, February). Congressional staffers witness miracle of touch. *APA Monitor*, 12–13.

90. Driscoll, M. S., Newman, D. L., & Seal, J. M. (1988). The effect of touch on the perception of counselors. *Counselor Education and Supervision, 27*, 344–354; Wilson, J. M. (1982). The value of touch in psychotherapy. *American Journal of Orthopsychiatry, 52*, 65–72.

91. Field, T., Lasko, D., Mundy, P., Henteleff, T., Kabat, S., Talpins, S., & Dowling, M. (1997). Brief report: Autistic children's attentiveness and responsivity improve after touch therapy. *Journal of Autism and Developmental Disorders, 27*, 333–338.

92. Kraus, M. W., Huang, C., & Keltner, D. (2010). Tactile communication, cooperation, and performance: An ethological study of the NBA. *Emotion, 10*, 745–749.

93. Patzer, G. (2008). *Looks: Why they matter more than you ever imagined*. New York: Amacon.

94. Dion, K. K. (1973). Young children's stereotyping of facial attractiveness. *Developmental Psychology, 9*, 183–188.

95. Ritts, V., Patterson, M. L., & Tubbs, M. E. (1992). Expectations, impressions, and judgments of physically attractive students: A review. *Review of Educational Research, 62*, 413–426.

96. Riniolo, T. C., Johnson, K. C., & Sherman, T. R. (2006). Hot or not: Do professors perceived as physically attractive receive higher student evaluations? *Journal of General Psychology, 133*, 19–35.

97. Hosoda, M., Stone-Romero, E. F., & Coats, G. (2003). The effects of physical attractiveness on job-related outcomes: A meta-analysis of experimental studies. *Personnel Psychology, 56*, 431–462.

98. Furnham, A. (April 22, 2014). Lookism at work. *Psychology Today*; Gordon, R., Crosnoe, R., & Wang, X. (2013). Physical attractiveness and the accumulation of social and human capital in adolescence and young adulthood. *Monographs of the Society for Research in Child Development, 78*, 1–137.

99. Agthe, M., Sporrle, M., & Maner, J. K. (2011). Does being attractive always help? Positive and negative effects of attractiveness on social decision making. *Personality and Social Psychology Bulletin, 37*, 1042–1054.

100. Frevert, T. K. & Walker, L. S. (2014). Physical attractiveness and social status. *Sociology Compass, 8*, 313–323.

101. Albada, K. F., Knapp, M. L., & Theune, K. E. (2002). Interaction appearance theory: Changing perceptions of physical attractiveness through social interaction. *Communication Theory, 12*, 8–40.

102. Thourlby, W. (1978). *You are what you wear* (p. 1). New York: New American Library.

103. Knapp, M. L. & Hall, J. A. (2010). *Nonverbal communication in human interaction* (7th ed., pp. 201–207). Boston: Wadsworth.

104. Hall, E. (1969). *The hidden dimension*. Garden City, NY: Anchor Books.

105. Hackman, M. & Walker, K. (1990). Instructional communication in the televised classroom: The effects of system design and teacher immediacy. *Communication Education, 39*, 196–206; McCroskey, J. C. & Richmond, V. P. (1992). Increasing teacher influence through immediacy. In V. P. Richmond & J. C. McCroskey (Eds.), *Power in the classroom: Communication, control, and concern* (pp. 101–119). Hillsdale, NJ: Erlbaum.

106. Conlee, C., Olvera, J., & Vagim, N. (1993). The relationships among physician nonverbal immediacy and measures of patient satisfaction with physician care. *Communication Reports, 6*, 25–33.

107. Kaya, N. & Burgess, B. (2007). Territoriality: Seat preferences in different types of classroom arrangements. *Environment and Behavior, 39*, 859–876.

108. Brown, G., Lawrence, T. B., & Robinson, S. L. (2005). Territoriality in organizations. *Academy of Management Review, 30*, 577–594.

109. Sadalla, E. (1987). Identity and symbolism in housing. *Environment and Behavior, 19*, 569–587.

110. Maslow, A. & Mintz, N. (1956). Effects of aesthetic surroundings: Initial effects of those aesthetic surroundings upon perceiving "energy" and "well-being" in faces. *Journal of Psychology, 41*, 247–254.

111. Teven, J. J. & Comadena, M. E. (1996). The effects of office aesthetic quality on students' perceptions of teacher credibility and communicator style. *Communication Research Reports, 13*, 101–108.

112. Sommer, R. (1969). *Personal space: The behavioral basis of design*. Englewood Cliffs, NJ: Prentice-Hall.

113. Sommer, R. & Augustin, S. (2007). Spatial orientation in the cubicle. *Journal of Facilities Management, 5*, 205–214.

114. Ballard, D. I. & Seibold, D. R. (2000). Time orientation and temporal variation across work groups: Implications for group and organizational communication. *Western Journal of Communication, 64*, 218–242.

115. Kalman, Y. M. & Rafaeli, S. (2011). Online pauses and silence: Chronemic expectancy violations in written computer-mediated communication. *Communication Research, 38*, 54–69.

116. Andersen, P. A., Guerrero, L. K., & Jones, S. M. (2006). Nonverbal behavior in intimate interactions and intimate relationships. In V. Manusov & M. L. Patterson (Eds.), *The Sage handbook of nonverbal communication* (pp. 259–278). Thousand Oaks, CA: Sage.

117. Egland, K. I., Stelzner, M. A., Andersen, P. A., & Spitzberg, B. S. (1997). Perceived understanding, nonverbal communication, and relational satisfaction. In J. E. Aitken & L. J. Shedletsky (Eds.), *Intrapersonal communication processes* (pp. 386–396). Annandale, VA: Speech Communication Association.

118. Walther, J. B. (2006). Nonverbal dynamics in computer-mediated communication. In V. Manusov & M. L. Patterson (Eds.), *The Sage handbook of nonverbal communication* (pp. 461–479). Thousand Oaks, CA: Sage.

119. Walther, J. B. & Bunz, U. (2005). The rules of virtual groups: Trust, liking, and performance in computer-mediated communication. *Journal of Communication, 55*, 828–846.

CHAPTER EIGHT

1. Emanuel, R., Adams, J., Baker, K., Daufin, E. K., Ellington, C., Fitts, E., Himsel, J., Holladay, L., & Okeowo, D. (2008). How college students spend their time communicating. *International Journal of Listening, 22*, 13–28; Barker, L., Edwards, R., Gaines, C., Gladney, K., & Holley, R. (1981). An investigation of proportional time spent in various communication activities by college students. *Journal of Applied Communication Research, 8*, 101–109.

2. Wolvin, A. D. & Coakley, C. G. (1981). A survey of the status of listening training in some Fortune 500 corporations. *Communication Education, 40*, 152–164.

3. Prager, K. J. & Buhrmester, D. (1998). Intimacy and need fulfillment in couple relationships. *Journal of Social and Personal Relationships, 15*, 435–469.

4. Vangelisti, A. L. (1994). Couples' communication problems: The counselor's perspective. *Journal of Applied Communication Research, 22*, 106–126.

5. Wolvin, A. D. (1984). Meeting the communication needs of the adult learners. *Communication Education, 33*, 267–271.

6. Beall, M. L., Gill-Rosier, J., Tate, J., & Matten, A. (2008). State of the context: Listening in education. *International Journal of Listening, 22*, 123–132.

7. Davis, J., Foley, A., Crigger, N., & Brannigan, M. C. (2008). Healthcare and listening: A relationship for caring. *International Journal of Listening, 22*, 168–175; Davis, J., Thompson, C. R., Foley, A., Bond, C. D., & DeWitt, J. (2008). An examination of listening concepts in the healthcare context: Differences among nurses, physicians, and administrators. *International Journal of Listening, 22*, 152–167.

8. Schnapp, D. C. (2008). Listening in context: Religion and spirituality. *International Journal of Listening, 22*, 133–140.

9. Flynn, J., Valikoski, T., & Grau, J. (2008). Listening in the business context: Reviewing the state of research. *International Journal of Listening, 22*, 141–151.

10. Keyton et al. (2013). Investigating verbal workplace communication behaviors. *Journal of Business Communication, 50*, 152–169.

11. Fernald, A. (2001). Hearing, listening, and understanding: Auditory development in infancy. In G. Bemner & A. Fogel (Eds.), *Blackwell handbook of infant development* (pp. 35–70). Malden, MA: Blackwell.

12. Burleson, B. R. (2010). Explaining recipient responses to supportive messages: Development and tests of a dual-process theory. In S. W. Smith & S. R. Wilson (Eds.), *New directions in interpersonal communication research* (pp. 159–179). Los Angeles: Sage; Bodie, G. D. & Burleson, B. R. (2008). Explaining variations in the effects of supportive messages: A dual-process framework. In C. S. Beck (Ed.), *Communication yearbook 32* (pp. 355–398). New York: Routledge.

13. Langer, E. (1990). *Mindfulness.* Reading, MA: Addison-Wesley; Burgoon, J. K., Berger, C. R., & Waldron, V. R. (2000). Mindfulness and interpersonal communication. *Journal of Social Issues, 56*, 105–127.

14. Burgoon, J. K., Berger, C. R., & Waldron, V. R. (2000). Mindfulness and interpersonal communication. *Journal of Social Issues, 56*, 105–127.

15. Langer, E. (1990). *Mindfulness* (p. 90). Reading, MA: Addison-Wesley.

16. Cooper, L. O. & Buchanan, T. (2010). Listening competency on campus: A psychometric analysis of student listening. *The International Journal of Listening, 24*, 141–163.

17. Kochkin, S. (2005). MarkeTrak VII: Hearing loss population tops 31 million. *Hearing Review, 12*, 16–29.

18. Flexer, C. (1997, February). Commonly asked questions about children with minimal hearing loss in the classroom. *Hearing Loss*, 8–12.

19. Smeltzer, L. R. & Watson, K. W. (1984). Listening: An empirical comparison of discussion length and level of incentive. *Central States Speech Journal, 35*, 166–170.

20. Pasupathi, M., Stallworth, L. M., & Murdoch, K. (1998). How what we tell becomes what we know: Listener effects on speakers' long-term memory for events. *Discourse Processes, 26*, 1–25.

21. Powers, W. G. & Witt, P. L. (2008). Expanding the theoretical framework of communication fidelity. *Communication Quarterly, 56*, 247–267; Fitch-Hauser, M., Powers, W. G., O'Brien, K., & Hanson, S. (2007). Extending the conceptualization of listening fidelity. *International Journal of Listening, 21*, 81–91; Powers, W. G. & Bodie, G. D. (2003). Listening fidelity: Seeking congruence between cognitions of the listener and the sender. *International Journal of Listening, 17*, 19–31.

22. Lewis, M. H. & Reinsch, N. L., Jr. (1988). Listening in organizational environments. *Journal of Business Communication, 23*, 49–67.

23. Imhof, M. (2002). In the eye of the beholder: Children's perception of good and poor listening behavior. *International Journal of Listening, 16*, 40–57.

24. Weger, H., Bell, G. C., Minei, E., M., & Robinson, M. C. (2014). The relative effectiveness of active listening in initial interactions. *International Journal of Listening, 28*, 13–31.

25. Barker, L. L. (1971). *Listening behavior.* Englewood Cliffs, NJ: Prentice-Hall.

26. Vangelisti, A. L., Knapp, M. L., & Daly, J. A. (1990). Conversational narcissism. *Communication Monographs, 57*, 251–274; McCroskey, J. C. & Richmond, V. P. (1993). Identifying compulsive communicators: The talkaholic scale. *Communication Research Reports, 10*, 107–114.

27. McComb, K. B. & Jablin, F. M. (1984). Verbal correlates of interviewer empathic listening and employment interview outcomes. *Communication Monographs, 51*, 367.

28. Hansen, J. (2007). *24/7: How cell phones and the Internet change the way we live, work, and play.* New York: Praeger; Turner, J. W. & Reinsch, N. L. (2007). The business communicator as presence allocator: Multicommunicating, equivocality, and status at work. *Journal of Business Communication, 44*, 36–58.

29. Wolvin, A. & Coakley, C. G. (1988). *Listening* (3rd ed., p. 208). Dubuque, IA: W. C. Brown.

30. Nichols, R. (1987, September). Listening is a ten-part skill. *Nation's Business, 75*, 40.

31. Golen, S. (1990). A factor analysis of barriers to effective listening. *Journal of Business Communication*, *27*, 25–36.

32. Nelson, P., Kohnert, K., Sabur, S., & Shaw, D. (2005). Noise and children learning through a second language: Double jeopardy? *Language, Speech, & Hearing Services in Schools*, *36*, 219–229.

33. Kline, N. (1999). *Time to think: Listening to ignite the human mind* (p. 21). London: Ward Lock.

34. Carrell, L. J. & Willmington, S. C. (1996). A comparison of self-report and performance data in assessing speaking and listening competence. *Communication Reports*, *9*, 185–191.

35. Nichols, R. G., Brown, J. I., & Keller, R. J. (2006). Measurement of communication skills. *International Journal of Listening*, *20*, 13–17; Spinks, N. & Wells, B. (1991). Improving listening power: The payoff. *Bulletin of the Association for Business Communication*, *54*, 75–77.

36. Listen to this: Hearing problems can stress relationships. (2008). Retrieved from http://www.energizer.com/livehealthy/#listentothis; Shafer, D. N. (2007). Hearing loss hinders relationships. *ASHA Leader*, *12*, 5–7.

37. Carbaugh, D. (1999). "Just listen": "Listening" and landscape among the Blackfeet. *Western Journal of Communication*, *63*, 250–270.

38. Bodie, G. D., St. Cyr, K., Pence, M., Rold, M., & Honeycutt, J. (2012). Listening competence in initial interactions I: Distinguishing between what listening is and what listeners do. *International Journal of Listening*, *26*, 1–28; Bippus, A. M. (2001). Recipients' criteria for evaluating the skillfulness of comforting communication and the outcomes of comforting interactions. *Communication Monographs*, *68*, 301–313.

39. Goodman, G. & Esterly, G. (1990). Questions—The most popular piece of language. In J. Stewart (Ed.), *Bridges not walls* (5th ed., pp. 69–77). New York: McGraw-Hill.

40. Chen, F. S., Minson, J. A., & Tormala, Z. L. (2010). Tell me more: The effects of expressed interest on receptiveness during dialog. *Journal of Experimental Social Psychology, 46*, 850–853.

41. Burleson, B. R. (1994). Comforting messages: Features, functions, and outcomes. In J. A. Daly & J. M. Wiemann (Eds.), *Strategic interpersonal communication* (p. 140). Hillsdale, NJ: Erlbaum.

42. Myers, S. (2000). Empathic listening: Reports on the experience of being heard. *Journal of Humanistic Psychology*, *40*, 148–173; Grant, S. G. (1998). A principal's active listening skills and teachers' perceptions of the principal's leader behaviors. *Dissertation Abstracts International Section A: Humanities and Social Sciences*, *58*, 2933; Van Hasselt, V. B., Baker, M. T., & Romano, S. J. (2006). Crisis (hostage) negotiation training: A preliminary evaluation of program efficacy. *Criminal Justice and Behavior*, *33*, 56–69.

43. Bruneau, J. (1989). Empathy and listening: A conceptual review and theoretical directions. *Journal of the International Listening Association*, *3*, 1–20; Cissna, K. N. & Anderson, R. (1990). The contributions of Carl R. Rogers to a philosophical praxis of dialogue. *Western Journal of Speech Communication*, *54*, 137–147.

44. Burleson, B. R. (2003). Emotional support skills. In J. O. Greene and B. R. Burleson (Eds.), *Handbook of communication and social interaction skills* (p. 552). Mahwah, NJ: Erlbaum.

45. Hample, D. (2006). Anti-comforting messages. In K. M. Galvin & P. J. Cooper (Eds.), *Making connections: Readings in relational communication* (4th ed., pp. 222–227). Los Angeles: Roxbury; Burleson, B. R. & MacGeorge, E. L. (2002). Supportive communication. In M. L. Knapp & J. A. Daly (Eds.), *Handbook of interpersonal communication* (3rd ed., pp. 374–422). Thousand Oaks, CA: Sage.

46. Singal, J. (June 25, 2014). Stop telling your depressed friends to cheer up. *New York Magazine*.

47. Samter, W., Burleson, B. R., & Murphy, L. B. (1987). Comforting conversations: The effects of strategy type on evaluations of messages and message producers. *Southern Speech Communication Journal*, *52*, 263–284.

48. Burleson, B. (2008). What counts as effective emotional support? In M. T. Motley (Ed.), *Studies in applied interpersonal communication* (pp. 207–227). Thousand Oaks, CA: Sage.

49. Davidowitz, M. & Myrick, R. D. (1984). Responding to the bereaved: An analysis of "helping" statements. *Death Education*, *8*, 1–10; Servaty-Seib, H. L. & Burleson, B. R. (2007). Bereaved adolescents' evaluations of the helpfulness of support-intended statements. *Journal of Social and Personal Relationships*, *24*, 207–223; Toller, P. (2011). Bereaved parents' experiences of supportive and unsupportive communication. *Southern Communication Journal, 76*, 17–34.

50. Miczo, N. & Burgoon, J. K. (2008). Facework and nonverbal behavior in social support interactions within romantic dyads. In M. T. Motley (Ed.), *Studies in applied interpersonal communication* (pp. 245–266). Thousand Oaks, CA: Sage.

51. Clark, R. A. & Delia, J. G. (1997). Individuals' preferences for friends' approaches to providing support in distressing situations. *Communication Reports*, *10*, 115–121.

52. Lewis, T., & Manusov, V. (2009). Listening to another's distress in everyday relationships. *Communication Quarterly, 57*, 282–301.

53. MacGeorge, E. L., Feng, B., & Thompson, E. R. (2008). "Good" and "bad" advice: How to advise more effectively." In M. T. Motley (Ed.), *Studies in applied interpersonal communication* (pp. 145–164). Thousand Oaks, CA: Sage; Notarius, C. J. & Herrick, L. R. (1988). Listener response strategies to a distressed other. *Journal of Social and Personal Relationships*, *5*, 97–108.

54. Messman, S. J., Canary, D. J., & Hause, K. S. (2000). Motives to remain platonic, equity, and the use of maintenance strategies in opposite-sex friendships. *Journal of Social and Personal Relationships*, *17*, 67–94.

55. Goldsmith, D. J. & Fitch, K. (1997). The normative context of advice as social support. *Human Communication Research*, *23*, 454–476; Goldsmith, D. J. & MacGeorge, E. L. (2000). The impact of politeness and relationship on perceived quality of advice about a problem. *Human Communication Research*, *26*, 234–263.

56. MacGeorge, E. L., Feng, B., & Thompson, E. R. (2008). "Good" and "bad" advice: How to advise more effectively." In M. T. Motley (Ed.), *Studies in applied interpersonal communication* (pp. 145–164). Thousand Oaks, CA: Sage.

57. Castro, D. R., Cohen, A., Tohar, G., & Kluger, A. N. (2013). The role of active listening in teacher-parent relations and the moderating role of attachment style. *International Journal of Listening, 27*, 136–145.

58. Miczo, N. & Burgoon, J. K. (2008). Facework and nonverbal behavior in social support interactions within romantic dyads. In M. T. Motley (Ed.), *Studies in applied interpersonal communication* (pp. 245–266). Thousand Oaks, CA: Sage.

59. Sillence, E. (2013). Giving and receiving peer advice in an online breast cancer support group. *Cyberpsychology, Behavior, and Social Networking, 16*, 480–485.

60. Silver, R. & Wortman, C. (1981). Coping with undesirable life events. In J. Garber & M. Seligman (Eds.), *Human helplessness: Theory and applications* (pp. 279–340). New York: Academic Press; Young, C. R., Giles, D. E., & Plantz, M. C. (1982). Natural networks: Help-giving and help-seeking in two rural communities. *American Journal of Community Psychology*, *10*, 457–469.

61. Clark, R. A. & Delia, J. G. (1997). Individuals' preferences for friends' approaches to providing support in distressing situations. *Communication Reports*, *10*, 115–121.

62. Burleson, B. (1994). Comforting messages: Their significance and effects. In J. A. Daly & J. M. Wiemann (Eds.), *Communicating strategically: Strategies in interpersonal communication* (pp. 135–161). Hillside, NJ: Erlbaum; Chesbro, J. L. (1999). The relationship between listening styles and conversational sensitivity. *Communication Research Reports, 16*, 233–238.

63. Sargent, S. L. & Weaver, J. B. (2003). Listening styles: Sex differences in perceptions of self and others. *International Journal of Listening, 17*, 5–18; Johnston, M. K., Weaver, J. B., Watson, K., & Barker, L. (2000). Listening styles: Biological or psychological differences? *International Journal of Listening, 14*, 32–47.

64. Samter, W. (2002). How gender and cognitive complexity influence the provision of emotional support: A study of indirect effects. *Communication Reports, 15*, 5–17; Hale, J. L., Tighe, M. R., & Mongeau, P. A. (1997). Effects of event type and sex on comforting messages. *Communication Research Reports, 14*, 214–220.

65. Burleson, B. R. (1982). The development of comforting communication skills in childhood and adolescence. *Child Development, 53*, 1578–1588.

66. Lemieux, R., & Tighe, M. R. (2004). Attachment styles and the evaluation of comforting responses: A receiver perspective. *Communication Research Reports, 21*, 144–153.

67. Burleson, B. R., Holmstrom, A. J., & Gilstrap, C. M. (2005). "Guys can't say that to guys:" Four experiments assessing the normative motivation account for deficiencies in the emotional support provided by men. *Communication Monographs, 72*, 468–501.

68. Woodward, M. S., Rosenfeld, L. B., & May, S. K. (1996). Sex differences in social support in sororities and fraternities. *Journal of Applied Communication Research, 24*, 260–272.

69. Burleson, B. R. & Kunkel, A. (2006). Revisiting the different cultures thesis: An assessment of sex differences and similarities in supportive communication. In K. Dindia & D. J. Canary (Eds.), *Sex differences and similarities in communication* (2nd ed., pp. 137–159). Mahwah, NJ: Erlbaum.

70. Horowitz, L. M., Krasnoperova, E. N., & Tatar, D. G. (2001). The way to console may depend on the goal: Experimental studies of social support. *Journal of Experimental Social Psychology, 37*, 49–61.

71. MacGeorge, E. L., Feng, B., & Thompson, E. R. (2008). "Good" and "bad" advice: How to advise more effectively. In M. T. Motley (Ed.), *Studies in applied interpersonal communication* (pp. 145–164). Thousand Oaks, CA: Sage; Young, R. W. & Cates, C. M. (2004). Emotional and directive listening in peer mentoring. *International Journal of Listening, 18*, 21–33.

72. Feng, B. & Lee, K. J. (2010). The influence of thinking styles on responses to supportive messages. *Communication Studies, 61*, 224–238.

CHAPTER NINE

1. Byrne, D. (2010). An overview (and underview) of research and theory within the attraction paradigm. In M. L. Knapp & J. A. Daly (Eds.), *Interpersonal communication* (pp. 77–94). Thousand Oaks, CA: Sage.

2. Hatfield, E. & Sprecher, S. (1986). *Mirror, mirror: The importance of looks in everyday life*. Albany: State University of New York Press.

3. Walster, E., Aronson, E., Abrahams, D., & Rottmann, L. (1966). Importance of physical attractiveness in dating behavior. *Journal of Personality and Social Psychology, 4*, 508–516.

4. Luo, S. & Zhang, G. (2009). What leads to romantic attraction: Similarity, reciprocity, security, or beauty? Evidence from a speed-dating study. *Journal of Personality, 77*, 933–964.

5. Hancock, J. T. & Toma, C. L. (2009). Putting your best face forward: The accuracy of online dating profile photographs. *Journal of Communication, 59*, 367–386.

6. Antheunis, M. L. & Schouten, A. P. (2011). The effects of other-generated and system-generated cues on adolescents' perceived attractiveness on social network sites. *Journal of Computer-Mediated Communication, 16*, 391–406; Jaschinski, C. & Kommers, P. (2012). Does beauty matter? The role of friends' attractiveness and gender on social attractiveness ratings of individuals on Facebook. *International Journal of Web Based Communities, 8*, 389–401.

7. Rodway, P., Schepman, A., & Lambert, J. (2013). The influence of position and context on facial attractiveness. *Acta Psychologica, 144*, 522–529.

8. Lewandowski, G. W., Aron, A., & Gee, J. (2007). Personality goes a long way: The malleability of opposite-sex physical attractiveness. *Personal Relationships, 14*, 571–585.

9. Zhang, Y., Kong, F., Zhong, Y., & Kou, H. (2014). Personality manipulations: Do they modulate facial attractiveness ratings? *Personality and Individual Differences, 70* 80–84; Albada, K. F. (2010). Interaction appearance theory: Changing perceptions of physical attractiveness through social interaction. In M. L. Knapp & J. A. Daly (Eds.), *Interpersonal communication* (pp. 99–130). Thousand Oaks, CA: Sage.

10. Barelds, D. & Dijkstra, P. (2009). Positive illusions about a partner's physical attractiveness and relationship quality. *Personal Relationships, 16*, 263–283.

11. Hamachek, D. (1982). *Encounters with others: Interpersonal relationships and you*. New York: Holt, Rinehart & Winston.

12. Yun, K. A. (2002). Similarity and attraction. In M. Allen, N. Burrell, B. M. Eayle, & R. W. Preiss (Eds.), *Interpersonal communication research: Advances through meta-analysis* (pp. 145–168). Mahwah, NJ: Erlbaum; Montoya, R., & Horton, R. S. (2013). A meta-analytic investigation of the processes underlying the similarity-attraction effect. *Journal of Social and Personal Relationships, 30*, 64–94.

13. Luo, S. & Klohnen, E. (2005). Assortative mating and marital quality in newlyweds: A couple-centered approach. *Journal of Personality and Social Psychology, 88*, 304–326; Amodio, D. M. & Showers, C. J. (2005). Similarity breeds liking revisited: The moderating role of commitment. *Journal of Social and Personal Relationships, 22*, 817–836.

14. Aboud, F. E. & Mendelson, M. J. (1998). Determinants of friendship selection and quality: Developmental perspectives. In W. M. Bukowski & A. F. Newcomb (Eds.), *The company they keep: Friendship in childhood and adolescence* (pp. 87–112). New York: Cambridge University Press.

15. Ledbetter, A. M., Griffin, E., & Sparks, G. G. (2007). Forecasting friends forever: A longitudinal investigation of sustained closeness between best friends. *Personal Relationships, 14*, 343–350.

16. Burleson, B. R. & Samter, W. (1996). Similarity in the communication skills of young adults: Foundations of attraction, friendship, and relationship satisfaction. *Communication Reports, 9*, 127–139.

17. Martin, A., Jacob, C., & Gueguen, N. (2013). Similarity facilitates relationships on social networks: A field experiment on Facebook. *Psychological Reports, 113*, 217–220.

18. Tidwell, N. D., Eastwick, P. W., & Finkel, E. J. (2013). Perceived, not actual, similarity predicts initial attraction in a live romantic context: Evidence from the speed-dating paradigm. *Personal Relationships, 20*, 199–215.

19. Sprecher, S. (2014). Effects of actual (manipulated) and perceived similarity on liking in get-acquainted interactions: The role of communication. *Communication Monographs, 81*, 4–27.

20. Jones, J. T., Pelham, B. W., & Carvallo, M. (2004). How do I love thee? Let me count the J's: Implicit egotism and interpersonal attraction. *Journal of Personality and Social Psychology, 87,* 665–683.

21. Ireland, M. E., Slatcher, R. B., Eastwick, P. W., Scissors, L. E., Finkel, E. J., & Pennebaker, J. W. (2011). Language style matching predicts relationship initiation and stability. *Psychological Science, 22,* 39–44; Scissors, L. E., Gill, A. J., Geraghty, K., & Gergle, D. (2009). In CMC we trust: The role of similarity. *Proceedings of CHI 2009,* 527–536. New York: ACM Press.

22. Alford, J. R., Hatemi, P. K., Hibbing, J. R., Martin, N. G., & Eaves, L. J. (2011). The politics of mate choice. *The Journal of Politics, 73,* 362–379.

23. Mette, D. & Taylor, S. (1971). When similarity breeds contempt. *Journal of Personality and Social Psychology, 20,* 75–81.

24. Fisher, H. (2007, May/June). The laws of chemistry. *Psychology Today, 40,* 76–81.

25. Heatherington, L., Escudero, V., & Friedlander, M. L. (2005). Couple interaction during problem discussions: Toward an integrative methodology. *Journal of Family Communication, 5,* 191–207.

26. Rick, S. I., Small, D. A., & Finkel, E. J. (2011). Fatal (fiscal) attraction: Spendthrifts and tightwads in marriage. *Journal of Marketing Research, 48,* 228–237.

27. Specher, S. (1998). Insiders' perspectives on reasons for attraction to a close other. *Social Psychology Quarterly, 61,* 287–300.

28. Aronson, E. (2004). *The social animal* (9th ed.). New York: Bedford, Freeman, & Worth.

29. Fiske, S. T., Cuddy, A. J. C., & Glick, P. (2007). Universal dimensions of social cognition: Warmth and competence. *Trends in Cognitive Sciences, 11,* 77–83.

30. Dindia, K. (2002). Self-disclosure research: Knowledge through meta-analysis. In M. Allen & R. W. Preiss (Eds.), *Interpersonal communication research: Advances through meta-analysis* (pp. 169–185). Mahwah, NJ: Erlbaum; Sprecher, S., Treger, S., & Wondra, J. D. (2013). Effects of self-disclosure role on liking, closeness, and other impressions in get-acquainted interactions. *Journal of Personal and Social Relationships, 30,* 497–514.

31. Ledbetter, A. M., Mazer, J. P., DeGroot, J. M., & Meyer, K. R. (2011). Attitudes toward online social connection and self-disclosure as predictors of Facebook communication and relational closeness. *Communication Research, 38,* 27–53; Sheldon, P. (2009). "I'll poke you. You'll poke me!" Self-disclosure, social attraction, predictability and trust as important predictors of Facebook relationships. *Cyberpsychology: Journal of Psychosocial Research on Cyberspace, 3*(2), article 1.

32. Dindia, K. (2002). Self-disclosure research: Knowledge through meta-analysis. In M. Allen & R. W. Preiss (Eds.), *Interpersonal communication research: Advances through meta-analysis* (pp. 169–185). Mahwah, NJ: Erlbaum.

33. Shirley, J. A., Powers, W. G., & Sawyer, C. R. (2007). Psychologically abusive relationships and self-disclosure orientations. *Human Communication, 10,* 289–301.

34. Flora, C. (2004, January/February). Close quarters. *Psychology Today, 37,* 15–16.

35. Haythornthwaite, C., Kazmer, M. M., & Robbins, J. (2000). Community development among distance learners: Temporal and technological dimensions. *Journal of Computer-Mediated Communication, 6*(1), article 2.

36. Stafford, L. (2008). Social exchange theories. In L. A. Baxter & D. O. Braithewaite (Eds.), *Engaging theories in interpersonal communication: Multiple perspectives* (pp. 377–389). Thousand Oaks, CA: Sage.

37. DeMaris, A. (2007). The role of relationship inequity in marital disruption. *Journal of Social and Personal Relationships, 24,* 177–195.

38. Knapp, M. L. & Vangelisti, A. L. (2006). *Interpersonal communication and human relationships* (6th ed.). Boston: Allyn & Bacon; Avtgis, T. A., West, D. V., & Anderson, T. L. (1998). Relationship stages: An inductive analysis identifying cognitive, affective, and behavioral dimensions of Knapp's relational stages model. *Communication Research Reports, 15,* 280–287; Welch, S. A. & Rubin, R. B. (2002). Development of relationship stage measures. *Communication Quarterly, 50,* 34–40.

39. Johnson, A. J., Wittenberg, E., Haigh, M., Wigley, S., Becker, J., Brown, K., & Craig, E. (2004). The process of relationship development and deterioration: Turning points in friendships that have terminated. *Communication Quarterly, 52,* 54–67.

40. Scharlott, B. W. & Christ, W. G. (1995). Overcoming relationship-initiation barriers: The impact of a computer-dating system on sex role, shyness, and appearance inhibitions. *Computers in Human Behavior, 11,* 191–204.

41. Urista, M. A., Dong, Q., & Day, K. D. (2009). Explaining why young adults use MySpace and Facebook through uses and gratifications theory. *Human Communication, 12,* 215–230.

42. Johnson, A. J., Wittenberg, E., Haigh, M., Wigley, S., Becker, J., Brown, K., & Craig, E. (2004). The process of relationship development and deterioration: Turning points in friendships that have terminated. *Communication Quarterly, 52,* 54–67.

43. Sobel, A. (2009, July 27). *Interview etiquette: Lessons from a first date.* The Ladders.

44. Berger, C. R. (1987). Communicating under uncertainty. In M. E. Roloff & G. R. Miller (Eds.), *Interpersonal processes: New directions in communication research* (pp. 39–62). Newbury Park, CA: Sage; Berger, C. R. & Calabrese, R. J. (1975). Some explorations in initial interaction and beyond: Toward a developmental theory of interpersonal communication. *Human Communication Research, 1,* 99–112.

45. Pratt, L., Wiseman, R. L., Cody, M. J., & Wendt, P. F. (1999). Interrogative strategies and information exchange in computer-mediated communication. *Communication Quarterly, 47,* 46–66.

46. Fox, J., Warber, K. M., & Makstaller, D. C. (2013). The role of Facebook in romantic relationship development: An exploration of Knapp's relational stage model. *Journal of Social and Personal Relationships, 30,* 771–794.

47. Levine, T. R., Aune, K., & Park, H. (2006). Love styles and communication in relationships: Partner preferences, initiation, and intensification. *Communication Quarterly, 54,* 465–486; Tolhuizen, J. H. (1989). Communication strategies for intensifying dating relationships: Identification, use and structure. *Journal of Social and Personal Relationships, 6,* 413–434.

48. Johnson, A. J., Wittenberg, E., Haigh, M., Wigley, S., Becker, J., Brown, K., & Craig, E. (2004). The process of relationship development and deterioration: Turning points in friendships that have terminated. *Communication Quarterly, 52,* 54–67.

49. Johnson, K. R. & Holmes, B. M. (2009). Contradictory messages: A content analysis of Hollywood-produced romantic comedy feature films. *Communication Quarterly, 57,* 352–373.

50. Baxter, L. A. (1987). Symbols of relationship identity in relationship culture. *Journal of Social and Personal Relationships, 4,* 261–280.

51. Buress, C. J. S. & Pearson, J. C. (1997). Interpersonal rituals in marriage and adult friendship. *Communication Monographs, 64,* 25–46.

52. Dunleavy, K. N. & Booth-Butterfield, M. (2009). Idiomatic communication in the stages of coming together and falling apart. *Communication Quarterly, 57,* 416–432; Bell, R. A. & Healey, J. G. (1992). Idiomatic communication and interpersonal solidarity in friends' relational cultures. *Human Communication Research, 18,* 307–335.

53. Fox, J., Warber, K. M., & Makstaller, D. C. (2013). The role of Facebook in romantic relationship development: An exploration of Knapp's relational stage model. *Journal of Social and Personal Relationships, 30,* 771–794.

54. Papp, L. M., Danielewicz, J., & Cayemberg, C. (2012). Are we Facebook Official? Implications of dating partners' Facebook use and profiles for intimate relationship satisfaction. *CyberPsychology, Behavior & Social Networking, 15*, 85–90.

55. Fox, J. & Warber, K. M. (2013). Romantic relationship development in the age of Facebook: An exploratory study of emerging adults' perceptions, motives, and behaviors. *Cyberpsychology, Behavior, and Social Networking, 16*, 3–7.

56. Foster, E. (2008). Commitment, communication, and contending with heteronormativity: An invitation to greater reflexivity in interpersonal research. *Southern Communication Journal, 73*, 84–101.

57. Rubin, L. (1985). *Just friends: The role of friendship in our lives*. New York: Harper & Row.

58. Skowron, E., Stanley, K., & Shapiro, M. (2009). A longitudinal perspective on differentiation of self, interpersonal and psychological well-being in young adulthood. *Contemporary Family Therapy: An International Journal, 31*, 3–18.

59. Harasymchuk, C. & Fehr, B. (2013). A prototype analysis of relational boredom. *Journal of Social and Personal Relationships, 30*, 627–646.

60. Courtright, J. A., Miller, F. E., Rogers, L. E., & Bagarozzi, D. (1990). Interaction dynamics of relational negotiation: Reconciliation versus termination of distressed relationships. *Western Journal of Speech Communication, 54*, 429–453.

61. Battaglia, D. M., Richard, F. D., Datteri, D. L., & Lord, C. G. (1998). Breaking up is (relatively) easy to do: A script for the dissolution of close relationships. *Journal of Social and Personal Relationships, 15*, 829–845.

62. Metts, S., Cupach, W. R., & Bejllovec, R. A. (1989). "I love you too much to ever start liking you": Redefining romantic relationships. *Journal of Social and Personal Relationships, 6*, 259–274.

63. Duck, S. (1982). A topography of relationship disengagement and dissolution. In S. Duck (Ed.), *Personal relationships 4: Dissolving personal relationships* (pp. 1–30). New York: Academic Press.

64. Weber, A. L., Harvey, J. H., & Orbuch, T. L. (1992). What went wrong: Communicating accounts of relationship conflict. In M. L. McLaughlin, M. J. Cody, & S. J. Read (Eds.), *Explaining one's self to others: Reason-giving in a social context* (pp. 261–280). Hillsdale, NJ: Erlbaum.

65. Chatel, A. (July 12, 2013). *You'll probably be dumped via text more than once in your life*. The Gloss.

66. Weisskirch, R. S. & Delevi, R. (2013). Attachment style and conflict resolution skills predicting technology use in relationship dissolution. *Computers in Human Behavior, 29*, 2530–2534.

67. Tong, S. (2013). Facebook use during relationship termination: Uncertainty reduction and surveillance. *Cyberpsychology, Behavior, and Social Networking, 16*, 788–793.

68. Marshall, T. (2012). Facebook surveillance of former romantic partners: Associations with postbreakup recovery and personal growth. *Cyberpsychology, Behavior, and Social Networking. 15*, 521–526.

69. Johnson, A. J., Wittenberg, E., Haigh, M., Wigley, S., Becker, J., Brown, K., & Craig, E. (2004). The process of relationship development and deterioration: Turning points in friendships that have terminated. *Communication Quarterly, 52*, 54–67.

70. Baxter, L. A. & Montgomery, B. M. (1992). *Relating: Dialogues and dialectics*. New York: Guilford; Rawlins, W. K. (1996). *Friendship matters: Communication, dialectics, and the life course*. New York: Aldine de Gruyter.

71. Baxter, L. A. (1994). A dialogic approach to relationship maintenance. In D. J. Canary & L. Stafford (Eds.), *Communication and relational maintenance* (pp. 233–254). San Diego, CA: Academic Press; Sahlstein, E., & Dun, T. (2008). "I wanted time to myself and he wanted to be together all the time": Constructing breakups as managing autonomy-connection. *Qualitative Research Reports in Communication, 9*, 37–45.

72. Sahlstein, E. & Dun, T. (2008). "I wanted time to myself and he wanted to be together all the time": Constructing breakups as managing autonomy-connection. *Qualitative Research Reports in Communication, 9*, 37–45.

73. Buunk, A. P. (2005). How do people respond to others with high commitment or autonomy in their relationships? *Journal of Social and Personal Relationships, 22*, 653–672.

74. Morris, D. (1997). *Intimate behavior* (pp. 21–29). New York: Kodansha USA.

75. Golish, T. D. (2000). Changes in closeness between adult children and their parents: A turning point analysis. *Communication Reports, 13*, 78–97.

76. Baxter, L. A. & Erbert, L. A. (1999). Perceptions of dialectical contradictions in turning points of development in heterosexual romantic relationships. *Journal of Social and Personal Relationships, 16*, 547–569.

77. Miller-Ott, A. E., Kelly, L., & Duran, R. L. (2012). The effects of cell phone usage rules on satisfaction in romantic relationships. *Communication Quarterly, 60*, 17–34; Duran, R. L., Kelly, L., & Rotaru, T. (2011). Mobile phones in romantic relationships and the dialectic of autonomy versus connection. *Communication Quarterly, 59*, 19–36.

78. Graham, E. E. (2003). Dialectic contradictions in postmarital relationships. *Journal of Family Communication, 3*, 193–215.

79. Baxter, L. A., Braithwaite, D. O., Golish, T. D., & Olson, L. N. (2002). Contradictions of interaction for wives of elderly husbands with adult dementia. *Journal of Applied Communication Research, 30*, 1–20.

80. Petronio, S. (2000). The boundaries of privacy: Praxis of everyday life. In S. Petronio (Ed.), *Balancing the secrets of private disclosures* (pp. 37–49). Mahwah, NJ: Erlbaum.

81. Debatin, B., Lovejoy, J. P., Horn, A., & Hughes, B. N. (2009). Facebook and online privacy: Attitudes, behaviors, and unintended consequences. *Journal of Computer-Mediated Communication, 15*, 83–108.

82. Barry, D. (1990). *Dave Barry turns 40* (p. 47). New York: Fawcett.

83. Pawlowski, D. R. (1998). Dialectical tensions in marital partners' accounts of their relationships. *Communication Quarterly, 46*, 396–416.

84. Griffin, E. M. (2000). *A first look at communication theory* (4th ed.). New York: McGraw-Hill.

85. Braithwaite, D. O. & Baxter, L. (2006). "You're my parent but you're not": Dialectical tensions in stepchildren's perceptions about communicating with the nonresident parent. *Journal of Applied Communication Research, 34*, 30–48.

86. Montgomery, B. M. (1993). Relationship maintenance versus relationship change: A dialectical dilemma. *Journal of Social and Personal Relationships, 10*, 205–223.

87. Braithwaite, D. O., Baxter, L. A., & Harper, A. M. (1998). The role of rituals in the management of the dialectical tension of "old" and "new" in blended families. *Communication Studies, 49*, 101–120.

88. Christensen, A. & Jacobson, J. (2000). *Reconcilable differences*. New York: Guilford.

89. Baxter, L. A. & Braithwaite, D. O. (2006). Social dialectics: The contradictions of relating. In B. Whaley & W. Samter (Eds.), *Explaining communication: Contemporary communication theories and exemplars* (pp. 305–324). Mahwah, NJ: Erlbaum.

90. Sahlstein, E. & Dun, T. (2008). "I wanted time to myself and he wanted to be together all the time": Constructing breakups as managing autonomy-connection. *Qualitative Research Reports in Communication, 9*, 37–45.

91. Conville, R. L. (1991). *Relational transitions: The evolution of personal relationships* (p. 80). New York: Praeger.

92. Brown, D. E. (1991). *Human universals*. New York: McGraw-Hill.

93. Hamon, R. R. & Ingoldsby, B. B. (Eds.). (2003). *Mate selection across cultures*. Thousand Oaks, CA: Sage.

94. Myers, J. E., Madathil, J., & Tingle, L. R. (2005). Marriage satisfaction and wellness in India and the United States: A preliminary comparison of arranged marriages and marriages of choice. *Journal of Counseling & Development*, *83*, 183–190; Yelsma, P. & Athappilly, K. (1988). Marriage satisfaction and communication practices: Comparisons among Indian and American couples. *Journal of Comparative Family Studies*, *19*, 37–54.

95. Kim, M. S. (2002). *Non-Western perspectives on human communication: Implications for theory and practice.* Thousand Oaks, CA: Sage.

96. Breitman, P. & Hatch, C. (2000). *How to say no without feeling guilty.* New York: Broadway Books.

97. Imami, M. (1981). *16 ways to avoid saying no.* Tokyo: Nihon Keizai Shimbun.

98. Watzlawick, P., Beavin, J. H., & Jackson, D. D. (1967). *Pragmatics of human communication.* New York: Norton; Lederer, W. J. & Jackson, D. D. (1968). *The mirages of marriage.* New York: Norton.

99. Bell, R. A. & Daly, J. A. (1995). The affinity-seeking function of communication. In M. V. Redmond (Ed.), *Interpersonal communication: Readings in theory and research* (pp. 155–192). Fort Worth, TX: Harcourt Brace.

100. Dainton, M. (1998). Everyday interaction in marital relationships: Variations in relative importance and event duration. *Communication Reports*, *11*, 101–143.

101. Myers, S. A. & Avtgis, T. A. (1997). The association of socio-communicative style and relational types on perceptions of nonverbal immediacy. *Communication Research Reports*, *14*, 339–349.

102. Richmond, V. P. & McCroskey, J. C. (2004). *Nonverbal behavior in interpersonal relationships* (5th ed., chapter 11). Boston: Allyn and Bacon.

103. Lim, T. S. & Bowers, J. W. (1991). Facework: Solidarity, approbation, and tact. *Human Communication Research*, *17*, 415–450.

104. Frei, J. R. & Shaver, P. R. (2002). Respect in close relationships: Prototype, definition, self-report assessment, and initial correlates. *Personal Relationships*, *9*, 121–139.

105. Palmer, M. T. (1989). Controlling conversations: Turns, topics, and interpersonal control. *Communication Monographs*, *56*, 1–18.

106. Watzlawick, P., Beavin, J. H., & Jackson, D. D. (1967). *Pragmatics of human communication.* New York: Norton.

107. Tannen, D. (1986). *That's not what I meant! How conversational style makes or breaks your relations with others* (p. 190). New York: Morrow.

108. Lydon, J. E. & Quinn, S. K. (2013). Relationship maintenance processes. In J. A. Simpson & L. Campbell (Eds.), *The Oxford handbook of close relationships* (pp. 573–588). New York: Oxford.

109. Dindia, K. (2003). Definitions and perspectives on relational maintenance communication. In D. J. Canary and M. Dainton (Eds.), *Maintaining relationships through communication* (pp. 1–30). Mahwah, NJ: Erlbaum.

110. Canary, D. J. & Stafford, L. (1992). Relational maintenance strategies and equity in marriage. *Communication Monographs*, *59*, 243–267; Ogolsky, B. G. & Bowers, J. R. (2013). A meta-analytic review of relationship maintenance and its correlates. *Journal of Social and Personal Relationships*, *30*, 343–367.

111. Johnson, A. J., Haigh, M. M., Becker, J. A. H., Craig, E. A., & Wigley, S. (2008). College students' use of relational management strategies in email in long-distance and geographically close relationships. *Journal of Computer-Mediated Communication*, *13*, 381–404.

112. Ledbetter, A. M. (2010). Assessing the measurement invariance of relational maintenance behavior when face-to-face and online. *Communication Research Reports, 27*, 30–37.

113. Craig, E. & Wright, B. (2012). Computer-mediated relational development and maintenance on Facebook. *Communication Research Reports*, *29*, 119–129; Dainton, M. (2013). Relationship maintenance on Facebook: Development of a measure, relationship to general maintenance, and relationship satisfaction. *College Student Journal, 47*, 112–121.

114. Utz, S. (2007). Media use in long-distance friendships. *Information, Communication & Society, 10*, 694–713.

115. Hunt, D. S., Lin, C. A., & Atkin, D. J. (2014). Communicating social relationships via the use of photo-messaging. *Journal of Broadcasting & Electronic Media, 58*, 234–252.

116. Houser, M. L., Fleuriet, C., & Estrada, D. (2012). The cyber factor: An analysis of relational maintenance through the use of computer-mediated communication. *Communication Research Reports*, *29*, 34–43.

117. Hall, J. A., Larson, K. A., & Watts, A. (2011). Satisfying friendship maintenance expectations: The role of friendship standards and biological sex. *Human Communication Research*, *37*, 529–552.

118. Merolla, A. J. (2010). Relational maintenance and noncopresence reconsidered: Conceptualizing geographic separation in close relationships. *Communication Theory, 20*, 169–193; Stafford, L. (2005). *Maintaining long-distance and cross residential relationships.* Mahwah, NJ: Erlbaum.

119. Johnson, A. J., Becker, J. A. H., Craig, E. A., Gilchrist, E. S., & Haigh, M. M. (2009). Changes in friendship commitment: Comparing geographically close and long-distance young-adult friendships. *Communication Quarterly*, *57*, 395–415.

120. McGuire, K. C. & Kinnery, T. A. (2010). When distance is problematic: Communication, coping, and relational satisfaction in female college students' long-distance dating relationships. *Journal of Applied Communication Research*, *38*, 27–46.

121. Johnson, A. J., Craig, E. A., Haigh, M. M., Becker, J. A. H., & Craig, E. A. (2009). Relational closeness: Comparing undergraduate college students' geographically close and long-distance friendships. *Personal Relationships*, *16*, 631–646.

122. Lakey, B. (2013). Social support processes in relationships. In J. A. Simpson & L. Campbell (Eds.), *The Oxford handbook of close relationships* (pp. 711–730). New York: Oxford.

123. MacGeorge, E. L., Feng, B., & Burleson, B. R. (2011). Supportive communication. In M. L. Knapp & J. A. Daly (Eds.), *The Sage handbook of interpersonal communication* (4th ed., pp. 317–354). Thousand Oaks, CA: Sage.

124. Reis, H. T. & Clark, M. S. (2013). Responsiveness. In J. A. Simpson & L. Campbell (Eds.), *The Oxford handbook of close relationships* (pp. 400–426). New York: Oxford.

125. High, A. C., & Dillard, J. P. (2012). A review and meta-analysis of person-centered messages and social support outcomes. *Communication Studies*, *53*, 99–118.

126. Semmer, N. K., Elfering, A., Jacobshagen, N., Perrot, T., Beehr, T. A., & Boos, N. (2008). The emotional meaning of instrumental social support. *International Journal of Stress Management, 15*, 235–251.

127. Barry, R. A., Bunde, M., Brock, R. L., & Lawrence, E. (2009). Validity and utility of a multidimensional model of received support in intimate relationships. *Journal of Family Psychology, 23*, 48–57.

128. Nauert, R. (February 1, 2010). *Support your partner, but not too much.* PsychCentral.

129. Oh, H. J., Ozkaya, E., & LaRose, R. (2014). How does online social networking enhance life satisfaction? The perceived relationships among online supportive interaction, affect, perceived social support, sense of community, and life satisfaction. *Computers in Human Behavior, 30*, 69–78.

130. Rusbult, C. E., Hannon, P. A., Stocker, S. L., & Finkel, E. J. (2005). Forgiveness and relational repair. In E. L. Worthington (Ed.), *Handbook of forgiveness* (pp. 185–206). New York: Routledge.

131. Emmers-Sommer, T. M. (2003). When partners falter: Repair after a transgression. In D. J. Canary & M. Dainton (Eds.), *Maintaining relationships through communication* (pp. 185–205). Mahwah, NJ: Erlbaum.

132. Dindia, K. & Baxter, L. A. (1987). Strategies for maintaining and repairing marital relationships. *Journal of Social and Personal Relationships, 4,* 143–159.

133. Park, H. S. (2009). Cross-cultural comparison of verbal and nonverbal strategies of apologizing. *Journal of International and Intercultural Communication, 2,* 66–87; Park, H. S. & Guan, X. (2006). The effects of national culture and face concerns on intention to apologize: A comparison of the USA and China. *Journal of Intercultural Communication Research, 35,* 183–204.

134. Exline, J. J., Deshea, L., & Holeman, V. T. (2007). Is apology worth the risk? Predictors, outcomes, and ways to avoid regret. *Journal of Social & Clinical Psychology, 26,* 479–504.

135. Wallace, H. M., Exline, J. J., & Baumeister, R. F. (2008). Interpersonal consequences of forgiveness: Does forgiveness deter or encourage repeat offenses? *Journal of Experimental Social Psychology, 44,* 453–460.

136. Chapman, G. D. & Thomas, J. M. (2006). *The five languages of apology.* Chicago: Northfield; Kelley, D. L. & Waldron, V. R. (2005). An investigation of forgiveness-seeking communication and relational outcomes. *Communication Quarterly, 53,* 339–359.

137. Merolla, A. J. (2008). Communicating forgiveness in friendships and dating relationships. *Communication Studies, 59,* 114–131.

138. Battistella, E. (2014). *Sorry about that: The language of public apology.* New York: Oxford University Press.

139. Orcutt, H. K. (2006). The prospective relationship of interpersonal forgiveness and psychological distress symptoms among college women. *Journal of Counseling Psychology, 53,* 350–361; Eaton, J. & Struthers, C. W. (2006). The reduction of psychological aggression across varied interpersonal contexts through repentance and forgiveness. *Aggressive Behavior, 32,* 195–206.

140. Lawler, K. A., Younger, J. W., Piferi, R. L., et al. (2003). A change of heart: Cardiovascular correlates of forgiveness in response to interpersonal conflict. *Journal of Behavioral Medicine, 26,* 373–393.

141. Fincham, F. D. & Beach, S. R. H. (2013). Gratitude and forgiveness in relationships. In J. A. Simpson & L. Campbell (Eds.), *The Oxford handbook of close relationships* (pp. 638–663). New York: Oxford; Waldron, V. R. & Kelley, D. L. (2005). Forgiving communication as a response to relational transgressions. *Journal of Social and Personal Relationships, 22,* 723–742.

142. Guerrero, L. K. & Bachman, G. F. (2010). Forgiveness and forgiving communication in dating relationships: An expectancy-investment explanation. *Journal of Social and Personal Relationships, 27,* 801–823.

143. Bachman, G. F. & Guerrero, L. K. (2006). Forgiveness, apology, and communicative responses to hurtful events. *Communication Reports, 19,* 45–56.

144. Henline, B. H., Lamke, L. K., & Howard, M. D. (2007). Exploring perceptions of online infidelity. *Personal Relationships, 14,* 113–129.

145. Takaku, S., Weiner, B., & Ohbuchi, K. (2001). A cross-cultural examination of the effects of apology and perspective-taking on forgiveness. *Journal of Language & Social Psychology, 20,* 144–167.

146. Kelley, D. (1998). The communication of forgiveness. *Communication Studies, 49,* 255–272.

CHAPTER TEN

1. Crowther, C. E. & Stone, G. (1986). *Intimacy: Strategies for successful relationships* (p. 13). Santa Barbara: Capra Press.

2. Peterson, C. (2006). *A primer in positive psychology.* New York: Oxford.

3. Berscheid, E., Schneider, M., & Omoto, A. M. (1989). Issues in studying close relationships: Conceptualizing and measuring closeness. In C. Hendrick (Ed.), *Close relationships* (pp. 63–91). Newbury Park, CA: Sage.

4. Morris, D. (1973). *Intimate behavior* (p. 7). New York: Bantam.

5. Manning, W. D., Giordano, P. C., & Longmore, M. A. (2006). Hooking up: The relationship contexts of "nonrelationship" sex. *Journal of Adolescent Research, 21,* 459–483.

6. Williams, L. & Russell, S. T. (2013). Shared social and emotional activities within adolescent romantic and non-romantic sexual relationships. *Archives of Sexual Behavior, 42,* 649–658.

7. Baxter, L. A. (1994). A dialogic approach to relationship maintenance. In D. Canary & L. Stafford (Eds.), *Communication and relational maintenance* (pp. 233–254). San Diego: Academic Press.

8. Vangelisti, A. L. & Beck, G. (2007). Intimacy and the fear of intimacy. In L. L'Abate (Ed.), *Low-cost approaches to promote physical and mental health: Theory, research, and practice* (pp. 395–414). New York: Springer.

9. Wood, J. T. & Inman, C. C. (1993). In a different mode: Masculine styles of communicating closeness. *Applied Communication Research, 21,* 279–295; Floyd, K. (1995). Gender and closeness among friends and siblings. *Journal of Psychology, 129,* 193–202.

10. Dindia, K. (2000). Sex differences in self-disclosure, reciprocity of self-disclosure, and self-disclosure and liking: Three meta-analyses reviewed. In S. Petronio (Ed.), *Balancing disclosure, privacy and secrecy* (pp. 21–37). Mahwah, NJ: Erlbaum.

11. Balswick, J. O. (1988). *The inexpressive male: A tragedy of American society.* Lexington, MA: Lexington Books.

12. Morman, M. T. & Floyd, K. (1999). Affection communication between fathers and young adult sons: Individual and relational-level correlates. *Communication Studies, 50,* 294–309.

13. Stafford, L., Dainton, M., & Haas, S. (2000). Measuring routine and strategic relational maintenance: Scale revision, sex versus gender roles, and the prediction of relational characteristics. *Communication Monographs, 67,* 306–323.

14. Reissman, C. K. (1990). *Divorce talk: Women and men make sense of personal relationships.* New Brunswick, NJ: Rutgers University Press.

15. Bowman, J. M. (2008). Gender role orientation and relational closeness: Self-disclosive behavior in same-sex male friendships. *Journal of Men's Studies, 16,* 316–330.

16. Good, G. E., Porter, M. J., & Dillon, M. G. (2002). When men divulge: Men's self-disclosure on prime time situation comedies. *Sex Roles, 46,* 419–427.

17. Morman, M. T. & Floyd, K. (2002). A "changing culture of fatherhood": Effects of affectionate communication, closeness, and satisfaction in men's relationships with their fathers and their sons. *Western Journal of Communication, 66,* 395–411.

18. Adamopoulos, J. (1991). The emergence of interpersonal behavior: Diachronic and cross-cultural processes in the evolution of intimacy. In S. Ting-Toomey & F. Korzenny (Eds.), *Cross-cultural interpersonal communication* (pp. 155–170). Newbury Park, CA: Sage; Fontaine, G. (1990). Cultural diversity in intimate intercultural relationships. In D. D. Cahn (Ed.), *Intimates in conflict: A communication perspective* (pp. 209–224). Hillsdale, NJ: Erlbaum.

19. Adamopoulos, J. & Bontempo, R. N. (1986). Diachronic universals in interpersonal structures. *Journal of Cross-Cultural Psychology, 17,* 169–189.

20. Argyle, M. & Henderson, M. (1985). The rules of relationships. In S. Duck & D. Perlman (Eds.), *Understanding personal relationships* (pp. 63–84). Beverly Hills, CA: Sage.

21. Triandis, H. C. (1994). *Culture and social behavior* (p. 230). New York: McGraw-Hill.

22. Lewin, K. (1936). *Principles of topological psychology*. New York: McGraw-Hill.

23. Hatfield, E. & Rapson, R. L. (2006). Passionate love, sexual desire, and mate selection: Cross-cultural and historical perspectives. In P. Noller & J. A. Feeney (Eds.), *Close relationships: Functions, forms, and processes* (pp. 227–243). Hove, England: Psychology Press/Taylor & Francis.

24. Finkel, E. J., Eastwick, P. W., Karney, B. R., Reis, H. T., & Sprecher, S. (2012). Online dating: A critical analysis from the perspective of psychological science. *Psychological Science in the Public Interest, 13*, 3–66; Hian, L. B., Chuan, S. L., Trevor, T. M. K., & Detenber, B. H. (2004). Getting to know you: Exploring the development of relational intimacy in computer-mediated communication. *Journal of Computer-Mediated Communication, 9*(3), 1–24.

25. Valkenberg, P. & Peter, J. (2009). The effects of instant messaging on the quality of adolescents' existing friendships: A longitudinal study. *Journal of Communication, 59*, 79–97; Ko, H. & Kuo, F. (2009). Can blogging enhance subjective well-being through self-disclosure? *CyberPsychology & Behavior, 12*, 75–79; Mazer, J. P., Murphy, R. E., & Simonds, C. J. (2008). The effects of teacher self-disclosure via "Facebook" on teacher credibility. *RCA Vestnik (Russian Communication Association)*, 30–37; Hu, Y., Wood, J. F., Smith, V., & Westbrook, N. (2004). Friendships through IM: Examining the relationship between instant messaging and intimacy. *Journal of Computer-Mediated Communication, 10*(1), 38–48.

26. Rosen, L. D. et al. (2008). The impact of emotionality and self-disclosure on online dating versus traditional dating. *Computers in Human Behavior, 24*, 2124–2157; Ben-Ze'ev, A. (2003). Privacy, emotional closeness, and openness in cyberspace. *Computers in Human Behavior, 19*, 451–467.

27. Boase, J., Horrigan, J. B., Wellman, B., & Rainie, L. (2006). The strength of Internet ties. *Pew Internet & American Life Project*. Retrieved from http://www.pewinternet.org/pdfs/PIP_Internet_ties.pdf

28. Henderson, S. & Gilding, M. (2004). "I've never clicked this much with anyone in my life": Trust and hyperpersonal communication in online friendships. *New Media & Society, 6*, 487–506.

29. Henline, B. H., Lamke, L. K., & Howard, M. D. (2007). Exploring perceptions of online infidelity. *Personal Relationships, 14*, 113–128; Whitty, M. T. (2005). The realness of cybercheating: Men's and women's representations of unfaithful Internet relationships. *Social Science Computer Review, 23*, 57–67.

30. Lewis, K., Kaufman, J., & Christakis, N. (2008). The taste for privacy: An analysis of college student privacy settings in an online social network. *Journal of Computer-Mediated Communication, 14*, 79–100; Tufekei, Z. (2008). Can you see me now? Audience and disclosure regulation in online social network sites. *Bulletin of Science, Technology & Society, 28*, 20–36.

31. Baumeister, R. F. (2005). *The cultural animal: Human nature, meaning, and social life*. New York: Oxford.

32. Bellah, R., Madsen, W. M., Sullivan, A., & Tipton, S. M. (1985). *Habits of the heart: Individualism and commitment in American life*. Berkeley: University of California Press; Sennett, R. (1974). *The fall of public man: On the social psychology of capitalism*. New York: Random House; Trenholm, S. & Jensen, A. (1990). *The guarded self: Toward a social history of interpersonal styles*. Paper presented at the Speech Communication Association meeting, San Juan, Puerto Rico.

33. Bombeck, E. (1987). *Family—The ties that bind...and gag!* (p. 11). New York: Random House.

34. Sillars, A. (1995). Communication and family culture. In M. A. Fitzpatrick & A. L. Vangelisti (Eds.), *Explaining family interactions* (pp. 375–399). Thousand Oaks, CA: Sage.

35. Kellas, J. (2010). Transmitting relational worldviews: The relationship between mother-daughter memorable messages and adult daughters' romantic relational schemata. *Communication Quarterly, 58*, 458–479.

36. Strom, R. E. & Boster, F. J. (2011). Dropping out of high school: Assessing the relationship between supportive messages from family and educational attainment. *Communication Reports, 24*, 25–37.

37. Simon, E. P. & Baxter, L. A. (1993). Attachment-style differences in relationship maintenance strategies. *Western Journal Of Communication, 57*, 416–430.

38. Fowler, C. & Dillow, M. R. (2011). Attachment dimensions and the Four Horsemen of the Apocalypse. *Communication Research Reports, 28*, 16–26.

39. Shochet, I. M., Smyth, T., & Homel, R. (2007). The impact of parental attachment on adolescent perception of the school environment and school connectedness. *Australian & New Zealand Journal of Family Therapy, 28*, 109–118.

40. Domingue, R. & Mollen, D. (2009). Attachment and conflict communication in adult romantic relationships. *Journal of Social & Personal Relationships, 26*, 678–696.

41. Rocca, K. A, Martin, M. M., & Dunleavy, K. N. (2010). Siblings' motives for talking to each other. *Journal of Psychology, 144*, 205–219.

42. Brody, L. R., Copeland, A. P., Sutton, L. S., Richardson, D. R., & Guyer, M. (1998). Mommy and daddy like you best: Perceived family favoritism in relation to affect, adjustment, and family process. *Journal of Family Therapy, 20*, 269–291.

43. Gillies, V. & Lucey, H. (2006). "It's a connection you can't get away from": Brothers, sisters, and social capital. *Journal of Youth Studies, 9*, 479–493.

44. Peisah, C., Brodaty, H., & Quadrio, C. (2006). Family conflict in dementia: Prodigal sons and black sheep. *International Journal of Geriatric Psychiatry, 21*, 485–492.

45. Suitor, J. J., Sechrist, J., Plikuhn, M., Pardo, S. T., Gilligan, M., & Pillemer, K. (2009). The role of perceived maternal favoritism in sibling relations in midlife. *Journal of Marriage and Family, 71*, 1026–1038.

46. Pyke, K. (2005). Generational deserters and "black sheep": Acculturative differences among siblings in Asian immigrant families. *Journal of Family Issues, 26*, 491–517.

47. Goetting, A. (1986). The developmental tasks of siblingship over the life cycle. *Journal of Marriage and the Family, 48*, 703–714.

48. Rittenour, C. E., Myers, S. A., & Brann, M. (2007). Commitment and emotional closeness in the sibling relationship. *Southern Communication Journal, 72*, 169–183.

49. Bryant, C. M., Conger, R. D., & Meehan, J. M. (2001). The influence of in-laws on change in marital success. *Journal of Marriage and Family, 63*, 614–626.

50. Ahrons, C. R. (1980). Divorce: A crisis of family transition and change. *Family Relations, 29*, 533–540.

51. Watzlawick, P., Beavin, J., & Jackson, D. (1967). *Pragmatics of human communication: A study of interactional patterns, pathologies, and paradoxes*. New York: Norton.

52. Sabourin, T. (2006). Theories and metatheories to explain family communication: An overview. In L. H. Turner & R. West (Eds.), *Family communication sourcebook* (pp. 43–60). Thousand Oaks, CA: Sage.

53. Galovan, A. M., Holmes, E. K., Schramm, D. G., & Lee, T. R. (2014). Father involvement, father-child relationship quality, and satisfaction with family work: Actor and partner influences on marital quality. *Journal of Family Issues, 35*, 1846–1867.

54. Thompson, E. H. & Trice-Black, S. (2012). School-based group interventions for children exposed to domestic violence. *Journal of Family Violence*, *27*, 233–241.

55. Wahl, K. & Metzner, C. (2012). Parental influences on the prevalence and development of child aggressiveness. *Journal of Child & Family Studies*, *21*, 344–355.

56. Barboza, G., Schiamberg, L. B., Oehmke, J., Korzeniewski, S. J., Post, L. A., & Heraux, C. G. (2009). Individual characteristics and the multiple contexts of adolescent bullying: An ecological perspective. *Journal of Youth & Adolescence*, *38*, 101–121.

57. Whitchurch, G. G. & Constantine, L. L. (1993). Systems theory. In P. G. Boss, W. J. Doherty, R. LaRossa, W. R. Schumm, & S. K. Steinmetz (Eds.), *Sourcebook of family theories and methods: A contextual approach* (pp. 325–349). New York: Plenum Press.

58. Koerner, A. F. & Fitzpatrick, M. A. (2002). Toward a theory of family communication. *Communication Theory*, *12*, 70–91. See also Koerner, A. F. & Schrodt, P. (2014). An introduction to the special issue on family communication patterns. *Journal of Family Communication*, *14*, 1–15.

59. Barbato, C. A., Graham, E. E., & Perse, E. M. (2003). Communicating in the family: An examination of the relationship of family communication climate and interpersonal communication motives. *Journal of Family Communication*, *3*, 123–148.

60. Sherman, S. M. & Dumlao, R. (2008). A cross-cultural comparison of family communication patterns and conflict between young adults and parents. *Journal of Family Communication*, *8*, 186–211.

61. Avtgis, T. A. (1999). The relationship between unwillingness to communicate and family communication patterns. *Communication Research Reports*, *16*, 333–338.

62. Koesten, J. (2004). Family communication patterns, sex of subject, and communication competence. *Communication Monographs*, *71*, 226–244.

63. Petronio, S. (1991). Communication boundary management: A theoretical model of managing disclosure of private information between marital couples. *Communication Theory*, *1*, 311–335.

64. Thorson, A. R. (2009). Adult children's experiences with their parent's infidelity: Communicative protection and access rules in the absence of divorce. *Communication Studies*, *60*, 32–48. doi:10.1080/10510970802623591

65. Sherman, S. M. & Dumlao, R. (2008). A cross-cultural comparison of family communication patterns and conflict between young adults and parents. *Journal of Family Communication*, *8*, 186–211.

66. Schrodt, P., Witt, P. L., & Messersmith, A. S. (2008). A meta-analytical review of family communication patterns and their associations with information processing, behavioral, and psychosocial outcomes. *Communication Monographs*, *75*, 248–269.

67. Ledbetter, A. M. & Schrodt, P. (2008). Family communication patterns and cognitive processing: Conversation and conformity orientations as predictors of informational reception apprehension. *Communication Studies*, *59*, 388–401.

68. Schrodt, P. & Carr, K. (2012). Trait verbal aggressiveness as a function of family communication patterns. *Communication Research Reports*, *29*, 54–63.

69. Ledbetter, A. M. & Vik, T. A. (2012). Parental invasive behaviors and emerging adults' privacy defenses: Instrument development and validation. *Journal of Family Communication*, *12*, 227–247.

70. Sillars, A., Holman, A. J., Richards, A., Jacobs, K. A., Koerner, A., & Reynolds-Dyk, A. (2014). Conversation and conformity orientations as predictors of observed conflict tactics in parent-adolescent discussions. *Journal of Family Communication*, *14*, 16–31.

71. Carvalho, J., Francisco, R., & Relvas, A. P. (2015). Family functioning and information and communication technologies: How do they relate? A literature review. *Computers in Human Behavior*, *45*, 99–108.

72. Crosswhite, J. M., Rice, D., & Asay, S. M. (2014). Texting among United States young adults: An exploratory study on texting and its use within families. *Social Science Journal*, *51*, 70–78.

73. Stern, M. J. & Messer, C. (2009). How family members stay in touch: A quantitative investigation of core family networks. *Marriage & Family Review*, *45*, 654–676.

74. Christofides, E., Muise, A., & Desmarais, S. (2012). Hey mom, what's on your Facebook? Comparing Facebook disclosure and privacy in adolescents and adults. *Social Psychological and Personality Sciences*, *3*, 48–54.

75. Coyne, S. M., Padilla-Walker, L. M., Day, R. D., Harper, J., & Stockdale, L. (2014). A friend request from dear old dad: Associations between parent-child social networking and adolescent outcomes. *Cyberpsychology, Behavior, and Social Networking*, *17*, 8–13.

76. Child, J. T. & Westermann, D. A. (2013). Let's be Facebook friends: Exploring parental Facebook friend requests from a Communication Privacy Management (CPM) perspective. *Journal of Family Communication*, *13*, 46–59.

77. Ball, H., Wanzer, M. B., & Servoss, T. J. (2013). Parent-child communication on Facebook: Family communication patterns and young adults' decisions to "friend" parents. *Communication Quarterly*, *61*, 615–629.

78. Johnson, A., Wittenberg, E., Haigh, M., Wigley, S., Becker, J., Brown, K., & Craig, E. (2004). The process of relationship development and deterioration: Turning points in friendships that have terminated. *Communication Quarterly*, *52*, 54–67.

79. Hartup, W. W. & Stevens, N. (1997). Friendships and adaptation in the life course. *Psychological Bulletin*, *121*, 355–370.

80. Pecchioni, L. (2005). Friendship throughout the life span. In L. Pecchioni, K. B. Wright, & J. F. Nussbaum (Eds.), *Lifespan communication* (pp. 97–116). Hillsdale, NJ: Erlbaum; Samter, W. (2003). Friendship interaction skills across the life-span. In J. O. Greene & B. R. Burleson (Eds.), *Handbook of communication and social interaction skills* (pp. 637–684). Mahwah, NJ: Erlbaum.

81. Rawlins, W. K. (1992). *Friendship matters, communication, dialectics, and the life course* (p. 105). New York: De Gruyter.

82. Kalmijn, M. (2003). Shared friendship networks and the life course: An analysis of survey data on married and cohabiting couples. *Social Networks*, *25*, 231–249.

83. Nussbaum, J. F., Pecchioni, L., Baringer, D., & Kundrat, A. (2002). Lifespan communication. In W. B. Gudykunst (Ed.), *Communication yearbook 26* (pp. 366–389). Mahwah, NJ: Erlbaum.

84. Utz, S. (2007). Media use in long-distance friendships. *Information, Communication & Society*, *10*, 694–713.

85. Solomon, S. & Knafo, A. (2007). Value similarity in adolescent friendships. In T. C. Rhodes (Ed.), *Focus on adolescent behavior research* (pp. 133–155). Hauppauge, NY: Nova Science Publishers.

86. Swain, S. (1989). Covert intimacy: Closeness in the same-sex friendships of men. In B. Risman & P. Schwartz (Eds.), *Gender in intimate relations: A microstructural approach* (pp. 75–87). Belmont, CA: Wadsworth.

87. Swain, S. (1989). Covert intimacy: Closeness in the same-sex friendships of men. In B. Risman & P. Schwartz (Eds.), *Gender in intimate relations: A microstructural approach* (pp. 75–87). Belmont, CA: Wadsworth.

88. Dindia, K. & Allen, M. (1992). Sex differences in self-disclosure: A meta-analysis. *Psychological Bulletin*, *112*, 106–124.

89. Bond, B. J. (2009). He posted, she posted: Gender differences in self-disclosure on social network sites. *Rocky Mountain Communicator*, *6*(2), 29–37.

90. Holmstrom, A. J. (2009). Sex and gender similarities and differences in communication values in same-sex and cross-sex friendships. *Communication Quarterly, 57*, 224–238.

91. Sapadin, L. A. (1988). Friendship and gender: Perspectives of professional men and women. *Journal of Social and Personal Relationships, 5*, 387–403.

92. Holmstrom, A. J. (2009). Sex and gender similarities and differences in communication values in same-sex and cross-sex friendships. *Communication Quarterly, 57*, 224–238.

93. Hand, L. & Furman, W. (2009). Rewards and costs in adolescent other-sex friendships: Comparisons to same-sex friendships and romantic relationships. *Social Development, 18*, 270–287.

94. Malachowski, C. C. & Dillow, M. R. (2011). An examination of relational uncertainty, romantic intent, and attraction on communicative and relational outcomes in cross-sex friendships. *Communication Research Reports, 28*, 356–368.

95. Halatsis, P. & Christakis, N. (2009). The challenge of sexual attraction within heterosexuals' cross-sex friendship. *Journal of Social and Personal Relationships, 26*, 919–937.

96. Sapadin, L. A. (1988). Friendship and gender: Perspectives of professional men and women. *Journal of Social and Personal Relationships, 5*, 387–403.

97. Bleske-Rechek, A. et al. (2012). Benefit or burden? Attraction in cross-sex friendship. *Journal of Social and Personal Relationships, 29*, 569–596.

98. Ledbetter, A. M., Mazer, J. P., DeGroot, J. M., & Meyer, K. R. (2011). Attitudes toward online social connection and self-disclosure as predictors of Facebook communication and relational closeness. *Communication Research, 38*, 27–53.

99. Mongeau, P. A., Knight, K., Williams, J., Eden, J., & Shaw, C. (2013). Identifying and explicating variation among friends with benefits relationships. *Journal of Sex Research, 50*, 37–47.

100. Wyndol, F. & Shaffer, L. (2011). Romantic partners, friends, friends with benefits, and casual acquaintances as sexual partners. *Journal of Sex Research, 48*, 554–564.

101. Owen, J. & Fincham, F. D. (2012). Friends with benefits relationships as a start to exclusive romantic relationships. *Journal of Social and Personal Relationships, 29*, 982–996.

102. Jonason, P. K. (2013). Four functions for four relationships: Consensus definitions of university students. *Archives of Sexual Behavior, 42*, 1407–1414.

103. Green, K. J. & Morman, M. T. (2011). The perceived benefits of the friends with benefits relationship. *Human Communication, 14*, 327–346.

104. Lehmiller, J., VanderDrift, L. E., & Kelly, J. R. (2011). Sex differences in approaching friends with benefits relationships. *Journal of Sex Research, 48*, 275–284.

105. Bisson, M. A. & Levine, T. R. (2009). Negotiating a friends with benefits relationship. *Archives of Sexual Behavior, 38*, 66–73; see also Knight, K. (2014). Communicative dilemmas in emerging adults' friends with benefits relationships: Challenge to relational talk. *Emerging Adulthood, 2*, 270–279.

106. Bisson, M. A. & Levine, T. R. (2009). Negotiating a friends with benefits relationship. *Archives of Sexual Behavior, 38*, 66–73.

107. Holmstrom, A. J. (2009). Sex and gender similarities and differences in communication values in same-sex and cross-sex friendships. *Communication Quarterly, 57*, 224–238.

108. Galupo, M. P. & Gonzalez, K. A. (2013). Friendship values and cross-category friendships: Understanding adult friendship patterns across gender, sexual orientation, and race. *Sex Roles, 68*, 779–790.

109. Hopcke, R. H. & Rafaty, L. (2001). *Straight women, gay men: Absolutely fabulous friendships*. Tulsa: Council Oak Books.

110. Bartlett, N. H., Patterson, H. M., VanderLaan, D. P., & Vasey, P. L. (2009). The relation between women's body esteem and friendships with gay men. *Body Image, 6*, 235–241.

111. Amichai-Hamburger, Y., Kingsbury, M., & Scheider, B. H. (2013). Friendship: An old concept with a new meaning? *Computers in Human Behavior, 29*, 33–39.

112. Smith, A. (February 3, 2014). 6 new facts about Facebook. *Pew Research Center*.

113. Tong, S. T., Van Der Heide, B., Langwell, L., & Walther, J. B. (2008). Too much of a good thing? The relationship between number of friends and interpersonal impressions on Facebook. *Journal of Computer-Mediated Communication, 13*, 531–549; Kim, J. & Lee, J. R. (2011). The Facebook paths to happiness: Effects of the number of Facebook friends and self-presentation on subjective well-being. *CyberPsychology, Behavior & Social Networking, 14*, 59–364.

114. Scott, G. G. (2014). More than friends: Popularity on Facebook and its role in impression formation. *Journal of Computer-Mediated Communication, 19*, 358–372.

115. Nabi, R. L., Prestin, A., & So, J. (2013). Facebook friends with (health) benefits? Exploring social network site use and perceptions of social support, stress, and well-being. *Cyberpsychology, Behavior, and Social Networking, 16*, 721–727.

116. Lee, J. R., Moore, D. C., Park, E., & Park, S. G. (2012). Who wants to be "friend rich"? Social compensatory friending on Facebook and the moderating role of public self-consciousness. *Computers in Human Behavior, 28*, 1036–1043; Kim, J. & Lee, J. R. (2011). The Facebook paths to happiness: Effects of the number of Facebook friends and self-presentation on subjective well-being. *Cyberpsychology, Behavior, and Social Networking, 14*, 359–364.

117. Bryant, E. M. & Marmo, J. (2012). The rules of Facebook friendship: A two-stage examination of interaction rules in close, casual, and acquaintance friendships. *Journal of Social and Personal Relationships, 29*, 1013–1035.

118. Anderson, B., Fagan, P., Woodnutt, T., & Chamorro-Premuzic, T. (2012). Facebook psychology: Popular questions answered by research. *Psychology of Popular Media Culture, 1*, 23–37; Ellison, N. B., Steinfield, C., & Lampe, C. (2007). The benefits of Facebook "friends": Social capital and college students' use of online social networks sites. *Journal of Computer-Mediated Communication, 12*, 1143–1168.

119. More than half of online friends go on to meet in person. (2008, December 17). *Daily Mail Reporter*. Retrieved from http://www.dailymail.co.uk/sciencetech/article-1096664/More-half-online-friends-meet-person.html

120. Ellison, N. B., Steinfield, C., & Lampe, C. (2007). The benefits of Facebook "friends": Social capital and college students' use of online social networks sites. *Journal of Computer-Mediated Communication, 12*, 1143–1168.

121. Loving, T. J. & Slatcher, R. B. (2013). Romantic relationships and health. In J. A. Simpson & L. Campbell (Eds.), *The Oxford handbook of close relationships* (pp. 617–637). New York: Oxford University Press.

122. Epstein, R., Warfel, R., Johnson, J., Smith, R., & McKinney, P. (2013). Which relationship skills count most? *Journal of Couple & Relationship Therapy, 12*, 297–313.

123. Sternberg, R. J. (2004). A triangular theory of love. In H. T. Reis & C. E. Rusbult (Eds.), *Close Relationships* (pp. 258–276). New York: Psychology Press.

124. Sumter, S. R., Valkenburg, P. M., & Peter, J. (2013). Perceptions of love across the lifespan: Differences in passion, intimacy, and commitment. *International Journal of Behavioral Development, 37*, 417–427.

125. Acevedo, B. P. & Aron, A. (2009). Does a long-term relationship kill romantic love? *Review of General Psychology, 13*, 59–65.

126. Weigel, D. J. (2008). Mutuality and the communication of commitment in romantic relationships. *Southern Communication Journal, 73*, 24–41.

127. Epstein, R., Pandit, M., & Thakar, M. (2013). How love emerges in arranged marriage: Two cross-cultural studies. *Journal of Comparative Family Studies, 43*, 341–360.

128. deOliveira, J. M., Costa, C. G., & Nogueira, C. (2013). The workings of homonormativity: Lesbian, gay, bisexual, and queer discourses on discrimination and public displays of affections in Portugal. *Journal of Homosexuality*, *60*, 1475–1493; Vaquera, E. & Kao, G. (2005). Private and public displays of affection among interracial and intra-racial adolescent couples. *Social Science Quarterly*, *86*, 484–508.

129. Floyd, K., Boren, J. P., Hannawa, A. F., Hesse, C., McEwan, B., & Veksler, A. E. (2009). Kissing in marital and cohabiting relationships: Effects on blood lipids, stress, and relationship satisfaction. *Western Journal of Communication*, *73*, 113–133.

130. Floyd, K. & Riforgiate, S. (2008). Affectionate communication received from spouses predicts stress hormone levels in healthy adults. *Communication Monographs*, *75*, 351–368.

131. Horan, S. M. (2012). Affection exchange theory and perceptions of relational transgressions. *Western Journal of Communication*, *76*, 109–126.

132. Horan, S. M. & Booth-Butterfield, M. (2013). Understanding the routine expression of deceptive affection in romantic relationships. *Communication Quarterly*, *61*, 195–216.

133. Epstein, R. (2010, January/February). How science can help you fall in love. *Scientific American Mind*, pp. 26–33.

134. Diamond, L. M. (2013). Sexuality in relationships. In J. A. Simpson & L. Campbell (Eds.), *The Oxford handbook of close relationships* (pp. 589–614). New York: Oxford University Press.

135. Byers, E. S. (2011). Beyond the birds and the bees and was it good for you?: Thirty years of research on sexual communication. *Canadian Psychology*, *52*, 20–28.

136. Theiss, J. A. & Solomon, D. H. (2007). Communication and the emotional, cognitive, and relational consequences of first sexual encounters between partners. *Communication Quarterly*, *55*, 179–206.

137. Miller-Ott, A. E. & Linder, A. (2013). Romantic partners' use of facework and humor to communicate about sex. *Qualitative Research Reports in Communication*, *14*, 69–78.

138. Baxter, L. A. (2001). Communicatively remembering turning points of relational development in heterosexual romantic relationships. *Communication Reports*, *14*, 1–17.

139. Becker, J. A. J., Johnson, A. J., Craig, E. A., Gilchrist, E. S., Haigh, M. M., & Lane, L. T. (2009). Friendships are flexible, not fragile: Turning points in geographically-close and long-distance friendships. *Journal of Social & Personal Relationships*, *4*, 347–369.

140. Mongeau, P. A., Serewicz, M. C. M., Henningsen, M. L. M., & Davis, K. L. (2006). Sex differences in the transition to a heterosexual romantic relationship. In K. Dindia & D. J. Canary (Eds.), *Sex differences and similarities in communication* (2nd ed., pp. 337–358). Mahwah, NJ: Erlbaum.

141. Papp, L. M., Danielewicz, J., & Cayemberg, C. (2012). Are we Facebook Official? Implications of dating partners' Facebook use and profiles for intimate relationship satisfaction. *CyberPsychology, Behavior & Social Networking*, *15*, 85–90.

142. Theiss, J. A. & Solomon, D. H. (2007). Communication and the emotional, cognitive, and relational consequences of first sexual encounters between partners. *Communication Quarterly*, *55*, 179–206.

143. Siegert, J. R. & Stamp, G. H. (1994). "Our first big fight" as a milestone in the development of close relationships. *Communication Monographs*, *61*, 345–361.

144. Dailey, R. M., Rossetto, K. R., McCracken, A. A., Jin, B., & Green, E. W. (2012). Negotiating breakups and renewals in on-again/off-again dating relationships: Traversing the transitions. *Communication Quarterly*, *60*, 165–189.

145. Baxter, L. A. & Bullis, C. (1986). Turning points in developing romantic relationships. *Human Communication Research*, *12*, 469–493.

146. Gottman, J. (1994). *Why marriages succeed or fail*. New York: Simon & Schuster.

147. Holman, T. B. & Jarvis, M. O. (2003). Hostile, volatile, avoiding, and validating couple-conflict types: An investigation of Gottman's couple-conflict types. *Personal Relationships*, *10*, 267–282.

148. Gottman, J. (1994). *Why marriages succeed or fail* (p. 41). New York: Simon & Schuster.

149. Gottman, J. (1994). *Why marriages succeed or fail* (p. 45). New York: Simon & Schuster.

150. Chapman, G. (2010). *The 5 love languages*. Chicago: Northfield.

151. Egbert, N. & Polk, D. (2006). Speaking the language of relational maintenance: A validity test of Chapman's (1992) five love languages. *Communication Research Reports*, *23*, 19–26.

152. Smith, A. & Duggan, M. (2013, October 21). *Online dating & relationships*. Pew Research Internet Project.

153. Lenhart, A. & Duggan, M. (2014, February 11). *Couples, the internet, and social media*. Pew Internet & American Life Project.

154. Jin, B. & Peña, J. F. (2010). Mobile communication in romantic relationships: Mobile phone use, relational uncertainty, love, commitment, and attachment styles. *Communication Reports*, *23*, 39–51.

155. Weisskirch, R. S. (2012). Women's adult romantic attachment style and communication by cell phone with romantic partners. *Psychological Reports*, *111*, 281–288; Duran, R. L., Kelly, L., & Rotaru, T. (2011). Mobile phones in romantic relationships and the dialectic of autonomy versus connection. *Communication Quarterly*, *59*, 19–36; Miller-Ott, A. E., Kelly, L., & Duran, R. L. (2012). The effects of cell phone usage rules on satisfaction in romantic relationships. *Communication Quarterly*, *60*, 17–34.

156. Schade, L. C., Sandberg, J., Bean, R., Busby, D., & Coyne, S. (2013). Using technology to connect in romantic relationships: Effects on attachment, relationship satisfaction, and stability in emerging adults. *Journal of Couple & Relationship Therapy*, *12*, 314–338; Coyne, S. M., Stockdale, L., Busby, D., Iverson, B., & Grant, D. M. "I luv u 🙂!": A descriptive study of the media use of individuals in romantic relationships. *Family Relationships*, *60*, 150–162.

157. Saslow, L. R., Muise, A., Impett, E. A., & Dubin, M. (2013). Can you see how happy we are? Facebook images and relationship satisfaction. *Social Psychological and Personality Science*, *4*, 411–418.

158. Hand, M. M., Thomas, D. B., Walter, C., Deemer, E. D., & Buyanjargal, M. (2013). Facebook and romantic relationships: Intimacy and couple satisfaction associated with online social network use. *Cyberpsychology, Behavior, and Social Networking*, *16*, 8–13.

159. Elphinston, R. A. & Noller, P. (2011). Time to face It! Facebook intrusion and the implications for romantic jealousy and relationship satisfaction. *Cyberpsychology, Behavior, and Social Networking*, *14*, 631–635.

160. Utz, S. & Beukeboom, C. J. (2011). The role of social network sites in romantic relationships: Effects on jealousy and relationship happiness. *Journal of Computer-Mediated Communication*, *16*, 511–527.

161. Valenzuela, S., Halpern, D., & Katz, J. E. (2014). Social network sites, marriage well-being and divorce: Survey and state-level evidence from the United States. *Computers in Human Behavior*, *36*, 94–101.

CHAPTER ELEVEN

1. Fitness, J. (2006).The emotionally intelligent marriage. In J. Ciarrochi, J. P. Forgas, & J. D. Mayer (Eds.), *Emotional intelligence in everyday life* (pp. 129–139). New York: Psychology Press.

2. Smith, E. E. (June 12, 2014). Masters of love. *The Atlantic*.

3. Barbato, C. A., Graham, E. E., & Perse, E. M. (2003). Communicating in the family: An examination of the relationship of family communication climate and interpersonal communication motives. *Journal of Family Communication*, *3*, 123–148.

4. Dailey, R. M. (2006). Confirmation in parent–adolescent relationships and adolescent openness: Toward extending confirmation theory. *Communication Monographs*, *73*, 434–458.

5. Teven, J. J., Martin, M. M., & Neupauer, N. C. (1998). Sibling relationships: Verbally aggressive messages and their effect on relational satisfaction. *Communication Reports*, *11*, 179–186.

6. Cooil, B., Aksoy, L., Keiningham, T. L., & Maryott, K. M. (2009). The relationship of employee perceptions of organizational climate to business-unit outcomes: An MPLS approach. *Journal of Service Research*, *11*, 277–294; Pincus, D. (1986). Communication satisfaction, job satisfaction, and job performance. *Human Communication Research*, *12*, 395–419.

7. Sopow, E. (2008). The communication climate change at RCMP. *Strategic Communication Management*, *12*, 20–23; Kassing, J. W. (2008). Consider this: A comparison of factors contributing to employees' expressions of dissent. *Communication Quarterly*, *56*, 342–355; Saunders, D. (2008). Create an open climate for communication. *Supervision*, *69*, 6–8; Beck, C. E. & Beck, E. A. (1996). The manager's open door and the communication climate. In K. M. Galvin & P. Cooper (Eds.), *Making connections: Readings in relational communication* (pp. 286–290). Los Angeles: Roxbury.

8. Goleman, D. (2006). *Social intelligence* (p. 279). New York: Random House.

9. Vangelisti, A. L. & Young, S. L. (2000). When words hurt: The effects of perceived intentionality on interpersonal relationships. *Journal of Social & Personal Relationships*, *17*, 393–424.

10. Sieberg, E. (1976). Confirming and disconfirming communication in an organizational setting. In J. Owen, P. Page, & G. Zimmerman (Eds.), *Communication in organizations* (pp. 129–149). St. Paul, MN: West.

11. Sieberg, E. & Larson, C. (1971). *Dimensions of interpersonal response*. Paper presented at the meeting of the International Communication Association, Phoenix.

12. Cox, S. A. (1999). Group communication and employee turnover: How coworkers encourage peers to voluntarily exit. *Southern Communication Journal*, *64*, 181–192.

13. Gottman, J. M. & Levenson, R. W. (2000). The timing of divorce: Predicting when a couple will divorce over a 14-year period. *Journal of Marriage and the Family*, *62*, 737–745.

14. Rancer, A. S. & Avtgis, T. A. (2006). *Argumentative and aggressive communication: Theory, research, and application*. Thousand Oaks, CA: Sage.

15. Bowes, L., Wolke, D., Joinson, C., Lereya, S. T., & Lewis, G. (2014). Sibling bullying and risk of depression, anxiety, and self-harm: A prospective cohort study. *Pediatrics*, *134*, 1032–1039.

16. Wade, A. & Beran, T. (2011). Cyberbullying: The new era of bullying. *Canadian Journal of School Psychology*, *26*, 44–61; Dempsey, A. G., Sulkowski, M. L., Dempsey, J., & Storch, E. A. (2011). Has cyber technology produced a new group of peer aggressors? *Cyberpsychology, Behavior, and Social Networking*, *14*, 297–302.

17. Duggan, M. (2014, October 22). *Online harassment*. Pew Research Internet Project.

18. Alberts, J. K. (1988). An analysis of couples' conversational complaints. *Communication Monographs*, *55*, 184–197.

19. Alberts, J. K. & Driscoll, G. (1992). Containment versus escalation: The trajectory of couples' conversational complaints. *Western Journal of Communication*, *56*, 394–412.

20. Gottman, J. M. & Silver, N. (1999). *The seven principles for making marriage work*. New York: Random House.

21. Johnson, A. J., Hample, D., & Cionea, I. A. (2014). Understanding argumentation in interpersonal communication. *Communication Yearbook*, *38*, 145–173; Rancer, A. S. & Avtgis, T. A. (2006). *Argumentative and aggressive communication: Theory, research, and application*. Thousand Oaks, CA: Sage.

22. Jordan-Jackson, F. F., Lin, Y., Rancer, A. S., & Infante, D. A. (2008). Perceptions of males and females' use of aggressive and nonaffirming messages in an interpersonal dispute: You've come a long way baby? *Western Journal of Communication*, *72*, 239–258.

23. Cissna, K. & Seiberg, E. (1995). Patterns of interactional confirmation and disconfirmation. In M. V. Redmond (Ed.), *Interpersonal communication: Readings in theory and research* (pp. 301–317—AU). Fort Worth, TX: Harcourt Brace.

24. Allen, M. W. (1995). Communication concepts related to perceived organizational support. *Western Journal of Communication*, *59*, 326–346.

25. Dailey, R. M. (2008). Assessing the contribution of nonverbal behaviors in displays of confirmation during parent–adolescent interactions: An actor–partner interdependence model. *Journal of Family Communication*, *8*, 62–91.

26. Wilmot, W. W. (1987). *Dyadic communication* (pp. 149–158). New York: Random House.

27. Burggraf, C. & Sillars, A. L. (1987). A critical examination of sex differences in marital communication. *Communication Monographs*, *54*, 276–294; Newton, D. A. & Burgoon, J. K. (1990). The use and consequences of verbal strategies during interpersonal disagreements. *Human Communication Research*, *16*, 477–518.

28. Hocker, J. L. & Wilmot, W. W. (1995). *Interpersonal conflict* (4th ed., p. 34). Dubuque, IA: Brown & Benchmark.

29. Hocker, J. L. & Wilmot, W. W. (1995). *Interpersonal conflict* (4th ed., p. 36). Dubuque, IA: Brown & Benchmark.

30. Gottman, J. M. & Levinson, R. W. (1999). Rebound for marital conflict and divorce prediction. *Family Process*, *38*, 387–292.

31. Domenici, K. & Littlejohn, S. (2006). *Facework: Bridging theory and practice*. Thousand Oaks, CA: Sage; Lapinski, M. K. & Boster, F. J. (2001). Modeling the ego-defensive function of attitudes. *Communication Monographs*, *68*, 314–324.

32. Lannin, D. G., Bittner, K. E., & Lorenz, F. O. (2013). Longitudinal effect of defensive denial on relationship instability. *Journal of Family Psychology*, *27*, 968–977.

33. Becker, J. A. H., Ellevold, B., & Stamp, G. H. (2008). The creation of defensiveness in social interaction II: A model of defensive communication among romantic couples. *Communication Monographs*, *75*, 86–110; Stamp, G. H., Vangelisti, A. L., & Daly, J. A. (1992). The creation of defensiveness in social interaction. *Communication Quarterly*, *40*, 177–190.

34. Turk, D. R. & Monahan, J. L. (1999). "Here I go again": An examination of repetitive behaviors during interpersonal conflicts. *Southern Communication Journal*, *64*, 232–244.

35. Cupach, W. R. & Messman, S. J. (1999). Face predilections and friendship solidarity. *Communication Reports*, *12*, 117–124.

36. Trees, A. R., Kerssen-Griefp, J., & Hess, J. A. (2009). Earning influence by communicating respect: Facework's contributions to effective instructional feedback. *Communication Education*, *58*, 397–416.

37. Kingsley Westerman, C. Y. & Westerman, D. (2010). Supervisor impression management: Message content and channel effects on impressions. *Communication Studies*, *61*, 585–601.

38. Gibb, J. (1961, September). Defensive communication. *Journal of Communication*, *11*, 141–148; Robertson, E. (2005). Placing leaders at the heart of organizational communication. *Communication Management*, *9*, 34–37.

39. Proctor, R. F. & Wilcox, J. R. (1993). An exploratory analysis of responses to owned messages in interpersonal communication. *ETC: A Review of General Semantics*, *50*, 201–220.

40. Seider, B. H., Hirschberger, G., Nelson, K. L., & Levenson, R. W. (2009). We can work it out: Age differences in relational pronouns, physiology, and behavior in marital conflict. *Psychology and Aging, 24*, 604–613.

41. Czech, K. & Forward, G. L. (2010). Leader communication: Faculty perceptions of the department chair. *Communication Quarterly, 58*, 431–457.

42. Hample, D., Richards, A. S., & Skubisz, C. (2013). Blurting. *Communication Monographs, 80*, 503–532.

43. Harwood, J., Ryan, E. B., Giles, H., & Tysoski, S. (1997). Evaluations of patronizing speech and three response styles in a non-service-providing context. *Journal of Applied Communication Research, 25*, 170–195.

44. Katt, J. A. & Collins, S. J. (2013). The power of provisional/immediate language revisited: Adding student personality traits to the mix. *Communication Research Reports, 30*, 85–95.

45. Miller, S., Nunnally, E. W., & Wackman, D. B. (1975). *Alive and aware: How to improve your relationships through better communication*. Minneapolis, MN: International Communication Programs; Remer, R. & deMesquita, P. (1990). Teaching and learning the skills of interpersonal confrontation. In D. D. Cahn (Ed.), *Intimates in conflict: A communication perspective* (pp. 225–252). Hillsdale, NJ: Erlbaum.

46. Smith, M. (1975). *When I say no, I feel guilty* (pp. 93–110). New York: Dial Press.

47. Benoit, W. L. & Drew, S. (1997). Appropriateness and effectiveness of image repair strategies. *Communication Reports, 10*, 153–163; Stamp, G. H., Vangelisti, A. L., & Daly, J. A. (1992). The creation of defensiveness in social interaction. *Communication Quarterly, 40*, 177–190.

CHAPTER TWELVE

1. Wilmot, W. & Hocker, J. L. (2010). *Interpersonal conflict* (8th ed., pp. 44–56). New York: McGraw-Hill; Buzzanell, P. M. & Burrell, N. A. (1997). Family and workplace conflict: Examining metaphorical conflict schemas and expressions across context and sex. *Human Communication Research, 24*, 109–146.

2. Metts, S. & Cupach, W. (1990). The influence of relationship beliefs and problem-solving responses on satisfaction in romantic relationships. *Human Communication Research, 17*, 170–185.

3. Wilmot, W. & Hocker, J. L. (2010). *Interpersonal conflict* (8th ed., pp. 11–19). New York: McGraw-Hill.

4. Cupach, W. R. & Canary, D. J. (1997). *Competence in interpersonal conflict* (pp. 5–6). New York: McGraw-Hill.

5. Benoit, W. L. & Benoit, P. J. (1987). Everyday argument practices of naive social actors. In J. Wenzel (Ed.), *Argument and critical practices* (pp. 465–474). Annandale, VA: Speech Communication Association.

6. Samter, W. & Cupach, W. R. (1998). Friendly fire: Topical variations in conflict among same- and cross-sex friends. *Communication Studies, 49*, 121–138.

7. Vuchinich, S. (1987). Starting and stopping spontaneous family conflicts. *Journal of Marriage and Family, 49*, 591–601.

8. Gottman, J. M. (1982). Emotional responsiveness in marital conversations. *Journal of Communication, 32*, 108–120; Cupach, W. R. (1982, May). *Communication satisfaction and interpersonal solidarity as outcomes of conflict message strategy use*. Paper presented at the International Communication Association conference, Boston.

9. Koren, K., Carlton, K., & Shaw, D. (1980). Marital conflict: Relations among behaviors, outcomes, and distress. *Journal of Consulting and Clinical Psychology, 48*, 460–468.

10. Wilmot, W. & Hocker, J. L. (2010). *Interpersonal conflict* (8th ed., p. 37). New York: McGraw-Hill.

11. Gottman, J. M. (1979). *Marital interaction: Experimental investigations*. New York: Academic Press; Infante, D. A., Myers, S. A., & Buerkel, R. A. (1994). Argument and verbal aggression in constructive and destructive family and organizational disagreements. *Western Journal of Communication, 58*, 73–84.

12. Crohan, S. E. (1992). Marital happiness and spousal consensus on beliefs about marital conflict: A longitudinal investigation. *Journal of Science and Personal Relationships, 9*, 89–102.

13. Canary, D. J., Weger, H., Jr., & Stafford, L. (1991). Couples' argument sequences and their associations with relational characteristics. *Western Journal of Speech Communication, 55*, 159–179.

14. Harper, M. S. & Welsh, D. P. (2007). Keeping quiet: Self-silencing and its association with relational and individual functioning among adolescent romantic couples. *Journal of Social and Personal Relationships, 24*, 99–116.

15. Afifi, T. D., McManus, T., Steuber, K., & Coho, A. (2009). Verbal avoidance and dissatisfaction in intimate conflict situations. *Human Communication Research, 35*, 357–383; Caughlin, J. P. & Golish, T. D. (2002). An analysis of the association between topic avoidance and dissatisfaction: Comparing perceptual and interpersonal explanations. *Communication Monographs, 69*, 275–295.

16. Caughlin, J. P. & Arr, T. D. (2004). When is topic avoidance unsatisfying? Examining moderators of the association between avoidance and dissatisfaction. *Human Communication Research, 30*, 479–513.

17. Cahn, D. D. (1992). *Conflict in intimate relationships* (p. 100). New York: Guilford.

18. Wilmot, W. & Hocker, J. L. (2010). *Interpersonal conflict* (8th ed., p. 159). New York: McGraw-Hill.

19. Oetzel, J. G. & Ting-Toomey, S. (2003). Face concerns in interpersonal conflict: A cross-cultural empirical test of the face negotiation theory. *Communication Research, 30*, 599–625; Dsilva, M. U. & Whyte, L. O. (1998). Cultural differences in conflict styles: Vietnamese refugees and established residents. *Howard Journal of Communication, 9*, 57–68.

20. Messman, S. J. & Mikesell, R. L. (2000). Competition and interpersonal conflict in dating relationships. *Communication Reports, 13*, 21–34.

21. Olson, L. N. & Braithwaite, D. O. (2004). "If you hit me again, I'll hit you back": Conflict management strategies of individuals experiencing aggression during conflicts. *Communication Studies, 55*, 271–285.

22. Warren, K., Schopplrey, S., & Moberg, D. (2005). A model of contagion through competition in the aggressive behaviors of elementary school students. *Journal of Abnormal Child Psychology, 33*, 283–292.

23. Infante, D. A. (1987). Aggressiveness. In J. C. McCroskey & J. A. Daly (Eds.), *Personality and interpersonal communication* (pp. 157–191). Newbury Park, CA: Sage.

24. Roloff, M. E. & Reznick, R. M. (2008). Communication during serial arguments: Connections with individuals' mental and physical well-being. In M. T. Motley (Ed.), *Studies in applied interpersonal communication* (pp. 97–120). Thousand Oaks, CA: Sage.

25. Infante, D. A., Rancer, A. S., & Jordan, F. F. (1996). Affirming and nonaffirming style, dyad sex, and the perception of argumentation and verbal aggression in an interpersonal dispute. *Human Communication Research, 22*, 315–334.

26. Infante, D. A., Chandler, T. A., & Rudd, J. E. (1989). Test of an argumentative skill deficiency model of interspousal violence. *Communication Monographs, 56*, 163–177.

27. Martin, M. M., Anderson, C. M., Burant, P. A., & Weber, K. (1997). Verbal aggression in sibling relationships. *Communication Quarterly, 45*, 304–317.

28. Kassing, J. W. & Infante, D. A. (1999). Aggressive communication in the coach-athlete relationship. *Communication Research Reports, 16*, 110–120.

29.   Beatty, M. J., Valencic, K. M., Rudd, J. E., & Dobos, J. A. (1999). A "dark side" of communication avoidance: Indirect interpersonal aggressiveness. *Communication Research Reports, 16,* 103–109.

30.   Filley, A. C. (1975). *Interpersonal conflict resolution* (p. 23). Glenview, IL: Scott, Foresman.

31.   Canary, D. (2003). Managing interpersonal conflict: A model of events related to strategic choices. In J. O. Greene & B. R. Burleson (Eds.), *Handbook of communication and social interaction skills* (pp. 515–549). Mahwah, NJ: Erlbaum.

32.   Wilmot, W. & Hocker, J. L. (2010). *Interpersonal conflict* (8th ed., pp. 13–16). New York: McGraw-Hill; Knapp, M. L., Putnam, L. L., & Davis, L. J. (1988). Measuring interpersonal conflict in organizations: Where do we go from here? *Management Communication Quarterly, 1,* 414–429.

33.   Burggraf, C. S. & Sillars, A. L. (1987). A critical examination of sex differences in marital communication. *Communication Monographs, 53,* 276–294.

34.   McGinn, M. M., McFarland, P. T., & Christensen, A. (2009). Antecedents and consequences of demand/withdraw. *Journal of Family Psychology, 23,* 749–757.

35.   Gottman, J. (1994). *Why marriages succeed or fail.* New York: Simon & Schuster; Fowler, C. & Dillow, M. R. (2011). Attachment dimensions and the Four Horsemen of the Apocalypse. *Communication Research Reports, 28,* 16–26; Holman, T. B. & Jarvis, M. O. (2003). Hostile, volatile, avoiding, and validating couple-conflict types: An investigation of Gottman's couple-conflict types. *Personal Relationships, 10,* 267–282.

36.   Rossel, J. & Collins, R. (2006). Conflict theory and interaction rituals: The microfoundations of conflict theory. In J. H. Turner (Ed.), *Handbook of sociological theory* (pp. 509–532). New York: Springer.

37.   Cupach, W. R. & Canary, D. J. (1997). *Competence in interpersonal conflict* (p. 109). New York: McGraw-Hill.

38.   Tannen, D. (1989). *You just don't understand: Women and men in conversation* (pp. 152–157, 162–165). New York: William Morrow.

39.   Tannen, D. (1989). *You just don't understand: Women and men in conversation* (pp. 152–157, 162–165). New York: William Morrow.

40.   Hess, N. H. & Hagen, E. H. (2006). Sex differences in indirect aggression: Psychological evidence from young adults. *Evolution and Human Behavior, 27,* 231–245; Underwood, M. K. (2003). *Social aggression among girls.* New York: Guilford.

41.   Wiseman, R. (2003). *Queen bees and wannabes: Helping your daughter survive cliques, gossip, boyfriends, and other realities of adolescence.* New York: Three Rivers Press.

42.   Collier, M. J. (1991). Conflict competence within African, Mexican, and Anglo-American friendships. In S. Ting-Toomey & F. Korzenny (Eds.), *Cross-cultural interpersonal communication* (pp. 132–154). Newbury Park, CA: Sage.

43.   Papa, M. J. & Natalle, E. J. (1989). Gender, strategy selection, and discussion satisfaction in interpersonal conflict. *Western Journal of Speech Communication, 52,* 260–272.

44.   Afifi, T. D, Joseph, A., & Aldeis, D. (2012). The "standards for openness hypothesis": Why women find (conflict) avoidance more dissatisfying than men. *Journal of Social and Personal Relationships, 29,* 102–125.

45.   Gayle, B. M., Preiss, R. W., & Allen, M. A. (2001). A meta-analytic interpretation of intimate and non-intimate interpersonal conflict. In M. A. Allen, R. W. Preiss, B. M. Gayle, & N. Burrell (Eds.), *Interpersonal communication: Advances through meta-analysis* (pp. 345–368). New York: Erlbaum.

46.   Allen, M. (1998). Methodological considerations when examining a gendered world. In D. Canary & K. Dindia (Eds.), *Handbook of sex differences and similarities in communication* (pp. 427–444). Mahwah, NJ: Erlbaum.

47.   Cupach, W. R. & Canary, D. J. (1997). *Competence in interpersonal conflict* (pp. 63–65). New York: McGraw-Hill.

48.   Burggraf, C. S. & Sillars, A. L. (1987). A critical examination of sex differences in marital communication. *Communication Monographs, 54,* 276–294.

49.   Gudykunst, W. B. & Ting-Toomey, S. (1988). *Culture and interpersonal communication* (pp. 153–160). Newbury Park, CA: Sage.

50.   Holt, J. L. & DeVore, C. J. (2005). Culture, gender, organizational role, and styles of conflict resolution: A meta-analysis. *International Journal of Intercultural Relations, 29,* 165–196.

51.   Ting-Toomey, S. (1988). Rhetorical sensitivity style in three cultures: France, Japan, and the United States. *Central States Speech Journal, 39,* 28–36.

52.   Okabe, K. (1987). Indirect speech acts of the Japanese. In L. Kincaid (Ed.), *Communication theory: Eastern and Western perspectives* (pp. 127–136). San Diego: Academic Press.

53.   Fontaine, G. (1991). Cultural diversity in intimate intercultural relationships. In D. D. Cahn (Ed.), *Intimates in conflict: A communication perspective* (pp. 209–224). Hillsdale, NJ: Erlbaum.

54.   Tannen, D. (1989). *You just don't understand: Women and men in conversation* (p. 160). New York: William Morrow.

55.   Collier, M. J. (1991). Conflict competence within African, Mexican, and Anglo-American friendships. In S. Ting-Toomey & F. Korzenny (Eds.), *Cross-cultural interpersonal communication* (pp. 132–154). Newbury Park, CA: Sage.

56.   Beatty, K. J. & McCroskey, J. C. (1997). It's in our nature: Verbal aggressiveness as temperamental expression. *Communication Quarterly, 45,* 446–460.

57.   Oetzel, J. G. (1998). Explaining individual communication processes in homogeneous and heterogeneous groups through individualism-collectivism and self-construal. *Human Communication Research, 25,* 202–224.

58.   Hahlweg, K. & Richter, D. (2010). Prevention of marital instability and distress: Results of an 11-year longitudinal follow-up study. *Behaviour Research and Therapy, 48,* 377–383.

59.   Gordon, T. (1970). *Parent effectiveness training* (pp. 236–264). New York: Wyden.

60.   Axelrod, R. (1984). *The evolution of cooperation.* New York: Basic Books.

FEATURE BOX NOTES

CHAPTER ONE

ON THE JOB

a. National Association of Colleges and Employers (October 24, 2012). *The skills and qualities employers want in their class of 2013 recruits*. NACE.
b. Winsor, J. L., Curtis, D. B., & Stephens, R. D. (1997). National preferences in business and communication education: An update. *Journal of the Association for Communication Administration, 3*, 170–179; Peterson, M. S. (1997). Personnel interviewers' perceptions of the importance and adequacy of applicants' communication skills. *Communication Education, 46*, 287–291.
c. Endicott, F. S. (1979). *The Endicott report: Trends in the employment of college and university graduates in business and industry*. Evanston, IL: Placement Center, Northwestern University.
d. Hindi, N. M., Miller, D. S., & Catt, S. E. (2004). Communication and miscommunication in corporate America: Evidence from Fortune 200 firms. *Journal of Organizational Culture, 8*, 13–26.
e. Darling, A. L. & Dannels, D. P. (2003). Practicing engineers talk about the importance of talk: A report on the role of oral communication in the workplace. *Communication Education, 52*, 1–16.
f. Gray, E. F. (2010). Specific oral communication skills desired in new accountancy graduates. *Business Communication Quarterly, 73*, 40–67.
g. Communication skills deemed vital. (1999, August 22). *Santa Barbara News-Press*, J1.
h. Richman, J. (2002, September 16). The news journal of the life scientist. *The Scientist, 16*, 42.

ETHICAL CHALLENGE

a. An English translation of Martin Buber's *I and Thou* was published in 1970 by Scribner's. For useful descriptions of its central themes, see Stewart, J. (2006). A philosopher's approach. In J. Stewart (Ed.), *Bridges not walls* (9th ed., pp. 679–696). New York: McGraw-Hill; Paton, H. J. (1955). *The modern predicament*. London: Allen & Unwin.

READING: ARTIFICIAL (UN)INTELLIGENCE AND COMMUNICATION (IN) COMPETENCE

http://www.ibtimes.com/ibms-watson-gets-swear-filter-after-learning-urban-dictionary-1007734

CHAPTER TWO

ON THE JOB

a. Adapted from Collins, S. D. (2003). *Communication in a virtual organization*. Cincinnati: Thomson Learning.

READING: VIRTUALLY SEPARATED

http://www.nytimes.com/2011/05/01/fashion/01Modern.html

READING: ALONE TOGETHER

http://www.nytimes.com/2012/04/22/opinion/sunday/the-flight-from-conversation.html

ETHICAL CHALLENGE

a. Bilton, R. (2014, April 14). Why some publishers are killing their comment sections. Digiday.
b. Dreyfus, H. (2004). Nihilism on the information highway: Anonymity versus commitment in the present age. In A. Feenberg and D. Barney (Eds.), *Community in the digital age: Philosophy and practice* (pp. 69–81). Lanham, MD: Rowman & Littlefield.

CHAPTER THREE

READING: TALKING WITH LITTLE GIRLS

http://www.huffingtonpost.com/lisa-bloom/how-to-talk-to-little-gir_b_882510.html

READING: WHAT I INSTAGRAMMED

http://www.bustle.com/articles/32177-what-i-instagrammed-vs-what-was-really-happening-or-my-entire-life-is-a-lie

ON THE JOB

a. Rosen, J. (July 25, 2010). The end of forgetting. *New York Times Magazine*.
b. Madden, M. & Smith, A. (2010, May 26). *Reputation management and social media*. Pew Internet & American Life Project; Berkelaar, B. L. & Buzzanell, P. M. (2014). Reconceptualizing fit (assessments) in personnel selection: Employers' sensemaking about cybervetting. *Journal of Applied Communication Research, 42*, 456–476.
c. Caron, A. H., Hwang, J. M., & Brummans, B. (2013). Business writing on the go: How executives manage impressions through e-mail communication in everyday work life. *Corporate Communications: An International Journal, 18*, 8–25.

ETHICAL CHALLENGE

a. Read Kant's own words on truth telling in the following works: On a supposed right to lie from altruistic motives. (1964). In L. W. Beck (Trans. and Ed.), *Critique of practical reason and other writings in moral philosophy*.

Chicago: University of Chicago Press; Paton, H. J. (Trans.). (1964). *Groundwork of the metaphysics of morals*. New York: Harper Torchbooks.

b. Fried, C. (1978). *Right and wrong*. Cambridge, MA: Harvard University Press; Bok, S. (1979). *Lying: Moral choice in public and private life*. New York: Vintage.

CHAPTER FOUR

ON THE JOB

a. Equal Employment Opportunity Commission. (2010). *Sexual harassment charges EEOC & FEPAs combined: FY 1997–FY 2010*.

b. Ohse, D. M. & Stockwell, M. S. (2008). Age comparisons in workplace sexual harassment perceptions. *Sex Roles, 59*, 240–253.

c. Fiedler, A. M. & Blanco, R. I. (2006). The challenge of varying perceptions of sexual harassment: An international study. *Journal of Behavioral and Applied Management, 7*, 274–292.

READING: AT FACEBOOK, CREATING EMPATHY

http://www.nytimes.com/2014/10/23/fashion/Facebook-Arturo-Bejar-Creating-Empathy-Among-Cyberbullying.html

ETHICAL CHALLENGE

a. For a discussion of the Golden and Platinum rules, see Bennett, M. (1979). Overcoming the Golden Rule: Sympathy and empathy. In D. Nimmo (Ed.), *Communication yearbook 3* (pp. 407–422). New Brunswick, NJ: Transaction Books; Johannesen, R. L. (2002). *Ethics in human communication*. Prospect Heights, IL: Waveland Press.

CHAPTER FIVE

READING: INTROVERTS: THOUGHTFUL, NOT SHY

http://www.psychologytoday.com/articles/201008/revenge-the-introvert

ON THE JOB

a. Scott, C. & Myers, K. K. (2005). The socialization of emotion: Learning emotion management at the fire station. *Journal of Applied Communication Research, 33*, 67–92.

b. Miller, K. I. & Koesten, J. (2008). Financial feeling: An investigation of emotion and communication in the workplace. *Journal of Applied Communication Research, 36*, 8–32.

c. Tracy, S. J. (2005). Locking up emotion: Moving beyond dissonance for understanding emotion labor discomfort. *Communication Monographs, 72*, 261–283.

READING: CRITIC'S MATH

https://www.facebook.com/notes/margaret-feinberg/guest-blogger-larry-david-the-3-problems-with-critics-math-by-jonacuff/346928495361285

CHAPTER SIX

READING: FINDING THE WORDS TO TALK ABOUT DISABILITY

http://www.huffingtonpost.com/amy-julia-becker/finding-the-words-to-talk_b_1449819.html

ON THE JOB

a. Jay, T. B. & Janschewitz, K. (2008). The pragmatics of swearing. *Journal of Politeness Research: Language, Behavior, Culture, 4*, 267–288.

b. Johnson, D. I. & Lewis, N. (2010). Perceptions of swearing in the work setting: An expectancy violations theory perspective. *Communication Reports, 23*, 106–118.

c. Sutton, R. I. (2010, June 18). Is it sometimes useful to cuss when you are at work?: The strategic use of swear words. *Psychology Today*.

READING: LANGUAGE AND HERITAGE

http://articles.latimes.com/1997/oct/26/opinion/op-46848

CHAPTER SEVEN

ON THE JOB

a. Goldberg, C. & Cohen, D. J. (2004). Walking the walk and talking the talk: Gender differences in the impact of interviewing skills on applicant assessments. *Group & Organization Management, 29*, 369–384.

b. Stewart, G. L., Dustin, S. L., Barrick, M. R., & Darnold, T. C. (2008). Exploring the handshake in employment interviews. *Journal of Applied Psychology, 93*, 1139–1146.

c. Riggio, R. E. & Throckmorton, B. (1988). The relative effects of verbal and nonverbal behavior, appearance, and social skills on evaluation made in hiring interviews. *Journal of Applied Social Psychology, 18*, 331–348; Gifford, R., Ng, C. F., & Wilkinson, M. (1985). Nonverbal cues in the employment interview: Links between applicant qualities and interviewer judgments. *Journal of Applied Psychology, 70*, 729–736.

d. Krumhuber, E., Manstead, A., Cosker, D., Marshall, D., & Rosin, P. (2009). Effects of dynamic attributes of smiles in human and synthetic faces: A simulated job interview setting. *Journal of Nonverbal Behavior, 33*, 1–15.

READING: THE EYES HAVE IT

http://www.nytimes.com/2014/05/17/sunday-review/the-eyes-have-it.html

READING: THE WAY YOU TALK CAN HURT YOU?

a. Hurka, T. (1994). *Principles: Short essays on ethics* (pp. 201–233).Toronto: Harcourt Brace.

CHAPTER EIGHT

ON THE JOB

a. Sypher, B. D., Bostrom, R. N., & Seibert, J. H. (1989). Listening communication abilities and success at work. *Journal of Business Communication, 26*, 293–303; Alexander, E. R., Penley, L. E., & Jernigan, I. E. (1992). The relationship of basic decoding skills to managerial effectiveness. *Management Communication Quarterly, 6*, 58–73.
b. Winsor, J. L., Curtis, D. B., & Stephens, R. D. (1999). National preferences in business and communication education: An update. *Journal of the Association for Communication Administration, 3*, 170–179.
c. Johnson, S. & Bechler, C. (1998). Examining the relationship between listening effectiveness and leadership emergence: Perceptions, behaviors, and recall. *Small Group Research, 29*, 452–471.
d. Christensen, D. & Rees, D. (2002, October). Communication skills needed by entry-level accountants. *The CPA letter, 82*. Retrieved from www.aicpa.org/pubs/cpaltr/Oct2002/AUDIT/audit.htm
e. Marchant, V. (1999, June 28). Listen up! *Time, 153*, 74; *Job Outlook 2006*. (2006). Retrieved from www.naceweb.org/press/display.asp?year=&prid=235
f. Brownell, J. (1990). Perceptions of effective listeners: A management study. *Journal of Business Communication, 27*, 401–415.

READING: TEXTING TO SAVE LIVES

http://www.newyorker.com/magazine/2015/02/09/r-u

READING: HOW TO HELP … AND NOT HELP

http://articles.latimes.com/2013/apr/07/opinion/la-oe-0407-silk-ring-theory-20130407

ETHICAL CHALLENGE

a. Rogers, C. (1961). *On becoming a person*. Boston: Houghton Mifflin.
b. High, A. C. & Dillard, J. P. (2012). A review and meta-analysis of person-centered messages and social support outcomes. *Communication Studies, 63*, 99–118.

CHAPTER NINE

READING: RELFIES: GOOD FOR YOU AND YOUR RELATIONSHIPS

http://www.scienceofrelationships.com/home/2014/7/1/the-top-8-reasons-why-relfies-are-good-for-you-your-relation.html

ON THE JOB

http://blogs.hbr.org/2014/06/how-to-repair-a-damaged-professional-relationship/

CHAPTER TEN

ON THE JOB

a. Studies summarized in University of Pennsylvania (2007, March 21). *More confident, less careful: Why office romances are hard to manage.* Knowledge@Wharton; Voo, J. (2007, August 30). *How to handle an office romance.* CNN.
b. University of Pennsylvania (2007, March 21). *More confident, less careful: Why office romances are hard to manage.* Knowledge@Wharton.

READING: WHEN FRIENDS GET IN THE WAY

http://time.com/7056/the-friendship-trap/

READING: HOW TO FALL IN LOVE

http://www.nytimes.com/2015/01/11/fashion/modern-love-to-fall-in-love-with-anyone-do-this.html

READING: LEARNING THE LANGUAGES OF LOVE

http://voxxi.com/the-five-love-languages-a-book-that-helps-couples-understand-each-other-mujer-voxpopuli

CHAPTER ELEVEN

READING: AN UNLIKELY FRIENDSHIP

http://www.huffingtonpost.com/shane-l-windmeyer/dan-cathy-chick-fil-a_b_2564379.html

ON THE JOB

a. Pasick, A. (June 20, 2013). *Google admits those infamous brainteasers were completely useless for hiring.* Quartz.
b. Bryant, A. (June 19, 2013). Head-hunting, big data may not be such a big deal. *New York Times*.

ETHICAL CHALLENGE

For more information on nonviolent strategies, see Ackerman, P. & Kruegler, C. (1994). *Strategic nonviolent conflict: The dynamics of people power in the twentieth century*. Westport, CT: Praeger; Holmes, R. L. (Ed.). (1990). *Nonviolence in theory and practice*. Belmont, CA: Wadsworth.

CHAPTER TWELVE

ON THE JOB

a. Shellenbarger, S. (2014, December 16). To fight, or not to fight? How to pick your battles in the workplace. *The Wall Street Journal*.

ETHICAL CHALLENGE

For more information about crazymaking, see Bach, G. & Wyden, P. (1968). *The intimate enemy*. New York: Avon; Bach, G. (1971). *Aggression lab: The fair fight manual*. Dubuque, IA: Kendall-Hunt.

READING: SOFTWARE TACKLES ROOMMATE CONFLICTS

http://college.usatoday.com/2014/07/30/start-up-tackles-roomie-conflicts-with-online-dorm-contracts

GLOSSARY

abstract language Language that is vague and general rather than concrete and specific. *See also* behavioral language.

abstraction ladder A range of more to less abstract terms describing an event or object.

accenting Nonverbal behaviors that emphasize part of a verbal message.

accommodating A lose–win conflict style in which the communicator submits to a situation rather than attempts to have his or her needs met.

adaptors Unconscious bodily movements in response to the environment.

advising A listening response in which the receiver offers suggestions about how the speaker should deal with a problem.

affinity The degree to which persons like or appreciate one another.

aggressiveness Verbal attacks that demean another's self-concept and inflict psychological pain.

ambiguous response A disconfirming response with more than one meaning, leaving the other party unsure of the responder's position.

ambushing A style in which the receiver listens carefully in order to gather information to use in an attack on the speaker.

analyzing A listening response in which the receiver offers an interpretation of a speaker's message.

androgynous Possessing both masculine and feminine traits.

argumentativeness Presenting and defending positions on issues while attacking positions taken by others.

assertive message format A direct expression of the sender's needs and thoughts delivered in a way that does not attack the receiver's dignity. A complete assertive message describes behavior, interpretation, feeling, consequence, and intention.

asynchronous communication Communication that occurs when there is a time gap between when the message is sent and when it is received. *See also* synchronous communication.

attending The process of filtering out some messages and focusing on others.

attribution The process of attaching meaning to behavior. *See also* interpretation statement.

avoiding (conflict style) A lose–lose conflict style in which the parties ignore the problem at hand.

avoiding (relational stage) A stage of relational deterioration immediately before terminating in which the parties minimize contact with one another.

behavioral description An account that refers only to observable phenomena.

behavioral language Language that describes observable behavior. *See also* abstract language.

benevolent lie A lie defined by the teller as not malicious, or even helpful, to the person to whom it is told.

body orientation A type of nonverbal communication characterized by the degree to which we face forward or away from someone.

bonding A stage of relational development in which the parties make symbolic public gestures to show that their relationship exists.

breadth A dimension of self-disclosure involving the range of subjects being discussed.

"but" statement A statement in which the word *but* cancels out the expression preceding it.

certainty An attitude behind messages that dogmatically implies that the speaker's position is correct and that the other person's ideas are not worth considering. Likely to generate a defensive response.

channel The medium through which a message passes from sender to receiver.

chronemics The study of how humans use and structure time.

circumscribing A stage of relational deterioration in which partners begin to reduce the scope of their contact and commitment to one another.

clichés Ritualized, stock statements delivered in response to a social situation.

co-culture A culture that exists within the larger culture of a country or society, such as subgroups defined by age, race or ethnicity, occupation, sexual orientation, physical disability, religion, avocation, and so on.

cognitive complexity The ability to construct a variety of frameworks for viewing an issue.

cognitive conservatism The tendency to seek and attend to information that conforms to an existing self-concept.

collaborating A conflict management style that seeks win–win solutions.

communication climate The emotional tone of a relationship between two or more individuals.

communication competence The ability to accomplish one's personal goals in a manner that maintains a relationship on terms that are acceptable to all parties.

competing A win–lose approach to conflicts that seeks to resolve them in one's own way.

complaining A disagreeing message that directly or indirectly communicates dissatisfaction with another person.

complementary conflict style A relational conflict style in which partners use different but mutually reinforcing behaviors.

complementing Nonverbal behavior that reinforces a verbal message.

compromising An approach to conflict resolution in which both parties attain at least part of what they wanted through self-sacrifice.

confirming communication A message that expresses caring or respect for another person.

conflict An expressed struggle between at least two interdependent parties who perceive incompatible goals, scarce resources, and interference from the other party in achieving their goals.

conflict ritual An unacknowledged repeating pattern of interlocking behavior used by participants in a conflict.

conformity orientation The degree to which a family enforces a uniformity of attitudes, values, and beliefs.

connection-autonomy dialectic The tension between the need for integration and the need for independence in a relationship.

consequence statement An explanation of the results that follow from either the behavior of the person to whom the message is addressed or the speaker's interpretation of the addressee's behavior. Consequence statements can describe what happens to the speaker, the addressee, or others.

content dimension The part of a message that communicates information about the subject being discussed. *See also* relational dimension.

contradicting Nonverbal behavior that is inconsistent with a verbal message.

control The social need to influence others.

controlling communication Messages in which the sender tries to impose some sort of outcome on the receiver, usually resulting in a defensive reaction.

convergence The process of adapting one's speech style to match that of others with whom the communicator wants to identify. *See also* divergence.

conversation orientation The degree of openness a family has in discussing a range of topics.

counterfeit questions Questions that disguise the speaker's true motives, which do not include a genuine desire to understand the other person. *See also* sincere questions.

crazymaking An indirect expression of aggression delivered in a way that allows the sender to maintain a façade of kindness. *Also called* passive aggression.

cyberbullying The aggressive harassment of others online.

cyberstalking Obsessive surveillance and pursuit of others online.

debilitative emotions Emotions that prevent a person from functioning effectively.

decode The process in which a receiver attaches meaning to a message.

de-escalatory conflict spiral A communication pattern in which the parties slowly lessen their dependence on one another, withdraw, and become less invested in the relationship. *See also* spiral.

defensive listening A response style in which the receiver perceives a speaker's comments as an attack.

defensiveness The attempt to protect a presenting image that a person believes is being attacked.

depth A dimension of self-disclosure involving a shift from relatively nonrevealing messages to more personal ones.

description Gibb's term for language that describes a complaint in behavioral terms rather than being judgmental, thereby creating a supportive communication climate. *See also* evaluation, "I" language.

dialectical tensions Inherent conflicts that arise when two opposing or incompatible forces exist simultaneously.

differentiating A relational stage in which the parties reestablish their individual identities after having bonded together.

direct aggression A criticism or demand that threatens the face of the person at whom it is directed.

disagreeing messages Messages that communicate to the other person, "You are wrong." Includes aggressiveness, complaining, and argumentativeness.

disconfirming communication A message that expresses a lack of caring or respect for another person.

disinhibition The tendency to transmit messages without considering their consequences; occurs more frequently in mediated communication.

divergence Language mannerisms that emphasize a communicator's differences from others. *See also* convergence.

dyad Two individuals communicating. The interaction may or may not be interpersonal in nature.

emblems Deliberate nonverbal behaviors with precise meanings that are known to virtually all members of a cultural group.

emotion labor Managing and even suppressing emotions when doing so is both appropriate and necessary.

emotional contagion The process by which emotions are transferred from one person to another.

emotional intelligence The ability to understand and manage one's own emotions and be sensitive to others' feelings.

emotive language Language that conveys the sender's attitude rather than simply offers an objective description.

empathy The ability to project oneself into another person's point of view so as to experience the other's thoughts and feelings. *See also* sympathy.

encode The process of putting thoughts into symbols, most commonly words.

environment The field of experiences that leads a person to make sense of another's behavior. Environments consist of physical characteristics, personal experiences, relational history, and cultural background.

equality A type of supportive communication described by Gibb that suggests that the sender regards the receiver as worthy of respect.

equivocal language Ambiguous language that has two or more equally plausible meanings.

escalatory conflict spiral A communication pattern in which one attack leads to another until the initial skirmish escalates into a full-fledged battle. *See also* spiral.

ethnocentrism The attitude that one's own culture is superior to others.

evaluation Gibb's term for judgmental assessments of another person's behavior, thereby increasing the odds of creating a defensive communication climate. *See also* description, "I" language.

experimenting An early stage in relational development consisting of a search for common ground. If the experimentation is successful, then the relationship will progress to intensifying. If not, it may go no further.

face The socially approved identity that a communicator tries to present. *See also* identity management.

face-threatening act Behavior by another that is perceived as attacking an individual's presenting image, or face.

facilitative emotions Emotions that contribute to effective functioning.

fallacy of approval The irrational belief that it is vital to win the approval of virtually every person a communicator deals with.

fallacy of catastrophic expectations The irrational belief that the worst possible outcome will probably occur.

fallacy of causation The irrational belief that emotions are caused by others and not by the person who has them.

fallacy of helplessness The irrational belief that satisfaction in life is determined by forces beyond one's control.

fallacy of overgeneralization Irrational beliefs in which (1) conclusions (usually negative) are based on limited evidence, or (2) communicators exaggerate their shortcomings.

fallacy of perfection The irrational belief that a worthwhile communicator should be able to handle every situation with complete confidence and skill.

fallacy of shoulds The irrational belief that people should behave in the most desirable way.

family communication pattern A mode of family interaction that involves a blending of conversation and conformity orientations. These include consensual, pluralistic, protective, and laissez-faire patterns.

family system A group of interdependent individuals who interact and adapt together as a whole.

feeling statement An expression of the sender's emotions that results from interpretation of sense data.

friends with benefits (FWB) A popular term for nonromantic heterosexual friendships that include sexual activity.

gender role Socially approved ways that men and women are expected to behave.

gestures Motions of the body, usually hands or arms, that have communicative value.

Gibb categories Six sets of contrasting styles of verbal and nonverbal behavior. Each set describes a communication style that is likely to arouse defensiveness and a contrasting style that is likely to prevent or reduce it. Developed by Jack Gibb.

halo effect The power of a first impression to influence subsequent perceptions.

haptics The study of touching.

hearing The physiological dimension of listening.

high-context cultures Cultures that avoid direct use of language, relying instead on the context of a message to convey meaning.

hyperpersonal communication An accelerated discussion of personal topics and relational development beyond what normally happens in face-to-face interactions.

"I" language A statement that clearly identifies the speaker as the source of a message. *See also* "you" language, description.

illustrators Nonverbal behaviors that accompany and support verbal messages.

immediacy The degree of interest and attention that we feel toward and communicate to others.

impersonal communication Behavior that treats others as objects rather than individuals. *See also* interpersonal communication.

impersonal response A disconfirming response that is superficial or trite.

impervious response A disconfirming response that ignores another person's attempt to communicate.

impression management The communication strategies people use to influence how others view them. *See also* face.

incongruous response A disconfirming response in which two messages, one of which is usually nonverbal, contradict each other.

initiating The first stage in relational development in which the parties express interest in one another.

insensitive listening Failure to recognize the thoughts or feelings that are not directly expressed by a speaker.

instrumental goals Goals aimed at getting others to behave in desired ways.

insulated listening A style in which the receiver ignores undesirable information.

integrating A stage of relational development in which the parties begin to take on a single identity.

intensifying A stage of relational development that precedes integrating in which the parties move toward integration by increasing the amount of contact and the breadth and depth of self-disclosure.

intention statement A description of where the speaker stands on an issue, what he or she wants, or how he or she plans to act in the future.

interpersonal communication A continuous, transactional process involving participants who occupy different but overlapping environments and create meaning and relationships through the exchange of messages, many of which are affected by external, physiological, and psychological noise.

interpretation The process of attaching meaning to sense data.

interpretation statement A statement that describes the speaker's interpretation of the meaning of another person's behavior. *See also* attribution.

interrupting response A disconfirming response in which one communicator interrupts another.

intimacy A state of closeness arising from physical, intellectual, or emotional contact or sometimes from shared activities.

intimate distance One of Hall's four distance zones, ranging from skin contact to 18 inches.

irrelevant response A disconfirming response in which one communicator's comments bear no relationship to the previous speaker's ideas.

"it" statements Statements that replace the personal pronoun "I" with the less immediate word "it," often reducing the speaker's acceptance of responsibility for the statement.

Johari Window A model that describes the relationship between self-disclosure and self-awareness.

judging A listening response in which the receiver evaluates the sender's message either favorably or unfavorably.

kinesics The study of body position and motion.

leakage Nonverbal behaviors that reveal information a communicator does not disclose verbally.

leanness Messages (usually electronic) that are stark from a lack of nonverbal information; opposite of richness.

linear communication model A characterization of communication as a one-way event in which a message flows from sender to receiver.

linguistic relativism The notion that the worldview of a culture is shaped and reflected by the language its members speak. *See also* Sapir-Whorf hypothesis.

listening Process that consists of hearing, attending, understanding, responding, and remembering others' messages.

listening fidelity The degree of congruence between what a listener understands and what the message sender was attempting to communicate.

love languages Modes of communicating affection in romantic relationships. These include words of affirmation, quality time, gifts, acts of service, and physical touch.

low-context cultures Cultures that use language primarily to express thoughts, feelings, and ideas as directly as possible.

manipulators A type of nonverbal adaptors involving self-touching behaviors.

mediated communication Communication between individuals that is conducted via electronic channels.

message Information sent from a sender to a receiver.

metacommunication Messages (usually relational) that refer to other messages; communication about communication.

microexpression A brief facial expression.

mindful listening Giving careful and thoughtful attention and responses to the messages we receive.

mindless listening Reacting to others' messages automatically and routinely without much mental investment.

mixed message Situation in which a person's words are incongruent with his or her nonverbal behavior.

monochronic Behavior emphasizing punctuality, schedules, and completing one task at a time.

narrative The stories used to describe one's personal world.

negotiation The sense making that occurs between and among people as they influence one another's perceptions

and try to achieve a shared perspective. Fourth stage in the perception process.

neutrality A defense-arousing behavior described by Gibb in which the sender expresses indifference toward a receiver.

noise External, physiological, and psychological distractions that interfere with the accurate transmission and reception of a message.

nonverbal communication Messages expressed by other than linguistic means.

online surveillance Monitoring the activities of unknowing targets through social media.

openness-privacy dialectic The tension between the need for disclosure and the need for secrecy in a relationship.

organization The second stage in the perception process in which selected information is arranged in some meaningful way.

paralanguage Nonlinguistic means of vocal expression: rate, pitch, tone, and so on.

parallel conflict style A relational conflict style in which the approach of the partners varies from one situation to another.

paraphrasing Restating a speaker's thoughts or feelings in the listener's own words.

passive aggression An indirect expression of aggression delivered in a way that allows the sender to maintain a façade of kindness. *Also called* crazymaking.

perceived self The person we believe ourselves to be in moments of candor. It may be identical to or different from the presenting and ideal self.

perception checking A three-part method for verifying the accuracy of interpretations, including a description of the sense data, two possible interpretations, and a request for confirmation of the interpretations.

personal distance One of Hall's four distance zones, ranging from 18 inches to 4 feet.

personality A relatively consistent set of traits exhibited by a person across a variety of situations.

pillow method A method for understanding an issue from several perspectives rather than with an egocentric "I'm right and you're wrong" attitude.

politeness Communicating in ways that save face for both senders and receivers.

polychronic An approach to the use of time that emphasizes flexibility and pursuing multiple tasks.

posture The way in which individuals carry themselves—erect, slumping, and so on.

powerless speech mannerisms Ways of speaking that may reduce perceptions of a communicator's power.

pragmatic rules Linguistic rules that help communicators understand how messages may be used and interpreted in a given context.

predictability-novelty dialectic The tension between the need for stability and the need for change in a relationship.

presenting self The image a person presents to others. It may be identical to or different from the perceived and ideal self.

privacy management The choices people make to reveal or conceal information about themselves.

problem orientation A supportive style of communication described by Gibb in which the communicators focus on working together to solve their problems instead of trying to impose their own solutions on one another.

prompting Using silences and brief statements of encouragement to draw out a speaker.

provisionalism A supportive style of communication described by Gibb in which the sender expresses a willingness to consider the other person's position.

proxemics The study of how people use interpersonal space and distance.

pseudolistening An imitation of true listening in which the receiver's mind is elsewhere.

public distance One of Hall's four distance zones, extending outward from 12 feet.

punctuation The process of determining the causal order of events.

questioning A listening response in which the receiver seeks additional information from the sender.

reappraisal Rethinking the meaning of emotionally charged events in ways that alter their emotional impact.

receiver One who notices and attends to a message.

reference groups Groups against which we compare ourselves, thereby influencing our self-concept and self-esteem.

reflected appraisal The theory that a person's self-concept mirrors the way the person believes others regard him or her.

regulating One function of nonverbal communication in which nonverbal cues control the flow of verbal communication among individuals.

relational commitment A promise—sometimes implied and sometimes explicit—to remain in a relationship and to make that relationship successful.

relational conflict style A pattern of managing disagreements that repeats itself over time in a relationship.

relational dimension The part of a message that expresses the social relationship between two or more individuals. *See also* content dimension.

relational maintenance Communication aimed at keeping relationships operating smoothly and satisfactorily.

relational transgression One partner's violation of the explicit or implicit terms of the relationship, letting the other one down in some important way.

relational turning point Transformative event that alters a relationship in a fundamental way.

relative words Words that gain their meaning by comparison.

remembering Ability to recall information.

repeating Nonverbal behaviors that duplicate the content of a verbal message.

respect The social need to be held in esteem by others.

responding Giving observable feedback to the speaker.

richness An abundance of nonverbal cues that add clarity to a verbal message; opposite of leanness.

role A set of expectations about how to communicate.

rumination Dwelling persistently on negative thoughts that, in turn, intensifies negative feelings.

Sapir-Whorf hypothesis Theory of linguistic relativity in which language shapes a culture's perceived reality. *See also* linguistic relativism.

selection The first stage in the perception process in which some data are chosen to attend to and others to ignore.

selective listening A listening style in which the receiver responds only to messages that interest him or her.

self-concept The relatively stable set of perceptions each individual holds of himself or herself.

self-disclosure The process of deliberately revealing information about oneself that is significant and that would not normally be known by others.

self-esteem The part of the self-concept that involves an individual's evaluations of his or her self-worth.

self-fulfilling prophecy An expectation of an event, followed by behaviors based on that expectation, that makes the outcome more likely to occur than would have been the case otherwise.

self-monitoring The process of attending to one's behavior and using these observations to shape the way one behaves.

self-serving bias The tendency to interpret and explain information in a way that casts the perceiver in the most favorable manner.

self-talk The nonvocal process of thinking; sometimes referred to as *intrapersonal communication*.

semantic rules Rules that govern the meaning of language as opposed to its structure. *See also* syntactic rules.

sender The creator of a message.

significant others People whose opinion is important enough to affect one's self-concept strongly.

sincere questions Attempts to elicit information that enable the asker to understand the other person. *See also* counterfeit questions.

social comparison Evaluation of oneself in terms of or by comparison to others.

social distance One of Hall's distance zones, ranging from 4 to 12 feet.

social media Forms of electronic communication through which users create online communities.

social penetration A model that describes relationships in terms of their breadth and depth.

social support Assistance for others provided through emotional, informational, or instrumental resources.

spiral A reciprocal communication pattern in which each person's message reinforces the other's. *See also* de-escalatory conflict spiral, escalatory conflict spiral.

spontaneity A supportive communication behavior described by Gibb in which the sender expresses a message without any attempt to manipulate the receiver.

stage-hogging A listening style in which the receiver is more concerned with making his or her own point than in understanding the speaker.

stagnating A stage of relational deterioration characterized by declining enthusiasm and by standardized forms of behavior.

static evaluation The tendency to view people or relation-ships as unchanging.

stereotyping Categorizing individuals according to a set of characteristics assumed to belong to all members of a group.

strategy A defense-arousing style of communication described by Gibb in which the sender tries to manipulate or deceive a receiver.

substituting Nonverbal behavior that takes the place of a verbal message.

superiority A defense-arousing style of communication described by Gibb in which the sender states or implies that the receiver is not worthy of respect.

supporting A listening response that demonstrates solidarity with a speaker's situation.

symmetrical conflict style A relational conflict style in which both partners use the same tactics.

sympathy Compassion for another's situation. *See also* empathy.

synchronous communication Communication that occurs in real time. *See also* asynchronous communication.

syntactic rules Rules that govern the ways symbols can be arranged, as opposed to the meanings of those symbols. *See also* semantic rules.

tangential response A disconfirming response that uses the speaker's remark as a starting point for a shift to a new topic.

terminating The concluding stage of relational deteriora-tion, characterized by the acknowledgment of one or both parties that the relationship is over.

territory A stationary area claimed by an individual.

transactional communication model A characterization of communication as the simultaneous sending and receiving of messages in an ongoing, irreversible process.

understanding Occurs when sense is made of a message.

"we" language Statement that implies that the issue is the concern and responsibility of both the speaker and receiver of a message. *See also* "I" language, "you" language.

"you" language A statement that expresses or implies a judgment of the other person. *See also* "I" language.

NAME INDEX

SUBJECT INDEX

Note: page references followed by *f* indicate figures; those followed by *t* indicate tables.